THE ONE YEAR NEW TESTAMENT

THE
ONE
YEAR

NEW
TESTAMENT

Arranged in 365 Daily Readings

THE LIVING BIBLE
A Thought-for-Thought Translation

KINGSWAY PUBLICATIONS
EASTBOURNE

This edition 1988

Total *Living Bibles* in print in 1986 over 33 million

ISBNs
Hardback   0 86065 702 7
Limp   0 86065 703 5

Printed and bound in Great Britain for
KINGSWAY PUBLICATIONS LTD
Lottbridge Drove, Eastbourne, E. Sussex BN23 6NT by
Richard Clay Ltd, Bungay, Suffolk

NOTE *(to be read!)*

This new edition of *The Living Bible* has been prepared especially for regular Bible readers who wish to read through the entire New Testament in one year.

There are three readings for each day: (1) a passage from the Gospels, Acts, or Revelation; (2) a passage from the Epistles; and (3) a selection from the book of Proverbs. *A Thought*—following each of the first two readings—provides fresh insight on applying that day's reading to daily life. This gives variety and freshness to your daily reading.

Instead of following a Bible reading chart and experiencing the delay of turning from place to place, you will find the text here in sequence, ready for your quiet reading and meditation.

Many Bible scholars have emphasized the importance of reading the Scriptures on a daily basis in order to experience anew the goodness and power of God's Word.

The Publishers

P.S. Although these daily readings begin January 1, you can as easily begin with today's date. Whenever you begin, you will finish the entire New Testament in one year. And it takes only ten minutes a day!

CONTENTS

JANUARY 1

The Ancestors of Jesus/ Matthew 1:1–17

These are the ancestors of Jesus Christ, a descendant of King David and of Abraham:

2Abraham was the father of Isaac; Isaac was the father of Jacob; Jacob was the father of Judah and his brothers.

3Judah was the father of Perez and Zerah (Tamar was their mother); Perez was the father of Hezron; Hezron was the father of Aram;

4Aram was the father of Amminadab; Amminadab was the father of Nahshon; Nahshon was the father of Salmon;

5Salmon was the father of Boaz (Rahab was his mother); Boaz was the father of Obed (Ruth was his mother); Obed was the father of Jesse;

6Jesse was the father of King David. David was the father of Solomon (his mother was the widow of Uriah);

7Solomon was the father of Rehoboam; Rehoboam was the father of Abijah; Abijah was the father of Asa;

8Asa was the father of Jehoshaphat; Jehoshaphat was the father of Joram; Joram was the father of Uzziah;

9Uzziah was the father of Jotham; Jotham was the father of Ahaz; Ahaz was the father of Hezekiah;

10Hezekiah was the father of Manasseh; Manasseh was the father of Amos; Amos was the father of Josiah;

11Josiah was the father of Jechoniah and his brothers (born at the time of the exile to Babylon).

12After the exile:

Jechoniah was the father of Shealtiel; Shealtiel was the father of Zerubbabel;

13Zerubbabel was the father of Abiud; Abiud was the father of Eliakim; Eliakim was the father of Azor;

14Azor was the father of Zadok; Zadok was the father of Achim; Achim was the father of Eliud;

15Eliud was the father of Eleazar; Eleazar was the father of Matthan; Matthan was the father of Jacob;

16Jacob was the father of Joseph (who was the husband of Mary, the mother of Jesus Christ the Messiah).

17These are fourteen of the generations from Abraham to King David; and fourteen from King David's time to the exile; and fourteen from the exile to Christ.

A THOUGHT: *In these first 17 verses we meet 46 people whose lives span 2,000 years. All were ancestors of Jesus, but they varied considerably in personality, spirituality, and experience. Some were heroes of faith—like Abraham, Isaac, Ruth, and David. Some had shady reputations—like Rahab and Tamar. Many were very ordinary—like Hezron, Aram, Nahshon, and Achim. And others were evil—like Manasseh and Abijah. God's work in history is not limited by human failures or sins, and he works through ordinary people. Just as God used all kinds of people to bring his Son into the world, he uses all kinds today to accomplish his will.*

The Good News Is about Jesus Christ/
Romans 1:1–7

Dear friends in Rome: 1This letter is from Paul, Jesus Christ's slave, chosen to be a missionary, and sent out to preach God's Good News. 2This Good News was promised long ago by God's prophets in the Old Testament. 3It is the Good News about his Son, Jesus Christ our Lord, who came as a human baby, born into King David's royal family line; 4and by being raised from the dead he was proved to be the mighty Son of God, with the holy nature of God himself.

5And now, through Christ, all the kindness of God has been poured out upon us undeserving sinners; and now he is sending us out around the world to tell all people everywhere the great things God has done for them, so that they, too, will believe and obey him.

6,7And you, dear friends in Rome, are among those he dearly loves; you, too, are invited by Jesus Christ to be

God's very own—yes, his holy people. May all God's mercies and peace be yours from God our Father and from Jesus Christ our Lord.

A THOUGHT: *Paul and the apostles received God's forgiveness as an undeserved privilege. But they also received the responsibility to share the message of God's forgiveness with others. God graciously forgives the sins of those who, by faith, believe in him as Lord. When we believe, we receive his forgiveness. In doing this, however, we are committing ourselves to live a new life. Paul's new life, a gift from God, also involved a call from God—a God-given responsibility—to witness to the world. God may or may not call you to be an overseas missionary, but he does call you (and all believers) to be a witness to Jesus Christ and his redemptive work.*

Proverbs for Today/ 1:1–6

These are the proverbs of King Solomon of Israel, David's son: He wrote them to teach his people how to live—how to act in every circumstance, for he wanted them to be understanding, just and fair in everything they did. "I want to make the simple-minded wise!" he said. "I want to warn young men about some problems they will face. I want those already wise to become the wiser and become leaders by exploring the depths of meaning in these nuggets of truth."

JANUARY 2

Jesus Is Born in Bethlehem/ Matthew 1:18–25

These are the facts concerning the birth of Jesus Christ: His mother, Mary, was engaged to be married to Joseph. But while she was still a virgin she became pregnant by the Holy Spirit. 19Then Joseph, her fiancé, being a man of stern principle, decided to break the engagement but to do it quietly, as he didn't want to publicly disgrace her.

20As he lay awake considering this, he fell into a dream, and saw an angel standing beside him. "Joseph, son of David," the angel said, "don't hesitate to take Mary as your wife! For the child within her has been conceived by the Holy Spirit. 21And she will have a Son, and you shall name him Jesus (meaning 'Savior'), for he will save his people from their sins. 22This will fulfill God's message through his prophets—

> 23*Listen! The virgin shall conceive a child!* She shall give birth to a Son, and he shall be called "Emmanuel" (meaning "God is with us").' "

24When Joseph awoke, he did as the angel commanded, and brought Mary home to be his wife, 25but she remained a virgin until her Son was born; and Joseph named him "Jesus."

A THOUGHT: *Why is the Virgin Birth so important to the Christian faith? In order to be the perfect sacrifice for sin, Jesus Christ had to be free from the sinful nature passed on from Adam to all other human beings. Because he was born of a woman, he was a human being; but because he was the Son of God, he was born without any trace of human sin. He was both fully human and fully divine.*

Because Jesus lived as a man, we know that he fully understands our experiences and struggles. Because he is God, he has the power and authority to deliver us from sin. We can tell him all our thoughts, feelings, and needs. He has been where we are now, and he has the ability to help.

Paul's Desire to Visit the Church in Rome/ Romans 1:8–15

Let me say first of all that wherever I go I hear you being talked about! For your faith in God is becoming known around the world. How I thank God through Jesus Christ for this good report, and for each one of you. 9God knows how often I pray for you. Day and night I bring you and your needs in prayer to the one I serve with all my might, telling others the Good News about his Son.

10And one of the things I keep on praying for is the opportunity, God willing, to come at last to see you and, if possible, that I will have a safe trip. 11,12For I long to visit you so that I can impart to you the faith that will help your church grow strong in the Lord. Then, too, I need your help, for I want not only to share my faith with you but to be encouraged by yours: Each of us will be a blessing to the other.

13I want you to know, dear brothers, that I planned to come many times before (but was prevented) so that I could work among you and see good results, just as I have among the other Gentile churches. 14For I owe a great debt to you and to everyone else, both to civilized people and uncivilized alike; yes, to the educated and uneducated alike. 15So, to the fullest extent of my ability, I am ready to come also to you in Rome to preach God's Good News.

A THOUGHT: *When you pray continually about a concern, don't be surprised at how God answers. Paul prayed to visit Rome so he could teach the Christians there. When he finally arrived in Rome, it was as a prisoner. Paul prayed for a safe trip, and he did arrive safely—after being arrested, slapped in the face, shipwrecked, and, among other things, bitten by a poisonous snake. God's ways of answering our prayers are often far from what we expect. When you pray, expect God to answer—although sometimes in ways you do not expect.*

Proverbs for Today/ 1:7–9

How does a man become wise? The first step is to trust and reverence the Lord! Only fools refuse to be taught. Listen to your father and mother. What you learn from them will stand you in good stead; it will gain you many honors.

JANUARY 3

Visitors from Eastern Lands/ Matthew 2:1–12

Jesus was born in the town of Bethlehem, in Judea, during the reign of King Herod.

At about that time some astrologers from eastern lands arrived in Jerusalem, asking, 2"Where is the newborn King of the Jews? for we have seen his star in far-off eastern lands, and have come to worship him."

3King Herod was deeply disturbed by their question, and all Jerusalem was filled with rumors. 4He called a meeting of the Jewish religious leaders.

"Did the prophets tell us where the Messiah would be born?" he asked.

5"Yes, in Bethlehem," they said, "for this is what the prophet Micah wrote:

⁶'O little town of Bethlehem, you are not just an unimportant Judean village, for a Governor shall rise from you to rule my people Israel.' "

⁷Then Herod sent a private message to the astrologers, asking them to come to see him; at this meeting he found out from them the exact time when they first saw the star. Then he told them, ⁸"Go to Bethlehem and search for the child. And when you find him, come back and tell me so that I can go and worship him too!"

⁹After this interview the astrologers started out again. And look! The star appeared to them again, standing over Bethlehem. ¹⁰Their joy knew no bounds!

¹¹Entering the house where the baby and Mary his mother were, they threw themselves down before him, worshiping. Then they opened their presents and gave him gold, frankincense and myrrh. ¹²But when they returned to their own land, they didn't go through Jerusalem to report to Herod, for God had warned them in a dream to go home another way.

A THOUGHT: *The astrologers traveled thousands of miles to see the King of the Jews. When they finally found him, they responded with joy, worship, and gifts. The astrologers worshiped Jesus for who he was. This is the essence of true worship—honoring Christ for who he is and being willing to give him what is valuable to you. How different from the approach people often take today. We expect God to come looking for us, to explain himself, prove who he is, and give us gifts. But those who are wise still seek and worship Jesus today, not for what they can get, but for who he is. Worship God because he is the perfect, just, and almighty Creator of the universe, worthy of the best you have to give.*

Paul Declares the Power of the Gospel/ Romans 1:16–19

For I am not ashamed of this Good News about Christ. It is God's powerful method of bringing all who believe it to heaven. This message was preached first to the Jews alone, but now everyone is invited to come to God in this same way. ¹⁷This Good News tells us that God makes us ready for heaven—makes us right in God's sight—when we put our faith and trust in Christ to save us. This is accomplished from start to finish by faith. As the Scripture says it, "The man who finds life will find it through trusting God."

¹⁸But God shows his anger from heaven against all sinful, evil men who push away the truth from them. ¹⁹For the truth about God is known to them instinctively; God has put this knowledge in their hearts.

A THOUGHT: *Paul was not ashamed, because his message was Good News. It was powerful, it was for everyone, and it was part of God's revealed plan. When you are tempted to be ashamed, remember what the Good News is all about. If you focus on God and on what God is doing in the world rather than on your own inadequacy, your embarrassment will soon disappear.*

Proverbs for Today/ 1:10–19

If young toughs tell you, "Come and join us"—turn your back on them! "We'll hide and rob and kill," they say. "Good or bad, we'll treat them all alike. And the loot we'll get! All kinds of stuff! Come on, throw in your lot with us; we'll split with you in equal shares." Don't do it, son! Stay far from men like that, for crime is their way of life, and murder is their specialty. When a bird sees a trap being set, it stays away, but not these men; they trap themselves! They lay a booby trap for their own lives. Such is the fate of all who live by violence and murder. They will die a violent death.

JANUARY 4

Mary and Joseph Flee to Egypt/ Matthew 2:13–23

After the astrologers were gone, an angel of the Lord appeared to Joseph in a dream. "Get up and flee to Egypt with the baby and his mother," the angel said, "and stay there until I tell you to return, for King Herod is going to try to kill the child." ¹⁴That same night he left for Egypt with Mary and the baby, ¹⁵and stayed there until King Herod's death. This fulfilled the prophet's prediction,

"I have called my Son from Egypt."

¹⁶Herod was furious when he learned that the astrologers had disobeyed him. Sending soldiers to Bethlehem, he ordered them to kill every baby boy two years old and

under, both in the town and on the nearby farms, for
the astrologers had told him the star first appeared to
them two years before. 17This brutal action of Herod's
fulfilled the prophecy of Jeremiah,

18"Screams of anguish come from Ramah,
Weeping unrestrained;
Rachel weeping for her children,
Uncomforted—
For they are dead."

19When Herod died, an angel of the Lord appeared in
a dream to Joseph in Egypt, and told him, 20"Get up and
take the baby and his mother back to Israel, for those
who were trying to kill the child are dead."

21So he returned immediately to Israel with Jesus and
his mother. 22But on the way he was frightened to learn
that the new king was Herod's son, Archelaus. Then, in
another dream, he was warned not to go to Judea, so
they went to Galilee instead, 23and lived in Nazareth. This
fulfilled the prediction of the prophets concerning the Messiah,

"He shall be called a Nazarene."

A THOUGHT: *Herod was afraid that this newborn king would one
day take his throne. He completely misunderstood the reason for
Christ's coming. Jesus didn't want Herod's throne, he wanted to
be king of Herod's life. He wanted to give him eternal life, not
take away his present life. Today people are often afraid that Christ
wants to take things away when, in reality, he wants to give them
real freedom, peace, and joy.*

The Depravity of Human Beings/ Romans 1:20–32

Since earliest times men have seen the earth and sky
and all God made, and have known of his existence and
great eternal power. So they will have no excuse [when
they stand before God at Judgment Day].

21Yes, they knew about him all right, but they wouldn't
admit it or worship him or even thank him for all his
daily care. And after awhile they began to think up silly
ideas of what God was like and what he wanted them to
do. The result was that their foolish minds became dark
and confused. 22Claiming themselves to be wise without
God, they became utter fools instead. 23And then, instead

of worshiping the glorious, ever-living God, they took wood and stone and made idols for themselves, carving them to look like mere birds and animals and snakes and puny men.

24So God let them go ahead into every sort of sex sin, and do whatever they wanted to—yes, vile and sinful things with each other's bodies. 25Instead of believing what they knew was the truth about God, they deliberately chose to believe lies. So they prayed to the things God made, but wouldn't obey the blessed God who made these things.

26That is why God let go of them and let them do all these evil things, so that even their women turned against God's natural plan for them and indulged in sex sin with each other. 27And the men, instead of having a normal sex relationship with women, burned with lust for each other, men doing shameful things with other men and, as a result, getting paid within their own souls with the penalty they so richly deserved.

28So it was that when they gave God up and would not even acknowledge him, God gave them up to doing everything their evil minds could think of. 29Their lives became full of every kind of wickedness and sin, of greed and hate, envy, murder, fighting, lying, bitterness, and gossip.

30They were backbiters, haters of God, insolent, proud braggarts, always thinking of new ways of sinning and continually being disobedient to their parents. 31They tried to misunderstand, broke their promises, and were heart-less—without pity. 32They were fully aware of God's death penalty for these crimes, yet they went right ahead and did them anyway, and encouraged others to do them, too.

A THOUGHT: *Paul clearly portrays the inevitable downward spiral into sin. First people reject God; next they make up their own ideas of what a god should be and do; then they fall into sin— sexual sin, greed, hatred, envy, murder, fighting, lying, bitterness, gossip. Finally they grow to hate God and encourage others to do so. God does not cause this steady progression toward evil. Rather, when people reject him, he allows them to live as they choose. Once caught in the downward spiral, no one can pull himself out. Sinners must trust Christ alone to put them on the path of escape.*

Proverbs for Today/ 1:20–23

Wisdom shouts in the streets for a hearing. She calls out to the crowds along Main Street, and to the judges in their courts, and to everyone in all the land: "You simpletons!" she cries. "How long will you go on being fools? How long will you scoff at wisdom and fight the facts? Come here and listen to me! I'll pour out the spirit of wisdom upon you, and make you wise.

JANUARY 5

John the Baptist Preaches Repentance/
Matthew 3:1–12

While Mary, Joseph, and Jesus were living in Nazareth, John the Baptist began preaching out in the Judean wilderness. His constant theme was, 2"Turn from your sins . . . turn to God . . . for the Kingdom of Heaven is coming soon." 3Isaiah the prophet had told about John's ministry centuries before! He had written,

> "I hear a shout from the wilderness, 'Prepare a road for the Lord—straighten out the path where he will walk.' "

4John's clothing was woven from camel's hair and he wore a leather belt; his food was locusts and wild honey. 5People from Jerusalem and from all over the Jordan Valley, and, in fact, from every section of Judea went out to the wilderness to hear him preach, 6and when they confessed their sins, he baptized them in the Jordan River.

7 But when he saw many Pharisees and Sadducees coming to be baptized, he denounced them.

"You sons of snakes!" he warned. "Who said that you could escape the coming wrath of God? 8Before being baptized, prove that you have turned from sin by doing worthy deeds. 9Don't try to get by as you are, thinking, 'We are safe for we are Jews—descendants of Abraham.'

That proves nothing. God can change these stones here into Jews!

10"And even now the axe of God's judgment is poised to chop down every unproductive tree. They will be chopped and burned.

11"With water I baptize those who repent of their sins; but someone else is coming, far greater than I am, so great that I am not worthy to carry his shoes! He shall baptize you with the Holy Spirit and with fire. 12He will separate the chaff from the grain, burning the chaff with never-ending fire, and storing away the grain."

A THOUGHT: *John the Baptist suddenly bursts onto the scene here in Matthew's Gospel (an event chronologically about 30 years after the birth narratives in chapter two). His theme was "turn from your sins; . . . turn to God." He meant that we must do an about–face—a 180–degree turn—from the kind of self–centeredness that leads to wrong actions such as lying, cheating, stealing, gossiping, revenge, abuse, and sexual immorality. Instead, we must follow God's prescribed way of living found in his Word. The first step in turning to God is to admit your sin, as John urged. Then God will receive you and help you live the way he wants you to. Remember that only God can get rid of sin. He doesn't expect us to clean up our lives before we come to him.*

God's Judgment on Sin/ Romans 2:1–16

"Well," you may be saying, "what terrible people you have been talking about!" But wait a minute! You are just as bad. When you say they are wicked and should be punished, you are talking about yourselves, for you do these very same things. 2And we know that God, in justice, will punish anyone who does such things as these. 3Do you think that God will judge and condemn others for doing them and overlook you when you do them, too? 4Don't you realize how patient he is being with you? Or don't you care? Can't you see that he has been waiting all this time without punishing you, to give you time to turn from your sin? His kindness is meant to lead you to repentance.

5But no, you won't listen; and so you are saving up terrible punishment for yourselves because of your stubbornness in refusing to turn from your sin; for there is going to come a day of wrath when God will be the just Judge of all the world. 6He will give each one whatever his deeds deserve. 7He will give eternal life to those who patiently do the will of God, seeking for the unseen glory and honor and eternal life that he offers. 8But he will terribly punish those who fight against the truth of God and walk in evil ways—God's anger will be poured out upon them. 9There will be sorrow and suffering for Jews and Gentiles alike who keep on sinning. 10But there will be glory and honor and peace from God for all who obey him, whether they are Jews or Gentiles. 11For God treats everyone the same.

12-15He will punish sin wherever it is found. He will punish the heathen when they sin, even though they never had God's written laws, for down in their hearts they know right from wrong. God's laws are written within them; their own conscience accuses them, or sometimes excuses them. And God will punish the Jews for sinning because they have his written laws but don't obey them. They know what is right but don't do it. After all, salvation is not given to those who know what to do, unless they do it. 16The day will surely come when at God's command Jesus Christ will judge the secret lives of everyone, their inmost thoughts and motives; this is all part of God's great plan which I proclaim.

A THOUGHT: *Whenever we find ourselves feeling justifiably angry about some sin we have observed in our community, we should be careful. We need to speak out against sin, but we must do so in a spirit of humility. Often the sins we see most clearly in others are the ones that have taken root in us. If we look closely at ourselves, we may find that we are committing the same sin in more socially acceptable forms.*

Proverbs for Today/ 1:24–28

I have called you so often but still you won't come. I have pleaded, but all in vain. For you have spurned my counsel and reproof. Some day you'll be in trouble, and I'll laugh! Mock me, will you?—I'll mock you! When a storm of terror surrounds you, and when you are engulfed by anguish and distress, then I will not answer your cry for help. It will be too late though you search for me ever so anxiously.

John Baptizes Jesus/ Matthew 3:13–17

Then Jesus went from Galilee to the Jordan River to be baptized there by John. 14John didn't want to do it.

"This isn't proper," he said. "I am the one who needs to be baptized by you."

15But Jesus said, "Please do it, for I must do all that is right." So then John baptized him.

16After his baptism, as soon as Jesus came up out of the water, the heavens were opened to him and he saw the Spirit of God coming down in the form of a dove. 17And a voice from heaven said, "This is my beloved Son, and I am wonderfully pleased with him."

A THOUGHT: *Put yourself in John's shoes. Your work is going well, people are taking notice, everything is growing. But you know that the purpose of your work is to prepare the hearts of the people for Jesus. Now Jesus has arrived, and with him, the real test of your integrity. Will you be able to turn your followers over to him? John passed the test by publicly baptizing Jesus. Soon he would say, "He must become greater and greater, and I must become less and less" (John 3:30). Can we, like John, put our egos and profitable work aside in order to point others to Jesus? Are we willing to lose some of our status so that others will benefit?*

Paul's Warning to Jews/ Romans 2:17–29

You Jews think all is well between yourselves and God because he gave his laws to you; you brag that you are his special friends. 18Yes, you know what he wants; you know right from wrong and favor the right because you have been taught his laws from earliest youth. 19You are so sure of the way to God that you could point it out to a blind man. You think of yourselves as beacon lights, directing men who are lost in darkness to God. 20You think that you can guide the simple and teach even children the affairs of God, for you really know his laws, which are full of all knowledge and truth.

21 Yes, you teach others—then why don't you teach yourselves? You tell others not to steal—do *you* steal? 22You say it is wrong to commit adultery—do *you* do it? You say, "Don't pray to idols," and then make money your god instead.

23You are so proud of knowing God's laws, *but you dishonor him by breaking them.* 24No wonder the Scriptures say that the world speaks evil of God because of you.

25Being a Jew is worth something if you obey God's laws; but if you don't, then you are no better off than the heathen. 26And if the heathen obey God's laws, won't God give them all the rights and honors he planned to give the Jews? 27In fact, those heathen will be much better off than you Jews who know so much about God and have his promises but don't obey his laws.

28For you are not real Jews just because you were born of Jewish parents or because you have gone through the Jewish initiation ceremony of circumcision. 29No, a real Jew is anyone whose heart is right with God. For God is not looking for those who cut their bodies in actual body circumcision, but he is looking for those with changed hearts and minds. Whoever has that kind of change in his life will get his praise from God, even if not from you.

A THOUGHT: *Paul explained to the Jews that they needed to judge themselves, not others, by their law. They knew the law so well that they had learned how to excuse their own actions while criticizing others. But the law is more than the "letter"—it is a guideline for living according to God's will, and it is also a reminder that we cannot live righteously without a relationship with God. As Jesus pointed out, even withholding what rightfully belongs to someone else is stealing, and looking on another person with lustful, adulterous intent is adultery. Before we accuse others, we must look at ourselves and see if that sin, in any form, exists within us.*

Proverbs for Today/ 1:29–33

"For you closed your eyes to the facts and did not choose to reverence and trust the Lord, and you turned your back on me, spurning my advice. That is why you must eat the bitter fruit of having your own way, and experience the full terrors of the pathway you have chosen. For you turned away from me—to death; your own complacency will kill you. Fools! But all who listen to me shall live in peace and safety, unafraid."

Satan Tempts Jesus in the Wilderness/
Matthew 4:1–11

Then Jesus was led out into the wilderness by the Holy
Spirit, to be tempted there by Satan. 2For forty days
and forty nights he ate nothing and became very hungry.
3Then Satan tempted him to get food by changing stones
into loaves of bread.

"It will prove you are the Son of God," he said.

4But Jesus told him, "No! For the Scriptures tell us
that bread won't feed men's souls: obedience to every
word of God is what we need."

5Then Satan took him to Jerusalem to the roof of the
Temple. 6"Jump off," he said, "and prove you are the
Son of God; for the Scriptures declare, 'God will send
his angels to keep you from harm,' . . . they will prevent
you from smashing on the rocks below."

7Jesus retorted, "It also says not to put the Lord your
God to a foolish test!"

8Next Satan took him to the peak of a very high mountain
and showed him the nations of the world and all their
glory. 9"I'll give it all to you," he said, "if you will only
kneel and worship me."

10"Get out of here, Satan," Jesus told him. "The Scriptures say, 'Worship only the Lord God. Obey only him.' "

11Then Satan went away, and angels came and cared
for Jesus.

A THOUGHT: *Satan's temptations focused on three areas: (1) physical
desires, (2) possessions and power, and (3) pride. Jesus was tempted
just like we are, but he never once gave in and sinned. He knows
firsthand what we are experiencing, and he is willing and able to
help us in our struggles. When tempted, turn to him for strength.*

The Advantage of Being Jewish/ Romans 3:1–8

Then what's the use of being a Jew? Are there any special
benefits for them from God? Is there any value in the
Jewish circumcision ceremony? 2Yes, being a Jew has many
advantages.

First of all, God trusted them with his laws [so that

they could know and do his will]. ³True, some of them were unfaithful, but just because they broke their promises to God, does that mean God will break his promises? ⁴Of course not! Though everyone else in the world is a liar, God is not. Do you remember what the book of Psalms says about this? That God's words will always prove true and right, no matter who questions them.

⁵"But," some say, "our breaking faith with God is good, our sins serve a good purpose, for people will notice how good God is when they see how bad we are. Is it fair, then, for him to punish us when our sins are helping him?" (That is the way some people talk.) ⁶God forbid! Then what kind of God would he be, to overlook sin? How could he ever condemn anyone? ⁷For he could not judge and condemn me as a sinner if my dishonesty brought him glory by pointing up his honesty in contrast to my lies. ⁸If you follow through with that idea you come to this: the worse we are, the better God likes it! But the damnation of those who say such things is just. Yet some claim that this is what I preach!

A THOUGHT: *What a depressing picture Paul painted! All of us—pagan Gentiles, humanitarians, or religious people—are condemned by our own actions. The law, which God gave to show the way to live, holds up our evil deeds to public view. Is there any hope for us? Yes, says Paul. The law condemns us, it is true, but the law is not the basis of our hope. God himself is our hope. He, in his righteousness and wonderful love, offers us eternal life. We receive our salvation not through law, but through faith in Jesus Christ. We do not—cannot—earn salvation, but we accept it as a gift from our loving heavenly Father.*

Proverbs for Today/ 2:1–5

Every young man who listens to me and obeys my instructions will be given wisdom and good sense. Yes, if you want better insight and discernment, and are searching for them as you would for lost money or hidden treasure, then wisdom will be given you, and knowledge of God himself; you will soon learn the importance of reverence for the Lord and of trusting him.

The Kingdom of Heaven Is Near/ Matthew 4:12–25

When Jesus heard that John had been arrested, he left Judea and returned home to Nazareth in Galilee; but soon he moved to Capernaum, beside the Lake of Galilee, close to Zebulun and Naphtali. ¹⁴This fulfilled Isaiah's prophecy:

> ¹⁵,¹⁶"The land of Zebulun and the land of Naphtali, beside the Lake, and the countryside beyond the Jordan River, and Upper Galilee where so many foreigners live—there the people who sat in darkness have seen a great Light; they sat in the land of death, and the Light broke through upon them."

¹⁷From then on, Jesus began to preach, "Turn from sin, and turn to God, for the Kingdom of Heaven is near."

¹⁸One day as he was walking along the beach beside the Lake of Galilee, he saw two brothers—Simon, also called Peter, and Andrew—out in a boat fishing with a net, for they were commercial fishermen.

¹⁹Jesus called out, "Come along with me and I will show you how to fish for the souls of men!" ²⁰And they left their nets at once and went with him.

²¹A little farther up the beach he saw two other brothers, James and John, sitting in a boat with their father Zebedee, mending their nets; and he called to them to come too. ²²At once they stopped their work and, leaving their father behind, went with him.

²³Jesus traveled all through Galilee teaching in the Jewish synagogues, everywhere preaching the Good News about the Kingdom of Heaven. And he healed every kind of sickness and disease. ²⁴The report of his miracles spread far beyond the borders of Galilee so that sick folk were soon coming to be healed from as far away as Syria. And whatever their illness and pain, or if they were possessed by demons, or were insane, or paralyzed—he healed them all. ²⁵Enormous crowds followed him wherever he went—people from Galilee, and the Ten Cities, and Jerusalem, and from all over Judea, and even from across the Jordan River.

A Thought: *Jesus started his ministry with the very words people had heard John the Baptist say, "Turn from sin and turn to God." The message is the same today as when Jesus and John gave it. Becoming a follower of Christ means turning away from our self-centeredness and "self" control and turning our lives over to Christ's direction and control.*

All People Are Sinners/ Romans 3:9–19

Well, then, are we Jews *better* than others? No, not at all, for we have already shown that all men alike are sinners, whether Jews or Gentiles. 10As the Scriptures say,

"No one is good—no one in all the world is innocent."

11No one has ever really followed God's paths, or even truly wanted to.

12Every one has turned away; all have gone wrong. No one anywhere has kept on doing what is right; not one.

13Their talk is foul and filthy like the stench from an open grave. Their tongues are loaded with lies. Everything they say has in it the sting and poison of deadly snakes.

14Their mouths are full of cursing and bitterness.

15They are quick to kill, hating anyone who disagrees with them.

16Wherever they go they leave misery and trouble behind them, 17and they have never known what it is to feel secure or enjoy God's blessing.

18They care nothing about God nor what he thinks of them.

19So the judgment of God lies very heavily upon the Jews, for they are responsible to keep God's laws instead of doing all these evil things; not one of them has any excuse; in fact, all the world stands hushed and guilty before Almighty God.

A Thought: *Paul uses these Old Testament references to show that humanity in general, in its present sinful condition, is unacceptable before God. Have you ever thought to yourself, "Well, I'm not too bad. I'm a pretty good person"? Look at these verses and see if any of them apply to you. Have you ever lied? Have you ever hurt someone's feelings by your words or tone of voice? Are you bitter toward anyone? Do you become angry with those who strongly disagree with you? In thought, word, and deed, we all stand guilty before God apart from the redemption of Jesus Christ. We must remember that apart from Jesus Christ we are alienated sinners in God's sight. Don't deny that you are a sinner. Instead, allow that knowledge to point you toward Christ.*

Proverbs for Today/ 2:6–15

For the Lord grants wisdom! His every word is a treasure of knowledge and understanding. He grants good sense to the godly—his saints. He is their shield, protecting them and guarding their pathway. He shows how to distinguish right from wrong, how to find the right decision every time. For wisdom and truth will enter the very center of your being, filling your life with joy. You will be given the sense to stay away from evil men who want you to be their partners in crime—men who turn from God's ways to walk down dark and evil paths, and exult in doing wrong, for they thoroughly enjoy their sins. Everything they do is crooked and wrong.

JANUARY 9

The Sermon on the Mount—the Beatitudes/ Matthew 5:1–16

One day as the crowds were gathering, Jesus went up the hillside with his disciples and sat down and taught them there.

3"Humble men are very fortunate!" he told them, "for the Kingdom of Heaven is given to them. 4Those who mourn are fortunate! for they shall be comforted. 5The meek and lowly are fortunate! for the whole wide world belongs to them.

6"Happy are those who long to be just and good, for they shall be completely satisfied. 7Happy are the kind and merciful, for they shall be shown mercy. 8Happy are those whose hearts are pure, for they shall see God. 9Happy are those who strive for peace—they shall be called the sons of God. 10Happy are those who are persecuted because they are good, for the Kingdom of Heaven is theirs.

11"When you are reviled and persecuted and lied about because you are my followers—wonderful! 12Be *happy* about it! Be *very glad!* for a *tremendous reward* awaits you up in heaven. And remember, the ancient prophets were persecuted too.

13"You are the world's seasoning, to make it tolerable. If you lose your flavor, what will happen to the world? And you yourselves will be thrown out and trampled underfoot as worthless. 14 You are the world's light—a city on a hill, glowing in the night for all to see. 15,16Don't hide your light! Let it shine for all; let your good deeds glow for all to see, so that they will praise your heavenly Father.

A THOUGHT: *Matthew 5—7 is called the "Sermon on the Mount" because Jesus gave it on a hillside near Capernaum. This "sermon" probably covered several days of preaching. In it, Jesus proclaimed his attitude toward the law. Position, authority, and money are not important in his Kingdom—what matters is faithful obedience from the heart.*

Jesus begins his sermon with a series of beatitudes which tell us how to be fortunate and happy. Other translations use the word blessed. These words don't mean laughter, pleasure, or earthly prosperity. Jesus turns the world's idea of happiness upside down. To Jesus, happiness means hope and joy, independent of outward circumstances. To find true hope and joy, get closer to God by serving and obeying him.

Salvation Is by Faith in Jesus Christ/ Romans 3:20–31

Now do you see it? No one can ever be made right in God's sight by doing what the law commands. For the more we know of God's laws, the clearer it becomes that we aren't obeying them; his laws serve only to make us see that we are sinners.

21,22But now God has shown us a different way to heaven —not by "being good enough" and trying to keep his laws, but by a new way (though not new, really, for the Scriptures told about it long ago). Now God says he will accept and acquit us—declare us "not guilty"—if we trust Jesus Christ to take away our sins. And we all can be saved in this same way, by coming to Christ, no matter who we are or what we have been like. 23Yes, all have sinned; all fall short of God's glorious ideal; 24yet now God declares us "not guilty" of offending him if we trust in Jesus Christ, who in his kindness freely takes away our sins.

25 For God sent Christ Jesus to take the punishment for our sins and to end all God's anger against us. He

used Christ's blood and our faith as the means of saving us from his wrath. In this way he was being entirely fair, even though he did not punish those who sinned in former times. For he was looking forward to the time when Christ would come and take away those sins. 26And now in these days also he can receive sinners in this same way, because Jesus took away their sins.

But isn't this unfair for God to let criminals go free, and say that they are innocent? No, for he does it on the basis of their trust in Jesus who took away their sins.

27Then what can we boast about doing, to earn our salvation? Nothing at all. Why? Because our acquittal is not based on our good deeds; it is based on what Christ has done and our faith in him. 28So it is that we are saved by faith in Christ and not by the good things we do.

29And does God save only the Jews in this way? No, the Gentiles, too, may come to him in this same manner. 30God treats us all the same; all, whether Jews or Gentiles, are acquitted if they have faith. 31Well then, if we are saved by faith, does this mean that we no longer need obey God's laws? Just the opposite! In fact, only when we trust Jesus can we truly obey him.

A THOUGHT: *After all this bad news about our sinfulness and God's condemnation, Paul now gives the wonderful news. There is a way to be declared not guilty—by trusting Jesus Christ to take away our sins. Trusting means putting our confidence in him to forgive our sins, to make us right with God, and to empower us to live the way he wants us to live. This is God's solution, and it is available to all of us regardless of our background or past behavior.*

Proverbs for Today/ 2:16–22

Only wisdom from the Lord can save a man from the flattery of prostitutes; these girls have abandoned their husbands and flouted the laws of God. Their houses lie along the road to death and hell. The men who enter them are doomed. None of these men will ever be the same again. Follow the steps of the godly instead, and stay on the right path, for only good men enjoy life to the full; evil men lose the good things they might have had, and they themselves shall be destroyed.

JANUARY 10

The Sermon on the Mount—Jesus Has Come to Fulfill the Law/ Matthew 5:17–48

"Don't misunderstand why I have come—it isn't to cancel the laws of Moses and the warnings of the prophets. No, I came to fulfill them, and to make them all come true. 18With all the earnestness I have I say: Every law in the Book will continue until its purpose is achieved. 19And so if anyone breaks the least commandment, and teaches others to, he shall be the least in the Kingdom of Heaven. But those who teach God's laws *and obey them* shall be great in the Kingdom of Heaven.

20"But I warn you—unless your goodness is greater than that of the Pharisees and other Jewish leaders, you can't get into the Kingdom of Heaven at all!

21"Under the laws of Moses the rule was, 'If you murder, you must die.' 22But I have added to that rule, and tell you that if you are only *angry*, even in your own home, you are in danger of judgment! If you call your friend an idiot, you are in danger of being brought before the court. And if you curse him, you are in danger of the fires of hell.

23"So if you are standing before the altar in the Temple, offering a sacrifice to God, and suddenly remember that a friend has something against you, 24 leave your sacrifice there beside the altar and go and apologize and be reconciled to him, and then come and offer your sacrifice to God. 25Come to terms quickly with your enemy before it is too late and he drags you into court and you are thrown into a debtor's cell, 26for you will stay there until you have paid the last penny.

27"The laws of Moses said, 'You shall not commit adultery.' 28But I say: Anyone who even looks at a woman with lust in his eye has already committed adultery with her in his heart. 29So if your eye—even if it is your best eye!—causes you to lust, gouge it out and throw it away. Better for part of you to be destroyed than for all of you to be cast into hell. 30And if your hand—even your right hand—causes you to sin, cut it off and throw it away. Better that than find yourself in hell.

31"The law of Moses says, 'If anyone wants to be rid of his wife, he can divorce her merely by giving her a letter of dismissal.' 32But I say that a man who divorces his wife, except for fornication, causes her to commit adultery if she marries again. And he who marries her commits adultery.

33"Again, the law of Moses says, 'You shall not break your vows to God, but must fulfill them all.' 34But I say: Don't make any vows! And even to say, 'By heavens!' is a sacred vow to God, for the heavens are God's throne. 35And if you say 'By the earth!' it is a sacred vow, for the earth is his footstool. And don't swear 'By Jerusalem!' for Jerusalem is the capital of the great King. 36Don't even swear 'By my head!' for you can't turn one hair white or black. 37Say just a simple 'Yes, I will' or 'No, I won't.' Your word is enough. To strengthen your promise with a vow shows that something is wrong.

38"The law of Moses says, 'If a man gouges out another's eye, he must pay with his own eye. If a tooth gets knocked out, knock out the tooth of the one who did it.' 39But I say: Don't resist violence! If you are slapped on one cheek, turn the other too. 40If you are ordered to court, and your shirt is taken from you, give your coat too. 41If the military demand that you carry their gear for a mile, carry it two. 42Give to those who ask, and don't turn away from those who want to borrow.

43"There is a saying, 'Love your *friends* and hate your enemies.' 44 But I say: Love your *enemies!* Pray for those who *persecute* you! 45In that way you will be acting as true sons of your Father in heaven. For he gives his sunlight to both the evil and the good, and sends rain on the just and on the unjust too. 46If you love only those who love you, what good is that? Even scoundrels do that much. 47If you are friendly only to your friends, how are you different from anyone else? Even the heathen do that. 48But you are to be perfect, even as your Father in heaven is perfect.

A THOUGHT: *The Pharisees were exacting and scrupulous in their attempts to follow the Law. So how could Jesus reasonably call us to a greater righteousness than theirs? The Pharisees' weakness was that they were content to obey the Law outwardly without allowing it to change their hearts (or attitudes). Jesus was saying that his listeners needed a different kind of goodness altogether, not just a more intense version of the Pharisees' goodness. Our goodness must (1) come from what God does in us, not what we can do by ourselves, (2) be God–centered, not self–centered, (3) be based on reverence for God, not the approval of people, and (4) go beyond merely keeping the Law to a loving obedience of the principles behind the Law. We can look pious and still be far from the Kingdom of God. God judges our hearts as well as our deeds, for it is in the heart where our real allegiance lies. Be just as concerned about your attitudes, which people don't see, as your actions, which are seen by all.*

Abraham Was Justified by Faith/ Romans 4:1–12

Abraham was, humanly speaking, the founder of our Jewish nation. What were his experiences concerning this question of being saved by faith? Was it because of his good deeds that God accepted him? If so, then he would have something to boast about. But from God's point of view Abraham had no basis at all for pride. 3For the Scriptures tell us Abraham *believed God,* and that is why God canceled his sins and declared him "not guilty."

4,5But didn't he earn his right to heaven by all the good things he did? No, for being saved is a gift; if a person could earn it by being good, then it wouldn't be free—but it is! It is *given* to those who do *not* work for it. For God declares sinners to be good in his sight if they have faith in Christ to save them from God's wrath.

6King David spoke of this, describing the happiness of an undeserving sinner who is declared "not guilty" by God. 7"Blessed, and to be envied," he said, "are those whose sins are forgiven and put out of sight. 8Yes, what joy there is for anyone whose sins are no longer counted against him by the Lord."

9Now then, the question: Is this blessing given only to those who have faith in Christ but also keep the Jewish laws, or is the blessing also given to those who do not keep the Jewish rules, but only trust in Christ? Well, what about Abraham? We say that he received these blessings through his faith. Was it by faith alone? Or because he also kept the Jewish rules?

10For the answer to that question, answer this one: *When* did God give this blessing to Abraham? It was *before he became a Jew*—before he went through the Jewish initiation ceremony of circumcision.

¹¹It wasn't until later on, *after* God had promised to bless him *because of his faith,* that he was circumcised. The circumcision ceremony was a sign that Abraham already had faith and that God had already accepted him and declared him just and good in his sight—before the ceremony took place. So Abraham is the spiritual father of those who believe and are saved without obeying Jewish laws. We see, then, that those who do not keep these rules are justified by God through faith. ¹²And Abraham is also the spiritual father of those Jews who have been circumcised. They can see from his example that it is not this ceremony that saves them, for Abraham found favor with God by faith alone, *before he was circumcised.*

A THOUGHT: *Some people, when they learn that we are saved through faith, start to worry. "Do I have enough faith?" they wonder, "Is my faith strong enough to save me?" These people miss the point. It is Jesus Christ who saves us, not our feelings or actions, and he is strong enough to save us no matter how weak our faith is. Jesus offers us salvation as a gift, because he loves us, not because we have earned it through our powerful faith. What, then, is the role of faith? Faith is believing and trusting in Jesus Christ, reaching out to accept his wonderful gift of salvation. Faith is effective whether it is great or small, timid or bold—because God loves us.*

Proverbs for Today/ 3:1–6

My son, never forget the things I've taught you. If you want a long and satisfying life, closely follow my instructions. Never tire of loyalty and kindness. Hold these virtues tightly. Write them deep within your heart. If you want favor with both God and man, and a reputation for good judgment and common sense, then trust the Lord completely; don't ever trust yourself. In everything you do, put God first, and he will direct you and crown your efforts with success.

JANUARY 11

The Sermon on the Mount—Religious Hypocrisy/
Matthew 6:1–18

"Take care! Don't do your good deeds publicly, to be admired, for then you will lose the reward from your Father in heaven. 2When you give a gift to a beggar, don't shout about it as the hypocrites do—blowing trumpets in the synagogues and streets to call attention to their acts of charity! I tell you in all earnestness, they have received all the reward they will ever get. 3But when you do a kindness to someone, do it secretly—don't tell your left hand what your right hand is doing. 4And your Father who knows all secrets will reward you.

5"And now about prayer. When you pray, don't be like the hypocrites who pretend piety by praying publicly on street corners and in the synagogues where everyone can see them. Truly, that is all the reward they will ever get. 6But when you pray, go away by yourself, all alone, and shut the door behind you and pray to your Father secretly, and your Father, who knows your secrets, will reward you.

7,8"Don't recite the same prayer over and over as the heathen do, who think prayers are answered only by repeating them again and again. Remember, your Father knows exactly what you need even before you ask him!

9"Pray along these lines: 'Our Father in heaven, we honor your holy name. 10We ask that your kingdom will come now. May your will be done here on earth, just as it is in heaven. 11Give us our food again today, as usual, 12and forgive us our sins, just as we have forgiven those who have sinned against us. 13Don't bring us into temptation, but deliver us from the Evil One. Amen.' 14,15Your heavenly Father will forgive you if you forgive those who sin against you; but if *you* refuse to forgive *them, he* will not forgive *you.*

16"And now about fasting. When you fast, declining your food for a spiritual purpose, don't do it publicly, as the hypocrites do, who try to look wan and disheveled so people will feel sorry for them. Truly, that is the only reward they will ever get. 17But when you fast, put on festive clothing, [18]so that no one will suspect you are hungry, except your Father who knows every secret. And he will reward you.

A THOUGHT: *It's easy to do right for recognition and praise. To insure that our motives are not selfish, we should do our good deeds quietly or in secret, with no thought of reward. Jesus says we should check our motives in three areas: generosity, prayer, and fasting. Those acts should not be self-centered, but God-centered. The reward God promises is not material, and it is never given to those who seek only the reward. Doing something only for ourselves is not a loving sacrifice. With your next good deed, ask, "Would I still do this if no one would ever know I did it?"*

Salvation Is the Free Gift of God/ Romans 4:13–17

It is clear, then, that God's promise to give the whole earth to Abraham and his descendants was not because Abraham obeyed God's laws but because he trusted God to keep his promise. [14]So if you still claim that God's blessings go to those who are "good enough," then you are saying that God's promises to those who have faith are meaningless, and faith is foolish. [15]But the fact of the matter is this: when we try to gain God's blessing and salvation by keeping his laws we always end up under his anger, for we always fail to keep them. The only way we can keep from breaking laws is not to have any to break!

[16]So God's blessings are given to us by faith, as a free gift; we are certain to get them whether or not we follow Jewish customs if we have faith like Abraham's, for Abraham is the father of us all when it comes to these matters of faith. [17]That is what the Scriptures mean when they say that God made Abraham the father of many nations. God will accept all people in every nation who trust God as Abraham did. And this promise is from God himself, who makes the dead live again and speaks of future events with as much certainty as though they were already past.

A THOUGHT: *Paul explains that Abraham was blessed through his faith alone, before he ever heard about the rituals that would become so important to the Jewish people. We too are saved by faith plus nothing. It is not by loving God and doing good that we are saved; neither is it by faith plus love or faith plus good works. Salvation is not a gift that we in any way coerce God into giving us—it is the free gift of his grace. We are saved only through faith in Christ, trusting him to forgive all our sins.*

Proverbs for Today/ 3:7–8

Don't be conceited, sure of your own wisdom. Instead, trust and reverence the Lord, and turn your back on evil; when you do that, then you will be given renewed health and vitality.

JANUARY 12

The Sermon on the Mount—Store Your Treasures in Heaven/ Matthew 6:19–34

"Don't store up treasures here on earth where they can erode away or may be stolen. 20Store them in heaven where they will never lose their value, and are safe from thieves. 21If your profits are in heaven your heart will be there too.

22"If your eye is pure, there will be sunshine in your soul. 23But if your eye is clouded with evil thoughts and desires, you are in deep spiritual darkness. And oh, how deep that darkness can be!

24"You cannot serve two masters: God and money. For you will hate one and love the other, or else the other way around.

25"So my counsel is: Don't worry about *things*—food, drink, and clothes. For you already have life and a body—and they are far more important than what to eat and wear. 26Look at the birds! They don't worry about what to eat—they don't need to sow or reap or store up food—for your heavenly Father feeds them. And you are far more valuable to him than they are. 27Will all your worries add a single moment to your life?

28"And why worry about your clothes? Look at the field lilies! They don't worry about theirs. 29Yet King Solomon in all his glory was not clothed as beautifully as they. 30And if God cares so wonderfully for flowers that are here today and gone tomorrow, won't he more surely care for you, O men of little faith?

31,32"So don't worry at all about having enough food and clothing. Why be like the heathen? For they take pride in all these things and are deeply concerned about them. But your heavenly Father already knows perfectly well that you need them, 33and he will give them to you if you give him first place in your life and live as he wants you to.

34"So don't be anxious about tomorrow. God will take care of your tomorrow too. Live one day at a time.

A THOUGHT: *Jesus says we can have only one master. We live in a materialistic society where many people serve money. People spend all their lives collecting and storing it, only to die and leave it behind. Their desire for money and what it can buy far outweighs their commitment to God and spiritual matters. Whatever you store up, you will spend all your time and energy thinking about. Don't fall into the materialistic trap, because "the love of money is the first step toward all kinds of sin" (1 Timothy 6:10). Can you honestly say that God is your Master, and not money? One test is to ask which one occupies more of your thoughts, time, and efforts.*

Abraham Believed God's Promise/ Romans 4:18–25

So, when God told Abraham that he would give him a son who would have many descendants and become a great nation, Abraham believed God even though such a promise just couldn't come to pass! 19And because his faith was strong, he didn't worry about the fact that he was too old to be a father, at the age of one hundred, and that Sarah his wife, at ninety, was also much too old to have a baby.

20But Abraham never doubted. He believed God, for his faith and trust grew ever stronger, and he praised God for this blessing even before it happened. 21He was completely sure that God was well able to do anything he promised. 22And because of Abraham's faith God forgave his sins and declared him "not guilty."

23Now this wonderful statement—that he was accepted and approved through his faith—wasn't just for Abraham's benefit. 24It was for us, too, assuring us that God will accept us in the same way he accepted Abraham—when we believe the promises of God who brought back Jesus our Lord from the dead. 25He died for our sins and rose again to make us right with God, filling us with God's goodness.

A THOUGHT: *Abraham never doubted that God would fulfill his promise. His life was marked by mistakes, sins, and failures as well as by wisdom and goodness, but he consistently trusted God. His life is an example of faith in action. If he had looked only at his own resources for subduing Canaan and founding a nation, he would have given up in despair. But he looked to God, obeyed him, and waited for God to fulfill his word to him. Abraham died without having seen descendants which were as numerous as the sands of the sea, and yet Abraham died believing in God's promise to him. This is genuine faith—a sincere trust in God in spite of all the circumstances.*

Proverbs for Today/ 3:9–10

Honor the Lord by giving him the first part of all your income, and he will fill your barns with wheat and barley and overflow your wine vats with the finest wines.

JANUARY 13

The Sermon on the Mount—Don't Criticize/ Matthew 7:1–5

"Don't criticize, and then you won't be criticized. 2For others will treat you as you treat them. 3And why worry about a speck in the eye of a brother when you have a board in your own? 4Should you say, 'Friend, let me help you get that speck out of your eye,' when you can't even see because of the board in your own? 5Hypocrite! First get rid of the board. Then you can see to help your brother.

A THOUGHT: *Jesus tells us to examine our own lives instead of criticizing others. The traits that bother us in others are often the habits we dislike in ourselves. Our unbroken bad habits and behavior patterns are the very ones we most want to change in others. Do you find it easy to magnify others' faults while ignoring your own? If you are ready to criticize someone, check to see if you deserve the same criticism. Judge yourself first, and then lovingly forgive and help your neighbor.*

Trials Are a Part of God's Redemptive Purpose/ Romans 5:1–5

So now, since we have been made right in God's sight by faith in his promises, we can have real peace with him because of what Jesus Christ our Lord has done for us. 2For because of our faith, he has brought us into this place of highest privilege where we now stand, and we confidently and joyfully look forward to actually becoming all that God has had in mind for us to be.

3We can rejoice, too, when we run into problems and

trials for we know that they are good for us—they help us learn to be patient. 4And patience develops strength of character in us and helps us trust God more each time we use it until finally our hope and faith are strong and steady. 5Then, when that happens, we are able to hold our heads high no matter what happens and know that all is well, for we know how dearly God loves us, and we feel this warm love everywhere within us because God has given us the Holy Spirit to fill our hearts with his love.

A THOUGHT: *There are two sides to our Christian life this side of heaven. On the one hand, we are complete in Christ (our acceptance with him is secure); on the other hand, we are growing in Christ (we are becoming more and more like him). At the same time we have the status of kings and the duties of slaves. We feel both the presence of Christ and the pressure of sin. We enjoy the peace that comes from being made right with God, but we still face daily problems that help us grow. If we remember these two sides of the Christian life, we will not grow discouraged as we face temptations and problems. Instead, we will learn to depend on the power available to us from Christ, through the Holy Spirit who lives in us.*

Proverbs for Today/ 3:11–12

Young man, do not resent it when God chastens and corrects you, for his punishment is proof of his love. Just as a father punishes a son he delights in to make him better, so the Lord corrects you.

JANUARY 14

The Sermon on the Mount—The Golden Rule/ Matthew 7:6–12

"Don't give holy things to depraved men. Don't give pearls to swine! They will trample the pearls and turn and attack you.

7"Ask, and you will be given what you ask for. Seek, and you will find. Knock, and the door will be opened. 8For everyone who asks, receives. Anyone who seeks, finds. If only you will knock, the door will open. 9If a child asks his father for a loaf of bread, will he be given a stone instead? 10If he asks for fish, will he be given a poisonous snake? Of course not! 11And if you hardhearted, sinful men know how to give good gifts to your children, won't your Father in heaven even more certainly give good gifts to those who ask him for them?

12"Do for others what you want them to do for you. This is the teaching of the laws of Moses in a nutshell.

A THOUGHT: *Jesus tells us to persist in pursuing God. People often give up after a few halfhearted efforts and conclude that God cannot be found. But knowing God takes effort, and Jesus assures us that our efforts will be rewarded. Don't give up in your efforts to seek God. Continue to ask him for more knowledge, patience, wisdom, love, and understanding. He will give them to you.*

God's Mercy Toward Sinners/ Romans 5:6–11

When we were utterly helpless with no way of escape, Christ came at just the right time and died for us sinners who had no use for him. 7Even if we were good, we really wouldn't expect anyone to die for us, though, of course, that might be barely possible. 8 But God showed his great love for us by sending Christ to die for us while we were still sinners. 9And since by his blood he did all this for us as sinners, how much more will he do for us now that he has declared us not guilty? Now he will save us from all of God's wrath to come. 10And since, when we were his enemies, we were brought back to God by the death of his Son, what blessings he must have for us now that we are his friends, and he is living within us!

11Now we rejoice in our wonderful new relationship with God—all because of what our Lord Jesus Christ has done in dying for our sins—making us friends of God.

A THOUGHT: *How does Christ's death make us friends with God? God is holy, and he will not be associated with sin. All people are sinful, and all sin deserves punishment. Instead of punishing us with the death we deserve, however, Christ took our sins upon himself and paid the price for them with his own death—while we were still sinners. Now the way to friendship with God has been opened. Through faith in Christ's work, we become his friends rather than enemies and outcasts.*

Proverbs for Today/ 3:13–15

The man who knows right from wrong and has good judgment and common sense is happier than the man who is immensely rich! For such wisdom is far more valuable than precious jewels. Nothing else compares with it.

The Sermon on the Mount—Enter by the Narrow Way/ Matthew 7:13–29

"Heaven can be entered only through the narrow gate! The highway to hell is broad, and its gate is wide enough for all the multitudes who choose its easy way. 14But the Gateway to Life is small, and the road is narrow, and only a few ever find it.

15"Beware of false teachers who come disguised as harmless sheep, but are wolves and will tear you apart. 16You can detect them by the way they act, just as you can identify a tree by its fruit. You need never confuse grapevines with thorn bushes or figs with thistles. 17Different kinds of fruit trees can quickly be identified by examining their fruit. 18A variety that produces delicious fruit never produces an inedible kind. And a tree producing an inedible kind can't produce what is good. 19So the trees having the inedible fruit are chopped down and thrown on the fire. 20Yes, the way to identify a tree or a person is by the kind of fruit produced.

21"Not all who sound religious are really godly people. They may refer to me as 'Lord,' but still won't get to heaven. For the decisive question is whether they obey my Father in heaven. 22At the Judgment many will tell me, 'Lord, Lord, we told others about you and used your name to cast out demons and to do many other great miracles.' 23But I will reply, 'You have never been mine. Go away, for your deeds are evil.'

24"All who listen to my instructions and follow them are wise, like a man who builds his house on solid rock. 25Though the rain comes in torrents, and the floods rise and the storm winds beat against his house, it won't collapse, for it is built on rock.

26"But those who hear my instructions and ignore them are foolish, like a man who builds his house on sand. 27For when the rains and floods come, and storm winds beat against his house, it will fall with a mighty crash." 28The crowds were amazed at Jesus' sermons, 29for he taught as one who had great authority, and not as their Jewish leaders.

A THOUGHT: *The gateway to heaven is indeed a narrow one. This means there are many ways to live your life, but only one way to live eternally with God. Believing in Jesus is the only way to heaven, because he alone died for our sins and made us right before God. At the Day of Judgment, only our relationship with Christ—our acceptance of him as Savior and our obedience to him—will matter. Many people think that if they are "good" and sound religious, they will be rewarded with eternal life. In reality, faith in Christ is what will count at the Judgment.*

Jesus and Adam/ Romans 5:12–19

When Adam sinned, sin entered the entire human race. His sin spread death throughout all the world, so everything began to grow old and die, for all sinned. 13[We know that it was Adam's sin that caused this] because although, of course, people were sinning from the time of Adam until Moses, God did not in those days judge them guilty of death for breaking his laws—because he had not yet given his laws to them, nor told them what he wanted them to do. 14So when their bodies died it was not for their own sins since they themselves had never disobeyed God's special law against eating the forbidden fruit, as Adam had.

What a contrast between Adam and Christ who was yet to come! 15And what a difference between man's sin and God's forgiveness!

For this one man, Adam, brought death to many through his *sin*. But this one man, Jesus Christ, brought forgiveness to many through God's *mercy*. 16Adam's *one* sin brought the penalty of death to many, while Christ freely takes away *many* sins and gives glorious life instead. 17The sin of this one man, Adam, caused *death to be king over all*, but all who will take God's gift of forgiveness and acquittal are *kings of life* because of this one man, Jesus Christ. 18Yes, Adam's *sin* brought *punishment* to all, but Christ's *righteousness* makes men *right with God*, so that they can live. 19Adam caused many to be sinners because he *disobeyed* God, and Christ caused many to be made acceptable to God because he *obeyed*.

A THOUGHT: *Paul has abundantly shown that keeping the law does not bring salvation. Now he adds that death is the result of Adam's sin and of the sins we all commit, even if they don't resemble Adam's. For thousands of years, Paul reminds his readers, the law had not yet been explicitly given, and yet people died. The law was added to help people see their sinfulness, to show them the seriousness of their offenses, and to drive them to God for mercy and pardon. This was true in Moses' day, and it is still true today. Sin is a profound disparity between who we are and who we were created to be. The law points out our sin and places the responsibility for it squarely on our shoulders, but the law offers no remedy for it. When we're convicted of sin, we must turn to Jesus Christ for healing.*

Proverbs for Today/ 3:16–18

Wisdom gives: a long, good life, riches, honor, pleasure, peace, wisdom is a tree of life to those who eat her fruit; happy is the man who keeps on eating it.

JANUARY 16

Jesus Performs Miracles of Healing/
Matthew 8:1–17

Large crowds followed Jesus as he came down the hillside.

2Look! A leper is approaching. He kneels before him, worshiping. "Sir," the leper pleads, "if you want to, you can heal me."

3Jesus touches the man. "I want to," he says. "Be healed." And instantly the leprosy disappears.

4Then Jesus says to him, "Don't stop to talk to anyone; go right over to the priest to be examined; and take with you the offering required by Moses' law for lepers who are healed—a public testimony of your cure."

5,6When Jesus arrived in Capernaum, a Roman army captain came and pled with him to come to his home and heal his servant boy who was in bed paralyzed and racked with pain.

7"Yes," Jesus said, "I will come and heal him."

8,9Then the officer said, "Sir, I am not worthy to have you in my home; [and it isn't necessary for you to come]. If you will only stand here and say, 'Be healed,' my servant will get well! I know, because I am under the authority of my superior officers and I have authority over my soldiers, and I say to one, 'Go,' and he goes, and to another, 'Come,' and he comes, and to my slave boy, 'Do this or that,' and he does it. And I know you have authority to tell his sickness to go—and it will go!"

10Jesus stood there amazed! Turning to the crowd he said, "I haven't seen faith like this in all the land of Israel! 11And I tell you this, that many Gentiles [like this Roman officer], shall come from all over the world and sit down in the Kingdom of Heaven with Abraham, Isaac, and Jacob. 12And many an Israelite—those for whom the Kingdom was prepared—shall be cast into outer darkness, into the place of weeping and torment."

13Then Jesus said to the Roman officer, "Go on home. What you have believed has happened!" And the boy was healed that same hour!

14When Jesus arrived at Peter's house, Peter's mother-in-law was in bed with a high fever. 15But when Jesus touched her hand, the fever left her; and she got up and prepared a meal for them!

16That evening several demon-possessed people were brought to Jesus; and when he spoke a single word, all the demons fled; and all the sick were healed. 17This fulfilled the prophecy of Isaiah, "He took our sicknesses and bore our diseases."

A THOUGHT: *Leprosy was a feared disease because there was no known cure. In Jesus' day, the word leprosy was used for a variety of similar diseases, and some forms were contagious. If a person contracted the contagious type, a priest declared him a leper and banished him from his home and city. He was sent to live in a community with other lepers until he either got better or died. Yet when the leper begged Jesus to heal him, Jesus reached out and touched him, even though his skin was covered with the dread disease.*

Through a single touch, Jesus heals; when he speaks a single word, demons flee his presence. Jesus has authority over all evil powers and all earthly disease. He also has power and authority to conquer sin. Sickness and evil are consequences of living in a fallen world. But in the future, when God cleanses the earth from sin, there will be no more sickness and death. Jesus' healing miracles were a taste of what will one day be experienced in the Kingdom of God.

Sin's Power over Us Is Broken/ Romans 5:20—6:11

The Ten Commandments were given so that all could see the extent of their failure to obey God's laws. But the more we see our sinfulness, the more we see God's abounding grace forgiving us. 21Before, sin ruled over all men and brought them to death, but now God's kindness rules instead, giving us right standing with God and resulting in eternal life through Jesus Christ our Lord.

6:1Well then, shall we keep on sinning so that God can keep on showing us more and more kindness and forgiveness?

2,3Of course not! Should we keep on sinning when we don't have to? For sin's power over us was broken when we became Christians and were baptized to become a part of Jesus Christ; through his death the power of your sinful nature was shattered. 4Your old sin-loving nature was buried with him by baptism when he died, and when God the Father, with glorious power, brought him back to life again, you were given his wonderful new life to enjoy.

5For you have become a part of him, and so you died with him, so to speak, when he died; and now you share his new life, and shall rise as he did. 6Your old evil desires were nailed to the cross with him; that part of you that loves to sin was crushed and fatally wounded, so that your sin-loving body is no longer under sin's control, no longer needs to be a slave to sin; 7 for when you are deadened to sin you are freed from all its allure and its power over you. 8And since your old sin-loving nature "died" with Christ, we know that you will share his new life. 9Christ rose from the dead and will never die again. Death no longer has any power over him. 10He died once for all to end sin's power, but now he lives forever in unbroken fellowship with God. 11So look upon your old sin nature as dead and unresponsive to sin, and instead be alive to God, alert to him, through Jesus Christ our Lord.

A THOUGHT: *The penalty of sin and its power over our lives died with Christ on the cross. Paul has already stated that through faith in Christ we stand acquitted, "not guilty" before God. Here Paul emphasizes that we need no longer live under sin's power. God does not take us out of the world or make us robots—we will still feel like sinning, and sometimes we will sin. The difference is that before we were saved, we were slaves to our sinful nature, but now we can choose to live for Christ.*

Proverbs for Today/ 3:19–20

The Lord's wisdom founded the earth; his understanding established all the universe and space. The deep fountains of the earth were broken open by his knowledge, and the skies poured down rain.

JANUARY 17

Follow Jesus Now/ Matthew 8:18–22

When Jesus noticed how large the crowd was growing, he instructed his disciples to get ready to cross to the other side of the lake.

19Just then one of the Jewish religious teachers said to him, "Teacher, I will follow you no matter where you go!"

20But Jesus said, "Foxes have dens and birds have nests, but I, the Messiah, have no home of my own—no place to lay my head."

21Another of his disciples said, "Sir, when my father is dead, then I will follow you."

22But Jesus told him, "Follow me *now!* Let those who are spiritually dead care for their own dead."

A THOUGHT: *Following Jesus is not always an easy or comfortable road. It means great cost and sacrifice, without necessarily receiving earthly rewards or having security. Jesus didn't have a place to call home. You may find that following Christ costs you popularity, friendships, leisure time, or treasured habits. But while the costs of following Christ may be high, the value of being Christ's disciple is an investment which lasts for eternity.*

No Longer Allow Sin to Be Your Master/ Romans 6:12–23

Do not let sin control your puny body any longer; do not give in to its sinful desires. 13Do not let any part of your bodies become tools of wickedness, to be used for sinning; but give yourselves completely to God—every part of you—for you are back from death and you want to be tools in the hands of God, to be used for his good purposes. 14Sin need never again be your master, for now you are no longer tied to the law where sin enslaves you, but you are free under God's favor and mercy.

15Does this mean that now we can go ahead and sin and not worry about it? (For our salvation does not depend on keeping the law, but on receiving God's grace!) Of course not!

16Don't you realize that you can choose your own master? You can choose sin (with death) or else obedience (with acquittal). The one to whom you offer yourself—he will take you and be your master and you will be his slave. 17Thank God that though you once chose to be slaves of sin, now you have obeyed with all your heart the teaching to which God has committed you. 18And now you are free from your old master, sin; and you have become slaves to your new master, righteousness.

19I speak this way, using the illustration of slaves and masters, because it is easy to understand: just as you used to be slaves to all kinds of sin, so now you must let yourselves be slaves to all that is right and holy.

20In those days when you were slaves of sin you didn't bother much with goodness. 21And what was the result? Evidently not good, since you are ashamed now even to think about those things you used to do, for all of them end in eternal doom. 22But now you are free from the power of sin and are slaves of God, and his benefits to you include holiness and everlasting life. 23For the wages of sin is death, but the free gift of God is eternal life through Jesus Christ our Lord.

A THOUGHT: *In certain skilled crafts, an apprentice trains under a "master," who shapes and molds his apprentice in the finer points of his craft. As spiritual people, we choose a master and pattern ourselves after him. Without Jesus, we would have no choice—we would have to apprentice ourselves to sin, and the results would be guilt, suffering, and separation from God. Thanks to Jesus, however, we can now choose God as our master. Following him, we can enjoy new life and learn the ways of the Kingdom. We are either following Christ or we are following sin—it is impossible to be neutral. A Christian is not someone who cannot sin or who never sins, but someone who is no longer a slave to sin. He belongs to God, not to sin. Have you apprenticed yourself to God?*

Proverbs for Today/ 3:21-26

Have two goals: wisdom—that is, knowing and doing right—and common sense. Don't let them slip away, for they fill you with living energy, and bring you honor and respect. They keep you safe from defeat and disaster and from stumbling off the trail. With them on guard you can sleep without fear; you need not be afraid of disaster or the plots of wicked men, for the Lord is with you; he protects you.

JANUARY 18

Jesus Demonstrates His Power over Nature and Demons/ Matthew 8:23–34

Then Jesus got into a boat and started across the lake with his disciples. 24Suddenly a terrible storm came up, with waves higher than the boat. But Jesus was asleep.

25The disciples went to him and wakened him, shouting, "Lord, save us! We're sinking!"

26But Jesus answered, "O you men of little faith! Why are you so frightened?" Then he stood up and rebuked the wind and waves, and the storm subsided and all was calm. 27The disciples just sat there, awed! "Who is this," they asked themselves, "that even the winds and the sea obey him?"

28When they arrived on the other side of the lake, in the country of the Gadarenes, two men with demons in them met him. They lived in a cemetery and were so dangerous that no one could go through that area.

29They began screaming at him, "What do you want with us, O Son of God? You have no right to torment us yet."

30A herd of pigs was feeding in the distance, 31so the demons begged, "If you cast us out, send us into that herd of pigs."

32"All right," Jesus told them. "Begone."

And they came out of the men and entered the pigs, and the whole herd rushed over a cliff and drowned in the water below. 33The herdsmen fled to the nearest city with the story of what had happened, 34and the entire population came rushing out to see Jesus, and begged him to go away and leave them alone.

A Thought: *Although the disciples had witnessed many miracles, they panicked in this storm. As experienced sailors, they knew the danger of storms; what they did not know was that Christ could control the forces of nature. The expectations of the disciples had blinded them. They did not realize that Jesus was more than a mere earthly conqueror—he was God in human flesh. Jesus demonstrates his power as Creator by calming this storm. With a word, God brought order to the universe, bringing it into being, and with a word, Jesus brings order to the chaos of this storm. There is nothing beyond his power. Let us worship Jesus as Creator and let us trust him as the sovereign King over all the affairs in the universe, including the situations in our life. We do not need to exclude him from any area of our lives.*

An Illustration from the Law/ Romans 7:1–6

Don't you understand yet, dear Jewish brothers in Christ, that when a person dies the law no longer holds him in its power?

2Let me illustrate: when a woman marries, the law binds her to her husband as long as he is alive. But if he dies, she is no longer bound to him; the laws of marriage no longer apply to her. 3Then she can marry someone else if she wants to. That would be wrong while he was alive, but it is perfectly all right after he dies.

4Your "husband," your master, used to be the Jewish law; but you "died," as it were, with Christ on the cross; and since you are "dead," you are no longer "married to the law," and it has no more control over you. Then you came back to life again when Christ did, and are a new person. And now you are "married," so to speak, to the one who rose from the dead, so that you can produce good fruit, that is, good deeds for God. 5When your old nature was still active, sinful desires were at work within you, making you want to do whatever God said not to, and producing sinful deeds, the rotting fruit of death. 6But now you need no longer worry about the Jewish laws and customs because you "died" while in their captivity, and now you can really serve God; not in the old way, mechanically obeying a set of rules, but in the new way, [with all of your hearts and minds].

A Thought: *Paul uses marriage to illustrate our relationship to the Law. When a spouse dies, the law of marriage no longer applies. Because we have died with Christ, the Law can no longer condemn us. The Law gave us no power to live a righteous life, but the Spirit enables us to produce good fruit for God. As new people living new lives in the power of the Spirit, we are bound to Christ and will serve him with our hearts and minds.*

Proverbs for Today/ 3:27–32

Don't withhold repayment of your debts. Don't say "some other time," if you can pay now. □ Don't plot against your neighbor; he is trusting you. Don't get into needless fights. □ Don't envy violent men. Don't copy their ways. For such men are an abomination to the Lord, but he gives his friendship to the godly.

JANUARY 19

Jesus Heals a Paralytic/ Matthew 9:1–8

So Jesus climbed into a boat and went across the lake to Capernaum, his home town.

2Soon some men brought him a paralyzed boy on a mat. When Jesus saw their faith, he said to the sick boy, "Cheer up, son! For I have forgiven your sins!"

3"Blasphemy! This man is saying he is God!" exclaimed some of the religious leaders to themselves.

4Jesus knew what they were thinking and asked them, "Why are you thinking such evil thoughts? 5,6I, the Messiah, have the authority on earth to forgive sins. But talk is cheap—anybody could say that. So I'll prove it to you by healing this man." Then, turning to the paralyzed man, he commanded, "Pick up your stretcher and go on home, for you are healed."

7And the boy jumped up and left!

8A chill of fear swept through the crowd as they saw this happen right before their eyes. How they praised God for giving such authority to a man!

A THOUGHT: *The first words Jesus said to the paralyzed man were "I have forgiven your sins." Then he healed the man. We must be careful not to concentrate on God's power to heal physical sickness more than on his power to forgive spiritual sickness in the form of sin. Jesus saw that in addition to needing physical health, this man needed spiritual health. Spiritual health comes only from Jesus' healing touch.*

God's Law Reveals Our Sin/ Romans 7:7–14

Well then, am I suggesting that these laws of God are evil? Of course not! No, the law is not sinful but it was the law that showed me my sin. I would never have known the sin in my heart—the evil desires that are hidden there—if the law had not said, "You must not have evil desires in your heart." 8But sin used this law against evil desires by reminding me that such desires are wrong and arousing all kinds of forbidden desires within me! Only if there were no laws to break would there be no sinning.

9That is why I felt fine so long as I did not understand what the law really demanded. But when I learned the truth, I realized that I had broken the law and was a sinner, doomed to die. 10So as far as I was concerned, the good law which was supposed to show me the way of life resulted instead in my being given the death penalty. 11Sin fooled me by taking the good laws of God and using them to make me guilty of death. 12But still, you see, the law itself was wholly right and good.

13But how can that be? Didn't the law cause my doom? How then can it be good? No, it was sin, devilish stuff that it is, that used what was good to bring about my condemnation. So you can see how cunning and deadly and damnable it is. For it uses God's good laws for its own evil purposes.

14The law is good, then, and the trouble is not there but with *me,* because I am sold into slavery with Sin as my owner.

A THOUGHT: *Paul gives three lessons he learned in trying to deal with his old sinful desires. (1) Knowledge is not the answer. Paul felt fine as long as he did not understand what the law demanded. When he learned the truth, he knew he was doomed. (2) Self-determination doesn't succeed. Paul found himself sinning in ways that weren't even attractive to him. (3) Even a profound Christian experience does not instantly stamp out all sin from the believer's life. Becoming like Christ is a lifelong process; Paul likens Christian growth to a strenuous race or fight. Thus, as Paul has been emphasizing since the beginning of his letter to the Romans, no one in the world is innocent; no one deserves to be saved—not the pagan who doesn't know God's laws, not the Christian or Jew who knows them and tries to keep them. All of us must depend totally on the work of Christ for our salvation. We cannot earn it by our good behavior.*

Proverbs for Today/ 3:33–35

The curse of God is on the wicked, but his blessing is on the upright. The Lord mocks at mockers, but helps the humble. The wise are promoted to honor, but fools are promoted to shame!

JANUARY 20

Jesus Calls Matthew to Be His Disciple/
Matthew 9:9–13

As Jesus was going on down the road, he saw a tax collector, Matthew, sitting at a tax collection booth. "Come and be my disciple," Jesus said to him, and Matthew jumped up and went along with him.

10Later, as Jesus and his disciples were eating dinner [at Matthew's house], there were many notorious swindlers there as guests!

11The Pharisees were indignant. "Why does your teacher associate with men like that?"

12"Because people who are well don't need a doctor! It's the sick people who do!" was Jesus' reply. 13Then he added, "Now go away and learn the meaning of this verse of Scripture,

'It isn't your sacrifices and your gifts I want—I want
  you to be merciful.'

For I have come to urge sinners, not the self-righteous, back to God."

A THOUGHT: *When Jesus called Matthew to be one of his disciples, Matthew jumped up and followed, leaving a lucrative career. When God calls you to follow or obey him, do you do it with as much abandon as Matthew? Sometimes the decision to follow Christ requires some difficult or painful choices. Like Matthew, we must decide to leave behind those things that would keep us from following Christ.*

The New and the Old Nature Are at War/
Romans 7:15–25

I don't understand myself at all, for I really want to do what is right, but I can't. I do what I don't want to—what I hate. 16I know perfectly well that what I am doing is wrong, and my bad conscience proves that I agree with these laws I am breaking. 17But I can't help myself, because I'm no longer doing it. It is sin inside me that is stronger than I am that makes me do these evil things.

18I know I am rotten through and through so far as my old sinful nature is concerned. No matter which way I turn I can't make myself do right. I want to but I can't. 19When I want to do good, I don't; and when I try not to do wrong, I do it anyway. 20Now if I am doing what I don't want to, it is plain where the trouble is: sin still has me in its evil grasp.

21It seems to be a fact of life that when I want to do what is right, I inevitably do what is wrong. 22I love to do God's will so far as my new nature is concerned; 23,24,25but there is something else deep within me, in my lower nature, that is at war with my mind and wins the fight and makes me a slave to the sin that is still within me. In my mind I want to be God's willing servant but instead I find myself still enslaved to sin.

So you see how it is: my new life tells me to do right, but the old nature that is still inside me loves to sin. Oh, what a terrible predicament I'm in! Who will free me from my slavery to this deadly lower nature? Thank God! It has been done by Jesus Christ our Lord. He has set me free.

A THOUGHT: *The inward confusion about sin we sometimes feel was as real for Paul as it is for us. From Paul we learn what to do about it. Whenever he felt lost, he would return to the beginning of his spiritual life, remembering that he had already been freed by Jesus Christ. When you feel confused, follow his example: thank God he has given you freedom through Jesus Christ. Let the reality of Christ's power lift you up to real victory over sin.*

Proverbs for Today/ 4:1–6

Young men, listen to me as you would to your father. Listen, and grow wise, for I speak the truth—don't turn away. For I, too, was once a son, tenderly loved by my mother as an only child, and the companion of my father. He told me never to forget his words. "If you follow them," he said, "you will have a long and happy life. *Learn to be wise,*" he said, "*and develop good judgment and common sense! I cannot overemphasize this point."* Cling to wisdom—she will protect you. Love her—she will guard you.

JANUARY 21

The Bridegroom and His Friends/ Matthew 9:14–17

One day the disciples of John the Baptist came to Jesus and asked him, "Why don't your disciples fast as we do and as the Pharisees do?"

15"Should the bridegroom's friends mourn and go without food while he is with them?" Jesus asked. "But the time is coming when I will be taken from them. Time enough then for them to refuse to eat.

16"And who would patch an old garment with unshrunk cloth? For the patch would tear away and make the hole worse. 17And who would use old wineskins to store new wine? For the old skins would burst with the pressure, and the wine would be spilled and skins ruined. Only new wineskins are used to store new wine. That way both are preserved."

A THOUGHT: *Jesus did not come to "patch up" the old religious system of Judaism with its rules and traditions. His purpose was to bring in something new, yet something that had been prophesied for centuries. This new message, the gospel, said that Jesus Christ, God's Son, came to earth to offer all people forgiveness of sins and restoration with God. This new message of faith and love did not fit in the old rigid legalistic system of religion. It needed a fresh start. The message will always remain "new" because it must be accepted and applied in every generation. When we follow Christ, we must be prepared for new ways to live, new ways to look at people, and new ways to serve.*

There Is No Condemnation in Christ/ Romans 8:1–11

So there is now no condemnation awaiting those who belong to Christ Jesus. 2For the power of the life-giving Spirit—and this power is mine through Christ Jesus—has freed me from the vicious circle of sin and death. 3We aren't saved from sin's grasp by knowing the commandments of God, because we can't and don't keep them, but God put into effect a different plan to save us. He sent his own Son in a human body like ours—except that ours are sinful—and destroyed sin's control over us by giving himself as a sacrifice for our sins. 4So now we can obey God's laws if we follow after the Holy Spirit and no longer obey the old evil nature within us.

5Those who let themselves be controlled by their lower natures live only to please themselves, but those who follow after the Holy Spirit find themselves doing those things that please God. 6Following after the Holy Spirit leads to life and peace, but following after the old nature leads to death, 7because the old sinful nature within us is against God. It never did obey God's laws and it never will. 8That's why those who are still under the control of their old sinful selves, bent on following their old evil desires, can never please God.

9But you are not like that. You are controlled by your new nature if you have the Spirit of God living in you. (And remember that if anyone doesn't have the Spirit of Christ living in him, he is not a Christian at all.) 10Yet, even though Christ lives within you, your body will die because of sin; but your spirit will live, for Christ has pardoned it. 11And if the Spirit of God, who raised up Jesus from the dead, lives in you, he will make your dying bodies live again after you die, by means of this same Holy Spirit living within you.

A THOUGHT: *"Not guilty; let him go free"—what would those words mean to you if you were on death row? The fact is, of course, that the whole human race is on death row, justly condemned for repeatedly breaking God's holy law. Without Jesus we would have no hope at all. But thank God! He has declared us not guilty and has offered us freedom from sin and power to do his will.*

Proverbs for Today/ 4:7–10

Getting wisdom is the most important thing you can do! And with your wisdom, develop common sense and good judgment. If you exalt wisdom, she will exalt you. Hold her fast and she will lead you to great honor; she will place a beautiful crown upon your head. My son, listen to me and do as I say, and you will have a long, good life.

JANUARY 22

Jesus Performs Miracles of Healing/ Matthew 9:18–26

As Jesus was saying this, the rabbi of the local synagogue came and worshiped him. "My little daughter has just died," he said, "but you can bring her back to life again if you will only come and touch her."

19As Jesus and the disciples were going to the rabbi's home, 20a woman who had been sick for twelve years with internal bleeding came up behind him and touched a tassel of his robe, 21for she thought, "If I only touch him, I will be healed."

22Jesus turned around and spoke to her. "Daughter," he said, "all is well! Your faith has healed you." And the woman was well from that moment.

23When Jesus arrived at the rabbi's home and saw the noisy crowds and heard the funeral music, 24he said, "Get them out, for the little girl isn't dead; she is only sleeping!" Then how they all scoffed and sneered at him!

25When the crowd was finally outside, Jesus went in where the little girl was lying and took her by the hand, and she jumped up and was all right again! 26The report of this wonderful miracle swept the entire countryside.

A THOUGHT: *Like lepers and those who were demon–possessed, this woman was considered unclean. For 12 years, she too had been one of the "untouchables" and had not been able to live a normal life. But Jesus changed that and restored her. Sometimes we are tempted to give up on people or situations which have not changed for many years. God can change what seems unchangeable, giving new life and hope.*

The Life of the Spirit/ Romans 8:12–23

So, dear brothers, you have no obligations whatever to your old sinful nature to do what it begs you to do. 13For if you keep on following it you are lost and will perish, but if through the power of the Holy Spirit you crush it and its evil deeds, you shall live. 14For all who are led by the Spirit of God are sons of God.

15And so we should not be like cringing, fearful slaves, but we should behave like God's very own children, adopted into the bosom of his family, and calling to him, "Father,

Father." 16For his Holy Spirit speaks to us deep in our hearts, and tells us that we really are God's children. 17And since we are his children, we will share his treasures—for all God gives to his Son Jesus is now ours too. But if we are to share his glory, we must also share his suffering.

18Yet what we suffer now is nothing compared to the glory he will give us later. 19For all creation is waiting patiently and hopefully for that future day when God will resurrect his children. 20,21For on that day thorns and thistles, sin, death, and decay—the things that overcame the world against its will at God's command—will all disappear, and the world around us will share in the glorious freedom from sin which God's children enjoy.

22For we know that even the things of nature, like animals and plants, suffer in sickness and death as they await this great event. 23And even we Christians, although we have the Holy Spirit within us as a foretaste of future glory, also groan to be released from pain and suffering. We, too, wait anxiously for that day when God will give us our full rights as his children, including the new bodies he has promised us—bodies that will never be sick again and will never die.

A THOUGHT: *Paul uses adoption to illustrate the believers' new relationship with God. In Roman culture, the adopted person gained all the rights of a legitimate child in his new family. He became a full heir to his new father's estate. Likewise, when a person becomes a Christian, he or she gains all the privileges and responsibilities of a child in God's family. We are the Master's children; we are no longer cringing and fearful slaves. What a privilege! Because we are God's children, we share in great treasures. God has given great gifts: his Son, forgiveness, the Holy Spirit, and eternal life.*

Proverbs for Today/ 4:11–13

I would have you learn this great fact: that a life of doing right is the wisest life there is. If you live that kind of life, you'll not limp or stumble as you run. Carry out my instructions; don't forget them, for they will lead you to real living.

JANUARY 23

Jesus Gives Sight to the Blind and Casts Out Demons/ Matthew 9:27–38

As Jesus was leaving her home, two blind men followed along behind, shouting, "O Son of King David, have mercy on us."

28They went right into the house where he was staying, and Jesus asked them, "Do you believe I can make you see?"

"Yes, Lord," they told him, "we do."

29Then he touched their eyes and said, "Because of your faith it will happen."

30And suddenly they could see! Jesus sternly warned them not to tell anyone about it, 31but instead they spread his fame all over the town.

32Leaving that place, Jesus met a man who couldn't speak because a demon was inside him. 33So Jesus cast out the demon, and instantly the man could talk. How the crowds marveled! "Never in all our lives have we seen anything like this," they exclaimed.

34But the Pharisees said, "The reason he can cast out demons is that he is demon-possessed himself—possessed by Satan, the demon king!"

35Jesus traveled around through all the cities and villages of that area, teaching in the Jewish synagogues and announcing the Good News about the Kingdom. And wherever he went he healed people of every sort of illness. 36And what pity he felt for the crowds that came, because their problems were so great and they didn't know what to do or where to go for help. They were like sheep without a shepherd.

37"The harvest is so great, and the workers are so few," he told his disciples. 38"So pray to the one in charge of the harvesting, and ask him to recruit more workers for his harvest fields."

A Thought: *Jesus didn't respond immediately to the pleas of the blind men. He waited to see how earnest they were. Not everyone who says he wants help really wants it badly enough to do something about it. Jesus may have waited and questioned these men to make their desire and faith stronger. If, in your prayers, it seems as if God is too slow in giving his answer, maybe he is testing you as he did the blind men. Do you believe God can help you? Do you really want his help?*

The Holy Spirit Intercedes for Us/ Romans 8:24–32

We are saved by trusting. And trusting means looking forward to getting something we don't yet have—for a man who already has something doesn't need to hope and trust that he will get it. 25But if we must keep trusting God for something that hasn't happened yet, it teaches us to wait patiently and confidently.

26And in the same way—by our faith—the Holy Spirit helps us with our daily problems and in our praying. For we don't even know what we should pray for, nor how to pray as we should; but the Holy Spirit prays for us with such feeling that it cannot be expressed in words. 27And the Father who knows all hearts knows, of course, what the Spirit is saying as he pleads for us in harmony with God's own will. 28And we know that all that happens to us is working for our good if we love God and are fitting into his plans.

29For from the very beginning God decided that those who came to him—and all along he knew who would—should become like his Son, so that his Son would be the First, with many brothers. 30And having chosen us, he called us to come to him; and when we came, he declared us "not guilty," filled us with Christ's goodness, gave us right standing with himself, and promised us his glory.

31What can we ever say to such wonderful things as these? If God is on our side, who can ever be against us? 32Since he did not spare even his own Son for us but gave him up for us all, won't he also surely give us everything else?

A THOUGHT: *Believers are not left to their own resources to cope with problems. Even when you don't have words to pray, the Holy Spirit prays with and for you, and God answers. With God helping you pray, you don't need to be afraid to come before him. Ask the Holy Spirit to plead for you "in harmony with God's own will." Then, when you bring your requests to God, trust that he will always do what is best.*

Proverbs for Today/ 4:14–19

Don't do as the wicked do. Avoid their haunts—turn away, go somewhere else, for evil men can't sleep until they've done their evil deed for the day. They can't rest unless they cause someone to stumble and fall. They eat and drink wickedness and violence! But the good man walks along in the ever-brightening light of God's favor; the dawn gives way to morning splendor, while the evil man gropes and stumbles in the dark.

JANUARY 24

Jesus Commissions the Twelve/ Matthew 10:1–18

Jesus called his twelve disciples to him, and gave them authority to cast out evil spirits and to heal every kind of sickness and disease.

2,3,4Here are the names of his twelve disciples:

Simon (also called Peter),
Andrew (Peter's brother),
James (Zebedee's son),
John (James' brother),
Philip,
Bartholomew,
Thomas,
Matthew (the tax collector),
James (Alphaeus' son),
Thaddaeus,
Simon (a member of "The Zealots," a subversive political party),
Judas Iscariot (the one who betrayed him).

5Jesus sent them out with these instructions: "Don't go to the Gentiles or the Samaritans, 6but only to the people of Israel—God's lost sheep. 7Go and announce to them that the Kingdom of Heaven is near. 8Heal the sick, raise the dead, cure the lepers, and cast out demons. Give as freely as you have received!

9"Don't take any money with you; 10don't even carry a duffle bag with extra clothes and shoes, or even a walking stick; for those you help should feed and care for you. 11Whenever you enter a city or village, search for a godly man and stay in his home until you leave for the next town. 12When you ask permission to stay, be friendly, 13and if it turns out to be a godly home, give it your blessing; if not, keep the blessing. 14Any city or home that doesn't welcome you—shake off the dust of that place from your feet as you leave. 15Truly, the wicked cities of Sodom and Gomorrah will be better off at Judgment Day than they.

16"I am sending you out as sheep among wolves. Be as wary as serpents and harmless as doves. 17But beware! For you will be arrested and tried, and whipped in the synagogues. 18Yes, and you must stand trial before governors and kings for my sake. This will give you the opportunity to tell them about me, yes, to witness to the world.

A Thought: *The list of Jesus' 12 disciples doesn't give us many details—probably because there weren't many impressive details to tell. Jesus called people from all walks of life—fishermen, political activists, tax collectors. He called common people and leaders; rich and poor; educated and uneducated. Today, many people discriminate about who is fit to follow Christ, but this was not the attitude of the Master himself. God can use anyone no matter how insignificant he or she feels. He uses ordinary people to do his extraordinary work.*

Nothing Can Separate Us from the Love of God/ Romans 8:33–39

Who dares accuse us whom God has chosen for his own? Will God? No! He is the one who has forgiven us and given us right standing with himself.

34Who then will condemn us? Will Christ? *No!* For he is the one who died for us and came back to life again for us and is sitting at the place of highest honor next to God, pleading for us there in heaven.

35Who then can ever keep Christ's love from us? When we have trouble or calamity, when we are hunted down or destroyed, is it because he doesn't love us anymore? And if we are hungry, or penniless, or in danger, or threatened with death, has God deserted us?

36No, for the Scriptures tell us that for his sake we must be ready to face death at every moment of the day—we are like sheep awaiting slaughter; 37but despite all this, overwhelming victory is ours through Christ who loved us enough to die for us. 38For I am convinced that nothing can ever separate us from his love. Death can't, and life can't. The angels won't, and all the powers of hell itself cannot keep God's love away. Our fears for today, our worries about tomorrow, 39or where we are—high above the sky, or in the deepest ocean—nothing will ever be able to separate us from the love of God demonstrated by our Lord Jesus Christ when he died for us.

A THOUGHT: *These verses contain one of the most comforting promises in all of Scripture. Believers have always had to face hardships in many forms: persecution, illness, imprisonment, even death. These might cause them to fear that they have been abandoned by Christ. But Paul exclaims that it is impossible to be separated from Christ. His death for us is proof of his unconquerable love. He is constantly present with us. God tells us how great his love is so that we will feel totally secure in him. If we believe these overwhelming assurances, we will not be afraid.*

Proverbs for Today/ 4:20–27

Listen, son of mine, to what I say. Listen carefully. Keep these thoughts ever in mind; let them penetrate deep within your heart, for they will mean real life for you, and radiant health.

Above all else, guard your affections. For they influence everything else in your life. Spurn the careless kiss of a prostitute. Stay far from her. Look straight ahead; don't even turn your head to look. Watch your step. Stick to the path and be safe. Don't sidetrack; pull back your foot from danger.

JANUARY 25

Take Up Your Cross and Follow Jesus/
Matthew 10:19—11:1

"When you are arrested, don't worry about what to say at your trial, for you will be given the right words at the right time. 20For it won't be you doing the talking—it will be the Spirit of your heavenly Father speaking through you!

21"Brother shall betray brother to death, and fathers shall betray their own children. And children shall rise against their parents and cause their deaths. 22Everyone shall hate you because you belong to me. But all of you who endure to the end shall be saved.

23"When you are persecuted in one city, flee to the next! I will return before you have reached them all!

24"A student is not greater than his teacher. A servant is not above his master. 25The student shares his teacher's fate. The servant shares his master's! And since I, the master of the household, have been called 'Satan,' how much more will you! 26But don't be afraid of those who threaten you. For the time is coming when the truth will be revealed: their secret plots will become public information.

27"What I tell you now in the gloom, shout abroad when daybreak comes. What I whisper in your ears, proclaim from the housetops!

28"Don't be afraid of those who can kill only your bodies—but can't touch your souls! Fear only God who can destroy both soul and body in hell. 29Not one sparrow (What do they cost? Two for a penny?) can fall to the ground without your Father knowing it. 30 And the very hairs of your head are all numbered. 31So don't worry! You are more valuable to him than many sparrows.

32"If anyone publicly acknowledges me as his friend, I will openly acknowledge him as my friend before my Father in heaven. 33But if anyone publicly denies me, I will openly deny him before my Father in heaven.

34"Don't imagine that I came to bring peace to the earth! No, rather, a sword. 35I have come to set a man against his father, and a daughter against her mother, and a daughter-in-law against her mother-in-law— 36a man's worst enemies will be right in his own home! 37If you love your father and mother more than you love me, you are not worthy of being mine; or if you love your son or daughter more than me, you are not worthy of being mine. 38If you refuse to take up your cross and follow me, you are not worthy of being mine.

39"If you cling to your life, you will lose it; but if you give it up for me, you will save it.

40"Those who welcome you are welcoming me. And when they welcome me they are welcoming God who sent me. 41If you welcome a prophet because he is a man of God, you will be given the same reward a prophet gets. And if you welcome good and godly men because of their godliness, you will be given a reward like theirs.

42"And if, as my representatives, you give even a cup of cold water to a little child, you will surely be rewarded."

11:1When Jesus had finished giving these instructions to his twelve disciples, he went off preaching in the cities where they were scheduled to go.

A THOUGHT: *Christian commitment may separate friends and loved ones. In saying this, Jesus was not encouraging disobedience to parents or conflict at home. Rather, he was showing that his presence demands a decision. Since some will follow him and some won't, inevitable conflict will arise. As we "take up our cross and follow him," our different values, morals, goals, and purposes inevitably will set us apart from others. We should be totally committed to God and willing to face anything, even suffering and death, for his sake. Don't neglect your family, but don't neglect your higher calling. God should be your first priority.*

Paul's Longing for the Salvation of the Jews/ Romans 9:1–5

Oh, Israel, my people! Oh, my Jewish brothers! How I long for you to come to Christ. My heart is heavy within me and I grieve bitterly day and night because of you. Christ knows and the Holy Spirit knows that it is no mere pretense when I say that I would be willing to be forever damned if that would save you. 4God has given you so much, but still you will not listen to him. He took you as his own special, chosen people and led you along with a bright cloud of glory and told you how very much he wanted to bless you. He gave you his rules for daily life so you would know what he wanted you to do. He let you worship him, and gave you mighty promises. 5Great men of God were your fathers, and Christ himself was one of you, a Jew so far as his human nature is concerned, he who now rules over all things. Praise God forever!

A THOUGHT: *Paul expressed concern for his people Israel by saying he would willingly take their punishment if that could save them. While the only one who can save us is Christ, Paul showed a rare depth of love. Like Jesus, he was willing to sacrifice for others. How concerned are you for those who don't know Christ? Are you willing to sacrifice your time, money, energy, comfort, and safety to see them come to faith in Jesus?*

Proverbs for Today/ 5:1–6

Listen to me, my son! I know what I am saying; *listen!*
Watch yourself, lest you be indiscreet and betray some
vital information. For the lips of a prostitute are as sweet
as honey, and smooth flattery is her stock in trade. But
afterwards only a bitter conscience is left to you, sharp
as a double-edged sword. She leads you down to death
and hell. For she does not know the path to life. She
staggers down a crooked trail, and doesn't even realize
where it leads.

JANUARY 26

Jesus Endorses John the Baptist's Ministry/
Matthew 11:2–19

John the Baptist, who was now in prison, heard about all
the miracles the Messiah was doing, so he sent his disciples
to ask Jesus, 3"Are you really the one we are waiting
for, or shall we keep on looking?"

4Jesus told them, "Go back to John and tell him about
the miracles you've seen me do— 5the blind people I've
healed, and the lame people now walking without help,
and the cured lepers, and the deaf who hear, and the
dead raised to life; and tell him about my preaching the
Good News to the poor. 6Then give him this message,
'Blessed are those who don't doubt me.'"

7When John's disciples had gone, Jesus began talking
about him to the crowds. "When you went out into the
barren wilderness to see John, what did you expect him
to be like? Grass blowing in the wind? 8Or were you
expecting to see a man dressed as a prince in a palace?
9Or a prophet of God? Yes, and he is more than just a
prophet. 10For John is the man mentioned in the Scriptures—a messenger to precede me, to announce my coming, and prepare people to receive me.

11"Truly, of all men ever born, none shines more brightly
than John the Baptist. And yet, even the lesser lights in
the Kingdom of Heaven will be greater than he is! 12And

from the time John the Baptist began preaching and baptizing until now, ardent multitudes have been crowding toward the Kingdom of Heaven, 13for all the laws and prophets looked forward [to the Messiah]. Then John appeared, 14and if you are willing to understand what I mean, he is Elijah, the one the prophets said would come [at the time the Kingdom begins]. 15If ever you were willing to listen, listen now!

16"What shall I say about this nation? These people are like children playing, who say to their little friends, 17'We played wedding and you weren't happy, so we played funeral but you weren't sad.' 18For John the Baptist doesn't even drink wine and often goes without food, and you say, 'He's crazy.' 19And I, the Messiah, feast and drink, and you complain that I am 'a glutton and a drinking man, and hang around with the worst sort of sinners!' But brilliant men like you can justify your every inconsistency!"

A THOUGHT: *As John sat in prison, he began to experience some doubts about whether Jesus really was the Messiah. If John's purpose was to prepare people for the coming Messiah, and if Jesus really was that Messiah, then why was John in prison when he could have been preaching to the crowds, preparing their hearts?*

Jesus answered John's doubts by pointing to his acts of healing the blind, lame, and deaf, curing the lepers, raising the dead, and preaching the Good News about God. With so much evidence, Jesus' identity was obvious. If you sometimes doubt your salvation, the forgiveness of your sins, or God's work in your life, look at the evidence in Scripture and the changes in your life. When you doubt, don't turn away from Christ, turn to him.

God Shows Mercy to Whomever He Wants/ Romans 9:6–18

Well then, has God failed to fulfill his promises to the Jews? No! [For these promises are only to those who are truly Jews.] And not everyone born into a Jewish family is truly a Jew! 7 Just the fact that they come from Abraham doesn't make them truly Abraham's children. For the Scriptures say that the promises apply only to Abraham's son Isaac and Isaac's descendants, though Abraham had other children too. 8This means that not all of Abraham's children are children of God, but only those who believe the promise of salvation which he made to Abraham.

9For God had promised, "Next year I will give you

and Sarah a son." 10-13And years later, when this son, Isaac, was grown up and married, and Rebecca his wife was about to bear him twin children, God told her that Esau, the child born first, would be a servant to Jacob, his twin brother. In the words of the Scripture, "I chose to bless Jacob, but not Esau." And God said this before the children were even born, before they had done anything either good or bad. This proves that God was doing what he had decided from the beginning; it was not because of what the children did but because of what God wanted and chose.

14Was God being unfair? Of course not. 15For God had said to Moses, "If I want to be kind to someone, I will. And I will take pity on anyone I want to." 16And so God's blessings are not given just because someone decides to have them or works hard to get them. They are given because God takes pity on those he wants to.

17Pharaoh, king of Egypt, was an example of this fact. For God told him he had given him the kingdom of Egypt for the very purpose of displaying the awesome power of God against him: so that all the world would hear about God's glorious name. 18 So you see, God is kind to some just because he wants to be, and he makes some refuse to listen.

A THOUGHT: *Was it right for God to choose Jacob, the younger, to be over Esau? Keep in mind the kind of God we worship: he is sovereign; he works for our good in everything; he is trustworthy; he will save all who believe in him. When we understand these qualities of God, we know his choices are good even if we don't understand all his reasons. Besides, if we wanted what was our due, we would deserve death for our sins; it is not "fair" for God to punish Christ in our place. But would you think of asking God to take back his offer of salvation because you don't deserve it?*

Proverbs for Today/ 5:7–14

Young men, listen to me, and never forget what I'm about to say: *Run from her! Don't go near her house,* lest you fall to her temptation and lose your honor, and give the remainder of your life to the cruel and merciless; lest strangers obtain your wealth, and you become a slave of foreigners. Lest afterwards you groan in anguish and in shame, when syphilis consumes your body, and you say,

"Oh, if only I had listened! If only I had not demanded my own way! Oh, why wouldn't I take advice? Why was I so stupid? For now I must face public disgrace."

JANUARY 27

Jesus Denounces Unrepentant Cities/
Matthew 11:20–30

Then Jesus began to pour out his denunciations against the cities where he had done most of his miracles, because they hadn't turned to God.

21"Woe to you, Chorazin, and woe to you, Bethsaida! For if the miracles I did in your streets had been done in wicked Tyre and Sidon their people would have repented long ago in shame and humility. 22Truly, Tyre and Sidon will be better off on the Judgment Day than you! 23And Capernaum, though highly honored, shall go down to hell! For if the marvelous miracles I did in you had been done in Sodom, it would still be here today. 24Truly, Sodom will be better off at the Judgment Day than you."

25And Jesus prayed this prayer: "O Father, Lord of heaven and earth, thank you for hiding the truth from those who think themselves so wise, and for revealing it to little children. 26Yes, Father, for it pleased you to do it this way! . . .

27"Everything has been entrusted to me by my Father. Only the Father knows the Son, and the Father is known only by the Son and by those to whom the Son reveals him. 28Come to me and I will give you rest—all of you who work so hard beneath a heavy yoke. 29,30Wear my yoke—for it fits perfectly—and let me teach you; for I am gentle and humble, and you shall find rest for your souls; for I give you only light burdens."

A THOUGHT: *A yoke is a heavy wooden harness that fits onto one or more oxen. It is attached to a piece of equipment the oxen are to pull. When an ox wears a yoke, it means that the animal is going to have a long day of hard work. The "heavy yoke" Jesus mentioned here can mean (1) the burden of sin, (2) the burden of the law (the excessive demands of the religious leaders), (3) government oppression, or (4) weariness in the search for God.*

Jesus frees people from all these burdens. The rest Jesus promises is love, healing, and peace with God, not the end of all effort. A relationship with God changes our meaningless toil into spiritual productivity and purpose.

God's Decisions Are Just and Merciful/ Romans 9:19–26

Well then, why does God blame them for not listening? Haven't they done what he made them do?

20No, don't say that. Who are you to criticize God? Should the thing made say to the one who made it, "Why have you made me like this?" 21When a man makes a jar out of clay, doesn't he have a right to use the same lump of clay to make one jar beautiful, to be used for holding flowers, and another to throw garbage into? 22Does not God have a perfect right to show his fury and power against those who are fit only for destruction, those he has been patient with for all this time? 23, 24And he has a right to take others such as ourselves, who have been made for pouring the riches of his glory into, whether we are Jews or Gentiles, and to be kind to us so that everyone can see how very great his glory is.

25Remember what the prophecy of Hosea says? There God says that he will find other children for himself (who are not from his Jewish family) and will love them, though no one had ever loved them before. 26And the heathen, of whom it once was said, "You are not my people," shall be called "sons of the Living God."

A Thought: *Paul is not saying that some of us are worth more than others, but simply that the Creator has control over the created object. The created object, therefore, has no right to demand anything from its Creator—its very existence depends on him. Keeping this perspective in mind removes any temptation to have pride in personal achievement.*

Proverbs for Today/ 5:15–21

Drink from your own well, my son—be faithful and true to your wife. Why should you beget children with women of the street? Why share your children with those outside your home? Be happy, yes, rejoice in the wife of your youth. Let her breasts and tender embrace satisfy you. Let her love alone fill you with delight. Why delight yourself with prostitutes, embracing what isn't yours? *For God is closely watching you,* and he weighs carefully everything you do.

JANUARY 28

Jesus Teaches about the Sabbath/ Matthew 12:1–21

About that time, Jesus was walking one day through some grainfields with his disciples. It was on the Sabbath, the Jewish day of worship, and his disciples were hungry; so they began breaking off heads of wheat and eating the grain.

2But some Pharisees saw them do it and protested, "Your disciples are breaking the law. They are harvesting on the Sabbath."

3But Jesus said to them, "Haven't you ever read what King David did when he and his friends were hungry? 4He went into the Temple and they ate the special bread permitted to the priests alone. That was breaking the law too. 5And haven't you ever read in the law of Moses how the priests on duty in the Temple may work on the Sabbath? 6And truly, one is here who is greater than the Temple! 7But if you had known the meaning of this Scripture verse, 'I want you to be merciful more than I want your offerings,' you would not have condemned those who aren't guilty! 8For I, the Messiah, am master even of the Sabbath."

9Then he went over to the synagogue, 10and noticed there a man with a deformed hand. The Pharisees asked Jesus, "Is it legal to work by healing on the Sabbath day?" (They were, of course, hoping he would say "Yes," so they could arrest him!) 11This was his answer: "If you had just one sheep, and it fell into a well on the Sabbath, would you work to rescue it that day? Of course you would. 12And how much more valuable is a person than a sheep! Yes, it is right to do good on the Sabbath." 13Then he said to the man, "Stretch out your arm." And as he did, his hand became normal, just like the other one!

14Then the Pharisees called a meeting to plot Jesus' arrest and death.

15But he knew what they were planning, and left the synagogue, with many following him. He healed all the sick among them, 16but he cautioned them against spreading the news about his miracles. 17This fulfilled the prophecy of Isaiah concerning him:

18"Look at my Servant.
See my Chosen One.
He is my Beloved, in whom my soul delights.
I will put my Spirit upon him,
And he will judge the nations.
19He does not fight nor shout;
He does not raise his voice!
20He does not crush the weak,
Or quench the smallest hope;
He will end all conflict with his final victory,
21And his name shall be the hope
Of all the world."

A THOUGHT: *The Ten Commandments prohibit work on the Sabbath. That was the letter of the Law. But because the purpose of the Sabbath is to rest and to worship God, the priests were allowed to work by performing sacrifices and conducting worship services. This "Sabbath work" was serving and worshiping God. Jesus always emphasized the intent of the Law, the meaning behind the letter. The Pharisees had lost the spirit of the Law and rigidly demanded that the letter (and their interpretation of it) be obeyed.*

As they pointed to the man with the deformed hand, the Pharisees tried to trick Jesus by asking him if it was legal to work by healing on the Sabbath. Their Sabbath rules said that people could be helped on the Sabbath only if their lives were in danger. Jesus healed on the Sabbath several times, and none of those healings could be classed as emergencies. If Jesus had waited until another day, he would have been submitting to the Pharisees' authority, showing that their petty rules were equal to God's Law. If he healed the man, the Pharisees could claim that because he broke their rules, his power was not from God. But Jesus made it clear to all those watching how ridiculous and petty their rules were. God is a God of people, not rules. The best time to reach out to someone is when they need help.

The Rock of Stumbling/ Romans 9:27–33

Isaiah the prophet cried out concerning the Jews that though there would be millions of them, only a small number would ever be saved. 28"For the Lord will execute his sentence upon the earth, quickly ending his dealings, justly cutting them short."

29And Isaiah says in another place that except for God's mercy all the Jews would be destroyed—all of them—just as everyone in the cities of Sodom and Gomorrah perished.

30Well then, what shall we say about these things? Just this, that God has given the Gentiles the opportunity to be acquitted by faith, even though they had not been really seeking God. 31But the Jews, who tried so hard to get right with God by keeping his laws, never succeeded. 32Why not? Because they were trying to be saved by keeping the law and being good instead of by depending on faith. They have stumbled over the great stumbling stone. 33God warned them of this in the Scriptures when he said, "I have put a Rock in the path of the Jews, and many will stumble over him (Jesus). Those who believe in him will never be disappointed."

A THOUGHT: *Sometimes we are like these people, trying "hard to get right with God by keeping his laws." We may think church attendance, church work, giving money, and being nice will be enough. After all, we've played by the rules, haven't we? But Paul's words sting—this approach never succeeds. Paul explains that God's plan is not for those who try to earn his favor by being good; it is for those who realize they can never be good enough and so must depend on Christ. Only by putting our faith in what Jesus Christ has done will we be saved. If we do that, we will "never be disappointed."*

Proverbs for Today/ 5:22–23

The wicked man is doomed by his own sins; they are ropes that catch and hold him. He shall die because he will not listen to the truth; he has let himself be led away into incredible folly.

The Kingdom of God Has Come with Power/
Matthew 12:22–37

Then a demon-possessed man—he was both blind and unable to talk—was brought to Jesus, and Jesus healed him so that he could both speak and see. 23The crowd was amazed. "Maybe Jesus is the Messiah!" they exclaimed.

24But when the Pharisees heard about the miracle they said, "He can cast out demons because he is Satan, king of devils."

25Jesus knew their thoughts and replied, "A divided kingdom ends in ruin. A city or home divided against itself cannot stand. 26And if Satan is casting out Satan, he is fighting himself, and destroying his own kingdom. 27And if, as you claim, I am casting out demons by invoking the powers of Satan, then what power do your own people use when they cast them out? Let them answer your accusation! 28But if I am casting out demons by the Spirit of God, then the Kingdom of God has arrived among you. 29One cannot rob Satan's kingdom without first binding Satan. Only then can his demons be cast out! 30Anyone who isn't helping me is harming me.

31,32"Even blasphemy against me or any other sin, can be forgiven—all except one: speaking against the Holy Spirit shall never be forgiven, either in this world or in the world to come.

33"A tree is identified by its fruit. A tree from a select variety produces good fruit; poor varieties don't. 34You brood of snakes! How could evil men like you speak what is good and right? For a man's heart determines his speech. 35A good man's speech reveals the rich treasures within him. An evil-hearted man is filled with venom, and his speech reveals it. 36And I tell you this, that you must give account on Judgment Day for every idle word you speak. 37Your words now reflect your fate then: either you will be justified by them or you will be condemned."

A THOUGHT: *It is impossible to be neutral about Christ. Anyone who is not actively following Jesus has chosen to reject him. Any person who tries to remain neutral in the cosmic struggle of good against evil is choosing to be separated from God, who alone is good. To refuse to follow Christ is to choose to play for Satan's team.*

We Are Reconciled to God through Faith in Christ/ Romans 10:1–12

Dear brothers, the longing of my heart and my prayer is that the Jewish people might be saved. 2I know what enthusiasm they have for the honor of God, but it is misdirected zeal. 3For they don't understand that Christ has died to make them right with God. Instead they are trying to make themselves good enough to gain God's favor by keeping the Jewish laws and customs, but that is not God's way of salvation. 4They don't understand that Christ gives to those who trust in him everything they are trying to get by keeping his laws. He ends all of that.

5For Moses wrote that if a person could be perfectly good and hold out against temptation all his life and never sin once, only then could he be pardoned and saved. 6But the salvation that comes through faith says, "You don't need to search the heavens to find Christ and bring him down to help you," and, 7"You don't need to go among the dead to bring Christ back to life again."

8For salvation that comes from trusting Christ—which is what we preach—is already within easy reach of each of us; in fact, it is as near as our own hearts and mouths. 9For if you tell others with your own mouth that Jesus Christ is your Lord, and believe in your own heart that God has raised him from the dead, you will be saved. 10For it is by believing in his heart that a man becomes right with God; and with his mouth he tells others of his faith, confirming his salvation.

11For the Scriptures tell us that no one who believes in Christ will ever be disappointed. 12Jew and Gentile are the same in this respect: they all have the same Lord who generously gives his riches to all those who ask him for them.

A THOUGHT: *What will happen to the Jewish people who believe in God but not in Christ? Since they believe in the same God, won't they be saved? If that were true, Paul would not have worked so hard and sacrificed so much to teach them about Christ. Since Jesus is the most complete revelation of God, and we cannot fully know God apart from Christ; and since God appointed Jesus to* bring God and man together, we cannot come to God by another path. The Jews, like everyone else, can find salvation only through Jesus Christ. Like Paul, we should wish that all Jews might be saved. We should pray for them and lovingly share the Good News with them.

Proverbs for Today/ 6:1–5

Son, if you endorse a note for someone you hardly know, guaranteeing his debt, you are in serious trouble. You may have trapped yourself by your agreement. Quick! Get out of it if you possibly can! Swallow your pride; don't let embarrassment stand in the way. Go and beg to have your name erased. Don't put it off. Do it now. Don't rest until you do. If you can get out of this trap you have saved yourself like a deer that escapes from a hunter, or a bird from the net.

JANUARY 30

The Sign of Jonah the Prophet/ Matthew 12:38–50

One day some of the Jewish leaders, including some Pharisees, came to Jesus asking him to show them a miracle.

39,40But Jesus replied, "Only an evil, faithless nation would ask for further proof; and none will be given except what happened to Jonah the prophet! For as Jonah was in the great fish for three days and three nights, so I, the Messiah, shall be in the heart of the earth three days and three nights. 41The men of Nineveh shall arise against this nation at the judgment and condemn you. For when Jonah preached to them, they repented and turned to God from all their evil ways. And now a greater than Jonah is here—and you refuse to believe him. 42The Queen of Sheba shall rise against this nation in the judgment, and condemn it; for she came from a distant land to hear the wisdom of Solomon; and now a greater than Solomon is here—and you refuse to believe him.

43,44,45"This evil nation is like a man possessed by a demon. For if the demon leaves, it goes into the deserts for a while, seeking rest but finding none. Then it says, 'I will return to the man I came from.' So it returns and finds the man's heart clean but empty! Then the demon finds seven other spirits more evil than itself, and all enter the man and live in him. And so he is worse off than before."

46,47As Jesus was speaking in a crowded house his mother and brothers were outside, wanting to talk with him. When someone told him they were there, 48he remarked, "Who is my mother? Who are my brothers?" 49He pointed to his disciples. "Look!" he said, "these are my mother and brothers." 50Then he added, "Anyone who obeys my Father in heaven is my brother, sister and mother!"

A THOUGHT: *Jonah was a prophet sent to the Assyrian city of Nineveh. Because Assyria was such a cruel and warlike nation, Jonah tried to run from his assignment and ended up spending three days in the belly of a great fish. When he got out, he grudgingly went to Nineveh, preached God's message, and saw the city repent. By contrast, when Jesus came to his people, they refused to repent. Here he is clearly saying that his resurrection would prove that he is the Messiah. Three days after his death he would come back to life, just as Jonah was given a new chance at life after three days in the fish.*

All Who Believe the Good News Will Be Saved/ Romans 10:13–21

Anyone who calls upon the name of the Lord will be saved.

14But how shall they ask him to save them unless they believe in him? And how can they believe in him if they have never heard about him? And how can they hear about him unless someone tells them? 15And how will anyone go and tell them unless someone sends him? That is what the Scriptures are talking about when they say, "How beautiful are the feet of those who preach the Gospel of peace with God and bring glad tidings of good things." In other words, how welcome are those who come preaching God's Good News!

16But not everyone who hears the Good News has welcomed it, for Isaiah the prophet said, "Lord, who has believed me when I told them?" 17Yet faith comes from listening to this Good News—the Good News about Christ.

18But what about the Jews? Have they heard God's Word? Yes, for it has gone wherever they are; the Good

News has been told to the ends of the earth. 19And did they understand [that God would give his salvation to others if they refused to take it]? Yes, for even back in the time of Moses, God had said that he would make his people jealous and try to wake them up by giving his salvation to the foolish heathen nations. 20And later on Isaiah said boldly that God would be found by people who weren't even looking for him. 21In the meantime, he keeps on reaching out his hands to the Jews, but they keep arguing and refusing to come.

A THOUGHT: *God's great message of salvation must be taken to others, so they can have the chance to respond to the Good News. How will your loved ones and neighbors hear it unless someone tells them? Is God calling you to take a part in making his message known in your community? Think of one person who needs to hear the Good News, and think of something you can do to help him or her hear it. Then bring the Good News to that person.*

Proverbs for Today/ 6:6–11

Take a lesson from the ants, you lazy fellow. Learn from their ways and be wise! For though they have no king to make them work, yet they labor hard all summer, gathering food for the winter. But you—all you do is sleep. When will you wake up? "Let me sleep a little longer!" Sure, just a little more! And as you sleep, poverty creeps upon you like a robber and destroys you; want attacks you in full armor.

JANUARY 31

The Parable of the Soils/ Matthew 13:1–23

Later that same day, Jesus left the house and went down to the shore, 2,3where an immense crowd soon gathered. He got into a boat and taught from it while the people listened on the beach. He used many illustrations such as this one in his sermon:

"A farmer was sowing grain in his fields. 4As he scattered the seed across the ground, some fell beside a path, and the birds came and ate it. 5And some fell on rocky soil where there was little depth of earth; the plants sprang up quickly enough in the shallow soil, 6but the hot sun soon scorched them and they withered and died, for they had so little root. 7Other seeds fell among thorns, and the thorns choked out the tender blades. 8But some fell on good soil, and produced a crop that was thirty, sixty, and even a hundred times as much as he had planted. 9If you have ears, listen!"

10His disciples came and asked him, "Why do you always use these hard-to-understand illustrations?"

11Then he explained to them that only they were permitted to understand about the Kingdom of Heaven, and others were not.

12,13"For to him who has will more be given," he told them, "and he will have great plenty; but from him who has not, even the little he has will be taken away. That is why I use these illustrations, so people will hear and see but not understand.

14"This fulfills the prophecy of Isaiah:

'They hear, but don't understand; they look, but don't see! 15For their hearts are fat and heavy, and their ears are dull, and they have closed their eyes in sleep, 16so they won't see and hear and understand and turn to God again, and let me heal them.'

But blessed are your eyes, for they see; and your ears, for they hear. 17Many a prophet and godly man has longed to see what you have seen, and hear what you have heard, but couldn't.

18"Now here is the explanation of the story I told about the farmer planting grain: 19The hard path where some of the seeds fell represents the heart of a person who hears the Good News about the Kingdom and doesn't understand it; then Satan comes and snatches away the seeds from his heart. 20The shallow, rocky soil represents the heart of a man who hears the message and receives it with real joy, 21but he doesn't have much depth in his life, and the seeds don't root very deeply, and after a while when trouble comes, or persecution begins because of his beliefs, his enthusiasm fades, and he drops out. 22The ground covered with thistles represents a man who hears the message, but the cares of this life and his longing for money choke out God's Word, and he does less and less for God. 23The good ground represents the heart of a man who listens to the message and understands it and goes out and brings thirty, sixty, or even a hundred others into the Kingdom."

A THOUGHT: *Jesus used many illustrations, or parables, when speaking to the crowds. A parable compares something familiar to something unfamiliar. It helps us understand spiritual truth by using everyday objects and relationships. Parables compel the listener to discover truth, while at the same time concealing the truth from those too lazy or too stubborn to see it. To those who are honestly searching, the truth becomes clear. We must be careful not to read too much into parables, forcing them to say what they don't mean.*

This is a parable about parables. The four types of soil in this parable represent the different responses we can have to God's message. We respond differently because we are in different states of readiness. Some people are hardened, others are shallow, others are contaminated by distracting cares, and some are receptive. How has God's Word taken root in your life? What kind of soil are you?

God Has Not Rejected the Jews/ Romans 11:1–6

I ask then, has God rejected and deserted his people the Jews? Oh no, not at all. Remember that I myself am a Jew, a descendant of Abraham and a member of Benjamin's family.

2,3No, God has not discarded his own people whom he chose from the very beginning. Do you remember what the Scriptures say about this? Elijah the prophet was complaining to God about the Jews, telling God how they had killed the prophets and torn down God's altars; Elijah claimed that he was the only one left in all the land who still loved God, and now they were trying to kill him too.

4And do you remember how God replied? God said, "No, you are not the only one left. I have seven thousand others besides you who still love me and have not bowed down to idols!"

5It is the same today. Not all the Jews have turned away from God; there are a few being saved as a result of God's kindness in choosing them. 6And if it is by God's kindness, then it is not by their being good enough. For in that case the free gift would no longer be free—it isn't free when it is earned.

A Thought: *God chose the Jews to be the people through whom the rest of the world could find salvation. But this did not mean the entire Jewish nation would be saved; only those who were faithful to God were considered true Jews. People are saved through faith in Christ, not because they are part of a nation, religion, or family. On what are you depending for salvation?*

Proverbs for Today/ 6:12–15

Let me describe for you a worthless and a wicked man; first, he is a constant liar; he signals his true intentions to his friends with eyes and feet and fingers. He is always thinking up new schemes to swindle people. He stirs up trouble everywhere. But he will be destroyed suddenly, broken beyond hope of healing.

FEBRUARY 1

Illustrations of the Kingdom of Heaven/ Matthew 13:24–35

Here is another illustration Jesus used: "The Kingdom of Heaven is like a farmer sowing good seed in his field; 25but one night as he slept, his enemy came and sowed thistles among the wheat. 26When the crop began to grow, the thistles grew too.

27"The farmer's men came and told him, 'Sir, the field where you planted that choice seed is full of thistles!'

28" 'An enemy has done it,' he exclaimed.

" 'Shall we pull out the thistles?' they asked.

29" 'No,' he replied. 'You'll hurt the wheat if you do. 30Let both grow together until the harvest, and I will tell the reapers to sort out the thistles and burn them, and put the wheat in the barn.' "

31,32Here is another of his illustrations: "The Kingdom of Heaven is like a tiny mustard seed planted in a field. It is the smallest of all seeds, but becomes the largest of plants, and grows into a tree where birds can come and find shelter."

33He also used this example:

"The Kingdom of Heaven can be compared to a woman

making bread. She takes a measure of flour and mixes in the yeast until it permeates every part of the dough."

34,35Jesus constantly used these illustrations when speaking to the crowds. In fact, because the prophets said that he would use so many, he never spoke to them without at least one illustration. For it had been prophesied, "I will talk in parables; I will explain mysteries hidden since the beginning of time."

A THOUGHT: *The young thistles and the young blades of wheat look the same and can't be distinguised until they are grown and ready for harvest. Thistles (unbelievers) and wheat (believers) must live side by side in this world. God is allowing unbelievers to remain for a while just as a farmer allows thistles to remain in his field so the surrounding wheat isn't uprooted with them. At the harvest, however, the thistles will be uprooted and thrown away. God's harvest (judgment) of all mankind is coming. We are to make ourselves ready by making sure our faith is sincere.*

A Stumbling Block to Jews/ Romans 11:7–12

So this is the situation: Most of the Jews have not found the favor of God they are looking for. A few have—the ones God has picked out—but the eyes of the others have been blinded. 8This is what our Scriptures refer to when they say that God has put them to sleep, shutting their eyes and ears so that they do not understand what we are talking about when we tell them of Christ. And so it is to this very day.

9King David spoke of this same thing when he said, "Let their good food and other blessings trap them into thinking all is well between themselves and God. Let these good things boomerang on them and fall back upon their heads to justly crush them. 10Let their eyes be dim," he said, "so that they cannot see, and let them walk bent-backed forever with a heavy load."

11Does this mean that God has rejected his Jewish people forever? Of course not! His purpose was to make his salvation available to the Gentiles, and then the Jews would be jealous and begin to want God's salvation for themselves. 12Now if the whole world became rich as a result of God's offer of salvation, when the Jews stumbled over it and turned it down, think how much greater a blessing the world will share in later on when the Jews, too, come to Christ.

A Thought: *These verses describe the punishment for hardened hearts predicted by the prophet Isaiah. If people constantly refuse to hear God's Good News, they eventually will be unable to understand it. Paul saw this happening in the synagogues he visited. But Paul had a vision for the church in which all Jews and Gentiles would be united in their love of God and obedience to Christ. While respecting God's Law, this ideal church would look to Christ alone for salvation and eternal life. One's ethnic background and social status would be irrelevant—what would matter would be one's faith in Christ.*

Proverbs for Today/ 6:16–19

For there are six things the Lord hates—no, seven: haughtiness, lying, murdering, plotting evil, eagerness to do wrong, a false witness, sowing discord among brothers.

FEBRUARY 2

Jesus Explains the Parable of the Thistles and Wheat/ Matthew 13:36–43

Then, leaving the crowds outside, Jesus went into the house. His disciples asked him to explain to them the illustration of the thistles and the wheat.

37"All right," he said, "I am the farmer who sows the choice seed. 38The field is the world, and the seed represents the people of the Kingdom; the thistles are the people belonging to Satan. 39The enemy who sowed the thistles among the wheat is the devil; the harvest is the end of the world, and the reapers are the angels.

40"Just as in this story the thistles are separated and burned, so shall it be at the end of the world: 41I will send my angels and they will separate out of the Kingdom every temptation and all who are evil, 42and throw them into the furnace and burn them. There shall be weeping and gnashing of teeth. 43Then the godly shall shine as the sun in their Father's Kingdom. Let those with ears, listen!

A Thought: *At the end of the world, angels will separate those who are evil from those who are good. There are true and false believers in churches today, but we should be cautious in our judg-*

ments because the final separation will be made by Christ himself.
If you start judging, you may damage some of the good "plants."
It's more important to judge our own response to God than to
analyze the spiritual condition of others.

God Has Grafted the Gentiles into His Family Tree/
Romans 11:13–21

As you know, God has appointed me as a special messenger
to you Gentiles. I lay great stress on this and remind
the Jews about it as often as I can, 14so that if possible I
can make them want what you Gentiles have and in that
way save some of them. 15And how wonderful it will be
when they become Christians! When God turned away
from them it meant that he turned to the rest of the
world to offer his salvation; and now it is even more wonderful when the Jews come to Christ. It will be like dead
people coming back to life. 16And since Abraham and the
prophets are God's people, their children will be too. For
if the roots of the tree are holy, the branches will be
too.

17But some of these branches from Abraham's tree,
some of the Jews, have been broken off. And you Gentiles
who were branches from, we might say, a wild olive tree,
were grafted in. So now you, too, receive the blessing
God has promised Abraham and his children, sharing in
God's rich nourishment of his own special olive tree.

18But you must be careful not to brag about being put
in to replace the branches that were broken off. Remember
that you are important only because you are now a part
of God's tree; you are just a branch, not a root.

19"Well," you may be saying, "those branches were
broken off to make room for me so I must be pretty
good."

20Watch out! Remember that those branches, the Jews,
were broken off because they didn't believe God, and
you are there only because you do. Do not be proud; be
humble and grateful—and careful. 21For if God did not
spare the branches he put there in the first place, he
won't spare you either.

A THOUGHT: *Paul, speaking to Gentile Christians, is warning
them not to feel superior because God rejected some Jews. The
Jewish religion, he says, is like the root of a tree, and the Jewish
people are the tree's natural branches. Gentile believers have been*

grafted into the tree, and now Jews and Gentiles share its nourish-ment. Both Jews and Gentiles depend on Christ for life. If there is to be boasting, it should be in the Lord who accomplished the redemption of his people. For our salvation rests upon the grace of God expressed in the giving of his Son for our sins and we can offer nothing from ourselves to bring about or add to this salvation.

Proverbs for Today/ 6:20–26

Young man, obey your father and your mother. Take to heart all of their advice; keep in mind everything they tell you. Every day and all night long their counsel will lead you and save you from harm; when you wake up in the morning, let their instructions guide you into the new day. For their advice is a beam of light directed into the dark corners of your mind to warn you of danger and to give you a good life. Their counsel will keep you far away from prostitutes with all their flatteries, and unfaithful wives of other men. Don't lust for their beauty. Don't let their coyness seduce you. For a prostitute will bring a man to poverty, and an adulteress may cost him his very life.

FEBRUARY 3

Illustrations of the Kingdom of Heaven/ Matthew 13:44–58

"The Kingdom of Heaven is like a treasure a man discovered in a field. In his excitement, he sold everything he owned to get enough money to buy the field—and get the treasure, too!

45"Again, the Kingdom of Heaven is like a pearl merchant on the lookout for choice pearls. 46 He discovered a real bargain—a pearl of great value—and sold everything he owned to purchase it!

47,48"Again, the Kingdom of Heaven can be illustrated by a fisherman—he casts a net into the water and gathers in fish of every kind, valuable and worthless. When the net is full, he drags it up onto the beach and sits down and sorts out the edible ones into crates and throws the others away. 49That is the way it will be at the end of the world—the angels will come and separate the wicked people from the godly, 50casting the wicked into the fire; there shall be weeping and gnashing of teeth. 51Do you understand?"

"Yes," they said, "we do."

52Then he added, "Those experts in Jewish law who are now my disciples have double treasures—from the Old Testament as well as from the New!"

53,54When Jesus had finished giving these illustrations, he returned to his home town, Nazareth in Galilee, and taught there in the synagogue and astonished everyone with his wisdom and his miracles.

55"How is this possible?" the people exclaimed. "He's just a carpenter's son, and we know Mary his mother and his brothers—James, Joseph, Simon, and Judas. 56And his sisters—they all live here. How can he be so great?" 57And they became angry with him!

Then Jesus told them, "A prophet is honored everywhere except in his own country, and among his own people!" 58And so he did only a few great miracles there, because of their unbelief.

A Thought: *The Kingdom of Heaven is more valuable than anything else we can have, so a person must be willing to give up everything to obtain it. The man who discovered the treasure in the field stumbled upon it by accident, but knew its value when he found it. The merchant was earnestly searching for the choice pearl and, when he found it, sold everything he had to purchase it. We too must seek the values of the Kingdom above everything else.*

The Kindness and Severity of God/
Romans 11:22–27

Notice how God is both kind and severe. He is very hard on those who disobey, but very good to you if you continue to love and trust him. But if you don't, you too will be cut off. 23On the other hand, if the Jews leave their unbelief behind them and come back to God, God will graft them back into the tree again. He has the power to do it.

24For if God was willing to take you who were so far away from him—being part of a wild olive tree—and graft you into his own good tree—a very unusual thing to do—don't you see that he will be far more ready to put the Jews back again, who were there in the first place?

25I want you to know about this truth from God, dear

brothers, so that you will not feel proud and start bragging. Yes, it is true that some of the Jews have set themselves against the Gospel now, but this will last only until all of you Gentiles have come to Christ—those of you who will. 26And then all Israel will be saved.

Do you remember what the prophets said about this? "There shall come out of Zion a Deliverer, and he shall turn the Jews from all ungodliness. 27At that time I will take away their sins, just as I promised."

A THOUGHT: *The fact that God has shown his kindness towards us does not mean that we have the freedom to presume upon his grace by disobeying him. God's true children will desire to obey God. Recognize that just as God judged the disobedience of the Jews who constantly refused to turn to God, so he will judge us if we constantly refuse to turn from our wicked ways. But if one who has lived a wicked life turns to God, God is able to graft that one into the family of God.*

Proverbs for Today/ 6:27–35

Can a man hold fire against his chest and not be burned? Can he walk on hot coals and not blister his feet? So it is with the man who commits adultery with another's wife. He shall not go unpunished for this sin. Excuses might even be found for a thief, if he steals when he is starving! But even so, he is fined seven times as much as he stole, though it may mean selling everything in his house to pay it back. But the man who commits adultery is an utter fool, for he destroys his own soul. Wounds and constant disgrace are his lot, for the woman's husband will be furious in his jealousy, and he will have no mercy on you in his day of vengeance. You won't be able to buy him off no matter what you offer.

FEBRUARY 4

King Herod Beheads John the Baptist/
Matthew 14:1–13

When King Herod heard about Jesus, 2he said to his men, "This must be John the Baptist, come back to life again.

That is why he can do these miracles." 3For Herod had arrested John and chained him in prison at the demand of his wife Herodias, his brother Philip's ex-wife, 4because John had told him it was wrong for him to marry her. 5He would have killed John but was afraid of a riot, for all the people believed John was a prophet.

6But at a birthday party for Herod, Herodias' daughter performed a dance that greatly pleased him, 7so he vowed to give her anything she wanted. 8Consequently, at her mother's urging, the girl asked for John the Baptist's head on a tray.

9The king was grieved, but because of his oath, and because he didn't want to back down in front of his guests, he issued the necessary orders.

10So John was beheaded in the prison, 11and his head was brought on a tray and given to the girl, who took it to her mother.

12Then John's disciples came for his body and buried it, and came to tell Jesus what had happened.

13As soon as Jesus heard the news, he went off by himself in a boat to a remote area to be alone. But the crowds saw where he was headed, and followed by land from many villages.

A THOUGHT: *Herod did not want to kill John the Baptist, but he gave the order so he wouldn't be embarrassed in front of his guests. How easy it is to give in to the pressure of the crowd and to let ourselves be coerced into doing wrong. Don't place yourself in a position where it is too embarrassing to do what is right. Do what is right no matter how embarrassing or painful it may be.*

God Will Not Go Back on His Promises/ Romans 11:28–36

Now many of the Jews are enemies of the Gospel. They hate it. But this has been a benefit to you, for it has resulted in God's giving his gifts to you Gentiles. Yet the Jews are still beloved of God because of his promises to Abraham, Isaac, and Jacob. 29For God's gifts and his call can never be withdrawn; he will never go back on his promises. 30Once you were rebels against God, but when the Jews refused his gifts God was merciful to you instead. 31And now the Jews are the rebels, but some day they, too, will share in God's mercy upon you. 32For

God has given them all up to sin so that he could have mercy upon all alike.

33Oh, what a wonderful God we have! How great are his wisdom and knowledge and riches! How impossible it is for us to understand his decisions and his methods! 34For who among us can know the mind of the Lord? Who knows enough to be his counselor and guide? 35And who could ever offer to the Lord enough to induce him to act? 36For everything comes from God alone. Everything lives by his power, and everything is for his glory. To him be glory evermore.

A THOUGHT: *In this passage Paul shows how the Jews and the Gentiles benefit from each other. Whenever God shows mercy on one group, the other shares the blessing. In God's original plan, the Jews would freely share their blessings with the Gentiles. When the Jews neglected to do this, God blessed the Gentiles anyway through the Jewish Messiah. Now it is the Gentiles' turn to bless the Jews. God's plans will not be thwarted: he will "have mercy upon all alike."*

Proverbs for Today/ 7:1–5

Follow my advice, my son; always keep it in mind and stick to it. Obey me and live! Guard my words as your most precious possession. Write them down, and also keep them deep within your heart. Love wisdom like a sweetheart; make her a beloved member of your family. Let her hold you back from affairs with other women—from listening to their flattery.

FEBRUARY 5

The Feeding of the Five Thousand/
Matthew 14:14–21

So when Jesus came out of the wilderness, a vast crowd was waiting for him and he pitied them and healed their sick.

15That evening the disciples came to him and said, "It is already past time for supper, and there is nothing to eat here in the desert; send the crowds away so they can go to the villages and buy some food."

16But Jesus replied, "That isn't necessary—you feed them!"

17"What!" they exclaimed. "We have exactly five small loaves of bread and two fish!"

18"Bring them here," he said.

19Then he told the people to sit down on the grass; and he took the five loaves and two fish, looked up into the sky and asked God's blessing on the meal, then broke the loaves apart and gave them to the disciples to place before the people. 20And everyone ate until full! And when the scraps were picked up afterwards, there were twelve basketfuls left over! 21(About 5,000 men were in the crowd that day, besides all the women and children.)

A THOUGHT: *Jesus multiplied five loaves and two fish to feed over 5,000 people. What he was originally given seemed insufficient, but in his hands it became more than enough. We often feel that our contribution to Jesus is meager, but he can use and multiply whatever we give him, whether it is talent, time, or treasure. It is when we give them to Jesus that our resources are multiplied.*

A Living Sacrifice to God/ Romans 12:1–5

And so, dear brothers, I plead with you to give your bodies to God. Let them be a living sacrifice, holy—the kind he can accept. When you think of what he has done for you, is this too much to ask? 2Don't copy the behavior and customs of this world, but be a new and different person with a fresh newness in all you do and think. Then you will learn from your own experience how his ways will really satisfy you.

3As God's messenger I give each of you God's warning: Be honest in your estimate of yourselves, measuring your value by how much faith God has given you. 4,5Just as there are many parts to our bodies, so it is with Christ's body. We are all parts of it, and it takes every one of us to make it complete, for we each have different work to do. So we belong to each other, and each needs all the others.

A THOUGHT: *When sacrificing an animal according to God's law, a priest killed the animal, cut it in pieces, and placed it on the altar. Sacrifice was important, but even in the Old Testament God made it clear that obedience from the heart was much more important. God wants us to offer ourselves, not animals, as living sacrifices—daily laying aside our own desires to follow him. We do this out of gratitude that our sins have been forgiven. He wants us to be new people with freshness of thought, alive to glorify him. Since he wants only what is best for us, and since he gave his Son to make our new lives possible, we should joyfully offer ourselves as living sacrifices to him.*

Proverbs for Today/ 7:6–23

I was looking out the window of my house one day, and saw a simple-minded lad, a young man lacking common sense, walking at twilight down the street to the house of this wayward girl, a prostitute. She approached him, saucy and pert, and dressed seductively. She was the brash, coarse type, seen often in the streets and markets, soliciting at every corner for men to be her lovers. She put her arms around him and kissed him, and with a saucy look she said, "I was just coming to look for you and here you are! Come home with me and I'll fix you a wonderful dinner, and after that—well, my bed is spread with lovely, colored sheets of finest linen imported from Egypt, perfumed with myrrh, aloes and cinnamon. Come on, let's take our fill of love until morning, for my husband is away on a long trip. He has taken a wallet full of money with him, and won't return for several days." So she seduced him with her pretty speech, her coaxing and her wheedling, until he yielded to her. He couldn't resist her flattery. He followed her as an ox going to the butcher, or as a stag that is trapped, waiting to be killed with an arrow through its heart. He was as a bird flying into a snare, not knowing the fate awaiting it there.

FEBRUARY 6

Jesus Walks on the Water/ Matthew 14:22–36

Immediately after this, Jesus told his disciples to get into their boat and cross to the other side of the lake while he stayed to get the people started home.

23,24Then afterwards he went up into the hills to pray. Night fell, and out on the lake the disciples were in trouble.

For the wind had risen and they were fighting heavy seas.

25About four o'clock in the morning Jesus came to them, walking on the water! 26They screamed in terror, for they thought he was a ghost.

27But Jesus immediately spoke to them, reassuring them. "Don't be afraid!" he said.

28Then Peter called to him: "Sir, if it is really you, tell me to come over to you, walking on the water."

29"All right," the Lord said, "come along!"

So Peter went over the side of the boat and walked on the water toward Jesus. 30But when he looked around at the high waves, he was terrified and began to sink. "Save me, Lord!" he shouted.

31Instantly Jesus reached out his hand and rescued him. "O man of little faith," Jesus said. "Why did you doubt me?" 32And when they had climbed back into the boat, the wind stopped.

33The others sat there, awestruck. "You really are the Son of God!" they exclaimed.

34They landed at Gennesaret. 35The news of their arrival spread quickly throughout the city, and soon people were rushing around, telling everyone to bring in their sick to be healed. 36The sick begged him to let them touch even the tassel of his robe, and all who did were healed.

A THOUGHT: *Although we start out with good intentions, sometimes our faith falters. This doesn't necessarily mean we have failed. When Peter's faith faltered, he reached out to Christ, the only one who could help. He was afraid, but he still looked to Christ. When we are apprehensive about the troubles around us and doubt Christ's presence or ability to help, we must remember that he is the only one who can really help.*

Gifts Are Given to Serve Others/ Romans 12:6–13

God has given each of us the ability to do certain things well. So if God has given you the ability to prophesy, then prophesy whenever you can—as often as your faith is strong enough to receive a message from God. 7If your gift is that of serving others, serve them well. If you are a teacher, do a good job of teaching. 8If you are a preacher, see to it that your sermons are strong and helpful. If God has given you money, be generous in helping others with it. If God has given you administrative ability and put you in charge of the work of others, take the responsibility seriously. Those who offer comfort to the sorrowing should do so with Christian cheer.

9Don't just pretend that you love others: really love them. Hate what is wrong. Stand on the side of the good. 10Love each other with brotherly affection and take delight in honoring each other. 11Never be lazy in your work but serve the Lord enthusiastically.

12Be glad for all God is planning for you. Be patient in trouble, and prayerful always. 13When God's children are in need, you be the one to help them out. And get into the habit of inviting guests home for dinner or, if they need lodging, for the night.

A THOUGHT: *Look at this list of gifts and imagine the kinds of people who would have each gift. Prophets are often bold and articulate. Servers are faithful and loyal. Teachers are clear thinkers. Preachers know how to motivate others. Givers are generous and trusting. Administrators are good organizers and managers. Comforters are caring people who are happy to give their time to others. It would be difficult for one person to embody all these gifts. An assertive prophet would not usually make a good counselor, and a generous giver might fail as an administrator. When you identify your own gifts (and you don't have to stop with this list—it is far from complete), ask how you can use them to God's glory. At the same time, realize that your gifts can't do the work of the church all alone. Be thankful for people whose gifts are completely different from yours. Let your strengths balance their weaknesses, and be grateful that their abilities make up for your deficiencies. Together we can build up the church.*

Proverbs for Today/ 7:24–27

Listen to me, young men, and not only listen but obey; don't let your desires get out of hand; don't let yourself think about her. Don't go near her; stay away from where she walks, lest she tempt you and seduce you. For she has been the ruin of multitudes—a vast host of men have been her victims. If you want to find the road to hell, look for her house.

Righteousness Is a Matter of the Heart/
Matthew 15:1–20

Some Pharisees and other Jewish leaders now arrived from Jerusalem to interview Jesus.

2"Why do your disciples disobey the ancient Jewish traditions?" they demanded. "For they ignore our ritual of ceremonial handwashing before they eat." 3He replied, "And why do your traditions violate the direct commandments of God? 4For instance, God's law is 'Honor your father and mother; anyone who reviles his parents must die.' 5,6But you say, 'Even if your parents are in need, you may give their support money to the church instead.' And so, by your man-made rule, you nullify the direct command of God to honor and care for your parents. 7You hypocrites! Well did Isaiah prophesy of you, 8 'These people say they honor me, but their hearts are far away. 9Their worship is worthless, for they teach their man-made laws instead of those from God.' "

10Then Jesus called to the crowds and said, "Listen to what I say and try to understand: 11You aren't made unholy by eating non-kosher food! It is what you *say* and *think* that makes you unclean."

12Then the disciples came and told him, "You offended the Pharisees by that remark."

13,14Jesus replied, "Every plant not planted by my Father shall be rooted up, so ignore them. They are blind guides leading the blind, and both will fall into a ditch."

15Then Peter asked Jesus to explain what he meant when he said that people are not defiled by non-kosher food.

16"Don't you understand?" Jesus asked him. 17"Don't you see that anything you eat passes through the digestive tract and out again? 18But evil words come from an evil heart, and defile the man who says them. 19For from the heart come evil thoughts, murder, adultery, fornication, theft, lying and slander. 20These are what defile; but there is no spiritual defilement from eating without first going through the ritual of ceremonial handwashing!"

A Thought: *We work hard to keep our outward appearance attractive, but what is in our hearts is even more important. The way we are deep down (where others can't see) matters much to God. What are you like inside? When people become Christians, God changes them and actually makes them different on the inside. He will continue to help change them if they only ask. God wants us to seek healthy thoughts and motives, not just healthy food and exercise.*

Conquer Evil by Doing Good/ Romans 12:14–21

If someone mistreats you because you are a Christian, don't curse him; pray that God will bless him. 15When others are happy, be happy with them. If they are sad, share their sorrow. 16Work happily together. Don't try to act big. Don't try to get into the good graces of important people, but enjoy the company of ordinary folks. And don't think you know it all!

17Never pay back evil for evil. Do things in such a way that everyone can see you are honest clear through. 18Don't quarrel with anyone. Be at peace with everyone, just as much as possible.

19Dear friends, never avenge yourselves. Leave that to God, for he has said that he will repay those who deserve it. [Don't take the law into your own hands.] 20Instead, feed your enemy if he is hungry. If he is thirsty give him something to drink and you will be "heaping coals of fire on his head." In other words, he will feel ashamed of himself for what he has done to you. 21Don't let evil get the upper hand but conquer evil by doing good.

A Thought: *In this day of constant lawsuits and incessant demands for legal rights, Paul's command sounds almost impossible. When someone hurts you deeply, instead of giving him what he deserves, Paul says to befriend him. Why does Paul tell us to forgive our enemies? (1) Forgiveness may break a cycle of retaliation and lead to mutual reconciliation. (2) It may make the enemy feel ashamed and change his ways. (3) Returning evil for evil hurts you just as much as it hurts your enemy. Even if your enemy never repents, forgiving him will free you of a heavy load of bitterness. For in loving our enemies in this way, we will be like our Lord Jesus Christ, who died for us while we were in a state of rebellion against him.*

Proverbs for Today/ 8:1–10

Can't you hear the voice of wisdom? She is standing at the city gates and at every fork in the road, and at the door of every house. Listen to what she says: "Listen, men!" she calls. "How foolish and naive you are! Let me give you understanding. O foolish ones, let me show you common sense! Listen to me! For I have important information for you. Everything I say is right and true, for I hate lies and every kind of deception. My advice is wholesome and good. There is nothing of evil in it. My words are plain and clear to anyone with half a mind—if it is only open! My instruction is far more valuable than silver or gold."

FEBRUARY 8

Jesus Heals a Canaanite Woman's Daughter/ Matthew 15:21–28

Jesus then left that part of the country and walked the fifty miles to Tyre and Sidon.

22A woman from Canaan who was living there came to him, pleading, "Have mercy on me, O Lord, King David's Son! For my daughter has a demon within her, and it torments her constantly."

23But Jesus gave her no reply—not even a word. Then his disciples urged him to send her away. "Tell her to get going," they said, "for she is bothering us with all her begging."

24Then he said to the woman, "I was sent to help the Jews—the lost sheep of Israel—not the Gentiles."

25But she came and worshiped him and pled again, "Sir, help me!"

26"It doesn't seem right to take bread from the children and throw it to the dogs," he said.

27"Yes, it is!" she replied, "for even the puppies beneath the table are permitted to eat the crumbs that fall."

28"Woman," Jesus told her, "your faith is large, and your request is granted." And her daughter was healed right then.

A THOUGHT: *The disciples asked Jesus to get rid of this Canaanite woman because she was bothering them with her begging. They showed no compassion for her or sensitivity to her needs. It is possible to become so occupied with spiritual matters that we miss real spiritual needs right around us, whether out of prejudice or simply the inconvenience they cause. Instead of being bothered, be aware of the opportunities that surround you. Be open to sharing God's message with all people, and do not to shut out those who are different from you.*

Obedience to the Government/ Romans 13:1–7

Obey the government, for God is the one who has put it there. There is no government anywhere that God has not placed in power. ²So those who refuse to obey the laws of the land are refusing to obey God, and punishment will follow. ³For the policeman does not frighten people who are doing right; but those doing evil will always fear him. So if you don't want to be afraid, keep the laws and you will get along well. ⁴The policeman is sent by God to help you. But if you are doing something wrong, of course you should be afraid, for he will have you punished. He is sent by God for that very purpose. ⁵Obey the laws, then, for two reasons: first, to keep from being punished, and second, just because you know you should.

⁶Pay your taxes too, for these same two reasons. For government workers need to be paid so that they can keep on doing God's work, serving you. ⁷Pay everyone whatever he ought to have: pay your taxes and import duties gladly, obey those over you, and give honor and respect to all those to whom it is due.

A THOUGHT: *Are there times when we should not obey the government? We can never allow government to force us to disobey God. Jesus and his apostles never disobeyed the government for personal reasons; when they disobeyed, it was in order to follow their higher loyalty to God. Their disobedience was not cheap: they were threatened, beaten, thrown into jail, tortured, and executed for their convictions. Like them, if we are compelled to disobey, we must disobey for the right reasons and we must be ready to accept the consequences.*

Proverbs for Today/ 8:11–13

For the value of wisdom is far above rubies; nothing can be compared with it. Wisdom and good judgment live together, for wisdom knows where to discover knowledge and understanding. If anyone respects and fears God, he will hate evil. For wisdom hates pride, arrogance, corruption and deceit of every kind.

The Feeding of the Four Thousand/
Matthew 15:29–39

Jesus now returned to the Sea of Galilee, and climbed a hill and sat there. 30And a vast crowd brought him their lame, blind, maimed, and those who couldn't speak, and many others, and laid them before Jesus, and he healed them all. 31What a spectacle it was! Those who hadn't been able to say a word before were talking excitedly, and those with missing arms and legs had new ones; the crippled were walking and jumping around, and those who had been blind were gazing about them! The crowds just marveled, and praised the God of Israel.

32Then Jesus called his disciples to him and said, "I pity these people—they've been here with me for three days now, and have nothing left to eat; I don't want to send them away hungry or they will faint along the road."

33The disciples replied, "And where would we get enough here in the desert for all this mob to eat?"

34Jesus asked them, "How much food do you have?" And they replied, "Seven loaves of bread and a few small fish!"

35Then Jesus told all of the people to sit down on the ground, 36and he took the seven loaves and the fish, and gave thanks to God for them, and divided them into pieces, and gave them to the disciples who presented them to the crowd. 37,38And everyone ate until full—4,000 men besides the women and children! And afterwards, when the scraps were picked up, there were seven basketfuls left over!

39Then Jesus sent the people home and got into the boat and crossed to Magadan.

A THOUGHT: *Jesus had already fed more than 5,000 people with five loaves and two fish. Now, in a similar situation, the disciples were again perplexed. How easily we throw up our hands in despair when faced with tough situations. Like the disciples, we often forget that if God has cared for us in the past, he will do the same now. If you are facing a difficult situation, remember when God cared for you and trust him to work faithfully again.*

FEBRUARY 9

Loving Others Is a Sure Way to Obey God/
Romans 13:8–14

Pay all your debts except the debt of love for others—
never finish paying that! For if you love them, you will
be obeying all of God's laws, fulfilling all his requirements.
⁹If you love your neighbor as much as you love yourself
you will not want to harm or cheat him, or kill him or
steal from him. And you won't sin with his wife or want
what is his, or do anything else the Ten Commandments
say is wrong. All ten are wrapped up in this one, to love
your neighbor as you love yourself. ¹⁰Love does no wrong
to anyone. That's why it fully satisfies all of God's requirements. It is the only law you need.

¹¹Another reason for right living is this: you know how
late it is; time is running out. Wake up, for the coming
of the Lord is nearer now than when we first believed.
¹²,¹³The night is far gone, the day of his return will soon
be here. So quit the evil deeds of darkness and put on
the armor of right living, as we who live in the daylight
should! Be decent and true in everything you do so that
all can approve your behavior. Don't spend your time in
wild parties and getting drunk or in adultery and lust, or
fighting, or jealousy. ¹⁴But ask the Lord Jesus Christ to
help you live as you should, and don't make plans to enjoy
evil.

A THOUGHT: *Somehow many of us have gotten the idea that self-
love is wrong. But if this were the case, it would be pointless to
love our neighbors as ourselves. But Paul explains what he means
by self-love. Even if you have low self-esteem, you probably don't
willingly let yourself go hungry. You clothe yourself reasonably
well. You make sure there's a roof over your head if you can.
You try not to let yourself be cheated or injured. And you get
angry if someone tries to ruin your marriage. This is the kind of
love we need to have for our neighbors. Do we see that others are
fed, clothed, and housed as well as they can be? Are we concerned
about issues of social justice? Are our morals above reproach?
Loving others as ourselves means to be actively working to see
that their needs are met. Interestingly, people who focus on others
rather than on themselves rarely suffer from low self-esteem.*

Proverbs for Today/ 8:14–26

"I, Wisdom, give good advice and common sense. Because
of my strength, kings reign in power, and rulers make
just laws. I love all who love me. Those who search for

me shall surely find me. Unending riches, honor, justice and righteousness are mine to distribute. My gifts are better than the purest gold or sterling silver! My paths are those of justice and right. Those who love and follow me are indeed wealthy. I fill their treasuries. The Lord formed me in the beginning, before he created anything else. From ages past, I am. I existed before the earth began. I lived before the oceans were created, before the springs bubbled forth their waters onto the earth; before the mountains and the hills were made. Yes, I was born before God made the earth and fields, and the first handfuls of soil.

FEBRUARY 10

Beware of the Teachings of the Pharisees and Sadducees/ Matthew 16:1–12

One day the Pharisees and Sadducees came to test Jesus' claim of being the Messiah by asking him to show them some great demonstrations in the skies.

2,3He replied, "You are good at reading the weather signs of the skies—red sky tonight means fair weather tomorrow; red sky in the morning means foul weather all day—but you can't read the obvious signs of the times! 4This evil, unbelieving nation is asking for some strange sign in the heavens, but no further proof will be given except the miracle that happened to Jonah." Then Jesus walked out on them.

5Arriving across the lake, the disciples discovered they had forgotten to bring any food.

6"Watch out!" Jesus warned them; "beware of the yeast of the Pharisees and Sadducees."

7They thought he was saying this because they had forgotten to bring bread.

8Jesus knew what they were thinking and told them, "O men of little faith! Why are you so worried about having no food? 9Won't you ever understand? Don't you remember at all the 5,000 I fed with five loaves, and the basketfuls left over? 10Don't you remember the 4,000 I fed, and all that was left? 11How could you even think I was talking about food? But again I say, 'Beware of the yeast of the Pharisees and Sadducees.' "

12Then at last they understood that by "yeast" he meant the *wrong teaching* of the Pharisees and Sadducees.

A THOUGHT: *The Pharisees and Sadducees were two different Jewish sects, and their views were diametrically opposed on many issues. The Pharisees carefully followed their religious rules and traditions, believing that this was the way to God. They also believed in the authority of all Scripture and in the resurrection of the dead. The Sadducees accepted only the books of Moses as Scripture and did not believe in life after death.*

Many people, like these Jewish leaders, want a miracle so they can believe. But Jesus knew that miracles would never convince them. Jesus had been healing, raising people from the dead, and feeding thousands, and still people wanted him to prove himself. Do you doubt Christ because you haven't seen a miracle? Do you expect God to prove himself to you personally before you believe? Jesus says, "Blessed are those who haven't seen me and believe anyway" (John 20:29). We have all the miracles recorded in the Old and New Testaments, 2,000 years of church history, and the witness of thousands. With all this evidence, those who don't believe are proud or stubborn. If you simply step forward in faith and believe, then you will begin to notice God at work in your own life!

God Is Master over the Weak and Strong Believer/ Romans 14:1–4

Give a warm welcome to any brother who wants to join you, even though his faith is weak. Don't criticize him for having different ideas from yours about what is right and wrong. 2For instance, don't argue with him about whether or not to eat meat that has been offered to idols. You may believe there is no harm in this, but the faith of others is weaker; they think it is wrong, and will go without any meat at all and eat vegetables rather than eat that kind of meat. 3Those who think it is all right to eat such meat must not look down on those who won't. And if you are one of those who won't, don't find fault with those who do. For God has accepted them to be his children. 4They are God's servants, not yours. They are responsible to him, not to you. Let him tell them whether they are right or wrong. And God is able to make them do as they should.

A THOUGHT: *Each person is ultimately accountable to Christ, not to others. While the church must be uncompromising in its stand against activities expressly forbidden by Scripture (adultery, homosexuality, murder, theft), it should not create additional rules and regulations and give them equal standing with God's Law. Many times Christians base their moral judgments on opinion, personal dislikes, or cultural bias rather than on the Word of God. When they do this, they show that their own faith is weak. They do not think God is powerful enough to guide his children without having to protect his "interests" by making additional requirements for the Christian life. Let us not become entangled in man–made rules. Instead, let us demonstrate our liberty in Christ by being sensitive to others and loving others unselfishly.*

Proverbs for Today/ 8:27–32

"I was there when he established the heavens and formed the great springs in the depths of the oceans. I was there when he set the limits of the seas and gave them his instructions not to spread beyond their boundaries. I was there when he made the blueprint for the earth and oceans. I was the craftsman at his side. I was his constant delight, rejoicing always in his presence. And how happy I was with what he created—his wide world and all his family of mankind! And so, young men, listen to me, for how happy are all who follow my instructions.

FEBRUARY 11

Jesus Predicts His Own Death/ Matthew 16:13–28

When Jesus came to Caesarea Philippi, he asked his disciples, "Who are the people saying I am?"

14"Well," they replied, "some say John the Baptist; some, Elijah; some, Jeremiah or one of the other prophets."

15Then he asked them, "Who do *you* think I am?"

16Simon Peter answered, "The Christ, the Messiah, the Son of the living God."

17"God has blessed you, Simon, son of Jonah," Jesus said, "for my Father in heaven has personally revealed this to you—this is not from any human source. 18You are Peter, a stone; and upon this rock I will build my church; and all the powers of hell shall not prevail against it. 19And I will give you the keys of the Kingdom of Heaven; whatever doors you lock on earth shall be locked in heaven; and whatever doors you open on earth shall be open in heaven!"

20Then he warned the disciples against telling others that he was the Messiah.

21From then on Jesus began to speak plainly to his disciples about going to Jerusalem, and what would happen to him there—that he would suffer at the hands of the Jewish leaders, that he would be killed, and that three days later he would be raised to life again.

22But Peter took him aside to remonstrate with him. "Heaven forbid, sir," he said. "This is not going to happen to you!"

23Jesus turned on Peter and said, "Get away from me, you Satan! You are a dangerous trap to me. You are thinking merely from a human point of view, and not from God's."

24Then Jesus said to the disciples, "If anyone wants to be a follower of mine, let him deny himself and take up his cross and follow me. 25For anyone who keeps his life for himself shall lose it; and anyone who loses his life for me shall find it again. 26What profit is there if you gain the whole world—and lose eternal life? What can be compared with the value of eternal life? 27For I, the Son of Mankind, shall come with my angels in the glory of my Father and judge each person according to his deeds. 28And some of you standing right here now will certainly live to see me coming in my Kingdom."

A THOUGHT: *The disciples answered Jesus' question with the common view people held—that Jesus was one of the great prophets who had come back to life. Peter, however, confesses that Jesus is the promised and long-awaited Messiah. If Jesus asked you this question, how would you answer? Is he your Lord and Messiah? Following Jesus means to be completely committed to him—to take up your cross and follow him—to risk even death, with no turning back.*

Jesus Is Our Lord in Both Life and Death/
Romans 14:5–9

Some think that Christians should observe the Jewish holidays as special days to worship God, but others say it is wrong and foolish to go to all that trouble, for every day alike belongs to God. On questions of this kind everyone must decide for himself. 6If you have special days for worshiping the Lord, you are trying to honor him; you are doing a good thing. So is the person who eats meat that has been offered to idols; he is thankful to the Lord for it; he is doing right. And the person who won't touch such meat, he, too, is anxious to please the Lord, and is thankful. 7We are not our own bosses to live or die as we ourselves might choose. 8Living or dying we follow the Lord. Either way we are his. 9Christ died and rose again for this very purpose, so that he can be our Lord both while we live and when we die.

A THOUGHT: *In all that we do we must remember that we live to obey Jesus Christ. We should see every part of our lives in relationship to God. This gives life meaning. When God is the central focus of all of life, all of life's goals, desires, wants, and activities can be seen in relation to taking joy in God's good gifts, obeying him, and working with the values of his Kingdom in mind.*

Proverbs for Today/ 8:33–36

"Listen to my counsel—oh, don't refuse it—and be wise. Happy is the man who is so anxious to be with me that he watches for me daily at my gates, or waits for me outside my home! For whoever finds me finds life and wins approval from the Lord. But the one who misses me has injured himself irreparably. Those who refuse me show that they love death."

FEBRUARY 12

Jesus Is Transfigured on the Mountain/ Matthew 17:1–13

Six days later Jesus took Peter, James, and his brother John to the top of a high and lonely hill, 2and as they watched, his appearance changed so that his face shone like the sun and his clothing became dazzling white.

3Suddenly Moses and Elijah appeared and were talking with him. 4Peter blurted out, "Sir, it's wonderful that we can be here! If you want me to, I'll make three shelters, one for you and one for Moses and one for Elijah."

5But even as he said it, a bright cloud came over them, and a voice from the cloud said, *"This* is my beloved Son, and I am wonderfully pleased with him. Obey *him."*

6At this the disciples fell face downward to the ground, terribly frightened. 7Jesus came over and touched them. "Get up," he said, "don't be afraid."

8And when they looked, only Jesus was with them.

9As they were going down the mountain, Jesus commanded them not to tell anyone what they had seen until after he had risen from the dead.

10His disciples asked, "Why do the Jewish leaders insist Elijah must return before the Messiah comes?"

11Jesus replied, "They are right. Elijah must come and set everything in order. 12And, in fact, he has already come, but he wasn't recognized, and was badly mistreated by many. And I, the Messiah, shall also suffer at their hands."

13Then the disciples realized he was speaking of John the Baptist.

A THOUGHT: *Moses and Elijah were two of the greatest prophets in the Old Testament. Moses represents the Law. He wrote the Pentateuch (the first five books of the Bible). Elijah represents the prophets who foretold the coming of the Messiah. Their presence with Jesus confirms his messianic mission—to fulfill God's Law and the words of God's prophets. Just as God's voice in the cloud over Mount Sinai confirmed the authority of the Mosaic law, God's voice at the transfiguration confirmed Jesus' authority as the Son of God.*

Be Sensitive to Others/ Romans 14:10–16

You have no right to criticize your brother or look down on him. Remember, each of us will stand personally before the Judgment Seat of God. 11For it is written, "As I live," says the Lord, "every knee shall bow to me and every tongue confess to God." 12Yes, each of us will give an account of himself to God.

13So don't criticize each other any more. Try instead to live in such a way that you will never make your brother stumble by letting him see you doing something he thinks is wrong.

14As for myself, I am perfectly sure on the authority of the Lord Jesus that there is nothing really wrong with eating meat that has been offered to idols. But if someone believes it is wrong, then he shouldn't do it because for him it is wrong. 15And if your brother is bothered by what you eat, you are not acting in love if you go ahead and eat it. Don't let your eating ruin someone for whom Christ died. 16Don't do anything that will cause criticism against yourself even though you know that what you do is right.

A THOUGHT: *Both "strong" and "weak" Christians can cause their brothers to stumble. The strong but insensitive Christian may flaunt his freedom and intentionally offend others' consciences. The scrupulous but weak Christian may fence in others with petty rules and regulations until they can't take it any longer. Paul wants his readers to be both strong in the faith and sensitive to the needs of others. Since we are all strong in some areas and weak in others, we need constantly to monitor the effect of our behavior on others.*

Proverbs for Today/ 9:1–6

Wisdom has built a palace supported on seven pillars, and has prepared a great banquet, and mixed the wines, and sent out her maidens inviting all to come. She calls from the busiest intersections in the city, "Come, you simple ones without good judgment; come to wisdom's banquet and drink the wines that I have mixed. Leave behind your foolishness and begin to live; learn how to be wise."

FEBRUARY 13

Jesus Heals a Demon–Possessed Boy/
Matthew 17:14–21

When Jesus, Peter, James, and John arrived at the bottom of the hill, a huge crowd was waiting for them. A man came and knelt before Jesus and said, 15"Sir, have mercy on my son, for he is mentally deranged, and in great trouble, for he often falls into the fire or into the water; 16so I brought him to your disciples, but they couldn't cure him."

17Jesus replied, "Oh, you stubborn, faithless people!

How long shall I bear with you? Bring him here to me." 18Then Jesus rebuked the demon in the boy and it left him, and from that moment the boy was well.

19Afterwards the disciples asked Jesus privately, "Why couldn't we cast that demon out?"

20"Because of your little faith," Jesus told them. "For if you had faith even as small as a tiny mustard seed you could say to this mountain, 'Move!' and it would go far away. Nothing would be impossible. 21But this kind of demon won't leave unless you have prayed and gone without food."

A THOUGHT: *The disciples were unable to cast out this demon, so they asked Jesus why. He pointed to their little faith which was small even in comparison with a mustard seed. The mustard seed produced a great plant, but their faith produced little. Perhaps they had tried to cast out the demon with their own ability rather than relying upon God's power. There is great power in even a little faith when God is with us. If we feel weak or powerless as Christians, we should examine our faith, making sure we are trusting not in our own abilities to produce results, but in God's power.*

Live to Build Each Other Up/ Romans 14:17–23

For, after all, the important thing for us as Christians is not what we eat or drink but stirring up goodness and peace and joy from the Holy Spirit. 18If you let Christ be Lord in these affairs, God will be glad; and so will others. 19In this way aim for harmony in the church and try to build each other up.

20Don't undo the work of God for a chunk of meat. Remember, there is nothing wrong with the meat, but it is wrong to eat it if it makes another stumble. 21The right thing to do is to quit eating meat or drinking wine or doing anything else that offends your brother or makes him sin. 22You may know that there is nothing wrong with what you do, even from God's point of view, but keep it to yourself; don't flaunt your faith in front of others who might be hurt by it. In this situation, happy is the man who does not sin by doing what he knows is right. 23But anyone who believes that something he wants to do is wrong shouldn't do it. He sins if he does, for he thinks it is wrong, and so for him it *is* wrong. Anything that is done apart from what he feels is right is sin.

A Thought: *Sin is not just a private matter. Everything we do affects others, and we have to think of others constantly. God created us to be interdependent, not independent. Let us seek to do all things out of love for God and out of a genuine desire to meet the needs of others. If we do this we will be building up the unity of the church.*

Proverbs for Today/ 9:7–8

If you rebuke a mocker, you will only get a smart retort; yes, he will snarl at you. So don't bother with him; he will only hate you for trying to help him. But a wise man, when rebuked, will love you all the more.

FEBRUARY 14

A Coin to Pay Taxes/ Matthew 17:22–27

One day while Jesus and the disciples were still in Galilee, Jesus told them, "I am going to be betrayed into the power of those who will kill me, and on the third day afterwards I will be brought back to life again." And the disciples' hearts were filled with sorrow and dread.

24On their arrival in Capernaum, the Temple tax collectors came to Peter and asked him, "Doesn't your master pay taxes?"

25"Of course he does," Peter replied.

Then he went into the house to talk to Jesus about it, but before he had a chance to speak, Jesus asked him, "What do you think, Peter? Do kings levy assessments against their own people, or against conquered foreigners?"

26,27"Against the foreigners," Peter replied.

"Well, then," Jesus said, "the citizens are free! However, we don't want to offend them, so go down to the shore and throw in a line, and open the mouth of the first fish you catch. You will find a coin to cover the taxes for both of us; take it and pay them."

A Thought: *The disciples didn't understand why Jesus kept talking about his death, because they expected him to set up a political, earthly kingdom—his death would dash their hopes. They didn't know that Jesus' death and resurrection would establish his Kingdom.*

As God's people, we are foreigners on earth because our loyalty is always to Jesus—whose Kingdom is not of this world. Still we have to cooperate with the governmental authorities and be responsible citizens. Ambassadors to another country keep the local laws in order to represent well the one who sent them. We are Christ's ambassadors. Are you being a good foreign ambassador for him to this world?

Adopt the Attitude of Christ/ Romans 15:1–6

Even if we believe that it makes no difference to the Lord whether we do these things, still we cannot just go ahead and do them to please ourselves; for we must bear the "burden" of being considerate of the doubts and fears of others—of those who feel these things are wrong. Let's please the other fellow, not ourselves, and do what is for his good and thus build him up in the Lord. 3Christ didn't please himself. As the Psalmist said, "He came for the very purpose of suffering under the insults of those who were against the Lord." 4These things that were written in the Scriptures so long ago are to teach us patience and to encourage us, so that we will look forward expectantly to the time when God will conquer sin and death.

5May God who gives patience, steadiness, and encouragement help you to live in complete harmony with each other—each with the attitude of Christ toward the other. 6And then all of us can praise the Lord together with one voice, giving glory to God, the Father of our Lord Jesus Christ.

A THOUGHT: *To accept Jesus' lordship in all areas of life means to share his values and his perspective. Just as we take Jesus' view on the authority of Scripture, the nature of heaven, and the resurrection, we are to have his attitude of love toward others as well. As we grow in faith and come to know Jesus better, we become more capable of maintaining this attitude throughout each day.*

Proverbs for Today/ 9:9–10

Teach a wise man, and he will be the wiser; teach a good man, and he will learn more. *For the reverence and fear of God are basic to all wisdom. Knowing God results in every other kind of understanding.*

How to Be Great in the Kingdom of God/
Matthew 18:1–20

About that time the disciples came to Jesus to ask which of them would be greatest in the Kingdom of Heaven!

2Jesus called a small child over to him and set the little fellow down among them, 3and said, "Unless you turn to God from your sins and become as little children, you will never get into the Kingdom of Heaven. 4Therefore anyone who humbles himself as this little child, is the greatest in the Kingdom of Heaven. 5And any of you who welcomes a little child like this because you are mine, is welcoming me and caring for me. 6But if any of you causes one of these little ones who trusts in me to lose his faith, it would be better for you to have a rock tied to your neck and be thrown into the sea.

7"Woe upon the world for all its evils. Temptation to do wrong is inevitable, but woe to the man who does the tempting. 8So if your hand or foot causes you to sin, cut it off and throw it away. Better to enter heaven crippled than to be in hell with both of your hands and feet. 9And if your eye causes you to sin, gouge it out and throw it away. Better to enter heaven with one eye than to be in hell with two.

10"Beware that you don't look down upon a single one of these little children. For I tell you that in heaven their angels have constant access to my Father. 11 And I, the Messiah, came to save the lost.

12"If a man has a hundred sheep, and one wanders away and is lost, what will he do? Won't he leave the ninety-nine others and go out into the hills to search for the lost one? 13And if he finds it, he will rejoice over it more than over the ninety-nine others safe at home! 14Just so, it is not my Father's will that even one of these little ones should perish.

15"If a brother sins against you, go to him privately and confront him with his fault. If he listens and confesses it, you have won back a brother. 16But if not, then take one or two others with you and go back to him again, proving everything you say by these witnesses. 17If he still refuses to listen, then take your case to the church, and if the church's verdict favors you, but he won't accept it, then the church should excommunicate him. [18]And I tell you this—whatever you bind on earth is bound in heaven, and whatever you free on earth will be freed in heaven.

[19]"I also tell you this—if two of you agree down here on earth concerning anything you ask for, my Father in heaven will do it for you. [20]For where two or three gather together because they are mine, I will be right there among them."

A THOUGHT: *Jesus points to the characteristics of a child to help his self-centered disciples get the message. We are not to be childish (like the disciples, arguing over petty issues), but rather, childlike, with humble and sincere hearts. The disciples had become so preoccupied with the organization of Jesus' earthly kingdom, they had lost sight of its divine purpose. Instead of seeking a place of service, they sought positions of advantage. How easy it is to lose our eternal perspective and to seek to fulfill our own ambitions. How hard it is to identify with the "little children"—weak and dependent people with no status or influence. Are you being childlike or childish?*

Gentiles Should Rejoice in God's Grace/ Romans 15:7–17

So, warmly welcome each other into the church, just as Christ has warmly welcomed you; then God will be glorified. [8]Remember that Jesus Christ came to show that God is true to his promises and to help the Jews. [9]And remember that he came also that the Gentiles might be saved and give glory to God for his mercies to them. That is what the Psalmist meant when he wrote: "I will praise you among the Gentiles, and sing to your name."

[10]And in another place, "Be glad, O you Gentiles, along with his people the Jews."

[11]And yet again, "Praise the Lord, O you Gentiles, let everyone praise him."

[12]And the prophet Isaiah said, "There shall be an Heir in the house of Jesse, and he will be King over the Gentiles; they will pin their hopes on him alone."

[13]So I pray for you Gentiles that God who gives you hope will keep you happy and full of peace as you believe in him. I pray that God will help you overflow with hope in him through the Holy Spirit's power within you.

¹⁴I know that you are wise and good, my brothers, and that you know these things so well that you are able to teach others all about them. ¹⁵,¹⁶But even so I have been bold enough to emphasize some of these points, knowing that all you need is this reminder from me; for I am, by God's grace, a special messenger from Jesus Christ to you Gentiles, bringing you the Gospel and offering you up as a fragrant sacrifice to God; for you have been made pure and pleasing to him by the Holy Spirit. ¹⁷So it is right for me to be a little proud of all Christ Jesus has done through me.

A Thought: *Paul was not proud of what he had done, but of what God had done through him. Being proud of God's work is not a sin—it is worship. If you are not sure whether your pride is selfish or holy, ask yourself this question: Are you just as proud of what God is doing through other people as of what he is doing through you?*

Proverbs for Today/ 9:11–12

"I, Wisdom, will make the hours of your day more profitable and the years of your life more fruitful." Wisdom is its own reward, and if you scorn her, you hurt only yourself.

FEBRUARY 16

Jesus Teaches on Forgiveness/ Matthew 18:21–35

Then Peter came to Jesus and asked, "Sir, how often should I forgive a brother who sins against me? Seven times?"

²²"No!" Jesus replied, "seventy times seven!

²³"The Kingdom of Heaven can be compared to a king who decided to bring his accounts up to date. ²⁴In the process, one of his debtors was brought in who owed him $10,000,000! ²⁵He couldn't pay, so the king ordered him sold for the debt, also his wife and children and everything he had.

²⁶"But the man fell down before the king, his face in the dust, and said, 'Oh, sir, be patient with me and I will pay it all.'

27"Then the king was filled with pity for him and released him and forgave his debt.

28"But when the man left the king, he went to a man who owed him $2,000 and grabbed him by the throat and demanded instant payment.

29"The man fell down before him and begged him to give him a little time. 'Be patient and I will pay it,' he pled.

30"But his creditor wouldn't wait. He had the man arrested and jailed until the debt would be paid in full.

31"Then the man's friends went to the king and told him what had happened. 32And the king called before him the man he had forgiven and said, 'You evil-hearted wretch! Here I forgave you all that tremendous debt, just because you asked me to— 33shouldn't you have mercy on others, just as I had mercy on you?'

34"Then the angry king sent the man to the torture chamber until he had paid every last penny due. 35So shall my heavenly Father do to you if you refuse to truly forgive your brothers."

A THOUGHT: *The rabbis taught that Jews should forgive those who offend them three times. Peter, in trying to be especially generous, asked Jesus if seven (the "perfect" number) was enough times to forgive someone. But Jesus answered, "Seventy times seven," meaning that we shouldn't even keep track of how many times we forgive someone.*

Realizing how completely Christ has forgiven us should produce a free and generous attitude of forgiveness toward others. When we don't forgive others, we are setting ourselves outside and above Christ's law of love.

Paul, Apostle to the Gentiles/ Romans 15:18–22

I dare not judge how effectively he has used others, but I know this: he has used me to win the Gentiles to God. 19I have won them by my message and by the good way I have lived before them, and by the miracles done through me as signs from God—all by the Holy Spirit's power. In this way I have preached the full Gospel of Christ all the way from Jerusalem clear over into Illyricum.

20But all the while my ambition has been to go still farther, preaching where the name of Christ has never yet been heard, rather than where a church has already been started by someone else. 21I have been following the plan spoken of in the Scriptures where Isaiah says that those who have never heard the name of Christ before will see and understand. 22In fact that is the very reason I have been so long in coming to visit you.

A THOUGHT: *Paul won people to Christ by: (1) boldly preaching the Good News, (2) living a life in accordance with the Good News, and (3) relying on the power of the Holy Spirit. This is a basic pattern that ought to be followed by all Christians in their evangelizing. All three elements are essential to effective Christian missions.*

Proverbs for Today/ 9:13–18

A prostitute is loud and brash, and never has enough of lust and shame. She sits at the door of her house or stands at the street corners of the city, whispering to men going by, and to those minding their own business. "Come home with me," she urges simpletons. "Stolen melons are the sweetest; stolen apples taste the best!" But they don't realize that her former guests are now citizens of hell.

FEBRUARY 17

Jesus Teaches about Divorce/ Matthew 19:1–12

After Jesus had finished this address, he left Galilee and circled back to Judea from across the Jordan River. 2Vast crowds followed him, and he healed their sick. 3Some Pharisees came to interview him, and tried to trap him into saying something that would ruin him.

"Do you permit divorce?" they asked.

4"Don't you read the Scriptures?" he replied. "In them it is written that at the beginning God created man and woman, 5,6and that a man should leave his father and mother, and be forever united to his wife. The two shall become one—no longer two, but one! And no man may divorce what God has joined together."

7"Then, why," they asked, "did Moses say a man may divorce his wife by merely writing her a letter of dismissal?"

8Jesus replied, "Moses did that in recognition of your hard and evil hearts, but it was not what God had originally intended. 9And I tell you this, that anyone who divorces his wife, except for fornication, and marries another, commits adultery."

10Jesus' disciples then said to him, "If that is how it is, it is better not to marry!"

11"Not everyone can accept this statement," Jesus said. "Only those whom God helps. 12Some are born without the ability to marry, and some are disabled by men, and some refuse to marry for the sake of the Kingdom of Heaven. Let anyone who can, accept my statement."

A THOUGHT: *John was put in prison and killed for his public opinions on marriage and divorce, and the Pharisees hoped to trap Jesus too. They were trying to trick Jesus by having him choose sides in a theological controversy. Two main groups had two opposing views on the issue of divorce. One group supported divorce for almost any reason. The other believed divorce could be allowed only for marital unfaithfulness. But in his answer, Jesus focused on marriage rather than on divorce. He pointed out that Scripture intended marriage to be permanent.*

Couples must decide against divorce from the start and build their marriage on mutual commitment. There are also many good reasons for not marrying, one of them being to have more time to work for God's Kingdom. Don't assume God wants everyone to marry. For many it may be better if they don't. But be sure you prayerfully seek God's will before you plunge into the lifelong commitment of marriage.

The Collection for the Jerusalem Church/
Romans 15:23–33

But now at last I am through with my work here, and I am ready to come after all these long years of waiting. 24For I am planning to take a trip to Spain, and when I do, I will stop off there in Rome; and after we have had a good time together for a little while, you can send me on my way again.

25But before I come, I must go down to Jerusalem to take a gift to the Jewish Christians there. 26For you see, the Christians in Macedonia and Achaia have taken up an offering for those in Jerusalem who are going through such hard times. 27They were very glad to do this, for they feel that they owe a real debt to the Jerusalem Christians. Why? Because the news about Christ came to these Gentiles from the church in Jerusalem. And since they received this wonderful spiritual gift of the Gospel from there, they feel that the least they can do in return is to give some material aid. 28As soon as I have delivered this money and completed this good deed of theirs, I will come to see you on my way to Spain. 29And I am sure that when I come the Lord will give me a great blessing for you.

30Will you be my prayer partners? For the Lord Jesus Christ's sake, and because of your love for me—given to you by the Holy Spirit—pray much with me for my work. 31Pray that I will be protected in Jerusalem from those who are not Christians. Pray also that the Christians there will be willing to accept the money I am bringing them. 32Then I will be able to come to you with a happy heart by the will of God, and we can refresh each other.

33And now may our God, who gives peace, be with you all. Amen.

A THOUGHT: *The Christians in Jerusalem at this time had experienced a severe drought so that many of them were struggling to keep food on the table. Paul had made a point of mentioning this to the Gentile congregations that he evangelized. The Gentile Christians responded in love by sending the necessary financial resources for the Jerusalem church to distribute goods to those in need. It was right that they meet the needs of the Jerusalem Christians because the Jerusalem church had been the source of missionaries who shared the Good News of salvation with the Gentiles. Our concern should also be to share what we have with those in need. God had called us to demonstrate his love in very practical everyday sorts of ways—such as feeding the hungry, clothing the naked, and caring for the sick. Let the love which God has put in our hearts become a reality in sacrificial sharing with those in need.*

Proverbs for Today/ 10:1–2

Happy is the man with a level-headed son; sad the mother of a rebel. □ Ill-gotten gain brings no lasting happiness; right living does.

FEBRUARY 18

Jesus Blesses the Little Children/
Matthew 19:13–15

Little children were brought for Jesus to lay his hands on them and pray. But the disciples scolded those who brought them. "Don't bother him," they said.

14But Jesus said, "Let the little children come to me, and don't prevent them. For of such is the Kingdom of Heaven." 15And he put his hands on their heads and blessed them before he left.

A Thought: *The disciples must have forgotten what Jesus had said about children. Jesus wanted little children to come because he loves them and because they have the kind of attitude needed to approach God. He didn't mean that heaven is only for children, but that people need childlike attitudes of trust in God. The receptiveness of little children was a great contrast to the stubbornness of the religious leaders who let their religious education and sophistication stand in the way of the simple faith needed to believe in Jesus.*

Paul Greets His Friends at Rome/ Romans 16:1–16

Phoebe, a dear Christian woman from the town of Cenchreae, will be coming to see you soon. She has worked hard in the church there. Receive her as your sister in the Lord, giving her a warm Christian welcome. Help her in every way you can, for she has helped many in their needs, including me. 3Tell Priscilla and Aquila "hello." They have been my fellow workers in the affairs of Christ Jesus. 4In fact, they risked their lives for me; and I am not the only one who is thankful to them: so are all the Gentile churches.

5Please give my greetings to all those who meet to worship in their home. Greet my good friend Epaenetus. He was the very first person to become a Christian in Asia. 6Remember me to Mary, too, who has worked so hard to help us. 7Then there are Andronicus and Junias, my relatives who were in prison with me. They are respected by the apostles, and became Christians before I did. Please give them my greetings. 8Say "hello" to Ampliatus, whom I love as one of God's own children, 9and Urbanus, our fellow worker, and beloved Stachys.

10Then there is Apelles, a good man whom the Lord approves; greet him for me. And give my best regards to those working at the house of Aristobulus. 11Remember me to Herodion my relative. Remember me to the Christian slaves over at Narcissus House. 12Say "hello" to Tryphaena and Tryphosa, the Lord's workers, and to dear Persis, who has worked so hard for the Lord. 13Greet Rufus for me, whom the Lord picked out to be his very own; and also his dear mother who has been such a mother to me. 14And please give my greetings to Asyncritus, Phlegon, Hermes, Patrobas, Hermas, and the other brothers who are with them. 15Give my love to Philologus, Julia, Nereus and his sister, and to Olympas, and all the Christians who are with them. 16Shake hands warmly with each other. All the churches here send you their greetings.

A THOUGHT: *Paul's personal greetings went to Romans and Greeks, Jews and Gentiles, men and women, prisoners and prominent citizens. The church's base was broad: it crossed cultural, social, and economic lines. From this list we learn that the Christian community was an incredibly diverse group. This is as it ought to be. The oneness we have in Christ should supercede all cultural barriers. The Good News is a great equalizer—it places us all on the same footing before the cross!*

Proverbs for Today/ 10:3–4

The Lord will not let a good man starve to death, nor will he let the wicked man's riches continue forever. □ Lazy men are soon poor; hard workers get rich.

FEBRUARY 19

Jesus and the Rich Man/ Matthew 19:16–30

Someone came to Jesus with this question: "Good master, what must I do to have eternal life?"

17"When you call me good you are calling me God," Jesus replied, "for God alone is truly good. But to answer your question, you can get to heaven if you keep the commandments."

18"Which ones?" the man asked.

And Jesus replied, "Don't kill, don't commit adultery, don't steal, don't lie, 19honor your father and mother, and love your neighbor as yourself!"

20"I've always obeyed every one of them," the youth replied. "What else must I do?"

21Jesus told him, "If you want to be perfect, go and

sell everything you have and give the money to the poor, and you will have treasure in heaven; and come, follow me." 22But when the young man heard this, he went away sadly, for he was very rich.

23Then Jesus said to his disciples, "It is almost impossible for a rich man to get into the Kingdom of Heaven. 24I say it again—it is easier for a camel to go through the eye of a needle than for a rich man to enter the Kingdom of God!"

25This remark confounded the disciples. "Then who in the world can be saved?" they asked.

26Jesus looked at them intently and said, "Humanly speaking, no one. But with God, everything is possible."

27Then Peter said to him, "We left everything to follow you. What will we get out of it?"

28And Jesus replied, "When I, the Messiah, shall sit upon my glorious throne in the Kingdom, you my disciples shall certainly sit on twelve thrones judging the twelve tribes of Israel. 29And anyone who gives up his home, brothers, sisters, father, mother, wife, children, or property, to follow me, shall receive a hundred times as much in return, and shall have eternal life. 30But many who are first now will be last then; and some who are last now will be first then."

A THOUGHT: *In response to the young man's question about how to have eternal life, Jesus told him to keep God's Ten Commandments. Jesus then listed six of them, all referring to relationships with others. When the young man replied that he had kept all of these laws, Jesus told him he must do something more—sell everything and give the money to the poor. This request showed the man's weakness. In reality, his wealth was his god, his "graven image," and he would not give it up. We cannot love God with all our hearts and keep our money to ourselves. We must use what God has given us to serve others.*

Avoid Divisive People/ Romans 16:17–27

And now there is one more thing to say before I end this letter. Stay away from those who cause divisions and are upsetting people's faith, teaching things about Christ that are contrary to what you have been taught. 18Such teachers are not working for our Lord Jesus, but only want gain for themselves. They are good speakers, and simple-minded people are often fooled by them. 19But everyone knows that you stand loyal and true. This makes me very happy. I want you always to remain very clear about what is right, and to stay innocent of any wrong. 20The God of peace will soon crush Satan under your feet. The blessings from our Lord Jesus Christ be upon you.

21Timothy my fellow-worker, and Lucius and Jason and Sosipater, my relatives, send you their good wishes. 22I, Tertius, the one who is writing this letter for Paul, send my greetings too, as a Christian brother. 23Gaius says to say "hello" to you for him. I am his guest, and the church meets here in his home. Erastus, the city treasurer, sends you his greetings and so does Quartus, a Christian brother. 24Goodbye. May the grace of our Lord Jesus Christ be with you all.

25,26,27I commit you to God, who is able to make you strong and steady in the Lord, just as the Gospel says, and just as I have told you. This is God's plan of salvation for you Gentiles, kept secret from the beginning of time. But now as the prophets foretold and as God commands, this message is being preached everywhere, so that people all around the world will have faith in Christ and obey him. To God, who alone is wise, be the glory forever through Jesus Christ our Lord. Amen.

Sincerely,
Paul

A THOUGHT: *The unity of the church was very important to Paul. He fought hard against those who wanted to bring division within the church. We also must be careful with those who want to split churches. The church should never be split over minor points of doctrine—as is too often the case. Let us be careful that we do not to end up dividing Christians from Christians—for in Christ we belong to one another. We should avoid those who wish to make such divisions between Christians.*

Proverbs for Today/ 10:5

A wise youth makes hay while the sun shines, but what a shame to see a lad who sleeps away his hour of opportunity.

FEBRUARY 20

The Parable of the Field Workers/
Matthew 20:1–19

Here is another illustration of the Kingdom of Heaven. "The owner of an estate went out early one morning to hire workers for his harvest field. ²He agreed to pay them $20 a day and sent them out to work.

³"A couple of hours later he was passing a hiring hall and saw some men standing around waiting for jobs, ⁴so he sent them also into his fields, telling them he would pay them whatever was right at the end of the day. ⁵At noon and again around three o'clock in the afternoon he did the same thing.

⁶"At five o'clock that evening he was in town again and saw some more men standing around and asked them, 'Why haven't you been working today?'

⁷" 'Because no one hired us,' they replied.

" 'Then go on out and join the others in my fields,' he told them.

⁸"That evening he told the paymaster to call the men in and pay them, beginning with the last men first. ⁹When the men hired at five o'clock were paid, each received $20. ¹⁰So when the men hired earlier came to get theirs, they assumed they would receive much more. But they, too, were paid $20.

¹¹,¹²"They protested, 'Those fellows worked only one hour, and yet you've paid them just as much as those of us who worked all day in the scorching heat.'

¹³" 'Friend,' he answered one of them, 'I did you no wrong! Didn't you agree to work all day for $20? ¹⁴Take it and go. It is my desire to pay all the same; ¹⁵is it against the law to give away my money if I want to? Should you be angry because I am kind?' ¹⁶And so it is that the last shall be first, and the first, last."

¹⁷As Jesus was on the way to Jerusalem, he took the twelve disciples aside, ¹⁸and talked to them about what would happen to him when they arrived.

"I will be betrayed to the chief priests and other Jewish leaders, and they will condemn me to die. ¹⁹And they will hand me over to the Roman government, and I will be mocked and crucified, and the third day I will rise to life again."

A Thought: *In this parable, God is the estate owner and believers are those who work for him. This parable was for those who felt superior because of heritage or favored position. This parable is not about rewards, but about salvation. It clarifies the membership rules of the Kingdom of Heaven—entrance is by God's grace alone. Do you resent God's gracious acceptance of the despised, the outcast, and the sinners who have turned to him for forgiveness? Are you ever jealous of what God has given to another person? Instead, focus on God's gracious benefits to you, and be thankful for what you have.*

God's Gifts to the Corinthian Church/
1 Corinthians 1:1–9

From: Paul, chosen by God to be Jesus Christ's missionary, and from brother Sosthenes.

²*To:* The Christians in Corinth, invited by God to be his people and made acceptable to him by Christ Jesus. *And to:* All Christians everywhere—whoever calls upon the name of Jesus Christ, our Lord and theirs.

³May God our Father and the Lord Jesus Christ give you all of his blessings, and great peace of heart and mind.

⁴I can never stop thanking God for all the wonderful gifts he has given you, now that you are Christ's: ⁵he has enriched your whole life. He has helped you speak out for him and has given you a full understanding of the truth; ⁶what I told you Christ could do for you has happened! ⁷Now you have every grace and blessing; every spiritual gift and power for doing his will are yours during this time of waiting for the return of our Lord Jesus Christ. ⁸And he guarantees right up to the end that you will be counted free from all sin and guilt on that day when he returns. ⁹God will surely do this for you, for he always does just what he says, and he is the one who invited you into this wonderful friendship with his Son, even Christ our Lord.

A Thought: *The Corinthian church members had all the spiritual gifts they needed to live the Christian life, to witness for Christ, and to stand against the paganism and immorality of Corinth. But instead of using what God had given them, they were arguing over which gifts were more important. God has not given us gifts to raise our status, but to give us the spiritual capacity to serve others. Let us not take pride in what has been given to us, rather, let us sacrifice ourselves in service to others.*

Proverbs for Today/ 10:6–7

The good man is covered with blessings from head to foot, but an evil man inwardly curses his luck. We all have happy memories of good men gone to their reward, but the names of wicked men stink after them.

FEBRUARY 21

The True Leader Is a Servant/ Matthew 20:20–28

Then the mother of James and John, the sons of Zebedee, brought her sons to Jesus and respectfully asked a favor.

21"What is your request?" he asked. She replied, "In your Kingdom, will you let my two sons sit on two thrones next to yours?"

22But Jesus told her, "You don't know what you are asking!" Then he turned to James and John and asked them, "Are you able to drink from the terrible cup I am about to drink from?"

"Yes," they replied, "we are able!"

23"You shall indeed drink from it," he told them. "But I have no right to say who will sit on the thrones next to mine. Those places are reserved for the persons my Father selects."

24The other ten disciples were indignant when they heard what James and John had asked for.

25But Jesus called them together and said, "Among the heathen, kings are tyrants and each minor official lords it over those beneath him. 26But among you it is quite different. Anyone wanting to be a leader among you must be your servant. 27And if you want to be right at the top, you must serve like a slave. 28Your attitude must be like my own, for I, the Messiah, did not come to be served, but to serve, and to give my life as a ransom for many."

A THOUGHT: *The disciples were upset because James and John were trying to grab the top positions. All the disciples wanted positions of greatness, but Jesus taught them that the greatest person in God's Kingdom is the servant of all. Jesus' purpose in life was to serve others and to give his life away. A real leader has a servant's heart. He appreciates the worth of others and realizes he's not above any job. If you see something that needs to be done, don't wait to be asked. Take the initiative and do it like a faithful servant.*

Divisions within the Corinthian Church/
1 Corinthians 1:10–17

But, dear brothers, I beg you in the name of the Lord Jesus Christ to stop arguing among yourselves. Let there be real harmony so that there won't be splits in the church. I plead with you to be of one mind, united in thought and purpose. 11For some of those who live at Chloe's house have told me of your arguments and quarrels, dear brothers. 12Some of you are saying, "I am a follower of Paul"; and others say that they are for Apollos or for Peter; and some that they alone are the true followers of Christ. 13And so, in effect, you have broken Christ into many pieces.

But did I, Paul, die for your sins? Were any of you baptized in my name? 14I am so thankful now that I didn't baptize any of you except Crispus and Gaius. 15For now no one can think that I have been trying to start something new, beginning a "Church of Paul." 16Oh, yes, and I baptized the family of Stephanas. I don't remember ever baptizing anyone else. 17For Christ didn't send me to baptize, but to preach the Gospel; and even my preaching sounds poor, for I do not fill my sermons with profound words and high sounding ideas, for fear of diluting the mighty power there is in the simple message of the cross of Christ.

A THOUGHT: *In this large and diverse Corinthian church, the believers favored different preachers. Because there was as yet no written New Testament, the believers depended heavily on preaching and teaching for spiritual insight into the meaning of the Old Testament. Some followed Paul, who had founded their church; some who had heard Peter in Jerusalem followed him; while others listened only to Apollos, an eloquent and popular preacher who had a dynamic ministry in Corinth. Although these three preachers were united in their message, their personalities attracted different people. Now the church was in danger of dividing. By mentioning Jesus Christ ten times in the first ten verses, Paul makes it clear what all preachers and teachers should emphasize—the Person and work of Jesus Christ. The message is more important than the messenger.*

Proverbs for Today/ 10:8–9

The wise man is glad to be instructed, but a self-sufficient fool falls flat on his face. A good man has firm footing, but a crook will slip and fall.

FEBRUARY 22

Jesus Heals Two Blind Men/ Matthew 20:29–34

As Jesus and the disciples left the city of Jericho, a vast crowd surged along behind.

30Two blind men were sitting beside the road and when they heard that Jesus was coming that way, they began shouting, "Sir, King David's Son, have mercy on us!"

31The crowd told them to be quiet, but they only yelled the louder.

32,33When Jesus came to the place where they were he stopped in the road and called, "What do you want me to do for you?"

"Sir," they said, "we want to see!"

34Jesus was moved with pity for them and touched their eyes. And instantly they could see, and followed him.

A THOUGHT: *The blind men called Jesus "King David's Son" because the Jews knew that the Messiah would be a descendant of King David. This poor blind beggar could see that Jesus was the long-awaited Messiah, while the religious leaders who witnessed Jesus' miracles were blind to his identity, refusing to open their eyes to the truth. Seeing with your eyes doesn't guarantee seeing with your heart.*

The "Foolishness" of God/ 1 Corinthians 1:18–25

I know very well how foolish it sounds to those who are lost, when they hear that Jesus died to save them. But we who are saved recognize this message as the very power of God. 19For God says, "I will destroy all human plans of salvation no matter how wise they seem to be, and ignore the best ideas of men, even the most brilliant of them."

20So what about these wise men, these scholars, these brilliant debaters of this world's great affairs? God has made them all look foolish, and shown their wisdom to be useless nonsense. 21For God in his wisdom saw to it that the world would never find God through human brilliance, and then he stepped in and saved all those who believed his message, which the world calls foolish and silly. 22It seems foolish to the Jews because they want a sign from heaven as proof that what is preached is true; and it is foolish to the Gentiles because they believe only what agrees with their philosophy and seems wise to them. 23So when we preach about Christ dying to save them, the Jews are offended and the Gentiles say it's all nonsense. 24But God has opened the eyes of those called to salvation, both Jews and Gentiles, to see that Christ is the mighty power of God to save them; Christ himself is the center of God's wise plan for their salvation. 25This so-called "foolish" plan of God is far wiser than the wisest plan of the wisest man, and God in his weakness—Christ dying on the cross—is far stronger than any man.

A THOUGHT: *The message of Christ's death for sins sounds foolish to those who don't believe. Death seems to be the end of the road, the ultimate weakness. But Jesus did not remain dead. His resurrection shows his power even over death, and he will save us from eternal death and give us everlasting life if we trust him as Savior and Lord. This sounds so simple that many people won't accept it. They try other ways to obtain eternal life (being good, being wise, etc.). But their attempts will not work. The 'foolish' people who simply accept Christ's offer are actually the wisest of all, because they alone will live eternally with God.*

Proverbs for Today/ 10:10

Winking at sin leads to sorrow; bold reproof leads to peace.

FEBRUARY 23

Jesus' Triumphal Entry into Jerusalem/ Matthew 21:1–17

As Jesus and the disciples approached Jerusalem, and were near the town of Bethphage on the Mount of Olives, Jesus sent two of them into the village ahead.

2"Just as you enter," he said, "you will see a donkey tied there, with its colt beside it. Untie them and bring them here. 3If anyone asks you what you are doing, just say, 'The Master needs them,' and there will be no trouble."

4This was done to fulfill the ancient prophecy, 5"Tell Jerusalem her King is coming to her, riding humbly on a donkey's colt!"

6The two disciples did as Jesus said, 7and brought the animals to him and threw their garments over the colt for him to ride on. 8And some in the crowd threw down their coats along the road ahead of him, and others cut branches from the trees and spread them out before him.

9Then the crowds surged on ahead and pressed along behind, shouting, "God bless King David's Son!" . . . "God's Man is here!" . . . Bless him, Lord!" . . . "Praise God in highest heaven!"

10The entire city of Jerusalem was stirred as he entered. "Who is this?" they asked.

11And the crowds replied, "It's Jesus, the prophet from Nazareth up in Galilee."

12Jesus went into the Temple, drove out the merchants, and knocked over the moneychangers' tables and the stalls of those selling doves.

13"The Scriptures say my Temple is a place of prayer," he declared, "but you have turned it into a den of thieves."

14And now the blind and crippled came to him and he healed them there in the Temple. 15But when the chief priests and other Jewish leaders saw these wonderful miracles, and heard even the little children in the Temple shouting, "God bless the Son of David," they were disturbed and indignant and asked him, "Do you hear what these children are saying?"

16"Yes," Jesus replied. "Didn't you ever read the Scriptures? For they say, 'Even little babies shall praise him!' "

17Then he returned to Bethany, where he stayed overnight.

A THOUGHT: *This event is celebrated by Christians on Palm Sunday, one week before Easter. It celebrates Jesus' entry into Jerusalem in fulfillment of Messianic prophecy. People lined the highway, praising God, waving palm branches, and throwing their cloaks in front of the colt as it passed before them. They were proclaiming that Jesus was the Messiah. Yet they believed that Jesus would be a political ruler who would throw off the yoke of Roman authority and restore Israel to its former glory (as in David's time). But the people were disappointed when their expectations were not fulfilled. A few days later these same people would bow to political pressure and demand that Jesus be crucified. How easy it is to change our loyalties when our expectations are not met.*

The Foolish Will Shame the Wise/
1 Corinthians 1:26–31

Notice among yourselves, dear brothers, that few of you who follow Christ have big names or power or wealth. 27Instead, God has deliberately chosen to use ideas the world considers foolish and of little worth in order to shame those people considered by the world as wise and great. 28He has chosen a plan despised by the world, counted as nothing at all, and used it to bring down to nothing those the world considers great, 29so that no one anywhere can ever brag in the presence of God.

30For it is from God alone that you have your life through Christ Jesus. He showed us God's plan of salvation; he was the one who made us acceptable to God; he made us pure and holy and gave himself to purchase our salvation. 31As it says in the Scriptures, "If anyone is going to boast, let him boast only of what the Lord has done."

A THOUGHT: *Paul continues to emphasize that the way to receive salvation is so ordinary and simple that any person who wants to can understand it. Skill does not get you into God's Kingdom— simple faith does. God planned it this way so no one could boast that his achievements helped him secure eternal life. Salvation is completely the work of God. Through Jesus' death, we become perfect in God's eyes. There is nothing we can do to become acceptable to God; we need only accept what Jesus has already done for us. He has done the work; we acknowledge that work, recognizing his position as God.*

Proverbs for Today/ 10:11–12

There is living truth in what a good man says, but the mouth of the evil man is filled with curses. □ Hatred stirs old quarrels, but love overlooks insults.

FEBRUARY 24

The Cursing of the Fig Tree/ Matthew 21:18–22

In the morning, as Jesus was returning to Jerusalem, he was hungry, 19and noticed a fig tree beside the road. He went over to see if there were any figs, but there were only leaves. Then he said to it, "Never bear fruit again!" And soon the fig tree withered up.

20The disciples were utterly amazed and asked, "How did the fig tree wither so quickly?"

21Then Jesus told them, "Truly, if you have faith, and don't doubt, you can do things like this and much more. You can even say to this Mount of Olives, 'Move over into the ocean,' and it will. 22You can get anything—*anything* you ask for in prayer—if you believe."

A Thought: *Why did Jesus curse the fig tree? This was not a thoughtless, angry act, but an acted–out parable. Jesus was showing his anger at religion without substance. Just as the fig tree looked good from a distance but was fruitless upon close examination, so the Temple looked impressive at first glance, but its sacrifices and other activities were hollow because they were not done to worship God sincerely. Genuine faith produces fruit for God's kingdom.*

The Preaching of the Cross/ 1 Corinthians 2:1–10

Dear brothers, even when I first came to you I didn't use lofty words and brilliant ideas to tell you God's message. 2For I decided that I would speak only of Jesus Christ and his death on the cross. 3I came to you in weakness—timid and trembling. 4And my preaching was very plain, not with a lot of oratory and human wisdom, but the Holy Spirit's power was in my words, proving to those who heard them that the message was from God. 5I did this because I wanted your faith to stand firmly upon God, not on man's great ideas.

6Yet when I am among mature Christians I do speak with words of great wisdom, but not the kind that comes from here on earth, and not the kind that appeals to the great men of this world, who are doomed to fall. 7Our words are wise because they are from God, telling of God's wise plan to bring us into the glories of heaven. This plan was hidden in former times, though it was made for our benefit before the world began. 8But the great men of the world have not understood it; if they had, they never would have crucified the Lord of Glory.

9That is what is meant by the Scriptures which say that no mere man has ever seen, heard or even imagined what wonderful things God has ready for those who love the Lord. 10But we know about these things because God has sent his Spirit to tell us, and his Spirit searches out and shows us all of God's deepest secrets.

A THOUGHT: *As a brilliant scholar, Paul could have overwhelmed his listeners with intellectual arguments and persuasive oratory. Instead he shared the simple message of Jesus Christ by allowing the Holy Spirit to guide his words. In sharing the gospel with others, we should follow Paul's example and keep our message simple and basic. The Holy Spirit will give power to our words and use them to bring glory to Jesus.*

Proverbs for Today/ 10:13–14

Men with common sense are admired as counselors; those without it are beaten as servants. □ A wise man holds his tongue. Only a fool blurts out everything he knows; that only leads to sorrow and trouble.

FEBRUARY 25

The Parable of the Disloyal Tenants/ Matthew 21:23–46

When Jesus had returned to the Temple and was teaching, the chief priests and other Jewish leaders came up to him and demanded to know by whose authority he had thrown out the merchants the day before.

24"I'll tell you if you answer one question first," Jesus replied. 25"Was John the Baptist sent from God, or not?"

They talked it over among themselves. "If we say, 'From God,'" they said, "then he will ask why we didn't believe what John said. 26And if we deny that God sent him, we'll be mobbed, for the crowd all think he was a prophet." 27So they finally replied, "We don't know!"

And Jesus said, "Then I won't answer your question either.

28"But what do you think about this? A man with two sons told the older boy, 'Son, go out and work on the farm today.' 29'I won't,' he answered, but later he changed his mind and went. 30Then the father told the youngest, 'You go!' and he said, 'Yes, sir, I will.' But he didn't. 31Which of the two was obeying his father?"

They replied, "The first, of course."

Then Jesus explained his meaning: "Surely evil men and prostitutes will get into the Kingdom before you do. 32For John the Baptist told you to repent and turn to God, and you wouldn't, while very evil men and prostitutes did. And even when you saw this happening, you refused to repent, and so you couldn't believe.

33"Now listen to this story: A certain landowner planted a vineyard with a hedge around it, and built a platform for the watchman, then leased the vineyard to some farmers on a sharecrop basis, and went away to live in another country.

34"At the time of the grape harvest he sent his agents to the farmers to collect his share. 35But the farmers attacked his men, beat one, killed one and stoned another.

36"Then he sent a larger group of his men to collect for him, but the results were the same. 37Finally the owner sent his son, thinking they would surely respect him.

38"But when these farmers saw the son coming they said among themselves, 'Here comes the heir to this estate; come on, let's kill him and get it for ourselves!' 39So they dragged him out of the vineyard and killed him.

40"When the owner returns, what do you think he will do to those farmers?"

41The Jewish leaders replied, "He will put the wicked men to a horrible death, and lease the vineyard to others who will pay him promptly."

42Then Jesus asked them, "Didn't you ever read in the Scriptures: 'The stone rejected by the builders has been made the honored cornerstone; how remarkable! what an amazing thing the Lord has done'?

43"What I mean is that the Kingdom of God shall be taken away from you, and given to a nation that will give God his share of the crop. 44All who stumble on this rock of truth shall be broken, but those it falls on will be scattered as dust."

45When the chief priests and other Jewish leaders realized that Jesus was talking about them—that they were the farmers in his story— 46they wanted to get rid of him, but were afraid to try because of the crowds, for they accepted Jesus as a prophet.

A THOUGHT: *The Pharisees demanded to know where Jesus got his authority. They didn't really want an answer to their question; they only wanted to trap him. Jesus answered them by asking a question concerning the source of John the Baptist's authority. Jesus' question forced the Pharisees into a dilemma. Whatever answer they would give would have negative consequences for their position. So they gave no answer. Since the Pharisees were unwilling to openly answer Jesus' question, Jesus gives his answer in the form of a parable. The main characters in this parable are (1) the landowner—God, (2) the vineyard—Israel, (3) the farmers—the Jewish religious leaders, (4) the landowner's men—the prophets and priests who remained faithful to God and preached to Israel, (5) the son—Jesus, and (6) the others—Gentiles. Jesus tells the parable to expose the religious leaders' hypocrisy and their plot to murder him.*

The Spirit Gives Us Wisdom/ 1 Corinthians 2:11–16

No one can really know what anyone else is thinking, or what he is really like, except that person himself. And no one can know God's thoughts except God's own Spirit. 12And God has actually given us his Spirit (not the world's spirit) to tell us about the wonderful free gifts of grace and blessing that God has given us. 13In telling you about these gifts we have even used the very words given to us by the Holy Spirit, not words that we as men might choose. So we use the Holy Spirit's words to explain the Holy Spirit's facts. 14 But the man who isn't a Christian can't understand and can't accept these thoughts from God, which the Holy Spirit teaches us. They sound foolish to him, because only those who have the Holy Spirit within them can understand what the Holy Spirit means. Others just can't take it in. 15But the spiritual man has insight into everything, and that bothers and baffles the man of the world, who can't understand him at all. 16How could he? For certainly he has never been one to know the Lord's thoughts, or to discuss them with him, or to move the hands of God by prayer. But, strange as it seems, we Christians actually do have within us a portion of the very thoughts and mind of Christ.

A THOUGHT: *No one can comprehend God by human effort, but by his Spirit many of his thoughts are revealed to us. Believers are spiritual people having insight into some of God's plans, thoughts, and actions. By his Holy Spirit we can begin to know his thoughts, discuss them with him, and expect his answers to our prayers. Are you spending enough time with Christ to have his very mind in you? An intimate relationship with Christ comes only from consistent time spent in his presence and in his Word.*

Proverbs for Today/ 10:15–16

The rich man's wealth is his only strength. The poor man's poverty is his only curse. □ The good man's earnings advance the cause of righteousness. The evil man squanders his on sin.

FEBRUARY 26

The Parable of the Wedding Dinner/ Matthew 22:1–14

Jesus told several other stories to show what the Kingdom of Heaven is like.

"For instance," he said, "it can be illustrated by the story of a king who prepared a great wedding dinner for his son. 3Many guests were invited, and when the banquet was ready he sent messengers to notify everyone that it was time to come. But all refused! 4So he sent other servants to tell them, 'Everything is ready and the roast is in the oven. Hurry!'

5"But the guests he had invited merely laughed and went on about their business, one to his farm, another to his store; 6others beat up his messengers and treated them shamefully, even killing some of them.

7"Then the angry king sent out his army and destroyed the murderers and burned their city. 8And he said to his servants, 'The wedding feast is ready, and the guests I invited aren't worthy of the honor. 9Now go out to the street corners and invite everyone you see.'

10"So the servants did, and brought in all they could find, good and bad alike; and the banquet hall was filled with guests. 11But when the king came in to meet the guests he noticed a man who wasn't wearing the wedding robe [provided for him].

12" 'Friend,' he asked, 'how does it happen that you are here without a wedding robe?' And the man had no reply.

13"Then the king said to his aides, 'Bind him hand and foot and throw him out into the outer darkness where there is weeping and gnashing of teeth.' 14For many are called, but few are chosen."

A THOUGHT: *In first–century Jewish culture, two invitations were expected when banquets were given. The first asked the guests to attend; the second announced that all was ready. Here the king, God, invited his guests three times—and each time they rejected his invitations. God wants us to join him at his banquet, which will last for eternity. That's why he sends us invitations again and again. Have you accepted his invitation?*

Paul Rebukes Divisive Church Members/
1 Corinthians 3:1–9

Dear brothers, I have been talking to you as though you were still just babies in the Christian life, who are not following the Lord, but your own desires; I cannot talk to you as I would to healthy Christians, who are filled with the Spirit. 2I have had to feed you with milk and not with solid food, because you couldn't digest anything stronger. And even now you still have to be fed on milk. 3For you are still only baby Christians, controlled by your own desires, not God's. When you are jealous of one another and divide up into quarreling groups, doesn't that prove you are still babies, wanting your own way? In fact, you are acting like people who don't belong to the Lord at all. 4There you are, quarreling about whether I am greater than Apollos, and dividing the church. Doesn't this show how little you have grown in the Lord?

5Who am I, and who is Apollos, that we should be the cause of a quarrel? Why, we're just God's servants, each of us with certain special abilities, and with our help you believed. 6My work was to plant the seed in your hearts, and Apollos' work was to water it, but it was God, not we, who made the garden grow in your hearts. 7The person who does the planting or watering isn't very important, but God is important because he is the one who makes things grow. 8Apollos and I are working as a team, with the same aim, though each of us will be rewarded for his own hard work. 9We are only God's co-workers. You are *God's* garden, not ours; you are *God's* building, not ours.

A THOUGHT: *Paul's work was to plant the seed of God's Word in people's hearts. He was a pioneer missionary, one who brought the message of salvation. Apollos' role was to water—to help the believers grow stronger in the faith Paul had helped them discover. Paul founded the church in Corinth, and Apollos built on that foundation. Tragically, the believers in Corinth had split into factions, pledging loyalty to different teachers. Paul wanted them to see that the preachers were merely their guides to point them to God.*

God's work in the world involves many different individuals with a variety of gifts and abilities. There are no superstars in this task, only team members performing their own special roles. We become useful members of God's team by setting aside the desire to receive glory for what we do. The praise that comes from people is comparatively worthless; invaluable approval comes from God.

Proverbs for Today/ 10:17

Anyone willing to be corrected is on the pathway to life. Anyone refusing has lost his chance.

FEBRUARY 27

Jesus Answers the Pharisees and the Sadducees/ Matthew 22:15–46

Then the Pharisees met together to try to think of some way to trap Jesus into saying something for which they could arrest him. 16They decided to send some of their men along with the Herodians to ask him this question: "Sir, we know you are very honest and teach the truth regardless of the consequences, without fear or favor. 17Now tell us, is it right to pay taxes to the Roman government or not?"

18But Jesus saw what they were after. "You hypocrites!" he exclaimed. "Who are you trying to fool with your trick questions? 19Here, show me a coin." And they handed him a penny.

20"Whose picture is stamped on it?" he asked them. "And whose name is this beneath the picture?"

21"Caesar's," they replied.

"Well, then," he said, "give it to Caesar if it is his, and give God everything that belongs to God."

22His reply surprised and baffled them and they went away.

23But that same day some of the Sadducees, who say there is no resurrection after death, came to him and asked, 24"Sir, Moses said that if a man died without children, his brother should marry the widow and their children would get all the dead man's property. 25Well, we had among us a family of seven brothers. The first of these men married and then died, without children, so his widow became the second brother's wife. 26This brother also died without children, and the wife was passed to the next brother, and so on until she had been the wife of each of them. 27And then she also died. 28So whose wife will she be in the resurrection? For she was the wife of all seven of them!"

29But Jesus said, "Your error is caused by your ignorance of the Scriptures and of God's power! 30For in the resurrection there is no marriage; everyone is as the angels in heaven. 31But now, as to whether there is a resurrection of the dead—don't you ever read the Scriptures? Don't you realize that God was speaking directly to you when he said, 32'I *am* the God of Abraham, Isaac, and Jacob'? So God is not the God of the dead, but of the *living*."

33The crowds were profoundly impressed by his answers— 34,35but not the Pharisees! When they heard that he had routed the Sadducees with his reply, they thought up a fresh question of their own to ask him. One of them, a lawyer, spoke up: 36"Sir, which is the most important command in the laws of Moses?"

37Jesus replied, " 'Love the Lord your God with all your heart, soul, and mind.' 38,39This is the first and greatest commandment. The second most important is similar: 'Love your neighbor as much as you love yourself.' 40All the other commandments and all the demands of the prophets stem from these two laws and are fulfilled if you obey them. Keep only these and you will find that you are obeying all the others."

41Then, surrounded by the Pharisees, he asked them a question: 42"What about the Messiah? Whose son is he?" "The son of David," they replied.

43"Then why does David, speaking under the inspiration of the Holy Spirit, call him 'Lord'?" Jesus asked. "For David said,

44'God said to my Lord, Sit at my right hand until I
    put your enemies beneath your feet.'

45Since David called him 'Lord,' how can he be merely his son?"

46They had no answer. And after that no one dared ask him any more questions.

A THOUGHT: *The Pharisees were a religious group opposed to the Roman occupation of Palestine. The Herodians were a Jewish political party who supported Herod Antipas and the policies instituted by Rome. Normally, these two groups were bitter enemies, but here they united against Jesus. Together, men from these two groups asked Jesus a question about paying Roman taxes, thinking they had a foolproof plan to corner him. If Jesus agreed that it was right to pay taxes to Caesar, the Pharisees would say he was opposed to God, the only king they recognized. If Jesus said the taxes should not be paid, the Herodians would hand him over to Rome for tax evasion. Jesus avoided this trap by showing that we have a dual citizenship. Our citizenship in the state requires that we pay money for the services and benefits we receive. Our citizenship in the Kingdom of Heaven requires that we pledge to God the obedience and commitment of our entire lives.*

After the Pharisees and Herodians failed to trap Jesus, the Sadducees smugly stepped in to try. They did not believe in the resurrection because the Pentateuch (Genesis—Deuteronomy) has no direct teaching on it. The Sadducees thought they had trapped Jesus for sure with their question on marriage. But Jesus answered that there wouldn't be marriage in the resurrection. In each of Jesus' answers, he exposed the evil motives of the questioners and demonstrated his great wisdom.

Everyone's Work Will Be Judged by God/
1 Corinthians 3:10–17

God, in his kindness, has taught me how to be an expert builder. I have laid the foundation and Apollos has built on it. But he who builds on the foundation must be very careful. 11And no one can ever lay any other real foundation than that one we already have—Jesus Christ. 12But there are various kinds of materials that can be used to build on that foundation. Some use gold and silver and jewels;

and some build with sticks, and hay, or even straw! 13There is going to come a time of testing at Christ's Judgment Day to see what kind of material each builder has used. Everyone's work will be put through the fire so that all can see whether or not it keeps its value, and what was really accomplished. 14Then every workman who has built on the foundation with the right materials, and whose work still stands, will get his pay. 15But if the house he has built burns up, he will have a great loss. He himself will be saved, but like a man escaping through a wall of flames.

16Don't you realize that all of you together are the house of God, and that the Spirit of God lives among you in his house? 17If anyone defiles and spoils God's home, God will destroy him. For God's home is holy and clean, and you are that home.

A Thought: *A building is only as solid as its foundation. The foundation of our lives is Jesus Christ; he is our base, our reason for being. Everything we are and do must fit into the pattern provided by Jesus Christ. Are you building your life on the only real and lasting foundation, or are you building on another foundation such as wealth, security, or success? What is your reason for living?*

Proverbs for Today/ 10:18
To hide hatred is to be a liar; to slander is to be a fool.

FEBRUARY 28

Jesus Condemns the Religious Leaders/ Matthew 23:1–12
Then Jesus said to the crowds, and to his disciples, 2"You would think these Jewish leaders and these Pharisees were Moses, the way they keep making up so many laws! 3And of course you should obey their every whim! It may be all right to do what they say, but above anything else, *don't follow their example.* For they don't do what they tell you to do. 4They load you with impossible demands that they themselves don't even try to keep.

5"Everything they do is done for show. They act holy

by wearing on their arms little prayer boxes with Scripture verses inside, and by lengthening the memorial fringes of their robes. 6And how they love to sit at the head table at banquets, and in the reserved pews in the synagogue! 7How they enjoy the deference paid them on the streets, and to be called 'Rabbi' and 'Master'! 8Don't ever let anyone call you that. For only God is your Rabbi and all of you are on the same level, as brothers. 9And don't address anyone here on earth as 'Father,' for only God in heaven should be addressed like that. 10And don't be called 'Master,' for only one is your master, even the Messiah.

11"The more lowly your service to others, the greater you are. To be the greatest, be a servant. 12But those who think themselves great shall be disappointed and humbled; and those who humble themselves shall be exalted.

A THOUGHT: *Jesus again exposed the hypocritical attitudes of the religious leaders. They knew the Scriptures, but did not live by them. They didn't care about being holy—just looking holy in order to receive the people's admiration and praise. Today, like the Pharisees, many people who know the Bible do not let it change their lives. They say they follow Jesus but don't live by his standards of love. People who live this way are hypocrites. We must make sure our actions match our beliefs.*

The "Foolishness" of God/ 1 Corinthians 3:18–23

Stop fooling yourselves. If you count yourself above average in intelligence, as judged by this world's standards, you had better put this all aside and be a fool rather than let it hold you back from the true wisdom from above. 19For the wisdom of this world is foolishness to God. As it says in the book of Job, God uses man's own brilliance to trap him; he stumbles over his own "wisdom" and falls. 20And again, in the book of Psalms, we are told that the Lord knows full well how the human mind reasons, and how foolish and futile it is.

21So don't be proud of following the wise men of this world. For God has already given you everything you need. 22He has given you Paul and Apollos and Peter as your helpers. He has given you the whole world to use, and life and even death are your servants. He has given you all of the present and all of the future. All are yours, 23and you belong to Christ, and Christ is God's.

A Thought: *Paul is not telling the Corinthian believers to neglect the pursuit of knowledge, but if one has to choose between earthly knowledge and heavenly wisdom, choose heavenly wisdom even though you may look foolish to the world. Worldly wisdom, if it holds you back from God, is no wisdom at all. The Corinthians were using so-called worldly wisdom to evaluate their leaders and teachers. Their pride made them value the presentation of the message more than its content.*

Proverbs for Today/ 10:19

Don't talk so much. You keep putting your foot in your mouth. Be sensible and turn off the flow!

MARCH 1

Jesus Denounces the Pharisees/ Matthew 23:13–39

"Woe to you, Pharisees, and you other religious leaders. Hypocrites! For you won't let others enter the Kingdom of Heaven, and won't go in yourselves. And you pretend to be holy, with all your long, public prayers in the streets, while you are evicting widows from their homes. Hypocrites! 15Yes, woe upon you hypocrites. For you go to all lengths to make one convert, and then turn him into twice the son of hell you are yourselves. 16Blind guides! Woe upon you! For your rule is that to swear 'By God's Temple' means nothing—you can break that oath, but to swear 'By the gold in the Temple' is binding! 17Blind fools! Which is greater, the gold, or the Temple that sanctifies the gold? 18And you say that to take an oath 'By the altar' can be broken, but to swear 'By the gifts on the altar' is binding! 19Blind! For which is greater, the gift on the altar, or the altar itself that sanctifies the gift? 20When you swear 'By the altar' you are swearing by it and everything on it, 21and when you swear 'By the Temple' you are swearing by it, and by God who lives in it. 22And when you swear 'By heavens' you are swearing by the Throne of God and by God himself.

23"Yes, woe upon you, Pharisees, and you other religious leaders—hypocrites! For you tithe down to the last mint leaf in your garden, but ignore the important things—justice and mercy and faith. Yes, you should tithe, but you shouldn't leave the more important things undone. 24Blind guides! You strain out a gnat and swallow a camel.

25"Woe to you, Pharisees, and you religious leaders—hypocrites! You are so careful to polish the outside of the cup, but the inside is foul with extortion and greed. 26Blind Pharisees! First cleanse the inside of the cup, and then the whole cup will be clean.

27"Woe to you, Pharisees, and you religious leaders! You are like beautiful mausoleums—full of dead men's bones, and of foulness and corruption. 28You try to look like saintly men, but underneath those pious robes of yours are hearts besmirched with every sort of hypocrisy and sin.

29,30"Yes, woe to you, Pharisees, and you religious leaders—hypocrites! For you build monuments to the prophets killed by your fathers and lay flowers on the graves of the godly men they destroyed, and say, 'We certainly would never have acted as our fathers did.'

31"In saying that, you are accusing yourselves of being the sons of wicked men. 32And you are following in their steps, filling up the full measure of their evil. 33Snakes! Sons of vipers! How shall you escape the judgment of hell?

34"I will send you prophets, and wise men, and inspired writers, and you will kill some by crucifixion, and rip open the backs of others with whips in your synagogues, and hound them from city to city, 35so that you will become guilty of all the blood of murdered godly men from righteous Abel to Zechariah (son of Barachiah), slain by you in the Temple between the altar and the sanctuary. 36Yes, all the accumulated judgment of the centuries shall break upon the heads of this very generation.

37"O Jerusalem, Jerusalem, the city that kills the prophets, and stones all those God sends to her! How often I have wanted to gather your children together as a hen gathers her chicks beneath her wings, but you wouldn't let me. 38And now your house is left to you, desolate. 39For I tell you this, you will never see me again until you are ready to welcome the one sent to you from God."

A THOUGHT: *Jesus condemned the Pharisees and religious leaders for appearing saintly and holy outwardly, but inwardly remaining full of corruption and greed. Likewise, Christianity which is merely a show for others is like washing a cup on the outside only. When we are clean on the inside, our cleanliness on the outside won't be a sham.*

Paul and Apollos—Servants of Christ/ 1 Corinthians 4:1–7

So Apollos and I should be looked upon as Christ's servants who distribute God's blessings by explaining God's secrets. ²Now the most important thing about a servant is that he does just what his master tells him to. ³What about me? Have I been a good servant? Well, I don't worry over what you think about this, or what anyone else thinks. I don't even trust my own judgment on this point. ⁴My conscience is clear, but even that isn't final proof. It is the Lord himself who must examine me and decide.

⁵So be careful not to jump to conclusions before the Lord returns as to whether someone is a good servant or not. When the Lord comes, he will turn on the light so that everyone can see exactly what each one of us is really like, deep down in our hearts. Then everyone will know why we have been doing the Lord's work. At that time God will give to each one whatever praise is coming to him.

⁶I have used Apollos and myself as examples to illustrate what I have been saying: that you must not have favorites. You must not be proud of one of God's teachers more than another. ⁷What are you so puffed up about? What do you have that God hasn't given you? And if all you have is from God, why act as though you are so great, and as though you have accomplished something on your own?

A THOUGHT: *It is tempting to judge a fellow Christian, evaluating whether or not he or she is a good follower of Christ. But only God knows a person's heart, and he is the only one with the right to judge. Paul's warning to the Corinthians should also warn us. We are to help those who are sinning, but we must not judge who is a better servant for Christ. When you judge someone, you automatically consider yourself better, and this is pride.*

Proverbs for Today/ 10:20–21

When a good man speaks, he is worth listening to, but the words of fools are a dime a dozen. A godly man gives good advice, but a rebel is destroyed by lack of common sense.

MARCH 2

Jesus Preaches about the End of the Age/
Matthew 24:1–31

As Jesus was leaving the Temple grounds, his disciples came along and wanted to take him on a tour of the various Temple buildings.

2 But he told them, "All these buildings will be knocked down, with not one stone left on top of another!"

3"When will this happen?" the disciples asked him later, as he sat on the slopes of the Mount of Olives. "What events will signal your return, and the end of the world?"

4Jesus told them, "Don't let anyone fool you. 5For many will come claiming to be the Messiah, and will lead many astray. 6When you hear of wars beginning, this does not signal my return; these must come, but the end is not yet. 7The nations and kingdoms of the earth will rise against each other and there will be famines and earthquakes in many places. 8But all this will be only the beginning of the horrors to come.

9"Then you will be tortured and killed and hated all over the world because you are mine, 10and many of you shall fall back into sin and betray and hate each other. 11And many false prophets will appear and lead many astray. 12Sin will be rampant everywhere and will cool the love of many. 13But those enduring to the end shall be saved.

14"And the Good News about the Kingdom will be preached throughout the whole world, so that all nations will hear it, and then, finally, the end will come.

15"So, when you see the horrible thing (told about by Daniel the prophet) standing in a holy place (Note to the reader: You know what is meant!), 16then those in Judea must flee into the Judean hills. 17Those on their porches must not even go inside to pack before they flee. 18Those in the fields should not return to their homes for their clothes.

19"And woe to pregnant women and to those with babies in those days. 20And pray that your flight will not be in winter, or on the Sabbath. 21For there will be persecution such as the world has never before seen in all its history, and will never see again.

22"In fact, unless those days are shortened, all mankind will perish. But they will be shortened for the sake of God's chosen people.

23"Then if anyone tells you, 'The Messiah has arrived at such and such a place, or has appeared here or there,' don't believe it. 24For false Christs shall arise, and false prophets, and will do wonderful miracles, so that if it were possible, even God's chosen ones would be deceived. 25See, I have warned you.

26"So if someone tells you the Messiah has returned and is out in the desert, don't bother to go and look. Or, that he is hiding at a certain place, don't believe it! 27For as the lightning flashes across the sky from east to west, so shall my coming be, when I, the Messiah, return. 28And wherever the carcass is, there the vultures will gather.

29"Immediately after the persecution of those days the sun will be darkened, and the moon will not give light, and the stars will seem to fall from the heavens, and the powers overshadowing the earth will be convulsed.

30"And then at last the signal of my coming will appear in the heavens and there will be deep mourning all around the earth. And the nations of the world will see me arrive in the clouds of heaven, with power and great glory. 31And I shall send forth my angels with the sound of a mighty trumpet blast, and they shall gather my chosen ones from the farthest ends of the earth and heaven.

A THOUGHT: *The Old Testament frequently mentions false prophets. They were people who claimed to receive messages from God, but who preached a "health and wealth" message. They told the people only what they wanted to hear, even when the nation was not following God as it should. There were false prophets in Jesus' day, and we have them today. They are the popular leaders who preach a false gospel, telling people what they want to hear—such as "God wants you to be rich," "Do whatever your desires tell you," or "There is no such thing as sin or hell." Jesus said false teachers would come, and he warned his disciples, as he warns us, not to listen to their dangerous words.*

The Corinthians' Pride and the Humility of Servants/
1 Corinthians 4:8–13

You seem to think you already have all the spiritual food you need. You are full and spiritually contented, rich kings on your thrones, leaving us far behind! I wish you really were already on your thrones, for when that time comes you can be sure that we will be there, too, reigning with you. 9Sometimes I think God has put us apostles at the very end of the line, like prisoners soon to be killed, put on display at the end of a victor's parade, to be stared at by men and angels alike.

10Religion has made us foolish, you say, but of course you are all such wise and sensible Christians! We are weak, but not you! You are well thought of, while we are laughed at. 11To this very hour we have gone hungry and thirsty, without even enough clothes to keep us warm. We have been kicked around without homes of our own. 12We have worked wearily with our hands to earn our living. We have blessed those who cursed us. We have been patient with those who injured us. 13We have replied quietly when evil things have been said about us. Yet right up to the present moment we are like dirt under foot, like garbage.

A THOUGHT: *The Corinthians had split into various cliques, each following its own superstar preacher (Paul, Apollos, Peter, etc.). Each clique really believed it was the only one who had the whole truth, and thus felt spiritually proud. But Paul told the groups not to boast about being tied to a particular preacher because even the superstars were simply humble servants who had each suffered many things for the same message of salvation in Jesus Christ. No preacher of God has more authority than another. The authority resides in the message and the Author of the message, not in the messenger.*

Proverbs for Today/ 10:22

The Lord's blessing is our greatest wealth. All our work adds nothing to it!

Be Prepared for the Lord's Coming/
Matthew 24:32–51

"Now learn a lesson from the fig tree. When her branch is tender and the leaves begin to sprout, you know that summer is almost here. 33Just so, when you see all these things beginning to happen, you can know that my return is near, even at the doors. 34Then at last this age will come to its close.

35"Heaven and earth will disappear, but my words remain forever. 36But no one knows the date and hour when the end will be—not even the angels. No, nor even God's Son. Only the Father knows.

37,38"The world will be at ease —banquets and parties and weddings—just as it was in Noah's time before the sudden coming of the flood; 39people wouldn't believe what was going to happen until the flood actually arrived and took them all away. So shall my coming be.

40"Two men will be working together in the fields, and one will be taken, the other left. 41Two women will be going about their household tasks; one will be taken, the other left.

42"So be prepared, for you don't know what day your Lord is coming.

43"Just as a man can prevent trouble from thieves by keeping watch for them, 44so you can avoid trouble by always being ready for my unannounced return.

45"Are you a wise and faithful servant of the Lord? Have I given you the task of managing my household, to feed my children day by day? 46Blessings on you if I return and find you faithfully doing your work. 47I will put such faithful ones in charge of everything I own!

48"But if you are evil and say to yourself, 'My Lord won't be coming for a while,' 49and begin oppressing your fellow servants, partying and getting drunk, 50your Lord will arrive unannounced and unexpected, 51and severely whip you and send you off to the judgment of the hypocrites; there will be weeping and gnashing of teeth.

A THOUGHT: *Knowing that Christ's return will be sudden should motivate us always to be prepared. We are not to live irresponsibly—(1) sitting and waiting, doing nothing; (2) seeking self-serving pleasure; (3) using his tarrying as an excuse not to do God's work of building his Kingdom; (4) developing a false security based on precise calculations of events; or (5) letting our curiosity about the end times divert us from doing God's work.*

Paul Counsels His Beloved Children/
1 Corinthians 4:14–21

I am not writing about these things to make you ashamed, but to warn and counsel you as beloved children. 15For although you may have ten thousand others to teach you about Christ, remember that you have only me as your father. For I was the one who brought you to Christ when I preached the Gospel to you. 16So I beg you to follow my example, and do as I do.

17That is the very reason why I am sending Timothy— to help you do this. For he is one of those I won to Christ, a beloved and trustworthy child in the Lord. He will remind you of what I teach in all the churches wherever I go.

18I know that some of you will have become proud, thinking that I am afraid to come to deal with you. 19But I will come, and soon, if the Lord will let me, and then I'll find out whether these proud men are just big talkers or whether they really have God's power. 20The Kingdom of God is not just talking; it is living by God's power. 21Which do you choose? Shall I come with punishment and scolding, or shall I come with quiet love and gentleness?

A THOUGHT: *Some people talk a lot about faith, but that's all it is—talk. They may know all the right words to say, but their lives are not examples of Christian living. Paul says the Kingdom of God is to be lived, not just discussed. There is a big difference between knowing the right words and living them out. Don't be content to have the right answers about Christ. Let your life put flesh on your words.*

Proverbs for Today/ 10:23

A fool's fun is being bad; a wise man's fun is being wise!

The Parable of the Ten Bridesmaids/
Matthew 25:1–13

"The Kingdom of Heaven can be illustrated by the story of ten bridesmaids who took their lamps and went to meet the bridegroom. 2,3,4But only five of them were wise enough to fill their lamps with oil, while the other five were foolish and forgot.

5,6"So, when the bridegroom was delayed, they lay down to rest until midnight, when they were roused by the shout, 'The bridegroom is coming! Come out and welcome him!'

7,8"All the girls jumped up and trimmed their lamps. Then the five who hadn't any oil begged the others to share with them, for their lamps were going out.

9"But the others replied, 'We haven't enough. Go instead to the shops and buy some for yourselves.'

10"But while they were gone, the bridegroom came, and those who were ready went in with him to the marriage feast, and the door was locked.

11"Later, when the other five returned, they stood outside, calling, 'Sir, open the door for us!'

12"But he called back, 'Go away! It is too late!'

13"So stay awake and be prepared, for you do not know the date or moment of my return.

A THOUGHT: *This parable is about a wedding. In Jewish culture, a couple was engaged for a long time before the actual marriage, and the engagement promise was just as binding as the marriage vows. On the wedding day the bridegroom went to the bride's house for the ceremony; then the bride and groom, along with a great parade, returned to the groom's house where a feast took place, often lasting a full week.*

These bridesmaids were waiting for the parade, and they hoped to take part in the wedding banquet. But when the groom didn't come when they expected, five of them let their lamps run out of oil. By the time they had purchased extra oil, it was too late to join the feast.

When Jesus returns to take his people to heaven, we must be ready. Spiritual preparation cannot be bought or borrowed at the last minute. Our relationship with God must be our own.

Paul Condemns Immorality in the Church/
1 Corinthians 5:1–8

Everyone is talking about the terrible thing that has happened there among you, something so evil that even the heathen don't do it: you have a man in your church who is living in sin with his father's wife. 2And are you still so conceited, so "spiritual"? Why aren't you mourning in sorrow and shame, and seeing to it that this man is removed from your membership?

3,4Although I am not there with you, I have been thinking a lot about this, and in the name of the Lord Jesus Christ I have already decided what to do, just as though I were there. You are to call a meeting of the church—and the power of the Lord Jesus will be with you as you meet, and I will be there in spirit— 5and cast out this man from the fellowship of the church and into Satan's hands, to punish him, in the hope that his soul will be saved when our Lord Jesus Christ returns.

6What a terrible thing it is that you are boasting about your purity, and yet you let this sort of thing go on. Don't you realize that if even one person is allowed to go on sinning, soon all will be affected? 7Remove this evil cancer—this wicked person—from among you, so that you can stay pure. Christ, God's Lamb, has been slain for us. 8So let us feast upon him and grow strong in the Christian life, leaving entirely behind us the cancerous old life with all its hatreds and wickedness. Let us feast instead upon the pure bread of honor and sincerity and truth.

A THOUGHT: *The church must discipline flagrant sin among its members—such actions, left unchecked, can polarize and paralyze a church. The correction, however, is never to be vengeful. Instead, it is intended to bring about a cure. The Corinthian church had a specific sin in their midst, but they had refused to deal with it. In this case, a man was having an affair with his mother (or stepmother), and the church members were trying to ignore the situation. Paul was telling the church that they had a responsibility to maintain the standards of morality found in God's Word. God tells us not to judge others, but he also tells us not to tolerate flagrant sin that opposes his holiness and has a dangerous influence on the lives of other believers.*

Proverbs for Today/ 10:24–25

The wicked man's fears will all come true, and so will the good man's hopes. Disaster strikes like a cyclone and the wicked are whirled away. But the good man has a strong anchor.

MARCH 5

Faithfulness in the Kingdom of Heaven/ Matthew 25:14–30

"Again, the Kingdom of Heaven can be illustrated by the story of a man going into another country, who called together his servants and loaned them money to invest for him while he was gone.

15"He gave $5,000 to one, $2,000 to another, and $1,000 to the last—dividing it in proportion to their abilities—and then left on his trip. 16The man who received the $5,000 began immediately to buy and sell with it and soon earned another $5,000. 17The man with $2,000 went right to work, too, and earned another $2,000.

18"But the man who received the $1,000 dug a hole in the ground and hid the money for safekeeping.

19"After a long time their master returned from his trip and called them to him to account for his money. 20The man to whom he had entrusted the $5,000 brought him $10,000.

21"His master praised him for good work. 'You have been faithful in handling this small amount,' he told him, 'so now I will give you many more responsibilities. Begin the joyous tasks I have assigned to you.'

22"Next came the man who had received the $2,000, with the report, 'Sir, you gave me $2,000 to use, and I have doubled it.'

23" 'Good work,' his master said. 'You are a good and faithful servant. You have been faithful over this small amount, so now I will give you much more.'

24,25"Then the man with the $1,000 came and said, 'Sir, I knew you were a hard man, and I was afraid you would rob me of what I earned, so I hid your money in the earth and here it is!'

26"But his master replied, 'Wicked man! Lazy slave! Since you knew I would demand your profit, 27you should at least have put my money into the bank so I could have some interest. 28Take the money from this man and give it to the man with the $10,000. 29For the man who uses well what he is given shall be given more, and he shall have abundance. But from the man who is unfaithful, even what little responsibility he has shall be taken from him. 30And throw the useless servant out into outer darkness: there shall be weeping and gnashing of teeth.'

A THOUGHT: *The master divided the money up among his servants according to their abilities—no one received more or less money than he could handle. If he failed in his master's assignment, his excuse could not be that he was overwhelmed. Failure could come only from laziness or hatred for the master. Money, as used here, represents any kind of resource we are given. God gives us time, abilities, gifts, and other resources, and he expects us to invest them wisely until he returns. We are responsible to use well what God has given us. The issue is not how much we have, but what we do with what we have.*

Be in the World, Not of the World/
1 Corinthians 5:9–13

When I wrote to you before I said not to mix with evil people. 10But when I said that I wasn't talking about unbelievers who live in sexual sin, or are greedy cheats and thieves and idol worshipers. For you can't live in this world without being with people like that. 11What I meant was that you are not to keep company with anyone who claims to be a brother Christian but indulges in sexual sins, or is greedy, or is a swindler, or worships idols, or is a drunkard, or abusive. Don't even eat lunch with such a person.

12It isn't our job to judge outsiders. But it certainly is our job to judge and deal strongly with those who are members of the church, and who are sinning in these ways. 13God alone is the Judge of those on the outside. But you yourselves must deal with this man and put him out of your church.

A THOUGHT: *Paul makes it clear that we should not dissociate ourselves from unbelievers—otherwise, we could not carry out*

Christ's command to tell them about salvation. But we are to distance ourselves from the person who claims to be a Christian, yet indulges in sins explicitly forbidden in Scripture and then rationalizes his or her actions. Those who continue in sin harm others for whom Christ died and dim the image of God in themselves. A church that includes greedy people and sexual sinners is hardly fit to be the light of the world. It is distorting the picture of Christ it presents to the world. Instead of joining Christ's Kingdom with its constant fight to replace darkness with light, it is adding to the darkness.

Proverbs for Today/ 10:26

A lazy fellow is a pain to his employers—like smoke in their eyes or vinegar that sets the teeth on edge.

MARCH 6

The Separation of the Sheep from the Goats/ Matthew 25:31–46

"But when I, the Messiah, shall come in my glory, and all the angels with me, then I shall sit upon my throne of glory. 32And all the nations shall be gathered before me. And I will separate the people as a shepherd separates the sheep from the goats, 33and place the sheep at my right hand, and the goats at my left.

34"Then I, the King, shall say to those at my right, 'Come, blessed of my Father, into the Kingdom prepared for you from the founding of the world. 35For I was hungry and you fed me; I was thirsty and you gave me water; I was a stranger and you invited me into your homes; 36naked and you clothed me; sick and in prison, and you visited me.'

37"Then these righteous ones will reply, 'Sir, when did we ever see you hungry and feed you? Or thirsty and give you anything to drink? 38Or a stranger, and help you? Or naked, and clothe you? 39When did we ever see you sick or in prison, and visit you?'

40"And I, the King, will tell them, 'When you did it to these my brothers you were doing it to me!' 41Then I will turn to those on my left and say, 'Away with you,

you cursed ones, into the eternal fire prepared for the devil and his demons. 42For I was hungry and you wouldn't feed me; thirsty, and you wouldn't give me anything to drink; 43a stranger, and you refused me hospitality; naked, and you wouldn't clothe me; sick, and in prison, and you didn't visit me.'

44"Then they will reply, 'Lord, when did we ever see you hungry or thirsty or a stranger or naked or sick or in prison, and not help you?'

45"And I will answer, 'When you refused to help the least of these my brothers, you were refusing help to me.'

46"And they shall go away into eternal punishment; but the righteous into everlasting life."

A THOUGHT: *This parable describes acts of mercy we all can do every day. These acts are not dependent on wealth, ability, or intelligence; they are simple acts freely given and freely received. We have no legitimate excuse for neglecting those who have deep needs, and we cannot hand over this responsibility to the church or the government. Jesus demands personal involvement in caring for others' needs.*

Believers Should Not Sue Each Other/ 1 Corinthians 6:1–9a

How is it that when you have something against another Christian, you "go to law" and ask a heathen court to decide the matter instead of taking it to other Christians to decide which of you is right? 2Don't you know that some day we Christians are going to judge and govern the world? So why can't you decide even these little things among yourselves? 3Don't you realize that we Christians will judge and reward the very angels in heaven? So you should be able to decide your problems down here on earth easily enough. 4Why then go to outside judges who are not even Christians? 5I am trying to make you ashamed. Isn't there anyone in all the church who is wise enough to decide these arguments? 6But, instead, one Christian sues another and accuses his Christian brother in front of unbelievers.

7To have such lawsuits at all is a real defeat for you as Christians. Why not just accept mistreatment and leave it at that? It would be far more honoring to the Lord to let yourselves be cheated. 8But, instead, you yourselves are the ones who do wrong, cheating others, even your own brothers.

9Don't you know that those doing such things have no share in the Kingdom of God?

A THOUGHT: *Why does Paul say it isn't good to sue another Christian? (1) If the judge and jury are not Christians, they are unlikely to be sensitive to Christian values. (2) The basis for going to court is often revenge; this should never be a Christian's motive. (3) Lawsuits make the church look bad, causing unbelievers to focus on its problems rather than its purpose. Paul says that disagreeing Christians should not have to go to a secular court to resolve their differences. As Christians we have the Holy Spirit and the mind of Christ, so why should we turn to those who lack God's wisdom? With all that we have been given as believers, and the power that we will have in the future to judge the world and the angels, we should be able to deal with the disputes between ourselves.*

Proverbs for Today/ 10:27–28

Reverence for God adds hours to each day; so how can the wicked expect a long, good life? □ The hope of good men is eternal happiness; the hopes of evil men are all in vain.

MARCH 7

The Priests Plot Jesus' Death/ Matthew 26:1–16

When Jesus had finished this talk with his disciples, he told them,

"As you know, the Passover celebration begins in two days, and I shall be betrayed and crucified."

3At that very moment the chief priests and other Jewish officials were meeting at the residence of Caiaphas the High Priest, 4to discuss ways of capturing Jesus quietly, and killing him. 5"But not during the Passover celebration," they agreed, "for there would be a riot."

6Jesus now proceeded to Bethany, to the home of Simon the leper. 7While he was eating, a woman came in with a bottle of very expensive perfume, and poured it over his head.

8,9The disciples were indignant. "What a waste of good

money," they said. "Why, she could have sold it for a fortune and given it to the poor."

10Jesus knew what they were thinking, and said, "Why are you criticizing her? For she has done a good thing to me. 11You will always have the poor among you, but you won't always have me. 12She has poured this perfume on me to prepare my body for burial. 13And she will always be remembered for this deed. The story of what she has done will be told throughout the whole world, wherever the Good News is preached."

14Then Judas Iscariot, one of the twelve apostles, went to the chief priests, 15and asked, "How much will you pay me to get Jesus into your hands?" And they gave him thirty silver coins. 16From that time on, Judas watched for an opportunity to betray Jesus to them.

A THOUGHT: *In the midst of the murderous plots of the Jewish religious leadership and Judas' betrayal, we find this woman who pours perfume over Jesus' head. It was this act of humble sacrifice, by an oppressed member of first–century Jewish society that Jesus accepted as the preparation for his burial. God has indeed chosen the humble of this world to shame the proud. Let us be numbered among the humble and the poor—true greatness is not found in the honor we find among others, but rather in the obedient and humble service to others where the servant seeks no reward.*

Christ's Blood Has Washed Away All Our Sins/ 1 Corinthians 6:9b–13a

Don't fool yourselves. Those who live immoral lives, who are idol worshipers, adulterers or homosexuals—will have no share in his Kingdom. Neither will thieves or greedy people, drunkards, slanderers, or robbers. 11There was a time when some of you were just like that but now your sins are washed away, and you are set apart for God, and he has accepted you because of what the Lord Jesus Christ and the Spirit of our God have done for you. 12I can do anything I want to if Christ has not said no, but some of these things aren't good for me. Even if I am allowed to do them, I'll refuse to if I think they might get such a grip on me that I can't easily stop when I want to.13For instance, take the matter of eating. God has given us an appetite for food and stomachs to digest it. But that doesn't mean we should eat more than we need. Don't think of eating as important, because some day God will do away with both stomachs and food.

A THOUGHT: *In a permissive society it is easy for Christians to overlook or accept immoral behavior (sexual sins, greed, drunkenness, gossip, etc.) because it is so widespread. Although it surrounds us, we cannot take part in it or condone it in any way. Staying away from generally accepted sin is difficult, but it is no harder for us than it was for the Corinthians. God expects his followers in any age to have high moral standards.*

Proverbs for Today/ 10:29–30
God protects the upright but destroys the wicked. The good shall never lose God's blessings, but the wicked shall lose everything.

MARCH 8

The Last Supper/ Matthew 26:17–35
On the first day of the Passover ceremonies, when bread made with yeast was purged from every Jewish home, the disciples came to Jesus and asked, "Where shall we plan to eat the Passover?"

18He replied, "Go into the city and see Mr. So-and-So, and tell him, 'Our Master says, my time has come, and I will eat the Passover meal with my disciples at your house.'" 19So the disciples did as he told them, and prepared the supper there.

20,21That evening as he sat eating with the Twelve, he said, "One of you will betray me."

22Sorrow chilled their hearts, and each one asked, "Am I the one?"

23He replied, "It is the one I served first. 24For I must die just as was prophesied, but woe to the man by whom I am betrayed. Far better for that one if he had never been born."

25Judas, too, had asked him, "Rabbi, am I the one?" And Jesus had told him, "Yes."

26As they were eating, Jesus took a small loaf of bread and blessed it and broke it apart and gave it to the disciples and said, "Take it and eat it, for this is my body."

27And he took a cup of wine and gave thanks for it and gave it to them and said, "Each one drink from it, 28for this is my blood, sealing the New Covenant. It is poured out to forgive the sins of multitudes. 29Mark my words—I will not drink this wine again until the day I drink it new with you in my Father's Kingdom."

30And when they had sung a hymn, they went out to the Mount of Olives.

31Then Jesus said to them, "Tonight you will all desert me. For it is written in the Scriptures that God will smite the Shepherd, and the sheep of the flock will be scattered. 32But after I have been brought back to life again I will go to Galilee, and meet you there."

33Peter declared, "If everyone else deserts you, I won't."

34Jesus told him, "The truth is that this very night, before the cock crows at dawn, you will deny me three times!"

35"I would die first!" Peter insisted. And all the other disciples said the same thing.

A THOUGHT: *This supper, which Jesus and his disciples observed to commemorate the Passover, the Church celebrates as one of its most holy sacraments. Each name we use for this sacrament brings out a different dimension of it. It is the Lord's Supper because it commemorates the Passover meal Jesus ate with his disciples; it is the Eucharist (thanksgiving) because in it we thank God for Christ's work for us; it is Communion because through it we commune with God and with other believers. As we eat the bread and drink the wine, we should reflect upon Jesus' suffering and death for the church, express our gratefulness to God for his wonderful grace towards us, and manifest in our actions towards others the grace of God which we have experienced.*

The Body Is the Home of the Holy Spirit/ 1 Corinthians 6:13b–20

But sexual sin is never right: our bodies were not made for that, but for the Lord, and the Lord wants to fill our bodies with himself. 14And God is going to raise our bodies from the dead by his power just as he raised up the Lord Jesus Christ. 15Don't you realize that your bodies are actually parts and members of Christ? So should I take part of Christ and join him to a prostitute? Never! 16And don't you know that if a man joins himself to a prostitute she becomes a part of him and he becomes a part of her? For God tells us in the Scripture that in his sight the two become one person. 17But if you give yourself to the Lord, you and Christ are joined together as one person.

18That is why I say to run from sex sin. No other sin affects the body as this one does. When you sin this sin it is against your own body. 19Haven't you yet learned that your body is the home of the Holy Spirit God gave you, and that he lives within you? Your own body does not belong to you. 20For God has bought you with a great price. So use every part of your body to give glory back to God, because he owns it.

A THOUGHT: *Many of the world's religions think the soul is important and the body is not, and Christianity has sometimes been influenced by them. In truth, however, Christianity is a very physical religion. We worship a God who created a physical world and pronounced it good. He promises us a new earth where real people continue to live physical lives—not a pink cloud where disembodied souls listen to harp music. At the heart of Christianity is the story of God himself taking on flesh and blood and coming to live with us.*
We humans, like Adam, are a combination of dust and spirit. Just as our spiritual lives affect our bodies, so our physical lives affect our souls. We cannot commit sin with our bodies without damaging our souls, because our bodies and souls are inseparably joined. In the new earth we will have resurrection bodies that are not corrupted by sin. Then we will enjoy the fullness of our salvation.

Proverbs for Today/ 10:31–32
The good man gives wise advice, but the liar's counsel is shunned. The upright speak what is helpful; the wicked speak rebellion.

MARCH 9

Jesus Is Betrayed at Gethsemane/ Matthew 26:36–56
Then Jesus brought them to a garden grove, Gethsemane, and told them to sit down and wait while he went on ahead to pray. 37He took Peter with him and Zebedee's

two sons James and John, and began to be filled with anguish and despair.

38Then he told them, "My soul is crushed with horror and sadness to the point of death . . . stay here . . . stay awake with me."

39He went forward a little, and fell face downward on the ground, and prayed, "My Father! If it is possible, let this cup be taken away from me. But I want your will, not mine."

40Then he returned to the three disciples and found them asleep. "Peter," he called, "couldn't you even stay awake with me one hour? 41Keep alert and pray. Otherwise temptation will overpower you. For the spirit indeed is willing, but how weak the body is!"

42Again he left them and prayed, "My Father! If this cup cannot go away until I drink it all, your will be done."

43He returned to them again and found them sleeping, for their eyes were heavy, 44so he went back to prayer the third time, saying the same things again.

45Then he came to the disciples and said, "Sleep on now and take your rest . . . but no! The time has come! I am betrayed into the hands of evil men! 46Up! Let's be going! Look! Here comes the man who is betraying me!"

47At that very moment while he was still speaking, Judas, one of the Twelve, arrived with a great crowd armed with swords and clubs, sent by the Jewish leaders. 48Judas had told them to arrest the man he greeted, for that would be the one they were after. 49So now Judas came straight to Jesus and said, "Hello, Master!" and embraced him in friendly fashion.

50Jesus said, "My friend, go ahead and do what you have come for." Then the others grabbed him.

51One of the men with Jesus pulled out a sword and slashed off the ear of the High Priest's servant.

52"Put away your sword," Jesus told him. "Those using swords will get killed. 53Don't you realize that I could ask my Father for thousands of angels to protect us, and he would send them instantly? 54But if I did, how would the Scriptures be fulfilled that describe what is happening now?" 55Then Jesus spoke to the crowd. "Am I some dangerous criminal," he asked, "that you had to arm yourselves with swords and clubs before you could arrest me?

I was with you teaching daily in the Temple and you didn't stop me then. 56But this is all happening to fulfill the words of the prophets as recorded in the Scriptures."

At that point, all the disciples deserted him and fled.

A Thought: *Jesus was in great anguish over his coming physical pain, separation from the Father, and death for the sins of the world. The divine course was set; but he, in his human nature, still struggled. Because of the anguish he faced, he can relate to our suffering. His strength to obey came from his relationship with God the Father, who is also the source of our strength.*

Paul's Advice to Married Couples/ 1 Corinthians 7:1–9

Now about those questions you asked in your last letter: my answer is that if you do not marry, it is good. 2But usually it is best to be married, each man having his own wife, and each woman having her own husband, because otherwise you might fall back into sin.

3The man should give his wife all that is her right as a married woman, and the wife should do the same for her husband: 4for a girl who marries no longer has full right to her own body, for her husband then has his rights to it, too; and in the same way the husband no longer has full right to his own body, for it belongs also to his wife. 5So do not refuse these rights to each other. The only exception to this rule would be the agreement of both husband and wife to refrain from the rights of marriage for a limited time, so that they can give themselves more completely to prayer. Afterwards, they should come together again so that Satan won't be able to tempt them because of their lack of self-control.

6I'm not saying you *must* marry; but you certainly *may* if you wish. 7I wish everyone could get along without marrying, just as I do. But we are not all the same. God gives some the gift of a husband or wife, and others he gives the gift of being able to stay happily unmarried. 8So I say to those who aren't married, and to widows— better to stay unmarried if you can, just as I am. 9But if you can't control yourselves, go ahead and marry. It is better to marry than to burn with lust.

A Thought: *Sexual temptations are difficult to withstand because they appeal to the normal and natural desires God has given us. Marriage is meant, in part, to satisfy these natural sexual desires and to strengthen the partners against temptation. Married couples have the responsibility to care for each other. Therefore, husbands and wives should not withhold themselves from one another, but should fulfill each other's needs and desires.*

Proverbs for Today/ 11:1–3

The Lord hates cheating and delights in honesty. □ Proud men end in shame, but the meek become wise. □ A good man is guided by his honesty; the evil man is destroyed by his dishonesty.

MARCH 10

Jesus Appears before the Jewish Supreme Court/ Matthew 26:57–75

Then the mob led Jesus to the home of Caiaphas the High Priest, where all the Jewish leaders were gathering. 58Meanwhile, Peter was following far to the rear, and came to the courtyard of the High Priest's house and went in and sat with the soldiers, and waited to see what was going to be done to Jesus.

59The chief priests and, in fact, the entire Jewish Supreme Court assembled there and looked for witnesses who would lie about Jesus, in order to build a case against him that would result in a death sentence. 60,61But even though they found many who agreed to be false witnesses, these always contradicted each other.

Finally two men were found who declared, "This man said, 'I am able to destroy the Temple of God and rebuild it in three days.' "

62Then the High Priest stood up and said to Jesus, "Well, what about it? Did you say that, or didn't you?" 63But Jesus remained silent.

Then the High Priest said to him, "I demand in the name of the living God that you tell us whether you claim to be the Messiah, the Son of God."

64"Yes," Jesus said, "I am. And in the future you will see me, the Messiah, sitting at the right hand of God and returning on the clouds of heaven."

65,66Then the High Priest tore at his own clothing, shouting, "Blasphemy! What need have we for other witnesses? You have all heard him say it! What is your verdict?"

They shouted, "Death!—Death!—Death!"

67Then they spat in his face and struck him and some slapped him, 68saying, "Prophesy to us, you Messiah! Who struck you that time?"

69Meanwhile, as Peter was sitting in the courtyard a girl came over and said to him, "You were with Jesus, for both of you are from Galilee."

70But Peter denied it loudly. "I don't even know what you are talking about," he angrily declared.

71Later, out by the gate, another girl noticed him and said to those standing around, "This man was with Jesus— from Nazareth."

72Again Peter denied it, this time with an oath. "I don't even know the man," he said.

73But after a while the men who had been standing there came over to him and said, "We know you are one of his disciples, for we can tell by your Galilean accent."

74Peter began to curse and swear. "I don't even know the man," he said.

And immediately the cock crowed. 75Then Peter remembered what Jesus had said, "Before the cock crows, you will deny me three times." And he went away, crying bitterly.

A THOUGHT: *After Judas singled out Jesus for arrest, the mob took Jesus to Caiaphas, the High Priest. The Jewish Supreme Court found two witnesses who distorted Jesus' teaching concerning the Temple. They claimed that Jesus had said he would destroy the Temple—a blasphemous boast. Actually, Jesus had said, "You destroy this temple and I will raise it up." Jesus, of course, was talking about his body, not a building. Ironically, the religious leaders were about to destroy Jesus' body just as he had said, and three days later he would rise from the dead.*

Jesus' trial, a mockery of justice, ended at daybreak with the decision of the court—to kill him. They needed Rome's permission for the death sentence, so Jesus was taken to Pilate who legally sentenced Jesus to die.

Paul's Advice on Divorce/ 1 Corinthians 7:10–17

Now, for those who are married I have a command, not just a suggestion. And it is not a command from me, for this is what the Lord himself has said: A wife must not leave her husband. 11But if she is separated from him, let her remain single or else go back to him. And the husband must not divorce his wife.

12Here I want to add some suggestions of my own. These are not direct commands from the Lord, but they seem right to me: If a Christian has a wife who is not a Christian, but she wants to stay with him anyway, he must not leave her or divorce her. 13And if a Christian woman has a husband who isn't a Christian, and he wants her to stay with him, she must not leave him. 14For perhaps the husband who isn't a Christian may become a Christian with the help of his Christian wife. And the wife who isn't a Christian may become a Christian with the help of her Christian husband. Otherwise, if the family separates, the children might never come to know the Lord; whereas a united family may, in God's plan, result in the children's salvation.

15But if the husband or wife who isn't a Christian is eager to leave, it is permitted. In such cases the Christian husband or wife should not insist that the other stay, for God wants his children to live in peace and harmony. 16For, after all, there is no assurance to you wives that your husbands will be converted if they stay; and the same may be said to you husbands concerning your wives.

17But be sure in deciding these matters that you are living as God intended, marrying or not marrying in accordance with God's direction and help, and accepting whatever situation God has put you into. This is my rule for all the churches.

A THOUGHT: *Because of their desire to serve Christ, some people in the Corinthian church thought they ought to divorce their pagan spouses and marry Christians. But Paul affirmed the marriage commitment. God's ideal is for marriages to stay together—even when one spouse is not a believer. The Christian spouse should try to win the other to Christ. It would be easy to rationalize leaving; however, Paul makes a strong case for staying with the unbelieving spouse and being a positive influence on the marriage. Paul, like Jesus, taught that marriage is to be a permanent relationship.*

Proverbs for Today/ 11:4
Your riches won't help you on Judgment Day; only righteousness counts then.

Judas Returns the Thirty Pieces of Silver/
Matthew 27:1–10

When it was morning, the chief priests and Jewish leaders met again to discuss how to induce the Roman government to sentence Jesus to death. ²Then they sent him in chains to Pilate, the Roman governor.

³About that time Judas, who betrayed him, when he saw that Jesus had been condemned to die, changed his mind and deeply regretted what he had done, and brought back the money to the chief priests and other Jewish leaders.

⁴"I have sinned," he declared, "for I have betrayed an innocent man."

"That's your problem," they retorted.

⁵Then he threw the money onto the floor of the Temple and went out and hanged himself. ⁶The chief priests picked the money up. "We can't put it in the collection," they said, "since it's against our laws to accept money paid for murder."

⁷They talked it over and finally decided to buy a certain field where the clay was used by potters, and to make it into a cemetery for foreigners who died in Jerusalem. ⁸That is why the cemetery is still called "The Field of Blood."

⁹This fulfilled the prophecy of Jeremiah which says,

"They took the thirty pieces of silver—the price at which he was valued by the people of Israel— ¹⁰and purchased a field from the potters as the Lord directed me."

A THOUGHT: *The religious leaders had to induce the Roman government to sentence Jesus to death because they did not have the authority to do it themselves. The Romans had taken away the religious leaders' authority to inflict capital punishment. Politically, it looked better for the religious leaders if someone else was responsible for killing Jesus. They wanted the death to appear to be the responsibility of the Romans so that the crowds couldn't blame them. They had arrested Jesus on theological grounds—blasphemy; but since this charge would be thrown out of a Roman court, they had to come up with a political reason for Jesus' death. Their strategy was to show Jesus as a rebel who claimed to be God and thus higher than Caesar.*

We Have Been Bought with a Price/
1 Corinthians 7:18–24

For instance, a man who already has gone through the Jewish ceremony of circumcision before he became a Christian shouldn't worry about it; and if he hasn't been circumcised, he shouldn't do it now. 19For it doesn't make any difference at all whether a Christian has gone through this ceremony or not. But it makes a lot of difference whether he is pleasing God and keeping God's commandments. That is the important thing.

20Usually a person should keep on with the work he was doing when God called him. 21Are you a slave? Don't let that worry you—but of course, if you get a chance to be free, take it. 22If the Lord calls you, and you are a slave, remember that Christ has set you free from the awful power of sin; and if he has called you and you are free, remember that you are now a slave of Christ. 23You have been bought and paid for by Christ, so you belong to him—be free now from all these earthly prides and fears. 24So, dear brothers, whatever situation a person is in when he becomes a Christian, let him stay there, for now the Lord is there to help him.

A THOUGHT: *Slavery was common throughout the Roman Empire. Some Christians in the Corinthian church were slaves. Paul said that although they were slaves to men, they were free from the power of sin in their lives. People today are slaves to sin until they commit their lives to Christ, who alone can conquer sin's power. Sin, pride, and fear no longer have claim over us, just as a slaveowner no longer has power over slaves he has sold. The Bible says we become Christ's slaves when we become Christians, but this actually means we gain our freedom, because sin no longer controls us. We have been bought with a high price—the shed blood of Jesus Christ. Our new status in Christ gives us the freedom to walk in righteousness through the power of the Holy Spirit. Therefore, let us walk in the Spirit and live in righteousness.*

Proverbs for Today/ 11:5–6

Good people are directed by their honesty; the wicked shall fall beneath their load of sins. The good man's goodness delivers him; the evil man's treachery is his undoing.

Jesus Appears before Pilate/ Matthew 27:11–30

Now Jesus was standing before Pilate, the Roman governor. "Are you the Jews' Messiah?" the governor asked him.

"Yes," Jesus replied.

12But when the chief priests and other Jewish leaders made their many accusations against him, Jesus remained silent.

13"Don't you hear what they are saying?" Pilate demanded.

14But Jesus said nothing, much to the governor's surprise.

15Now the governor's custom was to release one Jewish prisoner each year during the Passover celebration—anyone they wanted. 16This year there was a particularly notorious criminal in jail named Barabbas, 17and as the crowds gathered before Pilate's house that morning he asked them, "Which shall I release to you—Barabbas, or Jesus your Messiah?" 18For he knew very well that the Jewish leaders had arrested Jesus out of envy because of his popularity with the people.

19Just then, as he was presiding over the court, Pilate's wife sent him this message: "Leave that good man alone; for I had a terrible nightmare concerning him last night."

20Meanwhile the chief priests and Jewish officials persuaded the crowds to ask for Barabbas' release, and for Jesus' death. 21So when the governor asked again, "Which of these two shall I release to you?" the crowd shouted back their reply: "Barabbas!"

22"Then what shall I do with Jesus, your Messiah?" Pilate asked.

And they shouted, "Crucify him!"

23"Why?" Pilate demanded. "What has he done wrong?" But they kept shouting, "Crucify! Crucify!"

24When Pilate saw that he wasn't getting anywhere, and that a riot was developing, he sent for a bowl of water and washed his hands before the crowd, saying, "I am innocent of the blood of this good man. The responsibility is yours!"

25And the mob yelled back, "His blood be on us and on our children!"

26Then Pilate released Barabbas to them. And after he had whipped Jesus, he gave him to the Roman soldiers to take away and crucify.

27But first they took him into the armory and called out the entire contingent. 28They stripped him and put a scarlet robe on him, 29and made a crown from long thorns and put it on his head, and placed a stick in his right hand as a scepter and knelt before him in mockery. "Hail, King of the Jews," they yelled. 30And they spat on him and grabbed the stick and beat him on the head with it.

A THOUGHT: *Before Pilate, the religious leaders accused Jesus of different crimes from the ones for which they had arrested him. They arrested him for blasphemy (claiming to be God), but that charge would mean nothing to the Romans. So the religious leaders had to accuse Jesus of crimes that would have concerned the Roman government, such as encouraging the people not to pay taxes, claiming to be a king, and causing riots. These accusations were not true, but they were determined to kill Jesus; and they broke several commandments in order to carry out their murderous plot.*

At first Pilate hesitated to give the religious leaders permission to crucify Jesus. He thought they were simply jealous of a teacher who was more popular with the people than they were. But when the Jews threatened to report Pilate to Caesar, he became afraid. Historical records indicate that the Jews had already threatened to lodge a formal complaint against Pilate for his stubborn flouting of their traditions—and such a complaint would most likely have led to his recall by Rome. His job was in jeopardy. The Roman government could not afford to put large numbers of troops in all the regions under their control, so one of Pilate's main duties was to do whatever was necessary to maintain peace—in this case, allow the murder of an innocent man—the Son of God.

Paul's Advice to Unmarried Women/ 1 Corinthians 7:25–31

Now I will try to answer your other question. What about girls who are not yet married? Should they be permitted to do so? In answer to this question, I have no special command for them from the Lord. But the Lord in his kindness has given me wisdom that can be trusted, and I will be glad to tell you what I think.

26Here is the problem: We Christians are facing great dangers to our lives at present. In times like these I think it is best for a person to remain unmarried. 27Of course, if you already are married, don't separate because of this. But if you aren't, don't rush into it at this time. 28But if you men decide to go ahead anyway and get married now, it is all right; and if a girl gets married in times like these, it is no sin. However, marriage will bring extra problems that I wish you didn't have to face right now.

29The important thing to remember is that our remaining time is very short, [and so are our opportunities for doing the Lord's work]. For that reason those who have wives should stay as free as possible for the Lord; 30happiness or sadness or wealth should not keep anyone from doing God's work. 31Those in frequent contact with the exciting things the world offers should make good use of their opportunities without stopping to enjoy them; for the world in its present form will soon be gone.

A THOUGHT: *Many people naively think that marriage will solve all their problems. Here are some problems marriage won't solve: (1) loneliness, (2) sexual temptation, (3) satisfaction of one's deepest emotional needs, (4) elimination of life's difficulties. Marriage alone does not hold two people together, but commitment does—commitment to Christ and to each other despite conflicts and problems. As wonderful as it is, marriage does not solve problems. Whether married or single, we must be content with our situation and focus on Christ, not other people, to solve our problems.*

Proverbs for Today/ 11:7
When an evil man dies, his hopes all perish, for they are based upon this earthly life.

MARCH 13

The Crucifixion of Jesus/ Matthew 27:31–56
After the mockery, they took off the robe and put Jesus' own garment on him again, and took him out to crucify him.

32As they were on the way to the execution grounds they came across a man from Cyrene, in Africa—Simon was his name—and forced him to carry Jesus' cross. 33Then they went out to an area known as Golgotha, that is,

"Skull Hill," 34where the soldiers gave him drugged wine to drink; but when he had tasted it, he refused.

35After the crucifixion, the soldiers threw dice to divide up his clothes among themselves. 36Then they sat around and watched him as he hung there. 37And they put a sign above his head, "This is Jesus, the King of the Jews."

38Two robbers were also crucified there that morning, one on either side of him. 39And the people passing by hurled abuse, shaking their heads at him and saying, 40"So! You can destroy the Temple and build it again in three days, can you? Well, then, come on down from the cross if you are the Son of God!"

41,42,43And the chief priests and Jewish leaders also mocked him. "He saved others," they scoffed, "but he can't save himself! So you are the King of Israel, are you? Come down from the cross and we'll believe you! He trusted God—let God show his approval by delivering him! Didn't he say, 'I am God's Son'?"

44And the robbers also threw the same in his teeth.

45That afternoon, the whole earth was covered with darkness for three hours, from noon until three o'clock.

46About three o'clock, Jesus shouted, "Eli, Eli, lama sabachthani?" which means, "My God, my God, why have you forsaken me?"

47Some of the bystanders misunderstood and thought he was calling for Elijah. 48One of them ran and filled a sponge with sour wine and put it on a stick and held it up to him to drink. 49But the rest said, "Leave him alone. Let's see whether Elijah will come and save him."

50Then Jesus shouted out again, dismissed his spirit, and died.

51And look! The curtain secluding the Holiest Place in the Temple was split apart from top to bottom; and the earth shook, and rocks broke, 52and tombs opened, and many godly men and women who had died came back to life again. 53After Jesus' resurrection, they left the cemetery and went into Jerusalem, and appeared to many people there.

54The soldiers at the crucifixion and their sergeant were terribly frightened by the earthquake and all that happened. They exclaimed, "Surely this was God's Son."

55And many women who had come down from Galilee

with Jesus to care for him were watching from a distance. 56Among them were Mary Magdalene and Mary the mother of James and Joseph, and the mother of James and John (the sons of Zebedee).

A THOUGHT: *The Roman soldiers took Jesus to the armory, a part of the Praetorium, and mocked him, dressing him with a scarlet robe and a crown of thorns. They then led him to the crucifixion site outside the city. He was so weakened by his beatings that he could not carry his cross. So a man from Cyrene was forced to carry it to Golgotha.*

Christ's death was accompanied by at least four miraculous events: darkness, the splitting of the curtain in the Temple, an earthquake, and dead people rising from their tombs. The curtain in the Temple separated the Holy Place from the Holy of Holies. The fact that it was torn in two symbolized that the barrier between God and people was removed by Christ's death. Now all people are free to approach God because of Christ's sacrifice for our sins.

Paul's Advice to Unmarried Men/
1 Corinthians 7:32–40

In all you do, I want you to be free from worry. An unmarried man can spend his time doing the Lord's work and thinking how to please him. 33But a married man can't do that so well; he has to think about his earthly responsibilities and how to please his wife. 34His interests are divided. It is the same with a girl who marries. She faces the same problem. A girl who is not married is anxious to please the Lord in all she is and does. But a married woman must consider other things such as housekeeping and the likes and dislikes of her husband.

35I am saying this to help you, not to try to keep you from marrying. I want you to do whatever will help you serve the Lord best, with as few other things as possible to distract your attention from him.

36But if anyone feels he ought to marry because he has trouble controlling his passions, it is all right, it is not a sin; let him marry. 37But if a man has the willpower not to marry and decides that he doesn't need to and won't, he has made a wise decision. 38So the person who marries does well, and the person who doesn't marry does even better.

39The wife is part of her husband as long as he lives; if her husband dies, then she may marry again, but only if she marries a Christian. 40But in my opinion she will be happier if she doesn't marry again; and I think I am giving you counsel from God's Spirit when I say this.

A THOUGHT: *Some single people feel tremendous pressure to be married. They think their lives can be complete only with a spouse. But Paul underlines one advantage of being single—the potential of a greater focus on Christ and his work. If you are unmarried, use your special opportunity to serve Christ wholeheartedly.*

Proverbs for Today/ 11:8

God rescues good men from danger while letting the wicked fall into it.

MARCH 14

Jesus' Burial/ Matthew 27:57–66

When evening came, a rich man from Arimathea named Joseph, one of Jesus' followers, 58went to Pilate and asked for Jesus' body. And Pilate issued an order to release it to him. 59Joseph took the body and wrapped it in a clean linen cloth, 60and placed it in his own new rock-hewn tomb, and rolled a great stone across the entrance as he left. 61Both Mary Magdalene and the other Mary were sitting nearby watching.

62The next day—at the close of the first day of the Passover ceremonies—the chief priests and Pharisees went to Pilate, 63and told him, "Sir, that liar once said, 'After three days I will come back to life again.' 64So we request an order from you sealing the tomb until the third day, to prevent his disciples from coming and stealing his body and then telling everyone he came back to life! If that happens we'll be worse off than we were at first."

65"Use your own Temple police," Pilate told them. "They can guard it safely enough."

66So they sealed the stone and posted guards to protect it from intrusion.

A THOUGHT: *Joseph of Arimathea was a secret follower of Jesus. He was a religious leader, an honored member of the Jewish Supreme Court. In the past, Joseph had been afraid to speak against the religious leaders who opposed Jesus; now he was bold, courageously asking to take Jesus' body from the cross and bury it. The disciples who publicly followed Jesus had fled, but this Jewish leader, who followed Jesus in secret, came forward and did what was right.*

Teaching about Food Offered to Idols/
1 Corinthians 8:1–13

Next is your question about eating food that has been sacrificed to idols. On this question everyone feels that only his answer is the right one! But although being a "know-it-all" makes us feel important, what is really needed to build the church is love. 2If anyone thinks he knows all the answers, he is just showing his ignorance. 3But the person who truly loves God is the one who is open to God's knowledge.

4So now, what about it? Should we eat meat that has been sacrificed to idols? Well, we all know that an idol is not really a god, and that there is only one God, and no other. 5According to some people, there are a great many gods, both in heaven and on earth. 6But we know that there is only one God, the Father, who created all things and made us to be his own; and one Lord Jesus Christ, who made everything and gives us life.

7However, some Christians don't realize this. All their lives they have been used to thinking of idols as alive, and have believed that food offered to the idols is really being offered to actual gods. So when they eat such food it bothers them and hurts their tender consciences. 8Just remember that God doesn't care whether we eat it or not. We are no worse off if we don't eat it, and no better off if we do. 9But be careful not to use your freedom to eat it, lest you cause some Christian brother to sin whose conscience is weaker than yours.

10You see, this is what may happen: Someone who thinks it is wrong to eat this food will see you eating at a temple restaurant, for you know there is no harm in it. Then he will become bold enough to do it too, although all the time he still feels it is wrong. 11So because you "know it is all right to do it," you will be responsible for causing great spiritual damage to a brother with a tender conscience for whom Christ died. 12And it is a sin against Christ to sin against your brother by encouraging him to do something he thinks is wrong. 13So if eating meat offered to idols is going to make my brother sin, I'll not eat any of it as long as I live, because I don't want to do this to him.

A THOUGHT: *Christian freedom does not mean "anything goes." It means that our salvation is not determined by legalism, good works, or rules, but by the free gift of God. Christian freedom, then, is inseparably tied to Christian responsibility. New believers are often very sensitive to what is right or wrong, what they should or shouldn't do. Some actions may be perfectly all right for us to do, but may harm a Christian brother or sister who is still young in the faith and learning what the Christian life is all about. We must be careful not to offend a sensitive or younger Christian or, by our example, to cause him or her to sin. When we love others, our freedom to do certain things won't be as important to us as strengthening the faith of a brother or sister in Christ.*

Proverbs for Today/ 11:9–11

Evil words destroy. Godly skill rebuilds. □ The whole city celebrates a good man's success—and also the godless man's death. □ The good influence of godly citizens causes a city to prosper, but the moral decay of the wicked drives it downhill.

MARCH 15

Jesus Rises from the Grave/ Matthew 28:1–15

Early on Sunday morning, as the new day was dawning, Mary Magdalene and the other Mary went out to the tomb.

2Suddenly there was a great earthquake; for an angel of the Lord came down from heaven and rolled aside the stone and sat on it. 3His face shone like lightning and his clothing was a brilliant white. 4The guards shook with fear when they saw him, and fell into a dead faint.

5Then the angel spoke to the women. "Don't be frightened!" he said. "I know you are looking for Jesus, who was crucified, 6but he isn't here! For he has come back to life again, just as he said he would. Come in and see where his body was lying. . . . 7And now, go quickly and tell his disciples that he has risen from the dead, and that he is going to Galilee to meet them there. That is my message to them."

8The women ran from the tomb, badly frightened, but also filled with joy, and rushed to find the disciples to give them the angel's message. 9And as they were running, suddenly Jesus was there in front of them!

"Good morning!" he said. And they fell to the ground before him, holding his feet and worshiping him.

10Then Jesus said to them, "Don't be frightened! Go tell my brothers to leave at once for Galilee, to meet me there."

11As the women were on the way into the city, some of the Temple police who had been guarding the tomb went to the chief priests and told them what had happened. 12,13A meeting of all the Jewish leaders was called, and it was decided to bribe the police to say they had all been asleep when Jesus' disciples came during the night and stole his body.

14"If the governor hears about it," the Council promised, "we'll stand up for you and everything will be all right."

15So the police accepted the bribe and said what they were told to. Their story spread widely among the Jews, and is still believed by them to this very day.

A THOUGHT: *The angel who announced the Good News of the resurrection to the women gave them four messages: (1) Don't be frightened. The reality of the resurrection brings joy, not fear. When you are afraid, remember the empty tomb. (2) He isn't here. Jesus is not dead and is not to be looked for among the dead. He is alive, with his people. (3) Come in and see. The women could check the evidence themselves. The tomb was empty then, and is empty today. The resurrection is a historical fact. (4) Go quickly and tell. They were to spread the joy of the resurrection. We too are to spread the Good News about Jesus' resurrection.*

The Rights of an Apostle/ 1 Corinthians 9:1–10

I am an apostle, God's messenger, responsible to no mere man. I am one who has actually seen Jesus our Lord with my own eyes. And your changed lives are the result of my hard work for him. 2If in the opinion of others, I am not an apostle, I certainly am to you, for you have been won to Christ through me. 3This is my answer to those who question my rights.

4Or don't I have any rights at all? Can't I claim the same privilege the other apostles have of being a guest in your homes? 5If I had a wife, and if she were a believer, couldn't I bring her along on these trips just as the other disciples do, and as the Lord's brothers do, and as Peter does? 6And must Barnabas and I alone keep working for our living, while you supply these others? 7What soldier in the army has to pay his own expenses? And have you ever heard of a farmer who harvests his crop and doesn't have the right to eat some of it? What shepherd takes care of a flock of sheep and goats and isn't allowed to drink some of the milk? 8And I'm not merely quoting the opinions of men as to what is right. I'm telling you what God's law says. 9For in the law God gave to Moses he said that you must not put a muzzle on an ox to keep it from eating when it is treading out the wheat. Do you suppose God was thinking only about oxen when he said this? 10Wasn't he also thinking about us? Of course he was. He said this to show us that Christian workers should be paid by those they help. Those who do the plowing and threshing should expect some share of the harvest.

A THOUGHT: *Paul uses himself as an illustration of giving up personal rights. Paul had the right to hospitality, to be married, to bring guests, to be paid for his work; but he willingly gave up these rights to win people to Christ. When your focus is on living for Christ, your rights become comparatively unimportant. Obedience to God is far more important than maintaining our "rights."*

Proverbs for Today/ 11:12–13

To quarrel with a neighbor is foolish; a man with good sense holds his tongue. □ A gossip goes around spreading rumors, while a trustworthy man tries to quiet them.

MARCH 16

Jesus Commissions His Disciples/
Matthew 28:16–20

Then the eleven disciples left for Galilee, going to the mountain where Jesus had said they would find him. 17There they met him and worshiped him—but some of them weren't sure it really was Jesus!

18He told his disciples, "I have been given all authority

in heaven and earth. 19Therefore go and make disciples in all the nations, baptizing them into the name of the Father and of the Son and of the Holy Spirit, 20and then teach these new disciples to obey all the commands I have given you; and be sure of this—that I am with you always, even to the end of the world."

A Thought: *When someone is dying or leaving us, the last words spoken by that person are very important. Jesus left the disciples with these last words of instruction: they were under his authority; they were to make more disciples; they were to baptize and teach new disciples to obey Jesus; he would be with them always. Whereas in previous missions Jesus had sent his disciples only to the Jews, their mission from now on would be worldwide. Jesus is Lord of the earth, and he died for the sins of all people.*

We are to go—whether it is next door or to another country—and make disciples. It is not an option, but a command to all who call Jesus Lord. We are not all evangelists, but we have all received gifts that we can use in helping to fulfill the Great Commission. As we obey, we have comfort in the knowledge that Jesus is always with us.

The Good News Preached without Compensation/ 1 Corinthians 9:11–18

We have planted good spiritual seed in your souls. Is it too much to ask, in return, for mere food and clothing? 12You give them to others who preach to you, and you should. But shouldn't we have an even greater right to them? Yet we have *never* used this right, but supply our own needs without your help. We have never demanded payment of any kind for fear that, if we did, you might be less interested in our message to you from Christ.

13Don't you realize that God told those working in his temple to take for their own needs some of the food brought there as gifts to him? And those who work at the altar of God get a share of the food that is brought by those offering it to the Lord. 14In the same way the Lord has given orders that those who preach the Gospel should be supported by those who accept it.

15Yet I have never asked you for one penny. And I am not writing this to hint that I would like to start now. In fact, I would rather die of hunger than lose the satisfaction I get from preaching to you without charge. 16For just preaching the Gospel isn't any special credit to me—I couldn't keep from preaching it if I wanted to. I would be utterly miserable. Woe unto me if I don't.

17If I were volunteering my services of my own free will, then the Lord would give me a special reward; but that is not the situation, for God has picked me out and given me this sacred trust and I have no choice. 18Under this circumstance, what is my pay? It is the special joy I get from preaching the Good News without expense to anyone, never demanding my rights.

A THOUGHT: *Preaching the gospel was Paul's gift and calling, and he said he couldn't stop preaching if he wanted to. He was driven by the desire to do what God wanted, using his gifts for God's glory. He did not seek money or fame, rather he sought to know Christ and to bring him glory. This is true discipleship. What special gifts has God given you? Are you motivated, like Paul, to glorify God with your gifts?*

Proverbs for Today/ 11:14

Without wise leadership, a nation is in trouble; but with good counselors there is safety.

MARCH 17

John the Baptist Prepares the Way for Jesus/ Mark 1:1–8

Here begins the wonderful story of Jesus the Messiah, the Son of God.

2In the book written by the prophet Isaiah, God announced that he would send his Son to earth, and that a special messenger would arrive first to prepare the world for his coming.

3"This messenger will live out in the barren wilderness," Isaiah said, "and will proclaim that everyone must straighten out his life to be ready for the Lord's arrival."

4This messenger was John the Baptist. He lived in the wilderness and taught that all should be baptized as a public announcement of their decision to turn their backs on sin, so that God could forgive them. 5People from Jerusalem and from all over Judea traveled out into the Judean wastelands to see and hear John, and when they

confessed their sins he baptized them in the Jordan River.
6His clothes were woven from camel's hair and he wore
a leather belt; locusts and wild honey were his food. 7Here
is a sample of his preaching:

"Someone is coming soon who is far greater than I
am, so much greater that I am not even worthy to be
his slave. 8I baptize you with water but he will baptize
you with God's Holy Spirit!"

A THOUGHT: *The purpose of John's preaching was to prepare people
to accept Jesus as God's Son. When John challenged the people to
confess sin individually, he signaled the start of a new approach
to having a relationship with God.*

*Is change needed in your life before you can hear and understand
Jesus' message? People have to admit that they need forgiveness
before they can accept forgiveness; thus true repentance must come
before a person can have true faith in Jesus Christ. To prepare to
receive Christ, we must repent, denouncing the world's dead—end
attractions, sinful temptations, and harmful attitudes.*

Common Ground—the Context for Evangelism/
1 Corinthians 9:19–27

And this has a real advantage: I am not bound to obey
anyone just because he pays my salary; yet I have freely
and happily become a servant of any and all so that I can
win them to Christ. 20When I am with the Jews I seem
as one of them so that they will listen to the Gospel and
I can win them to Christ. When I am with Gentiles who
follow Jewish customs and ceremonies I don't argue, even
though I don't agree, because I want to help them. 21When
with the heathen I agree with them as much as I can,
except of course that I must always do what is right as
a Christian. And so, by agreeing, I can win their confidence
and help them too.

22When I am with those whose consciences bother them
easily, I don't act as though I know it all and don't say
they are foolish; the result is that they are willing to let
me help them. Yes, whatever a person is like, I try to
find common ground with him so that he will let me tell
him about Christ and let Christ save him. 23I do this to
get the Gospel to them and also for the blessing I myself
receive when I see them come to Christ.

24In a race, everyone runs but only one person gets
first prize. So run your race to win. 25To win the contest

you must deny yourselves many things that would keep you from doing your best. An athlete goes to all this trouble just to win a blue ribbon or a silver cup, but we do it for a heavenly reward that never disappears. 26So I run straight to the goal with purpose in every step. I fight to win. I'm not just shadow-boxing or playing around. 27Like an athlete I punish my body, treating it roughly, training it to do what it should, not what it wants to. Otherwise I fear that after enlisting others for the race, I myself might be declared unfit and ordered to stand aside.

A THOUGHT: *Paul gives several important principles for ministry: (1) find common ground with those you contact; (2) avoid a know-it-all attitude; (3) make others feel accepted; (4) be sensitive to their needs and concerns; and (5) look for opportunities to tell them about Christ. These principles are just as valid for us today as they were for Paul.*

Proverbs for Today/ 11:15
Be sure you know a person well before you vouch for his credit! Better refuse than suffer later.

MARCH 18

Jesus' Baptism and Temptation/ Mark 1:9–13
Then one day Jesus came from Nazareth in Galilee, and was baptized by John there in the Jordan River. 10The moment Jesus came up out of the water, he saw the heavens open and the Holy Spirit in the form of a dove descending on him, 11and a voice from heaven said, "You are my beloved Son; you are my Delight."

12,13Immediately the Holy Spirit urged Jesus into the desert. There, for forty days, alone except for desert animals, he was subjected to Satan's temptations to sin. And afterwards the angels came and cared for him.

A THOUGHT: *Jesus left the crowds and went into the desert where he was tempted by Satan. Temptation is bad for us only when we give in. Times of inner testing should not be hated and resented, because through them our character can be strengthened and God can teach us valuable lessons. When you face Satan and must deal with his temptations and the turmoil he brings, remember Jesus. He used God's Word against Satan and won. You can do the same.*

An Example for Christians/ 1 Corinthians 10:1–14

For we must never forget, dear brothers, what happened to our people in the wilderness long ago. God guided them by sending a cloud that moved along ahead of them; and he brought them all safely through the waters of the Red Sea. ²This might be called their "baptism"—baptized both in sea and cloud!—as followers of Moses—their commitment to him as their leader. ³,⁴And by a miracle God sent them food to eat and water to drink there in the desert; they drank the water that Christ gave them. He was there with them as a mighty Rock of spiritual refreshment. ⁵Yet after all this most of them did not obey God, and he destroyed them in the wilderness.

⁶From this lesson we are warned that we must not desire evil things as they did, ⁷nor worship idols as they did. (The Scriptures tell us, "The people sat down to eat and drink and then got up to dance" in worship of the golden calf.)

⁸Another lesson for us is what happened when some of them sinned with other men's wives, and 23,000 fell dead in one day. ⁹And don't try the Lord's patience— they did, and died from snake bites. ¹⁰And don't murmur against God and his dealings with you, as some of them did, for that is why God sent his Angel to destroy them.

¹¹All these things happened to them as examples—as object lessons to us—to warn us against doing the same things; they were written down so that we could read about them and learn from them in these last days as the world nears its end.

¹²So be careful. If you are thinking, "Oh, I would never behave like that"—let this be a warning to you. For you too may fall into sin. ¹³But remember this—the wrong desires that come into your life aren't anything new and different. Many others have faced exactly the same problems before you. And no temptation is irresistible. You can trust God to keep the temptation from becoming so strong that you can't stand up against it, for he has promised

this and will do what he says. He will show you how to escape temptation's power so that you can bear up patiently against it.

14So, dear friends, carefully avoid idol-worship of every kind.

A THOUGHT: *In a culture filled with moral depravity and pressures, Paul gave strong encouragement to the Corinthians about temptation. He said: wrong desires and temptations happen to everyone, so don't feel you've been singled out; others have resisted temptation, and so can you; any temptation can be resisted, because God will help you resist it. God helps you resist temptation by helping you (1) recognize those people and situations that give you trouble, (2) run from anything you know is wrong, (3) choose to do only what is right, (4) pray for God's help, and (5) seek friends who love God and can offer help in times of temptation. Running from a tempting situation is often the first step to victory.*

Proverbs for Today/ 11:16–17

Honor goes to kind and gracious women, mere money to cruel men. □ Your own soul is nourished when you are kind; it is destroyed when you are cruel.

MARCH 19

Jesus Calls His First Disciples/ Mark 1:14–20

Later on, after John was arrested by King Herod, Jesus went to Galilee to preach God's Good News.

15"At last the time has come!" he announced. "God's Kingdom is near! Turn from your sins and act on this glorious news!"

16One day as Jesus was walking along the shores of the Sea of Galilee, he saw Simon and his brother Andrew fishing with nets, for they were commercial fishermen.

17Jesus called out to them, "Come, follow me! And I will make you fishermen for the souls of men!" 18At once they left their nets and went along with him.

19A little farther up the beach, he saw Zebedee's sons, James and John, in a boat mending their nets. 20He called them too, and immediately they left their father Zebedee in the boat with the hired men and went with him.

A THOUGHT: *What is God's Good News? These first words spoken by Jesus in Mark's Gospel give the core of his teaching: that the long-awaited Messiah has come to begin God's personal reign on earth. Most of the people who heard this message were oppressed, poor, and without hope. Jesus' words were good news because they offered freedom, blessings, and promise.*

Communion—Sharing in the Lord's Death/ 1 Corinthians 10:15–22

You are intelligent people. Look now and see for yourselves whether what I am about to say is true. 16When we ask the Lord's blessing upon our drinking from the cup of wine at the Lord's Table, this means, doesn't it, that all who drink it are sharing together the blessing of Christ's blood? And when we break off pieces of the bread from the loaf to eat there together, this shows that we are sharing together in the benefits of his body. 17No matter how many of us there are, we all eat from the same loaf, showing that we are all parts of the one body of Christ. 18And the Jewish people, all who eat the sacrifices, are united by that act.

19What am I trying to say? Am I saying that the idols to whom the heathen bring sacrifices are really alive and are real gods, and that these sacrifices are of some value? No, not at all. 20What I am saying is that those who offer food to these idols are united together in sacrificing to demons, certainly not to God. And I don't want any of you to be partners with demons when you eat the same food, along with the heathen, that has been offered to these idols. 21You cannot drink from the cup at the Lord's Table and at Satan's table, too. You cannot eat bread both at the Lord's Table and at Satan's table.

22What? Are you tempting the Lord to be angry with you? Are you stronger than he is?

A THOUGHT: *As followers of Christ we must give him our total allegiance. We cannot, as Paul explains, eat "both at the Lord's table and at Satan's." Eating at the Lord's table means communing with Christ and identifying with his death. Eating at Satan's table means identifying with Satan by participating in evil actions. Are you trying to lead two lives, following the desires of both Christ and the crowd? The Bible says you can't do both at the same time. We must choose whom we will serve.*

Proverbs for Today/ 11:18–19

The evil man gets rich for the moment, but the good man's reward lasts forever. The good man finds life; the evil man, death.

MARCH 20

Jesus Demonstrates His Authority/ Mark 1:21–28

Jesus and his companions now arrived at the town of Capernaum and on Saturday morning went into the Jewish place of worship—the synagogue—where he preached. 22The congregation was surprised at his sermon because he spoke as an authority, and didn't try to prove his points by quoting others—quite unlike what they were used to hearing!

23A man possessed by a demon was present and began shouting, 24"Why are you bothering us, Jesus of Nazareth—have you come to destroy us demons? I know who you are—the holy Son of God!"

25Jesus curtly commanded the demon to say no more and to come out of the man. 26At that the evil spirit screamed and convulsed the man violently and left him. 27Amazement gripped the audience and they began discussing what had happened.

"What sort of new religion is this?" they asked excitedly. "Why, even evil spirits obey his orders!"

28The news of what he had done spread quickly through that entire area of Galilee.

A THOUGHT: *The Jewish teachers often quoted from well–known rabbis to give their words more authority. But Jesus didn't need to do that. Jesus' authority was not derived from the wisdom others, his authority was bound up with the fact that he is God's Son. He is the ultimate authority. Jesus demonstrated his power and authority by casting out demons and healing the sick. Jesus didn't have to conduct elaborate exorcism rituals. His word was enough to send out the demons.*

Do All to the Glory of God/
1 Corinthians 10:23—11:1

You are certainly free to eat food offered to idols if you want to; it's not against God's laws to eat such meat, but that doesn't mean that you should go ahead and do it. It may be perfectly legal, but it may not be best and helpful. 24 Don't think only of yourself. Try to think of the other fellow, too, and what is best for him.

25Here's what you should do. Take any meat you want that is sold at the market. Don't ask whether or not it was offered to idols, lest the answer hurt your conscience. 26For the earth and every good thing in it belongs to the Lord and is yours to enjoy.

27If someone who isn't a Christian asks you out to dinner, go ahead; accept the invitation if you want to. Eat whatever is on the table and don't ask any questions about it. Then you won't know whether or not it has been used as a sacrifice to idols, and you won't risk having a bad conscience over eating it. 28But if someone warns you that this meat has been offered to idols, then don't eat it for the sake of the man who told you, and of his conscience. 29In this case *his* feeling about it is the important thing, not yours.

But why, you may ask, must I be guided and limited by what someone else thinks? 30If I can thank God for the food and enjoy it, why let someone spoil everything just because he thinks I am wrong? 31Well, I'll tell you why. It is because you must do everything for the glory of God, even your eating and drinking. 32So don't be a stumbling block to anyone, whether they are Jews or Gentiles or Christians. 33That is the plan I follow, too. I try to please everyone in everything I do, not doing what I like or what is best for me, but what is best for them, so that they may be saved.

11:1And you should follow my example, just as I follow Christ's.

A THOUGHT: *Sometimes it's hard to know when to defer to the weaker brother. Paul gives a simple rule of thumb to help in making the decision—we should be sensitive and gracious. While we have freedom in Christ, we shouldn't exercise our freedom at the cost of hurting a Christian brother or sister. In all that we do, we must seek to obey God. Obedience to God is most clearly seen in our love for one another (which involves sacrificing our own desires for others).*

Proverbs for Today/ 11:20–21

The Lord hates the stubborn but delights in those who are good. You can be very sure the evil man will not go unpunished forever. And you can also be very sure God will rescue the children of the godly.

MARCH 21

Jesus Casts Out Demons and Heals Many/ Mark 1:29–39

Then, leaving the synagogue, Jesus and his disciples went over to Simon and Andrew's home, where they found Simon's mother-in-law sick in bed with a high fever. They told Jesus about her right away. 31He went to her bedside, and as he took her by the hand and helped her to sit up, the fever suddenly left, and she got up and prepared dinner for them!

32,33By sunset the courtyard was filled with the sick and demon-possessed, brought to him for healing; and a huge crowd of people from all over the city of Capernaum gathered outside the door to watch. 34So Jesus healed great numbers of sick folk that evening and ordered many demons to come out of their victims. (But he refused to allow the demons to speak, because they knew who he was.)

35The next morning he was up long before daybreak and went out alone into the wilderness to pray.

36,37Later, Simon and the others went out to find him, and told him, "Everyone is asking for you."

38But he replied, "We must go on to other towns as well, and give my message to them too, for that is why I came."

39So he traveled throughout the province of Galilee, preaching in the synagogues and releasing many from the power of demons.

A THOUGHT: *Jesus announced the presence of the Kingdom of God. He did this in both word and deed. In his words he announced God's Good News. In his deeds he demonstrated the power of God's rule through casting out demons and healing many. Ultimately, he established the entrance into the Kingdom of God by his death and resurrection for the redemption of God's people.*

Women in the Church/ 1 Corinthians 11:2–16

I am so glad, dear brothers, that you have been remembering and doing everything I taught you. 3But there is one matter I want to remind you about: that a wife is responsible to her husband, her husband is responsible to Christ, and Christ is responsible to God. 4That is why, if a man refuses to remove his hat while praying or preaching, he dishonors Christ. 5And that is why a woman who publicly prays or prophesies without a covering on her head dishonors her husband [for her covering is a sign of her subjection to him]. 6Yes, if she refuses to wear a head covering, then she should cut off all her hair. And if it is shameful for a woman to have her head shaved, then she should wear a covering. 7But a man should not wear anything on his head [when worshiping, for his hat is a sign of subjection to men].

God's glory is man made in his image, and man's glory is the woman. 8The first man didn't come from woman, but the first woman came out of man. 9And Adam, the first man, was not made for Eve's benefit, but Eve was made for Adam. 10So a woman should wear a covering on her head as a sign that she is under man's authority, a fact for all the angels to notice and rejoice in.

11But remember that in God's plan men and women need each other. 12For although the first woman came out of man, all men have been born from women ever since, and both men and women come from God their Creator.

13What do you yourselves really think about this? Is it right for a woman to pray in public without covering her head? 14,15Doesn't even instinct itself teach us that women's heads should be covered? For women are proud of their long hair, while a man with long hair tends to be ashamed. 16But if anyone wants to argue about this, all I can say is that we never teach anything else than this—that a woman should wear a covering when prophesying or praying publicly in the church, and all the churches feel the same way about it.

A THOUGHT: *This section focuses on attitudes toward worship, not on marriage or the role of women in the church. While Paul's specific instructions may be cultural (women wearing hats in worship), the principles behind his specific instructions are timeless,* including respect for spouse, reverence and appropriateness in worship, and focusing all of life on God. If anything you do can easily offend members and divide the church, then change your ways to promote church unity. Thus Paul told the women who were not wearing head coverings to wear them; not because it was a Scriptural command, but because it kept the congregation from dividing over a petty issue that served only to take people's minds off Christ.

Proverbs for Today/ 11:22
A beautiful woman lacking discretion and modesty is like a fine gold ring in a pig's snout.

MARCH 22

Jesus Heals a Leper/ Mark 1:40–45

Once a leper came and knelt in front of Jesus and begged to be healed. "If you want to, you can make me well again," he pled.

41And Jesus, moved with pity, touched him and said, "I want to! Be healed!" 42Immediately the leprosy was gone—the man was healed!

43,44Jesus then told him sternly, "Go and be examined immediately by the Jewish priest. Don't stop to speak to anyone along the way. Take along the offering prescribed by Moses for a leper who is healed, so that everyone will have proof that you are well again."

45But as the man went on his way he began to shout the good news that he was healed; as a result, such throngs soon surrounded Jesus that he couldn't publicly enter a city anywhere, but had to stay out in the barren wastelands. And people from everywhere came to him there.

A THOUGHT: *Jewish leaders declared lepers unclean. This meant they were unfit to participate in any religious or social activity. Because their law said that contact with any unclean person made them unclean too, some even threw rocks at lepers to keep them at a safe distance. But Jesus reached out in compassion and touched this leper.*

The real value of a person is on the inside, not what appears on the outside. Although a person's body may be diseased or deformed, the person inside is no less valuable to God than a physically healthy person. God's compassion reaches out to all without any such distinc-

*tions. In a sense, we are all lepers, because we have all been
deformed by the ugliness of sin. But God, by sending his Son
Jesus, has touched us, giving us the opportunity to be healed. When
you feel repulsed by someone, stop and remember how God feels
about that person—and about you.*

Gluttony at Communion Services/
1 Corinthians 11:17–22

Next on my list of items to write you about is something
else I cannot agree with. For it sounds as if more harm
than good is done when you meet together for your communion services. 18Everyone keeps telling me about the arguing that goes on in these meetings, and the divisions
developing among you, and I can just about believe it.
19But I suppose you feel this is necessary so that you
who are always right will become known and recognized!

20When you come together to eat, it isn't the Lord's
Supper you are eating, 21but your own. For I am told
that everyone hastily gobbles all the food he can without
waiting to share with the others, so that one doesn't get
enough and goes hungry while another has too much to
drink and gets drunk. 22What? Is this really true? Can't
you do your eating and drinking at home, to avoid disgracing
the church and shaming those who are poor and can bring
no food? What am I supposed to say about these things?
Do you want me to praise you? Well, I certainly do not!

A THOUGHT: *When the Lord's Supper was celebrated in the early
church, it included a feast or fellowship meal followed by communion.
In Corinth the fellowship meal had become a time of gluttony and
excessive drinking rather than a time of preparation for communion.
Although the feast was similar to a potluck, there was little sharing
and caring. This certainly did not demonstrate the unity and love
that should characterize the church, nor was it a preparation for
communion. Paul condemned these actions and reminded the church
of the real purpose of the Lord's Supper—participation in the Lord's
death. Christ should be the central focus of the communion service.*

Proverbs for Today/ 11:23

The good man can look forward to happiness, while the
wicked can expect only wrath.

MARCH 23

Jesus Heals a Paralytic/ Mark 2:1–12

Several days later Jesus returned to Capernaum, and the news of his arrival spread quickly through the city. 2Soon the house where he was staying was so packed with visitors that there wasn't room for a single person more, not even outside the door. And he preached the Word to them. 3Four men arrived carrying a paralyzed man on a stretcher. 4They couldn't get to Jesus through the crowd, so they dug through the clay roof above his head and lowered the sick man on his stretcher, right down in front of Jesus.

5When Jesus saw how strongly they believed that he would help, Jesus said to the sick man, "Son, your sins are forgiven!"

6But some of the Jewish religious leaders said to themselves as they sat there, 7"What? This is blasphemy! Does he think he is God? For only God can forgive sins."

8Jesus could read their minds and said to them at once, "Why does this bother you? 9,10,11I, the Messiah, have the authority on earth to forgive sins. But talk is cheap—anybody could say that. So I'll prove it to you by healing this man." Then, turning to the paralyzed man, he commanded, "Pick up your stretcher and go on home, for you are healed!"

12The man jumped up, took the stretcher, and pushed his way through the stunned onlookers! Then how they praised God. "We've never seen anything like this before!" they all exclaimed.

A THOUGHT: *Instead of saying to the paralyzed man, "You are healed," Jesus said, "Your sins are forgiven." To the Jewish leaders this was blasphemy, claiming to do something only God could do. According to Jewish law, this sin deserved death.*

The religious leaders understood correctly that Jesus was claiming to be the Messiah, but their judgment of him was wrong. Jesus was not blaspheming, because his claim was true. As God's Son, Jesus has the authority to forgive sin, and he proved his claim by healing the paralyzed man.

Share in the Lord's Table in a Worthy Manner/
1 Corinthians 11:23–34

For this is what the Lord himself has said about his Table, and I have passed it on to you before: That on the night when Judas betrayed him, the Lord Jesus took bread, 24and when he had given thanks to God for it, he broke it and gave it to his disciples and said, "Take this and eat it. This is my body, which is given for you. Do this to remember me." 25In the same way, he took the cup of wine after supper, saying, "This cup is the new agreement between God and you that has been established and set in motion by my blood. Do this in remembrance of me whenever you drink it." 26For every time you eat this bread and drink this cup you are re-telling the message of the Lord's death, that he has died for you. Do this until he comes again.

27So if anyone eats this bread and drinks from this cup of the Lord in an unworthy manner, he is guilty of sin against the body and the blood of the Lord. 28That is why a man should examine himself carefully before eating the bread and drinking from the cup. 29For if he eats the bread and drinks from the cup unworthily, not thinking about the body of Christ and what it means, he is eating and drinking God's judgment upon himself; for he is trifling with the death of Christ. 30That is why many of you are weak and sick, and some have even died.

31But if you carefully examine yourselves before eating you will not need to be judged and punished. 32Yet, when we are judged and punished by the Lord, it is so that we will not be condemned with the rest of the world. 33So, dear brothers, when you gather for the Lord's Supper—the communion service—wait for each other; 34if anyone is really hungry he should eat at home so that he won't bring punishment upon himself when you meet together.

I'll talk to you about the other matters after I arrive.

A THOUGHT: *Paul gives specific instructions on how the Lord's Supper should be observed. (1) We should take the Lord's Supper with a repentant attitude because we are remembering that Christ died for our sins. (2) We should take it after self–examination. We are to be prepared and ready, doing it only through our belief in and love for Christ. (3) We should take it in recognition of*

Jesus' act of love in taking away the punishment we deserve for our sins. (4) We should take it with mutual consideration, waiting until everyone is present and eating in an orderly and unified manner.

Proverbs for Today/ 11:24–26

It is possible to give away and become richer! It is also possible to hold on too tightly and lose everything. Yes, the liberal man shall be rich! By watering others, he waters himself. People curse the man who holds his grain for higher prices, but they bless the man who sells it to them in their time of need.

MARCH 24

Jesus Calls Levi to Be His Disciple/ Mark 2:13–17

Then Jesus went out to the seashore again, and preached to the crowds that gathered around him. ¹⁴As he was walking up the beach he saw Levi, the son of Alphaeus, sitting at his tax collection booth. "Come with me," Jesus told him. "Come be my disciple."

And Levi jumped to his feet and went along.

¹⁵That night Levi invited his fellow tax collectors and many other notorious sinners to be his dinner guests so that they could meet Jesus and his disciples. (There were many men of this type among the crowds that followed him.) ¹⁶But when some of the Jewish religious leaders saw him eating with these men of ill repute, they said to his disciples, "How can he stand it, to eat with such scum?"

¹⁷When Jesus heard what they were saying, he told them, "Sick people need the doctor, not healthy ones! I haven't come to tell good people to repent, but the bad ones."

A THOUGHT: *"Such scum," the self-righteous Pharisees said, describing the people with whom Jesus ate. But Jesus associated with sinners because he loved them and because he knew they needed to hear what he had to say. He spent time with whoever needed or wanted to hear his message—poor, rich, evil, and good. We, too, must befriend those who need Christ, even if they do not seem to* be ideal companions. *Are there people you have been neglecting because of their reputation? They may be the ones who most need to see and hear the message of Christ's love from you.*

Judging the Truthfulness of a Message/
1 Corinthians 12:1–3

And now, brothers, I want to write about the special abilities the Holy Spirit gives to each of you, for I don't want any misunderstanding about them. ²You will remember that before you became Christians you went around from one idol to another, not one of which could speak a single word. ³But now you are meeting people who claim to speak messages from the Spirit of God. How can you know whether they are really inspired by God or whether they are fakes? Here is the test: no one speaking by the power of the Spirit of God can curse Jesus, and no one can say, "Jesus is Lord," and really mean it, unless the Holy Spirit is helping him.

A THOUGHT: *Anyone can claim to speak for God, and the world is full of false teachers. Paul gives us a test to help us discern whether or not a messenger is really from God: does he or she confess Christ as Lord? Don't naively accept the words of all who claim to speak for God; test their credentials by finding out what they teach about Christ.*

Proverbs for Today/ 11:27

If you search for good you will find God's favor; if you search for evil you will find his curse.

MARCH 25

The Bridegroom and His Friends/ Mark 2:18–22

John's disciples and the Jewish leaders sometimes fasted, that is, went without food as part of their religion. One day some people came to Jesus and asked why his disciples didn't do this too.

¹⁹Jesus replied, "Do friends of the bridegroom refuse to eat at the wedding feast? Should they be sad while he is with them? ²⁰But some day he will be taken away from

them, and then they will mourn. 21[Besides, going without food is part of the old way of doing things.] It is like patching an old garment with unshrunk cloth! What happens? The patch pulls away and leaves the hole worse than before. 22You know better than to put new wine into old wineskins. They would burst. The wine would be spilled out and the wineskins ruined. New wine needs fresh wineskins."

A THOUGHT: *John the Baptist's ministry had two purposes: to announce to people that they needed to repent of their sin, and to prepare them for Christ's coming. This was a time of sober reflection, and so it included fasting, an outward sign of humility and regret for sin. Fasting is a turning away from food; repentance is a turning away from sin. Jesus' disciples did not need to fast to prepare for his coming, because he was with them. Jesus did not condemn fasting. He himself fasted for 40 days. Nevertheless, he emphasized fasting with the right motives. The Pharisees fasted twice a week to show how holy they were. Jesus explained that if people fast only to impress others, they have missed the purpose of fasting. Christian fasting should be a turning away from meeting our own needs—the time we normally set aside for eating—to pray, to worship God, or to serve God in serving others.*

Spiritual Gifts in the Church/ 1 Corinthians 12:4–11

Now God gives us many kinds of special abilities, but it is the same Holy Spirit who is the source of them all. 5There are different kinds of service to God, but it is the same Lord we are serving. 6There are many ways in which God works in our lives, but it is the same God who does the work in and through all of us who are his. 7The Holy Spirit displays God's power through each of us as a means of helping the entire church.

8To one person the Spirit gives the ability to give wise advice; someone else may be especially good at studying and teaching, and this is his gift from the same Spirit. 9He gives special faith to another, and to someone else the power to heal the sick. 10He gives power for doing miracles to some, and to others power to prophesy and preach. He gives someone else the power to know whether evil spirits are speaking through those who claim to be giving God's messages—or whether it is really the Spirit of God who is speaking. Still another person is able to speak in languages he never learned; and others, who do not know the language either, are given power to under stand what he is saying. [11]It is the same and only Holy Spirit who gives all these gifts and powers, deciding which each one of us should have.

A THOUGHT: *There is both unity and diversity in the body of Christ. There is unity in the fact that we all belong to the same Lord, we are all empowered by the same Spirit, and we all belong to the same community (the church). Within this great unity is a great diversity of gifts. Each of these gifts are given by the Holy Spirit to individuals for the building up of the whole body of Christ. Spiritual gifts should not be a source of contention over who has the "greater" gifts. God did not give the gifts to improve our status, but to allow us the opportunity to participate in the building up of the church. Therefore, let us employ our spiritual gifts as God intended them to be used—to build up the church.*

Proverbs for Today/ 11:28

Trust in your money and down you go! Trust in God and flourish as a tree!

MARCH 26

Jesus Has Authority over the Sabbath/ Mark 2:23—3:6

Another time, on a Sabbath day as Jesus and his disciples were walking through the fields, the disciples were breaking off heads of wheat and eating the grain.

[24]Some of the Jewish religious leaders said to Jesus, "They shouldn't be doing that! It's against our laws to work by harvesting grain on the Sabbath."

[25,26]But Jesus replied, "Didn't you ever hear about the time King David and his companions were hungry, and he went into the house of God—Abiathar was High Priest then—and they ate the special bread only priests were allowed to eat? That was against the law too. [27]But the Sabbath was made to benefit man, and not man to benefit the Sabbath. [28]And I, the Messiah, have authority even to decide what men can do on Sabbath days!"

[3:1]While in Capernaum Jesus went over to the synagogue again, and noticed a man there with a deformed hand.

[2]Since it was the Sabbath, Jesus' enemies watched him

closely. Would he heal the man's hand? If he did, they planned to arrest him!

3Jesus asked the man to come and stand in front of the congregation. 4Then turning to his enemies he asked, "Is it all right to do kind deeds on Sabbath days? Or is this a day for doing harm? Is it a day to save lives or to destroy them?" But they wouldn't answer him. 5Looking around at them angrily, for he was deeply disturbed by their indifference to human need, he said to the man, "Reach out your hand." He did, and instantly his hand was healed!

6At once the Pharisees went away and met with the Herodians to discuss plans for killing Jesus.

A THOUGHT: *Jesus used the example of King David to point out how ridiculous the Pharisees' accusations were. Jesus said that God created the Sabbath for our benefit, not his own. God derives no benefit from having us rest on the Sabbath, but we are restored both physically and spiritually when we take time to rest and focus on God. For the Pharisees, Sabbath laws had become more important than the reason for the Sabbath. Both David and Jesus understood that the true intent of God's Law is to promote love for God and for others. Don't blindly keep a law without looking carefully at the reasons for the law. Keeping the spirit of the law is more important than merely following the letter of the law.*

The Body of Christ Has Many Parts/
1 Corinthians 12:12–18

Our bodies have many parts, but the many parts make up only one body when they are all put together. So it is with the "body" of Christ. 13Each of us is a part of the one body of Christ. Some of us are Jews, some are Gentiles, some are slaves and some are free. But the Holy Spirit has fitted us all together into one body. We have been baptized into Christ's body by the one Spirit, and have all been given that same Holy Spirit.

14Yes, the body has many parts, not just one part. 15If the foot says, "I am not a part of the body because I am not a hand," that does not make it any less a part of the body. 16And what would you think if you heard an ear say, "I am not part of the body because I am only an ear, and not an eye"? Would that make it any less a part of the body? 17Suppose the whole body were an eye— then how would you hear? Or if your whole body were just one big ear, how could you smell anything?

18But that isn't the way God has made us. He has made many parts for our bodies and has put each part just where he wants it.

A THOUGHT: *Using the analogy of the body, Paul emphasizes the importance of each church member. If a seemingly insignificant part is taken away, the whole body becomes less effective. Thinking that your gift is more important than someone else's is spiritual pride. We should not look down on those who seem unimportant, and we should not be jealous of others who have impressive gifts. Instead, we must use the gifts we have been given and encourage others to use theirs. If we don't, the body of believers will be less effective.*

Proverbs for Today/ 11:29–31

The fool who provokes his family to anger and resentment will finally have nothing worthwhile left. He shall be the servant of a wiser man. □ Godly men are growing a tree that bears life-giving fruit, and all who win souls are wise. □ Even the godly shall be rewarded here on earth; how much more the wicked!

MARCH 27

Jesus Chooses His Twelve Disciples/ Mark 3:7–19

Meanwhile, Jesus and his disciples withdrew to the beach, followed by a huge crowd from all over Galilee, Judea, Jerusalem, Idumea, from beyond the Jordan River, and even from as far away as Tyre and Sidon. For the news about his miracles had spread far and wide and vast numbers came to see him for themselves.

9He instructed his disciples to bring around a boat and to have it standing ready to rescue him in case he was crowded off the beach. 10For there had been many healings that day and as a result great numbers of sick people were crowding around him, trying to touch him.

11And whenever those possessed by demons caught sight of him they would fall down before him shrieking, "You are the Son of God!" 12But he strictly warned them not to make him known.

13Afterwards he went up into the hills and summoned certain ones he chose, inviting them to come and join him there; and they did. 14,15Then he selected twelve of them to be his regular companions and to go out to preach and to cast out demons. 16–19These are the names of the twelve he chose:

Simon (he renamed him "Peter"),
James and John (the sons of Zebedee, but Jesus called them "Sons of Thunder"),
Andrew,
Philip,
Bartholomew,
Matthew,
Thomas,
James (the son of Alphaeus),
Thaddaeus,
Simon (a member of a political party advocating violent overthrow of the Roman government),
Judas Iscariot (who later betrayed him).

A THOUGHT: *Jesus was surrounded by followers, from whom he chose twelve to be his regular companions. He did not choose these twelve because of their faith, because their faith faltered. He didn't choose them because of their talent and ability, because no one stood out with unusual ability. The disciples represented a wide range of backgrounds and life experiences, but apparently they had no more leadership potential than those who were not chosen. The one characteristic they all shared was their willingness to obey and follow Jesus. After Jesus' ascension, they were filled with the Holy Spirit and carried out special roles in the early church. We should not disqualify ourselves from service to Christ because we do not have the right credentials. Being a good disciple is not a matter of credentials, but of following Jesus with a willing heart.*

All Parts of the Body Are Necessary/
1 Corinthians 12:19–27

What a strange thing a body would be if it had only one part! 20So he has made many parts, but still there is only one body.

21The eye can never say to the hand, "I don't need you." The head can't say to the feet, "I don't need you."

22And some of the parts that seem weakest and least important are really the most necessary. 23Yes, we are especially glad to have some parts that seem rather odd!

And we carefully protect from the eyes of others those parts that should not be seen, 24 while of course the parts that may be seen do not require this special care. So God has put the body together in such a way that extra honor and care are given to those parts that might otherwise seem less important. 25This makes for happiness among the parts, so that the parts have the same care for each other that they do for themselves. 26If one part suffers, all parts suffer with it, and if one part is honored, all the parts are glad.

27Now here is what I am trying to say: All of you together are the one body of Christ and each one of you is a separate and necessary part of it.

A THOUGHT: *What is your response when a fellow Christian is honored? When someone is suffering? We are called to rejoice with those who rejoice and weep with those who weep. Too often, unfortunately, we are jealous of those who rejoice and separate ourselves from those who weep. Believers are in the world together—there is no room in the church for an individualistic Christianity. We can't concern ourselves solely with our own relationship with God; we need to be concerned for the needs of others.*

Proverbs for Today/ 12:1
To learn, you must want to be taught. To refuse reproof is stupid.

MARCH 28

The Kingdom of God and the Kingdom of Satan/ Mark 3:20–35
When Jesus returned to the house where he was staying, the crowds began to gather again, and soon it was so full of visitors that he couldn't even find time to eat. 21When his friends heard what was happening they came to try to take him home with them.

"He's out of his mind," they said.

22But the Jewish teachers of religion who had arrived from Jerusalem said, "His trouble is that he's possessed by Satan, king of demons. That's why demons obey him."

23Jesus summoned these men and asked them (using proverbs they all understood), "How can Satan cast out Satan? 24A kingdom divided against itself will collapse. 25A home filled with strife and division destroys itself. 26And if Satan is fighting against himself, how can he accomplish anything? He would never survive. 27[Satan must be bound before his demons are cast out], just as a strong man must be tied up before his house can be ransacked and his property robbed.

28"I solemnly declare that any sin of man can be forgiven, even blasphemy against me; 29but blasphemy against the Holy Spirit can never be forgiven. It is an eternal sin."

30He told them this because they were saying he did his miracles by Satan's power [instead of acknowledging it was by the Holy Spirit's power].

31,32Now his mother and brothers arrived at the crowded house where he was teaching, and they sent word for him to come out and talk with them. "Your mother and brothers are outside and want to see you," he was told.

33He replied, "Who is my mother? Who are my brothers?" 34Looking at those around him he said, "These are my mother and brothers! 35Anyone who does God's will is my brother, and my sister, and my mother."

A THOUGHT: *God's family is open and doesn't exclude anyone. Although Jesus cared for his mother and brothers, he also cared for all those who loved him. Jesus did not show partiality; he allowed everyone the privilege of obeying God and becoming part of his family. He shows us how to relate to other believers in a new way. In our increasingly computerized, impersonal world, warm relationships among members of God's family take on major importance. The church can give loving, personalized care that many people find nowhere else.*

The Gifts of the Spirit/ 1 Corinthians 12:28-31

Here is a list of some of the parts he has placed in his Church, which is his body:

Apostles,
Prophets—those who preach God's Word,
Teachers,
Those who do miracles,
Those who have the gift of healing;
Those who can help others,

Those who can get others to work together,
Those who speak in languages they have never learned.

29Is everyone an apostle? Of course not. Is everyone a preacher? No. Are all teachers? Does everyone have the power to do miracles? 30Can everyone heal the sick? Of course not. Does God give all of us the ability to speak in languages we've never learned? Can just anyone understand and translate what those are saying who have that gift of foreign speech? 31No, but try your best to have the more important of these gifts.

First, however, let me tell you about something else that is better than any of them!

A THOUGHT: *The more important gifts are those that are more beneficial to the body of Christ. Paul has already made it clear that one gift is not superior to another, but he urges the believers to discover how they can serve Christ's body best with the gifts God has given them. Your spiritual gifts are not for your own self–advancement. They were given for serving God and enhancing the spiritual growth of the body.*

Proverbs for Today/ 12:2–3

The Lord blesses good men and condemns the wicked. Wickedness never brings real success; only the godly have that.

MARCH 29

The Parable of the Soils/ Mark 4:1–20

Once again an immense crowd gathered around Jesus on the beach as he was teaching, so he got into a boat and sat down and talked from there. 2His usual method of teaching was to tell the people stories. One of them went like this:

3"Listen! A farmer decided to sow some grain. As he scattered it across his field, 4some of it fell on a path, and the birds came and picked it off the hard ground and ate it. 5,6Some fell on thin soil with underlying rock. It grew up quickly enough, but soon wilted beneath the hot sun and died because the roots had no nourishment in the shallow soil. 7Other seeds fell among thorns that shot up and crowded the young plants so that they produced no grain. 8But some of the seeds fell into good soil and yielded thirty times as much as he had planted—some of it even sixty or a hundred times as much! 9If you have ears, listen!"

10Afterwards, when he was alone with the twelve and with his other disciples, they asked him, "What does your story mean?"

11,12He replied, "You are permitted to know some truths about the kingdom of God that are hidden to those outside the kingdom:

'Though they see and hear, they will not understand
    or turn to God, or be forgiven for their sins.'

13But if you can't understand *this* simple illustration, what will you do about all the others I am going to tell?

14"The farmer I talked about is anyone who brings God's message to others, trying to plant good seed within their lives. 15The hard pathway, where some of the seed fell, represents the hard hearts of some of those who hear God's message; Satan comes at once to try to make them forget it. 16The rocky soil represents the hearts of those who hear the message with joy, 17but, like young plants in such soil, their roots don't go very deep, and though at first they get along fine, as soon as persecution begins, they wilt.

18"The thorny ground represents the hearts of people who listen to the Good News and receive it, 19but all too quickly the attractions of this world and the delights of wealth, and the search for success and lure of nice things come in and crowd out God's message from their hearts, so that no crop is produced.

20"But the good soil represents the hearts of those who truly accept God's message and produce a plentiful harvest for God—thirty, sixty, or even a hundred times as much as was planted in their hearts."

A THOUGHT: *Jesus taught the people by telling stories, often called parables. A parable uses familiar scenes to explain deeper spiritual truth. This method of teaching compels the listener to think. It conceals the truth from those who are too stubborn or prejudiced to hear what is being taught. We hear with our ears, but there is a deeper kind of listening with the mind and heart that is necessary in order to gain spiritual understanding from Jesus' words. We must allow ourselves to be impacted by the truth of the story in order to be hearing with this deeper kind of listening. All of God's Word should impact us at this deeper level—where God's Word transforms our lives.*

The Characteristics of Love/ 1 Corinthians 13:1–7

If I had the gift of being able to speak in other languages without learning them, and could speak in every language there is in all of heaven and earth, but didn't love others, I would only be making noise. 2If I had the gift of prophecy and knew all about what is going to happen in the future, knew everything about *everything,* but didn't love others, what good would it do? Even if I had the gift of faith so that I could speak to a mountain and make it move, I would still be worth nothing at all without love. 3If I gave everything I have to poor people, and if I were burned alive for preaching the Gospel but didn't love others, it would be of no value whatever.

4Love is very patient and kind, never jealous or envious, never boastful or proud, 5never haughty or selfish or rude. Love does not demand its own way. It is not irritable or touchy. It does not hold grudges and will hardly even notice when others do it wrong. 6It is never glad about injustice, but rejoices whenever truth wins out. 7If you love someone you will be loyal to him no matter what the cost. You will always believe in him, always expect the best of him, and always stand your ground in defending him.

A Thought: *After discussing spiritual gifts in some detail, Paul comes to the core of spirituality—love. No matter what gift a person has, if he or she does not express love in using that gift, then whatever is done is empty. The greatest measure of spirituality is how much our lives are filled with Christlike love. This is not love that we can muster up within ourselves; it is a supernatural love that is produced by the Holy Spirit. Love is to be central to all that we do, for it is the most important part of spirituality. The more intimately we know Christ, the more we will unselfishly love others.*

Proverbs for Today/ 12:4

A worthy wife is her husband's joy and crown; the other kind corrodes his strength and tears down everything he does.

MARCH 30

Illustrations of the Kingdom of God/ Mark 4:21–34

Then Jesus asked them, "When someone lights a lamp, does he put a box over it to shut out the light? Of course not! The light couldn't be seen or used. A lamp is placed on a stand to shine and be useful.

22"All that is now hidden will someday come to light. 23If you have ears, listen! 24And be sure to put into practice what you hear. The more you do this, the more you will understand what I tell you. 25To him who has shall be given; from him who has not shall be taken away even what he has.

26"Here is another story illustrating what the Kingdom of God is like:

"A farmer sowed his field, 27and went away, and as the days went by, the seeds grew and grew without his help. 28For the soil made the seeds grow. First a leaf-blade pushed through, and later the wheat-heads formed and finally the grain ripened, 29and then the farmer came at once with his sickle and harvested it."

30Jesus asked, "How can I describe the Kingdom of God? What story shall I use to illustrate it? 31,32It is like a tiny mustard seed! Though this is one of the smallest of seeds, yet it grows to become one of the largest of plants, with long branches where birds can build their nests and be sheltered."

33He used many such illustrations to teach the people as much as they were ready to understand. 34In fact, he taught only by illustrations in his public teaching, but afterwards, when he was alone with his disciples, he would explain his meaning to them.

A THOUGHT: *Jesus adapted his methods to his audience's ability and desire to understand. He didn't speak in parables to confuse people, but to challenge sincere seekers to discover the true meaning of his words. These parables are about the Kingdom of God. They point to the fact that the Kingdom cannot be hidden, though it is small now, it will continue to grow and become a full harvest (or a very large plant). When you feel alone in your stand for Christ, realize that God is building a worldwide kingdom. He has faithful followers in every part of the world, and your faith, no matter how small, can join with that of others to accomplish great things.*

Love Is the Greatest Gift/ 1 Corinthians 13:8–13

All the special gifts and powers from God will someday come to an end, but love goes on forever. Someday prophecy, and speaking in unknown languages, and special knowledge—these gifts will disappear. 9Now we know so little, even with our special gifts, and the preaching of those most gifted is still so poor. 10But when we have been made perfect and complete, then the need for these inadequate special gifts will come to an end, and they will disappear.

11It's like this: when I was a child I spoke and thought and reasoned as a child does. But when I became a man my thoughts grew far beyond those of my childhood, and now I have put away the childish things. 12In the same way, we can see and understand only a little about God now, as if we were peering at his reflection in a poor mirror; but someday we are going to see him in his completeness, face to face. Now all that I know is hazy and blurred, but then I will see everything clearly, just as clearly as God sees into my heart right now.

13There are three things that remain—faith, hope, and love—and the greatest of these is love.

A THOUGHT: *In the morally corrupt society of Corinth, love had become a mixed-up term with little meaning. Today people are still confused about love. Love is the greatest of all human qualities. It involves unselfish service to others; therefore, it should permeate all that we do or think. We should constantly be called back to a recommitment to love as Christ loved.*

Proverbs for Today/ 12:5–7

A good man's mind is filled with honest thoughts; an evil man's mind is crammed with lies. □ The wicked accuse; the godly defend. The wicked shall perish; the godly shall stand.

MARCH 31

Jesus Calms the Storm/ Mark 4:35–41

As evening fell, Jesus said to his disciples, "Let's cross to the other side of the lake." 36So they took him just as he was and started out, leaving the crowds behind (though other boats followed). 37But soon a terrible storm arose. High waves began to break into the boat until it was nearly full of water and about to sink. 38Jesus was asleep at the back of the boat with his head on a cushion. Frantically they wakened him, shouting, "Teacher, don't you even care that we are all about to drown?"

39Then he rebuked the wind and said to the sea, "Quiet down!" And the wind fell, and there was a great calm!

40And he asked them, "Why were you so fearful? Don't you even yet have confidence in me?"

41And they were filled with awe and said among themselves, "Who is this man, that even the winds and seas obey him?"

A THOUGHT: *The disciples lived with Jesus, but they did not understand who he really was. They were expecting a political messiah who would deliver Israel from the power of Roman domination. They failed to see that Jesus was the divine Son of God. We should respond to Jesus' demonstrations of power with awe and worship. We should also be careful not to allow our cultural expectations blind us to the truth of God's Word before us.*

Prophecy and Tongues/ 1 Corinthians 14:1–5

Let love be your greatest aim; nevertheless, ask also for the special abilities the Holy Spirit gives, and especially the gift of prophecy, being able to preach the messages of God.

2But if your gift is that of being able to "speak in tongues," that is, to speak in languages you haven't learned, you will be talking to God but not to others, since they won't be able to understand you. You will be speaking by the power of the Spirit but it will all be a secret. 3But one who prophesies, preaching the messages of God, is helping others grow in the Lord, encouraging and comforting them. 4So a person "speaking in tongues" helps himself grow spiritually, but one who prophesies, preaching messages from God, helps the entire church grow in holiness and happiness.

5I wish you all had the gift of "speaking in tongues" but, even more, I wish you were all able to prophesy, preaching God's messages, for that is a greater and more useful power than to speak in unknown languages—unless, of course, you can tell everyone afterwards what you were saying, so that they can get some good out of it too.

A THOUGHT: *Paul makes several points about speaking in tongues: (1) it is a spiritual gift from God; (2) it is a desirable gift even though it isn't a requirement of faith; (3) it is less important than prophecy and teaching. Although Paul himself spoke in tongues, he stresses prophecy (preaching) because it benefits the whole church, while speaking in tongues primarily benefits the speaker. Public worship must be understandable and beneficial to the whole church.*

Proverbs for Today/ 12:8–9

Everyone admires a man with good sense, but a man with a warped mind is despised. □ It is better to get your hands dirty—and eat, than to be too proud to work—and starve.

APRIL 1

Jesus Casts Out Demons/ Mark 5:1–20

When Jesus and his disciples arrived at the other side of the lake a demon-possessed man ran out from a graveyard, just as Jesus was climbing from the boat.

3,4This man lived among the gravestones, and had such strength that whenever he was put into handcuffs and shackles—as he often was—he snapped the handcuffs from his wrists and smashed the shackles and walked away. No one was strong enough to control him. 5All day long and through the night he would wander among the tombs and in the wild hills, screaming and cutting himself with sharp pieces of stone.

6When Jesus was still far out on the water, the man

had seen him and had run to meet him, and fell down before him.

7,8Then Jesus spoke to the demon within the man and said, "Come out, you evil spirit."

It gave a terrible scream, shrieking, "What are you going to do to me, Jesus, Son of the Most High God? For God's sake, don't torture me!"

9"What is your name?" Jesus asked, and the demon replied, "Legion, for there are many of us here within this man."

10Then the demons begged him again and again not to send them to some distant land.

11Now as it happened there was a huge herd of hogs rooting around on the hill above the lake. 12"Send us into those hogs," the demons begged.

13And Jesus gave them permission. Then the evil spirits came out of the man and entered the hogs, and the entire herd plunged down the steep hillside into the lake and drowned.

14The herdsmen fled to the nearby towns and countryside, spreading the news as they ran. Everyone rushed out to see for themselves. 15And a large crowd soon gathered where Jesus was; but as they saw the man sitting there, fully clothed and perfectly sane, they were frightened. 16Those who saw what happened were telling everyone about it, 17and the crowd began pleading with Jesus to go away and leave them alone! 18So he got back into the boat. The man who had been possessed by the demons begged Jesus to let him go along. 19But Jesus said no.

"Go home to your friends," he told him, "and tell them what wonderful things God has done for you; and how merciful he has been."

20So the man started off to visit the Ten Towns of that region and began to tell everyone about the great things Jesus had done for him; and they were awestruck by his story.

A THOUGHT: *Jesus brings about the restoration of this demon-possessed man by commanding the legion of demons to come out. Jesus was demonstrating by this action the presence of the Kingdom of God in his own person. His work on the cross defeated Satan and his evil angels and, although the ultimate consummation of this defeat is yet to come, Satan's defeat is sure. While it is important to recognize situations or activities in which demons might be involved, so that we can stay away from them, we must avoid any curiosity about or involvement with demonic forces or the occult. If we resist the devil and his influences, he will flee from us, for the Lord Jesus Christ has overcome the Evil One.*

The Need for Understanding in the Church/
1 Corinthians 14:6–12

Dear friends, even if I myself should come to you talking in some language you don't understand, how would that help you? But if I speak plainly what God has revealed to me, and tell you the things I know, and what is going to happen, and the great truths of God's Word—that is what you need; that is what will help you. 7Even musical instruments—the flute, for instance, or the harp—are examples of the need for speaking in plain, simple English rather than in unknown languages. For no one will recognize the tune the flute is playing unless each note is sounded clearly. 8And if the army bugler doesn't play the right notes, how will the soldiers know that they are being called to battle? 9In the same way, if you talk to a person in some language he doesn't understand, how will he know what you mean? You might as well be talking to an empty room.

10I suppose that there are hundreds of different languages in the world, and all are excellent for those who understand them, 11but to me they mean nothing. A person talking to me in one of these languages will be a stranger to me and I will be a stranger to him. 12Since you are so anxious to have special gifts from the Holy Spirit, ask him for the very best, for those that will be of real help to the whole church.

A THOUGHT: *Since spiritual gifts are to be used to build up the body of Christ, all that we do should lead to the benefit of others. Gifts of speaking should always seek to edify the other person through helping them to understand. If a person cannot understand what we are attempting to communicate, they cannot be served. Let us seek to bring spiritual understanding in the use of speaking gifts in the church and not serve our selves.*

Proverbs for Today/ 12:10

A good man is concerned for the welfare of his animals, but even the kindness of godless men is cruel.

APRIL 2

Jesus Performs Miracles of Healing/ Mark 5:21–43

When Jesus had gone across by boat to the other side of the lake, a vast crowd gathered around him on the shore.

22The leader of the local synagogue, whose name was Jairus, came and fell down before him, 23pleading with him to heal his little daughter.

"She is at the point of death," he said in desperation. "Please come and place your hands on her and make her live."

24Jesus went with him, and the crowd thronged behind. 25In the crowd was a woman who had been sick for twelve years with a hemorrhage. 26She had suffered much from many doctors through the years and had become poor from paying them, and was no better but, in fact, was worse. 27She had heard all about the wonderful miracles Jesus did, and that is why she came up behind him through the crowd and touched his clothes.

28For she thought to herself, "If I can just touch his clothing, I will be healed." 29And sure enough, as soon as she had touched him, the bleeding stopped and she knew she was well!

30Jesus realized at once that healing power had gone out from him, so he turned around in the crowd and asked, "Who touched my clothes?"

31His disciples said to him, "All this crowd pressing around you, and you ask who touched you?"

32But he kept on looking around to see who it was who had done it. 33Then the frightened woman, trembling at the realization of what had happened to her, came and fell at his feet and told him what she had done. 34And he said to her, "Daughter, your faith has made you well; go in peace, healed of your disease."

35While he was still talking to her, messengers arrived from Jairus' home with the news that it was too late— his daughter was dead and there was no point in Jesus' coming now. 36But Jesus ignored their comments and said to Jairus, "Don't be afraid. Just trust me."

37Then Jesus halted the crowd and wouldn't let anyone go on with him to Jairus' home except Peter and James and John. 38When they arrived, Jesus saw that all was in great confusion, with unrestrained weeping and wailing. 39He went inside and spoke to the people.

"Why all this weeping and commotion?" he asked. "The child isn't dead; she is only asleep!"

40They laughed at him in bitter derision, but he told them all to leave, and taking the little girl's father and mother and his three disciples, he went into the room where she was lying.

41,42Taking her by the hand he said to her, "Get up, little girl!" (She was twelve years old.) And she jumped up and walked around! Her parents just couldn't get over it. 43Jesus instructed them very earnestly not to tell what had happened, and told them to give her something to eat.

A THOUGHT: *Jesus not only demonstrated great power; he also showed tremendous compassion. Jesus' power over nature, demons, and death was motivated by compassion—for a demonic man who lived among tombs, for a diseased woman, and for the family of a dead girl. The rabbis of the day considered such people unclean. Polite society avoided them. But Jesus reached out and helped anyone in need.*

Pray for the Ability to Interpret/
1 Corinthians 14:13–17

If someone is given the gift of speaking in unknown tongues, he should pray also for the gift of knowing what he has said, so that he can tell people afterwards, plainly. 14For if I pray in a language I don't understand, my spirit is praying but I don't know what I am saying.

15Well, then, what shall I do? I will do both. I will pray in unknown tongues and also in ordinary language that everyone understands. I will sing in unknown tongues and also in ordinary language, so that I can understand the praise I am giving; 16for if you praise and thank God with the spirit alone, speaking in another language, how can those who don't understand you be praising God along with you? How can they join you in giving thanks when they don't know what you are saying? 17You will be giving thanks very nicely, no doubt, but the other people present won't be helped.

A THOUGHT: *In order to promote unity and understanding in the church, if someone speaks in tongues there should always be someone to interpret the utterance. If there is no one to interpret the utterance, one should keep silent. For the purpose of employing a spiritual gift in the assembly is the upbuilding of all believers. In order for others to participate in what is being shared, people must understand. Therefore, when someone employs one of the speaking gifts, let there be interpreters to give understanding to the rest of the body.*

Proverbs for Today/ 12:11

Hard work means prosperity; only a fool idles away his time.

APRIL 3

A Prophet Is not Honored in His Hometown/ Mark 6:1-6

Soon afterwards Jesus left that section of the country and returned with his disciples to Nazareth, his home town. 2,3The next Sabbath he went to the synagogue to teach, and the people were astonished at his wisdom and his miracles because he was just a local man like themselves.

"He's no better than we are," they said. "He's just a carpenter, Mary's boy, and a brother of James and Joseph, Judas and Simon. And his sisters live right here among us." And they were offended!

4Then Jesus told them, "A prophet is honored everywhere except in his home town and among his relatives and by his own family." 5And because of their unbelief he couldn't do any mighty miracles among them except to place his hands on a few sick people and heal them. 6And he could hardly accept the fact that they wouldn't believe in him.

Then he went out among the villages, teaching.

A THOUGHT: *Jesus was teaching effectively and wisely, but the people of his hometown saw him as only a carpenter. "He's no better than us—he's just a common laborer," they said. They were offended that others could be impressed by him and follow him. They rejected his authority because he was one of their peers. They thought they knew him, but their preconceived notions about who he was made it impossible for them to accept his message. Don't let prejudice blind you to truth. As you learn more about Jesus, try to see him for who he really is.*

Tongues Is a Sign to Unbelievers/ 1 Corinthians 14:18–25

I thank God that I "speak in tongues" privately more than any of the rest of you. 19But in public worship I would much rather speak five words that people can understand and be helped by, than ten thousand words while "speaking in tongues" in an unknown language.

20Dear brothers, don't be childish in your understanding of these things. Be innocent babies when it comes to planning evil, but be men of intelligence in understanding matters of this kind. 21We are told in the ancient Scriptures that God would send men from other lands to speak in foreign languages to his people, but even then they would not listen. 22So you see that being able to "speak in tongues" is not a sign to God's children concerning his power, but is a sign to the unsaved. However, prophecy (preaching the deep truths of God) is what the Christians need, and unbelievers aren't yet ready for it. 23Even so, if an unsaved person, or someone who doesn't have these gifts, comes to church and hears you all talking in other languages, he is likely to think you are crazy. 24But if you prophesy, preaching God's Word, [even though such preaching is mostly for believers] and an unsaved person or a new Christian comes in who does not understand about these things, all these sermons will convince him of the fact that he is a sinner, and his conscience will be pricked by everything he hears. 25As he listens, his secret thoughts will be laid bare and he will fall down on his knees and worship God, declaring that God is really there among you.

A Thought: *The way the Corinthians were speaking in tongues was helping no one because believers did not understand what was being said and unbelievers thought the people speaking in tongues were crazy. Speaking in tongues was supposed to be a sign to unbelievers. After speaking in tongues, believers were supposed to explain what was said and give the credit to God. The unsaved people would then be convinced of a spiritual reality and motivated to search the Christian faith further. While this is one way to reach unbelievers, Paul says that clear preaching is usually better.*

Proverbs for Today/ 12:12–14

Crooks are jealous of each other's loot, while good men long to help each other. □ Lies will get any man into trouble, but honesty is its own defense. Telling the truth gives a man great satisfaction, and hard work returns many blessings to him.

APRIL 4

Jesus Commissions the Twelve Disciples/
Mark 6:7–13

And Jesus called his twelve disciples together and sent them out two by two, with power to cast out demons. 8,9He told them to take nothing with them except their walking sticks—no food, no knapsack, no money, not even an extra pair of shoes or a change of clothes.

10"Stay at one home in each village—don't shift around from house to house while you are there," he said. 11"And whenever a village won't accept you or listen to you, shake off the dust from your feet as you leave; it is a sign that you have abandoned it to its fate."

12So the disciples went out, telling everyone they met to turn from sin. 13And they cast out many demons, and healed many sick people, anointing them with olive oil.

A THOUGHT: *The disciples were sent out in pairs. Individually they could have reached more areas of the country, but this was not Christ's plan. One advantage in going out by twos was that they could strengthen and encourage each other, especially when they faced rejection. Our strength comes from God, but he meets many of our needs through our teamwork with others. As you serve him, don't try to go it alone.*

Use Your Gifts to Build Each Other Up/
1 Corinthians 14:26–33

Well, my brothers, let's add up what I am saying. When you meet together some will sing, another will teach, or tell some special information God has given him, or speak in an unknown language, or tell what someone else is saying who is speaking in the unknown language, but everything that is done must be useful to all, and build them up in the Lord. 27No more than two or three should speak in an unknown language, and they must speak one at a time, and someone must be ready to interpret what they are saying. 28But if no one is present who can interpret, they must not speak out loud. They must talk silently to themselves and to God in the unknown language but not publicly.

29,30Two or three may prophesy, one at a time, if they have the gift, while all the others listen. But if, while someone is prophesying, someone else receives a message or idea from the Lord, the one who is speaking should stop. 31In this way all who have the gift of prophecy can speak, one after the other, and everyone will learn and be encouraged and helped. 32Remember that a person who has a message from God has the power to stop himself or wait his turn. 33God is not one who likes things to be disorderly and upset. He likes harmony, and he finds it in all the other churches.

A THOUGHT: *Everything done in worship services must be beneficial to the worshipers. This principle touches every aspect—singing, preaching, and the exercise of spiritual gifts. Those contributing to the service (singers, speakers, readers) must have love as their chief motivation, giving useful words or help that will strengthen the faith of other believers.*

Proverbs for Today/ 12:15–17

A fool thinks he needs no advice, but a wise man listens to others. □ A fool is quick-tempered; a wise man stays cool when insulted. □ A good man is known by his truthfulness; a false man by deceit and lies.

APRIL 5

The Story of John the Baptist's Death/
Mark 6:14–29

King Herod soon heard about Jesus, for his miracles were talked about everywhere. The king thought Jesus was John the Baptist come back to life again. So the people

were saying, "No wonder he can do such miracles."
15Others thought Jesus was Elijah the ancient prophet,
now returned to life again; still others claimed he was a
new prophet like the great ones of the past.

16"No," Herod said, "it is John, the man I beheaded.
He has come back from the dead."

17,18For Herod had sent soldiers to arrest and imprison
John because he kept saying it was wrong for the king
to marry Herodias, his brother Philip's wife. 19Herodias
wanted John killed in revenge, but without Herod's approval
she was powerless. 20And Herod respected John, knowing
that he was a good and holy man, and so he kept him
under his protection. Herod was disturbed whenever he
talked with John, but even so he liked to listen to him.

21Herodias' chance finally came. It was Herod's birthday
and he gave a stag party for his palace aides, army officers,
and the leading citizens of Galilee. 22,23Then Herodias'
daughter came in and danced before them and greatly
pleased them all.

"Ask me for anything you like," the king vowed, "even
half of my kingdom, and I will give it to you!"

24She went out and consulted her mother, who told
her, "Ask for John the Baptist's head!"

25So she hurried back to the king and told him, "I want
the head of John the Baptist—right now—on a tray!"

26Then the king was sorry, but he was embarrassed
to break his oath in front of his guests. 27So he sent one
of his bodyguards to the prison to cut off John's head
and bring it to him. The soldier killed John in the prison,
28and brought back his head on a tray, and gave it to the
girl and she took it to her mother.

29When John's disciples heard what had happened, they
came for his body and buried it in a tomb.

A THOUGHT: *Herod, along with many others, wondered who Jesus
really was. Unable to accept Jesus' claim to be God's Son, many
people made up their own explanations for his power and authority.
Herod thought Jesus was John the Baptist come back to life; some
who were familiar with the Old Testament thought he was Elijah.
Still others believed he was a teaching prophet in the tradition of
Moses, Isaiah, or Jeremiah. Today people still have to make up
their minds about Jesus. Some think that if they can name what
he is—prophet, teacher, good man—they can weaken the power of*

his claim on their lives. But what they think does not change who Jesus is.

Let There Be Order in Christian Meetings/
1 Corinthians 14:34–40

Women should be silent during the church meetings. They are not to take part in the discussion, for they are subordinate to men as the Scriptures also declare. 35If they have any questions to ask, let them ask their husbands at home, for it is improper for women to express their opinions in church meetings.

36You disagree? And do you think that the knowledge of God's will begins and ends with you Corinthians? Well, you are mistaken! 37You who claim to have the gift of prophecy or any other special ability from the Holy Spirit should be the first to realize that what I am saying is a commandment from the Lord himself. 38But if anyone still disagrees—well, we will leave him in his ignorance.

39So, my fellow believers, long to be prophets so that you can preach God's message plainly; and never say it is wrong to "speak in tongues"; 40however, be sure that everything is done properly in a good and orderly way.

A THOUGHT: *Does this passage mean that women should not speak in church services today? It is clear from an earlier passage in this epistle that women can pray and prophesy in the church, apparently in public meetings. It is also clear in chapters 12—14 that women have spiritual gifts, and they are encouraged to exercise them in the body of Christ. Women have much to contribute and can participate in worship services.*

In the Corinthian culture, women were not allowed to confront men in public. Apparently some of the women who had become Christians thought their Christian freedom gave them the right to speak up in public worship and question the men. This was causing division in the church. In addition, women of that day did not receive formal religious education as did the men. Women may have been raising questions in the worship service which could have more easily been answered at home without disrupting the church service. To promote unity, Paul was asking the women not to flaunt their Christian freedom during the worship service. The purpose of Paul's words here was to promote unity, not to teach about women's role in the church.

Proverbs for Today/ 12:18

Some people like to make cutting remarks, but the words of the wise soothe and heal.

APRIL 6

The Feeding of the Five Thousand/ Mark 6:30–44

The apostles now returned to Jesus from their tour and told him all they had done and what they had said to the people they visited.

31Then Jesus suggested, "Let's get away from the crowds for a while and rest." For so many people were coming and going that they scarcely had time to eat. 32So they left by boat for a quieter spot. 33But many people saw them leaving and ran on ahead along the shore and met them as they landed. 34So the usual vast crowd was there as he stepped from the boat; and he had pity on them because they were like sheep without a shepherd, and he taught them many things they needed to know.

35,36Late in the afternoon his disciples came to him and said, "Tell the people to go away to the nearby villages and farms and buy themselves some food, for there is nothing to eat here in this desolate spot, and it is getting late."

37But Jesus said, *"You* feed them."

"With what?" they asked. "It would take a fortune to buy food for all this crowd!"

38"How much food do we have?" he asked. "Go and find out."

They came back to report that there were five loaves of bread and two fish. 39,40Then Jesus told the crowd to sit down, and soon colorful groups of fifty or a hundred each were sitting on the green grass.

41He took the five loaves and two fish and looking up to heaven, gave thanks for the food. Breaking the loaves into pieces, he gave some of the bread and fish to each disciple to place before the people. 42And the crowd ate until they could hold no more!

43,44There were about 5,000 men there for that meal, and afterwards twelve basketfuls of scraps were picked up off the grass!

A THOUGHT: *Jesus asked the disciples to provide food for over 5,000 people. They responded, "With what?" How do you react when you are given an impossible task? A situation that seems impossible with human means is simply an opportunity for God. The disciples did everything they could—they gathered the available food and organized the people into groups. Then, in answer to prayer, God did the impossible. When facing a seemingly impossible task, do what you can and ask God to do the rest. He may see fit to make the impossible happen.*

The Resurrection Appearances of the Lord/
1 Corinthians 15:1–11

Now let me remind you, brothers, of what the Gospel really is, for it has not changed—it is the same Good News I preached to you before. You welcomed it then and still do now, for your faith is squarely built upon this wonderful message; 2and it is this Good News that saves you if you still firmly believe it, unless of course you never really believed it in the first place.

3I passed on to you right from the first what had been told to me, that Christ died for our sins just as the Scriptures said he would, 4and that he was buried, and that three days afterwards he arose from the grave just as the prophets foretold. 5He was seen by Peter and later by the rest of "the Twelve." 6After that he was seen by more than five hundred Christian brothers at one time, most of whom are still alive, though some have died by now. 7Then James saw him and later all the apostles. 8Last of all I saw him too, long after the others, as though I had been born almost too late for this. 9For I am the least worthy of all the apostles, and I shouldn't even be called an apostle at all after the way I treated the church of God.

10But whatever I am now it is all because God poured out such kindness and grace upon me—and not without results: for I have worked harder than all the other apostles, yet actually I wasn't doing it, but God working in me, to bless me. 11It makes no difference who worked the hardest, I or they; the important thing is that we preached the Gospel to you, and you believed it.

A THOUGHT: *There will always be people who say Jesus didn't rise from the dead. Paul assures us that many people saw Jesus after his resurrection, including more than 500 Christian believers. The resurrection is a historical fact. Don't be discouraged by doubters who deny the resurrection. Be filled with hope by the knowledge that one day everyone will stand before the living Christ. We who are believers in Christ can take comfort in his promise of eternal life—an eternal life with a resurrected body like Christ's. For those who do not know Christ, judgment awaits them.*

Proverbs for Today/ 12:19–20
Truth stands the test of time; lies are soon exposed. Deceit fills hearts that are plotting for evil; joy fills hearts that are planning for good!

APRIL 7

Jesus Walks on the Water/ Mark 6:45–56
Immediately after this Jesus instructed his disciples to get back into the boat and strike out across the lake to Bethsaida, where he would join them later. He himself would stay and tell the crowds good-bye and get them started home.

46Afterwards he went up into the hills to pray. 47During the night, as the disciples in their boat were out in the middle of the lake, and he was alone on land, 48 he saw that they were in serious trouble, rowing hard and struggling against the wind and waves.

About three o'clock in the morning he walked out to them on the water. He started past them, 49but when they saw something walking along beside them they screamed in terror, thinking it was a ghost, 50for they all saw him.

But he spoke to them at once. "It's all right," he said. "It is I! Don't be afraid." 51Then he climbed into the boat and the wind stopped!

They just sat there, unable to take it in! 52For they still didn't realize who he was, even after the miracle the evening before! For they didn't want to believe!

53When they arrived at Gennesaret on the other side of the lake they moored the boat, 54and climbed out.

The people standing around there recognized him at once, 55and ran throughout the whole area to spread the news of his arrival, and began carrying sick folks to him on mats and stretchers. 56Wherever he went—in villages and cities, and out on the farms—they laid the sick in the market plazas and streets, and begged him to let them at least touch the fringes of his clothes; and as many as touched him were healed.

A THOUGHT: *The disciples were utterly amazed at Jesus walking on the water and his ability to calm the storm. Their conception of Messiah did not include such demonstrations of power. They did not transfer the truth they had already experienced about Jesus to new situations because they were blinded by their own expectations of what Messiah was supposed to be like. We worship Jesus whose power, compassion, and wisdom far exceed our expectations or wildest dreams. Let us worship the Lord Jesus Christ for who he is and remember that this same Jesus is present with us.*

The Resurrection—the Foundation of Faith/ 1 Corinthians 15:12–20

But tell me this! Since you believe what we preach, that *Christ* rose from the dead, why are some of you saying that dead people will never come back to life again? 13For if there is no resurrection of the dead, then Christ must still be dead. 14And if he is still dead, then all our preaching is useless and your trust in God is empty, worthless, hopeless; 15and we apostles are all liars because we have said that God raised Christ from the grave, and of course that isn't true if the dead do not come back to life again. 16If they don't, then Christ is still dead, 17and you are very foolish to keep on trusting God to save you, and you are still under condemnation for your sins; 18in that case all Christians who have died are lost! 19And if being a Christian is of value to us only now in this life, we are the most miserable of creatures.

20But the fact is that Christ did actually rise from the dead, and has become the first of millions who will come back to life again some day.

A THOUGHT: *Most Greeks did not believe that people's bodies would be resurrected after death. They saw the afterlife as something that happened only to the soul. According to Platonic philosophers, the soul was the real person, imprisoned in a physical body, and at death the soul was released. There was no immortality for the body, but the soul entered an eternal state. In Scripture, by contrast, the body and soul will be united after resurrection. The church at Corinth was in the heart of Greek culture. Thus many believers had a difficult time believing in a bodily resurrection. Paul wrote this part of his letter to solve this confusion about the resurrection.*

The resurrection of Christ is the center of the Christian faith. Because Christ rose from the dead, we know that what he said is true—he is God. Because he rose, his death for our sins was validated and we can be forgiven. Because he rose, he lives and makes intercession for us. Because he rose and defeated death, we know we will also rise.

Proverbs for Today/ 12:21–23

No real harm befalls the good, but there is constant trouble for the wicked. □ God delights in those who keep their promises, and abhors those who don't. □ A wise man doesn't display his knowledge, but a fool displays his foolishness.

APRIL 8

Inner Purity/ Mark 7:1–23

One day some Jewish religious leaders arrived from Jerusalem to investigate Jesus, 2and noticed that some of his disciples failed to follow the usual Jewish rituals before eating. 3(For the Jews, especially the Pharisees, will never eat until they have sprinkled their arms to the elbows, as required by their ancient traditions. 4So when they come home from the market they must always sprinkle themselves in this way before touching any food. This is but one of many examples of laws and regulations they have clung to for centuries, and still follow, such as their ceremony of cleansing for pots, pans and dishes.)

5So the religious leaders asked him, "Why don't your disciples follow our age-old customs? For they eat without first performing the washing ceremony."

6,7Jesus replied, "You bunch of hypocrites! Isaiah the prophet described you very well when he said, 'These people speak very prettily about the Lord but they have no love for him at all. Their worship is a farce, for they claim that God commands the people to obey their petty rules.' How right Isaiah was! 8For you ignore God's specific orders and substitute your own traditions. 9You are simply rejecting God's laws and trampling them under your feet for the sake of tradition.

10For instance, Moses gave you this law from God:

'Honor your father and mother.' And he said that anyone who speaks against his father or mother must die. 11But you say it is perfectly all right for a man to disregard his needy parents, telling them, 'Sorry, I can't help you! For I have given to God what I could have given to you.' 12,13And so you break the law of God in order to protect your man-made tradition. And this is only one example. There are many, many others."

14Then Jesus called to the crowd to come and hear. "All of you listen," he said, "and try to understand. 15,16Your souls aren't harmed by what you eat, but by what you think and say!"

17Then he went into a house to get away from the crowds, and his disciples asked him what he meant by the statement he had just made.

18"Don't you understand either?" he asked. "Can't you see that what you eat won't harm your soul? 19For food doesn't come in contact with your heart, but only passes through the digestive system." (By saying this he showed that every kind of food is kosher.)

20And then he added, "It is the thought-life that pollutes. 21For from within, out of men's hearts, come evil thoughts of lust, theft, murder, adultery, 22wanting what belongs to others, wickedness, deceit, lewdness, envy, slander, pride, and all other folly. 23All these vile things come from within; they are what pollute you and make you unfit for God."

A THOUGHT: *Hypocrisy is pretending to be something you are not. Jesus called the Pharisees hypocrites because they did not worship God out of love for him, but because it made them look holy, and it increased their status in the community. We become hypocrites when we (1) pay more attention to reputation than to character, (2) carefully follow certain religious practices while allowing our hearts to remain distant from God, and (3) emphasize our virtues (overlooking our own sins), but constantly point out sins in others.*

Death Will Be Defeated in the End/
1 Corinthians 15:21–28

Death came into the world because of what one man (Adam) did, and it is because of what this other man (Christ) has done that now there is the resurrection from the dead. 22Everyone dies because all of us are related to Adam, being members of his sinful race, and wherever there is sin, death results. But all who are related to Christ will rise again. 23Each, however, in his own turn: Christ rose first; then when Christ comes back, all his people will become alive again.

24After that the end will come when he will turn the Kingdom over to God the Father, having put down all enemies of every kind. 25For Christ will be King until he has defeated all his enemies, 26including the last enemy—death. This too must be defeated and ended. 27For the rule and authority over all things has been given to Christ by his Father; except, of course, Christ does not rule over the Father himself, who gave him this power to rule. 28When Christ has finally won the battle against all his enemies, then he, the Son of God, will put himself also under his Father's orders, so that God who has given him the victory over everything else will be utterly supreme.

A THOUGHT: *The redemption which Christ accomplished on the cross has reversed the consequences of the Fall. Adam brought death, Christ brings eternal life through the resurrection of the body. Adam brought sin; Christ brings forgiveness and righteousness. The final enemy to be defeated in this great reversal is death. The fullness of salvation will be experienced when death is ultimately defeated, to appear no more. In bringing about this great defeat, Christ will demonstrate that his authority is supreme in heaven and earth. Let us worship Christ for who he is—the Great Redeemer and King.*

Proverbs for Today/ 12:24
Work hard and become a leader; be lazy and never succeed.

APRIL 9

Jesus Demonstrates His Redemptive Power/
Mark 7:24–37
Then Jesus left Galilee and went to the region of Tyre and Sidon, and tried to keep it a secret that he was there, but couldn't. For as usual the news of his arrival spread fast.

25Right away a woman came to him whose little girl

was possessed by a demon. She had heard about Jesus and now she came and fell at his feet, 26and pled with him to release her child from the demon's control. (But she was Syrophoenician—a "despised Gentile!")

27Jesus told her, "First I should help my own family— the Jews. It isn't right to take the children's food and throw it to the dogs."

28She replied, "That's true, sir, but even the puppies under the table are given some scraps from the children's plates."

29"Good!" he said, "You have answered well—so well that I have healed your little girl. Go on home, for the demon has left her!"

30And when she arrived home, her little girl was lying quietly in bed, and the demon was gone.

31From Tyre he went to Sidon, then back to the Sea of Galilee by way of the Ten Towns. 32A deaf man with a speech impediment was brought to him, and everyone begged Jesus to lay his hands on the man and heal him.

33Jesus led him away from the crowd and put his fingers into the man's ears, then spat and touched the man's tongue with the spittle. 34Then, looking up to heaven, he sighed and commanded, "Open!" 35Instantly the man could hear perfectly and speak plainly!

36Jesus told the crowd not to spread the news, but the more he forbade them, the more they made it known, 37for they were overcome with utter amazement. Again and again they said, "Everything he does is wonderful; he even corrects deafness and stammering!"

A THOUGHT: *In this passage, Jesus demonstrates his compassion. In the setting of the Jewish culture of that day, this Syrophoenician woman had two strikes against her: (1) she was a woman (women were considered to be property to be bought and sold like cattle); and (2) she was a Gentile (Gentiles were generally considered to be beyond the grace of God). Here Jesus shows compassion to this woman, granting her request, and even commends her faith.*

True Meaning in Daily Life/ 1 Corinthians 15:29–34

If the dead will not come back to life again, then what point is there in people being baptized for those who are gone? Why do it unless you believe that the dead will some day rise again?

30And why should we ourselves be continually risking

our lives, facing death hour by hour? 31For it is a fact that I face death daily; that is as true as my pride in your growth in the Lord. 32And what value was there in fighting wild beasts—those men of Ephesus—if it was only for what I gain in this life down here? If we will never live again after we die, then we might as well go and have ourselves a good time: let us eat, drink, and be merry. What's the difference? For tomorrow we die, and that ends everything!

33Don't be fooled by those who say such things. If you listen to them you will start acting like them. 34Get some sense and quit your sinning. For to your shame I say it, some of you are not even Christians at all and have never really known God.

A THOUGHT: *If death ended it all, enjoying the moment would be all that mattered. But Christians know that there is life beyond the grave and that our life on earth is only a preparation for our life that will never end. What you do today matters for eternity. In light of eternity, sin is a foolish gamble.*

Proverbs for Today/ 12:25

Anxious hearts are very heavy but a word of encouragement does wonders!

APRIL 10

The Feeding of the Four Thousand/ Mark 8:1–9

One day about this time as another great crowd gathered, the people ran out of food again. Jesus called his disciples to discuss the situation.

"I pity these people," he said, "for they have been here three days, and have nothing left to eat. 3And if I send them home without feeding them, they will faint along the road! For some of them have come a long distance."

4"Are we supposed to find food for them here in the desert?" his disciples scoffed.

5"How many loaves of bread do you have?" he asked.

"Seven," they replied. 6So he told the crowd to sit down on the ground. Then he took the seven loaves, thanked God for them, broke them into pieces and passed them to his disciples; and the disciples placed them before the people. 7A few small fish were found, too, so Jesus also blessed these and told the disciples to serve them.

8,9And the whole crowd ate until they were full, and afterwards he sent them home. There were about 4,000 people in the crowd that day and when the scraps were picked up after the meal, there were seven very large basketfuls left over!

A THOUGHT: *Do you ever feel God is so busy with important concerns that he can't possibly be aware of your needs? Just as Jesus was concerned about these who needed food, he is concerned about our daily needs. At another time Jesus said, "Don't worry at all about having enough food and clothing. Your heavenly Father already knows perfectly well that you need them" (Matthew 6:31–32). Do you have concerns that you think would not interest God? There is no concern too large for him to handle and no need too small to escape his interest.*

Earthly Analogies for the Resurrection Body/ 1 Corinthians 15:35–44

But someone may ask, "How will the dead be brought back to life again? What kind of bodies will they have?" 36What a foolish question! You will find the answer in your own garden! When you put a seed into the ground it doesn't grow into a plant unless it "dies" first. 37And when the green shoot comes up out of the seed, it is very different from the seed you first planted. For all you put into the ground is a dry little seed of wheat, or whatever it is you are planting, 38then God gives it a beautiful new body—just the kind he wants it to have; a different kind of plant grows from each kind of seed. 39And just as there are different kinds of seeds and plants, so also there are different kinds of flesh. Humans, animals, fish, and birds are all different.

40The angels in heaven have bodies far different from ours, and the beauty and the glory of their bodies is different from the beauty and the glory of ours. 41The sun has one kind of glory while the moon and stars have another kind. And the stars differ from each other in their beauty and brightness.

42In the same way, our earthly bodies which die and decay are different from the bodies we shall have when we come back to life again, for they will never die. 43The bodies we have now embarrass us for they become sick and die; but they will be full of glory when we come back to life again. Yes, they are weak, dying bodies now, but when we live again they will be full of strength. 44They are just human bodies at death, but when they come back to life they will be superhuman bodies. For just as there are natural, human bodies, there are also supernatural, spiritual bodies.

A THOUGHT: *Paul launches into a discussion here about what our resurrected bodies will be like. If you could select your own body, what kind would you choose—strong, athletic, beautiful? Paul explains that we will be recognized in our resurrected bodies, yet they will be better than we can imagine, for they will be made to live forever. We will still have our own personalities and individualities, but these will be perfected through Christ's work. Scripture does not say what our resurrected bodies will be able to do, but we know they will be perfect, without sickness or disease.*

Proverbs for Today/ 12:26

The good man asks advice from friends; the wicked plunge ahead—and fall.

APRIL 11

Beware of the Teaching of Herod and the Pharisees/ Mark 8:10–21

Immediately after this Jesus got into a boat with his disciples and came to the region of Dalmanutha.

11When the local Jewish leaders learned of his arrival they came to argue with him.

"Do a miracle for us," they said. "Make something happen in the sky. Then we will believe in you."

12He sighed deeply when he heard this and he said, "Certainly not. How many more miracles do you people need?"

13So he got back into the boat and left them, and crossed

to the other side of the lake. 14But the disciples had forgotten to stock up on food before they left, and had only one loaf of bread in the boat.

15As they were crossing, Jesus said to them very solemnly, "Beware of the yeast of King Herod and of the Pharisees."

16"What does he mean?" the disciples asked each other. They finally decided that he must be talking about their forgetting to bring bread.

17Jesus realized what they were discussing and said, "No, that isn't it at all! Can't you understand? Are your hearts too hard to take it in? 18'Your eyes are to see with—why don't you look? Why don't you open your ears and listen?' Don't you remember anything at all?

19"What about the 5,000 men I fed with five loaves of bread? How many basketfuls of scraps did you pick up afterwards?"

"Twelve," they said.

20"And when I fed the 4,000 with seven loaves, how much was left?"

"Seven basketfuls," they said.

21"And yet you think I'm worried that we have no bread?"

A THOUGHT: *How could the disciples experience so many of Jesus' miracles and yet be so slow to comprehend his true identity? They had already seen Jesus feed over 5,000 people with five loaves and two fish, yet now they doubted whether he could feed another large group.*

Sometimes we are also slow to catch on. Although Christ has brought us through trials and temptations in the past, we are slow to believe he will do it in the future. Is your heart too closed to take in all that God can do for you? Don't be like the disciples. Remember what Christ has done, and have faith that he will do it again.

Adam Versus Christ/ 1 Corinthians 15:45–49

The Scriptures tell us that the first man, Adam, was given a natural, human body but Christ is more than that, for he was life-giving Spirit.

46First, then, we have these human bodies and later on God gives us spiritual, heavenly bodies. 47Adam was made from the dust of the earth, but Christ came from heaven above. 48Every human being has a body just like Adam's, made of dust, but all who become Christ's will have the same kind of body as his—a body from heaven. 49Just as each of us now has a body like Adam's, so we shall some day have a body like Christ's.

A THOUGHT: *When Christ rose from the dead, he became "life-giving Spirit." This means he entered into a new form of existence. Christ's new glorified human body now suits his new glorified life—just as Adam's human body was suitable to his natural life. When we will be resurrected, God will give us a glorified body suited to our new eternal life.*

Proverbs for Today/ 12:27–28

A lazy man won't even dress the game he gets while hunting, but the diligent man makes good use of everything he finds. □ The path of the godly leads to life. So why fear death?

APRIL 12

A Blind Man Has His Sight Restored/ Mark 8:22–26

When Jesus and his disciples arrived at Bethsaida, some people brought a blind man to him and begged him to touch and heal him. 23Jesus took the blind man by the hand and led him out of the village, and spat upon his eyes, and laid his hands over them.

"Can you see anything now?" Jesus asked him.

24The man looked around. "Yes!" he said, "I see men! But I can't see them very clearly; they look like tree trunks walking around!"

25Then Jesus placed his hands over the man's eyes again and as the man stared intently, his sight was completely restored, and he saw everything clearly, drinking in the sights around him.

26Jesus sent him home to his family. "Don't even go back to the village first," he said.

A THOUGHT: *Why did Jesus touch the man a second time before he could see? This miracle was not too difficult for Jesus, but he chose to do it in stages, possibly to show the disciples that some healing would be gradual rather than instantaneous or to demonstrate that spiritual truth is not always perceived clearly at first. Before Jesus left, however, the man was healed completely.*

Transformation in the Twinkling of an Eye/
1 Corinthians 15:50–58

I tell you this, my brothers: an earthly body made of flesh and blood cannot get into God's Kingdom. These perishable bodies of ours are not the right kind to live forever.

51But I am telling you this strange and wonderful secret: we shall not all die, but we shall all be given new bodies! 52It will all happen in a moment, in the twinkling of an eye, when the last trumpet is blown. For there will be a trumpet blast from the sky and all the Christians who have died will suddenly become alive, with new bodies that will never, never die; and then we who are still alive shall suddenly have new bodies too. 53For our earthly bodies, the ones we have now that can die, must be transformed into heavenly bodies that cannot perish but will live forever.

54When this happens, then at last this Scripture will come true—"Death is swallowed up in victory." 55,56O death, where then your victory? Where then your sting? For sin—the sting that causes death—will all be gone; and the law, which reveals our sins, will no longer be our judge. 57How we thank God for all of this! It is he who makes us victorious through Jesus Christ our Lord!

58So, my dear brothers, since future victory is sure, be strong and steady, always abounding in the Lord's work, for you know that nothing you do for the Lord is ever wasted as it would be if there were no resurrection.

A THOUGHT: *Paul said that because of the resurrection, nothing we do is wasted. Sometimes we hesitate to do good because we don't see any results. But if we can maintain a heavenly perspective, we understand that we don't often see the good that results from our efforts. If we truly believe that Christ has won the ultimate victory, it must affect the way we live right now. Don't let discouragement over an apparent lack of results keep you from working. Do the good that you have opportunity to do, knowing your work will have eternal results.*

Proverbs for Today/ 13:1
A wise youth accepts his father's rebuke; a young mocker doesn't.

Peter's Confession/ Mark 8:27–38

Jesus and his disciples now left Galilee and went out to the villages of Caesarea Philippi. As they were walking along he asked them, "Who do the people think I am? What are they saying about me?"

28"Some of them think you are John the Baptist," the disciples replied, "and others say you are Elijah or some other ancient prophet come back to life again."

29Then he asked, "Who do you think I am?" Peter replied, "You are the Messiah." 30But Jesus warned them not to tell anyone!

31Then he began to tell them about the terrible things he would suffer, and that he would be rejected by the elders and the Chief Priests and the other Jewish leaders—and be killed, and that he would rise again three days afterwards. 32He talked about it quite frankly with them, so Peter took him aside and chided him. "You shouldn't say things like that," he told Jesus.

33Jesus turned and looked at his disciples and then said to Peter very sternly, "Satan, get behind me! You are looking at this only from a human point of view and not from God's."

34Then he called his disciples and the crowds to come over and listen. "If any of you wants to be my follower," he told them, "you must put aside your own pleasures and shoulder your cross, and follow me closely. 35If you insist on saving your life, you will lose it. Only those who throw away their lives for my sake and for the sake of the Good News will ever know what it means to really live.

36"And how does a man benefit if he gains the whole world and loses his soul in the process? 37For is anything worth more than his soul? 38And anyone who is ashamed of me and my message in these days of unbelief and sin, I, the Messiah, will be ashamed of him when I return in the glory of my Father, with the holy angels."

A THOUGHT: *Jesus asked the disciples who others thought he was; then he focused on them: "Who do you think I am?" At this point Peter made his famous confession. However, it is clear from the rest of the story that Peter's conception of Messiah and Jesus' concep-*

tion were very different. Jesus went on to explain that he was going to die soon and that three days later he would be resurrected from the dead. Jesus calls all of his disciples to follow in his footsteps— to take up crosses and follow him. Commitment to Jesus involves sacrificing self–interests to love and serve others in obedience to him. The Christian life is not a paved road to wealth and ease. It often involves hard work, persecution, privation, and suffering.

The Jerusalem Church Collection/ 1 Corinthians 16:1–9

Now here are the directions about the money you are collecting to send to the Christians in Jerusalem; (and, by the way, these are the same directions I gave to the churches in Galatia). 2On every Lord's Day each of you should put aside something from what you have earned during the week, and use it for this offering. The amount depends on how much the Lord has helped you earn. Don't wait until I get there and then try to collect it all at once. 3When I come I will send your loving gift with a letter to Jerusalem, to be taken there by trustworthy messengers you yourselves will choose. 4And if it seems wise for me to go along too, then we can travel together.

5I am coming to visit you after I have been to Macedonia first, but I will be staying there only for a little while. 6It could be that I will stay longer with you, perhaps all winter, and then you can send me on to my next destination. 7This time I don't want to make just a passing visit and then go right on; I want to come and stay awhile, if the Lord will let me. 8I will be staying here at Ephesus until the holiday of Pentecost, 9for there is a wide open door for me to preach and teach here. So much is happening, but there are many enemies.

A THOUGHT: *The Christians in Jerusalem were suffering from poverty and famine, so Paul was collecting money for them. Paul suggested that believers set aside a certain amount of money each week until he arrived to take it on to Jerusalem. Paul had planned to go straight to Corinth from Ephesus, but he changed his mind. When he finally arrived in Jerusalem, he took the gift and delivered it to the Jerusalem church. Paul's concern for the poor should also motivate us to greater involvement in serving the poor.*

Proverbs for Today/ 13:2–3

The good man wins his case by careful argument; the evil-minded only wants to fight.   □ Self-control means controlling the tongue! A quick retort can ruin everything.

APRIL 14

The Transfiguration of Jesus/ Mark 9:1–13

Jesus went on to say to his disciples, "Some of you who are standing here right now will live to see the Kingdom of God arrive in great power!"

2Six days later Jesus took Peter, James and John to the top of a mountain. No one else was there.

Suddenly his face began to shine with glory, 3and his clothing became dazzling white, far more glorious than any earthly process could ever make it! 4Then Elijah and Moses appeared and began talking with Jesus!

5"Teacher, this is wonderful!" Peter exclaimed. "We will make three shelters here, one for each of you. . . . "

6He said this just to be talking, for he didn't know what else to say and they were all terribly frightened.

7But while he was still speaking these words, a cloud covered them, blotting out the sun, and a voice from the cloud said, *"This* is my beloved Son. Listen to *him."*

8Then suddenly they looked around and Moses and Elijah were gone, and only Jesus was with them.

9As they descended the mountainside he told them never to mention what they had seen until after he had risen from the dead. 10So they kept it to themselves, but often talked about it, and wondered what he meant by "rising from the dead."

11Now they began asking him about something the Jewish religious leaders often spoke of, that Elijah must return [before the Messiah could come]. 12,13Jesus agreed that Elijah must come first and prepare the way—and that he had, in fact, already come! And that he had been terribly mistreated, just as the prophets had predicted. Then Jesus asked them what the prophets could have been talking about when they predicted that the Messiah would suffer and be treated with utter contempt.

A THOUGHT: *The transfiguration revealed Christ's true nature as God's Son. God singled Jesus out from Moses and Elijah as the long-awaited Messiah with full divine authority. Moses represented the Law, and Elijah, the Prophets. Jesus was shown as the fulfillment of both the Old Testament Law and the prophetic promises.*

Jesus was not a reincarnation of Elijah or Moses. He was not merely one of the prophets. As God's only Son, he far surpasses their authority and power. Many voices try to tell us how to live and how to know God personally. Some of these are helpful; many are not. We must first listen to Jesus, and then evaluate all other authorities in light of his revelation.

Paul's Final Instructions/ 1 Corinthians 16:10–18

If Timothy comes make him feel at home, for he is doing the Lord's work just as I am. 11Don't let anyone despise or ignore him [because he is young], but send him back to me happy with his time among you; I am looking forward to seeing him soon, along with the others who are returning.

12I begged Apollos to visit you along with the others, but he thought that it was not at all God's will for him to go now; he will be seeing you later on when he has the opportunity.

13Keep your eyes open for spiritual danger; stand true to the Lord; act like men; be strong; 14and whatever you do, do it with kindness and love.

15Do you remember Stephanas and his family? They were the first to become Christians in Greece and they are spending their lives helping and serving Christians everywhere. 16 Please follow their instructions and do everything you can to help them as well as all others like them who work hard at your side with such real devotion. 17I am so glad that Stephanas, Fortunatus, and Achaicus have arrived here for a visit. They have been making up for the help you aren't here to give me. 18They have cheered me greatly and have been a wonderful encouragement to me, as I am sure they were to you, too. I hope you properly appreciate the work of such men as these.

A THOUGHT: *As the Corinthians awaited Paul's next visit, they were directed to (1) be alert to spiritual dangers, (2) stand true to the Lord, (3) behave maturely, (4) be strong, and (5) do all things with kindness and love. Today, as we await the return of Christ, we should follow the same instructions.*

Proverbs for Today/ 13:4

Lazy people want much but get little, while the diligent are prospering.

Jesus Casts Out a Demon/ Mark 9:14–29

At the bottom of the mountain Peter, James, and John found a great crowd surrounding the other nine disciples, as some Jewish leaders argued with them. 15The crowd watched Jesus in awe as he came toward them, and then ran to greet him. 16"What's all the argument about?" he asked.

17One of the men in the crowd spoke up and said, "Teacher, I brought my son for you to heal—he can't talk because he is possessed by a demon. 18And whenever the demon is in control of him it dashes him to the ground and makes him foam at the mouth and grind his teeth and become rigid. So I begged your disciples to cast out the demon, but they couldn't do it."

19Jesus said [to his disciples], "Oh, what tiny faith you have; how much longer must I be with you until you believe? How much longer must I be patient with you? Bring the boy to me."

20So they brought the boy, but when he saw Jesus the demon convulsed the child horribly, and he fell to the ground writhing and foaming at the mouth.

21"How long has he been this way?" Jesus asked the father.

And he replied, "Since he was very small, 22and the demon often makes him fall into the fire or into water to kill him. Oh, have mercy on us and do something if you can."

23"If I can?" Jesus asked. "*Anything* is possible if you have faith."

24The father instantly replied, "I *do* have faith; oh, help me to have *more!*"

25When Jesus saw the crowd was growing he rebuked the demon.

"O demon of deafness and dumbness," he said, "I command you to come out of this child and enter him no more!"

26Then the demon screamed terribly and convulsed the boy again and left him; and the boy lay there limp and motionless, to all appearance dead. A murmur ran through the crowd—"He is dead." 27But Jesus took him by the hand and helped him to his feet and he stood up and was all right! 28Afterwards, when Jesus was alone in the house with his disciples, they asked him, "Why couldn't we cast that demon out?"

29Jesus replied, "Cases like this require prayer."

A THOUGHT: *Faith is not something tangible to be taken like medicine. It is an attitude of trusting and believing. But even our ability to believe is a gift from God. No matter how much faith we have, we never reach the point of being self-sufficient. Faith is not stored away like money in the bank. Growing in faith is a constant process of daily renewing our trust in Jesus. Jesus was telling the disciples that they would face difficult situations that could be resolved only through prayer. Prayer is the key that unlocks faith in our lives. Effective prayer needs both an attitude—complete dependence—and an action—asking. Prayer demonstrates our reliance on God as we humbly invite God to fill us with faith and power. There is no substitute for prayer, especially in circumstances that seem unconquerable.*

Greetings from Other Believers/ 1 Corinthians 16:19–24

The churches here in Asia send you their loving greetings. Aquila and Priscilla send you their love and so do all the others who meet in their home for their church service. 20All the friends here have asked me to say "hello" to you for them. And give each other a loving handshake when you meet.

21I will write these final words of this letter with my own hand: 22if anyone does not love the Lord, that person is cursed. Lord Jesus, come! 23May the love and favor of the Lord Jesus Christ rest upon you. 24My love to all of you, for we all belong to Christ Jesus.

Sincerely,
Paul

A THOUGHT: *The Lord Jesus Christ is coming back to earth again. To Paul, this was a glad hope, the best he could look forward to. He was not afraid of seeing Christ—he could hardly wait! Do you share Paul's eager anticipation? Those who love Christ are looking forward to that wonderful time of his return.*

Proverbs for Today/ 13:5–6

A good man hates lies; wicked men lie constantly and come to shame. □ A man's goodness helps him all through life, while evil men are being destroyed by their wickedness.

APRIL 16

The Greatest Must Be the Servant of All/
Mark 9:30–37

Leaving that region Jesus and his disciples traveled through Galilee where Jesus tried to avoid all publicity in order to spend more time with his disciples, teaching them. He would say to them, "I, the Messiah, am going to be betrayed and killed and three days later I will return to life again."

32But they didn't understand and were afraid to ask him what he meant.

33And so they arrived at Capernaum. When they were settled in the house where they were to stay he asked them, "What were you discussing out on the road?"

34But they were ashamed to answer, for they had been arguing about which of them was the greatest!

35He sat down and called them around him and said, "Anyone wanting to be the greatest must be the least—the servant of all!"

36Then he placed a little child among them; and taking the child in his arms he said to them, 37"Anyone who welcomes a little child like this in my name is welcoming me, and anyone who welcomes me is welcoming my Father who sent me!"

A THOUGHT: *The disciples had been caught up in a constant struggle for personal success, and they were embarrassed to answer Jesus' question. It is always painful to compare our motives with Christ's. It is not wrong for believers to be industrious or ambitious, but inappropriate ambition is sin. Pride or insecurity can cause us to value position and prestige more than service. In God's kingdom, such motives are destructive. Our ambition should be for Christ's kingdom, not for our own advancement. What do you use as your measure of greatness—personal achievement or unselfish service?*

We Pass on God's Comfort to Others/
2 Corinthians 1:1–7

Dear friends, This letter is from me, Paul, appointed by God to be Jesus Christ's messenger; and from our dear brother Timothy. We are writing to all of you Christians there in Corinth and throughout Greece. 2May God our

Father and the Lord Jesus Christ mightily bless each one of you, and give you peace.

3,4What a wonderful God we have—he is the Father of our Lord Jesus Christ, the source of every mercy, and the one who so wonderfully comforts and strengthens us in our hardships and trials. And why does he do this? So that when others are troubled, needing our sympathy and encouragement, we can pass on to them this same help and comfort God has given us. 5You can be sure that the more we undergo sufferings for Christ, the more he will shower us with his comfort and encouragement. 6,7We are in deep trouble for bringing you God's comfort and salvation. But in our trouble God has comforted us— and this, too, to help you: to show you from our personal experience how God will tenderly comfort you when you undergo these same sufferings. He will give you the strength to endure.

A THOUGHT: *Many think that when God comforts us, our hardships should go away. But if that were always so, people would turn to God only to be relieved of pain and not out of love for him. We must understand that comfort can also mean receiving strength, encouragement, and hope to deal with our hardships. The more we suffer, the more comfort God gives us. If you are feeling overwhelmed, allow God to comfort you. Remember that every trial you endure will later become an opportunity to minister to other people suffering similar hardships.*

Proverbs for Today/ 13:7–8

Some rich people are poor, and some poor people have great wealth! □ Being kidnapped and held for ransom never worries the poor man!

APRIL 17

Entering God's Kingdom Requires Radical Change/ Mark 9:38–50

One of Jesus' disciples, John, told him one day, "Teacher, we saw a man using your name to cast out demons; but we told him not to, for he isn't one of our group."

³⁹"Don't forbid him!" Jesus said. "For no one doing miracles in my name will quickly turn against me. ⁴⁰Anyone who isn't against us is for us. ⁴¹If anyone so much as gives you a cup of water because you are Christ's—I say this solemnly—he won't lose his reward. ⁴²But if someone causes one of these little ones who believe in me to lose faith—it would be better for that man if a huge millstone were tied around his neck and he were thrown into the sea.

^{43,44}"If your hand does wrong, cut it off. Better live forever with one hand than be thrown into the unquenchable fires of hell with two! ^{45,46}If your foot carries you toward evil, cut it off! Better be lame and live forever than have two feet that carry you to hell.

⁴⁷"And if your eye is sinful, gouge it out. Better enter the Kingdom of God half blind than have two eyes and see the fires of hell, ⁴⁸where the worm never dies, and the fire never goes out— ⁴⁹where all are salted with fire.

⁵⁰"Good salt is worthless if it loses its saltiness; it can't season anything. So don't lose your flavor! Live in peace with each other."

A THOUGHT: *Jesus used startling language to stress the importance of cutting sin out of our lives. Painful discipline is required of his true followers. Giving up a relationship, job, or habit that is against God's will may seem just as painful as cutting off a hand. Our high goal, however, is worth any sacrifice; Christ is worth any possible loss. Nothing should stand in the way of faith. We must be ruthless in removing sins from our lives now in order to avoid being stuck with them for eternity. Make your choices from an eternal perspective.*

Paul's Ministry in Life and in Letters/ 2 Corinthians 1:8–14

I think you ought to know, dear brothers, about the hard time we went through in Asia. We were really crushed and overwhelmed, and feared we would never live through it. ⁹We felt we were doomed to die and saw how powerless we were to help ourselves; but that was good, for then we put everything into the hands of God, who alone could save us, for he can even raise the dead. ¹⁰And he did help us, and saved us from a terrible death; yes, and we expect him to do it again and again. ¹¹But you must help us too, by praying for us. For much thanks and praise will go to God from you who see his wonderful answers to your prayers for our safety!

12We are so glad that we can say with utter honesty that in all our dealings we have been pure and sincere, quietly depending upon the Lord for his help, and not on our own skills. And that is even more true, if possible, about the way we have acted toward you. 13,14My letters have been straightforward and sincere; nothing is written between the lines! And even though you don't know me very well (I hope someday you will), I want you to try to accept me and be proud of me, as you already are to some extent; just as I shall be of you on that day when our Lord Jesus comes back again.

A THOUGHT: *We often depend on our own skills and abilities when life seems easy, but when we feel powerless to help ourselves, we turn to God. We must recognize that even when life seems easy we are dependent upon God, for he upholds the universe with his power. Dependence is not defeat, but the realization that our source of truth and power is God. With this attitude, problems drive us to God rather than away from him. Learn how to depend on God daily.*

Proverbs for Today/ 13:9–10

The good man's life is full of light. The sinner's road is dark and gloomy. □ Pride leads to arguments; be humble, take advice and become wise.

APRIL 18

Jesus' Teachings on Divorce/ Mark 10:1–12

Then Jesus left Capernaum and went southward to the Judean borders and into the area east of the Jordan River. And as always there were the crowds; and as usual he taught them.

2Some Pharisees came and asked him, "Do you permit divorce?" Of course they were trying to trap him.

3"What did Moses say about divorce?" Jesus asked them.

4"He said it was all right," they replied. "He said that

all a man has to do is write his wife a letter of dismissal."

5"And why did he say that?" Jesus asked. "I'll tell you why—it was a concession to your hardhearted wickedness. 6,7But it certainly isn't God's way. For from the very first he made man and woman to be joined together permanently in marriage; therefore a man is to leave his father and mother, 8and he and his wife are united so that they are no longer two, but one. 9And no man may separate what God has joined together."

10Later, when he was alone with his disciples in the house, they brought up the subject again.

11He told them, "When a man divorces his wife to marry someone else, he commits adultery against her. 12And if a wife divorces her husband and remarries, she, too, commits adultery."

A THOUGHT: *God allowed divorce as a concession to people's sinfulness. Divorce was not approved, but it was instituted to protect the injured party in the midst of a bad situation. Unfortunately, many Pharisees had set up legal traditions to allow for divorce for almost any reason (the cause for divorce being left up to the discretion of the husband). Jesus explained that this was not God's intent; instead, God wants married people to consider their marriage permanent. Don't enter marriage with the option of getting out, but be committed to the permanence of the relationship. You'll stand a much better chance of making your marriage work. Don't be hard-hearted like these Pharisees, but be hardheaded in your determination, with God's help, to stay together.*

Paul's Plan to Visit the Corinthians/ 2 Corinthians 1:15-24

It was because I was so sure of your understanding and trust that I planned to stop and see you on my way to Macedonia, as well as afterwards when I returned, so that I could be a double blessing to you and so that you could send me on my way to Judea.

17Then why, you may be asking, did I change my plan? Hadn't I really made up my mind yet? Or am I like a man of the world who says "yes" when he really means "no"? 18Never! As surely as God is true, I am not that sort of person. My "yes" means "yes."

19Timothy and Silvanus and I have been telling you about Jesus Christ the Son of God. He isn't one to say "yes" when he means "no." He always does exactly what he says. 20He carries out and fulfills all of God's promises, no matter how many of them there are; and we have told everyone how faithful he is, giving glory to his name. 21It is this God who has made you and me into faithful Christians and commissioned us apostles to preach the Good News. 22He has put his brand upon us—his mark of ownership—and given us his Holy Spirit in our hearts as guarantee that we belong to him, and as the first installment of all that he is going to give us.

23I call upon this God to witness against me if I am not telling the absolute truth: the reason I haven't come to visit you yet is that I don't want to sadden you with a severe rebuke. 24When I come, although I can't do much to help your faith, for it is strong already, I want to be able to do something about your joy: I want to make you happy, not sad.

A THOUGHT: *Paul mentions two gifts God gives when we become believers: a "mark of ownership" to show who our master is, and the Holy Spirit as a guarantee that we belong to him. With the privilege of belonging to God comes the responsibility of identifying ourselves as faithful representatives and servants of our master. Don't be ashamed to let others know you are his.*

Proverbs for Today/ 13:11
Wealth from gambling quickly disappears; wealth from hard work grows.

APRIL 19

Enter the Kingdom of God like a Child/ Mark 10:13–16
Once when some mothers were bringing their children to Jesus to bless them, the disciples shooed them away, telling them not to bother him.

14But when Jesus saw what was happening he was very much displeased with his disciples and said to them, "Let the children come to me, for the Kingdom of God belongs to such as they. Don't send them away! 15I tell you as seriously as I know how that anyone who refuses to come to God as a little child will never be allowed into his Kingdom."

16Then he took the children into his arms and placed his hands on their heads and he blessed them.

A Thought: *Jesus was often criticized for spending too much time with the wrong people—children, sinners, tax collectors. Some, including the disciples, thought Jesus should be spending more time with important leaders and the devout, because this was the way to improve his position and avoid criticism. But Jesus reverses this whole conception of position and greatness by showing that the Kingdom of God belongs to those who have a childlike trust in God, not a confident trust in their own greatness. To become great in the Kingdom of God, the one of humble, childlike faith should become the servant of all.*

Paul's Sorrowful Letter/ 2 Corinthians 2:1–4

"No," I said to myself, "I won't do it. I'll not make them unhappy with another painful visit." 2For if I make you sad, who is going to make me happy? You are the ones to do it, and how can you if I cause you pain? 3That is why I wrote as I did in my last letter, so that you will get things straightened out before I come. Then, when I do come, I will not be made sad by the very ones who ought to give me greatest joy. I felt sure that your happiness was so bound up in mine that you would not be happy either, unless I came with joy.

4Oh, how I hated to write that letter! It almost broke my heart and I tell you honestly that I cried over it. I didn't want to hurt you, but I had to show you how very much I loved you and cared about what was happening to you.

A Thought: *Paul did not enjoy reprimanding his friends and fellow believers, but he cared enough for the Corinthians to confront them about their wrongdoing. Proverbs 27:6 says that "wounds from a friend are better than kisses from an enemy." Sometimes our friends make choices that we know are wrong. If we ignore their behavior and let them continue, we aren't showing love to them. Love means honestly sharing our concerns with those we love. When we don't move to help, we show that we are more concerned about what will happen to us than what will happen to them.*

Proverbs for Today/ 13:12–14

Hope deferred makes the heart sick; but when dreams come true at last, there is life and joy. □ Despise God's Word and find yourself in trouble. Obey it and succeed. □ The advice of a wise man refreshes like water from a mountain spring. Those accepting it become aware of the pitfalls on ahead.

APRIL 20

Jesus and the Rich Man/ Mark 10:17–31

As Jesus was starting out on a trip, a man came running to him and knelt down and asked, "Good Teacher, what must I do to get to heaven?"

18"Why do you call me good?" Jesus asked. "Only God is truly good! 19But as for your question—you know the commandments: don't kill, don't commit adultery, don't steal, don't lie, don't cheat, respect your father and mother."

20"Teacher," the man replied, "I've never once broken a single one of those laws."

21Jesus felt genuine love for this man as he looked at him. "You lack only one thing," he told him; "go and sell all you have and give the money to the poor—and you shall have treasure in heaven—and come, follow me."

22Then the man's face fell, and he went sadly away, for he was very rich.

23Jesus watched him go, then turned around and said to his disciples, "It's almost impossible for the rich to get into the Kingdom of God!"

24This amazed them. So Jesus said it again: "Dear children, how hard it is for those who trust in riches to enter the Kingdom of God. 25It is easier for a camel to go through the eye of a needle than for a rich man to enter the Kingdom of God."

26The disciples were incredulous! "Then who in the world can be saved, if not a rich man?" they asked.

27Jesus looked at them intently, then said, "Without God, it is utterly impossible. But with God everything is possible."

28Then Peter began to mention all that he and the other

disciples had left behind. "We've given up everything to follow you," he said.

29And Jesus replied, "Let me assure you that no one has ever given up anything—home, brothers, sisters, mother, father, children, or property—for love of me and to tell others the Good News, 30who won't be given back, a hundred times over, homes, brothers, sisters, mothers, children, and land—with persecutions!

"All these will be his here on earth, and in the world to come he shall have eternal life. 31But many people who seem to be important now will be the least important then; and many who are considered least here shall be greatest there."

A THOUGHT: *There was a barrier keeping this young man out of the Kingdom: his love of money. Money represented his pride of accomplishment and self-effort. Ironically, his attitude made him unable to keep the first commandment, to let nothing be more important than God. This man came to Jesus wondering what he could do; he left seeing what he was unable to do. Jesus said it was very difficult for the rich to get into the Kingdom of God because the rich have most of their basic physical needs met and thus often become self-reliant. When they feel empty, they can buy something new to dull the pain that was meant to drive them toward God. Their abundance becomes their deficiency. Jesus explained that in the world to come, the values of this world will be reversed. Those who seek status and importance here will have none in heaven. The person who has everything on earth can still lack what is most important—eternal life. What barriers are keeping you from turning your life over to Christ?*

Reinstate the Repentant Sinner/
2 Corinthians 2:5–11

Remember that the man I wrote about, who caused all the trouble, has not caused sorrow to me as much as to all the rest of you—though I certainly have my share in it too. I don't want to be harder on him than I should. He has been punished enough by your united disapproval. 7Now it is time to forgive him and comfort him. Otherwise he may become so bitter and discouraged that he won't be able to recover. 8Please show him now that you still do love him very much.

9I wrote to you as I did so that I could find out how far you would go in obeying me. 10When you forgive anyone, I do too. And whatever I have forgiven (to the extent that this affected me too) has been by Christ's authority, and for your good. 11A further reason for forgiveness is to keep from being outsmarted by Satan; for we know what he is trying to do.

A THOUGHT: *It was time to forgive the man who had been punished by the church and had subsequently repented. He now needed friendship and comfort. Church discipline should always allow for restoration. Two mistakes can be made in church discipline—being too lenient with sin and not correcting mistakes, or being too harsh and not forgiving. There is a time to confront and a time to comfort. We must remember that our purpose in discipline is to restore a person to the fellowship, not to destroy him or her. We must be cautious that personal anger is not vented under the guise of church discipline.*

Proverbs for Today/ 13:15–16

A man with good sense is appreciated. A treacherous man must walk a rocky road. □ A wise man thinks ahead; a fool doesn't, and even brags about it!

APRIL 21

The Greatest Must Be the Servant of All/ Mark 10:32–45

Now Jesus and his disciples were on the way to Jerusalem, and Jesus was walking along ahead; and as the disciples were following they were filled with terror and dread.

Taking them aside, Jesus once more began describing all that was going to happen to him when they arrived at Jerusalem.

33"When we get there," he told them, "I, the Messiah, will be arrested and taken before the chief priests and the Jewish leaders, who will sentence me to die and hand me over to the Romans to be killed. 34They will mock me and spit on me and flog me with their whips and kill me; but after three days I will come back to life again."

35Then James and John, the sons of Zebedee, came over and spoke to him in a low voice. "Master," they said, "we want you to do us a favor."

36"What is it?" he asked.

37"We want to sit on the thrones next to yours in your kingdom," they said, "one at your right and the other at your left!"

38But Jesus answered, "You don't know what you are asking! Are you able to drink from the bitter cup of sorrow I must drink from? Or to be baptized with the baptism of suffering I must be baptized with?"

39"Oh, yes," they said, "we are!"

And Jesus said, "You shall indeed drink from my cup and be baptized with my baptism, 40but I do not have the right to place you on thrones next to mine. Those appointments have already been made."

41When the other disciples discovered what James and John had asked, they were very indignant. 42So Jesus called them to him and said, "As you know, the kings and great men of the earth lord it over the people; 43but among you it is different. Whoever wants to be great among you must be your servant. 44And whoever wants to be greatest of all must be the slave of all. 45For even I, the Messiah, am not here to be served, but to help others, and to give my life as a ransom for many."

A THOUGHT: *James and John wanted the highest positions in Jesus' Kingdom. But Jesus told them that true greatness comes in serving others. Most businesses, organizations, and institutions in our world measure greatness by high personal achievement. In Christ's kingdom, however, service is the measure of greatness. The desire to be on top isn't a help but a hindrance to the Kingdom of God.*

The Fragrance of the Gospel/ 2 Corinthians 2:12–17

Well, when I got as far as the city of Troas, the Lord gave me tremendous opportunities to preach the Gospel. 13But Titus, my dear brother, wasn't there to meet me and I couldn't rest, wondering where he was and what had happened to him. So I said good-bye and went right on to Macedonia to try to find him.

14But thanks be to God! For through what Christ has done, he has triumphed over us so that now wherever we go he uses us to tell others about the Lord and to spread the Gospel like a sweet perfume. 15As far as God is concerned there is a sweet, wholesome fragrance in our lives. It is the fragrance of Christ within us, an aroma to both the saved and the unsaved all around us. 16To those who are not being saved, we seem a fearful smell of death and doom, while to those who know Christ we are a life-giving perfume. But who is adequate for such a task as this? 17Only those who, like ourselves, are men of integrity, sent by God, speaking with Christ's power, with God's eye upon us. We are not like those hucksters—and there are many of them—whose idea in getting out the Gospel is to make a good living out of it.

A THOUGHT: *Believers are to be like a sweet perfume whose fragrance others can't help but notice. Just as we cannot control a person's opinion about a perfume's fragrance, we cannot control a person's reaction to our Christian message and actions. But if we remain true to Christ, his Spirit working in us will attract others.*

Proverbs for Today/ 13:17–19

An unreliable messenger can cause a lot of trouble. Reliable communication permits progress. □ If you refuse criticism you will end in poverty and disgrace; if you accept criticism you are on the road to fame. □ It is pleasant to see plans develop. That is why fools refuse to give them up even when they are wrong.

APRIL 22

Jesus Heals Blind Bartimaeus/ Mark 10:46–52

And so Jesus and his disciples reached Jericho. Later, as they left town, a great crowd was following. Now it happened that a blind beggar named Bartimaeus (the son of Timaeus) was sitting beside the road as Jesus was going by.

47When Bartimaeus heard that Jesus from Nazareth was near, he began to shout out, "Jesus, Son of David, have mercy on me!"

48"Shut up!" some of the people yelled at him.

But he only shouted the louder, again and again, "O Son of David, have mercy on me!"

49When Jesus heard him he stopped there in the road and said, "Tell him to come here."

So they called the blind man. "You lucky fellow," they said, "come on, he's calling you!" 50Bartimaeus yanked off his old coat and flung it aside, jumped up and came to Jesus.

51"What do you want me to do for you?" Jesus asked.

"O Teacher," the blind man said, "I want to see!"

52And Jesus said to him, "All right, it's done. Your faith has healed you."

And instantly the blind man could see, and followed Jesus down the road!

A THOUGHT: *Beggars were a common sight in most towns in first-century Israel. Since most occupations of that day required physical labor, anyone with a crippling disease or handicap was at a severe disadvantage and was usually forced to beg, even though God's laws commanded care for such needy people. Blindness was considered a curse from God for sin; but Jesus refuted this idea when he reached out to heal those who were blind. It was to the ignored, oppressed, and despised of society that Jesus went to proclaim—in both word and deed—the Good News of the Kingdom. Our task is to reach out with God's love to the ignored, oppressed, and despised of our society.*

Law Brings Death, But the Spirit Gives Life/ 2 Corinthians 3:1–6

Are we beginning to be like those false teachers of yours who must tell you all about themselves and bring long letters of recommendation with them? I think you hardly need someone's letter to tell you about us, do you? And we don't need a recommendation from you, either! 2The only letter I need is you yourselves! By looking at the good change in your hearts, everyone can see that we have done a good work among you. 3They can see that you are a letter from Christ, written by us. It is not a letter written with pen and ink, but by the Spirit of the living God; not one carved on stone, but in human hearts.

4We dare to say these good things about ourselves only because of our great trust in God through Christ, that he will help us to be true to what we say, 5and not because we think we can do anything of lasting value by ourselves. Our only power and success comes from God. 6He is the one who has helped us tell others about his new agreement to save them. We do not tell them that they must obey every law of God or die; but we tell them there is life for them from the Holy Spirit. The old way, trying to be saved by keeping the Ten Command ments, ends in death; in the new way, the Holy Spirit gives them life.

A THOUGHT: *The last sentence of verse six can be translated "the letter kills, but the Spirit gives life." No one but Jesus has ever fulfilled the written law perfectly, and thus the whole world is condemned to death. The law makes people realize their sin, but it cannot give life. Eternal life comes from the Holy Spirit, who gives new life to all who believe in Christ. The moral law is still helpful to point out sin and show us how to live a life pleasing to God, but forgiveness comes only through the grace and mercy of Christ.*

Proverbs for Today/ 13:20–23

Be with wise men and become wise. Be with evil men and become evil. Curses chase sinners, while blessings chase the righteous! □ When a good man dies, he leaves an inheritance to his grandchildren; but when a sinner dies, his wealth is stored up for the godly. □ A poor man's farm may have good soil, but injustice robs him of its riches.

APRIL 23

Jesus' Triumphal Entry into Jerusalem/ Mark 11:1–11

As Jesus and his disciples neared Bethphage and Bethany on the outskirts of Jerusalem and came to the Mount of Olives, Jesus sent two of his disciples on ahead.

2"Go into that village over there," he told them, "and just as you enter you will see a colt tied up that has never been ridden. Untie him and bring him here. 3And if anyone asks you what you are doing, just say, 'Our Master needs him and will return him soon.'"

4,5Off went the two men and found the colt standing in the street, tied outside a house. As they were untying it, some who were standing there demanded, "What are you doing, untying that colt?"

6So they said what Jesus had told them to, and then the men agreed.

7So the colt was brought to Jesus and the disciples threw their cloaks across its back for him to ride on.

8Then many in the crowd spread out their coats along the road before him, while others threw down leafy branches from the fields.

9He was in the center of the procession with crowds ahead and behind, and all of them shouting, "Hail to the King!" "Praise God for him who comes in the name of the Lord!" . . . 10"Praise God for the return of our father David's kingdom . . . " "Hail to the King of the universe!"

11And so he entered Jerusalem and went into the Temple. He looked around carefully at everything and then left— for now it was late in the afternoon—and went out to Bethany with the twelve disciples.

A THOUGHT: *This was Sunday of the week Jesus would be crucified, and the great Passover festival was about to begin. Jews came to Jerusalem from all over the Roman world during this week-long celebration to remember the great Exodus from Egypt. Many in the crowds had heard of or seen Jesus and were hoping he would come to the Temple.*

Jesus did come, not as a conquering king on a white horse (symbolizing victory), but on a donkey's colt that had never been ridden (symbolizing humility). The people were anticipating that Jesus would become a great political Messiah who would overthrow Roman domination. A few days later these people who were shouting, "Hail to the king!" would cry out, "Crucify him!"

The Old and New Covenants Compared/ 2 Corinthians 3:7–18

Yet that old system of law that led to death began with such glory that people could not bear to look at Moses' face. For as he gave them God's law to obey, his face shone out with the very glory of God—though the brightness was already fading away. 8Shall we not expect far greater glory in these days when the Holy Spirit is giving life? 9If the plan that leads to doom was glorious, much more glorious is the plan that makes men right with God. 10In fact, that first glory as it shone from Moses' face is worth nothing at all in comparison with the overwhelming glory of the new agreement. 11 So if the old system that faded into nothing was full of heavenly glory, the glory of God's new plan for our salvation is certainly far greater, for it is eternal.

12Since we know that this new glory will never go away, we can preach with great boldness, 13and not as Moses did, who put a veil over his face so that the Israelis could not see the glory fade away.

¹⁴Not only Moses' face was veiled, but his people's minds and understanding were veiled and blinded too. Even now when the Scripture is read it seems as though Jewish hearts and minds are covered by a thick veil, because they cannot see and understand the real meaning of the Scriptures. For this veil of misunderstanding can be removed only by believing in Christ. ¹⁵Yes, even today when they read Moses' writings their hearts are blind and they think that obeying the Ten Commandments is the way to be saved.

¹⁶But whenever anyone turns to the Lord from his sins, then the veil is taken away. ¹⁷The Lord is the Spirit who gives them life, and where he is there is freedom [from trying to be saved by keeping the laws of God]. ¹⁸But we Christians have no veil over our faces; we can be mirrors that brightly reflect the glory of the Lord. And as the Spirit of the Lord works within us, we become more and more like him.

A THOUGHT: *When Moses came down Mount Sinai with the Ten Commandments, his face glowed from being in God's presence. He put on a veil to keep the people from being terrified by the brightness of his face. Paul adds that his veil kept them from seeing the glory fade away. The glory that the Spirit imparts to the believer is greater both in quality and longevity than that which Moses experienced. The glory experienced in the new covenant gradually transforms the believer into Christlikeness. Becoming Christlike is a progressive experience. The more closely we relate to him, the more we will be like him.*

Proverbs for Today/ 13:24–25

If you refuse to discipline your son, it proves you don't love him; for if you love him you will be prompt to punish him. □ The good man eats to live, while the evil man lives to eat.

APRIL 24

Jesus Cleanses the Temple/ Mark 11:12–25

The next morning as Jesus and his disciples left Bethany, he felt hungry. ¹³A little way off he noticed a fig tree in full leaf, so he went over to see if he could find any figs on it. But no, there were only leaves, for it was too early in the season for fruit.

14Then Jesus said to the tree, "You shall never bear fruit again!" And the disciples heard him say it.

15When they arrived back to Jerusalem he went to the Temple and began to drive out the merchants and their customers, and knocked over the tables of the money-changers and the stalls of those selling doves, 16and stopped everyone from bringing in loads of merchandise.

17He told them, "It is written in the Scriptures, 'My Temple is to be a place of prayer for all nations,' but you have turned it into a den of robbers."

18When the chief priests and other Jewish leaders heard what he had done they began planning how best to get rid of him. Their problem was their fear of riots because the people were so enthusiastic about Jesus' teaching.

19That evening as usual they left the city.

20Next morning, as the disciples passed the fig tree he had cursed, they saw that it was withered from the roots! 21Then Peter remembered what Jesus had said to the tree on the previous day, and exclaimed, "Look, Teacher! The fig tree you cursed has withered!"

22,23In reply Jesus said to the disciples, "If you only have faith in God—this is the absolute truth—you can say to this Mount of Olives, 'Rise up and fall into the Mediterranean,' and your command will be obeyed. All that's required is that you really believe and have no doubt! 24Listen to me! You can pray for *anything,* and *if you believe, you have it;* it's yours! 25But when you are praying, first forgive anyone you are holding a grudge against, so that your Father in heaven will forgive you your sins too."

A THOUGHT: *There are two parts to this unusual incident: the cursing of the fig tree and the cleansing of the Temple. The cursing of the fig tree was an acted–out parable related to the cleansing of the Temple. The Temple was supposed to be a place of worship, but true worship of God had virtually disappeared. The fig tree showed promise of fruit, but it produced none. Jesus was showing his anger at religious life without substance. If you "go through the motions" of faith without putting it to work in your life, you are like the fig tree that withered and died. Genuine faith has great potential; ask God to help you bear fruit for his Kingdom.*

Satan Blinds, But God Gives Light/
2 Corinthians 4:1–7

It is God himself, in his mercy, who has given us this wonderful work [of telling his Good News to others], and so we never give up. ²We do not try to trick people into believing—we are not interested in fooling anyone. We never try to get anyone to believe that the Bible teaches what it doesn't. All such shameful methods we forego. We stand in the presence of God as we speak and so we tell the truth, as all who know us will agree.

³If the Good News we preach is hidden to anyone, it is hidden from the one who is on the road to eternal death. ⁴Satan, who is the god of this evil world, has made him blind, unable to see the glorious light of the Gospel that is shining upon him, or to understand the amazing message we preach about the glory of Christ, who is God. ⁵We don't go around preaching about ourselves, but about Christ Jesus as Lord. All we say of ourselves is that we are your slaves because of what Jesus has done for us. ⁶For God, who said, "Let there be light in the darkness," has made us understand that it is the brightness of his glory that is seen in the face of Jesus Christ.

⁷But this precious treasure—this light and power that now shine within us —is held in a perishable container, that is, in our weak bodies. Everyone can see that the glorious power within must be from God and is not our own.

A Thought: *The supremely valuable message of salvation in Jesus Christ has been entrusted by God to frail and fallible human beings. Paul's focus, however, is not on the perishable container but on its priceless contents—God's power dwelling in us. Though we are weak, God uses us to spread his Good News and gives us power to do his work. Knowing that the power is his, not ours, keeps us from pride and motivates us to keep daily contact with God, our power source. Our responsibility is to let people see God through us.*

Proverbs for Today/ 14:1–2

A wise woman builds her house, while a foolish woman tears hers down by her own efforts.   □ To do right honors God; to sin is to despise him.

APRIL 25

The Parable of the Disloyal Tenants/
Mark 11:26—12:12

By this time Jesus and his disciples had arrived in Jerusalem again, and as he was walking through the Temple area, the chief priests and other Jewish leaders came up to him demanding, "What's going on here? Who gave you the authority to drive out the merchants?"

29Jesus replied, "I'll tell you if you answer one question! 30What about John the Baptist? Was he sent by God, or not? Answer me!"

31They talked it over among themselves. "If we reply that God sent him, then he will say, 'All right, why didn't you accept him?' 32But if we say God didn't send him, then the people will start a riot." (For the people all believed strongly that John was a prophet.)

33So they said, "We can't answer. We don't know."

To which Jesus replied, "Then I won't answer your question either!"

12:1Here are some of the story-illustrations Jesus gave to the people at that time:

"A man planted a vineyard and built a wall around it and dug a pit for pressing out the grape juice, and built a watchman's tower. Then he leased the farm to tenant farmers and moved to another country. 2At grape-picking time he sent one of his men to collect his share of the crop. 3But the farmers beat up the man and sent him back empty-handed.

4"The owner then sent another of his men, who received the same treatment, only worse, for his head was seriously injured. 5The next man he sent was killed; and later, others were either beaten or killed, until 6there was only one left—his only son. He finally sent him, thinking they would surely give him their full respect.

7"But when the farmers saw him coming they said, 'He will own the farm when his father dies. Come on, let's kill him—and then the farm will be ours!' 8So they caught him and murdered him and threw his body out of the vineyard.

9"What do you suppose the owner will do when he

hears what happened? He will come and kill them all, and lease the vineyard to others. 10Don't you remember reading this verse in the Scriptures? 'The Rock the builders threw away became the cornerstone, the most honored stone in the building! 11This is the Lord's doing and it is an amazing thing to see.' "

12The Jewish leaders wanted to arrest him then and there for using this illustration, for they knew he was pointing at them—they were the wicked farmers in his story. But they were afraid to touch him for fear of a mob. So they left him and went away.

A THOUGHT: *The Pharisees asked Jesus, who gave him the authority to chase away the merchants and moneychangers. Their request, however, was a trap. If Jesus said his authority was from God, they would accuse him of blasphemy; if he said his authority was his own, they would overrule him and dismiss him as a fanatic. To expose their real motives, Jesus countered their question with a question about John the Baptist. The Pharisees' silence proved they were not interested in the truth. In response to the silence of the Pharisees, Jesus tells this parable of the disloyal tenants to indicate: (1) that his source of authority is God (he is pictured as the son in the parable), and (2) that the Pharisees were really at odds with the landowner (God) when they should have been cultivating the vineyard.*

Suffering for the Gospel/ 2 Corinthians 4:8–17

We are pressed on every side by troubles, but not crushed and broken. We are perplexed because we don't know why things happen as they do, but we don't give up and quit. 9We are hunted down, but God never abandons us. We get knocked down, but we get up again and keep going. 10These bodies of ours are constantly facing death just as Jesus did; so it is clear to all that it is only the living Christ within [who keeps us safe].

11Yes, we live under constant danger to our lives because we serve the Lord, but this gives us constant opportunities to show forth the power of Jesus Christ within our dying bodies. 12Because of our preaching we face death, but it has resulted in eternal life for you.

13We boldly say what we believe [trusting God to care for us], just as the Psalm writer did when he said, "I believe and therefore I speak." 14We know that the same God who brought the Lord Jesus back from death will also bring us back to life again with Jesus, and present us to him along with you. [15]These sufferings of ours are for your benefit. And the more of you who are won to Christ, the more there are to thank him for his great kindness, and the more the Lord is glorified.

[16]That is why we never give up. Though our bodies are dying, our inner strength in the Lord is growing every day. [17]These troubles and sufferings of ours are, after all, quite small and won't last very long. Yet this short time of distress will result in God's richest blessing upon us forever and ever!

A THOUGHT: *Paul suffered many trials as he preached the Good News, but he knew that they would one day be over and he would obtain God's great blessings. As we face great troubles, it's easy to focus on the pain rather than on our ultimate goal. Just as athletes concentrate on the finish line and ignore their discomfort, we too must focus on the reward for our faith and the joy that lasts forever. No matter what happens to us in this life, we have the assurance of eternal life where all suffering will end.*

Proverbs for Today/ 14:3–4

A rebel's foolish talk should prick his own pride! But the wise man's speech is respected.   □ An empty stable stays clean—but there is no income from an empty stable.

APRIL 26

Jesus Answers the Pharisees and the Sadducees/ Mark 12:13–34

But the Jewish leaders sent other religious and political leaders to talk with Jesus and try to trap him into saying something he could be arrested for.

[14]"Teacher," these spies said, "we know you tell the truth no matter what! You aren't influenced by the opinions and desires of men, but sincerely teach the ways of God. Now tell us, is it right to pay taxes to Rome, or not?"

[15]Jesus saw their trick and said, "Show me a coin and I'll tell you."

[16]When they handed it to him he asked, "Whose picture and title is this on the coin?" They replied, "The emperor's."

17"All right," he said, "if it is his, give it to him. But everything that belongs to God must be given to God!" And they scratched their heads in bafflement at his reply.

18Then the Sadducees stepped forward—a group of men who say there is no resurrection. Here was their question:

19"Teacher, Moses gave us a law that when a man dies without children, the man's brother should marry his widow and have children in his brother's name. 20,21,22Well, there were seven brothers and the oldest married and died, and left no children. So the second brother married the widow, but soon he died too, and left no children. Then the next brother married her, and died without children, and so on until all were dead, and still there were no children; and last of all, the woman died too.

23"What we want to know is this: In the resurrection, whose wife will she be, for she had been the wife of each of them?"

24Jesus replied, "Your trouble is that you don't know the Scriptures, and don't know the power of God. 25For when these seven brothers and the woman rise from the dead, they won't be married—they will be like the angels.

26"But now as to whether there will be a resurrection— have you never read in the book of Exodus about Moses and the burning bush? God said to Moses, 'I *am* the God of Abraham, and I *am* the God of Isaac, and I *am* the God of Jacob.'

27"God was telling Moses that these men, though dead for hundreds of years, were still very much alive, for he would not have said, 'I *am* the God' of those who don't exist! You have made a serious error."

28One of the teachers of religion who was standing there listening to the discussion realized that Jesus had answered well. So he asked, "Of all the commandments, which is the most important?"

29Jesus replied, "The one that says, 'Hear, O Israel! The Lord our God is the one and only God. 30And you must love him with all your heart and soul and mind and strength.'

31"The second is: 'You must love others as much as yourself.' No other commandments are greater than these."

32The teacher of religion replied, "Sir, you have spoken

a true word in saying that there is only one God and no other. 33And I know it is far more important to love him with all my heart and understanding and strength, and to love others as myself, than to offer all kinds of sacrifices on the altar of the Temple."

34Realizing this man's understanding, Jesus said to him, "You are not far from the Kingdom of God." And after that, no one dared ask him any more questions.

A THOUGHT: *The Pharisees and Herodians thought they had the perfect question to trap Jesus. But Jesus answered wisely, once again exposing their self-interest and wrong motives. Jesus said that since the coin had the impression of the emperor's image, it should be given to the emperor. But whatever belongs to God—the earth and everyone who lives on the earth—should be offered up to God. Are you giving God all that is rightfully his? Make sure your life is wholly given to God.*

The Hope of the Resurrection/
2 Corinthians 4:18—5:10

So we do not look at what we can see right now, the troubles all around us, but we look forward to the joys in heaven which we have not yet seen. The troubles will soon be over, but the joys to come will last forever.

5:1For we know that when this tent we live in now is taken down—when we die and leave these bodies—we will have wonderful new bodies in heaven, homes that will be ours forevermore, made for us by God himself, and not by human hands. 2How weary we grow of our present bodies. That is why we look forward eagerly to the day when we shall have heavenly bodies which we shall put on like new clothes. 3For we shall not be merely spirits without bodies. 4These earthly bodies make us groan and sigh, but we wouldn't like to think of dying and having no bodies at all. We want to slip into our new bodies so that these dying bodies will, as it were, be swallowed up by everlasting life. 5This is what God has prepared for us and, as a guarantee, he has given us his Holy Spirit.

6Now we look forward with confidence to our heavenly bodies, realizing that every moment we spend in these earthly bodies is time spent away from our eternal home in heaven with Jesus. 7We know these things are true by believing, not by seeing. 8And we are not afraid, but are quite content to die, for then we will be at home with the Lord. 9So our aim is to please him always in everything we do, whether we are here in this body or away from this body and with him in heaven. 10For we must all stand before Christ to be judged and have our lives laid bare—before him. Each of us will receive whatever he deserves for the good or bad things he has done in his earthly body.

A THOUGHT: *The ultimate hope in terrible illness, persecution, or pain is realizing that this life is not all there is—there is life after death! Death is frightening for many people because it is mysterious and unknown. Paul was not afraid to die because he was confident of spending eternity with Christ. Of course, facing the unknown is cause for anxiety and leaving loved ones hurts deeply, but if we believe in Jesus Christ, we can share Paul's hope and confidence in the resurrection of the body and eternal life with Christ. Knowing that we will live forever with God in a place without sin and suffering helps us live above the pain we must face in this life.*

Proverbs for Today/ 14:5–6

A truthful witness never lies; a false witness always lies. □ A mocker never finds the wisdom he claims he is looking for, yet it comes easily to the man with common sense.

APRIL 27

Proud Teachers and a Humble Widow/ Mark 12:35–44

Later, as Jesus was teaching the people in the Temple area, he asked them this question:

"Why do your religious teachers claim that the Messiah must be a descendant of King David? 36For David himself said—and the Holy Spirit was speaking through him when he said it—'God said to my Lord, sit at my right hand until I make your enemies your footstool.' 37Since David called him his Lord, how can he be his *son?*"

(This sort of reasoning delighted the crowd and they listened to him with great interest.)

38Here are some of the other things he taught them at this time:

"Beware of the teachers of religion! For they love to wear the robes of the rich and scholarly, and to have everyone bow to them as they walk through the markets. 39They love to sit in the best seats in the synagogues, and at the places of honor at banquets— 40but they shamelessly cheat widows out of their homes and then, to cover up the kind of men they really are, they pretend to be pious by praying long prayers in public. Because of this, their punishment will be the greater."

41Then he went over to the collection boxes in the Temple and sat and watched as the crowds dropped in their money. Some who were rich put in large amounts. 42Then a poor widow came and dropped in two pennies.

43,44He called his disciples to him and remarked, "That poor widow has given more than all those rich men put together! For they gave a little of their extra fat, while she gave up her last penny."

A THOUGHT: *Jesus warned against the teachers of religion who loved to appear holy and receive honor when, in reality, they were phonies. Greatness is not measured by appearance, but by genuine obedience to God from a humble heart. In the Lord's eyes, the poor widow gave more than all the others put together, although her gift was by far the smallest. The value of a gift is not determined by its amount, but by the spirit in which it is given. In the same way, the value of acts of kindness or service should not be measured by quantity, nor by their value in the eyes of men, but by their value in the eyes of God.*

New Creations in Christ/ 2 Corinthians 5:11–21

It is because of this solemn fear of the Lord, which is ever present in our minds, that we work so hard to win others. God knows our hearts, that they are pure in this matter, and I hope that, deep within, you really know it too.

12Are we trying to pat ourselves on the back again? No, I am giving you some good ammunition! You can use this on those preachers of yours who brag about how well they look and preach, but don't have true and honest hearts. You can boast about us that we, at least, are well intentioned and honest.

13,14Are we insane [to say such things about ourselves]?

If so, it is to bring glory to God. And if we are in our right minds, it is for your benefit. Whatever we do, it is certainly not for our own profit, but because Christ's love controls us now. Since we believe that Christ died for all of us, we should also believe that we have died to the old life we used to live. 15He died for all so that all who live—having received eternal life from him—might live no longer for themselves, to please themselves, but to spend their lives pleasing Christ who died and rose again for them. 16So stop evaluating Christians by what the world thinks about them or by what they seem to be like on the outside. Once I mistakenly thought of Christ that way, merely as a human being like myself. How differently I feel now! 17When someone becomes a Christian he becomes a brand new person inside. He is not the same any more. A new life has begun!

18All these new things are from God who brought us back to himself through what Christ Jesus did. And God has given us the privilege of urging everyone to come into his favor and be reconciled to him. 19For God was in Christ, restoring the world to himself, no longer counting men's sins against them but blotting them out. This is the wonderful message he has given us to tell others. 20We are Christ's ambassadors. God is using us to speak to you: we beg you, as though Christ himself were here pleading with you, receive the love he offers you—be reconciled to God. 21For God took the sinless Christ and poured into him our sins. Then, in exchange, he poured God's goodness into us!

A Thought: *Christians are brand new people on the inside. The Holy Spirit gives them new life, and they are not the same any more. We are not reformed, rehabilitated, or reeducated—we are new creations, living in vital union with Christ. We are not merely turning over a new leaf; we are beginning a new life under a new master. The Christian life involves this continual process of transformation by the power of the Holy Spirit. Gradually we become more and more like Jesus Christ in our thoughts, attitudes, and actions.*

Proverbs for Today/ 14:7–8

If you are looking for advice, stay away from fools. The wise man looks ahead. The fool attempts to fool himself and won't face facts.

APRIL 28

Jesus Preaches about the End Times/ Mark 13:1–13

As Jesus was leaving the Temple that day, one of his disciples said, "Teacher, what beautiful buildings these are! Look at the decorated stonework on the walls."

2Jesus replied, "Yes, look! For not one stone will be left upon another, except as ruins."

3,4And as he sat on the slopes of the Mount of Olives across the valley from Jerusalem, Peter, James, John, and Andrew got alone with him and asked him, "Just when is all this going to happen to the Temple? Will there be some warning ahead of time?"

5So Jesus launched into an extended reply. "Don't let anyone mislead you," he said, 6"for many will come declaring themselves to be your Messiah, and will lead many astray. 7And wars will break out near and far, but this is not the signal of the end-time.

8"For nations and kingdoms will proclaim war against each other, and there will be earthquakes in many lands, and famines. These herald only the early stages of the anguish ahead. 9But when these things begin to happen, watch out! For you will be in great danger. You will be dragged before the courts, and beaten in the synagogues, and accused before governors and kings of being my followers. This is your opportunity to tell them the Good News. 10And the Good News must first be made known in every nation before the end-time finally comes. 11But when you are arrested and stand trial, don't worry about what to say in your defense. Just say what God tells you to. Then you will not be speaking, but the Holy Spirit will.

12"Brothers will betray each other to death, fathers will betray their own children, and children will betray their parents to be killed. 13And everyone will hate you because you are mine. But all who endure to the end without renouncing me shall be saved.

A THOUGHT: *What are the signs of the end times? There have been people in every generation since Christ's resurrection claiming to know exactly when Jesus would return. No one has yet been right. Christ will return on God's timetable, not man's. Jesus predicted that many would be misled before his return by false teachers claiming to have revelations from God.*

In Scripture, the one clear sign of Christ's return is that all mankind will see him coming in the clouds. In other words, you do not have to wonder whether a certain person is the Messiah or whether these are the "end times." When Jesus returns, you will know beyond a doubt that it is he. Beware of groups that claim special knowledge of the last days because no one knows when this time will be. Be cautious about saying, "This is it!" but be bold in your commitment to have your heart and life ready for his return.

Suffering for the Gospel/ 2 Corinthians 6:1–7

As God's partners we beg you not to toss aside this marvelous message of God's great kindness. 2For God says, "Your cry came to me at a favorable time, when the doors of welcome were wide open. I helped you on a day when salvation was being offered." Right now God is ready to welcome you. Today he is ready to save you.

3We try to live in such a way that no one will ever be offended or kept back from finding the Lord by the way we act, so that no one can find fault with us and blame it on the Lord. 4In fact, in everything we do we try to show that we are true ministers of God.

We patiently endure suffering and hardship and trouble of every kind. 5We have been beaten, put in jail, faced angry mobs, worked to exhaustion, stayed awake through sleepless nights of watching, and gone without food. 6We have proved ourselves to be what we claim by our wholesome lives and by our understanding of the Gospel and by our patience. We have been kind and truly loving and filled with the Holy Spirit. 7We have been truthful, with God's power helping us in all we do. All of the godly man's arsenal—weapons of defense, and weapons of attack—have been ours.

A THOUGHT: *In everything he did, Paul always considered what his actions communicated about Jesus Christ. If you are a believer, you are a minister for God. In the course of each day, non–Christians observe you. Consider whether your actions will keep anyone from God. Don't let your careless or undisciplined actions be another's excuse for rejecting God.*

Proverbs for Today/ 14:9–10

The common bond of rebels is their guilt. The common bond of godly people is good will. □ Only the person involved can know his own bitterness or joy—no one else can really share it.

APRIL 29

Be Prepared for the End/ Mark 13:14–37

"When you see the horrible thing standing in the Temple —reader, pay attention!—flee, if you can, to the Judean hills. 15,16Hurry! If you are on your rooftop porch, don't even go back into the house. If you are out in the fields, don't even return for your money or clothes.

17"Woe to pregnant women in those days, and to mothers nursing their children. 18And pray that your flight will not be in winter. 19For those will be days of such horror as have never been since the beginning of God's creation, nor will ever be again. 20And unless the Lord shortens that time of calamity, not a soul in all the earth will survive. But for the sake of his chosen ones he will limit those days.

21"And then if anyone tells you, 'This is the Messiah,' or, 'That one is,' don't pay any attention. 22For there will be many false Messiahs and false prophets who will do wonderful miracles that would deceive, if possible, even God's own children. 23Take care! I have warned you!

24"After the tribulation ends, then the sun will grow dim and the moon will not shine, 25and the stars will fall—the heavens will convulse.

26"Then all mankind will see me, the Messiah, coming in the clouds with great power and glory. 27And I will send out the angels to gather together my chosen ones from all over the world—from the farthest bounds of earth and heaven.

28"Now, here is a lesson from a fig tree. When its buds become tender and its leaves begin to sprout, you know that spring has come. 29And when you see these things happening that I've described, you can be sure that my return is very near, that I am right at the door.

30"Yes, these are the events that will signal the end of the age. 31Heaven and earth shall disappear, but my words stand sure forever.

32"However, no one, not even the angels in heaven, nor I myself, knows the day or hour when these things will happen; only the Father knows. 33 And since you don't know when it will happen, stay alert. Be on the watch [for my return].

34"My coming can be compared with that of a man who went on a trip to another country. He laid out his employees' work for them to do while he was gone, and told the gatekeeper to watch for his return.

35,36,37"Keep a sharp lookout! For you do not know when I will come, at evening, at midnight, early dawn or late daybreak. Don't let me find you sleeping. *Watch for my return!* This is my message to you and to everyone else."

A THOUGHT: *Is it possible for Christians to be deceived? Yes. So convincing will be the arguments and proofs from deceivers in the end times that it will be difficult not to fall away from Christ. If we are prepared, Jesus says, we can remain faithful, but if we are not prepared we will not endure. To penetrate the disguises of false teachers, we can ask: (1) Have their predictions come true, or do they have to revise them to fit what's already happened? (2) Does any teaching utilize a small section of the Bible to the neglect of the whole? (3) Does the teaching go against what is known in the Bible about God? (4) Are the practices meant to glorify the teacher or Christ? (5) Do the teachings promote hostility toward other Christians?*

Paul's Love for the Corinthians/ 2 Corinthians 6:8–13

We stand true to the Lord whether others honor us or despise us, whether they criticize us or commend us. We are honest, but they call us liars.

9The world ignores us, but we are known to God; we live close to death, but here we are, still very much alive. We have been injured but kept from death. 10Our hearts ache, but at the same time we have the joy of the Lord. We are poor, but we give rich spiritual gifts to others. We own nothing, and yet we enjoy everything.

11Oh, my dear Corinthian friends! I have told you all my feelings; I love you with all my heart. 12Any coldness still between us is not because of any lack of love on my part, but because your love is too small and does not reach out to me and draw me in. 13I am talking to you now as if you truly were my very own children. Open your hearts to us! Return our love!

A THOUGHT: *What a difference knowing Jesus can make! He turns everything around, caring for us in spite of what the world thinks. Christians don't have to give in to public opinion and pressure. Paul stood true to God whether people praised him or condemned him. He remained active, joyous, and content in the most difficult conditions. Don't let circumstances or people's expectations control you. Be firm as you stand true to God, and refuse to compromise on his standards for living.*

Proverbs for Today/ 14:11–12

The work of the wicked will perish; the work of the godly will flourish. Before every man there lies a wide and pleasant road that seems right but ends in death.

APRIL 30

Judas Iscariot Betrays Jesus/ Mark 14:1–11

The Passover observance began two days later—an annual Jewish holiday when no bread made with yeast was eaten. The chief priests and other Jewish leaders were still looking for an opportunity to arrest Jesus secretly and put him to death.

2"But we can't do it during the Passover," they said, "or there will be a riot."

3Meanwhile Jesus was in Bethany, at the home of Simon the leper; during supper a woman came in with a beautiful flask of expensive perfume. Then, breaking the seal, she poured it over his head.

4,5Some of those at the table were indignant among themselves about this "waste," as they called it.

"Why, she could have sold that perfume for a fortune and given the money to the poor!" they snarled.

6But Jesus said, "Let her alone; why berate her for doing a good thing? 7You always have the poor among you, and they badly need your help, and you can aid them whenever you want to; but I won't be here much longer.

8"She has done what she could, and has anointed my body ahead of time for burial. 9And I tell you this in solemn truth, that wherever the Good News is preached throughout the world, this woman's deed will be remembered and praised."

10Then Judas Iscariot, one of his disciples, went to the chief priests to arrange to betray Jesus to them.

11When the chief priests heard why he had come, they were excited and happy and promised him a reward. So he began looking for the right time and place to betray Jesus.

A Thought: *Why would Judas want to betray Jesus? Judas, like the other disciples, expected Jesus to start a political rebellion and overthrow Rome. As treasurer, Judas certainly assumed (as did the other disciples) that he would be given an important position in Jesus' new government. But when Jesus praised Mary for pouring out the perfume, thought to be worth half a year's salary, Judas finally realized that Jesus' kingdom was not physical or political, but spiritual. Judas' greedy desire for money and status could not be realized if he followed Jesus, so he betrayed him in exchange for money and favor from the religious leaders. We must be careful not to allow our expectations to be a barrier to hearing God's truth.*

Don't Become One with Unbelievers/
2 Corinthians 6:14—7:4

Don't be teamed with those who do not love the Lord, for what do the people of God have in common with the people of sin? How can light live with darkness? 15And what harmony can there be between Christ and the devil? How can a Christian be a partner with one who doesn't believe? 16And what union can there be between God's temple and idols? For you are God's temple, the home of the living God, and God has said of you, "I will live in them and walk among them, and I will be their God and they shall be my people." 17That is why the Lord has said, "Leave them; separate yourselves from them; don't touch their filthy things, and I will welcome you, 18and be a Father to you, and you will be my sons and daughters."

7:1Having such great promises as these, dear friends, let us turn away from everything wrong, whether of body or spirit, and purify ourselves, living in the wholesome fear of God, giving ourselves to him alone. 2Please open your hearts to us again, for not one of you has suffered any wrong from us. Not one of you was led astray. We have cheated no one nor taken advantage of anyone. ³I'm not saying this to scold or blame you, for, as I have said before, you are in my heart forever and I live and die with you. ⁴I have the highest confidence in you, and my pride in you is great. You have greatly encouraged me; you have made me so happy in spite of all my suffering.

A THOUGHT: *Paul urged believers not to form binding relationships with nonbelievers, because this might weaken their Christian commitment, integrity, or standards. Earlier, Paul had explained that this did not mean isolating themselves from nonbelievers, for we have been called to evangelize those who are not Christians. Paul wanted believers to be active in their witness for Christ to nonbelievers, but they should not lock themselves into personal or business relationships which could cause them to compromise their faith. Just as those in business should avoid conflicts of interest, all believers should avoid situations that would force them to divide their loyalties.*

Proverbs for Today/ 14:13–14

Laughter cannot mask a heavy heart. When the laughter ends, the grief remains. □ The backslider gets bored with himself; the godly man's life is exciting.

MAY 1

The Last Supper/ Mark 14:12–31

On the first day of the Passover, the day the lambs were sacrificed, the disciples asked Jesus where he wanted to go to eat the traditional Passover supper. ¹³He sent two of them into Jerusalem to make the arrangements.

"As you are walking along," he told them, "you will see a man coming toward you carrying a pot of water. Follow him. ¹⁴At the house he enters, tell the man in charge, 'Our Master sent us to see the room you have ready for us, where we will eat the Passover supper this evening!' ¹⁵He will take you upstairs to a large room all set up. Prepare our supper there."

¹⁶So the two disciples went on ahead into the city and found everything as Jesus had said, and prepared the Passover.

¹⁷In the evening Jesus arrived with the other disciples, ¹⁸and as they were sitting around the table eating, Jesus said, "I solemnly declare that one of you will betray me, one of you who is here eating with me."

¹⁹A great sadness swept over them, and one by one they asked him, "Am I the one?"

²⁰He replied, "It is one of you twelve eating with me now. ²¹I must die, as the prophets declared long ago; but, oh, the misery ahead for the man by whom I am betrayed. Oh, that he had never been born!"

²²As they were eating, Jesus took bread and asked God's blessing on it and broke it in pieces and gave it to them and said, "Eat it—this is my body."

²³Then he took a cup of wine and gave thanks to God for it and gave it to them; and they all drank from it. ²⁴And he said to them, "This is my blood, poured out for many, sealing the new agreement between God and man. ²⁵I solemnly declare that I shall never again taste wine until the day I drink a different kind in the Kingdom of God."

²⁶Then they sang a hymn and went out to the Mount of Olives.

²⁷"All of you will desert me," Jesus told them, "for God has declared through the prophets, 'I will kill the Shepherd, and the sheep will scatter.' ²⁸But after I am raised to life again, I will go to Galilee and meet you there."

²⁹Peter said to him, "I will never desert you no matter what the others do!"

³⁰"Peter," Jesus said, "before the cock crows a second time tomorrow morning you will deny me three times."

³¹"No!" Peter exploded. "Not even if I have to die with you! I'll *never* deny you!" And all the others vowed the same.

A THOUGHT: *Jesus' death for us on the cross seals a new agreement between God and mankind. The old agreement involved forgiveness of sins through the blood of an animal sacrifice. But, instead of a spotless lamb on the altar, Jesus came as the Lamb of God to sacrifice himself to bring forgiveness for sin once and for all. Jesus was the final sacrifice for sins, and his blood sealed the new agreement between God and us (also called the "new covenant" or "new testament"). Now all of us can come to God through Jesus, in full confidence that he will hear us and save us from our sins.*

The Good Report from Titus/ 2 Corinthians 7:5–10

When we arrived in Macedonia there was no rest for us; outside, trouble was on every hand and all around us; within us, our hearts were full of dread and fear. 6Then God who cheers those who are discouraged refreshed us by the arrival of Titus. 7Not only was his presence a joy, but also the news that he brought of the wonderful time he had with you. When he told me how much you were looking forward to my visit, and how sorry you were about what had happened, and about your loyalty and warm love for me, well, I overflowed with joy!

8I am no longer sorry that I sent that letter to you, though I was very sorry for a time, realizing how painful it would be to you. But it hurt you only for a little while. 9Now I am glad I sent it, not because it hurt you, but because the pain turned you to God. It was a good kind of sorrow you felt, the kind of sorrow God wants his people to have, so that I need not come to you with harshness. 10For God sometimes uses sorrow in our lives to help us turn away from sin and seek eternal life. We should never regret his sending it. But the sorrow of the man who is not a Christian is not the sorrow of true repentance and does not prevent eternal death.

A THOUGHT: *True repentance means being sorry for our sins and changing our behavior. Many people are sorry only for the effects of their sins or for being caught. Compare Peter's remorse and repentance with Judas' bitterness and suicide. Both denied Christ. One repented and was restored to faith and service; the other took his own life. True repentance should lead us into deeper relationship with God.*

Proverbs for Today/ 14:15–16

Only a simpleton believes everything he's told! A prudent man understands the need for proof. A wise man is cautious and avoids danger; a fool plunges ahead with great confidence.

Jesus Is Arrested in the Garden of Gethsemane/ Mark 14:32–52

And now Jesus and his disciples came to an olive grove called the Garden of Gethsemane, and he instructed his disciples, "Sit here, while I go and pray."

33He took Peter, James and John with him and began to be filled with horror and deepest distress. 34And he said to them, "My soul is crushed by sorrow to the point of death; stay here and watch with me."

35He went on a little further and fell to the ground and prayed that if it were possible the awful hour awaiting him might never come.

36"Father, Father," he said, "everything is possible for you. Take away this cup from me. Yet I want your will, not mine."

37Then he returned to the three disciples and found them asleep.

"Simon!" he said. "Asleep? Couldn't you watch with me even one hour? 38Watch with me and pray lest the Tempter overpower you. For though the spirit is willing enough, the body is weak."

39And he went away again and prayed, repeating his pleadings. 40Again he returned to them and found them sleeping, for they were very tired. And they didn't know what to say.

41The third time when he returned to them he said, "Sleep on; get your rest! But no! The time for sleep has ended! Look! I am betrayed into the hands of wicked men. 42Come! Get up! We must go! Look! My betrayer is here!"

43And immediately, while he was still speaking, Judas (one of his disciples) arrived with a mob equipped with swords and clubs, sent out by the chief priests and other Jewish leaders.

44Judas had told them, "You will know which one to arrest when I go over and greet him. Then you can take him easily." 45So as soon as they arrived he walked up to Jesus. "Master!" he exclaimed, and embraced him with a great show of friendliness. 46Then the mob arrested

Jesus and held him fast. 47But someone pulled a sword and slashed at the High Priest's servant, cutting off his ear.

48Jesus asked them, "Am I some dangerous robber, that you come like this, armed to the teeth to capture me? 49Why didn't you arrest me in the Temple? I was there teaching every day. But these things are happening to fulfill the prophecies about me."

50Meanwhile, all his disciples had fled. 51,52There was, however, a young man following along behind, clothed only in a linen nightshirt. When the mob tried to grab him, he escaped, though his clothes were torn off in the process, so that he ran away completely naked.

A THOUGHT: *Was Jesus trying to get out of his task by praying "Take this cup from me"? Jesus expressed his true feelings, but he did not deny or rebel against God's will. He reaffirmed his desire to do what God wanted—"Yet I want your will, not mine." His prayer highlights the terrible suffering he had to endure—an agony worse than dying, because he had to take on the sins of the whole world. This "cup" was the alienation Jesus knew would occur when he was separated from God, his Father, at the cross. The sinless Son of God took on our sins and was separated in that moment from God in order that we could be saved.*

Paul's Sorrowful Letter/ 2 Corinthians 7:11–16

Just see how much good this grief from the Lord did for you! You no longer shrugged your shoulders, but became earnest and sincere, and very anxious to get rid of the sin that I wrote you about. You became frightened about what had happened, and longed for me to come and help. You went right to work on the problem and cleared it up [punishing the man who sinned]. You have done everything you could to make it right.

12I wrote as I did so the Lord could show how much you really do care for us. That was my purpose even more than to help the man who sinned, or his father to whom he did the wrong.

13In addition to the encouragement you gave us by your love, we were made happier still by Titus' joy when you gave him such a fine welcome and set his mind at ease. 14I told him how it would be—told him before he left me of my pride in you—and you didn't disappoint me. I have always told you the truth and now my boasting to Titus has also proved true! 15He loves you more than ever when he remembers the way you listened to him so willingly and received him so anxiously and with such deep concern. 16How happy this makes me, now that I am sure all is well between us again. Once again I can have perfect confidence in you.

A THOUGHT: *It is difficult to hear that we have sinned, and even more difficult to get rid of sin. Paul praised the Corinthians for clearing up an especially troublesome situation. Do you tend to be defensive when confronted? Don't let pride keep you from admitting your sins. Accept confrontation as a tool for growth, and do all you can to correct problems that are pointed out to you.*

Proverbs for Today/ 14:17–19

A short-tempered man is a fool. He hates the man who is patient. □ The simpleton is crowned with folly; the wise man is crowned with knowledge. □ Evil men shall bow before the godly.

MAY 3

Jesus before the Jewish Supreme Court/ Mark 14:53–72

Jesus was led to the High Priest's home where all of the chief priests and other Jewish leaders soon gathered. 54Peter followed far behind and then slipped inside the gates of the High Priest's residence and crouched beside a fire among the servants.

55Inside, the chief priests and the whole Jewish Supreme Court were trying to find something against Jesus that would be sufficient to condemn him to death. But their efforts were in vain. 56Many false witnesses volunteered, but they contradicted each other.

57Finally some men stood up to lie about him and said, 58"We heard him say, 'I will destroy this Temple made with human hands and in three days I will build another, made without human hands!' " 59But even then they didn't get their stories straight!

60Then the High Priest stood up before the Court and asked Jesus, "Do you refuse to answer this charge? What do you have to say for yourself?"

61To this Jesus made no reply.

Then the High Priest asked him. "Are you the Messiah, the Son of God?"

62Jesus said, "I am, and you will see me sitting at the right hand of God, and returning to earth in the clouds of heaven."

63,64Then the High Priest tore at his clothes and said, "What more do we need? Why wait for witnesses? You have heard his blasphemy. What is your verdict?" And the vote for the death sentence was unanimous.

65Then some of them began to spit at him, and they blindfolded him and began to hammer his face with their fists.

"Who hit you that time, you prophet?" they jeered. And even the bailiffs were using their fists on him as they led him away.

66,67Meanwhile Peter was below in the courtyard. One of the maids who worked for the High Priest noticed Peter warming himself at the fire.

She looked at him closely and then announced, *"You were with Jesus, the Nazarene."*

68Peter denied it. "I don't know what you're talking about!" he said, and walked over to the edge of the courtyard.

Just then, a rooster crowed.

69The maid saw him standing there and began telling the others, "There he is! There's that disciple of Jesus!"

70Peter denied it again.

A little later others standing around the fire began saying to Peter, "You are, too, one of them, for you are from Galilee!"

71He began to curse and swear. "I don't even know this fellow you are talking about," he said.

72And immediately the rooster crowed the second time. Suddenly Jesus' words flashed through Peter's mind: "Before the cock crows twice, you will deny me three times." And he began to cry.

A THOUGHT: *This trial by the Jewish Supreme Court had two phases. A small group met at night, and then the full council met at daybreak. They tried Jesus for religious offenses such as calling himself the Son of God, which, according to law, was blasphemy. The trial was obviously fixed, because these religious leaders had already decided to kill Jesus.*

To the first question of the Sanhedrin, Jesus made no reply because the evidence itself was confusing and erroneous. In his response to the second question, Jesus predicted a powerful role reversal. That they would see the Jesus sitting at the right hand of God meant that on Judgment Day, Jesus would judge them and they would be answering his questions.

Generous Giving Glorifies the Lord/ 2 Corinthians 8:1–8

Now I want to tell you what God in his grace has done for the churches in Macedonia.

2Though they have been going through much trouble and hard times, they have mixed their wonderful joy with their deep poverty, and the result has been an overflow of giving to others. 3They gave not only what they could afford, but far more; and I can testify that they did it because they wanted to, and not because of nagging on my part. 4They begged us to take the money so they could share in the joy of helping the Christians in Jerusalem. 5Best of all, they went beyond our highest hopes, for their first action was to dedicate themselves to the Lord and to us, for whatever directions God might give to them through us. 6They were so enthusiastic about it that we have urged Titus, who encouraged your giving in the first place, to visit you and encourage you to complete your share in this ministry of giving. 7You people there are leaders in so many ways—you have so much faith, so many good preachers, so much learning, so much enthusiasm, so much love for us. Now I want you to be leaders also in the spirit of cheerful giving.

8I am not giving you an order; I am not saying you must do it, but others are eager for it. This is one way to prove that your love is real, that it goes beyond mere words.

A THOUGHT: *While making his third missionary journey, Paul was collecting money for the impoverished believers in Jerusalem. The churches in Macedonia—Philippi, Thessalonica, and Beroea— gave money even though they were poor, and they gave more than Paul expected. This was sacrificial giving—they were poor themselves, but they wanted to help. The point of giving is not so much the amount we give, but why and how we give. God does not want gifts given grudgingly. Instead, he wants us to give as these churches did—out of dedication to him, love for fellow believers, the joy of helping those in need, and because it was right to do so. How well does your giving measure up to the standards set by the Macedonian churches?*

Proverbs for Today/ 14:20–21

Even his own neighbors despise the poor man, while the rich have many "friends." But to despise the poor is to sin. Blessed are those who help them.

MAY 4

Jesus on Trial before Pilate/ Mark 15:1–21

Early in the morning the chief priests, elders and teachers of religion—the entire Supreme Court—met to discuss their next steps. Their decision was to send Jesus under armed guard to Pilate, the Roman governor.

2Pilate asked him, "Are you the King of the Jews?"

"Yes," Jesus replied, "it is as you say."

3,4Then the chief priests accused him of many crimes, and Pilate asked him, "Why don't you say something? What about all these charges against you?"

5But Jesus said no more, much to Pilate's amazement.

6Now, it was Pilate's custom to release one Jewish prisoner each year at Passover time—any prisoner the people requested. 7One of the prisoners at that time was Barabbas, convicted along with others for murder during an insurrection.

8Now a mob began to crowd in toward Pilate, asking him to release a prisoner as usual.

9"How about giving you the 'King of Jews'?" Pilate asked. "Is he the one you want released?" 10(For he realized by now that this was a frameup, backed by the chief priests because they envied Jesus' popularity.)

11But at this point the chief priests whipped up the mob to demand the release of Barabbas instead of Jesus.

12"But if I release Barabbas," Pilate asked them, "what shall I do with this man you call your king?"

13They shouted back, "Crucify him!"

14"But why?" Pilate demanded. "What has he done wrong?" They only roared the louder, "Crucify him!"

15Then Pilate, afraid of a riot and anxious to please the people, released Barabbas to them. And he ordered

Jesus flogged with a leaded whip, and handed him over to be crucified.

16,17Then the Roman soldiers took him into the barracks of the palace, called out the entire palace guard, dressed him in a purple robe, and made a crown of long, sharp thorns and put it on his head. 18Then they saluted, yelling, "Yea! King of the Jews!" 19And they beat him on the head with a cane, and spat on him and went down on their knees to "worship" him.

20When they finally tired of their sport, they took off the purple robe and put his own clothes on him again, and led him away to be crucified.

21Simon of Cyrene, who was coming in from the country just then, was pressed into service to carry Jesus' cross. (Simon is the father of Alexander and Rufus.)

A THOUGHT: *Although Jesus was innocent according to Roman law, Pilate caved in under political pressure. He abandoned what he knew was right. He tried to second–guess the Jewish leaders and give a decision that would please everyone while keeping himself safe. When we lay aside God's clear statements of right and wrong and make decisions based on our audience, we fall into compromise and lawlessness. God promises to honor those who do right; not those who make everyone happy.*

Christ Became Poor for Our Benefit/
2 Corinthians 8:9–15

You know how full of love and kindness our Lord Jesus was: though he was so very rich, yet to help you he became so very poor, so that by being poor he could make you rich.

10I want to suggest that you finish what you started to do a year ago, for you were not only the first to propose this idea, but the first to begin doing something about it. 11Having started the ball rolling so enthusiastically, you should carry this project through to completion just as gladly, giving whatever you can out of whatever you have. Let your enthusiastic idea at the start be equalled by your realistic action now. 12If you are really eager to give, then it isn't important how much you have to give. God wants you to give what you have, not what you haven't.

13Of course, I don't mean that those who receive your gifts should have an easy time of it at your expense, 14but you should divide with them. Right now you have plenty and can help them; then at some other time they can share with you when you need it. In this way each will have as much as he needs. 15Do you remember what the Scriptures say about this? "He that gathered much had nothing left over, and he that gathered little had enough." So you also should share with those in need.

A THOUGHT: *The Corinthian church had money, and Paul challenged them to share with the Jerusalem Christians just as the Macedonian churches had done. Four principles of giving emerge here: (1) your willingness to give cheerfully is more important than the amount you give; (2) you should strive to fulfill your financial commitments; (3) if you give to others in need, they will in turn help you when you are in need; (4) you should give as a response to Christ, not for anything you can get out of it. How you give reflects your devotion to Christ. These principles apply regardless of your financial condition.*

Proverbs for Today/ 14:22–24
Those who plot evil shall wander away and be lost, but those who plan good shall be granted mercy and quietness. □ Work brings profit; talk brings poverty! □ Wise men are praised for their wisdom; fools are despised for their folly.

MAY 5

Jesus Is Crucified/ Mark 15:22–32
And the Roman soldiers brought Jesus to a place called Golgotha. (Golgotha means skull.) 23Wine drugged with bitter herbs was offered to him there, but he refused it. 24 And then they crucified him—and threw dice for his clothes.

25It was about nine o'clock in the morning when the crucifixion took place.

26A signboard was fastened to the cross above his head, announcing his crime. It read, "The King of the Jews."

27Two robbers were also crucified that morning, their crosses on either side of his. 28And so the Scripture was fulfilled that said, "He was counted among evil men."

29,30The people jeered at him as they walked by, and wagged their heads in mockery.

"Ha! Look at you now!" they yelled at him. "Sure, you can destroy the Temple and rebuild it in three days! If you're so wonderful, save yourself and come down from the cross."

31The chief priests and religious leaders were also standing around joking about Jesus.

"He's quite clever at 'saving' others," they said, "but he can't save himself!"

32"Hey there, Messiah!" they yelled at him. "You 'King of Israel'! Come on down from the cross and we'll believe you!"

And even the two robbers dying with him, cursed him.

A THOUGHT: *Jesus could have saved himself, but he endured this suffering because of his love for us. He could have chosen not to take the pain and humiliation; he could have killed those who mocked him—but he suffered through it all because he loved even his enemies. We had a significant part in the drama that afternoon because our sin was on the cross too. Jesus died on that cross for us, and the penalty for our sin was paid by his death. The only adequate response we can make is to confess our sin and freely accept the fact that Jesus paid for it so we wouldn't have to. Don't insult God with indifference toward the greatest act of genuine love in history.*

The Ministry of Titus/ 2 Corinthians 8:16–24

I am thankful to God that he has given Titus the same real concern for you that I have. 17He is glad to follow my suggestion that he visit you again—but I think he would have come anyway, for he is very eager to see you! 18I am sending another well-known brother with him, who is highly praised as a preacher of the Good News in all the churches. 19In fact, this man was elected by the churches to travel with me to take the gift to Jerusalem. This will glorify the Lord and show our eagerness to help each other. 20By traveling together we will guard against any suspicion, for we are anxious that no one should find fault with the way we are handling this large gift. 21God knows we are honest, but I want everyone else to know it too. That is why we have made this arrangement.

22And I am sending you still another brother, whom

we know from experience to be an earnest Christian. He is especially interested, as he looks forward to this trip, because I have told him all about your eagerness to help.

23If anyone asks who Titus is, say that he is my partner, my helper in helping you, and you can also say that the other two brothers represent the assemblies here and are splendid examples of those who belong to the Lord.

24Please show your love for me to these men and do for them all that I have publicly boasted you would.

A THOUGHT: *Titus was a true disciple of Christ. He was eager to serve, he took joy in the growth of others, he had integrity, he was a servant, and he was concerned for the needs of others. Let us imitate Titus in his Christlikeness—this kind of character is what true Christian leadership is made of.*

Proverbs for Today/ 14:25
A witness who tells the truth saves good men from being sentenced to death, but a false witness is a traitor.

MAY 6

The Death and Burial of Jesus/ Mark 15:33–47
About noon, darkness fell across the entire land, lasting until three o'clock that afternoon.

34Then Jesus called out with a loud voice, "Eli, Eli, lama sabachthani?" ("My God, my God, why have you deserted me?")

35Some of the people standing there thought he was calling for the prophet Elijah. 36So one man ran and got a sponge and filled it with sour wine and held it up to him on a stick.

"Let's see if Elijah will come and take him down!" he said.

37Then Jesus uttered another loud cry, and dismissed his spirit.

38And the curtain in the Temple was split apart from top to bottom.

39When the Roman officer standing beside his cross saw how he dismissed his spirit, he exclaimed, "Truly, this was the Son of God!"

40Some women were there watching from a distance— Mary Magdalene, Mary (the mother of James the Younger and of Joses), Salome, and others. 41They and many other Galilean women who were his followers had ministered to him when he was up in Galilee, and had come with him to Jerusalem.

42,43This all happened the day before the Sabbath. Late that afternoon Joseph from Arimathea, an honored member of the Jewish Supreme Court (who personally was eagerly expecting the arrival of God's Kingdom), gathered his courage and went to Pilate and asked for Jesus' body.

44Pilate couldn't believe that Jesus was already dead so he called for the Roman officer in charge and asked him. 45The officer confirmed the fact, and Pilate told Joseph he could have the body.

46Joseph bought a long sheet of linen cloth and, taking Jesus' body down from the cross, wound it in the cloth and laid it in a rock-hewn tomb, and rolled a stone in front of the entrance.

47(Mary Magdalene and Mary the mother of Joses were watching as Jesus was laid away.)

A THOUGHT: *After Jesus died on the cross, Joseph of Arimathea asked for his body and then sealed it in a new tomb. Although an honored member of the Jewish Supreme Court, Joseph was a secret disciple of Jesus. Not all the religious leaders hated Jesus. Joseph risked his reputation as a religious leader to give a proper burial to the One he followed. It is frightening to risk one's reputation even for what is right. If your Christian witness endangers your reputation, consider Joseph. Today he is well known in the Christian church. How many of the other members of the Jewish Supreme Court can you name?*

Paul's Confidence in the Corinthians/ 2 Corinthians 9:1–5

I realize that I really don't even need to mention this to you, about helping God's people. 2For I know how eager you are to do it, and I have boasted to the friends in Macedonia that you were ready to send an offering a year ago. In fact, it was this enthusiasm of yours that stirred up many of them to begin helping. 3But I am sending these men just to be sure that you really are ready, as I told them you would be, with your money all collected; I don't want it to turn out that this time I was wrong in my boasting about you. 4I would be very much ashamed—and so would you—if some of these Macedonian people come with me, only to find that you still aren't ready after all I have told them!

5So I have asked these other brothers to arrive ahead of me to see that the gift you promised is on hand and waiting. I want it to be a real gift and not look as if it were being given under pressure.

A THOUGHT: *The example of giving here was at the heart of Jewish piety, for they showed their godliness by sharing with the poor. Christians today have forgotten this central idea of true godly living, largely because it is not tax-deductible! Of course, giving to organizations is still important, but we are urged to fulfill this biblical mandate by helping the poor, whether or not it is tax-deductible.*

Proverbs for Today/ 14:26–27

Reverence for God gives a man deep strength; his children have a place of refuge and security. Reverence for the Lord is a fountain of life; its waters keep a man from death.

MAY 7

The Resurrection of Jesus/ Mark 16:1–20

The next evening, when the Sabbath ended, Mary Magdalene and Salome and Mary the mother of James went out and purchased embalming spices.

Early the following morning, just at sunrise, they carried them out to the tomb. 3On the way they were discussing how they could ever roll aside the huge stone from the entrance.

4But when they arrived they looked up and saw that the stone—a *very* heavy one—was already moved away and the entrance was open! 5So they entered the tomb—and there on the right sat a young man clothed in white. The women were startled, 6but the angel said, "Don't be so surprised. Aren't you looking for Jesus, the Nazarene who was crucified? He isn't here! He has come back to life! Look, that's where his body was lying. 7Now go and give this message to his disciples including Peter:

" 'Jesus is going ahead of you to Galilee. You will see him there, just as he told you before he died!' "

8The women fled from the tomb, trembling and bewildered, too frightened to talk.

9It was early on Sunday morning when Jesus came back to life, and the first person who saw him was Mary Magdalene—the woman from whom he had cast out seven demons. 10,11She found the disciples wet-eyed with grief and exclaimed that she had seen Jesus, and he was alive! But they didn't believe her!

12Later that day he appeared to two who were walking from Jerusalem into the country, but they didn't recognize him at first because he had changed his appearance. 13When they finally realized who he was, they rushed back to Jerusalem to tell the others, but no one believed them.

14Still later he appeared to the eleven disciples as they were eating together. He rebuked them for their unbelief—their stubborn refusal to believe those who had seen him alive from the dead.

15And then he told them, "You are to go into all the world and preach the Good News to everyone, everywhere. 16Those who believe and are baptized will be saved. But those who refuse to believe will be condemned.

17"And those who believe shall use my authority to cast out demons, and they shall speak new languages. 18They will be able even to handle snakes with safety, and if they drink anything poisonous, it won't hurt them; and they will be able to place their hands on the sick and heal them."

19When the Lord Jesus had finished talking with them, he was taken up into heaven and sat down at God's right hand.

20And the disciples went everywhere preaching, and the Lord was with them and confirmed what they said by the miracles that followed their messages.

A THOUGHT: *The resurrection is vitally important for many reasons: (1) Jesus kept his promise to rise from the dead, so we can believe he will keep all his other promises. (2) The resurrection ensures that the ruler of God's eternal Kingdom will be the living Christ, not just an idea, hope, or dream. (3) Christ rose from the dead, giving us the assurance that we also will be resurrected. (4) The power of God that brought Christ's body back from the dead is available to us to bring our morally and spiritually dead selves back to life so we can change and grow. (5) The resurrection provides the substance of the church's witness to the world. We do not merely tell lessons from the life of a good teacher; we proclaim the reality of the resurrection of Jesus Christ.*

God Prizes Cheerful Givers/ 2 Corinthians 9:6–15

But remember this—if you give little, you will get little. A farmer who plants just a few seeds will get only a small crop, but if he plants much, he will reap much. 7Every one must make up his own mind as to how much he should give. Don't force anyone to give more than he really wants to, for cheerful givers are the ones God prizes. 8God is able to make it up to you by giving you everything you need and more, so that there will not only be enough for your own needs, but plenty left over to give joyfully to others. 9It is as the Scriptures say: "The godly man gives generously to the poor. His good deeds will be an honor to him forever."

10For God, who gives seed to the farmer to plant, and later on, good crops to harvest and eat, will give you more and more seed to plant and will make it grow so that you can give away more and more fruit from your harvest.

11Yes, God will give you much so that you can give away much, and when we take your gifts to those who need them they will break out into thanksgiving and praise to God for your help. 12So, two good things happen as a result of your gifts—those in need are helped, and they overflow with thanks to God. 13Those you help will be glad not only because of your generous gifts to themselves and to others, but they will praise God for this proof that your deeds are as good as your doctrine. 14And they will pray for you with deep fervor and feeling because of the wonderful grace of God shown through you.

15Thank God for his Son—his Gift too wonderful for words.

A THOUGHT: *People may hesitate to give generously to God if they worry about having enough money left over to meet their own needs.*

Paul assured the Corinthians that God is able to meet their needs. The person who gives only a little will receive only a little in return. Don't let a lack of faith keep you from giving freely and generously out of a love and concern for others and a desire to further the work of God's Kingdom.

Proverbs for Today/ 14:28–29

A growing population is a king's glory; a dwindling nation is his doom. □ A wise man controls his temper. He knows that anger causes mistakes.

MAY 8

An Angel Predicts John the Baptist's Birth/ Luke 1:1--25

Dear friend who loves God:

1,2Several biographies of Christ have already been written using as their source material the reports circulating among us from the early disciples and other eyewitnesses. 3However, it occurred to me that it would be well to recheck all these accounts from first to last and after thorough investigation to pass this summary on to you, 4to reassure you of the truth of all you were taught.

5My story begins with a Jewish priest, Zacharias, who lived when Herod was king of Judea. Zacharias was a member of the Abijah division of the Temple service corps. (His wife Elizabeth was, like himself, a member of the priest tribe of the Jews, a descendant of Aaron.) 6Zacharias and Elizabeth were godly folk, careful to obey all of God's laws in spirit as well as in letter. 7But they had no children, for Elizabeth was barren; and now they were both very old.

8,9One day as Zacharias was going about his work in the Temple—for his division was on duty that week—the honor fell to him by lot to enter the inner sanctuary and burn incense before the Lord. 10Meanwhile, a great crowd stood outside in the Temple court, praying as they always did during that part of the service when the incense was being burned.

11,12Zacharias was in the sanctuary when suddenly an angel appeared, standing to the right of the altar of incense! Zacharias was startled and terrified.

13But the angel said, "Don't be afraid, Zacharias! For I have come to tell you that God has heard your prayer, and your wife Elizabeth will bear you a son! And you are to name him John. 14You will both have great joy and gladness at his birth, and many will rejoice with you. 15For he will be one of the Lord's great men. He must never touch wine or hard liquor—and he will be filled with the Holy Spirit, even from before his birth! 16And he will persuade many a Jew to turn to the Lord his God. 17He will be a man of rugged spirit and power like Elijah, the prophet of old; and he will precede the coming of the Messiah, preparing the people for his arrival. He will soften adult hearts to become like little children's, and will change disobedient minds to the wisdom of faith."

18Zacharias said to the angel, "But this is impossible! I'm an old man now, and my wife is also well along in years."

19Then the angel said, "I am Gabriel! I stand in the very presence of God. It was he who sent me to you with this good news! 20And now, because you haven't believed me, you are to be stricken silent, unable to speak until the child is born. For my words will certainly come true at the proper time."

21Meanwhile the crowds outside were waiting for Zacharias to appear and wondered why he was taking so long. 22When he finally came out, he couldn't speak to them, and they realized from his gestures that he must have seen a vision in the Temple. 23He stayed on at the Temple for the remaining days of his Temple duties and then returned home. 24Soon afterwards Elizabeth his wife became pregnant and went into seclusion for five months.

25"How kind the Lord is," she exclaimed, "to take away my disgrace of having no children!"

A THOUGHT: *Zacharias, while offering incense on the altar, was also praying, perhaps for a son or for the coming of the Messiah. In either case, his prayer was answered. He would soon have a son who would prepare the way for the Messiah. God answers prayer in his own way and in his own time. He worked in an "impossible" situation—Zacharias' wife was barren—to bring about the fulfillment of all the prophecies concerning the coming of the*

Messiah. If we want to have our prayers answered, we must be open to what God can do in impossible situations. And we must wait for him to work in his way, in his time.

God's Mighty Weapons/ 2 Corinthians 10:1–6

I plead with you—yes, I, Paul—and I plead gently, as Christ himself would do. Yet some of you are saying, "Paul's letters are bold enough when he is far away, but when he gets here he will be afraid to raise his voice!"

2I hope I won't need to show you when I come how harsh and rough I can be. I don't want to carry out my present plans against some of you who seem to think my deeds and words are merely those of an ordinary man. 3It is true that I am an ordinary, weak human being, but I don't use human plans and methods to win my battles. 4I use God's mighty weapons, not those made by men, to knock down the devil's strongholds. 5These weapons can break down every proud argument against God and every wall that can be built to keep men from finding him. With these weapons I can capture rebels and bring them back to God, and change them into men whose hearts' desire is obedience to Christ. 6I will use these weapons against every rebel who remains after I have first used them on you yourselves, and you surrender to Christ.

A THOUGHT: *The Christian must choose whose methods to use, God's or man's. Paul assures us that God's mighty weapons— prayer, faith, hope, love, God's Word—are powerful and effective! When dealing with the pride that keeps people from a relationship with Christ, we may be tempted to use our own methods. But nothing can break down these barriers like God's weapons.*

Proverbs for Today/ 14:30–31

A relaxed attitude lengthens a man's life; jealousy rots it away. □ Anyone who oppresses the poor is insulting God who made them. To help the poor is to honor God.

MAY 9

Jesus' Birth Foretold to Mary/ Luke 1:26–56

The following month God sent the angel Gabriel to Nazareth, a village in Galilee, 27to a virgin, Mary, engaged to be married to a man named Joseph, a descendant of King David.

28Gabriel appeared to her and said, "Congratulations, favored lady! The Lord is with you!"

29Confused and disturbed, Mary tried to think what the angel could mean.

30"Don't be frightened, Mary," the angel told her, "for God has decided to wonderfully bless you! 31Very soon now, you will become pregnant and have a baby boy, and you are to name him 'Jesus.' 32He shall be very great and shall be called the Son of God. And the Lord God shall give him the throne of his ancestor David. 33And he shall reign over Israel forever; his Kingdom shall never end!"

34Mary asked the angel, "But how can I have a baby? I am a virgin."

35The angel replied, "The Holy Spirit shall come upon you, and the power of God shall overshadow you; so the baby born to you will be utterly holy—the Son of God. 36Furthermore, six months ago your Aunt Elizabeth— 'the barren one,' they called her—became pregnant in her old age! 37For every promise from God shall surely come true."

38Mary said, "I am the Lord's servant, and I am willing to do whatever he wants. May everything you said come true." And then the angel disappeared.

39,40A few days later Mary hurried to the highlands of Judea to the town where Zacharias lived, to visit Elizabeth.

41At the sound of Mary's greeting, Elizabeth's child leaped within her and she was filled with the Holy Spirit.

42She gave a glad cry and exclaimed to Mary, "You are favored by God above all other women, and your child is destined for God's mightiest praise. 43What an honor this is, that the mother of my Lord should visit me! 44When you came in and greeted me, the instant I heard your voice, my baby moved in me for joy! 45You believed that God would do what he said; that is why he has given you this wonderful blessing."

46Mary responded, "Oh, how I praise the Lord. 47How I rejoice in God my Savior! 48For he took notice of his lowly servant girl, and now generation after generation forever shall call me blest of God. 49For he, the mighty Holy One, has done great things to me. 50His mercy goes on from generation to generation, to all who reverence him.

51"How powerful is his mighty arm! How he scatters the proud and haughty ones! 52He has torn princes from their thrones and exalted the lowly. 53He has satisfied the hungry hearts and sent the rich away with empty hands. 54And how he has helped his servant Israel! He has not forgotten his promise to be merciful. 55For he promised our fathers—Abraham and his children—to be merciful to them forever."

56Mary stayed with Elizabeth about three months and then went back to her own home.

A THOUGHT: *A young unmarried girl who became pregnant risked disaster. Unless the father of the child agreed to marry her, she would probably remain unmarried for life. If her own father rejected her, she could be forced into begging or prostitution in order to earn her living. And Mary, with her story about being made pregnant by the Holy Spirit, risked being considered crazy as well. Still she said, despite the possible costs, "I am willing." When Mary said that, she didn't know about the tremendous blessing she would receive. She only knew God was asking her to serve him, and she willingly obeyed. Don't wait to see the bottom line before offering your life to God. Offer yourself willingly, even when the results of doing so look disastrous.*

The Shallow Vision of the Corinthians/
2 Corinthians 10:7–12

The trouble with you is that you look at me and I seem weak and powerless, but you don't look beneath the surface. Yet if anyone can claim the power and authority of Christ, I certainly can. 8I may seem to be boasting more than I should about my authority over you—authority to help you, not to hurt you—but I shall make good every claim. 9I say this so that you will not think I am just blustering when I scold you in my letters.

10"Don't bother about his letters," some say. "He sounds big, but it's all noise. When he gets here you will see that there is nothing great about him, and you have never heard a worse preacher!" 11This time my personal presence is going to be just as rough on you as my letters are!

12Oh, don't worry, I wouldn't dare say that I am as wonderful as these other men who tell you how good they are! Their trouble is that they are only comparing themselves with each other, and measuring themselves against their own little ideas. What stupidity!

A THOUGHT: *Paul criticized the false teachers who tried to prove their goodness by comparing themselves with others rather than with God. When we compare ourselves with others, we may feel proud because we think we're better. But when we measure ourselves against God's standards, it becomes obvious that we're not nearly good enough. Don't worry about how other people live. Instead, continually ask how your life measures up to what God wants you to be and how your life compares to that of Jesus Christ.*

Proverbs for Today/ 14:32–33

The godly have a refuge when they die, but the wicked are crushed by their sins. ▢ Wisdom is enshrined in the hearts of men of common sense, but it must shout loudly before fools will hear it.

MAY 10

The Birth of John the Baptist/ Luke 1:57–80

By now Elizabeth's waiting was over, for the time had come for the baby to be born—and it was a boy. 58The word spread quickly to her neighbors and relatives of how kind the Lord had been to her, and everyone rejoiced.

59When the baby was eight days old, all the relatives and friends came for the circumcision ceremony. They all assumed the baby's name would be Zacharias, after his father.

60But Elizabeth said, "No! He must be named John!"

61"What?" they exclaimed. "There is no one in all your family by that name." 62So they asked the baby's father, talking to him by gestures.

63He motioned for a piece of paper and to everyone's surprise wrote, "His name is *John!*" 64Instantly Zacharias could speak again, and he began praising God.

65Wonder fell upon the whole neighborhood, and the news of what had happened spread through the Judean hills. 66And everyone who heard about it thought long thoughts and asked, "I wonder what this child will turn out to be? For the hand of the Lord is surely upon him in some special way."

67Then his father Zacharias was filled with the Holy Spirit and gave this prophecy:

68"Praise the Lord, the God of Israel, for he has come to visit his people and has redeemed them. 69He is sending us a Mighty Savior from the royal line of his servant David, 70just as he promised through his holy prophets long ago— 71someone to save us from our enemies, from all who hate us.

72,73"He has been merciful to our ancestors, yes, to Abraham himself, by remembering his sacred promise to him, 74and by granting us the privilege of serving God fearlessly, freed from our enemies, 75and by making us holy and acceptable, ready to stand in his presence forever.

76"And you, my little son, shall be called the prophet of the glorious God, for you will prepare the way for the Messiah. 77You will tell his people how to find salvation through forgiveness of their sins. 78All this will be because the mercy of our God is very tender, and heaven's dawn is about to break upon us, 79to give light to those who sit in darkness and death's shadow, and to guide us to the path of peace."

80The little boy greatly loved God and when he grew up he lived out in the lonely wilderness until he began his public ministry to Israel.

A THOUGHT: *Zacharias praised God with his first words after months of silence. In a song that is often called the Benedictus, after its first words in the Latin translation of this passage, Zacharias prophesied the coming of a Savior who would redeem his people, and he predicted that his son John would prepare the Messiah's way. All the Old Testament prophecies were coming true—no wonder Zacharias praised God! The Messiah would come in his lifetime, and his son had been chosen to pave the way.*

Boast in the Lord/ 2 Corinthians 10:13–18

But we will not boast of authority we do not have. Our goal is to measure up to God's plan for us, and this plan includes our working there with you. 14We are not going too far when we claim authority over you, for we were the first to come to you with the Good News concerning Christ. 15It is not as though we were trying to claim credit for the work someone else has done among you. Instead, we hope that your faith will grow and that, still within the limits set for us, our work among you will be greatly enlarged.

16After that, we will be able to preach the Good News to other cities that are far beyond you, where no one else is working; then there will be no question about being in someone else's field. 17As the Scriptures say, "If anyone is going to boast, let him boast about what the Lord has done and not about himself." 18When someone boasts about himself and how well he has done, it doesn't count for much. But when the Lord commends him, that's different!

A THOUGHT: *When we do something well, we want to tell others and be recognized. But recognition is dangerous—it can lead to inflated pride. How much better to seek the praise of God rather than people. Interestingly, these two are usually opposites. To earn God's praise means giving up the praise of others. How should you live differently to receive God's commendation?*

Proverbs for Today/ 14:34–35

Godliness exalts a nation, but sin is a reproach to any people. □ A king rejoices in servants who know what they are doing; he is angry with those who cause trouble.

MAY 11

Jesus Is Born in Bethlehem/ Luke 2:1–20

About this time Caesar Augustus, the Roman Emperor, decreed that a census should be taken throughout the nation. 2(This census was taken when Quirinius was governor of Syria.)

3Everyone was required to return to his ancestral home for this registration. 4And because Joseph was a member of the royal line, he had to go to Bethlehem in Judea, King David's ancient home—journeying there from the

Galilean village of Nazareth. 5He took with him Mary, his fiancée, who was obviously pregnant by this time.

6And while they were there, the time came for her baby to be born; 7and she gave birth to her first child, a son. She wrapped him in a blanket and laid him in a manger, because there was no room for them in the village inn.

8That night some shepherds were in the fields outside the village, guarding their flocks of sheep. 9Suddenly an angel appeared among them, and the landscape shone bright with the glory of the Lord. They were badly frightened, 10but the angel reassured them.

"Don't be afraid!" he said. "I bring you the most joyful news ever announced, and it is for everyone! 11The Savior—yes, the Messiah, the Lord—has been born tonight in Bethlehem! 12How will you recognize him? You will find a baby wrapped in a blanket, lying in a manger!"

13Suddenly, the angel was joined by a vast host of others—the armies of heaven—praising God:

14"Glory to God in the highest heaven," they sang, "and peace on earth for all those pleasing him."

15When this great army of angels had returned again to heaven, the shepherds said to each other, "Come on! Let's go to Bethlehem! Let's see this wonderful thing that has happened, which the Lord has told us about."

16They ran to the village and found their way to Mary and Joseph. And there was the baby, lying in the manger. 17The shepherds told everyone what had happened and what the angel had said to them about this child. 18All who heard the shepherds' story expressed astonishment, 19but Mary quietly treasured these things in her heart and often thought about them.

20Then the shepherds went back again to their fields and flocks, praising God for the visit of the angels, and because they had seen the child, just as the angel had told them.

A Thought: *The greatest event in history had just happened! The Messiah was born! For ages the Jews had waited for this, and when it finally happened, the announcement came to humble shepherds. The good news about Jesus is that he comes to all, including the plain and the ordinary. He comes to anyone with a heart humble enough to accept him. Whoever you are, whatever you do, you can have Jesus in your life. Don't think you need extraordinary qualifications—he accepts you as you are.*

Paul's Concern for the Corinthians/ 2 Corinthians 11:1–6

I hope you will be patient with me as I keep on talking like a fool. Do bear with me and let me say what is on my heart. 2I am anxious for you with the deep concern of God himself—anxious that your love should be for Christ alone, just as a pure maiden saves her love for one man only, for the one who will be her husband. 3But I am frightened, fearing that in some way you will be led away from your pure and simple devotion to our Lord, just as Eve was deceived by Satan in the Garden of Eden. 4You seem so gullible: you believe whatever anyone tells you even if he is preaching about another Jesus than the one we preach, or a different spirit than the Holy Spirit you received, or shows you a different way to be saved. You swallow it all.

5Yet I don't feel that these marvelous "messengers from God," as they call themselves, are any better than I am. 6If I am a poor speaker, at least I know what I am talking about, as I think you realize by now, for we have proved it again and again.

A THOUGHT: *The Corinthians' pure and simple devotion to Christ was being threatened by false teaching. Paul did not want the believers to lose their single–minded love for Christ. Keeping Christ first in our lives can be very difficult when we have so many distractions threatening to sidetrack our faith. As Eve lost her focus by listening to the serpent, we too can lose our focus by letting our lives become overcrowded and confused. Is there anything that threatens your ability to keep Christ first in your life? How can you minimize the distractions that threaten your devotion to Christ?*

Proverbs for Today/ 15:1–3

A gentle answer turns away wrath, but harsh words cause quarrels. □ A wise teacher makes learning a joy; a rebellious teacher spouts foolishness. □ The Lord is watching everywhere and keeps his eye on both the evil and the good.

Simeon and Anna Recognize Jesus as the Messiah/
Luke 2:21–40

Eight days later, at the baby's circumcision ceremony, he was named Jesus, the name given him by the angel before he was even conceived.

22When the time came for Mary's purification offering at the Temple, as required by the laws of Moses after the birth of a child, his parents took him to Jerusalem to present him to the Lord; 23for in these laws God had said, "If a woman's first child is a boy, he shall be dedicated to the Lord."

24At that time Jesus' parents also offered their sacrifice for purification—"either a pair of turtledoves or two young pigeons" was the legal requirement. 25That day a man named Simeon, a Jerusalem resident, was in the Temple. He was a good man, very devout, filled with the Holy Spirit and constantly expecting the Messiah to come soon. 26For the Holy Spirit had revealed to him that he would not die until he had seen him—God's anointed King. 27The Holy Spirit had impelled him to go to the Temple that day; and so, when Mary and Joseph arrived to present the baby Jesus to the Lord in obedience to the law, 28Simeon was there and took the child in his arms, praising God.

29,30,31"Lord," he said, "now I can die content! For I have seen him as you promised me I would. I have seen the Savior you have given to the world. 32He is the Light that will shine upon the nations, and he will be the glory of your people Israel!"

33Joseph and Mary just stood there, marveling at what was being said about Jesus.

34,35Simeon blessed them but then said to Mary, "A sword shall pierce your soul, for this child shall be rejected by many in Israel, and this to their undoing. But he will be the greatest joy of many others. And the deepest thoughts of many hearts shall be revealed."

36,37Anna, a prophetess, was also there in the Temple that day. She was the daughter of Phanuel, of the Jewish tribe of Asher, and was very old, for she had been a widow for eighty-four years following seven years of marriage. She never left the Temple but stayed there night and day, worshiping God by praying and often fasting.

38She came along just as Simeon was talking with Mary and Joseph, and she also began thanking God and telling everyone in Jerusalem who had been awaiting the coming of the Savior that the Messiah had finally arrived.

39When Jesus' parents had fulfilled all the requirements of the Law of God they returned home to Nazareth in Galilee. 40There the child became a strong, robust lad, and was known for wisdom beyond his years; and God poured out his blessings on him.

A THOUGHT: *Although Simeon and Anna were very old, they still hoped to see the Messiah. Led by the Holy Spirit, they were among the first to bear witness to Jesus. In the Jewish culture, elders were respected, and Simeon's and Anna's prophecies carried extra weight because they were not young. Our society, however, values youthfulness over wisdom, and potential contributions by the elderly are often ignored. As Christians, we should reverse those values wherever we can. Encourage older people to share their wisdom and experience. Listen carefully when they speak. Offer them your friendship and help them find ways to continue to serve God.*

True and False Apostleship/ 2 Corinthians 11:7–15

Did I do wrong and cheapen myself and make you look down on me because I preached God's Good News to you without charging you anything? 8,9Instead I "robbed" other churches by taking what they sent me, and using it up while I was with you, so that I could serve you without cost. And when that was gone and I was getting hungry I still didn't ask you for anything, for the Christians from Macedonia brought me another gift. I have never yet asked you for one cent, and I never will. 10I promise this with every ounce of truth I possess—that I will tell everyone in Greece about it! 11Why? Because I don't love you? God knows I do. 12But I will do it to cut out the ground from under the feet of those who boast that they are doing God's work in just the same way we are.

13God never sent those men at all; they are "phonies" who have fooled you into thinking they are Christ's apostles. 14Yet I am not surprised! Satan can change himself into an angel of light, 15so it is no wonder his servants can do it too, and seem like godly ministers. In the end they will get every bit of punishment their wicked deeds deserve.

A THOUGHT: *The Corinthians may have thought that preachers could be judged by how much money they demanded. A good speaker would charge a large sum, a fair speaker would be a little cheaper, and a poor speaker would speak for free. The false teachers may have argued that because Paul asked no fee for his preaching, he must be an amateur, with little authority. Believers today must be careful not to assume that every speaker who is well known and receives large sums of money has something valuable to say. Don't be fooled by external appearances. Our impressions alone are not an accurate indicator of who is or isn't a true follower of Christ. It helps to ask these questions: (1) Do their teachings confirm Scripture? (2) Do the teachers affirm and proclaim that Jesus Christ is God who came into the world as a man to save people from their sins? (3) Is their lifestyle consistent with biblical morality?*

Proverbs for Today/ 15:4

Gentle words cause life and health; griping brings discouragement.

MAY 13

Jesus with the Teachers of the Law/ Luke 2:41–52

When Jesus was twelve years old he accompanied his parents to Jerusalem for the annual Passover Festival, which they attended each year. 43After the celebration was over they started home to Nazareth, but Jesus stayed behind in Jerusalem. His parents didn't miss him the first day, 44for they assumed he was with friends among the other travelers. But when he didn't show up that evening, they started to look for him among their relatives and friends; 45and when they couldn't find him, they went back to Jerusalem to search for him there.

46,47Three days later they finally discovered him. He was in the Temple, sitting among the teachers of Law, discussing deep questions with them and amazing everyone with his understanding and answers.

48His parents didn't know what to think. "Son!" his mother said to him. "Why have you done this to us? Your father and I have been frantic, searching for you everywhere."

⁴⁹"But why did you need to search?" he asked. "Didn't you realize that I would be here at the Temple, in my Father's House?" ⁵⁰But they didn't understand what he meant.

⁵¹Then he returned to Nazareth with them and was obedient to them; and his mother stored away all these things in her heart. ⁵²So Jesus grew both tall and wise, and was loved by God and man.

A THOUGHT: *At age 12, Jesus was considered almost an adult, and so he didn't spend a lot of time with his parents during the festival. Those who attended these festivals often traveled in caravans for protection from robbers along the roads throughout Israel. It was customary for the women and children to travel at the front of the caravan, with the men bringing up the rear. A 12–year–old boy could have been in either group, and Mary and Joseph assumed Jesus was with the others. But when the caravan left Jerusalem, Jesus stayed behind, absorbed in his discussion with the religious leaders, amazing them with his wisdom.*

Suffering for Christ—Paul's Validation of Apostleship/ 2 Corinthians 11:16–33

Again I plead, don't think that I have lost my wits to talk like this; but even if you do, listen to me anyway—a witless man, a fool—while I also boast a little as they do. ¹⁷Such bragging isn't something the Lord commanded me to do, for I am acting like a brainless fool. ¹⁸Yet those other men keep telling you how wonderful they are, so here I go: ¹⁹,²⁰(You think you are so wise—yet you listen gladly to those fools; you don't mind at all when they make you their slaves and take everything you have, and take advantage of you, and put on airs, and slap you in the face. ²¹I'm ashamed to say that I'm not strong and daring like that!

But whatever they can boast about—I'm talking like a fool again—I can boast about it, too.)

²²They brag that they are Hebrews, do they? Well, so am I. And they say that they are Israelites, God's chosen people? So am I. And they are descendants of Abraham? Well, I am too.

²³They say they serve Christ? But I have served him far more! (Have I gone mad to boast like this?) I have worked harder, been put in jail oftener, been whipped times without number, and faced death again and again

and again. 24 Five different times the Jews gave me their terrible thirty-nine lashes. 25Three times I was beaten with rods. Once I was stoned. Three times I was shipwrecked. Once I was in the open sea all night and the whole next day. 26I have traveled many weary miles and have been often in great danger from flooded rivers, and from robbers, and from my own people, the Jews, as well as from the hands of the Gentiles. I have faced grave dangers from mobs in the cities and from death in the deserts and in the stormy seas and from men who claim to be brothers in Christ but are not. 27I have lived with weariness and pain and sleepless nights. Often I have been hungry and thirsty and have gone without food; often I have shivered with cold, without enough clothing to keep me warm.

28Then, besides all this, I have the constant worry of how the churches are getting along: 29Who makes a mistake and I do not feel his sadness? Who falls without my longing to help him? Who is spiritually hurt without my fury rising against the one who hurt him?

30But if I must brag, I would rather brag about the things that show how weak I am. 31God, the Father of our Lord Jesus Christ, who is to be praised forever and ever, knows I tell the truth. 32For instance, in Damascus the governor under King Aretas kept guards at the city gates to catch me; 33but I was let down by rope and basket from a hole in the city wall, and so I got away! [What popularity!]

A THOUGHT: *Paul was angry that the false teachers had impressed and deceived the Corinthians. He had to reestablish his credibility and authority by listing the trials he had endured in his service for Christ. These trials showed that he was sacrificing his life for the gospel, something the false teachers would never do. The trials and hurts you have experienced for Christ's sake have built your character, demonstrated your faith, and prepared you to work for the Lord.*

Proverbs for Today/ 15:5–7

Only a fool despises his father's advice; a wise son considers each suggestion. □ There is treasure in being good, but trouble dogs the wicked. □ Only the good can give good advice. Rebels can't.

MAY 14

John the Baptist Warns of Coming Judgment/ Luke 3:1–18

In the fifteenth year of the reign of Emperor Tiberius Caesar, a message came from God to John (the son of Zacharias), as he was living out in the deserts. (Pilate was governor over Judea at that time; Herod, over Galilee; his brother Philip, over Iturea and Trachonitis; Lysanias, over Abilene; and Annas and Caiaphas were High Priests.) 3Then John went from place to place on both sides of the Jordan River, preaching that people should be baptized to show that they had turned to God and away from their sins, in order to be forgiven.

4In the words of Isaiah the prophet, John was "a voice shouting from the barren wilderness, 'Prepare a road for the Lord to travel on! Widen the pathway before him! 5Level the mountains! Fill up the valleys! Straighten the curves! Smooth out the ruts! 6And then all mankind shall see the Savior sent from God.' "

7Here is a sample of John's preaching to the crowds that came for baptism: "You brood of snakes! You are trying to escape hell without truly turning to God! That is why you want to be baptized! 8First go and prove by the way you live that you really have repented. And don't think you are safe because you are descendants of Abraham. That isn't enough. God can produce children of Abraham from these desert stones! 9The axe of his judgment is poised over you, ready to sever your roots and cut you down. Yes, every tree that does not produce good fruit will be chopped down and thrown into the fire."

10The crowd replied, "What do you want us to do?"

11"If you have two coats," he replied, "give one to the poor. If you have extra food, give it away to those who are hungry."

12Even tax collectors—notorious for their corruption— came to be baptized and asked, "How shall we prove to you that we have abandoned our sins?"

13"By your honesty," he replied. "Make sure you collect no more taxes than the Roman government requires you to."

14"And us," asked some soldiers, "what about us?"

John replied, "Don't extort money by threats and violence; don't accuse anyone of what you know he didn't do; and be content with your pay!"

15Everyone was expecting the Messiah to come soon, and eager to know whether or not John was he. This was the question of the hour, and was being discussed everywhere.

16John answered the question by saying, "I baptize only with water; but someone is coming soon who has far higher authority than mine; in fact, I am not even worthy of being his slave. He will baptize you with fire—with the Holy Spirit. 17He will separate chaff from grain, and burn up the chaff with eternal fire and store away the grain." 18He used many such warnings as he announced the Good News to the people.

A THOUGHT: *Repentance has two sides—turning away from sins, and turning toward God. To be forgiven, we must do both. We can't just say we believe and then live any way we want to, neither can we simply live a morally correct life without reference to God, because that alone cannot bring forgiveness from sin. Faith and works are inseparable. Faith without works is a lifeless faith. Jesus' harshest words were to the respectable religious leaders who lacked true faith. Repentance must be tied to action, or it isn't real. Is the fruit of your faith ripening as your faith grows, or is it rotting as you fail to act upon what God shows you?*

God's Grace Is Sufficient/ 2 Corinthians 12:1–10

This boasting is all so foolish, but let me go on. Let me tell about the visions I've had, and revelations from the Lord.

2,3Fourteen years ago I was taken up to heaven for a visit. Don't ask me whether my body was there or just my spirit, for I don't know; only God can answer that. But anyway, there I was in paradise, 4and heard things so astounding that they are beyond a man's power to describe or put in words (and anyway I am not allowed to tell them to others). 5That experience is something worth bragging about, but I am not going to do it. I am going to boast only about how weak I am and how great God is to use such weakness for his glory. 6I have plenty to boast about and would be no fool in doing it, but I don't want anyone to think more highly of me than he should from what he can actually see in my life and my message.

7I will say this: because these experiences I had were so tremendous, God was afraid I might be puffed up by them; so I was given a physical condition which has been a thorn in my flesh, a messenger from Satan to hurt and bother me, and prick my pride. 8Three different times I begged God to make me well again.

9Each time he said, "No. But I am with you; that is all you need. My power shows up best in weak people." Now I am glad to boast about how weak I am; I am glad to be a living demonstration of Christ's power, instead of showing off my own power and abilities. 10Since I know it is all for Christ's good, I am quite happy about "the thorn," and about insults and hardships, persecutions and difficulties; for when I am weak, then I am strong—the less I have, the more I depend on him.

A THOUGHT: *Although God did not remove Paul's physical affliction, he promised to demonstrate his power in Paul. The fact that God's power shows up in weak people should give us courage. When we are strong in abilities or resources, we are tempted to do God's work on our own, and that leads to pride. We must rely on God for our effectiveness rather than on our own energy, effort, or talent. Our weakness not only helps develop Christian character, it also deepens our worship. For in admitting our weakness, we affirm God's strength. When we are weak, when we allow God to fill us with his power, then we are stronger than we could ever be on our own. We must depend on God—only his power makes us effective for him and does work that has lasting value.*

Proverbs for Today/ 15:8–10
The Lord hates the gifts of the wicked, but delights in the prayers of his people. The Lord despises the deeds of the wicked, but loves those who try to be good. If they stop trying, the Lord will punish them; if they rebel against that punishment, they will die.

MAY 15

The Baptism of Jesus/ Luke 3:19–23a
(But after John had publicly criticized Herod, governor of Galilee, for marrying Herodias, his brother's wife, and

for many other wrongs he had done, Herod put John in prison, thus adding this sin to all his many others.)

21Then one day, after the crowds had been baptized, Jesus himself was baptized; and as he was praying, the heavens opened, 22and the Holy Spirit in the form of a dove settled upon him, and a voice from heaven said, "You are my much loved Son, yes, my delight."

23Jesus was about thirty years old when he began his public ministry.

A THOUGHT: *Luke emphasizes Jesus' humanness. He came to humble parents, unannounced except to shepherds and foreigners. This baptism was the first public declaration of his ministry. Instead of going to Jerusalem and identifying with the established religious leaders, Jesus went to a river and identified himself with those who were repenting of sin. When Jesus, at age 12, visited the Temple, he understood his mission. Eighteen years later, at his baptism, he began carrying it out. And as he prayed, God spoke to him and confirmed his decision to act. God broke into human history in Jesus Christ.*

Paul's Sacrifice for His Children/
2 Corinthians 12:11–15

You have made me act like a fool—boasting like this—for you people ought to be writing about me and not making me write about myself. There isn't a single thing these other marvelous fellows have that I don't have too, even though I am really worth nothing at all. 12When I was there I certainly gave you every proof that I was truly an apostle, sent to you by God himself: for I patiently did many wonders and signs and mighty works among you. 13The only thing I didn't do for you, that I do everywhere else in all other churches, was to become a burden to you—I didn't ask you to give me food to eat and a place to stay. Please forgive me for this wrong!

14Now I am coming to you again, the third time; and it is still not going to cost you anything, for I don't want your money. I want *you!* And anyway, you are my children, and little children don't pay for their father's and mother's food—it's the other way around; parents supply food for their children. 15I am glad to give you myself and all I have for your spiritual good, even though it seems that the more I love you, the less you love me.

A Thought: *Paul is not merely revealing his feelings, but defending his authority as an apostle of Jesus Christ. He was hurt that the church in Corinth was doubting and questioning him, but he was defending himself for the cause of the gospel, not to satisfy his ego. When you are "put on trial," do you think only about saving your reputation or are you more concerned about what people will think about Christ?*

Proverbs for Today/ 15:11

The depths of hell are open to God's knowledge. How much more the hearts of all mankind!

MAY 16

The Genealogy of Jesus/ Luke 3:23b–38

Jesus was known as the son of Joseph.
Joseph's father was Heli;
Heli's father was Matthat;
Matthat's father was Levi;
Levi's father was Melchi;
Melchi's father was Jannai;
Jannai's father was Joseph;
Joseph's father was Mattathias;
Mattathias' father was Amos;
Amos' father was Nahum;
Nahum's father was Esli;
Esli's father was Naggai;
Naggai's father was Maath;
Maath's father was Mattathias;
Mattathias' father was Semein;
Semein's father was Josech;
Josech's father was Joda;
Joda's father was Joanan;
Joanan's father was Rhesa;
Rhesa's father was Zerubbabel;
Zerubbabel's father was Shealtiel;
Shealtiel's father was Neri;
Neri's father was Melchi;
Melchi's father was Addi;

Addi's father was Cosam;
Cosam's father was Elmadam;
Elmadam's father was Er;
Er's father was Joshua;
Joshua's father was Eliezer;
Eliezer's father was Jorim;
Jorim's father was Matthat;
Matthat's father was Levi;
Levi's father was Simeon;
Simeon's father was Judah;
Judah's father was Joseph;
Joseph's father was Jonam;
Jonam's father was Eliakim;
Eliakim's father was Melea;
Melea's father was Menna;
Menna's father was Mattatha;
Mattatha's father was Nathan;
Nathan's father was David;
David's father was Jesse;
Jesse's father was Obed;
Obed's father was Boaz;
Boaz' father was Salmon;
Salmon's father was Nahshon;
Nahshon's father was Amminadab;
Amminadab's father was Admin;
Admin's father was Arni;
Arni's father was Hezron;
Hezron's father was Perez;
Perez' father was Judah;
Judah's father was Jacob;
Jacob's father was Isaac;
Isaac's father was Abraham;
Abraham's father was Terah;
Terah's father was Nahor;
Nahor's father was Serug;
Serug's father was Reu;
Reu's father was Peleg;
Peleg's father was Eber;
Eber's father was Shelah;
Shelah's father was Cainan;
Cainan's father was Arphaxad;
Arphaxad's father was Shem;

Shem's father was Noah;
Noah's father was Lamech;
Lamech's father was Methuselah;
Methuselah's father was Enoch;
Enoch's father was Jared;
Jared's father was Mahalaleel;
Mahalaleel's father was Cainan;
Cainan's father was Enos;
Enos's father was Seth;
Seth's father was Adam;
Adam's father was God.

A THOUGHT: *Here Jesus' genealogy is traced back through Mary. The genealogy recorded in Matthew 1:1–17 traces his line through Joseph, his legal, but not biological father. Matthew's genealogy goes back to Abraham and shows that Jesus was related to all Jews. Luke's goes back to Adam, showing he is related to all human beings. This is consistent with Luke's picture of Jesus as the Savior of the whole world.*

Paul Fears Another Sorrowful Visit/ 2 Corinthians 12:16–21

Some of you are saying, "It's true that his visits didn't seem to cost us anything, but he is a sneaky fellow, that Paul, and he fooled us. As sure as anything he must have made money from us some way."

17But how? Did any of the men I sent to you take advantage of you? 18When I urged Titus to visit you, and sent our other brother with him, did they make any profit? No, of course not. For we have the same Holy Spirit, and walk in each other's steps, doing things the same way.

19I suppose you think I am saying all this to get back into your good graces. That isn't it at all. I tell you, with God listening as I say it, that I have said this to help *you*, dear friends—to build you up spiritually and not to help myself. 20For I am afraid that when I come to visit you I won't like what I find, and then you won't like the way I will have to act. I am afraid that I will find you quarreling, and envying each other, and being angry with each other, and acting big, and saying wicked things about each other and whispering behind each other's backs, filled with conceit and disunity. 21Yes, I am afraid that when I come God will humble me before you and I will be sad and mourn because many of you who have sinned became sinners and don't even care about the wicked, impure things you have done: your lust and immorality, and the taking of other men's wives.

A THOUGHT: *After reading this catalog of sins, it is hard to believe that Paul is referring to the same group of people which he described as having "every spiritual gift and power for doing his will" (1 Corinthians 1:7). Paul feared that the practices of wicked Corinth had invaded the congregation, and he wrote sternly in hope that they would straighten up their lives before he arrived. We must live differently than unbelievers, not letting secular society dictate how we are to treat others.*

Proverbs for Today/ 15:12–14

A mocker stays away from wise men because he hates to be scolded. □ A happy face means a glad heart; a sad face means a breaking heart. □ A wise man is hungry for truth, while the mocker feeds on trash.

MAY 17

Jesus Is Tempted by Satan/ Luke 4:1–13

Then Jesus, full of the Holy Spirit, left the Jordan River, being urged by the Spirit out into the barren wastelands of Judea, where Satan tempted him for forty days. He ate nothing all that time, and was very hungry.

3Satan said, "If you are God's Son, tell this stone to become a loaf of bread."

4But Jesus replied, "It is written in the Scriptures, 'Other things in life are much more important than bread!' "

5Then Satan took him up and revealed to him all the kingdoms of the world in a moment of time; 6,7and the devil told him, "I will give you all these splendid kingdoms and their glory—for they are mine to give to anyone I wish—if you will only get down on your knees and worship me."

8Jesus replied, "We must worship God, and him alone. So it is written in the Scriptures."

9,10,11Then Satan took him to Jerusalem to a high roof

of the Temple and said, "If you are the Son of God, jump off! For the Scriptures say that God will send his angels to guard you and to keep you from crashing to the pavement below!"

12Jesus replied, "The Scriptures also say, 'Do not put the Lord your God to a foolish test.'"

13When the devil had ended all the temptations, he left Jesus for a while and went away.

A THOUGHT: *Knowing and obeying God's Word is an effective weapon against temptation. Jesus used Scripture to counter Satan's attacks, and you can too. But to use it effectively you must have faith in God's promises, because Satan also knows Scripture and is adept at twisting it to suit his purpose. Obeying the Scriptures is more important than simply having a verse to quote, so read them daily and apply them to your life. Then your "sword" will always be sharp.*

Paul's Warnings/ 2 Corinthians 13:1–6

This is the third time I am coming to visit you. The Scriptures tell us that if two or three have seen a wrong, it must be punished. [Well, this is my third warning, as I come now for this visit.] 2I have already warned those who had been sinning when I was there last; now I warn them again, and all others, just as I did then, that this time I come ready to punish severely and I will not spare them.

3I will give you all the proof you want that Christ speaks through me. Christ is not weak in his dealings with you, but is a mighty power within you. 4His weak, human body died on the cross, but now he lives by the mighty power of God. We, too, are weak in our bodies, as he was, but now we live and are strong, as he is, and have all of God's power to use in dealing with you.

5Check up on yourselves. Are you really Christians? Do you pass the test? Do you feel Christ's presence and power more and more within you? Or are you just pretending to be Christians when actually you aren't at all? 6I hope you can agree that I have stood that test and truly belong to the Lord.

A THOUGHT: *Just as we get physical check-ups, Paul urges us to give ourselves spiritual check-ups. We should look for a growing awareness of Christ's presence and power in our lives. Only then will we know if we are true Christians or imposters. If we're not taking active steps to grow closer to God, we are growing farther away from him.*

Proverbs for Today/ 15:15–17
When a man is gloomy, everything seems to go wrong; when he is cheerful, everything seems right! □ Better a little with reverence for God, than great treasure and trouble with it. It is better to eat soup with someone you love than steak with someone you hate.

MAY 18

Jesus Teaches in the Synagogues/ Luke 4:14–30
Then Jesus returned to Galilee, full of the Holy Spirit's power. Soon he became well known throughout all that region 15for his sermons in the synagogues; everyone praised him.

16When he came to the village of Nazareth, his boyhood home, he went as usual to the synagogue on Saturday, and stood up to read the Scriptures. 17The book of Isaiah the prophet was handed to him, and he opened it to the place where it says:

18,19"The Spirit of the Lord is upon me; he has appointed me to preach Good News to the poor; he has sent me to heal the brokenhearted and to announce that captives shall be released and the blind shall see, that the downtrodden shall be freed from their oppressors, and that God is ready to give blessings to all who come to him."

20He closed the book and handed it back to the attendant and sat down, while everyone in the synagogue gazed at him intently. 21Then he added, "These Scriptures came true today!"

22All who were there spoke well of him and were amazed by the beautiful words that fell from his lips. "How can this be?" they asked. "Isn't this Joseph's son?"

23Then he said, "Probably you will quote me that proverb, 'Physician, heal yourself'—meaning, 'Why don't you do miracles here in your home town like those you did in Capernaum?' 24But I solemnly declare to you that no prophet is accepted in his own home town! 25,26For example, remember how Elijah the prophet used a miracle to help the widow of Zarephath—a foreigner from the land of Sidon. There were many Jewish widows needing help in those days of famine, for there had been no rain for three and one-half years, and hunger stalked the land; yet Elijah was not sent to them. 27Or think of the prophet Elisha, who healed Naaman, a Syrian, rather than the many Jewish lepers needing help."

28These remarks stung them to fury; 29and jumping up, they mobbed him and took him to the edge of the hill on which the city was built, to push him over the cliff. 30But he walked away through the crowd and left them.

A THOUGHT: *Jesus quoted from Isaiah 61:1–2, stopping in the middle of verse two, just before "and the day of his wrath to their enemies." He did this because the time of God's blessings is fulfilled in Jesus' first coming, but the time of God's wrath awaits his Second Coming. His hearers were expecting just the opposite of the Messiah: they thought he would crush their enemies first, and then usher in God's blessings. Jesus was demonstrating from the Scriptures that he was the fulfillment of all that the prophets had spoken concerning Messiah. Two advents comprise Jesus' messiahship— one as suffering servant (Jesus' earthly ministry accomplishing mankind's redemption), and one at the end, as conquering King (bringing to fulfillment all the blessings of salvation for God's people).*

Paul's Final Advice and Greetings/ 2 Corinthians 13:7–14

I pray that you will live good lives, not because that will be a feather in our caps, proving that what we teach is right; no, for we want you to do right even if we ourselves are despised. 8Our responsibility is to encourage the right at all times, not to hope for evil. 9We are glad to be weak and despised if you are really strong. Our greatest wish and prayer is that you will become mature Christians.

10I am writing this to you now in the hope that I won't need to scold and punish when I come; for I want to use the Lord's authority which he has given me, not to punish you but to make you strong.

11I close my letter with these last words:

Be happy.

Grow in Christ.

Pay attention to what I have said.

Live in harmony and peace.

And may the God of love and peace be with you.

¹²Greet each other warmly in the Lord. ¹³All the Christians here send you their best regards. ¹⁴May the grace of our Lord Jesus Christ be with you all. May God's love and the Holy Spirit's friendship be yours.

Paul

A THOUGHT: *Paul's closing words—what he wants the Corinthians to remember about the needs for their church—are still fitting for the church today. When these qualities are not present, there are problems to be dealt with in the church. These traits do not come to a church by glossing over problems, conflicts, and difficulties. They are not produced by neglect, denial, withdrawal, or bitterness. They are traits which are the by-products of the extremely hard work of solving problems. Just as Paul and the Corinthians had to hammer out difficulties to bring peace, so we must receive and obey the principles of God's Word and not just hear them.*

Proverbs for Today/ 15:18–19

A quick-tempered man starts fights; a cool-tempered man tries to stop them. □ A lazy fellow has trouble all through life; the good man's path is easy!

MAY 19

Jesus Casts Out Demons and Heals Many/ Luke 4:31–44

Then Jesus returned to Capernaum, a city in Galilee, and preached there in the synagogue every Saturday. ³²Here, too, the people were amazed at the things he said. For he spoke as one who knew the truth, instead of merely quoting the opinions of others as his authority.

³³Once as he was teaching in the synagogue, a man possessed by a demon began shouting at Jesus, ³⁴"Go away! We want nothing to do with you, Jesus from Nazareth. You have come to destroy us. I know who you are—the Holy Son of God."

³⁵Jesus cut him short. "Be silent!" he told the demon. "Come out!" The demon threw the man to the floor as the crowd watched, and then left him without hurting him further.

³⁶Amazed, the people asked, "What is in this man's words that even demons obey him?" ³⁷The story of what he had done spread like wildfire throughout the whole region.

³⁸After leaving the synagogue that day, he went to Simon's home where he found Simon's mother-in-law very sick with a high fever. "Please heal her," everyone begged.

³⁹Standing at her bedside he spoke to the fever, rebuking it, and immediately her temperature returned to normal and she got up and prepared a meal for them!

⁴⁰As the sun went down that evening, all the villagers who had any sick people in their homes, no matter what their diseases were, brought them to Jesus; and the touch of his hands healed every one! ⁴¹Some were possessed by demons; and the demons came out at his command, shouting, "You are the Son of God." But because they knew he was the Christ, he stopped them and told them to be silent.

⁴²Early the next morning he went out into the desert. The crowds searched everywhere for him and when they finally found him they begged him not to leave them, but to stay at Capernaum. ⁴³But he replied, "I must preach the Good News of the Kingdom of God in other places too, for that is why I was sent." ⁴⁴So he continued to travel around preaching in synagogues throughout Judea.

A THOUGHT: *The people were amazed at Jesus' authority to cast out demons—evil spirits ruled by Satan and sent to tempt people to sin. Like their leader, demons are fallen angels who have joined him in rebellion against God. Demons can cause a person to become mute, deaf, blind, or insane. Jesus faced many demons during his time on earth, and he always exerted authority over them. Not only did the demon leave this man, Luke records that the man was not even hurt. By casting out this demon, Jesus was demonstrating the presence of the Kingdom of God in his own person. Jesus carries God's authority because he is God.*

Paul's Greeting and Prayer/ Galatians 1:1–5

From: Paul the missionary and all the other Christians here.

To: The churches of Galatia.

I was not called to be a missionary by any group or agency. My call is from Jesus Christ himself, and from God the Father who raised him from the dead. ³May peace and blessing be yours from God the Father and from the Lord Jesus Christ. 4He died for our sins just as God our Father planned, and rescued us from this evil world in which we live. 5All glory to God through all the ages of eternity. Amen.

A THOUGHT: *God's plan all along was to save us by Jesus' death. We have been rescued from the power of this evil world—a world ruled by Satan, full of cruelty, tragedy, temptation, and deception. Being rescued from this evil world doesn't mean we are taken out of it, but that we are no longer enslaved to it. We have been saved to live righteous lives for God, and we have been promised eternity with him.*

Proverbs for Today/ 15:20–21

A sensible son gladdens his father. A rebellious son saddens his mother. □ If a man enjoys folly, something is wrong! The sensible stay on the pathways of right.

MAY 20

The Miracle of a Great Catch/ Luke 5:1–11

One day as Jesus was preaching on the shore of Lake Gennesaret, great crowds pressed in on him to listen to the Word of God. 2He noticed two empty boats standing at the water's edge while the fishermen washed their nets. 3Stepping into one of the boats, Jesus asked Simon, its owner, to push out a little into the water, so that he could sit in the boat and speak to the crowds from there.

4When he had finished speaking, he said to Simon, "Now go out where it is deeper and let down your nets and you will catch a lot of fish!"

5"Sir," Simon replied, "we worked hard all last night and didn't catch a thing. But if you say so, we'll try again."

6And this time their nets were so full that they began to tear! 7A shout for help brought their partners in the other boat and soon both boats were filled with fish and on the verge of sinking.

8When Simon Peter realized what had happened, he fell to his knees before Jesus and said, "Oh, sir, please

leave us—I'm too much of a sinner for you to have around."
9For he was awestruck by the size of their catch, as were
the others with him, 10and his partners too—James and
John, the sons of Zebedee. Jesus replied, "Don't be afraid!
From now on you'll be fishing for the souls of men!"

11And as soon as they landed, they left everything and
went with him.

A THOUGHT: *Peter was awestruck at this miracle, and his first
response was to feel his own insignificance in comparison to Jesus'
greatness. Peter knew Jesus had healed the sick and cast out demons,
but he was amazed that Jesus cared about his day-to-day routine
and understood his needs. God's power reaches into every dimension
of our lives. As we come to recognize the greatness of God's power
expressed in the life of the church, we will find ourselves humbled
at the reality of who he is and at the magnitude of his grace towards
us.*

There Is No Other Gospel/ Galatians 1:6–12

I am amazed that you are turning away so soon from
God who, in his love and mercy, invited you to share
the eternal life he gives through Christ; you are already
following a different "way to heaven," which really doesn't
go to heaven at all. 7For there is no other way than the
one we showed you; you are being fooled by those who
twist and change the truth concerning Christ.

8Let God's curses fall on anyone, including myself, who
preaches any other way to be saved than the one we
told you about; yes, if an angel comes from heaven and
preaches any other message, let him be forever cursed.
9I will say it again: if anyone preaches any other Gospel
than the one you welcomed, let God's curse fall upon
him.

10You can see that I am not trying to please you by
sweet talk and flattery; no, I am trying to please God. If
I were still trying to please men I could not be Christ's
servant.

11Dear friends, I solemnly swear that the way to heaven
which I preach is not based on some mere human whim
or dream. 12For my message comes from no less a person
than Jesus Christ himself, who told me what to say. No
one else has taught me.

A THOUGHT: *The different "way to heaven" was preached by people
who wanted Gentile believers to follow Jewish laws in order to*

obtain salvation. Those proclaiming this different way believed that faith in Christ was not enough; a Christian must also follow the Jewish laws and customs, especially the rite of circumcision, in order to be saved. This message undermined the truth of the Good News that salvation is a gift, not a reward. Jesus Christ has made this gift available to all people, not just to those who are Jewish in orientation. Beware of people who say that more is needed for salvation than faith in Christ. When people set up additional requirements for salvation, they deny the power of Christ's redemptive work on the cross.

Proverbs for Today/ 15:22–23

Plans go wrong with too few counselors; many counselors bring success. □ Everyone enjoys giving good advice, and how wonderful it is to be able to say the right thing at the right time!

MAY 21

Jesus Heals a Leper/ Luke 5:12–16

One day in a certain village Jesus was visiting, there was a man with an advanced case of leprosy. When he saw Jesus he fell to the ground before him, face downward in the dust, begging to be healed.

"Sir," he said, "if you only will, you can clear me of every trace of my disease."

13Jesus reached out and touched the man and said, "Of course I will. Be healed." And the leprosy left him instantly! 14Then Jesus instructed him to go at once without telling anyone what had happened and be examined by the Jewish priest. "Offer the sacrifice Moses' law requires for lepers who are healed," he said. "This will prove to everyone that you are well." 15Now the report of his power spread even faster and vast crowds came to hear him preach and to be healed of their diseases. 16But he often withdrew to the wilderness for prayer.

A THOUGHT: *Leprosy was a feared disease because it was often highly contagious and there was no known cure for it. (Sometimes called Hansen's disease, leprosy still exists today in a less contagious form that can be treated.) The priests monitored the disease—banish-*

ing from the community those persons whose leprosy was active,
to prevent the spread of infection and readmitting lepers whose
disease was in remission. Since leprosy destroyed the nerve endings,
lepers often unknowingly damaged their fingers, toes, and noses.

Lepers were considered untouchable because people feared contracting their disease. Yet Jesus reached out and touched this leper to
heal him. We may consider certain people untouchable or repulsive.
We must not be afraid to reach out and touch them with God's
love. Who do you know that needs God's touch of love?

Paul Reviews His Conversion/ Galatians 1:13–24

You know what I was like when I followed the Jewish
religion—how I went after the Christians mercilessly, hunting them down and doing my best to get rid of them all.
14I was one of the most religious Jews of my own age in
the whole country, and tried as hard as I possibly could
to follow all the old, traditional rules of my religion.

15But then something happened! For even before I was
born God had chosen me to be his, and called me—what
kindness and grace— 16to reveal his Son within me so
that I could go to the Gentiles and show them the Good
News about Jesus.

When all this happened to me I didn't go at once and
talk it over with anyone else; 17I didn't go up to Jerusalem
to consult with those who were apostles before I was.
No, I went away into the deserts of Arabia, and then
came back to the city of Damascus. 18It was not until
three years later that I finally went to Jerusalem for a
visit with Peter, and stayed there with him for fifteen
days. 19And the only other apostle I met at that time
was James, our Lord's brother. 20(Listen to what I am
saying, for I am telling you this in the very presence of
God. This is exactly what happened—I am not lying to
you.) 21Then after this visit I went to Syria and Cilicia.
22And still the Christians in Judea didn't even know what
I looked like. 23All they knew was what people were saying,
that "our former enemy is now preaching the very faith
he tried to wreck." 24And they gave glory to God because
of me.

A THOUGHT: *Paul tells of his conversion to show that his message
came directly from God. God commissioned him to preach the Good
News to the Gentiles. After his call, Paul did not consult with
the apostles until he had spent three years in the desert. Then he
spoke with Peter and James, but he had no other contact with*

Jewish Christians for several more years. During those years, he was preaching to the Gentiles the message God gave him. His Good News did not ultimately come from man; it came from God.

Proverbs for Today/ 15:24–26

The road of the godly leads upward, leaving hell behind. □ The Lord destroys the possessions of the proud but cares for widows. □ The Lord hates the thoughts of the wicked but delights in kind words.

MAY 22

Jesus Heals a Paralytic/ Luke 5:17–26

One day while Jesus was teaching, some Jewish religious leaders and teachers of the Law were sitting nearby. (It seemed that these men showed up from every village in all Galilee and Judea, as well as from Jerusalem.) And the Lord's healing power was upon him.

18,19Then—look! Some men came carrying a paralyzed man on a sleeping mat. They tried to push through the crowd to Jesus but couldn't reach him. So they went up on the roof above him, took off some tiles and lowered the sick man down into the crowd, still on his sleeping mat, right in front of Jesus.

20Seeing their faith, Jesus said to the man, "My friend, your sins are forgiven!"

21"Who does this fellow think he is?" the Pharisees and teachers of the Law exclaimed among themselves. "This is blasphemy! Who but God can forgive sins?"

22Jesus knew what they were thinking, and he replied, "Why is it blasphemy? 23,24I, the Messiah, have the authority on earth to forgive sins. But talk is cheap—anybody could say that. So I'll prove it to you by healing this man." Then, turning to the paralyzed man, he commanded, "Pick up your stretcher and go on home, for you are healed!"

25And immediately, as everyone watched, the man jumped to his feet, picked up his mat and went home praising God! 26Everyone present was gripped with awe and fear. And they praised God, remarking over and over again, "We have seen strange things today."

A THOUGHT: *When Jesus told the paralyzed man his sins were forgiven, the Jewish leaders accused him of blasphemy—claiming to be God or to do what only God can do. In Jewish law, blasphemy was punishable by death. In labeling Jesus' claim to forgive sins blasphemous, the religious leaders did not understand that he is God, and he has God's power to heal both the body and the soul. Forgiveness of sins was a sign that the Messianic Age had come.*

Paul Stood Firm for the Gospel/ Galatians 2:1–5

Then fourteen years later I went back to Jerusalem again, this time with Barnabas; and Titus came along too. 2I went there with definite orders from God to confer with the brothers there about the message I was preaching to the Gentiles. I talked privately to the leaders of the church so that they would all understand just what I had been teaching and, I hoped, agree that it was right. 3And they did agree; they did not even demand that Titus, my companion, should be circumcised, though he was a Gentile.

4Even that question wouldn't have come up except for some so-called "Christians" there—false ones, really—who came to spy on us and see what freedom we enjoyed in Christ Jesus, as to whether we obeyed the Jewish laws or not. They tried to get us all tied up in their rules, like slaves in chains. 5But we did not listen to them for a single moment, for we did not want to confuse you into thinking that salvation can be earned by being circumcised and by obeying Jewish laws.

A THOUGHT: *Even though God had specifically sent Paul to the Gentiles, Paul was willing to discuss his gospel message with the leaders of the Jerusalem church. This meeting prevented a major split in the church, and it formally acknowledged the apostles' approval of Paul's preaching. Sometimes we avoid conferring with others because we fear that problems or arguments may develop. Instead, we should openly discuss our plans and actions with others. This helps everyone understand the situation better, it reduces gossip, and builds unity in the church.*

Proverbs for Today/ 15:27–28

Dishonest money brings grief to all the family, but hating bribes brings happiness. □ A good man thinks before he speaks; the evil man pours out his evil words without a thought.

Jesus Came to Save Sinners/ Luke 5:27–39

Later on as Jesus left the town he saw a tax collector—
with the usual reputation for cheating—sitting at a tax
collection booth. The man's name was Levi. Jesus said
to him, "Come and be one of my disciples!" 28So Levi
left everything, sprang up and went with him.

29Soon Levi held a reception in his home with Jesus
as the guest of honor. Many of Levi's fellow tax collectors
and other guests were there.

30But the Pharisees and teachers of the Law complained
bitterly to Jesus' disciples about his eating with such notorious sinners.

31Jesus answered them, "It is the sick who need a doctor,
not those in good health. 32My purpose is to invite sinners
to turn from their sins, not to spend my time with those
who think themselves already good enough."

33Their next complaint was that Jesus' disciples were
feasting instead of fasting. "John the Baptist's disciples
are constantly going without food, and praying," they declared, "and so do the disciples of the Pharisees. Why
are yours wining and dining?"

34Jesus asked, "Do happy men fast? Do wedding guests
go hungry while celebrating with the groom? 35But the
time will come when the bridegroom will be killed; then
they won't want to eat."

36Then Jesus used this illustration: "No one tears off a
piece of a new garment to make a patch for an old one.
Not only will the new garment be ruined, but the old
garment will look worse with a new patch on it! 37And
no one puts new wine into old wineskins, for the new
wine bursts the old skins, ruining the skins and spilling
the wine. 38New wine must be put into new wineskins.
39But no one after drinking the old wine seems to want
the fresh and the new. 'The old ways are best,' they say."

A THOUGHT: *The Pharisees wrapped their sin in respectability.
They made themselves appear good by publicly doing good deeds
and pointing out the sins of others. Jesus chose to spend time, not
with these self-righteous religious leaders, but with people who sensed
their own sin and knew they were not good enough for God. In*

order to come to God, you must repent; in order to repent, you must recognize your sin. As sinners, we can have hope because Jesus came to save sinners, not those who considered themselves righteous.

The Apostles Accepted Paul's Gospel/ Galatians 2:6–10

And the great leaders of the church who were there had nothing to add to what I was preaching. (By the way, their being great leaders made no difference to me, for all are the same to God.) 7,8,9In fact, when Peter, James, and John, who were known as the pillars of the church, saw how greatly God had used me in winning the Gentiles, just as Peter had been blessed so greatly in his preaching to the Jews—for the same God gave us each our special gifts—they shook hands with Barnabas and me and encouraged us to keep right on with our preaching to the Gentiles while they continued their work with the Jews. 10The only thing they did suggest was that we must always remember to help the poor, and I, too, was eager for that.

A THOUGHT: *Here the apostles were expressing their concern for the poor of Jerusalem. While many Gentile converts were financially comfortable, the Jerusalem church was suffering from a severe famine. Much of Paul's time was spent gathering funds for the Jewish Christians. The need for believers to care for the poor is a constant theme of Scripture, but often we do nothing about it. We get caught up in meeting our own needs and desires, or we just don't see enough poor people to remember their needs. Both in your own city and across the oceans there are people who need help. What can you do to show them tangible evidence of God's love?*

Proverbs for Today/ 15:29–30

The Lord is far from the wicked, but he hears the prayers of the righteous. ☐ Pleasant sights and good reports give happiness and health.

MAY 24

Jesus Is Master of the Sabbath/ Luke 6:1–11

One Sabbath as Jesus and his disciples were walking through some grainfields, they were breaking off the heads of wheat, rubbing off the husks in their hands and eating the grains.

2But some Pharisees said, "That's illegal! Your disciples are harvesting grain, and it's against the Jewish law to work on the Sabbath."

3Jesus replied, "Don't you read the Scriptures? Haven't you ever read what King David did when he and his men were hungry? 4He went into the Temple and took the shewbread, the special bread that was placed before the Lord, and ate it—illegal as this was—and shared it with others." 5And Jesus added, "I am master even of the Sabbath."

6On another Sabbath he was in the synagogue teaching, and a man was present whose right hand was deformed. 7The teachers of the Law and the Pharisees watched closely to see whether he would heal the man that day, since it was the Sabbath. For they were eager to find some charge to bring against him.

8How well he knew their thoughts! But he said to the man with the deformed hand, "Come and stand here where everyone can see." So he did.

9Then Jesus said to the Pharisees and teachers of the Law, "I have a question for you. Is it right to do good on the Sabbath day, or to do harm? To save life, or to destroy it?"

10He looked around at them one by one and then said to the man, "Reach out your hand." And as he did, it became completely normal again. 11At this, the enemies of Jesus were wild with rage, and began to plot his murder.

A THOUGHT: *The Pharisees had written in the Mishnah, their handbook of rabbinic law, 39 categories of activities that were forbidden on the Sabbath—and harvesting was one of them. The rabbinic religious leaders had also invented a law that said no healing could be done on the Sabbath. It was more important for the religious leaders to protect their laws than to free a person from painful suffering. For Jesus, practicing mercy towards another was to truly fulfill the purpose of the Sabbath command—which was to relieve people from their toil and suffering throughout the week.*

When Jesus said he was master of the Sabbath, he revealed to the Pharisees that he had the authority to overrule their traditions and regulations because he had created the Sabbath. The creator is always greater than the creation.

Paul Opposed Peter in Antioch/ Galatians 2:11–16

But when Peter came to Antioch I had to oppose him publicly, speaking strongly against what he was doing for it was very wrong. 12For when he first arrived he ate with the Gentile Christians [who don't bother with circumcision and the many other Jewish laws]. But afterwards when some Jewish friends of James came, he wouldn't eat with the Gentiles anymore because he was afraid of what these Jewish legalists, who insisted that circumcision was necessary for salvation, would say; 13and then all the other Jewish Christians and even Barnabas became hypocrites too, following Peter's example, though they certainly knew better. 14When I saw what was happening and that they weren't being honest about what they really believed, and weren't following the truth of the Gospel, I said to Peter in front of all the others, "Though you are a Jew by birth, you have long since discarded the Jewish laws; so why, all of a sudden, are you trying to make these Gentiles obey them? 15You and I are Jews by birth, not mere Gentile sinners, 16and yet we Jewish Christians know very well that we cannot become right with God by obeying our Jewish laws, but only by faith in Jesus Christ to take away our sins. And so we, too, have trusted Jesus Christ, that we might be accepted by God because of faith—and not because we have obeyed the Jewish laws. For no one will ever be saved by obeying them."

A THOUGHT: *The Judaizers accused Paul of watering down the gospel to make it easier for Gentiles to accept, while Paul accused the Judaizers of nullifying the truth of the gospel by adding conditions to it. The basis of salvation was the issue—is salvation through Christ alone, or does it come through Christ and adherence to the law? The argument came to a head when Peter, Paul, some Judaizers, and some Gentile Christians all gathered together in Antioch to share a meal. Peter probably thought that by staying aloof from the Gentiles, he was promoting harmony—he did not want to offend the friends of James. But Paul charged that Peter's action violated the gospel. By joining the Judaizers, Peter implicitly supported their claim that Christ was not sufficient for salvation. Compromise is an important element in getting along with others, but we should never compromise the truth of God's Word. If we feel we have to change our Christian beliefs to match those of our companions, we are on dangerous ground.*

Proverbs for Today/ 15:31–32

If you profit from constructive criticism you will be elected
to the wise men's hall of fame. But to reject criticism is
to harm yourself and your own best interests.

MAY 25

Jesus Chooses His Twelve Disciples/ Luke 6:12–16

One day soon afterwards Jesus went out into the mountains
to pray, and prayed all night. 13At daybreak he called
together his followers and chose twelve of them to be
the inner circle of his disciples. (They were appointed as
his "apostles," or "missionaries.") 14,15,16Here are their
names:

Simon (he also called him Peter),
Andrew (Simon's brother),
James,
John,
Philip,
Bartholomew,
Matthew,
Thomas,
James (the son of Alphaeus),
Simon (a member of the Zealots, a subversive political
    party),
Judas (son of James),
Judas Iscariot (who later betrayed him).

A THOUGHT: *Jesus selected ordinary people to be his disciples, and
they were a real mixture of backgrounds and personalities. They
were "ordinary" people with a high calling. Today, God calls "ordinary" people together to build his church, teach salvation's message,
and serve others out of love. Alone we may feel unqualified to
serve Christ effectively, but together we make up a group strong
enough to serve God in any way. Ask for patience to accept the
differences in people in your church, and build on the variety of
strengths represented in your group.*

Keeping the Law Cannot Bring Salvation/ Galatians 2:17–21

But what if we trust Christ to save us and then find that we are wrong, and that we cannot be saved without being circumcised and obeying all the other Jewish laws? Wouldn't we need to say that faith in Christ had ruined us? God forbid that anyone should dare to think such things about our Lord. 18Rather, we are sinners if we start rebuilding the old systems I have been destroying, of trying to be saved by keeping Jewish laws, 19for it was through reading the Scripture that I came to realize that I could never find God's favor by trying—and failing—to obey the laws. I came to realize that acceptance with God comes by believing in Christ.

20I have been crucified with Christ: and I myself no longer live, but Christ lives in me. And the real life I now have within this body is a result of my trusting in the Son of God, who loved me and gave himself for me. 21I am not one of those who treats Christ's death as meaningless. For if we could be saved by keeping Jewish laws, then there was no need for Christ to die.

A THOUGHT: *Through studying the Old Testament Scripture, Paul realized that he could not be saved by obeying God's laws. The prophets knew that God's plan of salvation did not rest upon keeping the Law. Because we have all been infected by sin, we cannot keep God's laws perfectly. Fortunately, God has provided a way of salvation that depends on Jesus Christ, not on our own efforts. We ignore God's system and try to earn our salvation whenever we think God accepts us because we do good things or because we are better than other people. In truth, only by trusting in Christ to take away our sin will we be acceptable to God.*

Proverbs for Today/ 15:33

Humility and reverence for the Lord will make you both wise and honored.

The Sermon on the Plain/ Luke 6:17–38

When they came down the slopes of the mountain, the disciples stood with Jesus on a large, level area, surrounded by many of his followers who, in turn, were surrounded by the crowds. For people from all over Judea and from Jerusalem and from as far north as the seacoasts of Tyre and Sidon had come to hear him or to be healed. And he cast out many demons. 19Everyone was trying to touch him, for when they did healing power went out from him and they were cured.

20Then he turned to his disciples and said, "What happiness there is for you who are poor, for the Kingdom of God is yours! 21What happiness there is for you who are now hungry, for you are going to be satisfied! What happiness there is for you who weep, for the time will come when you shall laugh with joy! 22What happiness it is when others hate you and exclude you and insult you and smear your name because you are mine! 23When that happens, rejoice! Yes, leap for joy! For you will have a great reward awaiting you in heaven. And you will be in good company— the ancient prophets were treated that way too!

24"But, oh, the sorrows that await the rich. For they have their only happiness down here. 25They are fat and prosperous now, but a time of awful hunger is before them. Their careless laughter now means sorrow for them. 26And what sadness is ahead for those praised by the crowds—for *false* prophets have *always* been praised.

27"Listen, all of you. Love your *enemies*. Do *good* to those who *hate* you. 28Pray for the happiness of those who *curse* you; implore God's blessing on those who *hurt* you.

29"If someone slaps you on one cheek, let him slap the other too! If someone demands your coat, give him your shirt besides. 30Give what you have to anyone who asks you for it; and when things are taken away from you, don't worry about getting them back. 31Treat others as you want them to treat you.

32"Do you think you deserve credit for merely loving those who love you? Even the godless do that! 33And if you do good only to those who do you good—is that so wonderful? Even sinners do that much! 34And if you lend money only to those who can repay you, what good is that? Even the most wicked will lend to their own kind for full return!

35"Love your *enemies!* Do good to *them!* Lend to *them!* And don't be concerned about the fact that they won't repay. Then your reward from heaven will be very great, and you will truly be acting as sons of God: for he is kind to the *unthankful* and to those who are *very wicked.*

36"Try to show as much compassion as your Father does.

37"Never criticize or condemn—or it will all come back on you. Go easy on others; then they will do the same for you. 38For if you give, you will get! Your gift will return to you in full and overflowing measure, pressed down, shaken together to make room for more, and running over. Whatever measure you use to give—large or small—will be used to measure what is given back to you."

A THOUGHT: *These "happiness" verses are called the Beatitudes, from the Latin word meaning "blessing." They describe what it means to be Christ's follower. They are a standard of conduct. They contrast Kingdom values with worldly values, showing what Christ's followers can expect from the world and what God will give them. They contrast fake piety with true humility. And finally, they show how the Old Testament expectations will be fulfilled in God's Kingdom.*

The True Children of Abraham/ Galatians 3:1–9

Oh, foolish Galatians! What magician has hypnotized you and cast an evil spell upon you? For you used to see the meaning of Jesus Christ's death as clearly as though I had waved a placard before you with a picture on it of Christ dying on the cross. 2Let me ask you this one question: Did you receive the Holy Spirit by trying to keep the Jewish laws? Of course not, for the Holy Spirit came upon you only after you heard about Christ and trusted him to save you. 3Then have you gone completely crazy? For if trying to obey the Jewish laws never gave you spiritual life in the first place, why do you think that trying to obey them now will make you stronger Christians? 4You have suffered so much for the Gospel. Now are you going to just throw it all overboard? I can hardly believe it!

5I ask you again, does God give you the power of the Holy Spirit and work miracles among you as a result of your trying to obey the Jewish laws? No, of course not. It is when you believe in Christ and fully trust him.

6Abraham had the same experience—God declared him fit for heaven only because he believed God's promises. 7You can see from this that the real children of Abraham are all the men of faith who truly trust in God.

8,9What's more, the Scriptures looked forward to this time when God would save the Gentiles also, through their faith. God told Abraham about this long ago when he said, "I will bless those in every nation who trust in me as you do." And so it is: all who trust in Christ share the same blessing Abraham received.

A THOUGHT: *The main argument of the Judaizers was that Gentiles had to become Jews in order to become Christians. Paul exposed the flaw in this argument by showing that real children of Abraham are those who have faith, not those who keep the Law. Abraham himself was saved by his faith. All believers of all time and from every nation share Abraham's blessing. This is a comforting promise, a great heritage, and a solid foundation for living.*

Proverbs for Today/ 16:1–3
We can make our plans, but the final outcome is in God's hands. We can always "prove" that we are right, but is the Lord convinced? Commit your work to the Lord, then it will succeed.

MAY 27

A Collection of Jesus' Parables/ Luke 6:39–49
Here are some of the story-illustrations Jesus used in his sermons: "What good is it for one blind man to lead another? He will fall into a ditch and pull the other down with him. 40How can a student know more than his teacher? But if he works hard, he may learn as much.

41"And why quibble about the speck in someone else's eye—his little fault —when a board is in your own? 42How can you think of saying to him, 'Brother, let me help you get rid of that speck in your eye,' when you can't see past the board in yours? Hypocrite! First get rid of the board, and then perhaps you can see well enough to deal with his speck!

43"A tree from good stock doesn't produce scrub fruit nor do trees from poor stock produce choice fruit. 44A tree is identified by the kind of fruit it produces. Figs never grow on thorns, or grapes on bramble bushes. 45A good man produces good deeds from a good heart. And an evil man produces evil deeds from his hidden wickedness. Whatever is in the heart overflows into speech.

46"So why do you call me 'Lord' when you won't obey me? 47,48But all those who come and listen and obey me are like a man who builds a house on a strong foundation laid upon the underlying rock. When the floodwaters rise and break against the house, it stands firm, for it is strongly built.

49"But those who listen and don't obey are like a man who builds a house without a foundation. When the floods sweep down against that house, it crumbles into a heap of ruins."

A THOUGHT: *This collection of parables centers upon the appropriate basis for judging the ethical character of oneself and others. We must be very aware of our own shortcomings when we approach another with the intent to "set them straight." We must recognize that we too have areas that need correcting. We should also take care that we are not attempting to correct the small faults in others when in reality we are the ones in greatest need of correction. Genuine humility is always appropriate when evaluating others.*

True spirituality must be from the heart and must be evidenced by good deeds ("choice fruit"). If our words do not match the true quality of our lives, it is time for self-examination.

Christ Became a Curse for Us/ Galatians 3:10–14

Yes, and those who depend on the Jewish laws to save them are under God's curse, for the Scriptures point out very clearly, "Cursed is everyone who at any time breaks a single one of these laws that are written in God's Book of the Law." 11Consequently, it is clear that no one can ever win God's favor by trying to keep the Jewish laws, because God has said that the only way we can be right in his sight is by faith. As the prophet Habakkuk says it, "The man who finds life will find it through trusting God." 12How different from this way of faith is the way of law which says that a man is saved by obeying every law of God, without one slip. 13But Christ has bought us out from under the doom of that impossible system by taking the curse for our wrongdoing upon himself. For it is written in the Scripture, "Anyone who is hanged on a tree is cursed" [as Jesus was hung upon a wooden cross].

14Now God can bless the Gentiles, too, with this same blessing he promised to Abraham; and all of us as Christians can have the promised Holy Spirit through this faith.

A THOUGHT: *Paul quotes Deuteronomy 27:26 to prove that, contrary to what the Judaizers claimed, the law cannot justify and save— it can only condemn. Breaking even one commandment brings a person under condemnation. Because everyone has broken the commandments, everyone is condemned, and the law can do nothing to reverse the condemnation. But Christ took the curse of the Law upon himself when he hung on the cross. He did this so we wouldn't have to bear our own punishment and so we could be saved through him. The only condition is that we accept Christ's work on the cross.*

Proverbs for Today/ 16:4–5

The Lord has made everything for his own purposes— even the wicked, for punishment. ☐ Pride disgusts the Lord. Take my word for it—*proud men shall be punished.*

MAY 28

Jesus Heals a Roman Soldier's Slave/ Luke 7:1–10

When Jesus had finished his sermon he went back into the city of Capernaum.

2Just at that time the highly prized slave of a Roman army captain was sick and near death. 3When the captain heard about Jesus, he sent some respected Jewish elders to ask him to come and heal his slave. 4So they began pleading earnestly with Jesus to come with them and help the man. They told him what a wonderful person the captain was.

"If anyone deserves your help, it is he," they said, 5"for he loves the Jews and even paid personally to build us a synagogue!"

6,7,8Jesus went with them; but just before arriving at the house, the captain sent some friends to say, "Sir, don't inconvenience yourself by coming to my home, for I am not worthy of any such honor or even to come and meet you. Just speak a word from where you are, and my servant boy will be healed! I know, because I am under the authority of my superior officers, and I have authority over my men. I only need to say 'Go!' and they go; or 'Come!' and they come; and to my slave, 'Do this or that,' and he does it. So just say, 'Be healed!' and my servant will be well again!"

9Jesus was amazed. Turning to the crowd he said, "Never among all the Jews in Israel have I met a man with faith like this."

10And when the captain's friends returned to his house, they found the slave completely healed.

A THOUGHT: *This Roman centurion recognized the authority of Jesus in a way that many of the religious leaders had not. When the centurion spoke a word, his soldiers and servants immediately responded with action. He recognized that Jesus' authority was far greater than his, so he was confident that Jesus could heal by just saying the word. Faith in Jesus must be this kind of implicit trust in his great power and ability, not only to deliver from physical ailment, but much more for his ability to transform our lives.*

The Fulfillment of God's Promise to Abraham/ Galatians 3:15–20

Dear brothers, even in everyday life a promise made by one man to another, if it is written down and signed, cannot be changed. He cannot decide afterward to do something else instead.

16Now, God gave some promises to Abraham and his Child. And notice that it doesn't say the promises were to his *children*, as it would if all his sons—all the Jews—were being spoken of, but to his *Child*—and that, of course, means Christ. 17Here's what I am trying to say: God's promise to save through faith—and God wrote this promise down and signed it—could not be canceled or changed four hundred and thirty years later when God gave the Ten Commandments. 18If *obeying those laws* could save us, then it is obvious that this would be a different way of gaining God's favor than Abraham's way, for he simply accepted God's promise.

¹⁹Well then, why were the laws given? They were added after the promise was given, to show men how guilty they are of breaking God's laws. But this system of law was to last only until the coming of Christ, the Child to whom God's promise was made. (And there is this further difference. God gave his laws to angels to give to Moses, who then gave them to the people; ²⁰but when God gave his promise to Abraham, he did it by himself alone, without angels or Moses as go-betweens.)

A THOUGHT: *Paul says that Jesus was the fulfillment of the Law. Jesus inaugurated a new order—the Kingdom of God. The Judaizers had misunderstood the nature of forgiveness and the Law, they saw the Law as a way to earn God's favor. But the Law was to be seen as a response to relationship with God (the covenant), not as an isolated code to be followed in order to gain God's favor. The Law was intended to flow from faith; it was not to be a prerequisite for faith. Similarly, right living is not the condition for faith, but the result of it. When we understand the transforming power of faith we will want to live in a way that demonstrates this transformation.*

Proverbs for Today/ 16:6–7

Iniquity is atoned for by mercy and truth; evil is avoided by reverence for God. □ When a man is trying to please God, God makes even his worst enemies to be at peace with him.

MAY 29

Jesus Raises a Young Boy from the Dead/ Luke 7:11–17

Not long afterwards Jesus went with his disciples to the village of Nain, with the usual great crowd at his heels. ¹²A funeral procession was coming out as he approached the village gate. The boy who had died was the only son of his widowed mother, and many mourners from the village were with her.

¹³When the Lord saw her, his heart overflowed with sympathy. "Don't cry!" he said. ¹⁴Then he walked over to the coffin and touched it, and the bearers stopped.

"Laddie," he said, "come back to life again."

15Then the boy sat up and began to talk to those around him! And Jesus gave him back to his mother.

16A great fear swept the crowd, and they exclaimed with praises to God, "A mighty prophet has risen among us," and, "We have seen the hand of God at work today."

17The report of what he did that day raced from end to end of Judea and even out across the borders.

A THOUGHT: *The widow's situation was serious. She had lost her husband, and now her only son was dead—her last means of support. The crowd of mourners would go home, and she would be left penniless and friendless. She was probably past the age of childbearing and would not marry again. Unless a relative came to her aid, her future was bleak. She would be an easy prey for swindlers, and she would likely be reduced to begging for food. In fact, as Luke repeatedly emphasizes, she was just the kind of person Jesus came to help—and help her he did. Jesus has the power to bring hope out of any tragedy.*

We Are All One in Christ/ Galatians 3:21–29

Well then, are God's laws and God's promises against each other? Of course not! If we could be saved by his laws, then God would not have had to give us a different way to get out of the grip of sin—for the Scriptures insist we are all its prisoners. The only way out is through faith in Jesus Christ; the way of escape is open to all who believe him.

23Until Christ came we were guarded by the law, kept in protective custody, so to speak, until we could believe in the coming Savior.

24Let me put it another way. The Jewish laws were our teacher and guide until Christ came to give us right standing with God through our faith. 25But now that Christ has come, we don't need those laws any longer to guard us and lead us to him. 26For now we are all children of God through faith in Jesus Christ, 27and we who have been baptized into union with Christ are enveloped by him. 28We are no longer Jews or Greeks or slaves or free men or even merely men or women, but we are all the same—we are Christians; we are one in Christ Jesus. 29And now that we are Christ's we are the true descendants of Abraham, and all of God's promises to him belong to us.

A THOUGHT: *It's our natural inclination to feel uncomfortable around those who are different from us and to gravitate toward those who resemble us. But when we allow our differences to separate us from our fellow believers, we are disregarding clear biblical teaching. We must remember that in Christ we have all been put on equal footing before the cross. No one has any greater value than anyone else. Make a point of seeking out and appreciating people who are not just like you and your friends. You may find that you and they have a lot in common.*

Proverbs for Today/ 16:8–9

A little, gained honestly, is better than great wealth gotten by dishonest means. We should make plans—counting on God to direct us.

MAY 30

Jesus Commends John the Baptist's Ministry/ Luke 7:18–35

The disciples of John the Baptist soon heard of all that Jesus was doing. When they told John about it, 19he sent two of his disciples to Jesus to ask him, "Are you really the Messiah? Or shall we keep on looking for him?"

20,21,22The two disciples found Jesus while he was curing many sick people of their various diseases—healing the lame and the blind and casting out evil spirits. When they asked him John's question, this was his reply: "Go back to John and tell him all you have seen and heard here today: how those who were blind can see. The lame are walking without a limp. The lepers are completely healed. The deaf can hear again. The dead come back to life. And the poor are hearing the Good News. 23And tell him, 'Blessed is the one who does not lose his faith in me.'"

24After they left, Jesus talked to the crowd about John. "Who is this man you went out into the Judean wilderness to see?" he asked. "Did you find him weak as grass, moved by every breath of wind? 25Did you find him dressed in expensive clothes? No! Men who live in luxury are found in palaces, not out in the wilderness. 26But did you find a prophet? Yes! And more than a prophet. 27He is the one to whom the Scriptures refer when they say, 'Look! I am sending my messenger ahead of you, to prepare the way before you.' 28In all humanity there is no one greater than John. And yet the least citizen of the Kingdom of God is greater than he."

29And all who heard John preach—even the most wicked of them—agreed that God's requirements were right, and they were baptized by him. 30All, that is, except the Pharisees and teachers of Moses' Law. They rejected God's plan for them and refused John's baptism.

31"What can I say about such men?" Jesus asked. "With what shall I compare them? 32They are like a group of children who complain to their friends, 'You don't like it if we play "wedding" and you don't like it if we play "funeral"'! 33For John the Baptist used to go without food and never took a drop of liquor all his life, and you said, 'He must be crazy!' 34But I eat my food and drink my wine, and you say, 'What a glutton Jesus is! And he drinks! And has the lowest sort of friends!' 35But I am sure you can always justify your inconsistencies."

A THOUGHT: *John was confused because the reports he received about Jesus were unexpected and incomplete. His doubts were natural, and Jesus didn't rebuke him for them. Instead, he responded in a way that John would understand—expaining that he had in fact accomplished those things that the Messiah was supposed to accomplish. God also can handle our doubts, and he welcomes our questions. Do you have questions about Jesus—about who he is or what he expects of you? Admit them to yourself and to God, and begin looking for answers. Only as you admit your doubts can you begin to resolve them.*

We Are God's Adopted Children/ Galatians 4:1–7

But remember this, that if a father dies and leaves great wealth for his little son, that child is not much better off than a slave until he grows up, even though he actually owns everything his father had. 2He has to do what his guardians and managers tell him to, until he reaches whatever age his father set.

3And that is the way it was with us before Christ came. We were slaves to Jewish laws and rituals for we thought they could save us. 4But when the right time came, the time God decided on, he sent his Son, born of a woman, born as a Jew, 5to buy freedom for us who were slaves to the law so that he could adopt us as his very own sons. 6And because we are his sons God has sent the Spirit of his Son into our hearts, so now we can rightly speak of God as our dear Father. 7Now we are no longer slaves, but God's own sons. And since we are his sons, everything he has belongs to us, for that is the way God planned.

A Thought: *Under Roman law, an adopted male child was guaranteed all legal rights to his father's property. He was not a second-class son; he was equal to all other sons, biological or adopted, in his father's family. As adopted children of God, we share with Jesus all rights to God's resources. As God's heirs, we can claim what he has provided for us—our full identity as his children.*

Proverbs for Today/ 16:10–11

God will help the king to judge the people fairly; there need be no mistakes. □ The Lord demands fairness in every business deal. He established this principle.

MAY 31

A Sinful Woman Anoints Jesus' Feet/ Luke 7:36–50

One of the Pharisees asked Jesus to come to his home for lunch and Jesus accepted the invitation. As they sat down to eat, 37a woman of the streets—a prostitute—heard he was there and brought an exquisite flask filled with expensive perfume. 38Going in, she knelt behind him at his feet, weeping, with her tears falling down upon his feet; and she wiped them off with her hair and kissed them and poured the perfume on them.

39When Jesus' host, a Pharisee, saw what was happening and who the woman was, he said to himself, "This proves that Jesus is no prophet, for if God had really sent him, he would know what kind of woman this one is!"

40Then Jesus spoke up and answered his thoughts. "Simon," he said to the Pharisee, "I have something to say to you."

"All right, Teacher," Simon replied, "go ahead."

41Then Jesus told him this story: "A man loaned money

to two people—$5,000 to one and $500 to the other. 42But neither of them could pay him back, so he kindly forgave them both, letting them keep the money! Which do you suppose loved him most after that?"

43"I suppose the one who had owed him the most," Simon answered.

"Correct," Jesus agreed.

44Then he turned to the woman and said to Simon, "Look! See this woman kneeling here! When I entered your home, you didn't bother to offer me water to wash the dust from my feet, but she has washed them with her tears and wiped them with her hair. 45You refused me the customary kiss of greeting, but she has kissed my feet again and again from the time I first came in. 46You neglected the usual courtesy of olive oil to anoint my head, but she has covered my feet with rare perfume. 47Therefore her sins—and they are many—are forgiven, for she loved me much; but one who is forgiven little, shows little love."

48And he said to her, "Your sins are forgiven."

49Then the men at the table said to themselves, "Who does this man think he is, going around forgiving sins?"

50And Jesus said to the woman, "Your faith has saved you; go in peace."

A THOUGHT: *Again the Pharisees are contrasted with sinners—and again the sinners come out ahead. Simon had committed a social error in neglecting to wash Jesus' feet (a courtesy that was extended to guests, because sandaled feet got very dirty), anoint his head with oil, and offer him the kiss of greeting. Did he perhaps feel he was too good to treat Jesus as an equal? The sinful woman, by contrast, lavished tears, expensive perfume, and kisses on her Savior. In this story it is the generous prostitute, not the stingy religious leader, whose sins are forgiven. Sinners who seek forgiveness will be accepted into God's Kingdom, while those who think they're too good to sin will not be accepted.*

Do Not Become Enslaved Again/ Galatians 4:8–11

Before you Gentiles knew God you were slaves to so-called gods that did not even exist. 9And now that you have found God (or I should say, now that God has found you) how can it be that you want to go back again and become slaves once more to another poor, weak, useless religion of trying to get to heaven by obeying God's laws?

¹⁰You are trying to find favor with God by what you do or don't do on certain days or months or seasons or years. ¹¹I fear for you. I am afraid that all my hard work for you was worth nothing.

A THOUGHT: *The legal traditions that had been handed down to the Jews by the rabbis had become oppressive to the people. They had become legalistic and were missing the real heart of the Law which was to love God and your neighbor. Paul is concerned for the Galatians. They were once again placing themselves under the oppressive legal system. Paul reminds them that perfection cannot be gained by keeping the Law. Perfection comes from the Perfect One—Jesus Christ. It is on the basis of Christ's sacrifice for sins that we will be acceptable to God. And it is the work of the Spirit, not our own good work, that transforms us into Christlikeness. To reject these two truths is to deny the very heart of Christianity.*

Proverbs for Today/ 16:12–13

It is a horrible thing for a king to do evil. His right to rule depends upon his fairness. The king rejoices when his people are truthful and fair.

JUNE 1

Some Disciples of Jesus/ Luke 8:1–3

Not long afterwards Jesus began a tour of the cities and villages of Galilee to announce the coming of the Kingdom of God, and took his twelve disciples with him. ²Some women went along, from whom he had cast out demons or whom he had healed; among them were Mary Magdalene (Jesus had cast out seven demons from her), ³Joanna, Chuza's wife (Chuza was King Herod's business manager and was in charge of his palace and domestic affairs), Susanna, and many others who were contributing from their private means to the support of Jesus and his disciples.

A THOUGHT: *Jesus raised women from the degradation and servitude imposed upon them by their male-dominated society, to fellowship and service. In Jewish culture, women were not supposed to learn from rabbis. By allowing these women to travel with him, Jesus was showing that all people are equal under God. These women supported Jesus' ministry with their own money. They owed a great debt to him, for he had cast demons out of some and healed others.*

Paul's Longing for Fellowship/ Galatians 4:12–20

Dear brothers, please feel as I do about these things, for I am as free from these chains as you used to be. You did not despise me then when I first preached to you, 13even though I was sick when I first brought you the Good News of Christ. 14But even though my sickness was revolting to you, you didn't reject me and turn me away. No, you took me in and cared for me as though I were an angel from God, or even Jesus Christ himself.

15Where is that happy spirit that we felt together then? For in those days I know you would gladly have taken out your own eyes and given them to replace mine if that would have helped me.

16And now have I become your enemy because I tell you the truth?

17Those false teachers who are so anxious to win your favor are not doing it for your good. What they are trying to do is to shut you off from me so that you will pay more attention to them. 18It is a fine thing when people are nice to you with good motives and sincere hearts, especially if they aren't doing it just when I am with you! 19Oh, my children, how you are hurting me! I am once again suffering for you the pains of a mother waiting for her child to be born—longing for the time when you will finally be filled with Christ. 20How I wish I could be there with you right now and not have to reason with you like this, for at this distance I frankly don't know what to do.

A THOUGHT: *Paul led many people to Christ and helped them mature spiritually. Perhaps one reason for his success as a spiritual father was the deep concern he felt for his spiritual children; he compared his pain over their faithlessness to the pain of childbirth. We should have the same intense care for those to whom we are spiritual parents. When you lead people to Christ, remember to stay by to help them grow.*

Proverbs for Today/ 16:14–15

The anger of the king is a messenger of death and a wise man will appease it. Many favors are showered on those who please the king.

The Parable of the Soils/ Luke 8:4–15

One day Jesus gave this illustration to a large crowd that was gathering to hear him—while many others were still on the way, coming from other towns.

⁵"A farmer went out to his field to sow grain. As he scattered the seed on the ground, some of it fell on a footpath and was trampled on; and the birds came and ate it as it lay exposed. ⁶Other seed fell on shallow soil with rock beneath. This seed began to grow, but soon withered and died for lack of moisture. ⁷Other seed landed in thistle patches, and the young grain stalks were soon choked out. ⁸Still other fell on fertile soil; this seed grew and produced a crop one hundred times as large as he had planted." (As he was giving this illustration he said, "If anyone has listening ears, use them now!")

⁹His apostles asked him what the story meant.

¹⁰He replied, "God has granted you to know the meaning of these parables, for they tell a great deal about the Kingdom of God. But these crowds hear the words and do not understand, just as the ancient prophets predicted.

¹¹"This is its meaning: The seed is God's message to men. ¹²The hard path where some seed fell represents the hard hearts of those who hear the words of God, but then the devil comes and steals the words away and prevents people from believing and being saved. ¹³The stony ground represents those who enjoy listening to sermons, but somehow the message never really gets through to them and doesn't take root and grow. They know the message is true, and sort of believe for awhile; but when the hot winds of persecution blow, they lose interest. ¹⁴The seed among the thorns represents those who listen and believe God's words but whose faith afterwards is choked out by worry and riches and the responsibilities and pleasures of life. And so they are never able to help anyone else to believe the Good News.

¹⁵"But the good soil represents honest, good-hearted people. They listen to God's words and cling to them and steadily spread them to others who also soon believe."

A Thought: *Hard-rock people, like the religious leaders, refused to believe God's message. Stony-ground people, like the crowds who followed Jesus, trusted God but never got around to doing anything about it. Thistle-patch people, overcome by materialism, left no room in their lives for God. Good-soil people, by contrast to all the other groups, followed God's Word no matter what the cost. Which type of soil are you?*

The Illustration of Sarah and Hagar/ Galatians 4:21–31

Listen to me, you friends who think you have to obey the Jewish laws to be saved: Why don't you find out what those laws really mean? 22For it is written that Abraham had two sons, one from his slavewife and one from his freeborn wife. 23There was nothing unusual about the birth of the slave-wife's baby. But the baby of the freeborn wife was born only after God had especially promised he would come.

24,25Now this true story is an illustration of God's two ways of helping people. One way was by giving them his laws to obey. He did this on Mount Sinai, when he gave the Ten Commandments to Moses. Mount Sinai, by the way, is called "Mount Hagar" by the Arabs—and in my illustration Abraham's slave-wife Hagar represents Jerusalem, the mother-city of the Jews, the center of that system of trying to please God by trying to obey the Commandments; and the Jews, who try to follow that system, are her slave children. 26But our mother-city is the heavenly Jerusalem, and she is not a slave to Jewish laws.

27That is what Isaiah meant when he prophesied, "Now you can rejoice, O childless woman; you can shout with joy though you never before had a child. For I am going to give you many children—more children than the slave-wife has."

28You and I, dear brothers, are the children that God promised, just as Isaac was. 29And so we who are born of the Holy Spirit are persecuted now by those who want us to keep the Jewish laws, just as Isaac the child of promise was persecuted by Ishmael the slave-wife's son.

30But the Scriptures say that God told Abraham to send away the slave-wife and her son, for the slave-wife's son could not inherit Abraham's home and lands along with the free woman's son. 31Dear brothers, we are not slave children, obligated to the Jewish laws, but children of the free woman, acceptable to God because of our faith.

A THOUGHT: *People are saved because of their faith in Christ, not because of what they do. Paul contrasts those who are enslaved to the Law (represented by Hagar, the slave woman) with those who are free from the Law (represented by Sarah, the free woman). Since we are joint-heirs with Christ, God's Son (the fulfillment of the Abrahamic promise), we are children of the promise. Our acceptance before God is the same as Abraham's—faith in the promise; but we have faith in the promise fulfilled (our faith is in Christ himself who has already come and accomplished our redemption).*

Proverbs for Today/ 16:16–17

How much better is wisdom than gold, and understanding than silver! □ The path of the godly leads away from evil; he who follows that path is safe.

JUNE 3

The Illustration of the Lamp/ Luke 8:16–18

[Another time Jesus asked,] "Who ever heard of someone lighting a lamp and then covering it up to keep it from shining? No, lamps are mounted in the open where they can be seen. 17This illustrates the fact that someday everything [in men's hearts] shall be brought to light and made plain to all. 18So be careful how you listen; for whoever has, to him shall be given more; and whoever does not have, even what he thinks he has shall be taken away from him."

A THOUGHT: *In God's eyes, people's hearts—their thoughts and motives—are as visible as a lamp mounted in the open. No matter how hard we try to cover up bad attitudes, deeds, or words, we cannot deceive God. Instead of hiding our faults, we should ask God to change our lives so we no longer have to be ashamed. If you are trying to hide anything from God it won't work. Only when you confess your hidden sins and seek God's forgiveness will you have the help you need to do right.*

Freedom from Slavery to Sin/ Galatians 5:1–6

So Christ has made us free. Now make sure that you stay free and don't get all tied up again in the chains of slavery to Jewish laws and ceremonies. 2Listen to me, for this is serious: *if you are counting on circumcision and keeping the Jewish laws to make you right with God, then Christ cannot save you.* 3I'll say it again. Anyone trying to find favor with God by being circumcised must always obey every other Jewish law or perish. 4Christ is useless to you if you are counting on clearing your debt to God by keeping those laws; you are lost from God's grace.

5But we by the help of the Holy Spirit are counting on Christ's death to clear away our sins and make us right with God. 6And we to whom Christ has given eternal life don't need to worry about whether we have been circumcised or not, or whether we are obeying the Jewish ceremonies or not; for all we need is faith working through love.

A THOUGHT: *Christ died to set us free from the bondage to sin and from a long list of laws and regulations. Christ came to set us free—not free to do whatever we want, for that would lead back into slavery to our selfish desires. Rather, thanks to Christ, we are now free and able to do what was impossible before—to live unselfishly. Those who appeal to their freedom in order to get their own way or indulge in selfish pursuits are falling back into sin. Do you use your freedom to serve yourself or others?*

Proverbs for Today/ 16:18

Pride goes before destruction and haughtiness before a fall.

JUNE 4

Those in the Family of God/ Luke 8:19–21

Once when Jesus' mother and brothers came to see him, they couldn't get into the house where he was teaching, because of the crowds. 20When Jesus heard they were standing outside and wanted to see him, 21he remarked, "My mother and my brothers are all those who hear the message of God and obey it."

A THOUGHT: *Jesus' true relatives are those who hear and obey his words. Hearing without obeying is not enough. As Jesus loved his mother, so he loves us. He offers us an intimate family relationship with him.*

Freedom to Serve One Another/ Galatians 5:7–15

You were getting along so well. Who has interfered with you to hold you back from following the truth? 8It certainly isn't God who has done it, for he is the one who has called you to freedom in Christ. 9But it takes only one wrong person among you to infect all the others.

10I am trusting the Lord to bring you back to believing as I do about these things. God will deal with that person, whoever he is, who has been troubling and confusing you.

11Some people even say that I myself am preaching that circumcision and Jewish laws are necessary to the plan of salvation. Well, if I preached that, I would be persecuted no more—for that message doesn't offend anyone. The fact that I am still being persecuted proves that I am still preaching salvation through faith in the cross of Christ alone.

12I only wish these teachers who want you to cut yourselves by being circumcised would cut themselves off from you and leave you alone!

13For, dear brothers, you have been given freedom: not freedom to do wrong, but freedom to love and serve each other. 14For the whole Law can be summed up in this one command: "Love others as you love yourself." 15But if instead of showing love among yourselves you are always critical and catty, watch out! Beware of ruining each other.

A THOUGHT: *Paul distinguished between freedom to sin and freedom to serve. Freedom to sin is no freedom at all, because it enslaves us to Satan, others, or our own evil desires. People who are slaves to sin are not free to live a righteous life. Christians, by contrast, should not be slaves to sin because they are free to do right and glorify God through their actions by the power of the Holy Spirit.*

Proverbs for Today/ 16:19–20

Better poor and humble than proud and rich. □ God blesses those who obey him; happy the man who puts his trust in the Lord.

JUNE 5

Jesus Calms the Storm/ Luke 8:22–25

One day about that time, as Jesus and his disciples were out in a boat, he suggested that they cross to the other side of the lake. 23On the way across he lay down for a nap, and while he was sleeping the wind began to rise. A fierce storm developed that threatened to swamp them, and they were in real danger.

24They rushed over and woke him up. "Master, Master, we are sinking!" they screamed.

So he spoke to the storm: "Quiet down," he said, and the wind and waves subsided and all was calm! 25Then he asked them, "Where is your faith?"

And they were filled with awe and fear of him and said to one another, "Who is this man, that even the winds and waves obey him?"

A THOUGHT: *The Sea of Galilee is still the scene of fierce storms, sometimes with waves as high as 20 feet. Jesus' disciples were not frightened without cause. Even though several of them were expert fishermen and knew how to handle a boat, their peril was real. We, like the disciples, should be awestruck at the immense power of Jesus—he can even calm fierce storms with a word. Jesus demonstrates his power over creation in a way that only the Creator could. Through this story we recognize that Jesus the Messiah is the Creator of the universe.*

The Spirit and the Flesh Are at War/ Galatians 5:16–21

I advise you to obey only the Holy Spirit's instructions. He will tell you where to go and what to do, and then you won't always be doing the wrong things your evil nature wants you to. 17For we naturally love to do evil things that are just the opposite from the things that the Holy Spirit tells us to do; and the good things we want to do when the Spirit has his way with us are just the opposite of our natural desires. These two forces within us are constantly fighting each other to win control over us, and our wishes are never free from their pressures. 18When you are guided by the Holy Spirit you need no longer force yourself to obey Jewish laws.

19But when you follow your own wrong inclinations your

lives will produce these evil results: impure thoughts, eagerness for lustful pleasure, 20idolatry, spiritism (that is, encouraging the activity of demons), hatred and fighting, jealousy and anger, constant effort to get the best for yourself, complaints and criticisms, the feeling that everyone else is wrong except those in your own little group—and there will be wrong doctrine, 21envy, murder, drunkenness, wild parties, and all that sort of thing. Let me tell you again as I have before, that anyone living that sort of life will not inherit the Kingdom of God.

A THOUGHT: *Paul describes the two forces at work within us— the Holy Spirit and our evil inclinations. Paul is not saying that these forces are equal. The Holy Spirit is infinitely stronger, but we are weak. Left to our own sinful ways, we will make wrong choices. Our only way to freedom from our natural evil desires is through the redemption of Christ and the empowering of the Holy Spirit.*

Proverbs for Today/ 16:21–23

The wise man is known by his common sense, and a pleasant teacher is the best. Wisdom is a fountain of life to those possessing it, but a fool's burden is his folly. From a wise mind comes careful and persuasive speech.

JUNE 6

Jesus Casts Out a Legion of Demons/ Luke 8:26–40

So Jesus and his disciples arrived at the other side, in the Gerasene country across the lake from Galilee. 27As he was climbing out of the boat a man from the city of Gadara came to meet him, a man who had been demon-possessed for a long time. Homeless and naked, he lived in a cemetery among the tombs. 28As soon as he saw Jesus he shrieked and fell to the ground before him, screaming, "What do you want with me, Jesus, Son of God Most High? Please, I beg you, oh, don't torment me!"

29For Jesus was already commanding the demon to leave him. This demon had often taken control of the man so that even when shackled with chains he simply broke them and rushed out into the desert, completely under the demon's power. 30"What is your name?" Jesus asked the demon. "Legion," they replied—for the man was filled with thousands of them! 31They kept begging Jesus not to order them into the Bottomless Pit.

32A herd of pigs was feeding on the mountainside nearby, and the demons pled with him to let them enter into the pigs. And Jesus said they could. 33So they left the man and went into the pigs, and immediately the whole herd rushed down the mountainside and fell over a cliff into the lake below, where they drowned. 34The herdsmen rushed away to the nearby city, spreading the news as they ran.

35Soon a crowd came out to see for themselves what had happened and saw the man who had been demon-possessed sitting quietly at Jesus' feet, clothed and sane! And the whole crowd was badly frightened. 36Then those who had seen it happen told how the demon-possessed man had been healed. 37And everyone begged Jesus to go away and leave them alone (for a deep wave of fear had swept over them). So he returned to the boat and left, crossing back to the other side of the lake.

38The man who had been demon-possessed begged to go too, but Jesus said no.

39"Go back to your family," he told him, "and tell them what a wonderful thing God has done for you."

So he went all through the city telling everyone about Jesus' mighty miracle.

40On the other side of the lake the crowds received him with open arms, for they had been waiting for him.

A Thought: *Why didn't Jesus just destroy these demons—or send them to the Bottomless Pit? Because his time for such work had not yet come. He healed many people of the destructive work of demon-possession, but he did not yet destroy demons. The same question could be asked today—why doesn't Jesus destroy or stop the evil in the world? His time for that has not yet come. But it will come. The book of Revelation records the future victory of Jesus over Satan, his demons, and all evil.*

The Fruit of the Spirit/ Galatians 5:22–26

But when the Holy Spirit controls our lives he will produce this kind of fruit in us: love, joy, peace, patience, kindness, goodness, faithfulness, 23gentleness and self-control; and here there is no conflict with Jewish laws.

24Those who belong to Christ have nailed their natural evil desires to his cross and crucified them there.

25If we are living now by the Holy Spirit's power, let us follow the Holy Spirit's leading in every part of our lives. 26Then we won't need to look for honors and popularity, which lead to jealousy and hard feelings.

A THOUGHT: *The Spirit produces character traits, not specific actions. We can't go out and do these things in our own power, and we can't obtain them by working to get them. If we want the fruit of the Spirit to develop in our lives, we must recognize that all of these characteristics are found in Christ. Thus the way to grow in them is to join our lives to his. We must know him, love him, remember him, imitate him. The result will be that we will fulfill the intended purpose of the Law—to love God and man. Which of these qualities need further development in your life?*

Proverbs for Today/ 16:24

Kind words are like honey—enjoyable and healthful.

JUNE 7

Jesus' Power over Sickness and Death/ Luke 8:41–56

And now a man named Jairus, a leader of a Jewish synagogue, came and fell down at Jesus' feet and begged him to come home with him, 42for his only child was dying, a little girl twelve years old. Jesus went with him, pushing through the crowds.

43,44As they went a woman who wanted to be healed came up behind and touched him, for she had been slowly bleeding for twelve years, and could find no cure (though she had spent everything she had on doctors). But the instant she touched the edge of his robe, the bleeding stopped.

45"Who touched me?" Jesus asked.

Everyone denied it, and Peter said, "Master, so many are crowding against you. . . ."

46But Jesus told him, "No, it was someone who

deliberately touched me, for I felt healing power go out from me."

47When the woman realized that Jesus knew, she began to tremble and fell to her knees before him and told why she had touched him and that now she was well.

48"Daughter," he said to her, "your faith has healed you. Go in peace."

49While he was still speaking to her, a messenger arrived from the Jairus' home with the news that the little girl was dead. "She's gone," he told her father; "there's no use troubling the Teacher now."

50But when Jesus heard what had happened, he said to the father, "Don't be afraid! Just trust me, and she'll be all right."

51When they arrived at the house Jesus wouldn't let anyone into the room except Peter, James, John, and the little girl's father and mother. 52The home was filled with mourning people, but he said, "Stop the weeping! She isn't dead; she is only asleep!" 53This brought scoffing and laughter, for they all knew she was dead.

54Then he took her by the hand and called, "Get up, little girl!" 55And at that moment her life returned and she jumped up! "Give her something to eat!" he said. 56Her parents were overcome with happiness, but Jesus insisted that they not tell anyone the details of what had happened.

A THOUGHT: *The bleeding woman acted upon her faith by reaching out to touch Jesus. When she did touch him, she was immediately healed. In the same way, Jairus came to Jesus asking him to heal his daughter. Jesus once again demonstrated his great power by raising Jairus' daughter from the dead. In both of these cases, God's compassion for the powerless of society is evident. God's grace reached down to a woman, who was considered unclean by her community, and to a little girl, who had little or no status in society, and restored them both to full health.*

We Will Reap What We Sow/ Galatians 6:1–10

Dear brothers, if a Christian is overcome by some sin, you who are godly should gently and humbly help him back onto the right path, remembering that next time it might be one of you who is in the wrong. 2Share each other's troubles and problems, and so obey our Lord's command. 3If anyone thinks he is too great to stoop to this, he is fooling himself. He is really a nobody.

4Let everyone be sure that he is doing his very best, for then he will have the personal satisfaction of work well done, and won't need to compare himself with someone else. 5Each of us must bear some faults and burdens of his own. For none of us is perfect!

6Those who are taught the Word of God should help their teachers by paying them.

7Don't be misled; remember that you can't ignore God and get away with it: a man will always reap just the kind of crop he sows! 8If he sows to please his own wrong desires, he will be planting seeds of evil and he will surely reap a harvest of spiritual decay and death; but if he plants the good things of the Spirit, he will reap the everlasting life which the Holy Spirit gives him. 9And let us not get tired of doing what is right, for after a while we will reap a harvest of blessing if we don't get discouraged and give up. 10That's why whenever we can we should always be kind to everyone, and especially to our Christian brothers.

A THOUGHT: *It would certainly be a surprise if you planted corn in the ground and pumpkins came up. But it probably would not be a surprise if you gossiped about your friends and soon found that you had no friends. It's a law of life—both physical and spiritual—that you reap what you sow. Every action has results. If you plant to please your own desires, you'll reap a crop of sorrow and evil; if you plant to please God, you'll reap joy and everlasting life. What kind of seeds are you sowing in the soil of your life?*

Proverbs for Today/ 16:25

Before every man there lies a wide and pleasant road he thinks is right, but it ends in death.

JUNE 8

Jesus Sends Out the Twelve/ Luke 9:1–9

One day Jesus called together his twelve apostles and gave them authority over all demons—power to cast them out—and to heal all diseases. 2Then he sent them away to tell everyone about the coming of the Kingdom of God and to heal the sick.

³"Don't even take along a walking stick," he instructed them, "nor a beggar's bag, nor food, nor money. Not even an extra coat. ⁴Be a guest in only one home at each village.

⁵"If the people of a town won't listen to you when you enter it, turn around and leave, demonstrating God's anger against it by shaking its dust from your feet as you go."

⁶So they began their circuit of the villages, preaching the Good News and healing the sick.

⁷When reports of Jesus' miracles reached Herod, the governor, he was worried and puzzled, for some were saying, "This is John the Baptist come back to life again"; ⁸and others, "It is Elijah or some other ancient prophet risen from the dead." These rumors were circulating all over the land.

⁹"I beheaded John," Herod said, "so who is this man about whom I hear such strange stories?" And he tried to see him.

A Thought: *Why did Jesus announce his Kingdom with preaching and healing? If he had limited himself to preaching, people might have seen his Kingdom as spiritual only. On the other hand, if he had healed without preaching, people might have not realized the spiritual importance of his mission. Most of his listeners expected a Messiah who would bring wealth and power to their nation; they preferred material blessings to spiritual discernment. The truth about Jesus is that he is both God and man, both spiritual and physical; and the salvation he offers is both for the soul and the body. Any group or teaching that emphasizes soul at the expense of body or body at the expense of soul is in danger of distorting Jesus' Good News.*

Paul's Closing Words/ Galatians 6:11–18

I will write these closing words in my own handwriting. See how large I have to make the letters! ¹²Those teachers of yours who are trying to convince you to be circumcised are doing it for just one reason: so that they can be popular and avoid the persecution they would get if they admitted that the cross of Christ alone can save. ¹³And even those teachers who submit to circumcision don't try to keep the other Jewish laws; but they want you to be circumcised in order that they can boast that you are their disciples.

¹⁴As for me, God forbid that I should boast about anything except the cross of our Lord Jesus Christ. Because of that cross my interest in all the attractive things of the

world was killed long ago, and the world's interest in me is also long dead. 15It doesn't make any difference now whether we have been circumcised or not; what counts is whether we really have been changed into new and different people.

16May God's mercy and peace be upon all of you who live by this principle and upon those everywhere who are really God's own.

17From now on please don't argue with me about these things, for I carry on my body the scars of the whippings and wounds from Jesus' enemies that mark me as his slave.

18Dear brothers, may the grace of our Lord Jesus Christ be with you all.

Sincerely,
Paul

A Thought: *Some of the Judaizers emphasized circumcision as proof of holiness, but ignored the other Jewish laws. People often choose a certain principle or prohibition and make it the measuring rod of faith. Some may abhor drunkenness but ignore gluttony. Others despise promiscuity but tolerate prejudice. The Bible in its entirety is our rule of faith and practice. We cannot pick and choose the mandates we will follow.*

Proverbs for Today/ 16:26–27

Hunger is good—if it makes you work to satisfy it!
□ Idle hands are the devil's workshop; idle lips are his mouthpiece.

JUNE 9

The Feeding of the Five Thousand/ Luke 9:10–17

After the apostles returned to Jesus and reported what they had done, he slipped quietly away with them toward the city of Bethsaida. 11But the crowds found out where he was going, and followed. And he welcomed them, teaching them again about the Kingdom of God and curing those who were ill.

12Late in the afternoon all twelve of the disciples came

and urged him to send the people away to the nearby villages and farms, to find food and lodging for the night. "For there is nothing to eat here in this deserted spot," they said.

13But Jesus replied, *"You* feed them!"

"Why, we have only five loaves of bread and two fish among the lot of us," they protested; "or are you expecting us to go and buy enough for this whole mob?" 14For there were about 5,000 men there!

"Just tell them to sit down on the ground in groups of about fifty each," Jesus replied. 15So they did.

16Jesus took the five loaves and two fish and looked up into the sky and gave thanks; then he broke off pieces for his disciples to set before the crowd. 17And everyone ate and ate; still, twelve basketfuls of scraps were picked up afterwards!

A THOUGHT: *The Kingdom of God was a focal point of Jesus' teaching. He explained that it was not just a future kingdom; it was among them, embodied in him, the Messiah. Even though the Kingdom will not be complete until Jesus comes again in glory, we do not have to wait to taste it. The Kingdom of God begins in the hearts of those who believe in Jesus. It is as present with us today as it was with the Judeans two thousand years ago.*

Jesus demonstrated the presence of the Kingdom of God through feeding all these people. Just as God had provided manna for Moses and the people of Israel in the wilderness so that they had more than they needed to eat, so Jesus provides food for these people to the point that they suffered no lack. Our sufficiency for all of life can be found in Jesus.

God's Overflowing Kindness to Us/ Ephesians 1:1–8

Dear Christian friends at Ephesus, ever loyal to the Lord: This is Paul writing to you, chosen by God to be Jesus Christ's messenger. 2May his blessings and peace be yours, sent to you from God our Father and Jesus Christ our Lord.

3How we praise God, the Father of our Lord Jesus Christ, who has blessed us with every blessing in heaven because we belong to Christ.

4Long ago, even before he made the world, God chose us to be his very own, through what Christ would do for us; he decided then to make us holy in his eyes, without a single fault—we who stand before him covered with his love. 5 His unchanging plan has always been to adopt us into his own family by sending Jesus Christ to die for us. And he did this because he wanted to!

6Now all praise to God for his wonderful kindness to us and his favor that he has poured out upon us, because we belong to his dearly loved Son. 7So overflowing is his kindness toward us that he took away all our sins through the blood of his Son, by whom we are saved; 8and he has showered down upon us the richness of his grace—for how well he understands us and knows what is best for us at all times.

A THOUGHT: *To speak of Jesus' blood was an important first-century way of speaking of Christ's death. His death points to two wonderful truths—redemption and forgiveness. Redemption was the price paid to gain freedom for a slave. Through his death, Jesus paid the price to release us from slavery to sin. Forgiveness was granted in Old Testament times on the basis of the shedding of animals' blood. Now we are forgiven on the basis of God's grace in the shedding of Jesus' blood, because he died as the perfect and final sacrifice for our sins. Grace is God's voluntary and loving favor given to those he saves. We can't earn it, nor do we deserve it. No religious or moral effort can gain it, for it comes only from God's mercy and love expressed in the death and resurrection of his Son for our redemption.*

Proverbs for Today/ 16:28–30

An evil man sows strife; gossip separates the best of friends. □ Wickedness loves company—and leads others into sin. The wicked man stares into space with pursed lips, deep in thought, planning his evil deeds.

JUNE 10

Peter's Confession/ Luke 9:18–22

One day as Jesus was alone, praying, with his disciples nearby, he came over and asked them, "Who are the people saying I am?"

19"John the Baptist," they told him, "or perhaps Elijah or one of the other ancient prophets risen from the dead."

20Then he asked them, "Who do you think I am?"

Peter replied, "The Messiah—the Christ of God!"

²¹He gave them strict orders not to speak of this to anyone. ²²"For I, the Messiah, must suffer much," he said, "and be rejected by the Jewish leaders—the elders, chief priests, and teachers of the Law—and be killed; and three days later I will come back to life again!"

A THOUGHT: *Jesus told his disciples not to tell anyone he was the Messiah because, at this point, they didn't fully understand the significance of that statement—nor did anyone else. God had revealed to Peter that Jesus was in fact the Messiah, but Peter, along with everyone else, still expected a messiah who would be a conquering king. But Jesus, as the Messiah, still had to suffer, be rejected by the leaders, be killed, and rise from the dead. Christians must confess with Peter that Jesus is indeed the Messiah, but the Suffering-Servant Messiah who accomplished the redemption of mankind and who will soon come to establish his kingdom on earth. The ultimate question for us as hearers of the Good News is the one that Jesus asked Peter, "Who do you think I am?"*

God's Eternal Plan of Redemption/ Ephesians 1:9–14

God has told us his secret reason for sending Christ, a plan he decided on in mercy long ago; ¹⁰and this was his purpose: that when the time is ripe he will gather us all together from wherever we are—in heaven or on earth— to be with him in Christ, forever. ¹¹Moreover, because of what Christ has done we have become gifts to God that he delights in, for as part of God's sovereign plan we were chosen from the beginning to be his, and all things happen just as he decided long ago. ¹²God's purpose in this was that we should praise God and give glory to him for doing these mighty things for us, who were the first to trust in Christ.

¹³And because of what Christ did, all you others too, who heard the Good News about how to be saved, and trusted Christ, were marked as belonging to Christ by the Holy Spirit, who long ago had been promised to all of us Christians. ¹⁴His presence within us is God's guarantee that he really will give us all that he promised; and the Spirit's seal upon us means that God has already purchased us and that he guarantees to bring us to himself. This is just one more reason for us to praise our glorious God.

A THOUGHT: *The Holy Spirit is God's guarantee to us that he will do what he has promised. He is like a down payment, a deposit, a validating signature on the contract. The presence of the Holy*

Spirit in our lives is our assurance of eternal life with all its blessings. His power at work in us now is transforming our lives, and is a taste of the total change we will experience in eternity.

Proverbs for Today/ 16:31–33

White hair is a crown of glory and is seen most among the godly.   □ It is better to be slow-tempered than famous; it is better to have self-control than to control an army. □ We toss the coin, but it is the Lord who controls its decision.

JUNE 11

Take Up Your Cross and Follow Jesus/ Luke 9:23–27

Then Jesus said to all, "Anyone who wants to follow me must put aside his own desires and conveniences and carry his cross with him every day and *keep close to me!* 24Whoever loses his life for my sake will save it, but whoever insists on keeping his life will lose it; 25and what profit is there in gaining the whole world when it means forfeiting one's self?

26"When I, the Messiah, come in my glory and in the glory of the Father and the holy angels, I will be ashamed then of all who are ashamed of me and of my words now. 27But this is the simple truth—some of you who are standing here right now will not die until you have seen the Kingdom of God."

A THOUGHT: *People are willing to pay a high price for something they value. Is it any surprise that Jesus should demand this much commitment from those who would follow him? There are at least three conditions that must be met by people who want to follow Jesus. They must be willing to deny self, to carry their crosses, and to give up control over their lives. Anything less is superficial lip service.*

Paul's Prayer for the Ephesians/ Ephesians 1:15–23

That is why, ever since I heard of your strong faith in the Lord Jesus and of the love you have for Christians everywhere, 16,17I have never stopped thanking God for you. I pray for you constantly, asking God, the glorious Father of our Lord Jesus Christ, to give you wisdom to see clearly and really understand who Christ is and all that he has done for you. 18I pray that your hearts will be flooded with light so that you can see something of the future he has called you to share. I want you to realize that God has been made rich because we who are Christ's have been given to him! 19I pray that you will begin to understand how incredibly great his power is to help those who believe him. It is that same mighty power 20that raised Christ from the dead and seated him in the place of honor at God's right hand in heaven, 21far, far above any other king or ruler or dictator or leader. Yes, his honor is far more glorious than that of anyone else either in this world or in the world to come. 22And God has put all things under his feet and made him the supreme Head of the Church— 23which is his body, filled with himself, the Author and Giver of everything everywhere.

A THOUGHT: *Paul's prayer for the Ephesians was that they might really understand who Christ is. Christ is our goal and our model, and the more we know of him, the more we will be like him. Study Jesus' life in the Bible to see what he was like on earth 2,000 years ago, and get to know him in prayer now. Personal knowledge of Christ is life-changing!*

Proverbs for Today/ 17:1

A dry crust eaten in peace is better than steak every day along with argument and strife.

JUNE 12

The Transfiguration of Jesus/ Luke 9:28–36

Eight days later Jesus took Peter, James, and John with him into the hills to pray. 29And as he was praying, his face began to shine, and his clothes became dazzling white and blazed with light. 30Then two men appeared and began talking with him—Moses and Elijah! 31They were splendid in appearance, glorious to see; and they were speaking of his death at Jerusalem, to be carried out in accordance with God's plan.

32Peter and the others had been very drowsy and had fallen asleep. Now they woke up and saw Jesus covered with brightness and glory, and the two men standing with him. 33As Moses and Elijah were starting to leave, Peter, all confused and not even knowing what he was saying, blurted out, "Master, this is wonderful! We'll put up three shelters—one for you and one for Moses and one for Elijah!"

34But even as he was saying this, a bright cloud formed above them; and terror gripped them as it covered them. 35And a voice from the cloud said, "*This* is my Son, my Chosen One; listen to *him.*"

36Then, as the voice died away, Jesus was there alone with his disciples. They didn't tell anyone what they had seen until long afterwards.

A THOUGHT: *Jesus took Peter, James, and John to the top of a mountain to show them who he really was—not just a great prophet, but God's own Son. Moses, representing the Law, and Elijah, representing the Prophets, appeared with Jesus. God's voice singled out Jesus as the long-awaited Messiah who possessed divine authority. The authority of Jesus superceded that of the Law and the Prophets represented by Moses and Elijah, for Jesus is the fulfillment of both the Law and the Prophets.*

As God's Son, Jesus has ultimate power and authority; thus his words should be our final authority. If a person's teaching is true, it will go along with Jesus' teachings. Test everything you hear against Jesus' words, and you will not be led astray.

We Were Dead and Doomed by Our Sins/ Ephesians 2:1–7

Once you were under God's curse, doomed forever for your sins. 2You went along with the crowd and were just like all the others, full of sin, obeying Satan, the mighty prince of the power of the air, who is at work right now in the hearts of those who are against the Lord. 3All of us used to be just as they are, our lives expressing the evil within us, doing every wicked thing that our passions or our evil thoughts might lead us into. We started out bad, being born with evil natures, and were under God's anger just like everyone else.

4But God is so rich in mercy; he loved us so much 5that even though we were spiritually dead and doomed by our sins, he gave us back our lives again when he raised Christ from the dead—only by his undeserved favor have we ever been saved— 6and lifted us up from the grave into glory along with Christ, where we sit with him in the heavenly realms—all because of what Christ Jesus did. 7And now God can always point to us as examples of how very, very rich his kindness is, as shown in all he has done for us through Jesus Christ.

A THOUGHT: *The fact that all people, without exception, commit sin proves that they share in the sinful nature. Does this mean there are no good people who are not Christians? Of course not. Many people do good to others. On a relative scale, many are moral, kind, keep the laws, and so on. Comparing these people to criminals, we would say they are very good indeed. But on God's absolute scale, no one is good. Only through uniting our lives to Christ's perfect life can we become good in God's sight.*

Proverbs for Today/ 17:2–3

A wise slave will rule his master's wicked sons and share their estate. □ Silver and gold are purified by fire, but God purifies hearts.

JUNE 13

Jesus Heals a Demon-Possesed Boy/ Luke 9:37–43a

The next day as Jesus and his disciples descended from the hill, a huge crowd met him, 38and a man in the crowd called out to him, "Teacher, this boy here is my only son, 39and a demon keeps seizing him, making him scream; and it throws him into convulsions so that he foams at the mouth; it is always hitting him and hardly ever leaves him alone. 40I begged your disciples to cast the demon out, but they couldn't."

41"O you stubborn faithless people," Jesus said [to his disciples], "how long should I put up with you? Bring him here."

42As the boy was coming the demon knocked him to the ground and threw him into a violent convulsion. But Jesus ordered the demon to come out, and healed the boy and handed him over to his father.

43Awe gripped the people as they saw this display of the power of God.

A THOUGHT: *This account is set in contrast to the transfiguration of Jesus which Peter, James, and John had just seen. The disciples were unable to cast out the demon from this boy because they lacked the faith. They did not recognize that the One who had commissioned them to preach the Good News, to heal, and to cast out demons, was the divine Son of God. Jesus demonstrated that he possessed the authority of God through casting out the demon from the boy— a sign that the Kingdom of God was present in the person of Jesus Christ himself. Recognizing God's great power should move us to worship him and live in humble obedience before him.*

We Have Been Saved by Grace through Faith/ Ephesians 2:8–13

Because of his kindness you have been saved through trusting Christ. And even trusting is not of yourselves; it too is a gift from God. 9Salvation is not a reward for the good we have done, so none of us can take any credit for it. 10It is God himself who has made us what we are and given us new lives from Christ Jesus; and long ages ago he planned that we should spend these lives in helping others.

11Never forget that once you were heathen, and that you were called godless and "unclean" by the Jews. (But their hearts, too, were still unclean, even though they were going through the ceremonies and rituals of the godly, for they circumcised themselves as a sign of godliness.) 12Remember that in those days you were living utterly apart from Christ; you were enemies of God's children and he had promised you no help. You were lost, without God, without hope.

13But now you belong to Christ Jesus, and though you once were far away from God, now you have been brought very near to him because of what Jesus Christ has done for you with his blood.

A THOUGHT: *We become Christians through God's unmerited gift to us, not as the result of any effort, ability, intelligent choice, or act of service to others on our part. However, out of gratitude for this free gift, we will seek to help and serve others with kindness, charity, and goodness, and not merely please ourselves. While no action or "work" we do can help us obtain salvation, God's intention is that our salvation will result in works of service. We are not*

saved merely for our own benefit but for his—to glorifying him
and build up the church.

Proverbs for Today/ 17:4–5

The wicked enjoy fellowship with others who are wicked;
liars enjoy liars. □ Mocking the poor is mocking the
God who made them. He will punish those who rejoice
at others' misfortunes.

JUNE 14

Servanthood Is the Measure of Greatness/
Luke 9:43b–50

Meanwhile, as the people were exclaiming over all the
wonderful things he was doing, Jesus said to his disciples,
44"Listen to me and remember what I say. I, the Messiah,
am going to be betrayed." 45But the disciples didn't know
what he meant, for their minds had been sealed and they
were afraid to ask him.

46Now came an argument among them as to which of
them would be greatest [in the coming Kingdom]! 47But
Jesus knew their thoughts, so he stood a little child beside
him 48and said to them, "Anyone who takes care of a
little child like this is caring for me! And whoever cares
for me is caring for God who sent me. Your care for
others is the measure of your greatness." 49His disciple
John came to him and said, "Master, we saw someone
using your name to cast out demons. And we told him
not to. After all, he isn't in our group."

50But Jesus said, "You shouldn't have done that! For
anyone who is not against you is for you."

A THOUGHT: *The disciples didn't understand Jesus' words about
his death. They still thought of Jesus as an earthly king, and they
were concerned about securing high places for themselves in his
kingdom. So they ignored his words about his death and began
arguing about who would be greatest. It is ironic that immediately
following Jesus' explanation of his betrayal—the Lord of glory offering
himself up as an atoning sacrifice for the sins of mankind—that
the disciples should be arguing about greatness. When we seek*

honor and glory for ourselves, we can be assured that it is not true greatness that we will find, for true greatness is marked by genuine self-sacrifice and obedience to God—true greatness is in Christlikeness.

Christ Is the Way of Peace/ Ephesians 2:14–22

For Christ himself is our way of peace. He has made peace between us Jews and you Gentiles by making us all one family, breaking down the wall of contempt that used to separate us. 15By his death he ended the angry resentment between us, caused by the Jewish laws which favored the Jews and excluded the Gentiles, for he died to annul that whole system of Jewish laws. Then he took the two groups that had been opposed to each other and made them parts of himself; thus he fused us together to become one new person, and at last there was peace. 16As parts of the same body, our anger against each other has disappeared, for both of us have been reconciled to God. And so the feud ended at last at the cross. 17And he has brought this Good News of peace to you Gentiles who were very far away from him, and to us Jews who were near. 18Now all of us, whether Jews or Gentiles, may come to God the Father with the Holy Spirit's help because of what Christ has done for us.

19Now you are no longer strangers to God and foreigners to heaven, but you are members of God's very own family, citizens of God's country, and you belong in God's household with every other Christian.

20What a foundation you stand on now: the apostles and the prophets; and the cornerstone of the building is Jesus Christ himself! 21We who believe are carefully joined together with Christ as parts of a beautiful, constantly growing temple for God. 22And you also are joined with him and with each other by the Spirit, and are part of this dwelling place of God.

A THOUGHT: *There are many barriers that can divide us from other Christians: age, appearance, intelligence, political persuasion, economic status, race, theological perspective. One of the best ways to stifle Christ's love is to cater only to those for whom we have natural affinity. Fortunately, Christ has knocked down the barriers and unified all believers in one family. His cross should be the focus of our unity. The Holy Spirit helps us look beyond the barriers to the unity we are called to enjoy.*

JUNE 15

Proverbs for Today/ 17:6
An old man's grandchildren are his crowning glory. A child's glory is his father.

JUNE 15

Would-Be Disciples/ Luke 9:51–62
As the time drew near for his return to heaven, Jesus moved steadily onward toward Jerusalem with an iron will.

52One day he sent messengers ahead to reserve rooms for them in a Samaritan village. 53But they were turned away! The people of the village refused to have anything to do with them because they were headed for Jerusalem.

54When word came back of what had happened, James and John said to Jesus, "Master, shall we order fire down from heaven to burn them up?" 55But Jesus turned and rebuked them, 56and they went on to another village.

57As they were walking along someone said to Jesus, "I will always follow you no matter where you go."

58But Jesus replied, "Remember, I don't even own a place to lay my head. Foxes have dens to live in, and birds have nests, but I, the Messiah, have no earthly home at all."

59Another time, when he invited a man to come with him and to be his disciple, the man agreed—but wanted to wait until his father's death.

60Jesus replied, "Let those without eternal life concern themselves with things like that. Your duty is to come and preach the coming of the Kingdom of God to all the world."

61Another said, "Yes, Lord, I will come, but first let me ask permission of those at home."

62But Jesus told him, "Anyone who lets himself be distracted from the work I plan for him is not fit for the Kingdom of God."

A Thought: *What does Jesus want from us? He wants total dedication, not halfhearted commitment. We can't pick and choose among*

Jesus' ideas and follow him selectively; we have to accept the cross along with the crown, judgment as well as mercy. We must count the cost and be willing to abandon everything else that has given us security. With our focus on Jesus, we should allow nothing to distract us from the manner of living he calls us to live out.

Paul's Special Mission to Gentiles/ Ephesians 3:1–7

I Paul, the servant of Christ, am here in jail because of you—for preaching that you Gentiles are a part of God's house. 2,3No doubt you already know that God has given me this special work of showing God's favor to you Gentiles, as I briefly mentioned before in one of my letters. God himself showed me this secret plan of his, that the Gentiles, too, are included in his kindness. 4I say this to explain to you how I know about these things. 5In olden times God did not share this plan with his people, but now he has revealed it by the Holy Spirit to his apostles and prophets.

6And this is the secret: that the Gentiles will have their full share with the Jews in all the riches inherited by God's sons; both are invited to belong to his Church, and all of God's promises of mighty blessings through Christ apply to them both when they accept the Good News about Christ and what he has done for them. 7God has given me the wonderful privilege of telling everyone about this plan of his; and he has given me his power and special ability to do it well.

A THOUGHT: *God gave the apostle Paul the ability to share effectively the gospel of Christ. You may not be an apostle or even an evangelist, but God will also give you opportunities to tell others about Christ— and with the opportunity he will provide the ability, courage, and power. Whenever an opportunity presents itself, make yourself available to God. As you focus on the other person and his or her needs, God will communicate your caring attitude, and your words will be natural, loving, and compelling.*

Proverbs for Today/ 17:7–8

Truth from a rebel or lies from a king are both unexpected. □ A bribe works like magic. Whoever uses it will prosper!

JUNE 16

Jesus Sends out Seventy Disciples/ Luke 10:1–24

The Lord now chose seventy other disciples and sent them on ahead in pairs to all the towns and villages he planned to visit later.

2These were Jesus' instructions to them: "Plead with the Lord of the harvest to send out more laborers to help you, for the harvest is so plentiful and the workers so few. 3Go now, and remember that I am sending you out as lambs among wolves. 4Don't take any money with you, or a beggar's bag, or even an extra pair of shoes. And don't waste time along the way.

5"Whenever you enter a home, give it your blessing. 6If it is worthy of the blessing, the blessing will stand; if not, the blessing will return to you.

7"When you enter a village, don't shift around from home to home, but stay in one place, eating and drinking without question whatever is set before you. And don't hesitate to accept hospitality, for the workman is worthy of his wages!

8,9"If a town welcomes you, follow these two rules:

(1) Eat whatever is set before you.
(2) Heal the sick; and as you heal them, say, 'The Kingdom of God is very near you now.'

10"But if a town refuses you, go out into its streets and say, 11'We wipe the dust of your town from our feet as a public announcement of your doom. Never forget how close you were to the Kingdom of God!' 12Even wicked Sodom will be better off than such a city on the Judgment Day. 13What horrors await you, you cities of Chorazin and Bethsaida! For if the miracles I did for you had been done in the cities of Tyre and Sidon, their people would have sat in deep repentance long ago, clothed in sackcloth and throwing ashes on their heads to show their remorse. 14Yes, Tyre and Sidon will receive less punishment on the Judgment Day than you. 15And you people of Capernaum, what shall I say about you? Will you be exalted to heaven? No, you shall be brought down to hell."

16Then he said to the disciples, "Those who welcome you are welcoming me. And those who reject you are rejecting me. And those who reject me are rejecting God who sent me."

17When the seventy disciples returned, they joyfully reported to him, "Even the demons obey us when we use your name."

18"Yes," he told them, "I saw Satan falling from heaven as a flash of lightning! 19And I have given you authority over all the power of the Enemy, and to walk among serpents and scorpions and to crush them. Nothing shall injure you! 20However, the important thing is not that demons obey you, but that your names are registered as citizens of heaven."

21Then he was filled with the joy of the Holy Spirit and said, "I praise you, O Father, Lord of heaven and earth, for hiding these things from the intellectuals and worldly wise and for revealing them to those who are as trusting as little children. Yes, thank you, Father, for that is the way you wanted it. 22I am the Agent of my Father in everything; and no one really knows the Son except the Father, and no one really knows the Father except the Son and those to whom the Son chooses to reveal him."

23Then, turning to the twelve disciples, he said quietly, "How privileged you are to see what you have seen. 24Many a prophet and king of old has longed for these days, to see and hear what you have seen and heard!"

A THOUGHT: *The disciples had seen tremendous results as they ministered in Jesus' name and with his authority. They were elated by the victories they had witnessed, and Jesus shared their enthusiasm. He brought them down to earth, however, by reminding them of their most important victory—that their names were registered among the citizens of heaven. This honor was more important than any of their accomplishments. As we see God's wonders at work in us and through us, we should not lose sight of the greatest wonder of all—the grace of God expressed in our heavenly citizenship.*

Jews and Gentiles Are One Family in the Church/ Ephesians 3:8–13

Just think! Though I did nothing to deserve it, and though I am the most useless Christian there is, yet I was the one chosen for this special joy of telling the Gentiles the

Glad News of the endless treasures available to them in Christ; 9and to explain to everyone that God is the Savior of the Gentiles too, just as he who made all things had secretly planned from the very beginning.

10And his reason? To show to all the rulers in heaven how perfectly wise he is when all of his family—Jews and Gentiles alike—are seen to be joined together in his Church, 11in just the way he had always planned it through Jesus Christ our Lord.

12Now we can come fearlessly right into God's presence, assured of his glad welcome when we come with Christ and trust in him.

13So please don't lose heart at what they are doing to me here. It is for you I am suffering and you should feel honored and encouraged.

A THOUGHT: *When Paul describes himself as a useless Christian, he is saying that without God's help, he would never be able to do God's work. Yet God chose him to share the gospel with the Gentiles and gave him the power to do this. If we feel useless, we may be right—except that we have forgotten what a difference God makes. How does God want to use you? Do your part and faithfully perform the special role you play in God's plan.*

Proverbs for Today/ 17:9–11

Love forgets mistakes; nagging about them parts the best of friends. □ A rebuke to a man of common sense is more effective than a hundred lashes on the back of a rebel. □ The wicked live for rebellion; they shall be severely punished.

JUNE 17

The Story of the Good Samaritan/ Luke 10:25–37

One day an expert on Moses' laws came to test Jesus' orthodoxy by asking him this question: "Teacher, what does a man need to do to live forever in heaven?"

26Jesus replied, "What does Moses' law say about it?"

27"It says," he replied, "that you must love the Lord your God with all your heart, and with all your soul, and with all your strength, and with all your mind. And you must love your neighbor just as much as you love yourself."

28"Right!" Jesus told him. *"Do* this and *you* shall live!"

29The man wanted to justify (his lack of love for some kinds of people), so he asked, "Which neighbors?"

30Jesus replied with an illustration: "A Jew going on a trip from Jerusalem to Jericho was attacked by bandits. They stripped him of his clothes and money and beat him up and left him lying half dead beside the road.

31"By chance a Jewish priest came along; and when he saw the man lying there, he crossed to the other side of the road and passed him by. 32A Jewish Temple-assistant walked over and looked at him lying there, but then went on.

33"But a despised Samaritan came along, and when he saw him, he felt deep pity. 34Kneeling beside him the Samaritan soothed his wounds with medicine and bandaged them. Then he put the man on his donkey and walked along beside him till they came to an inn, where he nursed him through the night. 35The next day he handed the innkeeper two twenty-dollar bills and told him to take care of the man. 'If his bill runs higher than that,' he said, 'I'll pay the difference the next time I am here.'

36"Now which of these three would you say was a neighbor to the bandits' victim?"

37The man replied, "The one who showed him some pity."

Then Jesus said, "Yes, now go and do the same."

A THOUGHT: *The legal experts treated the wounded man as a topic for discussion; the thieves, as an object to exploit; the priest, as a problem to avoid; and the temple assistant, as an object of curiosity. Only the Samaritan treated him as a person to love. From the parable we learn three principles about loving our neighbor: (1) lack of love is often easy to justify; (2) our neighbor is anyone of any race or creed or social background who is in need; and (3) love means acting to meet the need. Wherever you live, there are needy people close by. There is no good rationale for refusing to help.*

Paul Prays for the Ephesians/ Ephesians 3:14–21

When I think of the wisdom and scope of his plan I fall down on my knees and pray to the Father of all the great family of God—some of them already in heaven and some down here on earth— 16that out of his glorious, unlimited resources he will give you the mighty inner strengthening of his Holy Spirit. 17And I pray that Christ will be more and more at home in your hearts, living within you as you trust in him. May your roots go down deep into the soil of God's marvelous love; 18,19and may you be able to feel and understand, as all God's children should, how long, how wide, how deep, and how high his love really is; and to experience this love for yourselves, though it is so great that you will never see the end of it or fully know or understand it. And so at last you will be filled up with God himself.

20Now glory be to God who by his mighty power at work within us is able to do far more than we would ever dare to ask or even dream of—infinitely beyond our highest prayers, desires, thoughts, or hopes. 21May he be given glory forever and ever through endless ages because of his master plan of salvation for the Church through Jesus Christ.

A THOUGHT: *The great family of God includes all who have believed in him in the past, all who believe in the present, and all who will believe in the future. We are all a family because we have the same Father. He is the source of all creation, the rightful owner of everything. God promises his love and power to his family, the church; if we want to receive his blessings, it is important that we stay in living contact with other believers in the body of Christ. Those who isolate themselves from God's family and try to go it alone are cutting themselves off from the primary avenue through which God has chosen to work.*

Proverbs for Today/ 17:12–13

It is safer to meet a bear robbed of her cubs than a fool caught in his folly. □ If you repay evil for good, a curse is upon your home.

JUNE 18

Mary and Martha/ Luke 10:38–42

As Jesus and the disciples continued on their way to Jerusalem they came to a village where a woman named Martha welcomed them into her home. 39Her sister Mary sat on the floor, listening to Jesus as he talked.

⁴⁰But Martha was the jittery type, and was worrying over the big dinner she was preparing.

She came to Jesus and said, "Sir, doesn't it seem unfair to you that my sister just sits here while I do all the work? Tell her to come and help me."

⁴¹But the Lord said to her, "Martha, dear friend, you are so upset over all these details! ⁴²There is really only one thing worth being concerned about. Mary has discovered it—and I won't take it away from her!"

A THOUGHT: *Mary and Martha both loved Jesus. On this occasion they were both serving him. But Martha implied that Mary's style of serving was inferior to hers. She didn't realize that in her desire to serve, she was actually neglecting Jesus. Are you so busy doing things for Jesus that you're not spending any time with him? Don't let your service become self-serving. It is important to know whom you are serving.*

We Are One Body in Christ/ Ephesians 4:1–10

I beg you—I, a prisoner here in jail for serving the Lord— to live and act in a way worthy of those who have been chosen for such wonderful blessings as these. ²Be humble and gentle. Be patient with each other, making allowance for each other's faults because of your love. ³Try always to be led along together by the Holy Spirit, and so be at peace with one another.

⁴ We are all parts of one body, we have the same Spirit, and we have all been called to the same glorious future. ⁵For us there is only one Lord, one faith, one baptism, ⁶and we all have the same God and Father who is over us all and in us all, and living through every part of us. ⁷However, Christ has given each of us special abilities—whatever he wants us to have out of his rich storehouse of gifts.

⁸The Psalmist tells about this, for he says that when Christ returned triumphantly to heaven after his resurrection and victory over Satan, he gave generous gifts to men. ⁹Notice that it says he returned to heaven. This means that he had first come down from the heights of heaven, far down to the lowest parts of the earth. ¹⁰The same one who came down is the one who went back up, that he might fill all things everywhere with himself, from the very lowest to the very highest.

A THOUGHT: *"We are all parts of one body,"* says Paul, *and we have been given many gifts and abilities. Unity does not just happen; we have to work at it. Often differences among people can lead to division, but this should not be true in the church. Instead of concentrating on what divides us, we should remember what unites us: one body, one Spirit, one future, one Lord, one faith, one baptism, one God! Have you learned to appreciate people who are different from you? Can you see how their differing gifts and viewpoints can help the church as it does God's work? Learn to enjoy the way the members of Christ's body complement one another.*

Proverbs for Today/ 17:14–15

It is hard to stop a quarrel once it starts, so don't let it begin. □ The Lord despises those who say that bad is good, and good is bad.

JUNE 19

Jesus Instructs His Followers about Prayer/ Luke 11:1–13

Once when Jesus had been out praying, one of his disciples came to him as he finished and said, "Lord, teach us a prayer to recite just as John taught one to his disciples."

2And this is the prayer he taught them: "Father, may your name be honored for its holiness; send your Kingdom soon. 3Give us our food day by day. 4And forgive our sins—for we have forgiven those who sinned against us. And don't allow us to be tempted."

5,6Then, teaching them more about prayer, he used this illustration: "Suppose you went to a friend's house at midnight, wanting to borrow three loaves of bread. You would shout up to him, 'A friend of mine has just arrived for a visit and I've nothing to give him to eat.' 7He would call down from his bedroom, 'Please don't ask me to get up. The door is locked for the night and we are all in bed. I just can't help you this time.'

8"But I'll tell you this—though he won't do it as a friend, if you keep knocking long enough he will get up and give you everything you want—just because of your persistence. 9And so it is with prayer—keep on asking and you will keep on getting; keep on looking and you will keep on finding; knock and the door will be opened. 10Everyone who asks, receives; all who seek, find; and the door is opened to everyone who knocks.

11"You men who are fathers—if your boy asks for bread, do you give him a stone? If he asks for fish, do you give him a snake? 12If he asks for an egg, do you give him a scorpion? [Of course not!]

13"And if even sinful persons like yourselves give children what they need, don't you realize that your heavenly Father will do at least as much, and give the Holy Spirit to those who ask for him?"

A Thought: *When Jesus begins to teach his disciples about prayer, he gives them a pattern to follow—a model prayer. Notice the order in this prayer. First Jesus praises God; then he makes his requests. Praising God first puts us in the right frame of mind to tell him about our needs. Too often our prayers are more like shopping lists than conversations.*

Jesus also made forgiving others a central part of our relationship with God. God has forgiven our sins; we must forgive those who have wronged us. To remain unforgiving shows we have not understood that we, along with all other human beings, deeply need to be forgiven. Think of some people who have wronged you. Have you truly forgiven them, or do you still carry a grudge against them? Our communion with God in prayer is directly affected by our relationship with those around us.

God Has Gifted the Church/ Ephesians 4:11–16

Some of us have been given special ability as apostles; to others he has given the gift of being able to preach well; some have special ability in winning people to Christ, helping them to trust him as their Savior; still others have a gift for caring for God's people as a shepherd does his sheep, leading and teaching them in the ways of God.

12Why is it that he gives us these special abilities to do certain things best? It is that God's people will be equipped to do better work for him, building up the Church, the body of Christ, to a position of strength and maturity; 13until finally we all believe alike about our salvation and about our Savior, God's Son, and all become full-grown in the Lord—yes, to the point of being filled full with Christ.

14Then we will no longer be like children, forever changing our minds about what we believe because someone has told us something different, or has cleverly lied to us and made the lie sound like the truth. 15, 16Instead, we will lovingly follow the truth at all times—speaking truly, dealing truly, living truly —and so become more and more in every way like Christ who is the Head of his body, the Church. Under his direction the whole body is fitted together perfectly, and each part in its own special way helps the other parts, so that the whole body is healthy and growing and full of love.

A THOUGHT: *All believers in Christ belong to one body; all are united under one Head, who is Christ himself. Each believer has God-given abilities that can strengthen the whole body. Our oneness in Christ does not destroy our individuality. The Holy Spirit has given each Christian special gifts for building up the church. Now that we have these gifts, it is crucial to use them. Are you spiritually mature, exercising the gifts God has given you? If you know what your gifts are, look for opportunities to serve. If you don't know, ask God to show you what your gifts are. Then, as you begin to recognize your special area of service, use your gifts to strengthen and encourage the church.*

Proverbs for Today/ 17:16

It is senseless to pay tuition to educate a rebel who has no heart for truth.

JUNE 20

The Kingdom of God and the Kingdom of Satan/ Luke 11:14–28

Once, when Jesus cast out a demon from a man who couldn't speak, his voice returned to him. The crowd was excited and enthusiastic, 15but some said, "No wonder he can cast them out. He gets his power from Satan, the king of demons!" 16Others asked for something to happen in the sky to prove his claim of being the Messiah.

17He knew the thoughts of each of them, so he said, "Any kingdom filled with civil war is doomed; so is a home filled with argument and strife. 18Therefore, if what you say is true, that Satan is fighting against himself by empowering me to cast out his demons, how can his kingdom survive? 19And if I am empowered by Satan, what about your own followers? For they cast out demons! Do you think this proves they are possessed by Satan? Ask *them* if you are right! 20But if I am casting out demons because of power from God, it proves that the Kingdom of God has arrived.

21"For when Satan, strong and fully armed, guards his palace, it is safe— 22until someone stronger and better-armed attacks and overcomes him and strips him of his weapons and carries off his belongings.

23"Anyone who is not for me is against me; if he isn't helping me, he is hurting my cause.

24"When a demon is cast out of a man, it goes to the deserts, searching there for rest; but finding none, it returns to the person it left, 25and finds that its former home is all swept and clean. 26Then it goes and gets seven other demons more evil than itself, and they all enter the man. And so the poor fellow is seven times worse off than he was before."

27As he was speaking, a woman in the crowd called out, "God bless your mother—the womb from which you came, and the breasts that gave you suck!"

28He replied, "Yes, but even more blessed are all who hear the Word of God and put it into practice."

A THOUGHT: *Jesus proved to his listeners that the Kingdom of God had arrived in his person. Jesus was casting out the demons who belonged to the kingdom of darkness. This account, along with the many other accounts of casting out demons, pointed to Satan's defeat and the establishment of the Kingdom of God. God will bring about his ultimate victory over Satan in the end when he casts Satan and all of his followers into the Lake of Fire. Are we among those who recognize the power of God in Jesus Christ?*

Throw Off the Old and Clothe Yourself with the New/ Ephesians 4:17–24

Let me say this, then, speaking for the Lord: Live no longer as the unsaved do, for they are blinded and confused. Their closed hearts are full of darkness; they are far away from the life of God because they have shut their minds against him, and they cannot understand his ways. 19They don't care anymore about right and wrong and have given themselves over to impure ways. They stop at nothing, being driven by their evil minds and reckless lusts.

20But that isn't the way Christ taught you! 21If you have really heard his voice and learned from him the truths concerning himself, 22then throw off your old evil nature—the old you that was a partner in your evil ways—rotten through and through, full of lust and sham.

23Now your attitudes and thoughts must all be constantly changing for the better. 24Yes, you must be a new and different person, holy and good. Clothe yourself with this new nature.

A THOUGHT: *People should be able to see a difference between Christians and non-Christians because of the way Christians live. Paul tells the Ephesians to leave behind the old life of sin now that they are followers of Christ. The Christian life is a process. We don't automatically have all good thoughts and attitudes when we become new people in Christ. But if we keep listening to God, we will be changing all the time. As you look over the last year, do you see a process of change for the better in your thoughts, attitudes, and actions? Although change may be slow, it comes about if you trust God to change you.*

Proverbs for Today/ 17:17–18

A true friend is always loyal, and a brother is born to help in time of need. □ It is poor judgment to countersign another's note, to become responsible for his debts.

JUNE 21

The Sign of Jonah/ Luke 11:29–36

As the crowd pressed in upon Jesus, he preached them this sermon: "These are evil times, with evil people. They keep asking for some strange happening in the skies [to prove I am the Messiah], but the only proof I will give them is a miracle like that of Jonah, whose experiences proved to the people of Nineveh that God had sent him. My similar experience will prove that God has sent me to these people.

31"And at the Judgment Day the Queen of Sheba shall

arise and point her finger at this generation, condemning it, for she went on a long, hard journey to listen to the wisdom of Solomon; but one far greater than Solomon is here [and few pay any attention].

32"The men of Nineveh, too, shall arise and condemn this nation, for they repented at the preaching of Jonah; and someone far greater than Jonah is here [but this nation won't listen].

33"No one lights a lamp and hides it! Instead, he puts it on a lampstand to give light to all who enter the room. 34Your eyes light up your inward being. A pure eye lets sunshine into your soul. A lustful eye shuts out the light and plunges you into darkness. 35So watch out that the sunshine isn't blotted out. 36If you are filled with light within, with no dark corners, then your face will be radiant too, as though a floodlight is beamed upon you."

A THOUGHT: *The cruel, warlike men of Assyria repented when Jonah preached to them—and Jonah did not really care about them. The heathen Queen of Sheba praised the God of Israel when she heard Solomon's wisdom, and Solomon was full of faults. By contrast, Jesus, the perfect Son of God, came to people whom he loved dearly—and they rejected him. Thus God's chosen people made themselves more liable to judgment than either a notoriously wicked nation or a powerful pagan queen. The people of Nineveh and the Queen of Sheba had turned to God with far less evidence than Jesus was giving his listeners—and far less than we have today. We have eyewitness reports of the risen Jesus, the continuing power of the Holy Spirit, easy access to the Bible, and 2,000 years of church history recording Christ's redemptive activity. Do you take full advantage of your opportunities to know God?*

Paul's Commands for Christian Living/ Ephesians 4:25–32

Stop lying to each other; tell the truth, for we are parts of each other and when we lie to each other we are hurting ourselves. 26If you are angry, don't sin by nursing your grudge. Don't let the sun go down with you still angry— get over it quickly; 27for when you are angry you give a mighty foothold to the devil.

28If anyone is stealing he must stop it and begin using those hands of his for honest work so he can give to others in need. 29Don't use bad language. Say only what is good and helpful to those you are talking to, and what will give them a blessing.

30Don't cause the Holy Spirit sorrow by the way you live. Remember, he is the one who marks you to be present on that day when salvation from sin will be complete.

31Stop being mean, bad-tempered and angry. Quarreling, harsh words, and dislike of others should have no place in your lives. 32Instead, be kind to each other, tender-hearted, forgiving one another, just as God has forgiven you because you belong to Christ.

A THOUGHT: *We can cause the Holy Spirit sorrow by the way we live. Paul warns us against bad language, meanness, improper use of anger, quarrels, harsh words, and bad attitudes toward others. Instead of acting that way, we should be forgiving, just as God has forgiven us. Are you grieving or pleasing God with your attitudes and actions? Act in love toward your brothers and sisters in Christ, just as God acted in love by sending his Son to die for your sins.*

Proverbs for Today/ 17:19–21

Sinners love to fight; boasting is looking for trouble. □ An evil man is suspicious of everyone and tumbles into constant trouble. □ It's no fun to be a rebel's father.

JUNE 22

Jesus Denounces the Pharisees/ Luke 11:37–54

As Jesus was speaking, one of the Pharisees asked him home for a meal. When Jesus arrived, he sat down to eat without first performing the ceremonial washing required by Jewish custom. This greatly surprised his host.

39Then Jesus said to him, "You Pharisees wash the outside, but inside you are still dirty—full of greed and wickedness! 40Fools! Didn't God make the inside as well as the outside? 41Purity is best demonstrated by generosity.

42"But woe to you Pharisees! For though you are careful to tithe even the smallest part of your income, you completely forget about justice and the love of God. You should tithe, yes, but you should not leave these other things undone.

43"Woe to you Pharisees! For how you love the seats of honor in the synagogues and the respectful greetings from everyone as you walk through the markets! 44Yes, awesome judgment is awaiting you. For you are like hidden graves in a field. Men go by you with no knowledge of the corruption they are passing."

45"Sir," said an expert in religious law who was standing there, "you have insulted my profession, too, in what you just said."

46"Yes," said Jesus, "the same horrors await you! For you crush men beneath impossible religious demands— demands that you yourselves would never think of trying to keep. 47Woe to you! For you are exactly like your ancestors who killed the prophets long ago. 48Murderers! You agree with your fathers that what they did was right— you would have done the same yourselves.

49"This is what God says about you: 'I will send prophets and apostles to you, and you will kill some of them and chase away the others.'

50"And you of this generation will be held responsible for the murder of God's servants from the founding of the world— 51from the murder of Abel to the murder of Zechariah who perished between the altar and the sanctuary. Yes, it will surely be charged against you.

52"Woe to you experts in religion! For you hide the truth from the people. You won't accept it for yourselves, and you prevent others from having a chance to believe it."

53,54The Pharisees and legal experts were furious; and from that time on they plied him fiercely with a host of questions, trying to trap him into saying something for which they could have him arrested.

A THOUGHT: *Jesus criticized the Pharisees harshly because they (1) washed their hands but not their hearts, (2) remembered to tithe but forgot justice, (3) loved people's praise, (4) made impossible religious demands, and (5) would not accept the truth about Jesus and prevented others from believing it as well. They went wrong by focusing on outward appearances and ignoring the inner condition of their hearts. We do the same when our service is motivated by a desire to be seen rather than from a pure heart and love for others. Others may be fooled, but God isn't. Don't be a Christian on the outside only. Bring your inner life under God's control, and your outer life will naturally reflect him.*

Follow Christ's Example of Self-Sacrifice/
Ephesians 5:1–9

Follow God's example in everything you do just as a much loved child imitates his father. 2Be full of love for others, following the example of Christ who loved you and gave himself to God as a sacrifice to take away your sins. And God was pleased, for Christ's love for you was like sweet perfume to him.

3Let there be no sex sin, impurity or greed among you. Let no one be able to accuse you of any such things. 4Dirty stories, foul talk and coarse jokes—these are not for you. Instead, remind each other of God's goodness and be thankful.

5You can be sure of this: The Kingdom of Christ and of God will never belong to anyone who is impure or greedy, for a greedy person is really an idol worshiper— he loves and worships the good things of this life more than God. 6Don't be fooled by those who try to excuse these sins, for the terrible wrath of God is upon all those who do them. 7Don't even associate with such people. 8For though once your heart was full of darkness, now it is full of light from the Lord, and your behavior should show it! 9Because of this light within you, you should do only what is good and right and true.

A THOUGHT: *Just as children imitate their parents, we should imitate Christ. His great love for us led him to sacrifice himself so that we might live. Our love for others should be of the same kind—a love that goes beyond affection to self-sacrificing service.*

Proverbs for Today/ 17:22

A cheerful heart does good like medicine, but a broken spirit makes one sick.

JUNE 23

Jesus Gives Warnings/ Luke 12:1–12

Meanwhile the crowds grew until thousands upon thousands were milling about and crushing each other. Jesus turned now to his disciples and warned them, "More than anything else, beware of these Pharisees and the way they pretend to be good when they aren't. But such hypocrisy cannot be hidden forever. 2It will become as evident as yeast in dough. 3Whatever they have said in the dark shall be heard in the light, and what you have whispered in the inner rooms shall be broadcast from the housetops for all to hear!

4"Dear friends, don't be afraid of these who want to murder you. They can only kill the body; they have no power over your souls. 5But I'll tell you whom to fear— fear God who has the power to kill and then cast into hell.

6"What is the price of five sparrows? A couple of pennies? Not much more than that. Yet God does not forget a single one of them. 7And he knows the number of hairs on your head! Never fear, you are far more valuable to him than a whole flock of sparrows.

8"And I assure you of this: I, the Messiah, will publicly honor you in the presence of God's angels if you publicly acknowledge me here on earth as your Friend. 9But I will deny before the angels those who deny me here among men. 10(Yet those who speak against me may be forgiven— while those who speak against the Holy Spirit shall never be forgiven.)

11"And when you are brought to trial before these Jewish rulers and authorities in the synagogues, don't be concerned about what to say in your defense, 12for the Holy Spirit will give you the right words even as you are standing there."

A THOUGHT: *As Jesus watched the huge crowds approach to hear him, he warned his disciples against hypocrisy—trying to appear good when one's heart is far from God. The Pharisees could not keep their attitudes hidden forever. Their selfishness would grow like yeast, and soon they would expose themselves for what they really were—power-hungry impostors, not devoted religious leaders. We must be sure that we are more concerned with our relationship with God than we are with how we look to others. Our relationship with God will even involve facing opposition and ridicule in order to stand up for Christ.*

Do Things That Please God/ Ephesians 5:10–20

Learn as you go along what pleases the Lord. 11Take no part in the worthless pleasures of evil and darkness, but instead, rebuke and expose them. 12It would be shameful even to mention here those pleasures of darkness which the ungodly do. 13But when you expose them, the light shines in upon their sin and shows it up, and when they see how wrong they really are, some of them may even become children of light! 14That is why God says in the Scriptures, "Awake, O sleeper, and rise up from the dead; and Christ shall give you light."

15,16So be careful how you act; these are difficult days. Don't be fools; be wise: make the most of every opportunity you have for doing good. 17Don't act thoughtlessly, but try to find out and do whatever the Lord wants you to. 18Don't drink too much wine, for many evils lie along that path; be filled instead with the Holy Spirit, and controlled by him.

19Talk with each other much about the Lord, quoting psalms and hymns and singing sacred songs, making music in your hearts to the Lord. 20Always give thanks for everything to our God and Father in the name of our Lord Jesus Christ.

A THOUGHT: *It is not enough to know what God wants us to do; we must also do it. We must follow our beliefs with actions. We must seek to please God in all that we do. God is pleased when we obey him. Study God's Word in order to know what pleases God, and then in the power of the Spirit, obey!*

Proverbs for Today/ 17:23
It is wrong to accept a bribe to twist justice.

JUNE 24

Jesus Teaches in Parables/ Luke 12:13–34
Then someone called from the crowd, "Sir, please tell my brother to divide my father's estate with me."

14But Jesus replied, "Man, who made me a judge over you to decide such things as that? 15Beware! Don't always be wishing for what you don't have. For real life and real living are not related to how rich we are."

16Then he gave an illustration: "A rich man had a fertile farm that produced fine crops. 17In fact, his barns were full to overflowing—he couldn't get everything in. He thought about his problem, 18and finally exclaimed, 'I know—I'll tear down my barns and build bigger ones! Then I'll have room enough. 19And I'll sit back and say to myself, "Friend, you have enough stored away for years to come. Now take it easy! Wine, women, and song for you!"'

20"But God said to him, 'Fool! Tonight you die. Then who will get it all?'

21"Yes, every man is a fool who gets rich on earth but not in heaven."

22Then turning to his disciples he said, "Don't worry about whether you have enough food to eat or clothes to wear. 23For life consists of far more than food and clothes. 24Look at the ravens—they don't plant or harvest or have barns to store away their food, and yet they get along all right—for God feeds them. And you are far more valuable to him than any birds!

25"And besides, what's the use of worrying? What good does it do? Will it add a single day to your life? Of course not! 26And if worry can't even do such little things as that, what's the use of worrying over bigger things?

27"Look at the lilies! They don't toil and spin, and yet Solomon in all his glory was not robed as well as they are. 28And if God provides clothing for the flowers that are here today and gone tomorrow, don't you suppose that he will provide clothing for you, you doubters? 29And don't worry about food—what to eat and drink; don't worry at all that God will provide it for you. 30All mankind scratches for its daily bread, but your heavenly Father knows your needs. 31He will always give you all you need from day to day if you will make the Kingdom of God your primary concern.

32"So don't be afraid, little flock. For it gives your Father great happiness to give you the Kingdom. 33Sell what you have and give to those in need. This will fatten your purses in heaven! And the purses of heaven have no rips or holes in them. Your treasures there will never disappear;

no thief can steal them; no moth can destroy them.
34Wherever your treasure is, there your heart and thoughts will also be.

A THOUGHT: *Jesus says that the good life has nothing to do with being wealthy. This is the exact opposite of what our society usually tells us. Advertisers spend millions of dollars to entice us to think that if we buy more and more of their products, we will be happier, more in tune, more comfortable. How do you respond to the constant pressure to buy? Learn to tune out expensive enticements and concentrate on the truly good life—living in a relationship with God and doing his work.*

Submit to One Another/ Ephesians 5:21–33

Honor Christ by submitting to each other. 22You wives must submit to your husbands' leadership in the same way you submit to the Lord. 23For a husband is in charge of his wife in the same way Christ is in charge of his body the Church. (He gave his very life to take care of it and be its Savior!) 24So you wives must willingly obey your husbands in everything, just as the Church obeys Christ.

25And you husbands, show the same kind of love to your wives as Christ showed to the Church when he died for her, 26to make her holy and clean, washed by baptism and God's Word; 27so that he could give her to himself as a glorious Church without a single spot or wrinkle or any other blemish, being holy and without a single fault. 28That is how husbands should treat their wives, loving them as parts of themselves. For since a man and his wife are now one, a man is really doing himself a favor and loving himself when he loves his wife! 29,30No one hates his own body but lovingly cares for it, just as Christ cares for his body the Church, of which we are parts.

31(That the husband and wife are one body is proved by the Scripture which says, "A man must leave his father and mother when he marries, so that he can be perfectly joined to his wife, and the two shall be one.") 32I know this is hard to understand, but it is an illustration of the way we are parts of the body of Christ.

33So again I say, a man must love his wife as a part of himself; and the wife must see to it that she deeply respects her husband—obeying, praising and honoring him.

A Thought: *Submission is an often misused word. It does not mean becoming a doormat. Christ—at whose name "every knee shall bow in heaven and on earth and under the earth" (Philippians 2:10)—submitted his will to the Father, and we honor Christ by following his example. When we submit to God, we become more willing to obey his command to submit to others; that is, to subordinate our rights to theirs. In a marriage relationship both husband and wife are called to submit. For both the husband and the wife this means putting aside self-interests in order to care for the interests of the other. This kind of mutual submission preserves order and harmony in the family while it increases love and respect among family members.*

Proverbs for Today/ 17:24–25

Wisdom is the main pursuit of sensible men, but a fool's goals are at the ends of the earth! □ A rebellious son is a grief to his father and a bitter blow to his mother.

JUNE 25

Be Prepared for the Lord's Return/ Luke 12:35–48

"Be prepared—all dressed and ready— 36for your Lord's return from the wedding feast. Then you will be ready to open the door and let him in the moment he arrives and knocks. 37There will be great joy for those who are ready and waiting for his return. He himself will seat them and put on a waiter's uniform and serve them as they sit and eat! 38He may come at nine o'clock at night—or even at midnight. But whenever he comes there will be joy for his servants who are ready!

39"Everyone would be ready for him if they knew the exact hour of his return—just as they would be ready for a thief if they knew when he was coming. 40So be ready all the time. For I, the Messiah, will come when least expected."

41Peter asked, "Lord, are you talking just to us or to everyone?"

42,43,44And the Lord replied, "I'm talking to any faithful, sensible man whose master gives him the responsibility of feeding the other servants. If his master returns and finds that he has done a good job, there will be a reward— his master will put him in charge of all he owns.

45"But if the man begins to think, 'My Lord won't be back for a long time,' and begins to whip the men and women he is supposed to protect, and to spend his time at drinking parties and in drunkenness— 46well, his master will return without notice and remove him from his position of trust and assign him to the place of the unfaithful. 47He will be severely punished, for though he knew his duty he refused to do it.

48"But anyone who is not aware that he is doing wrong will be punished only lightly. Much is required from those to whom much is given, for their responsibility is greater.

A THOUGHT: *Christ's return at an unexpected time is not a trap, a trick by which God hopes to catch us off guard. In fact, God is delaying his return so more will have an opportunity to follow Christ. During this time before his return, we have the opportunity to live out our beliefs and to reflect Jesus' love as we relate to others.*

People who are ready for their Lord's return are (1) not hypocritical, but sincere; (2) not fearful, but ready to witness; (3) not anxious, but trusting; (4) not greedy, but generous; (5) not lazy, but diligent. Is your life growing more like Christ's so that when he comes, you will be ready to greet him joyfully?

Instructions to Parents and Children/ Ephesians 6:1–4

Children, obey your parents; this is the right thing to do because God has placed them in authority over you. 2Honor your father and mother. This is the first of God's Ten Commandments that ends with a promise. 3And this is the promise: that if you honor your father and mother, yours will be a long life, full of blessing.

4And now a word to you parents. Don't keep on scolding and nagging your children, making them angry and resentful. Rather, bring them up with the loving discipline the Lord himself approves, with suggestions and godly advice.

A THOUGHT: *If our faith in Christ is real, it will usually prove itself at home, in our relationships with those who know us best. Children and parents have a responsibility to each other. Children should honor their parents even if the parents are demanding and unfair. Parents should gently care for their children, even if the children are disobedient and unpleasant. Ideally, of course, Christian* parents and Christian children will relate to each other with thought-fulness and love. This will happen if parents and children put the others' interests above their own.

Proverbs for Today/ 17:26
How short-sighted to fine the godly for being good! And to punish nobles for being honest!

JUNE 26

Jesus Came to Bring Division/ Luke 12:49–59
"I have come to bring fire to the earth, and, oh, that my task were completed! 50There is a terrible baptism ahead of me, and how I am pent up until it is accomplished!

51"Do you think I have come to give peace to the earth? *No!* Rather, strife and division! 52From now on families will be split apart, three in favor of me, and two against— or perhaps the other way around. 53A father will decide one way about me; his son, the other; mother and daughter will disagree; and the decision of an honored mother-in-law will be spurned by her daughter-in-law."

54Then he turned to the crowd and said, "When you see clouds beginning to form in the west, you say, 'Here comes a shower.' And you are right.

55"When the south wind blows you say, 'Today will be a scorcher.' And it is. 56Hypocrites! You interpret the sky well enough, but you refuse to notice the warnings all around you about the crisis ahead. 57Why do you refuse to see for yourselves what is right?

58"If you meet your accuser on the way to court, try to settle the matter before it reaches the judge, lest he sentence you to jail; 59for if that happens you won't be free again until the last penny is paid in full."

A THOUGHT: *In these strange and unsettling words, Jesus revealed that his coming often results in conflict. He demands a response, and close groups can be torn apart when some choose to follow him and others refuse to do so. There is no middle ground with Jesus. Loyalties must be declared and commitments made, sometimes to the severing of other relationships. Life is easiest when a family*

is united in its belief in Christ, but this often does not happen.
Are you willing to risk your family's approval in order to gain
eternal life?

Instructions to Slaves and Masters/
Ephesians 6:5–9

Slaves, obey your masters; be eager to give them your
very best. Serve them as you would Christ. 6. 7Don't
work hard only when your master is watching and then
shirk when he isn't looking; work hard and with gladness
all the time, as though working for Christ, doing the will
of God with all your hearts. 8Remember, the Lord will
pay you for each good thing you do, whether you are
slave or free.

9And you slave owners must treat your slaves right,
just as I have told them to treat you. Don't keep threatening
them; remember, you yourselves are slaves to Christ;
you have the same Master they do, and he has no favorites.

A Thought: *Paul's instructions encourage responsibility and integ-*
rity on the job. Christian employees should do their jobs as if Jesus
Christ were their supervisor, and Christian employers should treat
their employees fairly and with respect. Are you trusted in any job
to do your best, whether or not the boss is around? Do you work
hard and with enthusiasm? Do you treat your employees as people,
not machines? Remember that no matter whom you work for, and
no matter who works for you, the One you ultimately want to
please is your Father in heaven.

Proverbs for Today/ 17:27–28

The man of few words and settled mind is wise; therefore,
even a fool is thought to be wise when he is silent. It
pays him to keep his mouth shut.

JUNE 27

Jesus Calls the People to Repent/ Luke 13:1–9

About this time Jesus was informed that Pilate had butch-
ered some Jews from Galilee as they were sacrificing at
the Temple in Jerusalem.

2"Do you think they were worse sinners than other

men from Galilee?" he asked. "Is that why they suffered? 3Not at all! And don't you realize that you also will perish unless you leave your evil ways and turn to God?

4"And what about the eighteen men who died when the Tower of Siloam fell on them? Were they the worst sinners in Jerusalem? 5Not at all! And you, too, will perish unless you repent."

6Then he used this illustration: "A man planted a fig tree in his garden and came again and again to see if he could find any fruit on it, but he was always disappointed. 7Finally he told his gardener to cut it down. 'I've waited three years and there hasn't been a single fig!' he said. 'Why bother with it any longer? It's taking up space we can use for something else.'

8" 'Give it one more chance,' the gardener answered. 'Leave it another year, and I'll give it special attention and plenty of fertilizer. 9If we get figs next year, fine; if not, I'll cut it down.' "

A THOUGHT: *In the Old Testament, a fruitful tree was often used as a symbol of godly living. Jesus pointed out what would happen to the other kind of tree—the kind that took up space, but produced nothing for the patient gardener. This was one way he warned his listeners that God would not tolerate their lack of productivity forever. Repentance is an essential part of Christian commitment. We must turn from our wicked ways and turn to God. Respond to the gardener's patient care and start preparing to bear fruit by living for God.*

The Whole Armor of God/ Ephesians 6:10–17

Last of all I want to remind you that your strength must come from the Lord's mighty power within you. 11Put on all of God's armor so that you will be able to stand safe against all strategies and tricks of Satan. 12For we are not fighting against people made of flesh and blood, but against persons without bodies—the evil rulers of the unseen world, those mighty satanic beings and great evil princes of darkness who rule this world; and against huge numbers of wicked spirits in the spirit world.

13So use every piece of God's armor to resist the enemy whenever he attacks, and when it is all over, you will still be standing up.

14But to do this, you will need the strong belt of truth and the breastplate of God's approval. 15Wear shoes that are able to speed you on as you preach the Good News of peace with God. 16In every battle you will need faith as your shield to stop the fiery arrows aimed at you by Satan. 17And you will need the helmet of salvation and the sword of the Spirit—which is the Word of God.

A THOUGHT: *In the Christian life, we battle against powerful evil forces, headed by Satan, a vicious fighter. To withstand his attacks, we must depend on God's strength and use every piece of his armor. Paul is giving this counsel to all individuals within the church. The whole body needs to be armed. As you do battle against "the evil rulers of the unseen world," fight in the strength of the church, whose power comes from the Holy Spirit.*

Proverbs for Today/ 18:1
The selfish man quarrels against every sound principle of conduct by demanding his own way.

JUNE 28

A Healing on the Sabbath/ Luke 13:10–17
One Sabbath as Jesus was teaching in a synagogue, 11he saw a seriously handicapped woman who had been bent double for eighteen years and was unable to straighten herself.

12Calling her over to him Jesus said, "Woman, you are healed of your sickness!" 13He touched her, and instantly she could stand straight. How she praised and thanked God!

14But the local Jewish leader in charge of the synagogue was very angry about it because Jesus had healed her on the Sabbath day. "There are six days of the week to work," he shouted to the crowd. "Those are the days to come for healing, not on the Sabbath!"

15But the Lord replied, "You hypocrite! You work on the Sabbath! Don't you untie your cattle from their stalls on the Sabbath and lead them out for water? 16And is it wrong for me, just because it is the Sabbath day, to free this Jewish woman from the bondage in which Satan has held her for eighteen years?"

¹⁷This shamed his enemies. And all the people rejoiced at the wonderful things he did.

A Thought: *Why was healing considered work? The religious leaders saw healing as part of a doctor's profession, and practicing one's profession on the Sabbath was prohibited. The synagogue leader could not see beyond the law to Jesus' compassion in healing this handicapped woman. Jesus shamed him and the other leaders by pointing out their hypocrisy. The Pharisees hid behind their own set of laws to avoid love's obligations. We too can use the letter of the law to rationalize away our obligation to care for others (for example, tithing regularly then refusing to give help to a needy neighbor). But peoples' needs are more important than laws. Take time to lovingly help others, even if doing so might make you look less spiritual.*

Pray Earnestly in the Spirit/ Ephesians 6:18–24

Pray all the time. Ask God for anything in line with the Holy Spirit's wishes. Plead with him, reminding him of your needs, and keep praying earnestly for all Christians everywhere. ¹⁹Pray for me, too, and ask God to give me the right words as I boldly tell others about the Lord, and as I explain to them that his salvation is for the Gentiles too. ²⁰I am in chains now for preaching this message from God. But pray that I will keep on speaking out boldly for him even here in prison, as I should.

²¹Tychicus, who is a much loved brother and faithful helper in the Lord's work, will tell you all about how I am getting along. ²²I am sending him to you for just this purpose, to let you know how we are and be encouraged by his report.

²³May God give peace to you, my Christian brothers, and love, with faith from God the Father and the Lord Jesus Christ. ²⁴May God's grace and blessing be upon all who sincerely love our Lord Jesus Christ.

Sincerely,
Paul

A Thought: *How can anyone pray all the time? One way to pray constantly is to make quick, brief prayers your habitual response to every situation you meet throughout the day. Another way is to order your life around God's desires and teachings so that your very life becomes a prayer. You don't have to isolate yourself from other people and from daily work in order to pray constantly. You can make prayer your life and your life a prayer while living in a world that needs God's powerful influence.*

Proverbs for Today/ 18:2–3

A rebel doesn't care about the facts. All he wants to do is yell. □ Sin brings disgrace.

JUNE 29

Illustrations of the Kingdom of God/ Luke 13:18–22

Now Jesus began teaching them again about the Kingdom of God: "What is the Kingdom like?" he asked. "How can I illustrate it? 19It is like a tiny mustard seed planted in a garden; soon it grows into a tall bush and the birds live among its branches.

20,21"It is like yeast kneaded into dough, which works unseen until it has risen high and light."

22He went from city to city and village to village, teaching as he went, always pressing onward toward Jerusalem.

A THOUGHT: *The general expectation among Jesus' hearers was that the Messiah would come as a great king and leader, freeing Israel from Roman domination and restoring Israel's former glory. But Jesus said his Kingdom was beginning small and quietly. Like the tiny mustard seed that grows into an enormous bush or the spoonful of yeast that doubles the bread dough, the Kingdom of God would eventually push outward until the whole world was changed.*

God Will Finish the Work He Began/ Philippians 1:1–6

From: Paul and Timothy, slaves of Jesus Christ.

To: The pastors and deacons and all the Christians in the city of Philippi.

2May God bless you all. Yes, I pray that God our Father and the Lord Jesus Christ will give each of you his fullest blessings, and his peace in your hearts and your lives. 3All my prayers for you are full of praise to God! 4When I pray for you, my heart is full of joy, 5because of all your wonderful help in making known the Good News about Christ from the time you first heard it until now. 6And I am sure that God who began the good work within you will keep right on helping you grow in his grace until his task within you is finally finished on that day when Jesus Christ returns.

A THOUGHT: *The God who begins his good work in us continues it through our lives and will finish it when we meet him face to face. God's work for us began when Christ died on the cross to forgive our sins. His work in us begins when the Holy Spirit comes into our hearts, enabling us to be more like Christ every day. Paul is describing the process of Christian growth and maturity that begins when we accept Jesus and continues until Christ returns. Do you sometimes feel as if you'll never make progress in your spiritual life? When God starts a project, he finishes it! Trust God to keep his promise.*

Proverbs for Today/ 18:4–5

A wise man's words express deep streams of thought.
□ It is wrong for a judge to favor the wicked and condemn the innocent.

JUNE 30

The Narrow Way/ Luke 13:23–30

Someone asked Jesus, "Will only a few be saved?"

And he replied, 24,25"The door to heaven is narrow. Work hard to get in, for the truth is that many will try to enter but when the head of the house has locked the door, it will be too late. Then if you stand outside knocking, and pleading, 'Lord, open the door for us,' he will reply, 'I do not know you.'

26" 'But we ate with you, and you taught in our streets,' you will say.

27"And he will reply, 'I tell you, I don't know you. You can't come in here, guilty as you are. Go away.'

28"And there will be great weeping and gnashing of teeth as you stand outside and see Abraham, Isaac, Jacob, and all the prophets within the Kingdom of God— 29for people will come from all over the world to take their places there. 30And note this: some who are despised now will be greatly honored then; and some who are highly thought of now will be least important then."

A THOUGHT: *There will be many surprises in God's Kingdom. Some who are despised now will be greatly honored then; some influential people here will be left outside the gates. Many "great" people on this earth (in God's eyes) are virtually ignored by the rest of the world. What matters to God is not one's earthly popularity, status, wealth, heritage, or power, but one's commitment to Christ. How do your values and actions match what the Bible tells us to do and to value? Make sure you put God in first place so you will join the people from all over the world who will take their places in the Kingdom of Heaven.*

Paul's Love for the Philippians/ Philippians 1:7–11

How natural it is that I should feel as I do about you, for you have a very special place in my heart. We have shared together the blessings of God, both when I was in prison and when I was out, defending the truth and telling others about Christ. 8Only God knows how deep is my love and longing for you—with the tenderness of Jesus Christ. 9My prayer for you is that you will overflow more and more with love for others, and at the same time keep on growing in spiritual knowledge and insight, 10for I want you always to see clearly the difference between right and wrong, and to be inwardly clean, no one being able to criticize you from now until our Lord returns. 11May you always be doing those good, kind things which show that you are a child of God, for this will bring much praise and glory to the Lord.

A THOUGHT: *Have you ever longed to see a friend with whom you share fond memories? Paul had such a longing to see the Christians at Philippi. His love and affection for them was based, not merely on past experiences, but upon the unity that comes when believers draw upon Christ's love. All Christians are part of God's family and thus share equally in the transforming power of his love. Do you feel a deep love for fellow Christians, friends and strangers alike? Let Christ's love for you motivate you to love other Christians.*

Proverbs for Today/ 18:6–7

A fool gets into constant fights. His mouth is his undoing! His words endanger him.

JULY 1

Jesus Laments over Jerusalem/ Luke 13:31–35

A few minutes later some Pharisees said to Jesus, "Get out of here if you want to live, for King Herod is after you!"

32Jesus replied, "Go tell that fox that I will keep on casting out demons and doing miracles of healing today and tomorrow; and the third day I will reach my destination. 33Yes, today, tomorrow, and the next day! For it wouldn't do for a prophet of God to be killed except in Jerusalem!

34"O Jerusalem, Jerusalem! The city that murders the prophets. The city that stones those sent to help her. How often I have wanted to gather your children together even as a hen protects her brood under her wings, but you wouldn't let me. 35And now—now your house is left desolate. And you will never again see me until you say, 'Welcome to him who comes in the name of the Lord.'"

A THOUGHT: *Why was Jesus aiming for Jerusalem? Jerusalem, the city of God, symbolized the entire nation. It was Israel's largest city and the nation's spiritual and political capital, and Jews from around the world visited it frequently. But Jerusalem had a history of rejecting the prophets sent by God, and it would reject the Messiah just as it had rejected his forerunners. God's love and grace have been shown to mankind in the midst of rebellion against him. His supreme act of love can be seen in Jesus Christ, who was rejected by those who followed him and yet died to redeem people from their sins. Truly God's grace is amazing!*

Paul Rejoices at the Preaching of the Good News/ Philippians 1:12–18

And I want you to know this, dear brothers: Everything that has happened to me here has been a great boost in getting out the Good News concerning Christ. 13For everyone around here, including all the soldiers over at the barracks, knows that I am in chains simply because I am a Christian. 14And because of my imprisonment many of the Christians here seem to have lost their fear of chains! Somehow my patience has encouraged them and they have become more and more bold in telling others about Christ.

15Some, of course, are preaching the Good News because

they are jealous of the way God has used me. They want reputations as fearless preachers! But others have purer motives, 16,17preaching because they love me, for they know that the Lord has brought me here to use me to defend the Truth. And some preach to make me jealous, thinking that their success will add to my sorrows here in jail! 18But whatever their motive for doing it, the fact remains that the Good News about Christ is being preached and I am glad.

A THOUGHT: *Being imprisoned would cause many people to become bitter or to give up, but Paul saw it as one more opportunity to spread the Good News of Christ. Paul realized that his current circumstances weren't as important as what he did with them. Turning a bad situation into a good one, Paul reached out to the Roman soldiers who were assigned to guard him and encouraged those Christians who were afraid of persecution. We may not be in prison, but we still have plenty of opportunities to be discouraged— times of indecision, financial burdens, family conflict, church conflict, or the loss of our jobs. How we act in such situations reflects what we believe. Like Paul, look for opportunities to demonstrate your faith even in bad situations. Whether or not the situation improves, your faith will grow stronger.*

Proverbs for Today/ 18:8
What dainty morsels rumors are. They are eaten with great relish!

JULY 2

Jesus Heals on the Sabbath/ Luke 14:1–6
One Sabbath as Jesus was in the home of a member of the Jewish Council, the Pharisees were watching him like hawks to see if he would heal a man who was present who was suffering from dropsy.

3Jesus said to the Pharisees and legal experts standing around, "Well, is it within the Law to heal a man on the Sabbath day, or not?"

4And when they refused to answer, Jesus took the sick man by the hand and healed him and sent him away.

5Then he turned to them: "Which of you doesn't work

on the Sabbath?" he asked. "If your cow falls into a pit, don't you proceed at once to get it out?"

6Again they had no answer.

A THOUGHT: *By healing this man who had dropsy on the Sabbath, Jesus was rejecting the Pharisaic tradition which did not allow for this. The Pharisees were more concerned for their traditions than they were for following the intent of God's Sabbath law. The Sabbath law was intended for restoration, not oppression. Jesus was giving this man rest by restoring him to full health—relieving him from the toil of his disease. Showing mercy should always take precedence over a rigid keeping of rules.*

Honor Christ in Both Life and Death/
Philippians 1:19–30

I am going to keep on being glad, for I know that as you pray for me, and as the Holy Spirit helps me, this is all going to turn out for my good. 20For I live in eager expectation and hope that I will never do anything that will cause me to be ashamed of myself but that I will always be ready to speak out boldly for Christ while I am going through all these trials here, just as I have in the past; and that I will always be an honor to Christ, whether I live or whether I must die. 21For to me, living means opportunities for Christ, and dying—well, that's better yet! 22But if living will give me more opportunities to win people to Christ, then I really don't know which is better, to live or die! 23Sometimes I want to live and at other times I don't, for I long to go and be with Christ. How much happier for *me* than being here! 24But the fact is that I can be of more help to *you* by staying!

25Yes, I am still needed down here and so I feel certain I will be staying on earth a little longer, to help you grow and become happy in your faith; 26my staying will make you glad and give you reason to glorify Christ Jesus for keeping me safe, when I return to visit you again.

27But whatever happens to me, remember always to live as Christians should, so that, whether I ever see you again or not, I will keep on hearing good reports that you are standing side by side with one strong purpose—to tell the Good News 28fearlessly, no matter what your enemies may do. They will see this as a sign of their downfall, but for you it will be a clear sign from God that he is with you, and that he has given you eternal

life with him. 29For to you has been given the privilege
not only of trusting him but also of suffering for him.
30We are in this fight together. You have seen me suffer
for him in the past; and I am still in the midst of a great
and terrible struggle now, as you know so well.

A THOUGHT: *To those who don't believe in God, life on earth is
all there is, and so it is natural for them to strive for the things
that this world values—money, popularity, power, and prestige.
For Paul, however, life meant developing eternal values and telling
others about Christ, who alone can help us see life from an eternal
perspective. Paul's whole purpose in life was to speak out boldly
for Christ and to become more like him. Thus Paul could confidently
say that dying would be even better than living because in death
he would be spared from the troubles of the world and see Christ
face to face. If you're not ready to die, then you're not ready to
live. Once you know your eternal purpose, then you're free to serve—
devoting your life to what really counts without fear of dying.*

Proverbs for Today/ 18:9–10
A lazy man is brother to the saboteur. □ The Lord is
a strong fortress. The godly run to him and are safe.

JULY 3

The Privilege of Entering the Kingdom of God/
Luke 14:7–24
When Jesus noticed that all who came to the dinner were
trying to sit near the head of the table, he gave them
this advice: 8"If you are invited to a wedding feast, don't
always head for the best seat. For if someone more respected than you shows up, 9the host will bring him over
to where you are sitting and say, 'Let this man sit here
instead.' And you, embarrassed, will have to take whatever
seat is left at the foot of the table!

10"Do this instead—start at the foot; and when your
host sees you he will come and say, 'Friend, we have a
better place than this for you!' Thus you will be honored
in front of all the other guests. 11For everyone who tries
to honor himself shall be humbled; and he who humbles
himself shall be honored." 12Then he turned to his host.
"When you put on a dinner," he said, "don't invite friends,

brothers, relatives, and rich neighbors! For they will return the invitation. 13Instead, invite the poor, the crippled, the lame, and the blind. 14Then at the resurrection of the godly, God will reward you for inviting those who can't repay you."

15Hearing this, a man sitting at the table with Jesus exclaimed, "What a privilege it would be to get into the Kingdom of God!"

16Jesus replied with this illustration: "A man prepared a great feast and sent out many invitations. 17When all was ready, he sent his servant around to notify the guests that it was time for them to arrive. 18But they all began making excuses. One said he had just bought a field and wanted to inspect it, and asked to be excused. 19Another said he had just bought five pair of oxen and wanted to try them out. 20Another had just been married and for that reason couldn't come.

21"The servant returned and reported to his master what they had said. His master was angry and told him to go quickly into the streets and alleys of the city and to invite the beggars, crippled, lame, and blind. 22But even then, there was still room.

23" 'Well, then,' said his master, 'go out into the country lanes and out behind the hedges and urge anyone you find to come, so that the house will be full. 24For none of those I invited first will get even the smallest taste of what I had prepared for them.' "

A THOUGHT: *Jesus taught two lessons here. First he spoke to the guests, telling them not to seek places of honor. Service is more important in God's Kingdom than status. Second he told the host not to be exclusive about whom he invites. God opens his Kingdom to everyone—especially to those who can never repay his invitation. Entering the Kingdom of God comes by God's grace alone. In response to the experience of God's grace in our own lives, we should share the grace of God with others.*

Christ Is Our Model of Humility/ Philippians 2:1–11

Is there any such thing as Christians cheering each other up? Do you love me enough to want to help me? Does it mean anything to you that we are brothers in the Lord, sharing the same Spirit? Are your hearts tender and sympathetic at all? 2Then make me truly happy by loving each other and agreeing wholeheartedly with each other, working together with one heart and mind and purpose.

3Don't be selfish; don't live to make a good impression on others. Be humble, thinking of others as better than yourself. 4Don't just think about your own affairs, but be interested in others, too, and in what they are doing.

5Your attitude should be the kind that was shown us by Jesus Christ, 6who, though he was God, did not demand and cling to his rights as God, 7but laid aside his mighty power and glory, taking the disguise of a slave and becoming like men. 8And he humbled himself even further, going so far as actually to die a criminal's death on a cross.

9Yet it was because of this that God raised him up to the heights of heaven and gave him a name which is above every other name, 10that at the name of Jesus every knee shall bow in heaven and on earth and under the earth, 11and every tongue shall confess that Jesus Christ is Lord, to the glory of God the Father.

A THOUGHT: *Many people—even Christians—live only to make a good impression on others or to please themselves. This is self-centered living; if people are concerned only for themselves, seeds of discord are sown. Paul therefore stresses spiritual unity, asking the Philippians to love one another and to work together with one heart and purpose. When we work together, caring for the problems of others as if they were our own, we are demonstrating Christ's example of putting others first. This brings unity. Don't be concerned about making a good impression or pleasing yourself to the point where you strain your relationship with others in God's family. Let the Spirit of God work through you to attract fellow believers to himself.*

Proverbs for Today/ 18:11–12

The rich man thinks of his wealth as an impregnable defense, a high wall of safety. What a dreamer! □ Pride ends in destruction; humility ends in honor.

JULY 4

The Cost of Discipleship/ Luke 14:25–35

Great crowds were following Jesus. He turned around and addressed them as follows: 26"Anyone who wants to be my follower must love me far more than he does his

own father, mother, wife, children, brothers, or sisters—
yes, more than his own life—otherwise he cannot be my
disciple. 27And no one can be my disciple who does not
carry his own cross and follow me.

28 "But don't begin until you count the cost. For who
would begin construction of a building without first getting
estimates and then checking to see if he has enough money
to pay the bills? 29Otherwise he might complete only the
foundation before running out of funds. And then how
everyone would laugh!

30" 'See that fellow there?' they would mock. 'He started
that building and ran out of money before it was finished!'

31"Or what king would ever dream of going to war without
first sitting down with his counselors and discussing whether
his army of 10,000 is strong enough to defeat the 20,000
men who are marching against him?

32"If the decision is negative, then while the enemy
troops are still far away, he will send a truce team to
discuss terms of peace. 33So no one can become my disciple
unless he first sits down and counts his blessings—and
then renounces them all for me.

34"What good is salt that has lost its saltiness?
35Flavorless salt is fit for nothing—not even for fertilizer.
It is worthless and must be thrown out. Listen well, if
you would understand my meaning."

A THOUGHT: *Jesus' audience was well aware of what it meant to
carry one's own cross. When the Romans led a criminal to his
execution site, he was forced to carry the cross on which he was
to be hanged. Following Christ does not mean that we will have
a trouble-free life. On the contrary, following Christ costs us a
great deal—discipleship demands that we follow Christ with complete
commitment. We must carefully count the cost of becoming Christ's
disciples so that we know what we are getting into and are not
later tempted to turn back. Following Christ means total submission
to him—perhaps even to death.*

Be a Light to the World/ Philippians 2:12–18

Dearest friends, when I was there with you, you were
always so careful to follow my instructions. And now that
I am away you must be even more careful to do the
good things that result from being saved, obeying God
with deep reverence, shrinking back from all that might
displease him. 13For God is at work within you, helping

you want to obey him, and then helping you do what he wants.

14In everything you do, stay away from complaining and arguing, 15so that no one can speak a word of blame against you. You are to live clean, innocent lives as children of God in a dark world full of people who are crooked and stubborn. Shine out among them like beacon lights, 16 holding out to them the Word of Life.

Then when Christ returns how glad I will be that my work among you was so worthwhile. 17And if my lifeblood is, so to speak, to be poured out over your faith which I am offering up to God as a sacrifice—that is, if I am to die for you—even then I will be glad, and will share my joy with each of you. 18For you should be happy about this, too, and rejoice with me for having this privilege of dying for you.

A THOUGHT: *Our lives should be characterized by purity, patience, and peacefulness, so that we will shine out "like beacon lights." A transformed life is an effective witness to the power of God's Word. Is your light shining brightly, or is it clouded by complaints and arguing? Be a clean, radiant light shining out for God.*

Proverbs for Today/ 18:13
What a shame—yes, how stupid!—to decide before knowing the facts!

JULY 5

A Lost Sheep and a Lost Coin/ Luke 15:1–10
Dishonest tax collectors and other notorious sinners often came to listen to Jesus' sermons; 2but this caused complaints from the Jewish religious leaders and the experts on Jewish law because he was associating with such despicable people—even eating with them!

3,4So Jesus used this illustration: "If you had a hundred sheep and one of them strayed away and was lost in the wilderness, wouldn't you leave the ninety-nine others to go and search for the lost one until you found it? 5And then you would joyfully carry it home on your shoulders.

6When you arrived you would call together your friends and neighbors to rejoice with you because your lost sheep was found.

7"Well, in the same way heaven will be happier over one lost sinner who returns to God than over ninety-nine others who haven't strayed away!

8"Or take another illustration: A woman has ten valuable silver coins and loses one. Won't she light a lamp and look in every corner of the house and sweep every nook and cranny until she finds it? 9And then won't she call in her friends and neighbors to rejoice with her? 10In the same way there is joy in the presence of the angels of God when one sinner repents."

A THOUGHT: *It seems foolish for the shepherd to leave the 99 sheep to search for just one which is missing. But God's love for each individual is so great that he seeks each one out and rejoices when he or she is "found." God values the lost one so much that, like the woman searching for the lost coin, he searches diligently until the lost one is found. Jesus associated with sinners—those who were lost and assumed to be beyond the grace of God—in order to bring them the Good News of God's Kingdom. The amazing truth is that God, in his great love, searches for sinners and then forgives them. This is the kind of extraordinary love God has for you. If you feel far from God, don't despair. He is searching for you.*

Timothy and Epaphroditus/ Philippians 2:19—3:1

If the Lord is willing, I will send Timothy to see you soon. Then when he comes back he can cheer me up by telling me all about you and how you are getting along. 20There is no one like Timothy for having a real interest in you; 21everyone else seems to be worrying about his own plans and not those of Jesus Christ. 22But you know Timothy. He has been just like a son to me in helping me preach the Good News. 23I hope to send him to you just as soon as I find out what is going to happen to me here. 24And I am trusting the Lord that soon I myself may come to see you.

25Meanwhile, I thought I ought to send Epaphroditus back to you. You sent him to help me in my need; well, he and I have been real brothers, working and battling side by side. 26Now I am sending him home again, for he has been homesick for all of you and upset because you heard that he was ill. 27And he surely was; in fact, he almost died. But God had mercy on him, and on me too, not allowing me to have this sorrow on top of everything else.

28So I am all the more anxious to get him back to you again, for I know how thankful you will be to see him, and that will make me happy and lighten all my cares. 29Welcome him in the Lord with great joy, and show your appreciation, 30for he risked his life for the work of Christ and was at the point of death while trying to do for me the things you couldn't do because you were far away.

3:1Whatever happens, dear friends, be glad in the Lord. I never get tired of telling you this and it is good for you to hear it again and again.

A THOUGHT: *Timothy and Epaphroditus serve as examples of Christian living for us. Timothy was faithful in the work of the Lord, with a constant, genuine concern for those he was serving. Epaphroditus was also faithful in the work of the Lord—he risked his life for Christ. True discipleship includes such self-sacrifice. Let us follow in the footsteps of these servants of God in our service to others.*

Proverbs for Today/ 18:14–15

A man's courage can sustain his broken body, but when courage dies, what hope is left? □ The intelligent man is always open to new ideas. In fact, he looks for them.

JULY 6

The Prodigal Son/ Luke 15:11–32

To further illustrate the point, Jesus told the crowds this story: "A man had two sons. 12When the younger told his father, 'I want my share of your estate now, instead of waiting until you die!' his father agreed to divide his wealth between his sons.

13"A few days later this younger son packed all his belongings and took a trip to a distant land, and there wasted all his money on parties and prostitutes. 14About the time his money was gone a great famine swept over the land, and he began to starve. 15He persuaded a local farmer to hire him to feed his pigs. 16The boy became so hungry that even the pods he was feeding the swine looked good to him. And no one gave him anything.

17"When he finally came to his senses, he said to himself, 'At home even the hired men have food enough and to spare, and here I am, dying of hunger! 18I will go home to my father and say, "Father, I have sinned against both heaven and you, 19and am no longer worthy of being called your son. Please take me on as a hired man." '

20"So he returned home to his father. And while he was still a long distance away, his father saw him coming, and was filled with loving pity and ran and embraced him and kissed him.

21"His son said to him, 'Father, I have sinned against heaven and you, and am not worthy of being called your son—'

22"But his father said to the slaves, 'Quick! Bring the finest robe in the house and put it on him. And a jeweled ring for his finger; and shoes! 23And kill the calf we have in the fattening pen. We must celebrate with a feast, 24 for this son of mine was dead and has returned to life. He was lost and is found.' So the party began.

25"Meanwhile, the older son was in the fields working; when he returned home, he heard dance music coming from the house, 26and he asked one of the servants what was going on.

27" 'Your brother is back,' he was told, 'and your father has killed the calf we were fattening and has prepared a great feast to celebrate his coming home again unharmed.'

28"The older brother was angry and wouldn't go in. His father came out and begged him, 29but he replied, 'All these years I've worked hard for you and never once refused to do a single thing you told me to; and in all that time you never gave me even one young goat for a feast with my friends. 30Yet when this son of yours comes back after spending your money on prostitutes, you celebrate by killing the finest calf we have on the place.'

31" 'Look, dear son,' his father said to him, 'you and I are very close, and everything I have is yours. 32But it is right to celebrate. For he is your brother; and he was dead and has come back to life! He was lost and is found!' "

A THOUGHT: *Some people need to hit bottom in order to come to their senses. The younger son's attitude was based on a desire to* be free to live as he pleased. That is not so different from the desires of most people in our society today. It may take great sorrow and tragedy to cause them to look up to the only One who can help them. Are you trying to live life your way, selfishly pushing aside anything that gets in your way? Don't take leave of your senses—stop and look before you hit bottom, and save yourself and your family much grief.

Paul's Jewish Heritage/ Philippians 3:2–7

Watch out for those wicked men—dangerous dogs, I call them—who say you must be circumcised to be saved. ³For it isn't the *cutting of our bodies* that makes us children of God; it is *worshiping him with our spirits*. That is the only true "circumcision." We Christians glory in what Christ Jesus has done for us and realize that we are helpless to save ourselves.

⁴Yet if anyone ever had reason to hope that he could save himself, it would be I. If others could be saved by what they are, certainly I could! ⁵For I went through the Jewish initiation ceremony when I was eight days old, having been born into a pure-blooded Jewish home that was a branch of the old original Benjamin family. So I was a real Jew if there ever was one! What's more, I was a member of the Pharisees who demand the strictest obedience to every Jewish law and custom. ⁶And sincere? Yes, so much so that I greatly persecuted the Church; and I tried to obey every Jewish rule and regulation right down to the very last point.

⁷But all these things that I once thought very worthwhile—now I've thrown them all away so that I can put my trust and hope in Christ alone.

A THOUGHT: *At first glance, it seems that Paul is boasting about his achievements. But he is actually doing the opposite, showing that human achievements, no matter how impressive, cannot earn a person salvation and eternal life with God. Paul had impressive credentials: upbringing, nationality, family background, inheritance, orthodoxy, activity, and morality. But when he was converted to faith in Christ, it wasn't based upon his credentials, but upon the grace of Christ. Paul did not depend on his credentials to please God, because even the most impressive credentials fall short of God's holy standards. Are you depending on Christian parents, church affiliation, or just being good to make you right with God? Credentials, accomplishments, or reputation cannot earn salvation. Like Paul, you must realize that salvation comes only through faith in Christ.*

Proverbs for Today/ 18:16–18
A gift does wonders; it will bring you before men of importance! □ Any story sounds true until someone tells the other side and sets the record straight. □ A coin toss ends arguments and settles disputes between powerful opponents.

JULY 7

**The Story of the Dishonest Accountant/
Luke 16:1–14**
Jesus now told this story to his disciples: "A rich man hired an accountant to handle his affairs, but soon a rumor went around that the accountant was thoroughly dishonest.

2"So his employer called him in and said, 'What's this I hear about your stealing from me? Get your report in order, for you are to be dismissed.'

3"The accountant thought to himself, 'Now what? I'm through here, and I haven't the strength to go out and dig ditches, and I'm too proud to beg. 4I know just the thing! And then I'll have plenty of friends to take care of me when I leave!'

5,6"So he invited each one who owed money to his employer to come and discuss the situation. He asked the first one, 'How much do you owe him?' 'My debt is 850 gallons of olive oil,' the man replied. 'Yes, here is the contract you signed,' the accountant told him. 'Tear it up and write another one for half that much!'

7" 'And how much do you owe him?' he asked the next man. 'A thousand bushels of wheat,' was the reply. 'Here,' the accountant said, 'take your note and replace it with one for only 800 bushels!'

8"The rich man had to admire the rascal for being so shrewd. And it is true that the citizens of this world are more clever [in dishonesty!] than the godly are. 9But shall I tell *you* to act that way, to buy friendship through cheating? Will this ensure your entry into an everlasting home in heaven? 10*No!* For unless you are honest in small matters, you won't be in large ones. If you cheat even a little, you won't be honest with greater responsibilities. 11And if you are untrustworthy about worldly wealth, who will trust you with the true riches of heaven? 12And if you are not faithful with other people's money, why should you be entrusted with money of your own?

13"For neither you nor anyone else can serve two masters. You will hate one and show loyalty to the other, or else the other way around—you will be enthusiastic about one and despise the other. You cannot serve both God and money."

14The Pharisees, who dearly loved their money, naturally scoffed at all this.

A THOUGHT: *Our integrity often meets its match in money matters. God calls us to be honest even in small details we could rationalize away. Heaven's riches are far more valuable than earthly wealth, but if we are untrustworthy with our earthly wealth (no matter how much or little we have), we are unfit to handle the vast riches of God's Kingdom. Don't let your integrity slip in small matters, and it will not fail you in crucial decisions either.*

The Value of Knowing Christ/ Philippians 3:8–12

Yes, everything else is worthless when compared with the priceless gain of knowing Christ Jesus my Lord. I have put aside all else, counting it worth less than nothing, in order that I can have Christ, 9and become one with him, no longer counting on being saved by being good enough or by obeying God's laws, but by trusting Christ to save me; for God's way of making us right with himself depends on faith—counting on Christ alone. 10Now I have given up everything else—I have found it to be the only way to really know Christ and to experience the mighty power that brought him back to life again, and to find out what it means to suffer and to die with him. 11So, whatever it takes, I will be one who lives in the fresh newness of life of those who are alive from the dead.

12I don't mean to say I am perfect. I haven't learned all I should even yet, but I keep working toward that day when I will finally be all that Christ saved me for and wants me to be.

A THOUGHT: *After Paul considered everything he had accomplished in his life, he said that it was all worthless when compared with knowing Christ. This is a profound statement about values: a person's relationship with Christ is more important than anything*

else. To know Christ should be our ultimate goal. Consider your
values. Do you place anything above your relationship with Christ?
If your priorities are wrong, how can you reorder them?

Proverbs for Today/ 18:19

It is harder to win back the friendship of an offended
brother than to capture a fortified city. His anger shuts
you out like iron bars.

JULY 8

Lazarus and the Rich Man/ Luke 16:15–31

Then Jesus said to the Pharisees, "You wear a noble,
pious expression in public, but God knows your evil hearts.
Your pretense brings you honor from the people, but it
is an abomination in the sight of God. 16Until John the
Baptist began to preach, the laws of Moses and the messages of the prophets were your guides. But John introduced
the Good News that the Kingdom of God would come
soon. And now eager multitudes are pressing in. 17But
that doesn't mean that the Law has lost its force in even
the smallest point. It is as strong and unshakable as heaven
and earth.

18"So anyone who divorces his wife and marries someone
else commits adultery, and anyone who marries a divorced
woman commits adultery."

19"There was a certain rich man," Jesus said, "who
was splendidly clothed and lived each day in mirth and
luxury. 20One day Lazarus, a diseased beggar, was laid
at his door. 21As he lay there longing for scraps from
the rich man's table, the dogs would come and lick his
open sores. 22Finally the beggar died and was carried by
the angels to be with Abraham in the place of the righteous
dead. The rich man also died and was buried, 23and his
soul went into hell. There, in torment, he saw Lazarus
in the far distance with Abraham.

24" 'Father Abraham,' he shouted, 'have some pity! Send
Lazarus over here if only to dip the tip of his finger in

water and cool my tongue, for I am in anguish in these flames.'

25"But Abraham said to him, 'Son, remember that during your lifetime you had everything you wanted, and Lazarus had nothing. So now he is here being comforted and you are in anguish. 26And besides, there is a great chasm separating us, and anyone wanting to come to you from here is stopped at its edge; and no one over there can cross to us.'

27"Then the rich man said, 'O Father Abraham, then please send him to my father's home— 28for I have five brothers—to warn them about this place of torment lest they come here when they die.'

29"But Abraham said, 'The Scriptures have warned them again and again. Your brothers can read them any time they want to.'

30"The rich man replied, 'No, Father Abraham, they won't bother to read them. But if someone is sent to them from the dead, then they will turn from their sins.'

31"But Abraham said, 'If they won't listen to Moses and the prophets, they won't listen even though someone rises from the dead.'"

A THOUGHT: *The Pharisees considered wealth evidence of God's blessing. Jesus startled them with this story in which a diseased beggar is rewarded and a rich man is punished. The rich man did not go to hell because of his wealth, but because he was selfish with it. He did not feed Lazarus, take him in, or care for his health. He was hard-hearted in spite of his great blessings. The amount of money we have is not so important as the way we use it. Rich people can be generous or stingy—and so can poor people. What is your attitude toward your possessions? Do you hoard them selfishly, or do you use them to bless others?*

Forget the Past and Strive for the Goal/ Philippians 3:13–16

No, dear brothers, I am still not all I should be but I am bringing all my energies to bear on this one thing: Forgetting the past and looking forward to what lies ahead, 14I strain to reach the end of the race and receive the prize for which God is calling us up to heaven because of what Christ Jesus did for us.

15I hope all of you who are mature Christians will see eye-to-eye with me on these things, and if you disagree on some point, I believe that God will make it plain to you— 16if you fully obey the truth you have.

A THOUGHT: *Paul said his goal was to know Christ, to be like Christ, and to be all Christ has in mind for him. This goal absorbed all his energy. This is an example for us. We should not let anything take our eyes off our goal—Christ. With the singlemindedness of an athlete in training, we must lay aside everything harmful and forsake even the good things that may distract us from being effective Christians.*

Proverbs for Today/ 18:20–21

Ability to give wise advice satisfies like a good meal! □ Those who love to talk will suffer the consequences. Men have died for saying the wrong thing!

JULY 9

Temptation and Forgiveness/ Luke 17:1–4

"There will always be temptations to sin," Jesus said one day to his disciples, "but woe to the man who does the tempting. 2,3If he were thrown into the sea with a huge rock tied to his neck, he would be far better off than facing the punishment in store for those who harm these little children's souls. I am warning you!

"Rebuke your brother if he sins, and forgive him if he is sorry. 4Even if he wrongs you seven times a day and each time turns again and asks forgiveness, forgive him."

A THOUGHT: *To rebuke does not mean to point out every sin we see, it means to bring sin to a person's attention with the purpose of restoring him or her to God and to fellow believers. When you feel you must rebuke another Christian for a sin, check your own attitudes before opening your mouth. Do you love the person? Are you willing to forgive? Unless rebuke is tied to forgiveness, it will not help the sinning person.*

Our Homeland Is in Heaven/ Philippians 3:17–21

Dear brothers, pattern your lives after mine and notice who else lives up to my example. 18For I have told you often before, and I say it again now with tears in my eyes, there are many who walk along the Christian road who are really enemies of the cross of Christ. 19Their future is eternal loss, for their god is their appetite: they are proud of what they should be ashamed of; and all they think about is this life here on earth. 20But our homeland is in heaven, where our Savior the Lord Jesus Christ is; and we are looking forward to his return from there. 21When he comes back he will take these dying bodies of ours and change them into glorious bodies like his own, using the same mighty power that he will use to conquer all else everywhere.

A THOUGHT: *Citizens of Philippi had the same rights and privileges as the citizens of Rome because Philippi was a Roman colony. Likewise we Christians will one day experience all the special privileges of our heavenly citizenship because we belong to Christ. Knowing that our ultimate home is in heaven with God should shape the way we live today. To be truly heavenly minded, we will live like Christ on earth.*

Proverbs for Today/ 18:22
The man who finds a wife finds a good thing; she is a blessing to him from the Lord.

JULY 10

Jesus Teaches about Faith/ Luke 17:5–10
One day the apostles said to the Lord, "We need more faith; tell us how to get it."

6"If your faith were only the size of a mustard seed," Jesus answered, "it would be large enough to uproot that mulberry tree over there and send it hurtling into the sea! Your command would bring immediate results! 7,8,9When a servant comes in from plowing or taking care of sheep, he doesn't just sit down and eat, but first prepares his master's meal and serves him his supper before he eats his own. And he is not even thanked, for he is merely doing what he is supposed to do. 10Just so, if you merely obey me, you should not consider yourselves worthy of praise. For you have simply done your duty!"

A THOUGHT: *A mustard seed is small, but it has great potential for growth. Like this tiny seed, a small amount of genuine faith* in God will take root and grow. The amount of faith is not as important as its object and its genuineness. What is faith? It is total dependence on God and a willingness to do his will. It is not something we use to put on a show for others. It is complete and humble obedience to God's will, readiness to do whatever he calls us to do. The amount of faith isn't as important as the right kind of faith—faith in our all-powerful God.

Rejoice in the Lord Always/ Philippians 4:1–7

Dear brother Christians, I love you and long to see you, for you are my joy and my reward for my work. My beloved friends, stay true to the Lord.

²And now I want to plead with those two dear women, Euodias and Syntyche. Please, please, with the Lord's help, quarrel no more—be friends again. ³And I ask you, my true teammate, to help these women, for they worked side by side with me in telling the Good News to others; and they worked with Clement, too, and the rest of my fellow workers whose names are written in the Book of Life.

⁴Always be full of joy in the Lord; I say it again, rejoice! ⁵Let everyone see that you are unselfish and considerate in all you do. Remember that the Lord is coming soon. ⁶Don't worry about anything; instead, pray about everything; tell God your needs and don't forget to thank him for his answers. ⁷If you do this you will experience God's peace, which is far more wonderful than the human mind can understand. His peace will keep your thoughts and your hearts quiet and at rest as you trust in Christ Jesus.

A THOUGHT: *It seems strange that a man in prison would be telling a church to be joyful. Paul's attitude serves to teach us an important lesson—our inner attitudes do not have to reflect our outward circumstances. Paul was full of joy because he knew that no matter what happened to him, Jesus Christ was with him. Several times in this letter, Paul urges the Philippians to be joyful, probably because they needed to hear this. It's easy to get discouraged about unpleasant circumstances or to take unimportant events too seriously. If you haven't been joyful lately, you may not be looking at life from the right perspective.*

Proverbs for Today/ 18:23–24

The poor man pleads and the rich man answers with insults. □ There are "friends" who pretend to be friends, but there is a friend who sticks closer than a brother.

JULY 11

Jesus Heals Ten Lepers/ Luke 17:11–19

As Jesus and his disciples continued onward toward Jerusalem, they reached the border between Galilee and Samaria, 12and as they entered a village there, ten lepers stood at a distance, 13crying out, "Jesus, sir, have mercy on us!"

14He looked at them and said, "Go to the Jewish priest and show him that you are healed!" And as they were going, their leprosy disappeared.

15One of them came back to Jesus, shouting, "Glory to God, I'm healed!" 16He fell flat on the ground in front of Jesus, face downward in the dust, thanking him for what he had done. This man was a despised Samaritan.

17Jesus asked, "Didn't I heal ten men? Where are the nine? 18Does only this foreigner return to give glory to God?"

19And Jesus said to the man, "Stand up and go; your faith has made you well."

A THOUGHT: *Lepers were required to stay apart from other people and to announce their presence by yelling "Unclean, unclean!" if they had to come near. Sometimes leprosy went into remission; if a leper thought his leprosy had gone away, he was supposed to present himself to a priest who could declare him clean. Jesus sent the ten lepers to the priest before they were healed—and they went! They responded in faith, and Jesus healed them on the way. Is your trust in God so strong that you act on what he says even before it happens?*

Jesus healed all ten lepers, but only one returned to thank him. It is possible to receive God's great gifts with an ungrateful spirit— nine of the lepers did so. Only the thankful leper, however, learned that his faith had played a role in his healing. God does not demand that we thank him, but he is pleased when we do so, and he uses our spirit of thankfulness to teach us more about his Kingdom.

Think about Pure and Lovely Things/
Philippians 4:8–14

And now, brothers, as I close this letter let me say this one more thing: Fix your thoughts on what is true and good and right. Think about things that are pure and lovely, and dwell on the fine, good things in others. Think about all you can praise God for and be glad about. 9Keep putting into practice all you learned from me and saw me doing, and the God of peace will be with you.

10How grateful I am and how I praise the Lord that you are helping me again. I know you have always been anxious to send what you could, but for a while you didn't have the chance. 11Not that I was ever in need, for I have learned how to get along happily whether I have much or little. 12I know how to live on almost nothing or with everything. I have learned the secret of contentment in every situation, whether it be a full stomach or hunger, plenty or want; 13for I can do everything God asks me to with the help of Christ who gives me the strength and power. 14But even so, you have done right in helping me in my present difficulty.

A THOUGHT: *What we put into our minds determines what comes out in our words and actions. Paul tells us to fill our minds with thoughts that are "true and good and right." Do you have problems with impure thoughts and daydreams? Examine what you are putting into your mind through television, books, movies, and magazines. Replace harmful input with wholesome material. Above all, read God's Word and pray. Ask him to help you focus your mind on what is good and pure. It takes practice, but it can be done.*

Proverbs for Today/ 19:1–3

Better be poor and honest than rich and dishonest. □ It is dangerous and sinful to rush into the unknown. A man may ruin his chances by his own foolishness and then blame it on the Lord!

JULY 12

Instructions about the Last Days/ Luke 17:20–37

One day the Pharisees asked Jesus, "When will the Kingdom of God begin?" Jesus replied, "The Kingdom of God isn't ushered in with visible signs. 21You won't be able to say, 'It has begun here in this place or there in that part of the country.' For the Kingdom of God is within you."

22Later he talked again about this with his disciples. "The time is coming when you will long for me to be with you even for a single day, but I won't be here," he said. 23"Reports will reach you that I have returned and that I am in this place or that; don't believe it or go out to look for me. 24For when I return, you will know it beyond all doubt. It will be as evident as the lightning that flashes across the skies. 25But first I must suffer terribly and be rejected by this whole nation.

26"[When I return] the world will be [as indifferent to the things of God] as the people were in Noah's day. 27They ate and drank and married—everything just as usual right up to the day when Noah went into the ark and the flood came and destroyed them all.

28"And the world will be as it was in the days of Lot: people went about their daily business—eating and drinking, buying and selling, farming and building— 29until the morning Lot left Sodom. Then fire and brimstone rained down from heaven and destroyed them all. 30Yes, it will be 'business as usual' right up to the hour of my return.

31"Those away from home that day must not return to pack; those in the fields must not return to town— 32remember what happened to Lot's wife! 33Whoever clings to his life shall lose it, and whoever loses his life shall save it. 34That night two men will be asleep in the same room, and one will be taken away, the other left. 35,36Two women will be working together at household tasks; one will be taken, the other left; and so it will be with men working side by side in the fields."

37"Lord, where will they be taken?" the disciples asked. Jesus replied, "Where the body is, the vultures gather!"

A THOUGHT: *Life will be going on as usual on the day that Christ returns. There will be no prior warning. People will be going about their everyday tasks, indifferent to the things of God. They will be as surprised by Christ's return as the people in Noah's day were by the flood or the people in Lot's day by the destruction of Sodom. We don't know the day or the hour of Christ's return, but we do know he is coming. It may be today, or tomorrow, or centuries in the future. Whenever it is, we must be ready. Live as if Jesus were coming today, and then you will be ready for his return.*

Paul Thanks the Philippians for Their Gift/ Philippians 4:15–23

As you well know, when I first brought the Gospel to you and then went on my way, leaving Macedonia, only you Philippians became my partners in giving and receiving.

No other church did this. 16Even when I was over in Thessalonica you sent help twice. 17But though I appreciate your gifts, what makes me happiest is the well-earned reward you will have because of your kindness.

18At the moment I have all I need—more than I need! I am generously supplied with the gifts you sent me when Epaphroditus came. They are a sweet-smelling sacrifice that pleases God well. 19And it is he who will supply all your needs from his riches in glory, because of what Christ Jesus has done for us. 20Now unto God our Father be glory forever and ever. Amen.

Sincerely,
Paul

P.S.
21Say "hello" for me to all the Christians there; the brothers with me send their greetings too. 22And all the other Christians here want to be remembered to you, especially those who work in Caesar's palace. 23The blessings of our Lord Jesus Christ be upon your spirits.

A THOUGHT: *We can trust that God will always meet our needs, but we must remember that he may not supply them all in this life. Christians suffer and die (tradition says Paul himself was beheaded), and God does not always intervene to spare them. We must also be careful not to confuse needs with wants and desires. In our materialistic society we often consider many luxuries necessities. God has promised to meet our needs, but he has not promised that he will meet our evil indulgent desires. Our hope is in relationship with God, not in the accumulation of goods! What goods we have we must be willing to share with others sacrificially.*

Proverbs for Today/ 19:4–5
A wealthy man has many "friends"; the poor man has none left. □ Punish false witnesses. Track down liars.

JULY 13

An Illustration on Prayer/ Luke 18:1–8
One day Jesus told his disciples a story to illustrate their need for constant prayer and to show them that they

must keep praying until the answer comes.

2"There was a city judge," he said, "a very godless man who had great contempt for everyone. 3A widow of that city came to him frequently to appeal for justice against a man who had harmed her. 4,5The judge ignored her for a while, but eventually she got on his nerves.

" 'I fear neither God nor man,' he said to himself, 'but this woman bothers me. I'm going to see that she gets justice, for she is wearing me out with her constant coming!' "

6Then the Lord said, "If even an evil judge can be worn down like that, 7don't you think that God will surely give justice to his people who plead with him day and night? 8Yes! He will answer them quickly! But the question is: When I, the Messiah, return, how many will I find who have faith [and are praying]?"

A THOUGHT: *To repeat our prayers until the answer comes does not mean endless repetition or painfully long prayer sessions. Constant prayer means keeping our requests constantly before God as we live for him day by day, always believing he will answer. When we thus live by faith, we are not to give up. God may delay answering, but his delays always have good reasons, and we must not confuse them with neglect. As we persist in prayer we grow in character, faith, and hope.*

Paul Thanks God for the Colossians/
Colossians 1:1–6

From: Paul, chosen by God to be Jesus Christ's messenger, and from Brother Timothy.

2*To:* The faithful Christian brothers—God's people—in the city of Colosse.

May God our Father shower you with blessings and fill you with his great peace.

3Whenever we pray for you we always begin by giving thanks to God the Father of our Lord Jesus Christ, 4for we have heard how much you trust the Lord, and how much you love his people. 5And you are looking forward to the joys of heaven, and have been ever since the Gospel first was preached to you. 6The same Good News that came to you is going out all over the world and changing lives everywhere, just as it changed yours that very first day you heard it and understood about God's great kindness to sinners.

A Thought: *Wherever Paul went, he preached the gospel—to Gentile audiences, to hostile Jewish leaders, and even to his Roman guards. Whenever people believed in the message he spoke, they were changed. God's Word is not just for our information, it is for our transformation! Becoming a Christian means beginning a whole new relationship with God, not just turning over a new leaf or determining to do right. New believers have a changed purpose, direction, attitude, and behavior. They no longer seek to serve themselves, but to serve God. Can you point to any areas where hearing God's Word has changed your life, or where it should do so?*

Proverbs for Today/ 19:6–7

Many beg favors from a man who is generous; everyone is his friend! □ A poor man's own brothers turn away from him in embarrassment; how much more his friends! He calls after them, but they are gone.

JULY 14

The Pharisee and the Tax Collector/ Luke 18:9–17

Then Jesus told this story to some who boasted of their virtue and scorned everyone else:

10"Two men went to the Temple to pray. One was a proud, self-righteous Pharisee, and the other a cheating tax collector. 11The proud Pharisee 'prayed' this prayer: 'Thank God, I am not a sinner like everyone else, especially like that tax collector over there! For I never cheat, I don't commit adultery, 12I go without food twice a week, and I give to God a tenth of everything I earn.'

13"But the corrupt tax collector stood at a distance and dared not even lift his eyes to heaven as he prayed, but beat upon his chest in sorrow, exclaiming, 'God, be merciful to me, a sinner.' 14I tell you, this sinner, not the Pharisee, returned home forgiven! For the proud shall be humbled, but the humble shall be honored."

15One day some mothers brought their babies to him to touch and bless. But the disciples told them to go away.

16,17Then Jesus called the children over to him and said to the disciples, "Let the little children come to me! Never send them away! For the Kingdom of God belongs to men who have hearts as trusting as these little children's. And anyone who doesn't have their kind of faith will never get within the Kingdom's gates."

A THOUGHT: *The Pharisee did not go to the Temple to pray to God but to announce to all within earshot how good he was. The tax collector went recognizing his sin and begging for mercy. Self-righteousness is sin. It leads to pride, causes a person to despise others, and prevents him or her from learning anything from God. The tax collector's prayer should be our prayer because we all need God's mercy every day. Don't let pride get in the way of your relationship with God or with others.*

Epaphras' Good Report/ Colossians 1:7–10

Epaphras, our much-loved fellow worker, was the one who brought you this Good News. He is Jesus Christ's faithful slave, here to help us in your place. 8And he is the one who has told us about the great love for others which the Holy Spirit has given you.

9So ever since we first heard about you we have kept on praying and asking God to help you understand what he wants you to do; asking him to make you wise about spiritual things; 10and asking that the way you live will always please the Lord and honor him, so that you will always be doing good, kind things for others, while all the time you are learning to know God better and better.

A THOUGHT: *The Colossians had a great love for others because the Holy Spirit had transformed their lives. The ability to love others in the same way Christ loved us comes through the working of the Holy Spirit. The Bible speaks of love as an action and attitude, not just an emotion. It is a by-product of our new life in Christ. Christians have no excuse for failing to love others, because Christian love is not a feeling but a decision to act in the best interests of others.*

Proverbs for Today/ 19:8–9

He who loves wisdom loves his own best interest and will be a success. □ A false witness shall be punished and a liar shall be caught.

Jesus and the Rich Man/ Luke 18:18–30

Once a Jewish religious leader asked Jesus this question: "Good sir, what shall I do to get to heaven?"

19"Do you realize what you are saying when you call me 'good'?" Jesus asked him. "Only God is truly good, and no one else.

20"But as to your question, you know what the ten commandments say—don't commit adultery, don't murder, don't steal, don't lie, honor your parents, and so on."

21The man replied, "I've obeyed every one of these laws since I was a small child."

22"There is still one thing you lack," Jesus said. "Sell all you have and give the money to the poor—it will become treasure for you in heaven—and come, follow me."

23But when the man heard this he went sadly away, for he was very rich.

24Jesus watched him go and then said to his disciples, "How hard it is for the rich to enter the Kingdom of God! 25It is easier for a camel to go through the eye of a needle than for a rich man to enter the Kingdom of God."

26Those who heard him say this exclaimed, "If it is that hard, how can *anyone* be saved?"

27He replied, "God can do what men can't!"

28And Peter said, "We have left our homes and followed you."

29"Yes," Jesus replied, "and everyone who has done as you have, leaving home, wife, brothers, parents, or children for the sake of the Kingdom of God, 30will be repaid many times over now, as well as receiving eternal life in the world to come."

A THOUGHT: *This man's wealth gave him power and prestige. When Jesus told him to sell everything he owned, he was touching this man's very security. Because money represents power, authority, and success, it is often difficult for wealthy people to realize their need for God and their powerlessness to save themselves. Unless God reaches down into their lives, they will not come to him. Jesus surprised some of his hearers by offering salvation to the poor; he may surprise some people today by offering it to the rich. It is difficult for a rich person to realize his need and come to Jesus, but "God can do what men can't!" Jesus asks us all to get rid of anything that has become more important to us than God. What is the ultimate source of your security?*

Prayerful Response to Epaphras' Report/ Colossians 1:11–14

We are praying, too, that you will be filled with his mighty, glorious strength so that you can keep going no matter what happens—always full of the joy of the Lord, 12and always thankful to the Father who has made us fit to share all the wonderful things that belong to those who live in the Kingdom of light. 13For he has rescued us out of the darkness and gloom of Satan's kingdom and brought us into the Kingdom of his dear Son, 14who bought our freedom with his blood and forgave us all our sins.

A THOUGHT: *Sometimes we wonder how to pray for missionaries and other leaders we have never met. Paul had never met the Colossians, but he faithfully prayed for them. His prayers teach us how to pray for others, whether we know them or not. We can request that they (1) understand God's will, (2) gain spiritual wisdom, (3) live lives pleasing and honoring to God, (4) do kind things for others, (5) know God better and better, (6) be filled with God's strength, (7) endure in faith, (8) stay full of Christ's joy, and (9) always be thankful. All believers have these same basic needs. When you don't know how to pray for someone, remember the pattern of Paul's prayer for the Colossians.*

Proverbs for Today/ 19:10–12

It doesn't seem right for a fool to succeed or for a slave to rule over princes! □ A wise man restrains his anger and overlooks insults. This is to his credit. □ The king's anger is as dangerous as a lion's. But his approval is as refreshing as the dew on grass.

JULY 16

Jesus Predicts His Death/ Luke 18:31–34

Gathering the Twelve around him, Jesus told them, "As you know, we are going to Jerusalem. And when we get there, all the predictions of the ancient prophets concerning me will come true. 32I will be handed over to the Gentiles to be mocked and treated shamefully and spat upon, 33and lashed and killed. And the third day I will rise again."

34But they didn't understand a thing he said. He seemed to be talking in riddles.

A THOUGHT: *Although the disciples had spent a great deal of time with Jesus, they did not understand his statements concerning suffering and death. Their expectations for a conquering king were so great that they could not fathom Jesus' words. Despite the fact that no one on earth understood what Jesus was going through— his disciples all abandoned him when he was crucified—Jesus went to Jerusalem this last time fully knowing what was ahead of him. He willingly submitted to the misunderstandings, the mockings, the shame, the crucifixion, and death in order to redeem mankind.*

The Exact Image of the Unseen God/ Colossians 1:15–19

Christ is the exact likeness of the unseen God. He existed before God made anything at all, and, in fact, 16Christ himself is the Creator who made everything in heaven and earth, the things we can see and the things we can't; the spirit world with its kings and kingdoms, its rulers and authorities; all were made by Christ for his own use and glory. 17He was before all else began and it is his power that holds everything together. 18He is the Head of the body made up of his people—that is, his Church— which he began; and he is the Leader of all those who arise from the dead, so that he is first in everything; 19for God wanted all of himself to be in his Son.

A THOUGHT: *This is one of the strongest statements about the divine nature of Christ found anywhere in the Bible. Jesus is not only equal to God, he is God. He not only reflects God, but he reveals God to us. He came from heaven, not from the dust of the ground, and is Lord of all. He is completely holy, and he has authority to judge the world. Therefore, he is supreme over all creation, including the spirit world. We, like the Colossian believers, must believe in the deity of Jesus Christ (that Jesus is God), or our Christian faith is hollow, misdirected, and meaningless. The deity of Christ is a central truth of Christianity.*

Proverbs for Today/ 19:13–14

A rebellious son is a calamity to his father, and a nagging wife annoys like constant dripping. □ A father can give his sons homes and riches, but only the Lord can give them understanding wives.

JULY 17

Jesus Heals a Blind Man/ Luke 18:35–43

As Jesus and his disciples approached Jericho, a blind man was sitting beside the road, begging from travelers. 36When he heard the noise of a crowd going past, he asked what was happening. 37He was told that Jesus from Nazareth was going by, 38so he began shouting, "Jesus, Son of David, have mercy on me!"

39The crowds ahead of Jesus tried to hush the man, but he only yelled the louder, "Son of David, have mercy on me!"

40When Jesus arrived at the spot, he stopped. "Bring the blind man over here," he said. 41Then Jesus asked the man, "What do you want?"

"Lord," he pleaded, "I want to see!"

42And Jesus said, "All right, begin seeing! Your faith has healed you."

43And instantly the man could see, and followed Jesus, praising God. And all who saw it happen praised God too.

A THOUGHT: *Beggars often waited along the roads near cities because that was where they would be able to contact the most people. Usually handicapped in some way, these beggars were unable to earn a living. Medical help was not available for their problems, and others tended to ignore their obligation to care for the needy. Thus beggars had little hope of escaping their degrading way of life. But this blind beggar took hope in the Messiah. He shamelessly cried out for Jesus' attention, and Jesus said his faith made him see. No matter how desperate your situation may seem, if you call out to Jesus in faith, he will help you.*

The Reconciling Cross of Christ/ Colossians 1:20–23

It was through what his Son did that God cleared a path for everything to come to him—all things in heaven and on earth—for Christ's death on the cross has made peace with God for all by his blood. 21This includes you who were once so far away from God. You were his enemies and hated him and were separated from him by your evil thoughts and actions, yet now he has brought you back as his friends. 22He has done this through the death on the cross of his own human body, and now as a result

Christ has brought you into the very presence of God, and you are standing there before him with nothing left against you—nothing left that he could even chide you for; 23the only condition is that you fully believe the Truth, standing in it steadfast and firm, strong in the Lord, convinced of the Good News that Jesus died for you, and never shifting from trusting him to save you. This is the wonderful news that came to each of you and is now spreading all over the world. And I, Paul, have the joy of telling it to others.

A THOUGHT: *Christ's death provided a way for all people to come to God. It cleared away the sin that keeps us from having a right relationship with our Creator. This does not mean that everyone has been saved, but that the way has been cleared for anyone who will trust Christ to be saved. God gives salvation to all those who by faith accept Christ's death for themselves. Salvation reconciles people to God and to each other, thus the cross of Christ brings peace.*

Proverbs for Today/ 19:15–16

A lazy man sleeps soundly—and he goes hungry! □ Keep the commandments and keep your life; despising them means death.

JULY 18

Salvation Comes to Zacchaeus' Home/ Luke 19:1–10

As Jesus was passing through Jericho, a man named Zacchaeus, one of the most influential Jews in the Roman tax-collecting business (and, of course, a very rich man), 3tried to get a look at Jesus, but he was too short to see over the crowds. 4 So he ran ahead and climbed into a sycamore tree beside the road, to watch from there.

5When Jesus came by he looked up at Zacchaeus and called him by name! "Zacchaeus!" he said. "Quick! Come down! For I am going to be a guest in your home today!"

6Zacchaeus hurriedly climbed down and took Jesus to his house in great excitement and joy.

7But the crowds were displeased. "He has gone to be

the guest of a notorious sinner," they grumbled.

8Meanwhile, Zacchaeus stood before the Lord and said, "Sir, from now on I will give half my wealth to the poor, and if I find I have overcharged anyone on his taxes, I will penalize myself by giving him back four times as much!"

9,10Jesus told him, "This shows that salvation has come to this home today. This man was one of the lost sons of Abraham, and I, the Messiah, have come to search for and to save such souls as his."

A THOUGHT: *To finance their great world empire, the Romans levied heavy taxes against all nations under their control. The Jews opposed these taxes because they supported a secular government and its pagan gods, but they were still forced to pay. Tax collectors— Jews by birth who chose to work for Rome—were considered traitors among the people of Israel. Besides, it was common knowledge that tax collectors made themselves rich by gouging their fellow Jews of extra tax money which they kept for themselves. No wonder the crowds were displeased when Jesus went home with the tax collector Zacchaeus. But despite the fact that Zacchaeus was both dishonest and a turncoat, Jesus loved him, and in response, the little tax collector was converted. In every society certain groups of people are considered "untouchable" because of their politics, their immoral behavior, or their lifestyle. We should not give in to social pressure to avoid these people. Jesus loves them, and they need to hear his Good News.*

Christ in You, the Hope of Glory/
Colossians 1:24–29

But part of my work is to suffer for you; and I am glad, for I am helping to finish up the remainder of Christ's sufferings for his body, the Church.

25God has sent me to help his Church and to tell his secret plan to you Gentiles. 26,27He has kept this secret for centuries and generations past, but now at last it has pleased him to tell it to those who love him and live for him, and the riches and glory of his plan are for you Gentiles too. And this is the secret: *that Christ in your hearts is your only hope of glory.*

28So everywhere we go we talk about Christ to all who will listen, warning them and teaching them as well as we know how. We want to be able to present each one to God, perfect because of what Christ has done for each of them. 29This is my work, and I can do it only because Christ's mighty energy is at work within me.

A THOUGHT: *The false teachers in the Colossian church believed spiritual perfection was a secret and hidden plan that only a few privileged people would discover. Their secret plan was meant to be exclusive. Paul calls God's plan a secret, not because only a few would understand, but because it was hidden until Christ came. Who could have imagined that God's secret plan was to have his Son, Jesus Christ, live in the hearts of all who believe in him?*

Proverbs for Today/ 19:17

When you help the poor you are lending to the Lord—and he pays wonderful interest on your loan!

JULY 19

The Nobleman and His Assistants/ Luke 19:11–27

And because Jesus was nearing Jerusalem, he told a story to correct the impression that the Kingdom of God would begin right away.

12"A nobleman living in a certain province was called away to the distant capital of the empire to be crowned king of his province. 13Before he left he called together ten assistants and gave them each $2,000 to invest while he was gone. 14But some of his people hated him and sent him their declaration of independence, stating that they had rebelled and would not acknowledge him as their king.

15"Upon his return he called in the men to whom he had given the money, to find out what they had done with it, and what their profits were.

16"The first man reported a tremendous gain—ten times as much as the original amount!

17" 'Fine!' the king exclaimed. 'You are a good man. You have been faithful with the little I entrusted to you, and as your reward, you shall be governor of ten cities.'

18"The next man also reported a splendid gain—five times the original amount.

19" 'All right!' his master said. 'You can be governor over five cities.'

20"But the third man brought back only the money he had started with. 'I've kept it safe,' he said, 21'because I was afraid [you would demand my profits], for you are a hard man to deal with, taking what isn't yours and even confiscating the crops that others plant.' 22'You vile and wicked slave,' the king roared. 'Hard, am I? That's exactly how I'll be toward you! If you knew so much about me and how tough I am, 23then why didn't you deposit the money in the bank so that I could at least get some interest on it?'

24"Then turning to the others standing by he ordered, 'Take the money away from him and give it to the man who earned the most.'

25" 'But, sir,' they said, 'he has enough already!'

26" 'Yes,' the king replied, 'but it is always true that those who have, get more, and those who have little, soon lose even that. 27And now about these enemies of mine who revolted—bring them in and execute them before me.' "

A THOUGHT: *Why was the king so hard on this man who had not increased the money entrusted to him? He punished the man because (1) he didn't share his master's interest in the kingdom; (2) he didn't trust his master's intentions; and (3) his only loyalty was to himself. Like the king in this story, God has given us gifts to use for the benefit of his Kingdom. Jesus expects us to use these talents so that people will be drawn into the Kingdom. He asks each of us, "What are you doing with what I have given you?" While awaiting the coming of the Kingdom of God in glory, we must do his work.*

Treasures of Wisdom and Knowledge/
Colossians 2:1–10

I wish you could know how much I have struggled in prayer for you and for the church at Laodicea, and for my many other friends who have never known me personally. 2This is what I have asked of God for you: that you will be encouraged and knit together by strong ties of love, and that you will have the rich experience of knowing Christ with real certainty and clear understanding. *For God's secret plan, now at last made known, is Christ himself.* 3In him lie hidden all the mighty, untapped treasures of wisdom and knowledge.

4I am saying this because I am afraid that someone

may fool you with smooth talk. 5For though I am far away from you my heart is with you, happy because you are getting along so well, happy because of your strong faith in Christ. 6And now just as you trusted Christ to save you, trust him, too, for each day's problems; live in vital union with him. 7Let your roots grow down into him and draw up nourishment from him. See that you go on growing in the Lord, and become strong and vigorous in the truth you were taught. Let your lives overflow with joy and thanksgiving for all he has done.

8Don't let others spoil your faith and joy with their philosophies, their wrong and shallow answers built on men's thoughts and ideas, instead of on what Christ has said. 9For in Christ there is all of God in a human body; 10*so you have everything when you have Christ,* and you are filled with God through your union with Christ. He is the highest Ruler, with authority over every other power.

A THOUGHT: *The problem Paul was combatting in the Colossian church was similar to gnosticism (from the Greek word for "knowledge"). This heresy (a teaching contrary to biblical doctrine) attacked Christianity in several basic ways: (1) It insisted that important hidden knowledge was a secret kept from most believers; Paul, however, said that in Christ we see all we need to see of God's provision for us. (2) It taught that the body was evil; Paul countered this by saying that God himself dwelt in a body—that is, he was embodied in Jesus Christ. (3) It said that Christ seemed to be human, but was not. Paul insisted that in Jesus we see one who is fully human and fully God.*

Gnosticism became fashionable in the second century. Even in Paul's day, these ideas sounded attractive to many and could easily seduce a church that didn't know Christian doctrine well. Aspects of this early heresy still pose significant problems for many in the church today. The antidote for heretical ideas is a thorough acquaintance with God's Word through personal study and sound Bible teaching.

Proverbs for Today/ 19:18–19

Discipline your son in his early years while there is hope. If you don't you will ruin his life. □ A short-tempered man must bear his own penalty; you can't do much to help him. If you try once you must try a dozen times!

JULY 20

Jesus' Triumphal Entry into Jerusalem/
Luke 19:28–40

After telling this story, Jesus went on toward Jerusalem, walking along ahead of his disciples. 29As they came to the towns of Bethphage and Bethany, on the Mount of Olives, he sent two disciples ahead, 30with instructions to go to the next village, and as they entered they were to look for a donkey tied beside the road. It would be a colt, not yet broken for riding.

"Untie him," Jesus said, "and bring him here. 31And if anyone asks you what you are doing, just say, 'The Lord needs him.'"

32They found the colt as Jesus said, 33and sure enough, as they were untying it, the owners demanded an explanation.

"What are you doing?" they asked. "Why are you untying our colt?"

34And the disciples simply replied, "The Lord needs him!" 35So they brought the colt to Jesus and threw some of their clothing across its back for Jesus to sit on.

36,37Then the crowds spread out their robes along the road ahead of him, and as they reached the place where the road started down from the Mount of Olives, the whole procession began to shout and sing as they walked along, praising God for all the wonderful miracles Jesus had done.

38"God has given us a King!" they exulted. "Long live the King! Let all heaven rejoice! Glory to God in the highest heavens!"

39But some of the Pharisees among the crowd said, "Sir, rebuke your followers for saying things like that!"

40He replied, "If they keep quiet, the stones along the road will burst into cheers!"

A THOUGHT: *This is the event Christians celebrate on Palm Sunday. The people lined the highway, praising God, waving palm branches, and throwing their cloaks in front of the colt as it passed before them. "Long live the King" was the meaning of their joyful shouts, because they knew Jesus was intentionally fulfilling the prophecy in Zechariah 9:9: "Your King is coming! He is the Righteous One, the Victor! Yet he is lowly, riding on a donkey's colt!" To announce that he was indeed the Messiah, Jesus chose a time when all Israel would be gathered at Jerusalem, a place where huge crowds could see him, and a way of proclaiming his mission that was unmistakable. Now the people were sure their liberation was at hand. They were praising God for giving them a king, but they had the wrong idea about Jesus' ministry. They were sure he would be a national leader who would restore their nation to its former glory, and thus they were deaf to the words of their prophets and blind to Jesus' real mission. When it became apparent that Jesus was not going to fulfill their hopes, many people turned against him.*

Our Sins Have Been Nailed to the Cross/ Colossians 2:11–15

When you came to Christ he set you free from your evil desires, not by a bodily operation of circumcision but by a spiritual operation, the baptism of your souls. 12For in baptism you see how your old, evil nature died with him and was buried with him; and then you came up out of death with him into a new life because you trusted the Word of the mighty God who raised Christ from the dead.

13You were dead in sins, and your sinful desires were not yet cut away. Then he gave you a share in the very life of Christ, for he forgave all your sins, 14and blotted out the charges proved against you, the list of his commandments which you had not obeyed. He took this list of sins and destroyed it by nailing it to Christ's cross. 15In this way God took away Satan's power to accuse you of sin, and God openly displayed to the whole world Christ's triumph at the cross where your sins were all taken away.

A THOUGHT: *Before we believed in Christ, our nature was evil. The Christian, however, has a new nature. God has crucified the old rebellious nature and given us a new, loving nature. The penalty of sin died with Christ on the cross. God has declared us not guilty, and we need no longer live under sin's power. God does not take us out of the world or make us robots—we will still feel like sinning, and sometimes we will sin. The difference is that before we were saved, we were slaves to our sinful nature, but now we can choose to live for Christ.*

Proverbs for Today/ 19:20–21

Get all the advice you can and be wise the rest of your life. □ Man proposes, but God disposes.

JULY 21

Jesus Weeps over Jerusalem/ Luke 19:41–48

But as Jesus and his disciples came closer to Jerusalem and he saw the city ahead, he began to cry. 42"Eternal peace was within your reach and you turned it down," he wept, "and now it is too late. 43Your enemies will pile up earth against your walls and encircle you and close in on you, 44and crush you to the ground, and your children within you; your enemies will not leave one stone upon another—for you have rejected the opportunity God offered you."

45Then he entered the Temple and began to drive out the merchants from their stalls, 46saying to them, "The Scriptures declare, 'My Temple is a place of prayer; but you have turned it into a den of thieves.'"

47After that he taught daily in the Temple, but the chief priests and other religious leaders and the business community were trying to find some way to get rid of him. 48But they could think of nothing, for he was a hero to the people—they hung on every word he said.

A THOUGHT: *Why would the business community—which included the leading political, commercial, and judicial men among the people—want to get rid of Jesus? Obviously he had damaged business in the Temple by driving the merchants out. In addition, he preached against injustice, and his teachings often favored the poor over the rich. Further, his great popularity was in danger of attracting Rome's attention, and the leaders of Israel wanted as little as possible to do with Rome. These leaders not only refused God's offer of salvation, they sought to kill the Savior! God continues to offer salvation to the people he loves, both Jews and Gentiles. Eternal peace is within your reach—accept it before it is too late.*

Don't Allow Yourself to Be Enslaved by Legalism/ Colossians 2:16–23

So don't let anyone criticize you for what you eat or drink, or for not celebrating Jewish holidays and feasts or new moon ceremonies or Sabbaths. 17For these were only temporary rules that ended when Christ came. They were only shadows of the real thing—of Christ himself. 18Don't let anyone declare you lost when you refuse to worship angels, as they say you must. They have seen a vision, they say, and know you should. These proud men (though they claim to be so humble) have a very clever imagination. 19But they are not connected to Christ, the Head to which all of us who are his body are joined; for we are joined together by his strong sinews and we grow only as we get our nourishment and strength from God.

20Since you died, as it were, with Christ and this has set you free from following the world's ideas of how to be saved—by doing good and obeying various rules—why do you keep right on following them anyway, still bound by such rules as 21not eating, tasting, or even touching certain foods? 22Such rules are mere human teachings, for food was made to be eaten and used up. 23These rules may seem good, for rules of this kind require strong devotion and are humiliating and hard on the body, but they have no effect when it comes to conquering a person's evil thoughts and desires. They only make him proud.

A THOUGHT: *We cannot reach up to God by following rules and rituals or by practicing religion. Paul isn't saying all rules are bad. But no keeping of laws or rules will earn salvation. The Good News is that God reaches down to man, and we respond. Man-made religions focus on human effort; Christianity focuses on Christ's work. Paul agrees that believers must put aside sinful desires, but that is the by-product of our new life in Christ, not the cause of it. Our salvation does not depend on our own discipline and rule-keeping, but on the power of Christ's death and resurrection.*

We can guard against man-made religions by asking these questions of any religious group: (1) Does it stress man-made rules and taboos rather than God's grace? (2) Does it foster a critical spirit about others, or does it exercise discipline discreetly and lovingly? (3) Does it stress formulas, secret knowledge, or special visions more than the Word of God? (4) Does it elevate self-righteousness, honoring those who keep the rules, rather than elevating Christ? (5) Does it neglect Christ's universal church, claiming to be an elite group? (6) Does it teach humiliation of the body as a means to spiritual growth rather than focusing on the growth of the whole person? (7) Does it disregard the family rather than holding it in high regard as the Bible does?

Proverbs for Today/ 19:22–23

Kindness makes a man attractive. And it is better to be poor than dishonest. □ Reverence for God gives life, happiness, and protection from harm.

JULY 22

The Story of the Disloyal Tenants/ Luke 20:1–19

On one of those days when Jesus was teaching and preaching the Good News in the Temple, he was confronted by the chief priests and other religious leaders and councilmen. 2They demanded to know by what authority he had driven out the merchants from the Temple.

3"I'll ask you a question before I answer," he replied. 4"Was John sent by God, or was he merely acting under his own authority?"

5They talked it over among themselves. "If we say his message was from heaven, then we are trapped because he will ask, 'Then why didn't you believe him?' 6But if we say John was not sent from God, the people will mob us, for they are convinced that he was a prophet." 7Finally they replied, "We don't know!"

8And Jesus responded, "Then I won't answer your question either."

9Now he turned to the people again and told them this story: "A man planted a vineyard and rented it out to some farmers, and went away to a distant land to live for several years. 10When harvest time came, he sent one of his men to the farm to collect his share of the crops. But the tenants beat him up and sent him back empty-handed. 11Then he sent another, but the same thing happened; he was beaten up and insulted and sent away without collecting. 12A third man was sent and the same thing happened. He, too, was wounded and chased away.

13" 'What shall I do?' the owner asked himself. 'I know! I'll send my cherished son. Surely they will show respect for him.'

14"But when the tenants saw his son, they said, 'This is our chance! This fellow will inherit all the land when his father dies. Come on. Let's kill him, and then it will be ours.' 15So they dragged him out of the vineyard and killed him.

"What do you think the owner will do? 16I'll tell you— he will come and kill them and rent the vineyard to others."

"But they would never do a thing like that," his listeners protested.

17Jesus looked at them and said, "Then what does the Scripture mean where it says, 'The Stone rejected by the builders was made the cornerstone'?" 18And he added, "Whoever stumbles over that Stone shall be broken; and those on whom it falls will be crushed to dust."

19When the chief priests and religious leaders heard about this story he had told, they wanted him arrested immediately, for they realized that he was talking about them. They were the wicked tenants in his illustration. But they were afraid that if they themselves arrested him there would be a riot. So they tried to get him to say something that could be reported to the Roman governor as reason for arrest by him.

A THOUGHT: *This group of religious leaders wanted to get rid of Jesus, so they tried to trap him with their question. If Jesus answered that his authority came from God, then they would accuse him of blasphemy—claiming to be the Son of God—and bring him to trial. Jesus did not let himself be caught. Instead, he turned the question on them. Thus he exposed their motives and avoided their trap by answering them in a parable.*

The characters in this parable are easily identified. The religious leaders understood it. The landowner is God; the vineyard is Israel; the tenant farmers are the religious leaders; the landowner's men are the prophets and priests God sent to Israel to denounce their sins; the son is the Messiah, Jesus; and the others are the Gentiles. Jesus' parable indirectly answered the religious leaders' question about his authority; it also showed them that he knew their plan to kill him.

Set Your Heart on Heaven Where Christ Is/ Colossians 3:1–8

Since you became alive again, so to speak, when Christ arose from the dead, now set your sights on the rich treasures and joys of heaven where he sits beside God in the place of honor and power. 2Let heaven fill your thoughts; don't spend your time worrying about things down here. 3You should have as little desire for this world as a dead person does. Your real life is in heaven with Christ and God. 4And when Christ who is our real life comes back again, you will shine with him and share in all his glories.

5Away then with sinful, earthly things; deaden the evil desires lurking within you; have nothing to do with sexual sin, impurity, lust and shameful desires; don't worship the good things of life, for that is idolatry. 6God's terrible anger is upon those who do such things. 7You used to do them when your life was still part of this world; 8but now is the time to cast off and throw away all these rotten garments of anger, hatred, cursing, and dirty language.

A THOUGHT: *The Christian's real home is where Christ lives. This gives us a different perspective on our lives here on earth. To let heaven fill your thoughts means to look at life from God's perspective. This is the antidote to materialism; we gain the proper perspective on material goods when we take God's view of them. The more we see the life around us as God sees it, the more we live in harmony with him. We must not become too attached to what is only temporary.*

Proverbs for Today/ 19:24–25

Some men are so lazy they won't even feed themselves! □ Punish a mocker and others will learn from his example. Reprove a wise man and he will be the wiser.

JULY 23

It Is Right to Pay Taxes/ Luke 20:20–26

Watching their opportunity, the religious leaders sent secret agents pretending to be honest men. 21They said to Jesus, "Sir, we know what an honest teacher you are. You always tell the truth and don't budge an inch in the face of what others think, but teach the ways of God. 22Now tell us—is it right to pay taxes to the Roman government or not?"

23He saw through their trickery and said, 24"Show me a coin. Whose portrait is this on it? And whose name?"

They replied, "Caesar's—the Roman emperor's."

25He said, "Then give the emperor all that is his—and give to God all that is his!"

26Thus their attempt to outwit him before the people failed; and marveling at his answer, they were silent.

A THOUGHT: *This question concerning taxes was indeed a loaded question. The Jews were enraged at having to pay taxes to Rome which supported the pagan government and its gods. They hated the system which allowed tax collectors to charge exorbitant rates and keep the extra for themselves. If Jesus said they should pay taxes, they would call him a traitor to their nation and their religion. But if he said they should not pay taxes, they could report him to Rome as a rebel. Jesus' questioners thought they had him this time, but he outwitted them again. Jesus turned his enemies' attempt to trap him into a powerful lesson: God's followers have legitimate obligations to both God and the government. But what is important is to keep our priorities straight. When the two authorities conflict, our duty to God always comes before our duty to the government.*

Principles for Holy Living/ Colossians 3:9–13

Don't tell lies to each other; it was your old life with all its wickedness that did that sort of thing; now it is dead and gone. 10You are living a brand new kind of life that is continually learning more and more of what is right, and trying constantly to be more and more like Christ who created this new life within you. 11In this new life one's nationality or race or education or social position is unimportant; such things mean nothing. Whether a person has Christ is what matters, and he is equally available to all.

12Since you have been chosen by God who has given you this new kind of life, and because of his deep love and concern for you, you should practice tenderhearted mercy and kindness to others. Don't worry about making a good impression on them but be ready to suffer quietly and patiently. 13Be gentle and ready to forgive; never hold grudges. Remember, the Lord forgave you, so you must forgive others.

A THOUGHT: *The Christian is in a continuing education program. The more we know of Christ and his work, the more we are being changed to be like him. Because this process is lifelong, we must never cease learning and obeying. There is no justification for drifting along, but there is an incentive to find the rich treasures of growing in him. It takes practice, review, patience, and concentration to keep in line with God's will.*

Proverbs for Today/ 19:26

A son who mistreats his father or mother is a public disgrace.

Jesus Answers the Religious Leaders/
Luke 20:27–47

Then some Sadducees—men who believed that death is the end of existence, that there is no resurrection— 28came to Jesus with this:

"The laws of Moses state that if a man dies without children, the man's brother shall marry the widow and their children will legally belong to the dead man, to carry on his name. 29We know of a family of seven brothers. The oldest married and then died without any children. 30His brother married the widow and he, too, died. Still no children. 31And so it went, one after the other, until each of the seven had married her and died, leaving no children. 32Finally the woman died also. 33Now here is our question: Whose wife will she be in the resurrection? For all of them were married to her!"

34,35Jesus replied, "Marriage is for people here on earth, but when those who are counted worthy of being raised from the dead get to heaven, they do not marry. 36And they never die again; in these respects they are like angels, and are sons of God, for they are raised up in new life from the dead.

37,38"But as to your real question—whether or not there is a resurrection—why, even the writings of Moses himself prove this. For when he describes how God appeared to him in the burning bush, he speaks of God as 'the God of Abraham, the God of Isaac, and the God of Jacob.' To say that the Lord *is* some person's God means that person is *alive*, not dead! So from God's point of view, all men are living."

39"Well said, sir!" remarked some of the experts in the Jewish law who were standing there. 40And that ended their questions, for they dared ask no more!

41Then he presented *them* with a question. "Why is it," he asked, "that Christ, the Messiah, is said to be a descendant of King David? 42,43For David himself wrote in the book of Psalms: 'God said to my Lord, the Messiah, "Sit at my right hand until I place your enemies beneath your feet." ' 44How can the Messiah be both David's son and David's God at the same time?"

45Then, with the crowds listening, he turned to his disciples and said, 46"Beware of these experts in religion, for they love to parade in dignified robes and to be bowed to by the people as they walk along the street. And how they love the seats of honor in the synagogues and at religious festivals! 47But even while they are praying long prayers with great outward piety, they are planning schemes to cheat widows out of their property. Therefore God's heaviest sentence awaits these men."

A Thought: *The Sadducees, a group of conservative religious leaders, honored only the Pentateuch—Genesis through Deuteronomy—as Scripture and did not believe in a resurrection of the dead because they could find no mention of it in these books. They decided to try their hand at tricking Jesus, so they brought him a question that had always stumped the Pharisees. After addressing their question about marriage, Jesus answered their real question about resurrection. Basing his answer on the writings of Moses—an authority they respected—he upheld belief in resurrection.*

Let the Peace of Christ Rule in Your Hearts/ Colossians 3:14–17

Most of all, let love guide your life, for then the whole church will stay together in perfect harmony. 15Let the peace of heart which comes from Christ be always present in your hearts and lives, for this is your responsibility and privilege as members of his body. And always be thankful.

16Remember what Christ taught and let his words enrich your lives and make you wise; teach them to each other and sing them out in psalms and hymns and spiritual songs, singing to the Lord with thankful hearts. 17And whatever you do or say, let it be as a representative of the Lord Jesus, and come with him into the presence of God the Father to give him your thanks.

A Thought: *Christians should live in perfect harmony. This does not mean there cannot be differences in opinion, but loving Christians will work together despite their differences. Such love is not a feeling, but a decision to meet others' needs. It leads to peace between individuals and among the members of the body of believers. Do problems in your relationship with other Christians cause open conflicts or mutual silence? Consider what you can do to heal those relationships with selfless acts of love.*

Proverbs for Today/ 19:27–29

Stop listening to teaching that contradicts what you know is right. □ A worthless witness cares nothing for truth—he enjoys his sinning too much. □ Mockers and rebels shall be severely punished.

JULY 25

The Poor Widow/ Luke 21:1–4

As Jesus stood in the Temple, he was watching the rich tossing their gifts into the collection box. 2Then a poor widow came by and dropped in two small copper coins.

3"Really," he remarked, "this poor widow has given more than all the rest of them combined. 4For they have given a little of what they didn't need, but she, poor as she is, has given everything she has."

A THOUGHT: *Jesus was probably in the area of the Temple called the Court of the Women, where it is thought that the treasury was located. In this area were seven boxes in which men could deposit their Temple tax and six boxes for freewill offerings like the one this woman gave. Not only was she poor; as a widow she had few resources for making money. Her small gift was a sacrifice, but she gave it willingly. This widow gave all she had, in stark contrast to the way most of us handle our money. When we consider giving a certain percentage of our income a great accomplishment, we resemble "the rest of them" who gave only a little of what they didn't need. Here, Jesus is admiring sacrifical giving. As believers, we should increase our giving—whether of money, time, or talents—to a point beyond that which is convenient or safe.*

Paul's Commands for Community Life/ Colossians 3:18—4:1

You wives, submit yourselves to your husbands, for that is what the Lord has planned for you. 19And you husbands must be loving and kind to your wives and not bitter against them, nor harsh.

20You children must always obey your fathers and mothers, for that pleases the Lord. 21Fathers, don't scold your children so much that they become discouraged and quit trying.

²²You slaves must always obey your earthly masters, not only trying to please them when they are watching you but all the time; obey them willingly because of your love for the Lord and because you want to please him. ²³Work hard and cheerfully at all you do, just as though you were working for the Lord and not merely for your masters, ²⁴remembering that it is the Lord Christ who is going to pay you, giving you your full portion of all he owns. He is the one you are really working for. ²⁵And if you don't do your best for him, he will pay you in a way that you won't like—for he has no special favorites who can get away with shirking.

⁴:¹You slave owners must be just and fair to all your slaves. Always remember that you, too, have a Master in heaven who is closely watching you.

A THOUGHT: *Paul describes three relationships: (1) husbands and wives, (2) parents and children, and (3) masters and slaves. In each case there is mutual responsibility to submit and love, to obey and encourage, to work hard and be fair. Examine your family and work relationships. Do you relate to others as God intended?*

Proverbs for Today/ 20:1
Wine gives false courage; hard liquor leads to brawls; what fools men are to let it master them, making them reel drunkenly down the street!

JULY 26

The Signs of the Last Days/ Luke 21:5–19
Some of Jesus' disciples began talking about the beautiful stonework of the Temple and the memorial decorations on the walls.

⁶ But Jesus said, "The time is coming when all these things you are admiring will be knocked down, and not one stone will be left on top of another; all will become one vast heap of rubble."

⁷"Master!" they exclaimed. "When? And will there be any warning ahead of time?"

8He replied, "Don't let anyone mislead you. For many will come announcing themselves as the Messiah, and saying, 'The time has come.' But don't believe them! 9And when you hear of wars and insurrections beginning, don't panic. True, wars must come, but the end won't follow immediately—10for nation shall rise against nation and kingdom against kingdom, 11and there will be great earthquakes, and famines in many lands, and epidemics, and terrifying things happening in the heavens.

12"But before all this occurs, there will be a time of special persecution, and you will be dragged into synagogues and prisons and before kings and governors for my name's sake. 13But as a result, the Messiah will be widely known and honored. 14Therefore, don't be concerned about how to answer the charges against you, 15for I will give you the right words and such logic that none of your opponents will be able to reply! 16Even those closest to you—your parents, brothers, relatives, and friends will betray you and have you arrested; and some of you will be killed. 17And everyone will hate you because you are mine and are called by my name. 18But not a hair of your head will perish! 19For if you stand firm, you will win your souls.

A THOUGHT: *Jesus did not leave his disciples unprepared for the difficult years ahead. He warned them against false messiahs and persecutions, but he assured them he would be with them to protect them and make his Kingdom known through them. In the end, he promised, he would return in power and glory to save them. Jesus' warnings and promises to his disciples still apply to us as we look forward to his return.*

Be Diligent in Prayer/ Colossians 4:2–6

Don't be weary in prayer; keep at it; watch for God's answers and remember to be thankful when they come. 3Don't forget to pray for us too, that God will give us many chances to preach the Good News of Christ for which I am here in jail. 4Pray that I will be bold enough to tell it freely and fully, and make it plain, as, of course, I should.

5Make the most of your chances to tell others the Good News. Be wise in all your contacts with them. 6Let your conversation be gracious as well as sensible, for then you will have the right answer for everyone.

A THOUGHT: *Have you ever grown tired of praying for something or someone? Paul says, "Keep at it." Persistence demonstrates our faith that God answers our prayers. Faith shouldn't die if the answers don't come immediately, for the delay may be God's way of working his will in your life. When you feel weary in your prayers, know that God is present, always listening, always acting— maybe not in ways you had hoped, but in ways that are best.*

Proverbs for Today/ 20:2–3

The king's fury is like that of a roaring lion; to rouse his anger is to risk your life. ☐ It is an honor for a man to stay out of a fight. Only fools insist on quarreling.

JULY 27

Be Ready for Christ's Return/ Luke 21:20–38

"But when you see Jerusalem surrounded by armies, then you will know that the time of its destruction has arrived. 21Then let the people of Judea flee to the hills. Let those in Jerusalem try to escape, and those outside the city must not attempt to return. 22For those will be days of God's judgment, and the words of the ancient Scriptures written by the prophets will be abundantly fulfilled. 23Woe to expectant mothers in those days, and those with tiny babies. For there will be great distress upon this nation and wrath upon this people. 24They will be brutally killed by enemy weapons, or sent away as exiles and captives to all the nations of the world; and Jerusalem shall be conquered and trampled down by the Gentiles until the period of Gentile triumph ends in God's good time.

25"Then there will be strange events in the skies—warnings, evil omens and portents in the sun, moon and stars; and down here on earth the nations will be in turmoil, perplexed by the roaring seas and strange tides. 26The courage of many people will falter because of the fearful fate they see coming upon the earth, for the stability of the very heavens will be broken up. 27Then the peoples of the earth shall see me, the Messiah, coming in a cloud with power and great glory. 28So when all these things begin to happen, stand straight and look up! For your salvation is near."

29Then he gave them this illustration: "Notice the fig tree, or any other tree. 30When the leaves come out, you know without being told that summer is near. 31In the same way, when you see the events taking place that I've described you can be just as sure that the Kingdom of God is near.

32"I solemnly declare to you that when these things happen, the end of this age has come. 33And though all heaven and earth shall pass away, yet my words remain forever true.

34,35"Watch out! Don't let my sudden coming catch you unawares; don't let me find you living in careless ease, carousing and drinking, and occupied with the problems of this life, like all the rest of the world. 36Keep a constant watch. And pray that if possible you may arrive in my presence without having to experience these horrors."

37,38Every day Jesus went to the Temple to teach, and the crowds began gathering early in the morning to hear him. And each evening he returned to spend the night on the Mount of Olives.

A THOUGHT: *Jesus told the disciples to keep a constant watch for his return. Although nearly two thousand years have passed since he spoke these words, their truth remains: he is coming again, and we need to watch and be ready. This means faithfully working at the tasks God has given us. Our attitude toward all we do should be colored with our joyful expectation of Christ's return.*

Greetings from Paul's Christian Friends/ Colossians 4:7–18

Tychicus, our much loved brother, will tell you how I am getting along. He is a hard worker and serves the Lord with me. 8I have sent him on this special trip just to see how you are, and to comfort and encourage you. 9I am also sending Onesimus, a faithful and much loved brother, one of your own people. He and Tychicus will give you all the latest news.

10Aristarchus, who is with me here as a prisoner, sends you his love, and so does Mark, a relative of Barnabas. And as I said before, give Mark a hearty welcome if he comes your way. 11Jesus Justus also sends his love. These are the only Jewish Christians working with me here, and what a comfort they have been!

12Epaphras, from your city, a servant of Christ Jesus, sends you his love. He is always earnestly praying for you, asking God to make you strong and perfect and to help you know his will in everything you do. 13I can assure you that he has worked hard for you with his prayers, and also for the Christians in Laodicea and Hierapolis.

14Dear doctor Luke sends his love, and so does Demas.

15Please give my greeting to the Christian friends at Laodicea, and to Nymphas, and to those who meet in his home. 16By the way, after you have read this letter will you pass it on to the church at Laodicea? And read the letter I wrote to them. 17And say to Archippus, "Be sure that you do all the Lord has told you to."

18Here is my own greeting in my own handwriting: Remember me here in jail. May God's blessings surround you.

Sincerely,
Paul

A THOUGHT: *Tychicus was one of Paul's personal respresentatives and probably the bearer of the letters to the Colossians and Ephesians. He accompanied Paul to Jerusalem with the collection for the church.*

Mark went with Paul and Barnabas on their first missionary journey, but then left in the middle of the trip for unknown reasons. Barnabas and Mark were relatives, and when Paul refused to take Mark on another journey, Barnabas and Mark journeyed together to preach the Good News. Mark also worked with Peter. Later, Mark and Paul were reconciled. Mark wrote the Gospel which bears his name.

Epaphras founded the Colossian church, and his report to Paul in Rome caused Paul to write this letter. Epaphras was a hero of the Colossian church, one of the believers who helped keep the church together in spite of growing troubles. His earnest prayers for the believers show his deep love and concern for them.

Luke spent much time with Paul, not only accompanying him on most of his third missionary journey, but sitting with him in the prison at Rome. Luke wrote the Gospel which bears his name and the book of Acts. Demas was faithful to Paul for a while, but then left him.

Proverbs for Today/ 20:4–6

If you won't plow in the cold, you won't eat at the harvest. ☐ Though good advice lies deep within a counselor's heart, the wise man will draw it out. ☐ Most people will tell you what loyal friends they are, but are they telling the truth?

JULY 28

The Last Supper/ Luke 22:1-23

And now the Passover celebration was drawing near— the Jewish festival when only bread made without yeast was used. 2The chief priests and other religious leaders were actively plotting Jesus' murder, trying to find a way to kill him without starting a riot—a possibility they greatly feared.

3Then Satan entered into Judas Iscariot, who was one of the twelve disciples, 4and he went over to the chief priests and captains of the Temple guards to discuss the best way to betray Jesus to them. 5They were, of course, delighted to know that he was ready to help them and promised him a reward. 6So he began to look for an opportunity for them to arrest Jesus quietly when the crowds weren't around.

7Now the day of the Passover celebration arrived, when the Passover lamb was killed and eaten with the unleavened bread. 8Jesus sent Peter and John ahead to find a place to prepare their Passover meal.

9"Where do you want us to go?" they asked.

10And he replied, "As soon as you enter Jerusalem, you will see a man walking along carrying a pitcher of water. Follow him into the house he enters, 11and say to the man who lives there, 'Our Teacher says for you to show us the guest room where he can eat the Passover meal with his disciples.' 12He will take you upstairs to a large room all ready for us. That is the place. Go ahead and prepare the meal there."

13They went off to the city and found everything just as Jesus had said, and prepared the Passover supper.

14Then Jesus and the others arrived, and at the proper time all sat down together at the table; 15and he said, "I have looked forward to this hour with deep longing, anxious to eat this Passover meal with you before my suffering begins. 16For I tell you now that I won't eat it again until what it represents has occurred in the Kingdom of God."

17Then he took a glass of wine, and when he had given thanks for it, he said, "Take this and share it among yourselves. 18For I will not drink wine again until the Kingdom of God has come."

19Then he took a loaf of bread; and when he had thanked God for it, he broke it apart and gave it to them, saying, "This is my body, given for you. Eat it in remembrance of me."

20After supper he gave them another glass of wine, saying, "This wine is the token of God's new agreement to save you—an agreement sealed with the blood I shall pour out to purchase back your souls. 21But here at this table, sitting among us as a friend, is the man who will betray me. 22I must die. It is part of God's plan. But, oh, the horror awaiting that man who betrays me."

23Then the disciples wondered among themselves which of them would ever do such a thing.

A THOUGHT: *The Passover commemorated Israel's escape from Egypt when the blood of a lamb, painted on their doorposts, saved them from the angel of death who was killing the firstborn in all the homes in Egypt. This event foreshadowed Jesus' work on the cross. As the spotless Lamb of God, his blood would be spilled in order to save his people from the death brought by sin and judgment.*

Jesus asked the disciples to eat the bread and drink the wine "in remembrance of me." He wanted them to remember his sacrifice, which is the basis for forgiveness of sins, and also his friendship, which they could continue to enjoy through the work of the Holy Spirit. Although the exact meaning of communion has been strongly debated almost since the church began, Christians still take bread and wine in remembrance of their Lord, Savior, and friend, Jesus Christ. Do not neglect participating in the Lord's Supper. Let it remind you what Christ did for you.

Paul Commends the Thessalonians' Faith/
1 Thessalonians 1:1–10

From: Paul, Silas and Timothy.

To: The Church at Thessalonica—to you who belong to God the Father and the Lord Jesus Christ: May blessing and peace of heart be your rich gifts from God our Father, and from Jesus Christ our Lord.

2We always thank God for you and pray for you constantly.

³We never forget your loving deeds as we talk to our God and Father about you, and your strong faith and steady looking forward to the return of our Lord Jesus Christ.

⁴We know that God has chosen you, dear brothers, much beloved of God. ⁵For when we brought you the Good News, it was not just meaningless chatter to you; no, you listened with great interest. What we told you produced a powerful effect upon you, for the Holy Spirit gave you great and full assurance that what we said was true. And you know how our very lives were further proof to you of the truth of our message. ⁶So you became our followers and the Lord's; for you received our message with joy from the Holy Spirit in spite of the trials and sorrows it brought you.

⁷Then you yourselves became an example to all the other Christians in Greece. ⁸And now the Word of the Lord has spread out from you to others everywhere, far beyond your boundaries, for wherever we go we find people telling us about your remarkable faith in God. We don't need to tell *them* about it, ⁹for *they* keep telling *us* about the wonderful welcome you gave us, and how you turned away from your idols to God so that now the living and true God only is your Master. ¹⁰And they speak of how you are looking forward to the return of God's Son from heaven—Jesus, whom God brought back to life— and he is our only Savior from God's terrible anger against sin.

A THOUGHT: *The Good News produced a powerful effect upon the Thessalonians. These Christians stood firm when they were persecuted. Paul commends these young believers for their loving deeds, strong faith, and deep commitment to Christ. These characteristics are the marks of an effective Christian. Whenever the Word of God is heard and obeyed, lives are changed! Christianity is more than a collection of interesting facts; it is the power of God for salvation to every one who believes. What has God's power done in your life since you first put your faith in Christ?*

Proverbs for Today/ 20:7

It is a wonderful heritage to have an honest father.

A Leader Must Be a Servant/ Luke 22:24–30

And the disciples began to argue among themselves as to who would have the highest rank [in the coming Kingdom].

25Jesus told them, "In this world the kings and great men order their slaves around, and the slaves have no choice but to like it! 26But among you, the one who serves you best will be your leader. 27Out in the world the master sits at the table and is served by his servants. But not here! For I am your servant. 28Nevertheless, because you have stood true to me in these terrible days, 29and because my Father has granted me a Kingdom, I, here and now, grant you the right 30to eat and drink at my table in that Kingdom; and you will sit on thrones judging the twelve tribes of Israel.

A THOUGHT: *The world's system of leadership is very different from the Kingdom's. Worldly leaders are often selfish and arrogant as they claw their way to the top. But among Christians, the leader is to be the one who serves best. There are different styles of leadership—some lead through public speaking, some through administering, some through relationships—but all leaders need a servant's heart. Ask the people you lead how you can serve them better.*

Paul Reviews His Ministry to the Thessalonians/ 1 Thessalonians 2:1–8

You yourselves know, dear brothers, how worthwhile that visit was. 2You know how badly we had been treated at Philippi just before we came to you, and how much we suffered there. Yet God gave us the courage to boldly repeat the same message to you, even though we were surrounded by enemies. 3So you can see that we were not preaching with any false motives or evil purposes in mind; we were perfectly straightforward and sincere.

4For we speak as messengers from God, trusted by him to tell the truth; we change his message not one bit to suit the taste of those who hear it; for we serve God alone, who examines our hearts' deepest thoughts. 5Never once did we try to win you with flattery, as you very well know, and God knows we were not just pretending to be your friends so that you would give us money! 6As for praise, we have never asked for it from you or anyone else, although as apostles of Christ we certainly had a right to some honor from you. 7But we were as gentle among you as a mother feeding and caring for her own children. 8We loved you dearly—so dearly that we gave you not only God's message, but our own lives too.

A THOUGHT: *When Paul was with the Thessalonians, he didn't flatter them, didn't take their money, didn't seek their praise, and wasn't a burden to them. He and Silas completely focused their efforts on presenting God's message of salvation to the Thessalonians. This was important! The Thessalonian believers had their lives changed by God, not Paul; it was Christ's message they believed, not Paul's. When we witness for Christ, our focus should not be on the impression we make. As true ministers of Christ, we should point to him, not to ourselves. In trying to persuade people, we often alter our position just enough to make our message more palatable. Paul never changed his message to make it more acceptable, but he did tailor his presentation to each audience. Although our presentation must be altered to be appropriate to the situation, the truth of the gospel must never be compromised.*

Proverbs for Today/ 20:8–10

A king sitting as judge weighs all the evidence carefully, distinguishing the true from false. □ Who can ever say, "I have cleansed my heart; I am sinless"? □ The Lord despises every kind of cheating.

JULY 30

Jesus Predicts Peter's Denial/ Luke 22:31–34

"Simon, Simon, Satan has asked to have you, to sift you like wheat, 32but I have pleaded in prayer for you that your faith should not completely fail. So when you have repented and turned to me again, strengthen and build up the faith of your brothers."

33Simon said, "Lord, I am ready to go to jail with you, and even to die with you."

34But Jesus said, "Peter, let me tell you something. Between now and tomorrow morning when the rooster crows, you will deny me three times, declaring that you don't even know me."

A Thought: *Satan wanted to crush Peter like a grain of wheat. He hoped to find only chaff and blow it away. But Jesus assured Peter that his faith, although it would falter, would not be destroyed. It would be renewed, and he would become a powerful leader. In the same way, we often fall short of what God demands of us. But when we turn to God, he will restore us and deepen our faith.*

Paul's Work among the Thessalonians/
1 Thessalonians 2:9–13

Don't you remember, dear brothers, how hard we worked among you? Night and day we toiled and sweated to earn enough to live on so that our expenses would not be a burden to anyone there, as we preached God's Good News among you. 10You yourselves are our witnesses—as is God—that we have been pure and honest and faultless toward every one of you. 11We talked to you as a father to his own children—don't you remember?—pleading with you, encouraging you and even demanding 12that your daily lives should not embarrass God, but bring joy to him who invited you into his Kingdom to share his glory.

13And we will never stop thanking God for this: that when we preached to you, you didn't think of the words we spoke as being just our own, but you accepted what we said as the very Word of God—which, of course, it was—and it changed your lives when you believed it.

A Thought: *No loving father would neglect the safety of his children, allowing them to walk into circumstances that might prove fatal or permanently damaging. In the same way, we must take new believers under our wing until they are mature enough to stand firm in their faith. When new Christians are strong enough to influence others for the gospel, rather than be influenced by others to practices contrary to the gospel, they are ready to be out from under our wings.*

Proverbs for Today/ 20:11

The character of even a child can be known by the way he acts—whether what he does is pure and right.

JULY 31

Jesus Prepares the Disciples for His Death/
Luke 22:35–38

Then Jesus asked his disciples, "When I sent you out to preach the Good News and you were without money, duffle bag, or extra clothing, how did you get along?"

"Fine," they replied.

36"But now," he said, "take a duffle bag if you have one, and your money. And if you don't have a sword, better sell your clothes and buy one! 37For the time has come for this prophecy about me to come true: 'He will be condemned as a criminal!' Yes, everything written about me by the prophets will come true."

38"Master," they replied, "we have two swords among us."

"Enough!" he said.

A THOUGHT: *Now Jesus reverses his earlier advice regarding how to travel. The disciples were to bring a bag, money, and a sword. They would be facing hatred and persecution and would need to be prepared. When Jesus said "Enough," he may have meant that two swords were enough or that they had talked enough. In either case, their need for a sword vividly communicated the trials they were soon to face.*

Persecuted for Spreading the Gospel/
1 Thessalonians 2:14—3:4

And then, dear brothers, you suffered what the churches in Judea did, persecution from your own countrymen, just as they suffered from their own people the Jews. 15After they had killed their own prophets, they even executed the Lord Jesus; and now they have brutally persecuted us and driven us out. They are against both God and man, 16trying to keep us from preaching to the Gentiles for fear some might be saved; and so their sins continue to grow. But the anger of God has caught up with them at last.

17Dear brothers, after we left you and had been away from you but a very little while (though our hearts never left you), we tried hard to come back to see you once more. 18We wanted very much to come and I, Paul, tried again and again, but Satan stopped us. 19For what is it we live for, that gives us hope and joy and is our proud reward and crown? It is you! Yes, you will bring us much joy as we stand together before our Lord Jesus Christ when he comes back again. 20For you are our trophy and joy.

3:1Finally, when I could stand it no longer, I decided to stay alone in Athens 2,3and send Timothy, our brother and fellow worker, God's minister, to visit you to strengthen your faith and encourage you, and to keep you from becoming fainthearted in all the troubles you were going through. (But of course you know that such troubles are a part of God's plan for us Christians. 4Even while we were still with you we warned you ahead of time that suffering would soon come—and it did.)

A THOUGHT: *Just as the Jewish Christians in Jerusalem were persecuted by their own people, so the Gentile Christians in Thessalonica were persecuted by their fellow Gentiles. It is discouraging to face persecution, especially when it comes from your own people. But when we take a stand for Christ, we must face opposition, disapproval, ridicule, and even persecution from our neighbors, friends, and even family members.*

Proverbs for Today/ 20:12
If you have good eyesight and good hearing, thank God who gave them to you.

AUGUST 1

Judas Betrays Jesus/ Luke 22:39–54
Then, accompanied by the disciples, Jesus left the upstairs room and went as usual to the Mount of Olives. 40There he told them, "Pray God that you will not be overcome by temptation."

41,42He walked away, perhaps a stone's throw, and knelt down and prayed this prayer: "Father, if you are willing, please take away this cup of horror from me. But I want your will, not mine." 43Then an angel from heaven appeared and strengthened him, 44for he was in such agony of spirit that he broke into a sweat of blood, with great drops falling to the ground as he prayed more and more earnestly.

45At last he stood up again and returned to the disciples—only to find them asleep, exhausted from grief.

46"Asleep!" he said. "Get up! Pray God that you will not fall when you are tempted."

47But even as he said this, a mob approached, led by Judas, one of his twelve disciples. Judas walked over to Jesus and kissed him on the cheek in friendly greeting.

48But Jesus said, "Judas, how can you do this—betray the Messiah with a kiss?"

49When the other disciples saw what was about to happen, they exclaimed, "Master, shall we fight? We brought along the swords!" 50And one of them slashed at the High Priest's servant, and cut off his right ear.

51But Jesus said, "Don't resist any more." And he touched the place where the man's ear had been and restored it. 52Then Jesus addressed the chief priests and captains of the Temple guards and the religious leaders who headed the mob. "Am I a robber," he asked, "that you have come armed with swords and clubs to get me? 53Why didn't you arrest me in the Temple? I was there every day. But this is your moment—the time when Satan's power reigns supreme."

54So they seized him and led him to the High Priest's residence, and Peter followed at a distance.

A THOUGHT: *Jesus asked the disciples to pray that they would not be overcome by temptation because he knew he would soon be leaving them. He also knew they would need extra strength to face the temptations ahead—temptations to run away, or to deny their relationship with him. Also, they were about to see him die—would they still think he was the Messiah? Their strongest temptation would be to think they had been deceived.*

Timothy's Good Report/ 1 Thessalonians 3:5–8

As I was saying, when I could bear the suspense no longer I sent Timothy to find out whether your faith was still strong. I was afraid that perhaps Satan had gotten the best of you and that all our work had been useless. 6And now Timothy has just returned and brings the welcome news that your faith and love are as strong as ever, and that you remember our visit with joy and want to see us just as much as we want to see you. 7So we are greatly comforted, dear brothers, in all of our own crushing troubles and suffering here, now that we know you are standing true to the Lord. 8We can bear anything as long as we know that you remain strong in him.

A THOUGHT: *Paul is encouraged by Timothy's report concerning the Thessalonian Christians. These young believers were standing firm in the faith despite fierce persecution. In the midst of persecution or pressure, believers should encourage each other. Compliments, expressions of thanks, and support for those who are wavering in the faith help to build up fellow believers.*

Proverbs for Today/ 20:13–15

If you love sleep, you will end in poverty. Stay awake, work hard, and there will be plenty to eat! □ "Utterly worthless!" says the buyer as he haggles over the price. But afterwards he brags about his bargain! □ Good sense is far more valuable than gold or precious jewels.

AUGUST 2

Peter's Denials/ Luke 22:55–62

The soldiers lit a fire in the courtyard and sat around it for warmth, and Peter joined them there.

56A servant girl noticed him in the firelight and began staring at him. Finally she spoke: "This man was with Jesus!"

57Peter denied it. "Woman," he said, "I don't even know the man!"

58After a while someone else looked at him and said, "You must be one of them!"

"No sir, I am not!" Peter replied.

59About an hour later someone else flatly stated, "I know this fellow is one of Jesus' disciples, for both are from Galilee."

60But Peter said, "Man, I don't know what you are talking about." And as he said the words, a rooster crowed.

61At that moment Jesus turned and looked at Peter. Then Peter remembered what he had said—"Before the rooster crows tomorrow morning, you will deny me three times." 62And Peter walked out of the courtyard, crying bitterly.

A THOUGHT: *Peter wept bitterly, not only because he realized that he had denied his Lord, the Messiah, but also because he had turned away from a very dear friend, a person who had loved and taught him for three years. Peter had said he would never deny Christ—despite Jesus' prediction—but when frightened, he went against all he had boldly promised. Unable to stand up for his Lord for even 12 hours, he had failed as a disciple and as a friend. We need to be aware of our own breaking points and not become overconfident or self-sufficient. If we fail, we must remember that Christ can use those who recognize their failure. From this humiliating experience Peter learned much that would help him in the leadership responsibilities he would soon assume.*

Paul Prays for the Thessalonians/ 1 Thessalonians 3:9–13

How can we thank God enough for you and for the joy and delight you have given us in our praying for you? 10For night and day we pray on and on for you, asking God to let us see you again, to fill up any little cracks there may yet be in your faith.

11May God our Father himself and our Lord Jesus send us back to you again. 12And may the Lord make your love to grow and overflow to each other and to everyone else, just as our love does toward you. 13This will result in your hearts being made strong, sinless and holy by God our Father, so that you may stand before him guiltless on that day when our Lord Jesus Christ returns with all those who belong to him.

A THOUGHT: *It is a great joy for Christians to see another person come to faith in Christ and mature in that faith. Paul experienced this joy countless times. He thanked God for those who had come to know Christ and prayed for their continued growth in faith. If there are new Christians who have brought you joy, thank God for them and support them as they continue to grow in their walk with God.*

Proverbs for Today/ 20:16–18

It is risky to make loans to strangers! ☐ Some men enjoy cheating, but the cake they buy with such ill-gotten gain will turn to gravel in their mouths. ☐ Don't go ahead with your plans without the advice of others; don't go to war until they agree.

Jesus Is Tried before the Jewish Supreme Court/
Luke 22:63–71

Now the guards in charge of Jesus began mocking him.
They blindfolded him and hit him with their fists and asked,
"Who hit you that time, prophet?" 65And they threw all
sorts of other insults at him.

66Early the next morning at daybreak the Jewish Supreme
Court assembled, including the chief priests and all the
top religious authorities of the nation. Jesus was led before
this Council, 67,68and instructed to state whether or not
he claimed to be the Messiah.

But he replied, "If I tell you, you won't believe me or
let me present my case. 69But the time is soon coming
when I, the Messiah, shall be enthroned beside Almighty
God."

70They all shouted, "Then you claim you are the Son
of God?"

And he replied, "Yes, I am."

71"What need do we have for other witnesses?" they
shouted. "For we ourselves have heard him say it."

A THOUGHT: *Jesus identified himself with God by using a familiar
title for God found in the Old Testament: "I Am." The High Priest
recognized Jesus' claim and accused him of blasphemy. Although
claiming to be God is blasphemy, blasphemy includes attacks on
God as well as claiming to have his attributes. For any other
man this claim would have been blasphemy, but in this case it
was true. Blasphemy, the sin of claiming to be God, was punishable
by death. The Jewish leaders had the evidence they wanted, but
they were about to bring about the greatest injustice ever perpetrated
on earth. Jesus willingly submitted to this great injustice to make
salvation available to all who genuinely want to be reconciled to
God.*

God's People Should Be Holy/
1 Thessalonians 4:1–8

Let me add this, dear brothers: You already know how
to please God in your daily living, for you know the commands we gave you from the Lord Jesus himself. Now
we beg you—yes, we demand of you in the name of the
Lord Jesus—that you live more and more closely to that
ideal. 3,4For God wants you to be holy and pure, and to

keep clear of all sexual sin so that each of you will marry in holiness and honor— 5not in lustful passion as the heathen do, in their ignorance of God and his ways.

6And this also is God's will: that you never cheat in this matter by taking another man's wife, because the Lord will punish you terribly for this, as we have solemnly told you before. 7For God has not called us to be dirty-minded and full of lust, but to be holy and clean. 8If anyone refuses to live by these rules he is not disobeying the rules of men but of God who gives his *Holy* Spirit to you.

A THOUGHT: *Sexual desires and activities must be placed under Christ's control. God created sex for procreation, pleasure, and as an expression of love between a husband and wife. Sexual experience must be limited to the marriage relationship to avoid hurting ourselves, our relationship with God, and our relationships with others.*

Proverbs for Today/ 20:19

Don't tell your secrets to a gossip unless you want them broadcast to the world.

AUGUST 4

Pilate Sentences Jesus to Death/ Luke 23:1–25

Then the entire Council took Jesus over to Pilate, the governor. 2They began at once accusing him: "This fellow has been leading our people to ruin by telling them not to pay their taxes to the Roman government and by claiming he is our Messiah—a King."

3So Pilate asked him, "Are you their Messiah—their King?"

"Yes," Jesus replied, "it is as you say."

4Then Pilate turned to the chief priests and to the mob and said, "So? That isn't a crime!"

5Then they became desperate. "But he is causing riots against the government everywhere he goes, all over Judea, from Galilee to Jerusalem!"

6"Is he then a Galilean?" Pilate asked.

7When they told him yes, Pilate said to take him to King Herod, for Galilee was under Herod's jurisdiction;

and Herod happened to be in Jerusalem at the time. 8Herod was delighted at the opportunity to see Jesus, for he had heard a lot about him and had been hoping to see him perform a miracle.

9He asked Jesus question after question, but there was no reply. 10Meanwhile, the chief priests and the other religious leaders stood there shouting their accusations.

11Now Herod and his soldiers began mocking and ridiculing Jesus; and putting a kingly robe on him, they sent him back to Pilate. 12That day Herod and Pilate—enemies before—became fast friends.

13Then Pilate called together the chief priests and other Jewish leaders, along with the people, 14and announced his verdict:

"You brought this man to me, accusing him of leading a revolt against the Roman government. I have examined him thoroughly on this point and find him innocent. 15Herod came to the same conclusion and sent him back to us— nothing this man has done calls for the death penalty. 16I will therefore have him scourged with leaded thongs, and release him."

17,18But now a mighty roar rose from the crowd as with one voice they shouted. "Kill him, and release Barabbas to us!" 19(Barabbas was in prison for starting an insurrection in Jerusalem against the government, and for murder.) 20Pilate argued with them, for he wanted to release Jesus. 21But they shouted, "Crucify him! Crucify him!"

22Once more, for the third time, he demanded, "Why? What crime has he committed? I have found no reason to sentence him to death. I will therefore scourge him and let him go." 23But they shouted louder and louder for Jesus' death, and their voices prevailed.

24So Pilate sentenced Jesus to die as they demanded. 25And he released Barabbas, the man in prison for insurrection and murder, at their request. But he delivered Jesus over to them to do with as they would.

A THOUGHT: *Pilate wanted to release Jesus, but the crowd loudly demanded his death, so Pilate sentenced Jesus to die. No doubt Pilate did not want to risk losing his position (which may already have been shaky), by allowing a riot to occur in his province. As a career politician, he knew the importance of compromise, and he saw Jesus more as a political threat than as a human being with rights and dignity.*

When the stakes are high, it is hard to stand up for what is right, and it is easy to see our opponents as problems to be solved rather than as people to be respected. Had Pilate been a man of real courage, he would have released Jesus no matter what the consequences. But the crowd roared, and Pilate buckled. When you have a difficult decision to make, don't discount the effects of peer pressure. Realize beforehand that the right decision could have unpleasant consequences: social rejection, career derailment, public ridicule. Then think of Pilate and resolve to stand up for what is right no matter what other people pressure you to do.

Christian Ambition/ 1 Thessalonians 4:9–12

But concerning the pure brotherly love that there should be among God's people, I don't need to say very much, I'm sure! For God himself is teaching you to love one another. 10Indeed, your love is already strong toward all the Christian brothers throughout your whole nation. Even so, dear friends, we beg you to love them more and more. 11This should be your ambition: to live a quiet life, minding your own business and doing your own work, just as we told you before. 12As a result, people who are not Christians will trust and respect you, and you will not need to depend on others for enough money to pay your bills.

A THOUGHT: *Ambition is a characteristic that people in our society value greatly. However, society's view of ambition is "getting ahead," "grabbing all the gusto," "living for number one." All of these ambitions center on pursuits for the self. The Christian's ambition, however, is to strive for the Kingdom of God. Christians do not live to be flashy; instead, they seek to be obedient servants of Jesus Christ who is Lord of the church. Whatever we do, let us do it faithfully, as unto the Lord, and let us be a positive force in society— serving those around us rather than stepping on people to get to the top.*

Proverbs for Today/ 20:20–21

God puts out the light of the man who curses his father or mother. □ Quick wealth is not a blessing in the end.

AUGUST 5

Jesus Is Crucified/ Luke 23:26–43

As the crowd led Jesus away to his death, Simon of Cyrene, who was just coming into Jerusalem from the country, was forced to follow, carrying Jesus' cross. 27Great crowds trailed along behind, and many grief-stricken women.

28But Jesus turned and said to them, "Daughters of Jerusalem, don't weep for me, but for yourselves and for your children. 29For the days are coming when the women who have no children will be counted fortunate indeed. 30Mankind will beg the mountains to fall on them and crush them, and the hills to bury them. 31For if such things as this are done to me, the Living Tree, what will they do to you?"

32,33Two others, criminals, were led out to be executed with him at a place called "The Skull." There all three were crucified—Jesus on the center cross, and the two criminals on either side.

34"Father, forgive these people," Jesus said, "for they don't know what they are doing."

And the soldiers gambled for his clothing, throwing dice for each piece. 35The crowd watched. And the Jewish leaders laughed and scoffed. "He was so good at helping others," they said, "let's see him save himself if he is really God's Chosen One, the Messiah."

36The soldiers mocked him, too, by offering him a drink— of sour wine. 37And they called to him, "If you are the King of the Jews, save yourself!"

38A signboard was nailed to the cross above him with these words: "This is the King of the Jews."

39One of the criminals hanging beside him scoffed, "So you're the Messiah, are you? Prove it by saving yourself— and us, too, while you're at it!"

40,41But the other criminal protested. "Don't you even fear God when you are dying? We deserve to die for our evil deeds, but this man hasn't done one thing wrong." 42Then he said, "Jesus, remember me when you come into your Kingdom."

43And Jesus replied, "Today you will be with me in Paradise. This is a solemn promise."

A THOUGHT: *As Jesus was led away through the streets of Jerusalem, he could no longer carry his cross, and Simon of Cyrene was given the burden. Jesus was crucified, along with common criminals, on a hill outside Jerusalem. When James and John asked Jesus for the places of honor next to him in his Kingdom, he told them they didn't know what they were asking. Now that Jesus was inaugurating his Kingdom through his death, the places on his right and on his left were taken by dying men—criminals. As Jesus explained to his two power-hungry disciples, a person who wants to be close to Jesus must be prepared to suffer and die as he himself was doing. The way to greatness in the Kingdom is the way of the cross.*

The Hope of the Resurrection/
1 Thessalonians 4:13—5:3

And now, dear brothers, I want you to know what happens to a Christian when he dies so that when it happens, you will not be full of sorrow, as those are who have no hope. 14For since we believe that Jesus died and then came back to life again, we can also believe that when Jesus returns, God will bring back with him all the Christians who have died.

15I can tell you this directly from the Lord: that we who are still living when the Lord returns will not rise to meet him ahead of those who are in their graves. 16For the Lord himself will come down from heaven with a mighty shout and with the soul-stirring cry of the archangel and the great trumpet-call of God. And the believers who are dead will be the first to rise to meet the Lord. 17Then we who are still alive and remain on the earth will be caught up with them in the clouds to meet the Lord in the air and remain with him forever. 18So comfort and encourage each other with this news.

5:1When is all this going to happen? I really don't need to say anything about that, dear brothers, 2for you know perfectly well that no one knows. That day of the Lord will come unexpectedly like a thief in the night. 3When people are saying, "All is well, everything is quiet and peaceful"—then, all of a sudden, disaster will fall upon them as suddenly as a woman's birth pains begin when her child is born. And these people will not be able to get away anywhere—there will be no place to hide.

A THOUGHT: *Because Jesus Christ came back to life, so will all believers. All Christians, including those living when he returns, will live with Jesus forever. Therefore, we need not despair when Christian loved ones die or world events take a tragic turn. For God will turn our tragedies to triumphs, our pain to glory, and our defeat to victory. All believers throughout history will stand reunited in God's very presence, safe and secure. As Paul comforted the Thessalonians with the promise of the resurrection, so we should comfort and reassure one another with this great hope.*

Proverbs for Today/ 20:22–23

Don't repay evil for evil. Wait for the Lord to handle the matter. □ The Lord loathes all cheating and dishonesty.

AUGUST 6

Jesus' Death and Burial/ Luke 23:44–56

By now it was noon, and darkness fell across the whole land for three hours, until three o'clock. 45The light from the sun was gone—and suddenly the thick veil hanging in the Temple split apart.

46Then Jesus shouted, "Father, I commit my spirit to you," and with those words he died.

47When the captain of the Roman military unit handling the executions saw what had happened, he was stricken with awe before God and said, "Surely this man was innocent."

48And when the crowd that came to see the crucifixion saw that Jesus was dead they went home in deep sorrow. 49Meanwhile, Jesus' friends, including the women who had followed him down from Galilee, stood in the distance watching.

50,51,52Then a man named Joseph, a member of the Jewish Supreme Court, from the city of Arimathea in Judea, went to Pilate and asked for the body of Jesus. He was a godly man who had been expecting the Messiah's coming and had not agreed with the decision and actions of the other Jewish leaders. 53So he took down Jesus' body and wrapped it in a long linen cloth and laid it in a new, unused tomb hewn into the rock [at the side of a hill]. 54This was done late on Friday afternoon, the day of preparation for the Sabbath.

55As the body was taken away, the women from Galilee followed and saw it carried into the tomb. 56Then they went home and prepared spices and ointments to embalm him; but by the time they were finished it was the Sabbath, so they rested all that day as required by the Jewish law.

A Thought: *Darkness covered the entire land for about three hours in the middle of the day. All nature seemed to mourn over the stark tragedy of the death of God's Son. In the midst of this darkness, the curtain separating the Holy of Holies from the Holy place was torn in two. This significant event symbolized Christ's work on the cross. The Temple had three parts: the courtyard area; the Holy Place, where only priests could enter; and the Holy of Holies, where the High Priest alone could enter once a year to atone for the sins of the people. It was in the Holy of Holies that the Ark of the Covenant (the symbol of God's presence) rested. The curtain that split was the one that closed off the Holy of Holies from view. At Christ's death, the barrier between God and man was torn apart. Now all people are able to approach God directly through Christ.*

Live in the Light of Jesus' Coming/
1 Thessalonians 5:4–11

But, dear brothers, you are not in the dark about these things, and you won't be surprised as by a thief when that day of the Lord comes. 5For you are all children of the light and of the day, and do not belong to darkness and night. 6So be on your guard, not asleep like the others. Watch for his return and stay sober. 7Night is the time for sleep and the time when people get drunk. 8But let us who live in the light keep sober, protected by the armor of faith and love, and wearing as our helmet the happy hope of salvation.

9For God has not chosen to pour out his anger upon us, but to save us through our Lord Jesus Christ; 10he died for us so that we can live with him forever, whether we are dead or alive at the time of his return. 11So encourage each other to build each other up, just as you are already doing.

A Thought: *As you near the end of a foot race, your legs ache, your throat burns, and your whole body cries out for you to stop. This is when supporters are most valuable. Their encouragement helps you push through the pain to the finish. In the same way, Christians are to encourage one another. A word of encouragement offered at the right moment can be the difference between finishing well and collapsing along the way. Look around you. Be sensitive to another's need for encouragement and offer supportive words or actions.*

Proverbs for Today/ 20:24–25

Since the Lord is directing our steps, why try to understand everything that happens along the way? □ It is foolish and rash to make a promise to the Lord before counting the cost.

AUGUST 7

Jesus Rises from the Dead/ Luke 24:1–12

But very early on Sunday morning the women from Galilee took the ointments to the tomb— 2and found that the huge stone covering the entrance had been rolled aside. 3So they went in—but the Lord Jesus' body was gone.

4They stood there puzzled, trying to think what could have happened to it. Suddenly two men appeared before them, clothed in shining robes so bright their eyes were dazzled. 5The women were terrified and bowed low before them.

Then the men asked, "Why are you looking in a tomb for someone who is alive? 6,7He isn't here! He has come back to life again! Don't you remember what he told you back in Galilee—that the Messiah must be betrayed into the power of evil men and be crucified and that he would rise again the third day?"

8Then they remembered, 9and rushed back to Jerusalem to tell his eleven disciples—and everyone else—what had happened. 10(The women who went to the tomb were Mary Magdalene and Joanna and Mary the mother of James, and several others.) 11But the story sounded like a fairy tale to the men—they didn't believe it.

12However, Peter ran to the tomb to look. Stooping, he peered in and saw the empty linen wrappings; and then he went back home again, wondering what had happened.

A THOUGHT: *The resurrection of Jesus from the dead is central to the Christian faith. Why is the resurrection so important? (1) Because Christ was raised from the dead, we know that the Kingdom of Heaven has broken into earth's history. (2) Because of the resurrection, we know that death has been conquered, and we too will be raised from the dead to live forever with Christ. (3) The resurrection gives meaning to the church's regular feast, the Lord's Supper. Like the disciples on the Emmaus Road, we break bread with our* risen Lord, who comes in power to save us. (4) The resurrection helps us find meaning even in the midst of great tragedy. No matter what happens to us as we walk with the Lord, the resurrection gives us hope for the future. (5) God's power that brought Jesus back from the dead is available to us so that we can live for him in an evil world.

Christians can look very different from one another; they can hold widely varying beliefs about politics, lifestyle, and even some aspects of theology. But one central belief unites all true Christians—Jesus Christ rose from the dead!

Paul's Commands for Holy Living/ 1 Thessalonians 5:12–22

Dear brothers, honor the officers of your church who work hard among you and warn you against all that is wrong. 13Think highly of them and give them your whole-hearted love because they are straining to help you. And remember, no quarreling among yourselves.

14Dear brothers, warn those who are lazy; comfort those who are frightened; take tender care of those who are weak; and be patient with everyone. 15See that no one pays back evil for evil, but always try to do good to each other and to everyone else. 16Always be joyful. 17Always keep on praying. 18No matter what happens, always be thankful, for this is God's will for you who belong to Christ Jesus.

19Do not smother the Holy Spirit. 20Do not scoff at those who prophesy, 21but test everything that is said to be sure it is true, and if it is, then accept it. 22Keep away from every kind of evil.

A THOUGHT: Don't lie down with the lazy; warn them. Don't yell at the frightened; comfort them. At times it's difficult to distinguish between laziness and fear. Two people may be doing nothing—one because he is lazy and the other out of fear of doing something wrong. The key to ministry is sensitivity: sensing the condition of each person and offering the appropriate remedy for each situation. You can't effectively help until you know the problem. You can't apply the right medicine until you know what kind of wound there is that needs to be treated.

Proverbs for Today/ 20:26–27

A wise king stamps out crime by severe punishment. □
A man's conscience is the Lord's searchlight exposing his hidden motives.

Jesus' Emmaus Road Appearance/ Luke 24:13–34

That same day, Sunday, two of Jesus' followers were walking to the village of Emmaus, seven miles out of Jerusalem. 14As they walked along they were talking of Jesus' death, 15when suddenly Jesus himself came along and joined them and began walking beside them. 16But they didn't recognize him, for God kept them from it.

17"You seem to be in a deep discussion about something," he said. "What are you so concerned about?" They stopped short, sadness written across their faces. 18And one of them, Cleopas, replied, "You must be the only person in Jerusalem who hasn't heard about the terrible things that happened there last week."

19"What things?" Jesus asked.

"The things that happened to Jesus, the Man from Nazareth," they said. "He was a Prophet who did incredible miracles and was a mighty Teacher, highly regarded by both God and man. 20But the chief priests and our religious leaders arrested him and handed him over to the Roman government to be condemned to death, and they crucified him. 21We had thought he was the glorious Messiah and that he had come to rescue Israel.

"And now, besides all this—which happened three days ago — 22,23some women from our group of his followers were at his tomb early this morning and came back with an amazing report that his body was missing, and that they had seen some angels there who told them Jesus is alive! 24Some of our men ran out to see, and sure enough, Jesus' body was gone, just as the women had said."

25Then Jesus said to them, "You are such foolish, foolish people! You find it so hard to believe all that the prophets wrote in the Scriptures! 26Wasn't it clearly predicted by the prophets that the Messiah would have to suffer all these things before entering his time of glory?"

27Then Jesus quoted them passage after passage from the writings of the prophets, beginning with the book of Genesis and going right on through the Scriptures, explain ing what the passages meant and what they said about himself.

28By this time they were nearing Emmaus and the end of their journey. Jesus would have gone on, 29but they begged him to stay the night with them, as it was getting late. So he went home with them. 30As they sat down to eat, he asked God's blessing on the food and then took a small loaf of bread and broke it and was passing it over to them, 31when suddenly—it was as though their eyes were opened—they recognized him! And at that moment he disappeared!

32They began telling each other how their hearts had felt strangely warm as he talked with them and explained the Scriptures during the walk down the road. 33,34Within the hour they were on their way back to Jerusalem, where the eleven disciples and the other followers of Jesus greeted them with these words, "The Lord has really risen! He appeared to Peter!"

A THOUGHT: *The two disciples returning to Emmaus missed the significance of history's greatest event because they focused on their disappointments and problems—so much so that they didn't recognize that it was Jesus walking beside them. To compound the problem, they were walking in the wrong direction—away from the fellowship of believers in Jerusalem. We are likely to miss Jesus and withdraw from the strength found in other believers when we become preoccupied with our dashed hopes and frustrated plans. Only when we are looking for Jesus in our midst will we experience the power and help he can bring.*

Paul's Prayer and Final Greetings/ 1 Thessalonians 5:23–28

May the God of peace himself make you entirely pure and devoted to God; and may your spirit and soul and body be kept strong and blameless until that day when our Lord Jesus Christ comes back again. 24God, who called you to become his child, will do all this for you, just as he promised. 25Dear brothers, pray for us. 26Shake hands for me with all the brothers there. 27I command you in the name of the Lord to read this letter to all the Christians. 28And may rich blessings from our Lord Jesus Christ be with you, every one.

Sincerely,
Paul

A THOUGHT: *The spirit, soul, and body are integral parts of a person. This expression is Paul's way of saying that God must be involved in every aspect of our lives. It is wrong to think we can separate our spiritual lives from everything else, obeying God only in some ethereal sense or living for him only one day each week. Christ must control all of us, not just a "religious" part.*

Proverbs for Today/ 20:28–30

If a king is kind, honest and fair, his kingdom stands secure. □ The glory of young men is their strength; of old men, their experience. □ Punishment that hurts chases evil from the heart.

AUGUST 9

The Ascension of Jesus/ Luke 24:35–53

Then the two from Emmaus told their story of how Jesus had appeared to them as they were walking along the road and how they had recognized him as he was breaking the bread.

36And just as they were telling about it, Jesus himself was suddenly standing there among them, and greeted them. 37But the whole group was terribly frightened, thinking they were seeing a ghost!

38"Why are you frightened?" he asked. "Why do you doubt that it is really I? 39Look at my hands! Look at my feet! You can see that it is I, myself! Touch me and make sure that I am not a ghost! For ghosts don't have bodies, as you see that I do!" 40As he spoke, he held out his hands for them to see [the marks of the nails], and showed them [the wounds in] his feet.

41Still they stood there undecided, filled with joy and doubt.

Then he asked them, "Do you have anything here to eat?"

42They gave him a piece of broiled fish, 43and he ate it as they watched!

44Then he said, "When I was with you before, don't you remember my telling you that everything written about me by Moses and the prophets and in the Psalms must all come true?" 45Then he opened their minds to understand at last these many Scriptures! 46And he said, "Yes, it was written long ago that the Messiah must suffer and die and rise again from the dead on the third day; 47and that this message of salvation should be taken from Jerusalem to all the nations: *There is forgiveness of sins for all who turn to me.* 48You have seen these prophecies come true.

49"And now I will send the Holy Spirit upon you, just as my Father promised. Don't begin telling others yet— stay here in the city until the Holy Spirit comes and fills you with power from heaven."

50Then Jesus led them out along the road to Bethany, and lifting his hands to heaven, he blessed them, 51and then began rising into the sky, and went on to heaven. 52And they worshiped him, and returned to Jerusalem filled with mighty joy, 53and were continually in the Temple, praising God.

A THOUGHT: *As the disciples stood and watched, Jesus began rising into the air, and soon he disappeared into heaven. Seeing Jesus leave must have been frightening, but they knew he would keep his promise to be with them in the Spirit. This same Jesus who lived with the disciples, who died and rose from the dead, and who loves us, promises to be with us always. We can get to know him better through studying the Scriptures, praying, and allowing the Holy Spirit to make us more like him.*

Paul Encourages the Thessalonians/
2 Thessalonians 1:1–12

From: Paul, Silas and Timothy.

To: The church of Thessalonica—kept safe in God our Father and in the Lord Jesus Christ.

2May God the Father and the Lord Jesus Christ give you rich blessings and peace-filled hearts and minds.

3Dear brothers, giving thanks to God for you is not only the right thing to do, but it is our duty to God, because of the really wonderful way your faith has grown, and because of your growing love for each other. 4We are happy to tell other churches about your patience and complete faith in God, in spite of all the crushing troubles and hardships you are going through.

⁵This is only one example of the fair, just way God does things, for he is using your sufferings to make you ready for his Kingdom, ⁶while at the same time he is preparing judgment and punishment for those who are hurting you.

⁷And so I would say to you who are suffering, God will give you rest along with us when the Lord Jesus appears suddenly from heaven in flaming fire with his mighty angels, ⁸bringing judgment on those who do not wish to know God, and who refuse to accept his plan to save them through our Lord Jesus Christ. ⁹They will be punished in everlasting hell, forever separated from the Lord, never to see the glory of his power, ¹⁰when he comes to receive praise and admiration because of all he has done for his people, his saints. And you will be among those praising him, because you have believed what we told you about him.

¹¹And so we keep on praying for you that our God will make you the kind of children he wants to have—will make you as good as you wish you could be!—rewarding your faith with his power. ¹²Then everyone will be praising the name of the Lord Jesus Christ because of the results they see in you; and your greatest glory will be that you belong to him. The tender mercy of our God and of the Lord Jesus Christ has made all this possible for you.

A THOUGHT: *As we live for Christ, we will experience troubles and hardships. Some say troubles are a result of sin or lack of faith. But Paul teaches that they may be a part of God's plan for believers. Our problems help us look upward and forward, not inward; they help build strong character; and they help us be sensitive to others who also struggle. Problems are unavoidable for godly people in an ungodly world. Your troubles may well be a sign of effective Christian living.*

Proverbs for Today/ 21:1–2

Just as water is turned into irrigation ditches, so the Lord directs the king's thoughts. He turns them wherever he wants to. □ We can justify our every deed but God looks at our motives.

AUGUST 10

Christ, the Word Made Flesh/ John 1:1–14

Before anything else existed, there was Christ, with God. He has always been alive and is himself God. 3He created everything there is—nothing exists that he didn't make. 4Eternal life is in him, and this life gives light to all mankind. 5His life is the light that shines through the darkness— and the darkness can never extinguish it.

6,7God sent John the Baptist as a witness to the fact that Jesus Christ is the true Light. 8John himself was not the Light; he was only a witness to identify it.

9Later on, the one who is the true Light arrived to shine on everyone coming into the world.

10But although he made the world, the world didn't recognize him when he came. 11,12Even in his own land and among his own people, the Jews, he was not accepted. Only a few would welcome and receive him. But to all who received him, he gave the right to become children of God. All they needed to do was to trust him to save them. 13All those who believe this are reborn!—not a physical rebirth resulting from human passion or plan— but from the will of God.

14And Christ became a human being and lived here on earth among us and was full of loving forgiveness and truth. And some of us have seen his glory—the glory of the only Son of the heavenly Father!

A THOUGHT: *When Jesus Christ was born, God became a man. He was not part man and part God; he was completely human and completely divine. Before Christ came, people could know God partially. After Christ came, people could know God fully because he became visible and tangible in Christ. Christ is the perfect expression of God in human form. The two most common errors are to minimize Jesus' humanity or to minimize his divinity. Jesus is both God and man. We can be comforted with the knowledge that our great God and Savior has walked among us and experienced the struggles and difficulties we experience. Jesus went far beyond merely sharing our experiences here on earth—he died in our stead to make intimate relationship with God the Father possible.*

Don't Be Deceived/ 2 Thessalonians 2:1–6

And now, what about the coming again of our Lord Jesus Christ, and our being gathered together to meet him?

Please don't be upset and excited, dear brothers, by the rumor that this day of the Lord has already begun. If you hear of people having visions and special messages from God about this, or letters that are supposed to have come from me, don't believe them. 3Don't be carried away and deceived regardless of what they say.

For that day will not come until two things happen: first, there will be a time of great rebellion against God, and then the man of rebellion will come—the son of hell. 4He will defy every god there is, and tear down every other object of adoration and worship. He will go in and sit as God in the temple of God, claiming that he himself is God. 5Don't you remember that I told you this when I was with you? 6And you know what is keeping him from being here already; for he can come only when his time is ready.

A THOUGHT: *Here Paul launches into a discussion about the end of the world and Christ's Second Coming. He says that great suffering and trouble lie ahead, but evil will not prevail, because Christ will return to judge all people. Although Paul presents a few signs of the end times, his emphasis, like Jesus', is not on specific or current events but on each person's need to prepare for Christ's return by living rightly day by day. If we are ready, we won't have to be concerned about what will happen or when it will happen. Our confidence is that God is in control of all events.*

Proverbs for Today/ 21:3
God is more pleased when we are just and fair than when we give him gifts.

AUGUST 11

John Proclaims Jesus as the Messiah/ John 1:15–34
John pointed Jesus out to the people, telling the crowds, "This is the one I was talking about when I said, 'Someone is coming who is greater by far than I am—for he existed long before I did!' " 16We have all benefited from the rich blessings he brought to us—blessing upon blessing heaped upon us! 17For Moses gave us only the Law with its rigid

demands and merciless justice, while Jesus Christ brought us loving forgiveness as well. 18No one has ever actually seen God, but, of course, his only Son has, for he is the companion of the Father and has told us all about him.

19The Jewish leaders sent priests and assistant priests from Jerusalem to ask John whether he claimed to be the Messiah.

20He denied it flatly. "I am not the Christ," he said.

21"Well then, who are you?" they asked. "Are you Elijah?"

"No," he replied.

"Are you the Prophet?"

"No."

22"Then who are you? Tell us, so we can give an answer to those who sent us. What do you have to say for yourself?"

23He replied, "I am a voice from the barren wilderness, shouting as Isaiah prophesied, 'Get ready for the coming of the Lord!' "

24,25Then those who were sent by the Pharisees asked him, "If you aren't the Messiah or Elijah or the Prophet, what right do you have to baptize?"

26John told them, "I merely baptize with water, but right here in the crowd is someone you have never met, 27who will soon begin his ministry among you, and I am not even fit to be his slave."

28This incident took place at Bethany, a village on the other side of the Jordan River where John was baptizing.

29The next day John saw Jesus coming toward him and said, "Look! There is the Lamb of God who takes away the world's sin! 30He is the one I was talking about when I said, 'Soon a man far greater than I am is coming, who existed long before me!' 31I didn't know he was the one, but I am here baptizing with water in order to point him out to the nation of Israel."

32Then John told about seeing the Holy Spirit in the form of a dove descending from heaven and resting upon Jesus.

33"I didn't know he was the one," John said again, "but at the time God sent me to baptize he told me, 'When you see the Holy Spirit descending and resting upon someone—he is the one you are looking for. He is the one who baptizes with the Holy Spirit.' 34I saw it happen to this man, and I therefore testify that he is the Son of God."

A THOUGHT: *In the Pharisees' minds, there were four options regarding John the Baptist's identity: he was (1) the Prophet who would speak God's words, (2) Elijah, (3) the Messiah, or (4) a false prophet. John denied being the first three personages, and instead referred to himself, in the words of the Old Testament prophet Isaiah, as the voice shouting in the wilderness. The leaders kept pressing him to say who he was, because people were expecting the Messiah to come. But John emphasized only why he had come— to prepare the way for the Messiah. The Pharisees missed the point. They wanted to know who John was, but John wanted them to know who Jesus was.*

John the Baptist's job was to point people to Jesus, the Messiah for whom they were looking. Today people are looking for someone to give them security in an insecure world. Our job is to point them to Christ and to show that he is the One they seek.

The Man of Rebellion/ 2 Thessalonians 2:7–17

As for the work this man of rebellion and hell will do when he comes, it is already going on, but he himself will not come until the one who is holding him back steps out of the way. 8Then this wicked one will appear, whom the Lord Jesus will burn up with the breath of his mouth and destroy by his presence when he returns. 9This man of sin will come as Satan's tool, full of satanic power, and will trick everyone with strange demonstrations, and will do great miracles. 10He will completely fool those who are on their way to hell because they have said "no" to the Truth; they have refused to believe it and love it, and let it save them, 11so God will allow them to believe lies with all their hearts, 12and all of them will be justly judged for believing falsehood, refusing the Truth, and enjoying their sins. 13But we must forever give thanks to God for you, our brothers loved by the Lord, because God chose from the very first to give you salvation, cleansing you by the work of the Holy Spirit and by your trusting in the Truth. 14Through us he told you the Good News. Through us he called you to share in the glory of our Lord Jesus Christ.

15With all these things in mind, dear brothers, stand firm and keep a strong grip on the truth that we taught you in our letters and during the time we were with you.

16May our Lord Jesus Christ himself and God our Father, who has loved us and given us everlasting comfort and hope which we don't deserve, 17comfort your hearts with all comfort, and help you in every good thing you say and do.

A THOUGHT: *Paul knew that the Thessalonians would face persecutions, false teachers, worldliness, apathy, and the temptation to wander from the truth and to leave the faith; so he urged them to keep a "grip on the truth" and to stand firm. We are also confronted with temptations to turn away from God. We should hold on to the truth found in Christ's teachings because our lives depend on it. Never forget the reality of his life and love!*

Proverbs for Today/ 21:4
Pride, lust, and evil actions are all sin.

AUGUST 12

Jesus Calls Some of His Disciples/ John 1:35–51
The following day as John was standing with two of his disciples, 36Jesus walked by. John looked at him intently and then declared, "See! There is the Lamb of God!"

37Then John's two disciples turned and followed Jesus.

38Jesus looked around and saw them following. "What do you want?" he asked them.

"Sir," they replied, "where do you live?"

39"Come and see," he said. So they went with him to the place where he was staying and were with him from about four o'clock that afternoon until the evening. 40(One of these men was Andrew, Simon Peter's brother.)

41Andrew then went to find his brother Peter and told him, "We have found the Messiah!" 42And he brought Peter to meet Jesus.

Jesus looked intently at Peter for a moment and then said, "You are Simon, John's son—but you shall be called Peter, the rock!"

43The next day Jesus decided to go to Galilee. He found Philip and told him, "Come with me." 44(Philip was from Bethsaida, Andrew and Peter's home town.)

45Philip now went off to look for Nathanael and told him, "We have found the Messiah!—the very person Moses and the prophets told about! His name is Jesus, the son of Joseph from Nazareth!"

46"Nazareth!" exclaimed Nathanael. "Can anything good come from there?"

"Just come and see for yourself," Philip declared.

47As they approached, Jesus said, "Here comes an honest man—a true son of Israel."

48"How do you know what I am like?" Nathanael demanded.

And Jesus replied, "I could see you under the fig tree before Philip found you."

49Nathanael replied, "Sir, you are the Son of God—the King of Israel!"

50Jesus asked him, "Do you believe all this just because I told you I had seen you under the fig tree? You will see greater proofs than this. 51You will even see heaven open and the angels of God coming back and forth to me, the Messiah."

A THOUGHT: *These new disciples used several names for Jesus: Lamb of God, Rabbi or Teacher, Messiah, Son of God, King of Israel. As they got to know Jesus, their appreciation for him grew. The more time we spend getting to know Christ, the more we understand and appreciate who he is. We may be drawn to him for his teaching, but we will come to know him as the Son of God. Although these disciples made this verbal shift in a few days, they would not fully understand until three years later. What they so easily professed had to be worked out in experience. We may find that words of faith come easily, but deep appreciation for Christ comes with living by faith.*

Paul Requests Prayer/ 2 Thessalonians 3:1–5

Finally, dear brothers, as I come to the end of this letter I ask you to pray for us. Pray first that the Lord's message will spread rapidly and triumph wherever it goes, winning converts everywhere as it did when it came to you. 2Pray too that we will be saved out of the clutches of evil men, for not everyone loves the Lord. 3But the Lord is faithful; he will make you strong and guard you from satanic attacks of every kind. 4And we trust the Lord that you are putting into practice the things we taught you, and that you always will. 5May the Lord bring you into an ever deeper under standing of the love of God and of the patience that comes from Christ.

A THOUGHT: *Beneath the surface of the routine of daily life, a fierce struggle among invisible spiritual powers is being waged. Like the wind, the power of evil forces can be devastating. Our main defense is prayer that God will protect us and that he will make us strong. The following guidelines can help you prepare for satanic attacks: (1) take the threat of spiritual attack seriously; (2) pray for strength and help from God; (3) study the Bible to recognize Satan's style and tactics, (4) memorize Scripture so it will be a source of help no matter where you are; (5) associate with those who speak the truth; and (6) practice what you are taught by spiritual leaders.*

Proverbs for Today/ 21:5–7

Steady plodding brings prosperity; hasty speculation brings poverty. □ Dishonest gain will never last, so why take the risk? □ Because the wicked are unfair, their violence boomerangs and destroys them.

AUGUST 13

Jesus Turns Water into Wine/ John 2:1–12

Two days later Jesus' mother was a guest at a wedding in the village of Cana in Galilee, 2and Jesus and his disciples were invited too. 3The wine supply ran out during the festivities, and Jesus' mother came to him with the problem.

4"I can't help you now," he said. "It isn't yet my time for miracles."

5But his mother told the servants, "Do whatever he tells you to."

6Six stone waterpots were standing there; they were used for Jewish ceremonial purposes and held perhaps twenty to thirty gallons each. 7,8Then Jesus told the servants to fill them to the brim with water. When this was done he said, "Dip some out and take it to the master of ceremonies."

9When the master of ceremonies tasted the water that was now wine, not knowing where it had come from (though, of course, the servants did), he called the bridegroom over.

10"This is wonderful stuff!" he said. "You're different from most. Usually a host uses the best wine first, and afterwards, when everyone is full and doesn't care, then he brings out the less expensive brands. But you have kept the best for the last!"

11This miracle at Cana in Galilee was Jesus' first public demonstration of his heaven-sent power. And his disciples believed that he really was the Messiah.

12After the wedding he left for Capernaum for a few days with his mother, brothers, and disciples.

A THOUGHT: *Miracles are not merely superhuman happenings, but happenings that demonstrate God's power. Jesus performed miracles to renew people—restoring sight, making the lame to walk, even restoring life to the dead. Believe in him, not because he is a superman, but because he is God, graciously renewing his creation. Although God does not always choose to bring full restoration this side of heaven, God does have a special concern for the poor, the weak, the crippled, the orphaned, the blind, the lame, and the oppressed. Our concern should be like God's—to care for the powerless in society by bringing Christ's message of redemption in both our words and actions.*

An Admonishment against Laziness/
2 Thessalonians 3:6–18

Now here is a command, dear brothers, given in the name of our Lord Jesus Christ by his authority: Stay away from any Christian who spends his days in laziness and does not follow the ideal of hard work we set up for you. 7For you well know that you ought to follow our example: you never saw us loafing; 8we never accepted food from anyone without buying it; we worked hard day and night for the money we needed to live on, in order that we would not be a burden to any of you. 9It wasn't that we didn't have the right to ask you to feed us, but we wanted to show you, firsthand, how you should work for your living. 10Even while we were still there with you we gave you this rule: "He who does not work shall not eat."

11Yet we hear that some of you are living in laziness, refusing to work, and wasting your time in gossiping. 12In the name of the Lord Jesus Christ we appeal to such people—we command them—to quiet down, get to work, and earn their own living. 13And to the rest of you I say, dear brothers, never be tired of doing right.

14If anyone refuses to obey what we say in this letter, notice who he is and stay away from him, that he may be ashamed of himself. 15Don't think of him as an enemy, but speak to him as you would to a brother who needs to be warned.

16May the Lord of peace himself give you his peace no matter what happens. The Lord be with you all.

17Now here is my greeting which I am writing with my own hand, as I do at the end of all my letters, for proof that it really is from me. This is in my own handwriting. 18May the blessing of our Lord Jesus Christ be upon you all.

Sincerely,
Paul

A THOUGHT: *Some people in the Thessalonian church were falsely teaching that since Christ's Second Coming could happen any day, people should set aside their responsibilities, quit work, do no future planning, and just wait for Christ. But their lack of activity only led them into sin. They became a burden to the church, which was supporting them; they wasted time that could have been used for helping others; and they gossiped. They may have thought they were being more spiritual by not working, but Paul told them to be responsible and get back to work. Being ready for Christ means obeying him in every area of life. Because we know Christ is coming, we must do everything we can to live in a way that will please him when he arrives.*

Proverbs for Today/ 21:8–10

A man is known by his actions. An evil man lives an evil life; a good man lives a godly life. □ It is better to live in the corner of an attic than with a crabby woman in a lovely home. □ An evil man loves to harm others; being a good neighbor is out of his line.

Jesus Clears the Temple/ John 2:13–25

Then it was time for the annual Jewish Passover celebration, and Jesus went to Jerusalem.

¹⁴In the Temple area he saw merchants selling cattle, sheep, and doves for sacrifices, and moneychangers behind their counters. ¹⁵Jesus made a whip from some ropes and chased them all out, and drove out the sheep and oxen, scattering the moneychangers' coins over the floor and turning over their tables! ¹⁶Then, going over to the men selling doves, he told them, "Get these things out of here. Don't turn my Father's House into a market!"

¹⁷Then his disciples remembered this prophecy from the Scriptures: "Concern for God's House will be my undoing."

¹⁸"What right have you to order them out?" the Jewish leaders demanded. "If you have this authority from God, show us a miracle to prove it."

¹⁹"All right," Jesus replied, "this is the miracle I will do for you: Destroy this sanctuary and in three days I will raise it up!"

²⁰"What!" they exclaimed. "It took forty-six years to build this Temple, and you can do it in three days?" ²¹But by "this sanctuary" he meant his body. ²²After he came back to life again, the disciples remembered his saying this and realized that what he had quoted from the Scriptures really did refer to him, and had all come true!

²³Because of the miracles he did in Jerusalem at the Passover celebration, many people were convinced that he was indeed the Messiah. ²⁴,²⁵But Jesus didn't trust them, for he knew mankind to the core. No one needed to tell him how changeable human nature is!

A THOUGHT: *The Passover celebration took place yearly at the Temple in Jerusalem. Every Jewish male was expected to make a pilgrimage to Jerusalem during this time. This was a week-long festival—the Passover was one day, and the Feast of Unleavened Bread lasted the rest of the week. The entire week commemorated the freeing of the Jews from slavery in Egypt. To Jews, the Passover was the most important celebration of the year. Yet in the midst of this holy celebration merchants were using God's Temple as a market-place. They forgot, or didn't care, that God's house is a place of worship, not a marketplace for making a profit. Our attitude toward the church is wrong if we see it as a place for personal or business contacts. Make sure your purpose for attending a church meeting is to worship God.*

Paul Warns about False Teachers/ 1 Timothy 1:1–5

From: Paul, a missionary of Jesus Christ, sent out by the direct command of God our Savior and by Jesus Christ our Lord—our only hope.

2 *To:* Timothy.

Timothy, you are like a son to me in the things of the Lord. May God our Father and Jesus Christ our Lord show you his kindness and mercy and give you great peace of heart and mind.

3,4As I said when I left for Macedonia, please stay there in Ephesus and try to stop the men who are teaching such wrong doctrine. Put an end to their myths and fables, and their idea of being saved by finding favor with an endless chain of angels leading up to God—wild ideas that stir up questions and arguments instead of helping people accept God's plan of faith. 5What I am eager for is that all the Christians there will be filled with love that comes from pure hearts, and that their minds will be clean and their faith strong.

A THOUGHT: *The church at Ephesus was probably plagued by the same heresy that threatened the church at Colosse, the false doctrine that to be acceptable to God one had to find favor with angels. To aid in their salvation, some Ephesians constructed lists and biographies of angels. The false teachers mentioned here were motivated by their own interests rather than Christ's. They embroiled the church in endless and irrelevant disputes. Today we have many opportunities to enter into such worthless and irrelevant discussions. Such disputes crowd out the life-changing message of Christ. Stay away from religious speculation and theological haggling. It may seem harmless at first, but it has a way of sidetracking us from the central message of the gospel—the person and work of Jesus Christ.*

Proverbs for Today/ 21:11–12

The wise man learns by listening; the simpleton can learn only by seeing scorners punished. □ God, the Righteous One, knows what is going on in the homes of the wicked, and will bring the wicked to judgment.

Nicodemus Visits Jesus at Night/ John 3:1–21

After dark one night a Jewish religious leader named Nicodemus, a member of the sect of the Pharisees, came for an interview with Jesus. "Sir," he said, "we all know that God has sent you to teach us. Your miracles are proof enough of this."

3Jesus replied, "With all the earnestness I possess I tell you this: Unless you are born again, you can never get into the Kingdom of God."

4"Born again!" exclaimed Nicodemus. "What do you mean? How can an old man go back into his mother's womb and be born again?"

5Jesus replied, "What I am telling you so earnestly is this: Unless one is born of water and the Spirit, he cannot enter the Kingdom of God. 6Men can only reproduce human life, but the Holy Spirit gives new life from heaven; 7so don't be surprised at my statement that you must be born again! 8Just as you can hear the wind but can't tell where it comes from or where it will go next, so it is with the Spirit. We do not know on whom he will next bestow this life from heaven."

9"What do you mean?" Nicodemus asked.

10,11Jesus replied, "You, a respected Jewish teacher, and yet you don't understand these things? I am telling you what I know and have seen—and yet you won't believe me. 12But if you don't even believe me when I tell you about such things as these that happen here among men, how can you possibly believe if I tell you what is going on in heaven? 13For only I, the Messiah, have come to earth and will return to heaven again. 14And as Moses in the wilderness lifted up the bronze image of a serpent on a pole, even so I must be lifted up upon a pole, 15so that anyone who believes in me will have eternal life. 16For God loved the world so much that he gave his only Son so that anyone who believes in him shall not perish but have eternal life. 17God did not send his Son into the world to condemn it, but to save it.

18"There is no eternal doom awaiting those who trust him to save them. But those who don't trust him have already been tried and condemned for not believing in the only Son of God. 19Their sentence is based on this fact: that the Light from heaven came into the world, but they loved the darkness more than the Light, for their deeds were evil. 20They hated the heavenly Light because they wanted to sin in the darkness. They stayed away from that Light for fear their sins would be exposed and they would be punished. 21But those doing right come gladly to the Light to let everyone see that they are doing what God wants them to."

A THOUGHT: *What did Nicodemus know about the Kingdom? From the Bible he knew it would be ruled by God, it would be restored on earth, and it would incorporate God's people. Jesus revealed to this devout Pharisee that the Kingdom would come to the whole world, not just the Jews, and that Nicodemus wouldn't be a part of it unless he was personally born again. This was a revolutionary concept; the Kingdom is personal, not national or ethnic, and its entrance requirements are repentance and spiritual rebirth. Jesus later taught that God's Kingdom has already begun in the hearts of believers through the presence of the Holy Spirit. It will be fully realized when Jesus returns again to judge the world and abolish evil forever.*

The Purpose of the Law/ 1 Timothy 1:6–11

But these teachers have missed this whole idea and spend their time arguing and talking foolishness. 7They want to become famous as teachers of the laws of Moses when they haven't the slightest idea what those laws really show us. 8Those laws are good when used as God intended. 9But they were not made for us, whom God has saved; they are for sinners who hate God, have rebellious hearts, curse and swear, attack their fathers and mothers, and murder. 10,11Yes, these laws are made to identify as sinners all who are immoral and impure: homosexuals, kidnappers, liars, and all others who do things that contradict the glorious Good News of our blessed God, whose messenger I am.

A THOUGHT: *Theological hairsplitting—arguing about tiny details of Scripture—can take us into interesting, but irrelevant bypaths and cause us to miss the intent of God's message. The false teachers at Ephesus constructed vast speculative systems and then argued about the minor details of their wholly imaginary ideas. We should allow nothing to distract us from the Good News of Jesus Christ, the main point of Scripture. We need to know what the Scriptures*

say, apply them to our lives daily, and teach them to others. When
we do this we will be able to evaluate all teachings in light of the
central truth about Jesus. Don't spend so much time on the minute
details of Scripture that you miss the main point of what God is
trying to teach you.

Proverbs for Today/ 21:13

He who shuts his ears to the cries of the poor will be
ignored in his own time of need.

AUGUST 16

John the Baptist Testifies of Jesus/ John 3:22–36

Afterwards Jesus and his disciples left Jerusalem and stayed
for a while in Judea and baptized there.

23,24At this time John the Baptist was not yet in prison.
He was baptizing at Aenon, near Salim, because there
was plenty of water there. 25One day someone began an
argument with John's disciples, telling them that Jesus'
baptism was best. 26So they came to John and said, "Master,
the man you met on the other side of the Jordan River—
the one you said was the Messiah—he is baptizing too,
and everybody is going over there instead of coming here
to us."

27John replied, "God in heaven appoints each man's work.
28My work is to prepare the way for that man so that
everyone will go to him. You yourselves know how plainly
I told you that I am not the Messiah. I am here to prepare
the way for him—that is all. 29The crowds will naturally
go to the main attraction —the bride will go where the
bridegroom is! A bridegroom's friends rejoice with him.
I am the Bridegroom's friend, and I am filled with joy at
his success. 30 He must become greater and greater, and
I must become less and less.

31"He has come from heaven and is greater than anyone
else. I am of the earth, and my understanding is limited
to the things of earth. 32He tells what he has seen and
heard, but how few believe what he tells them! 33,34Those

who believe him discover that God is a fountain of truth. For this one—sent by God—speaks God's words, for God's Spirit is upon him without measure or limit. 35The Father loves this man because he is his Son, and God has given him everything there is. 36And all who trust him—God's Son—to save them have eternal life; those who don't believe and obey him shall never see heaven, but the wrath of God remains upon them."

A THOUGHT: *John the Baptist's disciples were disturbed because people were following Jesus instead of John. It is easy to grow jealous of the popularity of another person's ministry. But we must remember that our true mission is to win people to follow Christ, not us—Christ must become greater and greater to those we minister to, and we must become less and less. Beware of those leaders who put more emphasis on their own achievements than on God's Kingdom.*

The Greatest of Sinners/ 1 Timothy 1:12–17

How thankful I am to Christ Jesus our Lord for choosing me as one of his messengers, and giving me the strength to be faithful to him, 13even though I used to scoff at the name of Christ. I hunted down his people, harming them in every way I could. But God had mercy on me because I didn't know what I was doing, for I didn't know Christ at that time. 14Oh, how kind our Lord was, for he showed me how to trust him and become full of the love of Christ Jesus.

15How true it is, and how I long that everyone should know it, that Christ Jesus came into the world to save sinners—and I was the greatest of them all. 16But God had mercy on me so that Christ Jesus could use me as an example to show everyone how patient he is with even the worst sinners, so that others will realize that they, too, can have everlasting life. 17Glory and honor to God forever and ever. He is the King of the ages, the unseen one who never dies; he alone is God, and full of wisdom. Amen.

A THOUGHT: *People can feel so guilt-ridden by their past that they think God could never forgive and accept them. But consider Paul's past. He had hunted down and murdered God's own people before coming to faith in Christ. God forgave Paul and he can forgive you.*

Proverbs for Today/ 21:14–16

An angry man is silenced by giving him a gift! □ A good man loves justice, but it is a calamity to evil-doers. □ The man who strays away from common sense will end up dead!

AUGUST 17

Jesus Talks to a Woman at the Well/ John 4:1–30

When the Lord knew that the Pharisees had heard about the greater crowds coming to him than to John to be baptized and to become his disciples—(though Jesus himself didn't baptize them, but his disciples did)— 3he left Judea and returned to the province of Galilee.

4He had to go through Samaria on the way, 5,6and around noon as he approached the village of Sychar, he came to Jacob's Well, located on the parcel of ground Jacob gave to his son Joseph. Jesus was tired from the long walk in the hot sun and sat wearily beside the well.

7Soon a Samaritan woman came to draw water, and Jesus asked her for a drink. 8He was alone at the time as his disciples had gone into the village to buy some food. 9The woman was surprised that a Jew would ask a "despised Samaritan" for anything—usually they wouldn't even speak to them!—and she remarked about this to Jesus.

10He replied, "If you only knew what a wonderful gift God has for you, and who I am, you would ask me for some *living* water!"

11"But you don't have a rope or a bucket," she said, "and this is a very deep well! Where would you get this living water? 12And besides, are you greater than our ancestor Jacob? How can you offer better water than this which he and his sons and cattle enjoyed?"

13Jesus replied that people soon became thirsty again after drinking this water. 14"But the water I give them," he said, "becomes a perpetual spring within them, watering them forever with eternal life."

15"Please, sir," the woman said, "give me some of that water! Then I'll never be thirsty again and won't have to make this long trip out here every day."

16"Go and get your husband," Jesus told her.

17,18"But I'm not married," the woman replied.

"All too true!" Jesus said. "For you have had five husbands, and you aren't even married to the man you're living with now."

19"Sir," the woman said, "you must be a prophet. 20But say, tell me, why is it that you Jews insist that Jerusalem is the only place of worship, while we Samaritans claim it is here [at Mount Gerazim], where our ancestors worshiped?"

21-24Jesus replied, "The time is coming, ma'am, when we will no longer be concerned about whether to worship the Father here or in Jerusalem. For it's not *where* we worship that counts, but *how* we worship—is our worship spiritual and real? Do we have the Holy Spirit's help? For God is Spirit, and we must have his help to worship as we should. The Father wants this kind of worship from us. But you Samaritans know so little about him, worshiping blindly, while we Jews know all about him, for salvation comes to the world through the Jews."

25The woman said, "Well, at least I know that the Messiah will come—the one they call Christ—and when he does, he will explain everything to us."

26Then Jesus told her, "I am the Messiah!"

27Just then his disciples arrived. They were surprised to find him talking to a woman, but none of them asked him why, or what they had been discussing.

28,29Then the woman left her waterpot beside the well and went back to the village and told everyone, "Come and meet a man who told me everything I ever did! Can this be the Messiah?" 30So the people came streaming from the village to see him.

A THOUGHT: *This woman (1) was a Samaritan, a member of a hated mixed race, (2) had a bad reputation, and (3) was in a public place. No respectable Jewish man would talk to a woman under such circumstances. But Jesus did. The gospel is for every person, no matter what his or her race, social position, or past sins. We must be prepared to share this gospel at any time in any place. Jesus crossed all barriers to share the Good News, and we who follow him must do no less.*

Fight the Lord's Battles/ 1 Timothy 1:18–20

Now, Timothy, my son, here is my command to you:
Fight well in the Lord's battles, just as the Lord told us
through his prophets that you would. 19Cling tightly to
your faith in Christ and always keep your conscience clear,
doing what you know is right. For some people have disobeyed their consciences and have deliberately done what
they knew was wrong. It isn't surprising that soon they
lost their faith in Christ after defying God like that.
20Hymenaeus and Alexander are two examples of this. I
had to give them over to Satan to punish them until they
could learn not to bring shame to the name of Christ.

A THOUGHT: *How can you keep your conscience clear? Treasure
your faith in Christ more than anything else and do what you
know is right. Each time you deliberately ignore your conscience,
you are hardening your heart. Soon your capacity to tell right from
wrong will disappear. But when you walk with God, he is able to
speak to you through your conscience, letting you know the difference
between right and wrong. Be sure to act on those inner tugs to do
what is right—then your conscience will remain clear.*

Proverbs for Today/ 21:17–18

A man who loves pleasure becomes poor; wine and luxury
are not the way to riches! □ The wicked will finally
lose; the righteous will finally win.

AUGUST 18

The Harvest/ John 4:31–42

Meanwhile, the disciples were urging Jesus to eat. 32"No,"
he said, "I have some food you don't know about."

33"Who brought it to him?" the disciples asked each
other.

34Then Jesus explained: "My nourishment comes from
doing the will of God who sent me, and from finishing
his work. 35Do you think the work of harvesting will
not begin until the summer ends four months from now?
Look around you! Vast fields of human souls are ripening
all around us, and are ready now for reaping. 36The reapers
will be paid good wages and will be gathering eternal souls

into the granaries of heaven! What joys await the sower and the reaper, both together! 37For it is true that one sows and someone else reaps. 38I sent you to reap where you didn't sow; others did the work, and you received the harvest."

39Many from the Samaritan village believed he was the Messiah because of the woman's report: "He told me everything I ever did!" 40,41When they came out to see him at the well, they begged him to stay at their village; and he did, for two days, long enough for many of them to believe in him after hearing him. 42Then they said to the woman, "Now we believe because we have heard him ourselves, not just because of what you told us. He is indeed the Savior of the world."

A THOUGHT: *Sometimes Christians excuse themselves from witnessing by saying their family or friends aren't ready to believe. Jesus, however, makes it clear that around us a continual harvest waits to be reaped. Don't let Jesus find you making excuses. Look around. You will find people ready to hear God's Word.*

Instructions for Worship/ 1 Timothy 2:1–8

Here are my directions: Pray much for others; plead for God's mercy upon them; give thanks for all he is going to do for them.

2Pray in this way for kings and all others who are in authority over us, or are in places of high responsibility, so that we can live in peace and quietness, spending our time in godly living and thinking much about the Lord. 3This is good and pleases God our Savior, 4for he longs for all to be saved and to understand this truth: 5*That God is on one side and all the people on the other side, and Christ Jesus, himself man, is between them to bring them together, 6by giving his life for all mankind.*

This is the message which at the proper time God gave to the world. 7And I have been chosen—this is the absolute truth—as God's minister and missionary to teach this truth to the Gentiles, and to show them God's plan of salvation through faith.

8So I want men everywhere to pray with holy hands lifted up to God, free from sin and anger and resentment.

A THOUGHT: *Although God is all-powerful and all-knowing, he has chosen to let us help him change the world through our prayers. How this works is a mystery to us because of our limited understand ing, but it is a reality. Paul urges us to pray for each other and for our leaders in government. Our earnest prayers will have powerful results.*

Proverbs for Today/ 21:19–20

Better to live in the desert than with a quarrelsome, complaining woman. □ The wise man saves for the future, but the foolish man spends whatever he gets.

AUGUST 19

Jesus Heals the Son of a Government Official/ John 4:43–54

At the end of the two days' stay Jesus went on into Galilee. Jesus used to say, "A prophet is honored everywhere except in his own country!" 45But the Galileans welcomed him with open arms, for they had been in Jerusalem at the Passover celebration and had seen some of his miracles.

46,47In the course of his journey through Galilee he arrived at the town of Cana, where he had turned the water into wine. While he was there, a man in the city of Capernaum, a government official, whose son was very sick, heard that Jesus had come from Judea and was traveling in Galilee. This man went over to Cana, found Jesus, and begged him to come to Capernaum with him and heal his son, who was now at death's door.

48Jesus asked, "Won't any of you believe in me unless I do more and more miracles?"

49The official pled, "Sir, please come now before my child dies."

50Then Jesus told him, "Go back home. Your son is healed!" And the man believed Jesus and started home. 51While he was on his way, some of his servants met him with the news that all was well—his son had recovered. 52He asked them when the lad had begun to feel better, and they replied, "Yesterday afternoon at about one o'clock his fever suddenly disappeared!" 53Then the father realized it was the same moment that Jesus had told him, "Your son is healed." And the officer and his entire household believed that Jesus was the Messiah.

54This was Jesus' second miracle in Galilee after coming from Judea.

A THOUGHT: *This government official not only believed Jesus could heal; he also obeyed Jesus by returning home, thus demonstrating his faith. It isn't enough for us to say we believe Jesus can take care of our problems. We need to act as if he can. When you pray about a need or problem, live as though you believe Jesus can do what he says.*

Women in the Church/ 1 Timothy 2:9–15

And the women should be the same way, quiet and sensible in manner and clothing. Christian women should be noticed for being kind and good, not for the way they fix their hair or because of their jewels or fancy clothes. 11Women should listen and learn quietly and humbly.

12I never let women teach men or lord it over them. Let them be silent in your church meetings. 13Why? Because God made Adam first, and afterwards he made Eve. 14And it was not Adam who was fooled by Satan, but Eve, and sin was the result. 15So God sent pain and suffering to women when their children are born, but he will save their souls if they trust in him, living quiet, good, and loving lives.

A THOUGHT: *To understand this passage, we must understand the situation in which Paul and Timothy worked. In first-century Jewish culture, women were not allowed to study. When Paul said women should learn quietly and humbly, he was offering them new opportunities. Paul did not want the Ephesian women to teach because they didn't yet have enough knowledge or experience. The Ephesian church had a particular problem with false teachers. Evidently the women were especially susceptible to their teaching, because they did not yet have enough biblical knowledge to see through the false claims. In addition, some of the women were apparently flaunting their new-found Christian freedom by wearing inappropriate clothing. Paul was telling Timothy not to put anyone (in this case, women) into positions of leadership who were not yet mature in the faith. The same principle applies to churches today.*

Proverbs for Today/ 21:21–22

The man who tries to be good, loving and kind finds life, righteousness and honor. □ The wise man conquers the strong man and levels his defenses.

AUGUST 20

A Healing at Bethesda Pool/ John 5:1–24

Afterwards Jesus returned to Jerusalem for one of the Jewish religious holidays. 2Inside the city, near the Sheep Gate, was Bethesda Pool, with five covered platforms or porches surrounding it. 3Crowds of sick folks—lame, blind, or with paralyzed limbs—lay on the platforms (waiting for a certain movement of the water, 4for an angel of the Lord came from time to time and disturbed the water, and the first person to step down into it afterwards was healed).

5One of the men lying there had been sick for thirty-eight years. 6When Jesus saw him and knew how long he had been ill, he asked him, "Would you like to get well?"

7"I can't," the sick man said, "for I have no one to help me into the pool at the movement of the water. While I am trying to get there, someone else always gets in ahead of me."

8Jesus told him, "Stand up, roll up your sleeping mat and go on home!"

9Instantly, the man was healed! He rolled up the mat and began walking!

But it was on the Sabbath when this miracle was done. 10So the Jewish leaders objected. They said to the man who was cured, "You can't work on the Sabbath! It's illegal to carry that sleeping mat!"

11"The man who healed me told me to," was his reply.

12"Who said such a thing as that?" they demanded.

13The man didn't know, and Jesus had disappeared into the crowd. 14But afterwards Jesus found him in the Temple and told him, "Now you are well; don't sin as you did before, or something even worse may happen to you."

15Then the man went to find the Jewish leaders and told them it was Jesus who had healed him.

16So they began harassing Jesus as a Sabbath breaker.

17But Jesus replied, "My Father constantly does good, and I'm following his example."

18Then the Jewish leaders were all the more eager to kill him because in addition to disobeying their Sabbath laws, he had spoken of God as his Father, thereby making himself equal with God.

19Jesus replied, "The Son can do nothing by himself. He does only what he sees the Father doing, and in the same way. 20For the Father loves the Son, and tells him everything he is doing; and the Son will do far more awesome miracles than this man's healing. 21He will even raise from the dead anyone he wants to, just as the Father does. 22And the Father leaves all judgment of sin to his Son, 23so that everyone will honor the Son, just as they honor the Father. But if you refuse to honor God's Son, whom he sent to you, then you are certainly not honoring the Father.

24"I say emphatically that anyone who listens to my message and believes in God who sent me has eternal life, and will never be damned for his sins, but has already passed out of death into life.

A THOUGHT: *A man who hadn't walked for 38 years was healed, but the Pharisees were more concerned about their petty rules than the life and health of a human being. It is easy to get so caught up in our man-made structures and rules that we forget the people involved. Are your guidelines for living, God-made or man-made? Are they helping people, or have they become needless stumbling blocks?*

Requirements for Church Leadership/
1 Timothy 3:1–7

It is a true saying that if a man wants to be a pastor he has a good ambition. 2For a pastor must be a good man whose life cannot be spoken against. He must have only one wife, and he must be hard working and thoughtful, orderly, and full of good deeds. He must enjoy having guests in his home, and must be a good Bible teacher. 3He must not be a drinker or quarrelsome, but he must be gentle and kind, and not be one who loves money. 4He must have a well-behaved family, with children who obey quickly and quietly. 5For if a man can't make his own little family behave, how can he help the whole church?

6The pastor must not be a new Christian, because he might be proud of being chosen so soon, and pride comes before a fall. (Satan's downfall is an example.) 7Also, he must be well spoken of by people outside the church—those who aren't Christians—so that Satan can't trap him with many accusations, and leave him without freedom to lead his flock.

A THOUGHT: *It is good to want to be a spiritual leader, but the standards are high. Paul enumerates some of the qualifications here. Do you hold a position of spiritual leadership, or would you like to be a leader some day? Check yourself against Paul's standard of excellence. Those with great responsibility must meet high expectations.*

Proverbs for Today/ 21:23–24

Keep your mouth closed and you'll stay out of trouble.
□ Mockers are proud, haughty and arrogant.

AUGUST 21

Jesus Is the Son of God/ John 5:25–47

"And I solemnly declare that the time is coming, in fact, it is here, when the dead shall hear my voice—the voice of the Son of God—and those who listen shall live. 26The Father has life in himself, and has granted his Son to have life in himself, 27and to judge the sins of all mankind because he is the Son of Man. 28Don't be so surprised! Indeed the time is coming when all the dead in their graves shall hear the voice of God's Son, 29and shall rise again—those who have done good, to eternal life; and those who have continued in evil, to judgment.

30"But I pass no judgment without consulting the Father. I judge as I am told. And my judgment is absolutely fair and just, for it is according to the will of God who sent me and is not merely my own.

31"When I make claims about myself they aren't believed, 32,33but someone else, yes, John the Baptist, is making these claims for me too. You have gone out to listen to his preaching, and I can assure you that all he says about me is true! 34But the truest witness I have is not from a man, though I have reminded you about John's witness so that you will believe in me and be saved. 35John shone brightly for a while, and you benefited and rejoiced, 36but I have a greater witness than John. I refer to the miracles

I do; these have been assigned me by the Father, and they prove that the Father has sent me. 37And the Father himself has also testified about me, though not appearing to you personally, or speaking to you directly. 38But you are not listening to him, for you refuse to believe me—the one sent to you with God's message.

39"You search the Scriptures, for you believe they give you eternal life. And the Scriptures point to me! 40Yet you won't come to me so that I can give you this life eternal!

41,42"Your approval or disapproval means nothing to me, for as I know so well, you don't have God's love within you. 43I know, because I have come to you representing my Father and you refuse to welcome me, though you readily enough receive those who aren't sent from him, but represent only themselves! 44No wonder you can't believe! For you gladly honor each other, but you don't care about the honor that comes from the only God!

45"Yet it is not I who will accuse you of this to the Father—Moses will! Moses, on whose laws you set your hopes of heaven. 46For you have refused to believe Moses. He wrote about me, but you refuse to believe him, so you refuse to believe in me. 47And since you don't believe what he wrote, no wonder you don't believe me either."

A THOUGHT: *Whose approval do you seek? The religious leaders enjoyed great prestige in Israel, but their stamp of approval meant nothing to Jesus. He was concerned about God's approval. This is a good principle for us. If even the highest officials in the world approve of our actions and God does not, we should be greatly concerned. But if God approves, even though others don't, we should be content.*

The Requirements for Deacons/ 1 Timothy 3:8–15

The deacons must be the same sort of good, steady men as the pastors. They must not be heavy drinkers and must not be greedy for money. 9They must be earnest, wholehearted followers of Christ who is the hidden Source of their faith. 10Before they are asked to be deacons they should be given other jobs in the church as a test of their character and ability, and if they do well, then they may be chosen as deacons.

11Their wives must be thoughtful, not heavy drinkers, not gossipers, but faithful in everything they do. 12Deacons should have only one wife and they should have happy, obedient families. 13Those who do well as deacons will be well rewarded both by respect from others and also by developing their own confidence and bold trust in the Lord.

14I am writing these things to you now, even though I hope to be with you soon, 15so that if I don't come for awhile you will know what kind of men you should choose as officers for the church of the living God, which contains and holds high the truth of God.

A THOUGHT: *Deacon means "one who serves." This position was begun by the apostles in the Jerusalem church to care for the physical needs of the congregation, especially the needs of the Greek-speaking widows. Deacons were leaders in the church and their qualifications resemble those of elders. In some churches today, the office of deacon has become a catch-all position in which new and young Christians are often asked to serve. That is not the New Testament pattern. Paul says people are to be tested with lesser responsibilities before being made deacons.*

Proverbs for Today/ 21:25–26

The lazy man longs for many things but his hands refuse to work. He is greedy to get, while the godly love to give!

AUGUST 22

The Feeding of the Five Thousand/ John 6:1–15

After this, Jesus crossed over the Sea of Galilee, also known as the Sea of Tiberias. 2-5And a huge crowd, many of them pilgrims on their way to Jerusalem for the annual Passover celebration, were following him wherever he went, to watch him heal the sick. So when Jesus went up into the hills and sat down with his disciples around him, he soon saw a great multitude of people climbing the hill, looking for him.

Turning to Philip he asked, "Philip, where can we buy bread to feed all these people?" 6(He was testing Philip, for he already knew what he was going to do.)

7Philip replied, "It would take a fortune to begin to do it!"

8,9Then Andrew, Simon Peter's brother, spoke up. "There's a youngster here with five barley loaves and a couple of fish! But what good is that with all this mob?"

10"Tell everyone to sit down," Jesus ordered. And all of them—the approximate count of the men only was 5,000—sat down on the grassy slopes. 11Then Jesus took the loaves and gave thanks to God and passed them out to the people. Afterwards he did the same with the fish. And everyone ate until full!

12"Now gather the scraps," Jesus told his disciples, "so that nothing is wasted." 13And twelve baskets were filled with the leftovers!

14When the people realized what a great miracle had happened, they exclaimed, "Surely, he is the Prophet we have been expecting!"

15Jesus saw that they were ready to take him by force and make him their king, so he went higher into the mountains alone.

A THOUGHT: *Jesus asked Philip where they could buy a great amount of bread. Philip started assessing the probable cost. Jesus wanted to teach him that financial resources are not the most important ones. We can limit what God does in our lives by assuming what is and is not possible. Is there some impossible task you feel God wants you to do? Don't let your estimate of what can't be done keep you from taking on the task. God can do the miraculous; trust him to provide the resources.*

Godly Living in the Last Times/
1 Timothy 3:16—4:6

It is quite true that the way to live a godly life is not an easy matter. But the answer lies in Christ, who came to earth as a man, was proved spotless and pure in his Spirit, was served by angels, was preached among the nations, was accepted by men everywhere and was received up again to his glory in heaven.

4:1But the Holy Spirit tells us clearly that in the last times some in the church will turn away from Christ and become eager followers of teachers with devil-inspired ideas. 2These teachers will tell lies with straight faces and do it so often that their consciences won't even bother them.

³They will say it is wrong to be married and wrong to eat meat, even though God gave these things to well-taught Christians to enjoy and be thankful for. ⁴For everything God made is good, and we may eat it gladly if we are thankful for it, ⁵and if we ask God to bless it, for it is made good by the Word of God and prayer.

⁶If you explain this to the others you will be doing your duty as a worthy pastor who is fed by faith and by the true teaching you have followed.

A THOUGHT: *In opposition to the false teachers, Paul affirms that everything God made is good. We should ask his blessing on his created gifts that give us pleasure and we should thank him for them. This doesn't mean we should abuse what God has made (for example gluttony abuses God's gift of good food, lust abuses God's gift of love, and murder abuses God's gift of life). We should not abuse what God has made, but enjoy these gifts by using them to serve and honor God. Have you thanked God for the good things he has made? Are you using them in a way that is pleasing to God?*

Proverbs for Today/ 21:27

God loathes the gifts of evil men, especially if they are trying to bribe him!

AUGUST 23

Jesus Walks on the Water/ John 6:16–21

That evening Jesus' disciples went down to the shore to wait for him. ¹⁷But as darkness fell and Jesus still hadn't come back, they got into the boat and headed out across the lake toward Capernaum. ¹⁸,¹⁹But soon a gale swept down upon them as they rowed, and the sea grew very rough. They were three or four miles out when suddenly they saw Jesus walking toward the boat! They were terrified, ²⁰but he called out to them and told them not to be afraid. ²¹Then they were willing to let him in, and immediately the boat was where they were going!

A THOUGHT: *The Sea of Galilee is 650 feet below sea level, 150 feet deep, and surrounded by hills. These physical features often lead to sudden windstorms causing extremely high waves. Such storms were part of life on this sea, but nevertheless frightening. When Jesus came to the disciples during a storm, walking on the water, he told them not to be afraid. In this difficult circumstance, Jesus displayed his great power in the middle of this great storm, by immediately bringing the disciples to their destination. Jesus intervened for the disciples when they really needed it. We often experience God's grace in the midst of difficult times. Jesus never leaves us to face difficulty on our own. Let us trust in God and his power when we face hard times.*

Exercise Yourself Spiritually/ 1 Timothy 4:7–11

Don't waste time arguing over foolish ideas and silly myths and legends. Spend your time and energy in the exercise of keeping spiritually fit. 8Bodily exercise is all right, but spiritual exercise is much more important and is a tonic for all you do. So exercise yourself spiritually and practice being a better Christian, because that will help you not only now in this life, but in the next life too. 9,10This is the truth and everyone should accept it. We work hard and suffer much in order that people will believe it, for our hope is in the living God who died for all, and particularly for those who have accepted his salvation.

11Teach these things and make sure everyone learns them well.

A THOUGHT: *Are you in shape physically and spiritually? In our society, much emphasis is placed on physical fitness, but Paul declared that spiritual health is even more important than physical health. We must develop our faith through using the abilities God has given us in the service of the church.*

Proverbs for Today/ 21:28–29

No one believes a liar, but everyone respects the words of an honest man. □ An evil man is stubborn, but a godly man will reconsider.

AUGUST 24

Jesus Is the True Bread from Heaven/ John 6:22–46

The next morning, back across the lake, crowds began gathering on the shore [waiting to see Jesus]. For they knew that he and his disciples had come over together and that the disciples had gone off in their boat, leaving him behind. Several small boats from Tiberias were nearby, 24so when the people saw that Jesus wasn't there, nor his disciples, they got into the boats and went across to Capernaum to look for him.

25When they arrived and found him, they said, "Sir, how did you get here?" 26Jesus replied, "The truth of the matter is that you want to be with me because I fed you, not because you believe in me. 27But you shouldn't be so concerned about perishable things like food. No, spend your energy seeking the eternal life that I, the Messiah, can give you. For God the Father has sent me for this very purpose."

28They replied, "What should we do to satisfy God?" 29Jesus told them, "This is the will of God, that you believe in the one he has sent."

30,31They replied, "You must show us more miracles if you want us to believe you are the Messiah. Give us free bread every day, like our fathers had while they journeyed through the wilderness! As the Scriptures say, 'Moses gave them bread from heaven.'"

32Jesus said, "Moses didn't give it to them. My Father did. And now he offers you true Bread from heaven. 33The true Bread is a Person—the one sent by God from heaven, and he gives life to the world."

34"Sir," they said, "give us that bread every day of our lives!"

35Jesus replied, "I am the Bread of Life. No one coming to me will ever be hungry again. Those believing in me will never thirst. 36But the trouble is, as I have told you before, you haven't believed even though you have seen me. 37But some will come to me—those the Father has given me—and I will never, never reject them. 38For I have come here from heaven to do the will of God who sent me, not to have my own way. 39And this is the will of God, that I should not lose even one of all those he has given me, but that I should raise them to eternal life at the Last Day. 40For it is my Father's will that everyone who sees his Son and believes on him should have eternal life—that I should raise him at the Last Day."

41Then the Jews began to murmur against him because

he claimed to be the Bread from heaven.

42"What?" they exclaimed. "Why, he is merely Jesus the son of Joseph, whose father and mother we know. What is this he is saying, that he came down from heaven?"

43But Jesus replied, "Don't murmur among yourselves about my saying that. 44For no one can come to me unless the Father who sent me draws him to me, and at the Last Day I will cause all such to rise again from the dead. 45As it is written in the Scriptures, 'They shall all be taught of God.' Those the Father speaks to, who learn the truth from him, will be attracted to me. 46(Not that anyone actually sees the Father, for only I have seen him.)

A THOUGHT: *People eat bread to satisfy physical hunger and to sustain physical life. We can satisfy spiritual hunger and sustain spiritual life only by a right relationship with Jesus Christ. No wonder he called himself the Bread of Life. But bread must be eaten to give life, and Christ must be invited into our daily walk to give spiritual life. Jesus criticized those who followed him merely for the physical and temporal benefits they received rather than seeking after relationship with God. We should follow Christ because we need the truth. Many people use religion to gain prestige, comfort, or votes. But those are self-centered motives. True believers follow Jesus simply because they know his way is true life—eternal life.*

Role Models for God's Flock/ 1 Timothy 4:12—5:2

Don't let anyone think little of you because you are young. Be their ideal; let them follow the way you teach and live; be a pattern for them in your love, your faith, and your clean thoughts. 13Until I get there, read and explain the Scriptures to the church; preach God's Word.

14Be sure to use the abilities God has given you through his prophets when the elders of the church laid their hands upon your head. 15Put these abilities to work; throw yourself into your tasks so that everyone may notice your improvement and progress. 16Keep a close watch on all you do and think. Stay true to what is right and God will bless you and use you to help others.

5:1Never speak sharply to an older man, but plead with him respectfully just as though he were your own father. Talk to the younger men as you would to much loved brothers. 2Treat the older women as mothers, and the girls as your sisters, thinking only pure thoughts about them.

A Thought: *Timothy was a young leader. It would be easy for older Christians to look down on him because of his youth. He had to earn the respect of his elders by setting an example in his teaching and living, of love, faith, and purity. Regardless of your age, God can use you. Whether you are young or old, don't think of your age as a handicap. Live so others can see Christ in you.*

Proverbs for Today/ 21:30–31

No one, regardless of how shrewd or well-advised he is, can stand against the Lord. □ Go ahead and prepare for the conflict, but victory comes from God.

AUGUST 25

Jesus Alone Has the Words of Eternal Life/
John 6:47–71

"How earnestly I tell you this—anyone who believes in me already has eternal life! 48-51Yes, I am the Bread of Life! When your fathers in the wilderness ate bread from the skies, they all died. But the Bread from heaven gives eternal life to everyone who eats it. I am that Living Bread that came down out of heaven. Anyone eating this Bread shall live forever; this Bread is my flesh given to redeem humanity."

52Then the Jews began arguing with each other about what he meant. "How can this man give us his flesh to eat?" they asked.

53So Jesus said it again, "With all the earnestness I possess I tell you this: Unless you eat the flesh of the Messiah and drink his blood, you cannot have eternal life within you. 54But anyone who does eat my flesh and drink my blood has eternal life, and I will raise him at the Last Day. 55For my flesh is the true food, and my blood is the true drink. 56Everyone who eats my flesh and drinks my blood is in me, and I in him. 57I live by the power of the living Father who sent me, and in the same way those who partake of me shall live because of me! 58I am the true Bread from heaven; and anyone who eats this Bread shall live forever, and not die as your fathers did—though they ate bread from heaven." 59(He preached this sermon in the synagogue in Capernaum.)

60Even his disciples said, "This is very hard to understand. Who can tell what he means?"

61Jesus knew within himself that his disciples were complaining and said to them, "Does *this* offend you? 62Then what will you think if you see me, the Messiah, return to heaven again? 63Only the Holy Spirit gives eternal life. Those born only once, with physical birth, will never receive this gift. But now I have told you how to get this true spiritual life. 64But some of you don't believe me." (For Jesus knew from the beginning who didn't believe and knew the one who would betray him.)

65And he remarked, "That is what I meant when I said that no one can come to me unless the Father attracts him to me."

66At this point many of his disciples turned away and deserted him.

67Then Jesus turned to the Twelve and asked, "Are you going too?"

68Simon Peter replied, "Master, to whom shall we go? You alone have the words that give eternal life, 69and we believe them and know you are the holy Son of God."

70Then Jesus said, "I chose the twelve of you, and one is a devil." 71He was speaking of Judas, son of Simon Iscariot, one of the Twelve, who would betray him.

A THOUGHT: *There is no middle ground with Jesus. When he asked the disciples if they would also leave, Jesus was showing that they could either accept or reject him. Jesus was not trying to repel people with his teachings. He was simply telling the truth. The more the people heard Jesus' real message, the more they divided into two camps—the honest seekers who wanted to understand more, and those who rejected Jesus because they didn't like what they heard.*

Helping Older Widows in the Church/
1 Timothy 5:3–10

The church should take loving care of women whose husbands have died, if they don't have anyone else to help them. 4But if they have children or grandchildren, these are the ones who should take the responsibility, for kindness should begin at home, supporting needy parents. This is something that pleases God very much.

⁵The church should care for widows who are poor and alone in the world, if they are looking to God for his help and spending much time in prayer; ⁶but not if they are spending their time running around gossiping, seeking only pleasure and thus ruining their souls. ⁷This should be your church rule so that the Christians will know and do what is right.

⁸But anyone who won't care for his own relatives when they need help, especially those living in his own family, has no right to say he is a Christian. Such a person is worse than the heathen.

⁹A widow who wants to become one of the special church workers should be at least sixty years old and have been married only once. ¹⁰She must be well thought of by everyone because of the good she has done. Has she brought up her children well? Has she been kind to strangers as well as to other Christians? Has she helped those who are sick and hurt? Is she always ready to show kindness?

A THOUGHT: *Because there were no pensions, no social security, no life insurance, and few honorable jobs for women, widows were usually unable to support themselves. If a widow had no children or other family members to support her, she was doomed to poverty. From the beginning the church took care of its widows, who in turn gave valuable service to the church.*

The responsibility for caring for the helpless naturally falls first on their families, the people whose lives are closely linked with theirs. But families cannot always provide all the necessary care. The church should support those who have no families, and it should also help others—whether elderly, young, handicapped, ill, or poverty stricken—with their emotional and spiritual needs. Often families who are caring for their own helpless members have heavy burdens. They may need extra money, a listening ear, a helping hand, or a word of encouragement. Interestingly, those who are helped often turn around and help others so that the church turns into a circle of caring.

Proverbs for Today/ 22:1

If you must choose, take a good name rather than great riches; for to be held in loving esteem is better than silver and gold.

AUGUST 26

Jesus at the Feast of Tabernacles/ John 7:1–13

After this, Jesus went to Galilee, going from village to village, for he wanted to stay out of Judea where the Jewish leaders were plotting his death. 2But soon it was time for the Tabernacle Ceremonies, one of the annual Jewish holidays, 3and Jesus' brothers urged him to go to Judea for the celebration.

"Go where more people can see your miracles!" they scoffed. 4"You can't be famous when you hide like this! If you're so great, prove it to the world!" 5For even his brothers didn't believe in him.

6Jesus replied, "It is not the right time for me to go now. But you can go anytime and it will make no difference, 7for the world can't hate you; but it does hate me, because I accuse it of sin and evil. 8You go on, and I'll come later when it is the right time." 9So he remained in Galilee.

10But after his brothers had left for the celebration, then he went too, though secretly, staying out of the public eye. 11The Jewish leaders tried to find him at the celebration and kept asking if anyone had seen him. 12There was a lot of discussion about him among the crowds. Some said, "He's a wonderful man," while others said, "No, he's duping the public." 13But no one had the courage to speak out for him in public for fear of reprisals from the Jewish leaders.

A THOUGHT: *Jesus' brothers had a difficult time believing in him. Some of these brothers would eventually become leaders in the church, but here they are still wondering if Jesus will prove once and for all his messianic claims. After Jesus died and rose again, they finally believed. Today we have every reason to believe, because we have the full record of Jesus' miracles, death, and resurrection. We also have the evidence of what the gospel has done in people's lives for hundreds of years. Don't miss this opportunity to believe in God's Son.*

Instructions to Younger Widows/ 1 Timothy 5:11–16

The younger widows should not become members of this special group because after awhile they are likely to disregard their vow to Christ and marry again. 12And so they will stand condemned because they broke their first promise. 13Besides, they are likely to be lazy and spend their time gossiping around from house to house, getting into other people's business. 14So I think it is better for these younger widows to marry again and have children, and take care of their own homes; then no one will be able to say anything against them. 15For I am afraid that some of them have already turned away from the church and been led astray by Satan.

16Let me remind you again that a widow's relatives must take care of her, and not leave this to the church to do. Then the church can spend its money for the care of widows who are all alone and have nowhere else to turn.

A THOUGHT: *Apparently older widows took a vow by which they committed themselves to work for the church in exchange for financial support. Three out of four women today eventually are widowed, and most of the older women in our churches have lost their husbands. Does your church provide an avenue of service for these women? Could you help match their gifts and abilities with your church's needs?*

Proverbs for Today/ 22:2–4

The rich and the poor are alike before the Lord who made them all. □ A prudent man foresees the difficulties ahead and prepares for them; the simpleton goes blindly on and suffers the consequences. □ True humility and respect for the Lord lead a man to riches, honor and long life.

AUGUST 27

Jesus Preaches in the Temple/ John 7:14–36

Then, midway through the festival, Jesus went up to the Temple and preached openly. 15The Jewish leaders were surprised when they heard him. "How can he know so much when he's never been to our schools?" they asked.

16So Jesus told them, "I'm not teaching you my own thoughts, but those of God who sent me. 17If any of you really determines to do God's will, then you will certainly know whether my teaching is from God or is merely my own. 18Anyone presenting his own ideas is looking for praise for himself, but anyone seeking to honor the one who sent him is a good and true person. 19None of *you* obeys the laws of Moses! So why pick on *me* for breaking them? Why kill *me* for this?"

20The crowd replied, "You're out of your mind! Who's trying to kill you?"

21,22,23Jesus replied, "I worked on the Sabbath by healing a man, and you were surprised. But you work on the Sabbath, too, whenever you obey Moses' law of circumcision (actually, however, this tradition of circumcision is older than the Mosaic law); for if the correct time for circumcising your children falls on the Sabbath, you go ahead and do it, as you should. So why should I be condemned for making a man completely well on the Sabbath? 24Think this through and you will see that I am right."

25Some of the people who lived there in Jerusalem said among themselves, "Isn't this the man they are trying to kill? 26But here he is preaching in public, and they say nothing to him. Can it be that our leaders have learned, after all, that he really is the Messiah? 27But how could he be? For we know where this man was born; when Christ comes, he will just appear and no one will know where he comes from."

28So Jesus, in a sermon in the Temple, called out, "Yes, you know me and where I was born and raised, but I am the representative of one you don't know, and he is Truth. 29I know him because I was with him, and he sent me to you."

30Then the Jewish leaders sought to arrest him; but no hand was laid on him, for God's time had not yet come.

31Many among the crowds at the Temple believed on him. "After all," they said, "what miracles do you expect the Messiah to do that this man hasn't done?"

32When the Pharisees heard that the crowds were in this mood, they and the chief priests sent officers to arrest Jesus. 33But Jesus told them, "[Not yet!] I am to be here a little longer. Then I shall return to the one who sent me. 34You will search for me but not find me. And you won't be able to come where I am!"

35The Jewish leaders were puzzled by this statement. "Where is he planning to go?" they asked. "Maybe he is thinking of leaving the country and going as a missionary among the Jews in other lands, or maybe even to the Gentiles! 36What does he mean about our looking for him and not being able to find him, and, 'You won't be able to come where I am'?"

A THOUGHT: *The Pharisees spent their lives trying to appear holy by keeping the meticulous rules they had added to God's Law. Jesus' accusation that they didn't keep Moses' laws stung them deeply. In spite of their pompous pride in themselves and their rules, they did not even fulfill a legalistic religion, for they were living far below what the law of Moses required. Jesus' followers should do more than the moral law requires, going beyond and beneath the mere do's and don'ts of the Law to the spirit of the Law. The spirit of God's Law is captured in love for God and one's neighbor. We must never allow rules to keep us from following the true intent of God's Law. Obedience to God must be from the heart.*

Honor Church Leaders/ 1 Timothy 5:17–25

Pastors who do their work well should be paid well and should be highly appreciated, especially those who work hard at both preaching and teaching. 18For the Scriptures say, "Never tie up the mouth of an ox when it is treading out the grain—let him eat as he goes along!" And in another place, "Those who work deserve their pay!"

19Don't listen to complaints against the pastor unless there are two or three witnesses to accuse him. 20If he has really sinned, then he should be rebuked in front of the whole church so that no one else will follow his example.

21I solemnly command you in the presence of God and the Lord Jesus Christ and of the holy angels to do this whether the pastor is a special friend of yours or not. All must be treated exactly the same. 22Never be in a hurry about choosing a pastor; you may overlook his sins and it will look as if you approve of them. Be sure that you yourself stay away from all sin. 23(By the way, this doesn't mean you should completely give up drinking wine. You ought to take a little sometimes as medicine for your stomach because you are sick so often.)

24Remember that some men, even pastors, lead sinful lives and everyone knows it. In such situations you can do something about it. But in other cases only the judgment day will reveal the terrible truth. 25In the same way, everyone knows how much good some pastors do, but sometimes their good deeds aren't known until long afterward.

A THOUGHT: *Faithful, diligent church leaders should be supported and appreciated. Too often they are targets for criticism because the congregation has unrealistic expectations. How do you treat your church leaders? Do you enjoy finding fault, or do you show your appreciation? Do they receive enough financial support to allow them to live without worry and provide for the needs of their families? Jesus and Paul emphasized the importance of supporting ministers who lead and teach us.*

Proverbs for Today/ 22:5–6

The rebel walks a thorny, treacherous road; the man who values his soul will stay away. Teach a child to choose the right path, and when he is older he will remain upon it.

AUGUST 28

Rivers of Living Water/ John 7:37–53

On the last day, the climax of the holidays, Jesus shouted to the crowds, "If anyone is thirsty, let him come to me and drink. 38For the Scriptures declare that rivers of living water shall flow from the inmost being of anyone who believes in me." 39(He was speaking of the Holy Spirit, who would be given to everyone believing in him; but the Spirit had not yet been given, because Jesus had not yet returned to his glory in heaven.)

40When the crowds heard him say this, some of them declared, "This man surely is the prophet who will come just before the Messiah." 41,42Others said, "He *is* the Messiah." Still others, "But he *can't* be! Will the Messiah come from *Galilee?* For the Scriptures clearly state that the Messiah will be born of the royal line of David, in *Bethlehem,* the village where David was born." 43So the crowd was divided about him. 44And some wanted him arrested, but no one touched him.

45The Temple police who had been sent to arrest him returned to the chief priests and Pharisees. "Why didn't you bring him in?" they demanded.

⁴⁶"He says such wonderful things!" they mumbled. "We've never heard anything like it."

⁴⁷"So you also have been led astray?" the Pharisees mocked. ⁴⁸"Is there a single one of us Jewish rulers or Pharisees who believes he is the Messiah? ⁴⁹These stupid crowds do, yes; but what do they know about it? A curse upon them anyway!"

⁵⁰Then Nicodemus spoke up. (Remember him? He was the Jewish leader who came secretly to interview Jesus.) ⁵¹"Is it legal to convict a man before he is even tried?" he asked.

⁵²They replied, "Are you a wretched Galilean too? Search the Scriptures and see for yourself—no prophets will come from Galilee!"

⁵³Then the meeting broke up and everybody went home.

A THOUGHT: *The crowd was asking questions about Jesus. As a result, some believed, others were hostile, and others disqualified Jesus as the Messiah because he was from Nazareth, not Bethlehem (according to the prophets, the Messiah would come from Bethlehem, the city of David). But Jesus was born in Bethlehem, although he grew up in Nazareth. We, along with the crowd, are left to decide what we believe about Jesus—Is he the Son of God, the Savior of the world or not? If we claim that he is the Son of God, we are called to be completely committed to following him.*

Instructions to Masters and Slaves/ 1 Timothy 6:1–5

Christian slaves should work hard for their owners and respect them; never let it be said that Christ's people are poor workers. Don't let the name of God or his teaching be laughed at because of this. ²If their owner is a Christian, that is no excuse for slowing down; rather they should work all the harder because a brother in the faith is being helped by their efforts.

Teach these truths, Timothy, and encourage all to obey them.

³Some may deny these things, but they are the sound, wholesome teachings of the Lord Jesus Christ and are the foundation for a godly life. ⁴Anyone who says anything different is both proud and stupid. He is quibbling over the meaning of Christ's words and stirring up arguments ending in jealousy and anger, which only lead to

name-calling, accusations, and evil suspicions. 5These arguers—their minds warped by sin—don't know how to tell the truth; to them the Good News is just a means of making money. Keep away from them.

A THOUGHT: *In Paul's culture there was a great social and legal gulf separating masters and slaves. But as Christians, masters and slaves became spiritual equals, brothers or sisters in the faith. Here Paul gives guidelines for how Christian slaves and Christian masters should relate to one another. His counsel for the master/slave relationship can be applied to the employer/ employee relationship today. Employees should work hard, showing respect for their employers. In turn, employers should be fair. Our work should reflect our faithfulness to and love for Christ.*

Proverbs for Today/ 22:7
Just as the rich rule the poor, so the borrower is servant to the lender.

AUGUST 29

Jesus Forgives an Adulterous Woman/ John 8:1–11
Jesus returned to the Mount of Olives, 2but early the next morning he was back again at the Temple. A crowd soon gathered, and he sat down and talked to them. 3As he was speaking, the Jewish leaders and Pharisees brought a woman caught in adultery and placed her out in front of the staring crowd.

4"Teacher," they said to Jesus, "this woman was caught in the very act of adultery. 5Moses' law says to kill her. What about it?"

6They were trying to trap him into saying something they could use against him, but Jesus stooped down and wrote in the dust with his finger. 7They kept demanding an answer, so he stood up again and said, "All right, hurl the stones at her until she dies. But only he who never sinned may throw the first!"

8Then he stooped down again and wrote some more in the dust. 9And the Jewish leaders slipped away one by one, beginning with the eldest, until only Jesus was left in front of the crowd with the woman.

10Then Jesus stood up again and said to her, "Where are your accusers? Didn't even one of them condemn you?"

11"No, sir," she said.

And Jesus said, "Neither do I. Go and sin no more."

A THOUGHT: *By mentioning the throwing of stones, Jesus could not be accused of being against the Law. But by saying that only a sinless person could throw the first stone, he highlighted the importance of compassion and forgiveness. When others are caught in sin, are you quick to pass judgment? To do so is to act as though you have never sinned. It is God's role to judge, not ours. Our role is to show forgiveness and compassion.*

Paul Defines True Riches/ 1 Timothy 6:6–12

Do you want to be truly rich? You already are if you are happy and good. 7After all, we didn't bring any money with us when we came into the world, and we can't carry away a single penny when we die. 8So we should be well satisfied without money if we have enough food and clothing. 9But people who long to be rich soon begin to do all kinds of wrong things to get money, things that hurt them and make them evil-minded and finally send them to hell itself. 10For the love of money is the first step toward all kinds of sin. Some people have even turned away from God because of their love for it, and as a result have pierced themselves with many sorrows.

11Oh, Timothy, you are God's man. Run from all these evil things and work instead at what is right and good, learning to trust him and love others, and to be patient and gentle. 12Fight on for God. Hold tightly to the eternal life which God has given you, and which you have confessed with such a ringing confession before many witnesses.

A THOUGHT: *Despite almost overwhelming evidence to the contrary, most people still believe that money brings happiness. Rich people craving greater riches can be caught in an endless cycle which only ends in ruin and destruction. How can you keep away from the love of money? Paul gives us some principles: (1) realize that one day riches will all be gone; (2) be content with what you have; (3) monitor what you are willing to do to get more money; (4) love people more than money; (5) love God's work more than money; (6) freely share what you have with others.*

Proverbs for Today/ 22:8–9

The unjust tyrant will reap disaster and his reign of terror shall end. □ Happy is the generous man, the one who feeds the poor.

AUGUST 30

Jesus' Testimony Is from God the Father/ John 8:12–31a

Later, in one of his talks, Jesus said to the people, "I am the Light of the world. So if you follow me, you won't be stumbling through the darkness, for living light will flood your path."

13The Pharisees replied, "You are boasting—and lying!"

14Jesus told them, "These claims are true even though I make them concerning myself. For I know where I came from and where I am going, but you don't know this about me. 15You pass judgment on me without knowing the facts. I am not judging you now; 16but if I were, it would be an absolutely correct judgment in every respect, for I have with me the Father who sent me. 17Your laws say that if two men agree on something that has happened, their witness is accepted as fact. 18Well, I am one witness, and my Father who sent me is the other."

19"Where is your father?" they asked.

Jesus answered, "You don't know who I am, so you don't know who my Father is. If you knew me, then you would know him too."

20Jesus made these statements while in the section of the Temple known as the Treasury. But he was not arrested, for his time had not yet run out.

21Later he said to them again, "I am going away; and you will search for me, and die in your sins. And you cannot come where I am going."

22The Jews asked, "Is he planning suicide? What does he mean, 'You cannot come where I am going'?"

23Then he said to them, "You are from below; I am from above. You are of this world; I am not. 24That is why I said that you will die in your sins; for unless you believe that I am the Messiah, the Son of God, you will die in your sins."

25"Tell us who you are," they demanded.

He replied, "I am the one I have always claimed to be. 26I could condemn you for much and teach you much, but I won't, for I say only what I am told to by the one who sent me; and he is Truth." 27But they still didn't understand that he was talking to them about God.

28So Jesus said, "When you have killed the Messiah, then you will realize that I am he and that I have not been telling you my own ideas, but have spoken what the Father taught me. 29And he who sent me is with me—he has not deserted me—for I always do those things that are pleasing to him."

30,31Then many of the Jewish leaders who heard him say these things began believing him to be the Messiah.

A THOUGHT: *People will die in their sins if they reject Christ because they are rejecting the only way to be rescued from sin. Sadly, many are so taken up with the values of this world that they are blind to the priceless gift Christ offers. Where are you looking for meaning and value? Don't focus on this world's values and miss what is most valuable—eternal life with God.*

Fulfill Your Calling/ 1 Timothy 6:13–16

I command you before God who gives life to all, and before Christ Jesus who gave a fearless testimony before Pontius Pilate, 14that you fulfill all he has told you to do, so that no one can find fault with you from now until our Lord Jesus Christ returns. 15For in due season Christ will be revealed from heaven by the blessed and only Almighty God, the King of kings and Lord of lords, 16who alone can never die, who lives in light so terrible that no human being can approach him. No mere man has ever seen him, nor ever will. Unto him be honor and everlasting power and dominion forever and ever. Amen.

A THOUGHT: *God has called each Christian to a particular sphere of ministry in this life. God has called some to be plumbers, lawyers, doctors, and carpenters, others he has called to be teachers, mothers, bankers, and artists. Whatever calling in life God has given us we must be diligent to fulfill it. True contentment in life can be found in serving others through the calling God has given each one of us. God will call us into account for the degree of faithfulness we show in our calling. Let us strive to be found faithful.*

Proverbs for Today/ 22:10–12

Throw out the mocker, and you will be rid of tension, fighting and quarrels. ▢ He who values grace and truth is the king's friend. ▢ The Lord preserves the upright but ruins the plans of the wicked.

AUGUST 31

Jesus Is the Eternal Son Sent from God/ John 8:31b–59

Jesus said to them, "You are truly my disciples if you live as I tell you to, 32and you will know the truth, and the truth will set you free."

33"But we are descendants of Abraham," they said, "and have never been slaves to any man on earth! What do you mean, 'set free'?"

34Jesus replied, "You are slaves of sin, every one of you. 35And slaves don't have rights, but the Son has every right there is! 36So if the Son sets you free, you will indeed be free—37(Yes, I realize that you are descendants of Abraham!) And yet some of you are trying to kill me because my message does not find a home within your hearts. 38I am telling you what I saw when I was with my Father. But you are following the advice of *your* father."

39"Our father is Abraham," they declared.

"No!" Jesus replied, "for if he were, you would follow his good example. 40But instead you are trying to kill me—and all because I told you the truth I heard from God. Abraham wouldn't do a thing like that! 41No, you are obeying your *real* father when you act that way."

They replied, "We were not born out of wedlock—our true Father is God himself."

42Jesus told them, "If that were so, then you would love me, for I have come to you from God. I am not here on my own, but he sent me. 43Why can't you understand what I am saying? It is because you are prevented from doing so! 44For you are the children of your father the devil and you love to do the evil things he does. He was a murderer from the beginning and a hater of truth—there is not an iota of truth in him. When he lies, it is perfectly normal; for he is the father of liars. 45And so when I tell the truth, you just naturally don't believe it!

46"Which of you can truthfully accuse me of one single sin? [No one!] And since I am telling you the truth, why don't you believe me? 47Anyone whose Father is God listens gladly to the words of God. Since you don't, it proves you aren't his children."

48"You Samaritan! Foreigner! Devil!" the Jewish leaders snarled. "Didn't we say all along you were possessed by a demon?"

49"No," Jesus said, "I have no demon in me. For I honor my Father—and you dishonor me. 50And though I have no wish to make myself great, God wants this for me and judges [those who reject me]. 51With all the earnestness I have I tell you this—no one who obeys me shall ever die!"

52The leaders of the Jews said, "Now we know you are possessed by a demon. Even Abraham and the mightiest prophets died, and yet you say that obeying you will keep a man from dying! 53So you are greater than our father Abraham, who died? And greater than the prophets, who died? Who do you think you are?" 54Then Jesus told them this: "If I am merely boasting about myself, it doesn't count. But it is my Father—and you claim him as your God—who is saying these glorious things about me. 55But you do not even know him. I do. If I said otherwise, I would be as great a liar as you! But it is true—I know him and fully obey him. 56Your father Abraham rejoiced to see my day. He knew I was coming and was glad."

57*The Jewish leaders:* "You aren't even fifty years old—sure, you've seen Abraham!"

58*Jesus:* "The absolute truth is that I was in existence before Abraham was ever born!"

59At that point the Jewish leaders picked up stones to kill him. But Jesus was hidden from them, and walked past them and left the Temple.

A THOUGHT: *Jesus himself is the truth that sets us free. He is the source of truth, the perfect standard of what is right. He frees us from the consequences of sin, from self-deception, and from the deception of Satan. He shows us clearly the way to eternal life with God.*

Thus Jesus does not give us freedom to do what we want, but freedom to follow God. As we seek to live for God, Jesus' perfect truth frees us to be all that God meant us to be.

Paul's Instructions to the Rich/ 1 Timothy 6:17–21

Tell those who are rich not to be proud and not to trust in their money, which will soon be gone, but their pride and trust should be in the living God who always richly gives us all we need for our enjoyment. 18Tell them to use their money to do good. They should be rich in good works and should give happily to those in need, always being ready to share with others whatever God has given them. 19By doing this they will be storing up real treasure for themselves in heaven—it is the only safe investment for eternity! And they will be living a fruitful Christian life down here as well.

20Oh, Timothy, don't fail to do these things that God entrusted to you. Keep out of foolish arguments with those who boast of their "knowledge" and thus prove their lack of it. 21Some of these people have missed the most important thing in life—they don't know God. May God's mercy be upon you.

Sincerely,
Paul

A THOUGHT: *Ephesus was a wealthy city and the Ephesian church probably had many wealthy members. Paul advised Timothy to deal with that potential problem by teaching that the possession of riches carries great responsibility. Those who have money must be generous, not arrogant because they have a lot to give. They must be careful not to put their trust in money instead of in the living God for their security. Even if we don't have material wealth, we can be rich in good works toward others. No matter how poor we are, we have something to share with someone.*

Proverbs for Today/ 22:13

The lazy man is full of excuses. "I can't go to work!" he says. "If I go outside I might meet a lion in the street and be killed!"

Jesus Heals a Blind Man/ John 9:1–12

As Jesus was walking along, he saw a man blind from birth.

2"Master," his disciples asked him, "why was this man born blind? Was it a result of his own sins or those of his parents?"

3"Neither," Jesus answered. "But to demonstrate the power of God. 4All of us must quickly carry out the tasks assigned us by the one who sent me, for there is little time left before the night falls and all work comes to an end. 5But while I am still here in the world, I give it my light."

6Then he spat on the ground and made mud from the spittle and smoothed the mud over the blind man's eyes, 7and told him, "Go and wash in the Pool of Siloam" (the word "Siloam" means "Sent"). So the man went where he was sent and washed and came back seeing!

8His neighbors and others who knew him as a blind beggar asked each other, "Is this the same fellow—that beggar?"

9Some said yes, and some said no. "It can't be the same man," they thought, "but he surely looks like him!"

And the beggar said, "I *am* the same man!"

10Then they asked him how in the world he could see. What had happened?

11And he told them, "A man they call Jesus made mud and smoothed it over my eyes and told me to go to the Pool of Siloam and wash off the mud. I did, and I can see!"

12"Where is he now?" they asked.

"I don't know," he replied.

A THOUGHT: *A common belief in Jewish culture was that calamity or suffering was the result of some great sin. But Christ used this man's suffering to teach about faith and to glorify God. We live in a fallen world where good behavior is not always rewarded and bad behavior not always punished. Therefore, innocent people often suffer. If God took suffering away whenever we asked, we would follow him for comfort and convenience, not out of love and devotion. Regardless of the reasons for our suffering, Jesus has the power to help us deal with it. When you suffer from a disease, tragedy, or a handicap, try not to ask, "Why did this happen to me?" or "What did I do wrong?" Instead, ask God to give you strength and offer you a deeper perspective on what is happening.*

Paul Encourages Timothy to Be Faithful/ 2 Timothy 1:1–8

From: Paul, Jesus Christ's missionary, sent out by God to tell men and women everywhere about the eternal life he has promised them through faith in Jesus Christ.

²*To:* Timothy, my dear son. May God the Father and Christ Jesus our Lord shower you with his kindness, mercy and peace.

³How I thank God for you, Timothy. I pray for you every day, and many times during the long nights I beg my God to bless you richly. He is my fathers' God, and mine, and my only purpose in life is to please him.

⁴How I long to see you again. How happy I would be, for I remember your tears as we left each other.

⁵I know how much you trust the Lord, just as your mother Eunice and your grandmother Lois do; and I feel sure you are still trusting him as much as ever.

⁶This being so, I want to remind you to stir into flame the strength and boldness that is in you, that entered into you when I laid my hands upon your head and blessed you. ⁷For the Holy Spirit, God's gift, does not want you to be afraid of people, but to be wise and strong, and to love them and enjoy being with them.

⁸If you will stir up this inner power, you will never be afraid to tell others about our Lord, or to let them know that I am your friend even though I am here in jail for Christ's sake. You will be ready to suffer with me for the Lord, for he will give you strength in suffering.

A THOUGHT: *At the time of his ordination, Timothy received special gifts of the Spirit to enable him to serve the church. In telling Timothy to stir those gifts into flames, Paul was encouraging him to persevere. Timothy did not need new revelations or new gifts; he needed the courage and self–discipline to hang onto the truth and use the gifts he had already received. If he would step out boldly in faith and proclaim the gospel once again, the Holy Spirit would go with him and give him power. The power of the Holy Spirit is also available to us who believe. We too can be effective and faithful servants in the area God has called us, by relying on the power of the Spirit.*

Proverbs for Today/ 22:14

A prostitute is a dangerous trap; those cursed of God are caught in it.

SEPTEMBER 2

A Pharisaic Investigation/ John 9:13–41

Then some people took the man [whom Jesus had healed] to the Pharisees. 14Now as it happened, this all occurred on a Sabbath. 15Then the Pharisees asked him all about it. So he told them how Jesus had smoothed the mud over his eyes, and when it was washed away, he could see!

16Some of them said, "Then this fellow Jesus is not from God, because he is working on the Sabbath."

Others said, "But how could an ordinary sinner do such miracles?" So there was a deep division of opinion among them.

17Then the Pharisees turned on the man who had been blind and demanded, "This man who opened your eyes— who do you say he is?"

"I think he must be a prophet sent from God," the man replied.

18The Jewish leaders wouldn't believe he had been blind, until they called in his parents 19and asked them, "Is this your son? Was he born blind? If so, how can he see?"

20His parents replied, "We know this is our son and that he was born blind, 21but we don't know what happened to make him see, or who did it. He is old enough to speak for himself. Ask him."

22,23They said this in fear of the Jewish leaders who had announced that anyone saying Jesus was the Messiah would be excommunicated.

24So for the second time they called in the man who had been blind and told him, "Give the glory to God, not to Jesus, for we know Jesus is an evil person."

25"I don't know whether he is good or bad," the man replied, "but I know this: *I was blind, and now I see!*"

26"But what did he do?" they asked. "How did he heal you?"

27"Look!" the man exclaimed. "I told you once; didn't you listen? Why do you want to hear it again? Do you want to become his disciples too?"

28Then they cursed him and said, "You are his disciple, but we are disciples of Moses. 29We know God has spoken to Moses, but as for this fellow, we don't know anything about him."

30"Why, that's very strange!" the man replied. "He can heal blind men, and yet you don't know anything about him! 31Well, God doesn't listen to evil men, but he has open ears to those who worship him and do his will. 32Since the world began there has never been anyone who could open the eyes of someone born blind. 33If this man were not from God, he couldn't do it."

34"You illegitimate bastard, you!" they shouted. "Are you trying to teach *us?*" And they threw him out.

35When Jesus heard what had happened, he found the man and said, "Do you believe in the Messiah?"

36The man answered, "Who is he, sir, for I want to."

37"You have seen him," Jesus said, "and he is speaking to you!"

38"Yes, Lord," the man said, "I believe!" And he worshiped Jesus.

39Then Jesus told him, "I have come into the world to give sight to those who are spiritually blind and to show those who think they see that they are blind."

40The Pharisees who were standing there asked, "Are you saying we are blind?"

41"If you were blind, you wouldn't be guilty," Jesus replied. "But your guilt remains because you claim to know what you are doing.

A THOUGHT: *The Pharisees sought every angle they could think of to discredit Jesus' healing of this blind man. But the overwhelming evidence clearly showed that Jesus had healed the man. Jesus' healing ministry pointed to the fact that he was the Messiah. Faced with the same evidence—along with the rest of the New Testament— who do you say is the Messiah?*

Stand Firm for the Gospel/ 2 Timothy 1:9–14

It is he who saved us and chose us for his holy work, not because we deserved it but because that was his plan long before the world began—to show his love and kindness to us through Christ. 10And now he has made all of this plain to us by the coming of our Savior Jesus Christ, who broke the power of death and showed us the way of everlasting life through trusting him. 11And God has chosen me to be his missionary, to preach to the Gentiles and teach them.

12That is why I am suffering here in jail and I am certainly not ashamed of it, for I know the one in whom I trust, and I am sure that he is able to safely guard all that I have given him until the day of his return.

13Hold tightly to the pattern of truth I taught you, especially concerning the faith and love Christ Jesus offers you. 14Guard well the splendid, God-given ability you received as a gift from the Holy Spirit who lives within you.

A THOUGHT: *Timothy was in a time of transition. He had been Paul's bright young helper; soon he would be on his own as leader of a difficult, but critically important church. Although his responsibilities were changing, Timothy was not without help. He had everything he needed to face the future, if he would hold tightly onto it. When you are facing difficult transitions, it is good to follow Paul's advice to Timothy and look back at your experience. Who is the foundation of your faith? What gifts has the Holy Spirit given you? How can you build on the foundation that has already been laid, using the gifts you have already been given?*

Proverbs for Today/ 22:15

A youngster's heart is filled with rebellion, but punishment will drive it out of him.

SEPTEMBER 3

Jesus Is the Good Shepherd/ John 10:1–21

"Anyone refusing to walk through the gate into a sheepfold, who sneaks over the wall, must surely be a thief! 2For a shepherd comes through the gate. 3The gatekeeper opens the gate for him, and the sheep hear his voice and come to him; and he calls his own sheep by name and leads them out. 4He walks ahead of them; and they follow him, for they recognize his voice. 5They won't follow a stranger but will run from him, for they don't recognize his voice."

6Those who heard Jesus use this illustration didn't understand what he meant, 7so he explained it to them.

"I am the Gate for the sheep," he said. 8"All others who came before me were thieves and robbers. But the true sheep did not listen to them. 9Yes, I am the Gate. Those who come in by way of the Gate will be saved and will go in and out and find green pastures. 10The thief's purpose is to steal, kill and destroy. My purpose is to give life in all its fullness.

11"I am the Good Shepherd. The Good Shepherd lays down his life for the sheep. 12A hired man will run when he sees a wolf coming and will leave the sheep, for they aren't his and he isn't their shepherd. And so the wolf leaps on them and scatters the flock. 13The hired man runs because he is hired and has no real concern for the sheep.

14"I am the Good Shepherd and know my own sheep, and they know me, 15just as my Father knows me and I know the Father; and I lay down my life for the sheep. 16I have other sheep, too, in another fold. I must bring them also, and they will heed my voice; and there will be one flock with one Shepherd.

17"The Father loves me because I lay down my life that I may have it back again. 18No one can kill me without my consent—I lay down my life voluntarily. For I have the right and power to lay it down when I want to and also the right and power to take it again. For the Father has given me this right."

19When he said these things, the Jewish leaders were again divided in their opinions about him. 20Some of them said, "He has a demon or else is crazy. Why listen to a man like that?"

21Others said, "This doesn't sound to us like a man possessed by a demon! Can a demon open the eyes of blind men?"

A THOUGHT: *At night, sheep were often gathered into a sheepfold to protect them from thieves, weather, or wild animals. The sheepfolds were caves, sheds, or open areas surrounded by walls made of stones or branches. The shepherd often slept in the fold to protect the sheep. Just as a shepherd cares for his sheep, Jesus, the Good Shepherd, cares for his flock (those who follow him). In speaking of himself as the Good Shepherd, Jesus was casting himself in the role of Yahweh (the special Old Testament name for God), who in Psalm 23 is pictured as a shepherd caring for his sheep.*

The Blessing of Onesiphorus/ 2 Timothy 1:15–18

As you know, all the Christians who came here from Asia have deserted me; even Phygellus and Hermogenes are gone. 16May the Lord bless Onesiphorus and all his family, because he visited me and encouraged me often. His visits revived me like a breath of fresh air, and he was never ashamed of my being in jail. 17In fact, when he came to Rome he searched everywhere trying to find me, and finally did. 18May the Lord give him a special blessing at the day of Christ's return. And you know better than I can tell you how much he helped me at Ephesus.

A THOUGHT: *Onesiphorus is an model for us of Christlike living. He visited Paul in prison many times in order to encourage him. He was not ashamed to be associated with this prisoner. "'For I was hungry and you fed me; I was thirsty and you gave me water; I was a stranger and you invited me into your homes; naked and you clothed me; sick and in prison and you visited me.'" (Matthew 25:35–36). We meet Christ in serving those in need. Let us be like Onesiphorus, serving with genuine love and concern those in need without being ashamed.*

Proverbs for Today/ 22:16

He who gains by oppressing the poor or by bribing the rich shall end in poverty.

SEPTEMBER 4

Jesus Is God's Son/ John 10:22–42

It was winter, and Jesus was in Jerusalem at the time of the Dedication Celebration. He was at the Temple, walking through the section known as Solomon's Hall. 24The Jewish leaders surrounded him and asked, "How long are you going to keep us in suspense? If you are the Messiah, tell us plainly."

25"I have already told you, and you don't believe me," Jesus replied. "The proof is in the miracles I do in the name of my Father. 26But you don't believe me because you are not part of my flock. 27My sheep recognize my voice, and I know them, and they follow me. 28I give them eternal life and they shall never perish. No one shall snatch them away from me, 29for my Father has given them to me, and he is more powerful than anyone else, so no one can kidnap them from me. 30I and the Father are one."

31Then again the Jewish leaders picked up stones to kill him.

32Jesus said, "At God's direction I have done many a miracle to help the people. For which one are you killing me?"

33They replied, "Not for any good work, but for blasphemy; you, a mere man, have declared yourself to be God."

34,35,36"In your own Law it says that men are gods!" he replied. "So if the Scripture, which cannot be untrue, speaks of those as gods to whom the message of God came, do you call it blasphemy when the one sanctified and sent into the world by the Father says, 'I am the Son of God'? 37Don't believe me unless I do miracles of God. 38But if I do, believe them even if you don't believe me. Then you will become convinced that the Father is in me, and I in the Father."

39Once again they started to arrest him. But he walked away and left them, 40and went beyond the Jordan River to stay near the place where John was first baptizing. 41And many followed him.

"John didn't do miracles," they remarked to one another, "but all his predictions concerning this man have come true." 42And many came to the decision that he was the Messiah.

A THOUGHT: *These Jewish leaders were waiting for the signs and answers they thought would convince them of Jesus' identity. Thus they couldn't hear the truth Jesus was giving them. Jesus tried to correct their mistaken ideas, but they clung to the wrong idea of what kind of Messiah God would send. Such blindness still keeps people away from Jesus. They want him on their own terms; they do not want him if it means changing their whole lives.*

Suffer As a Good Soldier of Christ/ 2 Timothy 2:1–7

Oh, Timothy, my son, be strong with the strength Christ Jesus gives you. ²For you must teach others those things you and many others have heard me speak about. Teach these great truths to trustworthy men who will, in turn, pass them on to others.

³Take your share of suffering as a good soldier of Jesus Christ, just as I do, ⁴and as Christ's soldier do not let yourself become tied up in worldly affairs, for then you cannot satisfy the one who has enlisted you in his army. ⁵Follow the Lord's rules for doing his work, just as an athlete either follows the rules or is disqualified and wins no prize. ⁶Work hard, like a farmer who gets paid well if he raises a large crop. ⁷Think over these three illustrations, and may the Lord help you to understand how they apply to you.

A THOUGHT: *Timothy would face suffering as he preached and taught, but Paul told him that he should be willing to take it for the sake of Christ. Christian leaders are not the only ones to suffer. Soldiers, athletes, and farmers all must discipline themselves and be willing to sacrifice to achieve the results they want. Like soldiers, we have to give up worldly security and endure rigorous discipline. Like athletes, we must train hard and follow the rules. Like farmers, we must work extremely hard. We keep going in spite of suffering because of the hope of victory, the vision of winning, and the hope of harvest. All our suffering is made worthwhile by our goal of glorifying God, winning people to Christ, and one day living eternally with him.*

Proverbs for Today/ 22:17–19

Listen to this wise advice; follow it closely, for it will do you good, and you can pass it on to others: *Trust in the Lord.*

SEPTEMBER 5

Lazarus Dies/ John 11:1–29

Do you remember Mary, who poured the costly perfume on Jesus' feet and wiped them with her hair? Well, her brother Lazarus, who lived in Bethany with Mary and her sister Martha, was sick. 3So the two sisters sent a message to Jesus telling him, "Sir, your good friend is very, very sick."

4But when Jesus heard about it he said, "The purpose of his illness is not death, but for the glory of God. I, the Son of God, will receive glory from this situation."

5Although Jesus was very fond of Martha, Mary, and Lazarus, 6he stayed where he was for the next two days and made no move to go to them. 7Finally, after the two days, he said to his disciples, "Let's go to Judea."

8But his disciples objected. "Master," they said, "only a few days ago the Jewish leaders in Judea were trying to kill you. Are you going there again?"

9Jesus replied, "There are twelve hours of daylight every day, and during every hour of it a man can walk safely and not stumble. 10Only at night is there danger of a wrong step, because of the dark." 11Then he said, "Our friend Lazarus has gone to sleep, but now I will go and waken him!"

12,13The disciples, thinking Jesus meant Lazarus was having a good night's rest, said, "That means he is getting better!" But Jesus meant Lazarus had died.

14Then he told them plainly, "Lazarus is dead. 15And for your sake, I am glad I wasn't there, for this will give you another opportunity to believe in me. Come, let's go to him."

16Thomas, nicknamed "The Twin," said to his fellow disciples, "Let's go too—and die with him."

17When they arrived at Bethany, they were told that Lazarus had already been in his tomb for four days. 18Bethany was only a couple of miles down the road from Jerusalem, 19and many of the Jewish leaders had come to pay their respects and to console Martha and Mary on their loss. 20When Martha got word that Jesus was coming, she went to meet him. But Mary stayed at home.

21Martha said to Jesus, "Sir, if you had been here, my brother wouldn't have died. 22And even now it's not too late, for I know that God will bring my brother back to life again, if you will only ask him to."

23Jesus told her, "Your brother will come back to life again."

24"Yes," Martha said, "when everyone else does, on Resurrection Day."

25Jesus told her, "I am the one who raises the dead and gives them life again. Anyone who believes in me, even though he dies like anyone else, shall live again. 26 He is given eternal life for believing in me and shall never perish. Do you believe this, Martha?"

27"Yes, Master," she told him. "I believe you are the Messiah, the Son of God, the one we have so long awaited."

28Then she left him and returned to Mary and, calling her aside from the mourners, told her, "He is here and wants to see you." 29So Mary went to him at once.

A THOUGHT: *Jesus loved this family and often stayed with them. He knew their pain, but did not respond immediately. His delay had a specific purpose. God's timing, especially his delays, may make us think he is not answering or is not answering the way we want. But he will meet all our needs according to his perfect schedule and purpose. Patiently await his timing.*

Suffering for Christ/ 2 Timothy 2:8–15a

Don't ever forget the wonderful fact that Jesus Christ was a Man, born into King David's family; and that he was God, as shown by the fact that he rose again from the dead. 9It is because I have preached these great truths that I am in trouble here and have been put in jail like a criminal. But the Word of God is not chained, even though I am. 10I am more than willing to suffer if that will bring salvation and eternal glory in Christ Jesus to those God has chosen.

11I am comforted by this truth, that when we suffer and die for Christ it only means that we will begin living with him in heaven. 12And if we think that our present service for him is hard, just remember that some day we are going to sit with him and rule with him. But if we give up when we suffer, and turn against Christ, then he must turn against us. 13Even when we are too weak to have any faith left, he remains faithful to us and will help us, for he cannot disown us who are part of himself, and he will always carry out his promises to us.

14Remind your people of these great facts, and command them in the name of the Lord not to argue over unimportant things. Such arguments are confusing and useless, and even harmful. 15Work hard so God can say to you, "Well done."

A Thought: *We are called to suffer for Christ—it is part of our identification with him. God is faithful to his children, and although we may suffer great hardships here, he promises that someday we will live eternally with him. We must remember that we are God's servants—we belong to him. We are to take up our crosses and follow him, no matter what comes our way. Living out the Good News in serving others will involve suffering. True discipleship is very costly. Are we willing to follow Christ to the point of suffering for him?*

Proverbs for Today/ 22:20–21

In the past, haven't I been right? Then believe what I am telling you now, and share it with others.

SEPTEMBER 6

Jesus Raises Lazarus from the Dead/ John 11:30–46

Now Jesus had stayed outside the village, at the place where Martha met him. 31When the Jewish leaders who were at the house trying to console Mary saw her leave so hastily, they assumed she was going to Lazarus' tomb to weep; so they followed her.

32When Mary arrived where Jesus was, she fell down at his feet, saying, "Sir, if you had been here, my brother would still be alive."

33When Jesus saw her weeping and the Jewish leaders wailing with her, he was moved with indignation and deeply troubled. 34"Where is he buried?" he asked them.

They told him, "Come and see." 35Tears came to Jesus' eyes.

36"They were close friends," the Jewish leaders said. "See how much he loved him."

37,38But some said, "This fellow healed a blind man— why couldn't he keep Lazarus from dying?"

And again Jesus was moved with deep anger. Then they came to the tomb. It was a cave with a heavy stone rolled across its door.

39"Roll the stone aside," Jesus told them.

But Martha, the dead man's sister, said, "By now the smell will be terrible, for he has been dead four days."

40"But didn't I tell you that you will see a wonderful miracle from God if you believe?" Jesus asked her.

41So they rolled the stone aside. Then Jesus looked up to heaven and said, "Father, thank you for hearing me. 42(You always hear me, of course, but I said it because of all these people standing here, so that they will believe you sent me.)" 43Then he shouted, "Lazarus, come out!"

44And Lazarus came—bound up in the gravecloth, his face muffled in a head swath. Jesus told them, "Unwrap him and let him go!"

45And so at last many of the Jewish leaders who were with Mary and saw it happen, finally believed on him. 46But some went away to the Pharisees and reported it to them.

A THOUGHT: *Jesus has power over life and death because he is the Creator of life. He who is Life can surely restore life. In this passage, Jesus heals Lazarus, his good friend. This demonstration of power should cause us to recognize the One sent from the Father— the Creator of life. Let us worship the Father, Son, and Spirit in wonder at such marvelous and gracious acts as this—the raising of a dead man to life. Let us also take hope in the resurrection, for Jesus here demonstrates that he holds the power of the resurrection—a power he secured by his own death and resurrection— forever conquering death.*

Be a Good Student of God's Word/
2 Timothy 2:15b–21

Be a good workman, one who does not need to be ashamed when God examines your work. Know what his Word says and means. 16Steer clear of foolish discussions which lead people into the sin of anger with each other. 17Things will be said that will burn and hurt for a long time to come. Hymenaeus and Philetus, in their love of argument, are men like that. 18They have left the path of truth, preaching the lie that the resurrection of the dead has already occurred; and they have weakened the faith of some who believe them.

19But God's truth stands firm like a great rock, and nothing can shake it. It is a foundation stone with these words written on it: "The Lord knows those who are really his," and "A person who calls himself a Christian should not be doing things that are wrong."

20In a wealthy home there are dishes made of gold and silver as well as some made from wood and clay. The expensive dishes are used for guests, and the cheap ones are used in the kitchen or to put garbage in. 21If you stay away from sin you will be like one of these dishes made of purest gold—the very best in the house— so that Christ himself can use you for his highest purposes.

A THOUGHT: *Life on earth is not a script which we meaninglessly act out. It is a time of deciding whether we will live for God or not, and then living out what we have decided. Because God will examine what kinds of workers we have been for him, we should build our lives on his Word and build his Word into our lives. God's Word alone tells us how to live for him and serve him. Believers who ignore the Bible will certainly be ashamed at the judgment. Consistent and diligent study of God's Word is vital, or else we will be lulled into neglecting relationship with God— our true purpose for living.*

Proverbs for Today/ 22:22–23

Don't rob the poor and sick! For the Lord is their defender. If you injure them he will punish you.

SEPTEMBER 7

The Prophecy of the High Priest/ John 11:47–57

Then the chief priests and Pharisees convened a council to discuss the situation.

"What are we going to do?" they asked each other. "For this man certainly does miracles. 48If we let him alone the whole nation will follow him—and then the Roman army will come and kill us and take over the Jewish government."

49And one of them, Caiaphas, who was High Priest that year, said, "You stupid idiots— 50let this one man die for the people—why should the whole nation perish?"

51This prophecy that Jesus should die for the entire

nation came from Caiaphas in his position as High Priest—he didn't think of it by himself, but was inspired to say it. 52It was a prediction that Jesus' death would not be for Israel only, but for all the children of God scattered around the world. 53So from that time on the Jewish leaders began plotting Jesus' death.

54Jesus now stopped his public ministry and left Jerusalem; he went to the edge of the desert, to the village of Ephraim, and stayed there with his disciples.

55The Passover, a Jewish holy day, was near, and many country people arrived in Jerusalem several days early so that they could go through the cleansing ceremony before the Passover began. 56They wanted to see Jesus, and as they gossiped in the Temple, they asked each other, "What do you think? Will he come for the Passover?" 57Meanwhile the chief priests and Pharisees had publicly announced that anyone seeing Jesus must report him immediately so that they could arrest him.

A THOUGHT: *The Jewish leaders knew that if they didn't stop Jesus, the Romans would discipline them. Rome gave partial freedom to the Jews as long as they were quiet and obedient. Jesus' miracles often caused a disturbance. The leaders feared that Rome's displeasure would cause them to lose their jobs or be punished. Caiaphas had the solution for their dilemma—let Jesus be put to death on behalf of the nation. Little did he realize that he was inspired by God to predict Jesus' death.*

Flee Evil Desires/ 2 Timothy 2:22–26

Run from anything that gives you the evil thoughts that young men often have, but stay close to anything that makes you want to do right. Have faith and love, and enjoy the companionship of those who love the Lord and have pure hearts.

23Again I say, don't get involved in foolish arguments which only upset people and make them angry. 24God's people must not be quarrelsome; they must be gentle, patient teachers of those who are wrong. 25Be humble when you are trying to teach those who are mixed up concerning the truth. For if you talk meekly and courteously to them they are more likely, with God's help, to turn away from their wrong ideas and believe what is true. 26Then they will come to their senses and escape from

Satan's trap of slavery to sin which he uses to catch them whenever he likes, and then they can begin doing the will of God.

A THOUGHT: *Running away is sometimes considered cowardly. But wise people realize that removing oneself physically from temptation is often prudent. Timothy, a young man, was warned to run from anything that produced evil thoughts. Perhaps you experience a recurring temptation that is difficult to resist. Remove yourself physically from the situation. Knowing when to run is as important in spiritual battle as knowing when and how to fight.*

Proverbs for Today/ 22:24–25

Keep away from angry, short-tempered men, lest you learn to be like them and endanger your soul.

SEPTEMBER 8

Mary Anoints Jesus' Feet/ John 12:1–11

Six days before the Passover ceremonies began, Jesus arrived in Bethany where Lazarus was—the man he had brought back to life. 2A banquet was prepared in Jesus' honor. Martha served, and Lazarus sat at the table with him. 3Then Mary took a jar of costly perfume made from essence of nard, and anointed Jesus' feet with it and wiped them with her hair. And the house was filled with fragrance.

4But Judas Iscariot, one of his disciples—the one who would betray him—said, 5"That perfume was worth a fortune. It should have been sold and the money given to the poor." 6Not that he cared for the poor, but he was in charge of the disciples' funds and often dipped into them for his own use!

7Jesus replied, "Let her alone. She did it in preparation for my burial. 8You can always help the poor, but I won't be with you very long."

9When the ordinary people of Jerusalem heard of his arrival, they flocked to see him and also to see Lazarus— the man who had come back to life again. 10Then the chief priests decided to kill Lazarus too, 11for it was because of him that many of the Jewish leaders had deserted and believed in Jesus as their Messiah.

A THOUGHT: *Nard was a fragrant ointment imported from the mountains of India. Thus it was very expensive. The amount Mary used was worth a year's wages. Nard was used to anoint kings; Mary may have been anointing Jesus as her kingly Messiah. This act and Jesus' response to it do not teach us to ignore the poor so we can do extravagant things for Christ. This was a unique act for a specific occasion—an anointing for Jesus' burial and a public declaration of faith in him as Messiah. Jesus' words should have taught Judas a valuable lesson about the worth of money. Unfortunately, he did not take heed; soon he would sell his Master's life for 30 pieces of silver.*

The Character of the Last Days/ 2 Timothy 3:1–10a

You may as well know this too, Timothy, that in the last days it is going to be very difficult to be a Christian. ²For people will love only themselves and their money; they will be proud and boastful, sneering at God, disobedient to their parents, ungrateful to them, and thoroughly bad. ³They will be hardheaded and never give in to others; they will be constant liars and troublemakers and will think nothing of immorality. They will be rough and cruel, and sneer at those who try to be good. ⁴They will betray their friends; they will be hotheaded, puffed up with pride, and prefer good times to worshiping God. ⁵They will go to church, yes, but they won't really believe anything they hear. Don't be taken in by people like that.

⁶They are the kind who craftily sneak into other people's homes and make friendships with silly, sin-burdened women and teach them their new doctrines. ⁷Women of that kind are forever following new teachers, but they never understand the truth. ⁸And these teachers fight truth just as Jannes and Jambres fought against Moses. They have dirty minds, warped and twisted, and have turned against the Christian faith.

⁹But they won't get away with all this forever. Some day their deceit will be well known to everyone, as was the sin of Jannes and Jambres.

¹⁰But you know from watching me that I am not that kind of person.

A THOUGHT: *In many parts of the world today it does not seem especially difficult to be a Christian. No one is jailed for reading the Bible or executed for preaching Christ. But when we read Paul's descriptive list of behavior in the last days, we recognize it as a description of our society—even, unfortunately, of many*

Christians. There is a comfortable acceptance of a superficial Christianity that should cause us to be uncomfortable. Check your life against this list. Don't give in to society's pressures. Stand up against its evil ways by living as God would have his people live.

Proverbs for Today/ 22:26–27

Unless you have the extra cash on hand, don't countersign a note. Why risk everything you own? They'll even take your bed!

SEPTEMBER 9

The Crowd Hails Jesus As King/ John 12:12–19

The next day, the news that Jesus was on the way to Jerusalem swept through the city, and a huge crowd of Passover visitors 13took palm branches and went down the road to meet him, shouting, "The Savior! God bless the King of Israel! Hail to God's Ambassador!"

14Jesus rode along on a young donkey, fulfilling the prophecy that said: 15"Don't be afraid of your King, people of Israel, for he will come to you meekly, sitting on a donkey's colt!"

16(His disciples didn't realize at the time that this was a fulfillment of prophecy; but after Jesus returned to his glory in heaven, then they noticed how many prophecies of Scripture had come true before their eyes.)

17And those in the crowd who had seen Jesus call Lazarus back to life were telling all about it. 18That was the main reason why so many went out to meet him—because they had heard about this mighty miracle.

19Then the Pharisees said to each other, "We've lost. Look—the whole world has gone after him!"

A THOUGHT: *The people who were praising God for giving them a king had the wrong idea about Jesus. They were sure he would be a national leader who would restore their nation to its former glory, and thus they were deaf to the words of their prophets and blind to Jesus' real mission. When it became apparent that Jesus was not going to fulfill their hopes, many people turned against him. Loyalties change all to quickly in accordance with unfulfilled expectations. We must remain loyal to Jesus in spite of circumstances, for genuine faith goes beyond what can be seen and felt to trust in what God has promised.*

God's Word Can Equip Us for Righteousness/
2 Timothy 3:10b–17

You know what I believe and the way I live and what I want. You know my faith in Christ and how I have suffered. You know my love for you, and my patience. 11You know how many troubles I have had as a result of my preaching the Good News. You know about all that was done to me while I was visiting in Antioch, Iconium and Lystra, but the Lord delivered me. 12Yes, and those who decide to please Christ Jesus by living godly lives will suffer at the hands of those who hate him. 13In fact, evil men and false teachers will become worse and worse, deceiving many, they themselves having been deceived by Satan.

14But you must keep on believing the things you have been taught. You know they are true for you know that you can trust those of us who have taught you. 15You know how, when you were a small child, you were taught the holy Scriptures; and it is these that make you wise to accept God's salvation by trusting in Christ Jesus. 16The whole Bible was given to us by inspiration from God and is useful to teach us what is true and to make us realize what is wrong in our lives; it straightens us out and helps us do what is right. 17It is God's way of making us well prepared at every point, fully equipped to do good to everyone.

A THOUGHT: *In our zeal for the truth of Scripture, we must never forget its purpose—to equip us to do good to others. We do not study God's Word simply to increase our own knowledge or to prepare us to win arguments. We do not even study it primarily to learn how to save our own souls (most people are Christians before they begin intensively studying the Bible). We study Scripture so that we will know how to do Christ's work in the world. Our knowledge of God's Word is not useful unless we use it to do good to others.*

Proverbs for Today/ 22:28–29

Do not move the ancient boundary marks. That is stealing. □ Do you know a hard-working man? He shall be successful and stand before kings!

SEPTEMBER 10

Jesus Predicts His Death/ John 12:20–36

Some Greeks who had come to Jerusalem to attend the Passover 21paid a visit to Philip, who was from Bethsaida, and said, "Sir, we want to meet Jesus." 22Philip told Andrew about it, and they went together to ask Jesus.

23,24Jesus replied that the time had come for him to return to his glory in heaven, and that "I must fall and die like a kernel of wheat that falls into the furrows of the earth. Unless I die I will be alone—a single seed. But my death will produce many new wheat kernels—a plentiful harvest of new lives. 25If you love your life down here—you will lose it. If you despise your life down here— you will exchange it for eternal glory.

26"If these Greeks want to be my disciples, tell them to come and follow me, for my servants must be where I am. And if they follow me, the Father will honor them. 27Now my soul is deeply troubled. Shall I pray, 'Father, save me from what lies ahead'? But that is the very reason why I came! 28Father, bring glory and honor to your name."

Then a voice spoke from heaven saying, "I have already done this, and I will do it again." 29When the crowd heard the voice, some of them thought it was thunder, while others declared an angel had spoken to him.

30Then Jesus told them, "The voice was for your benefit, not mine. 31The time of judgment for the world has come— and the time when Satan, the prince of this world, shall be cast out. 32 And when I am lifted up [on the cross], I will draw everyone to me." 33He said this to indicate how he was going to die.

34"Die?" asked the crowd. "We understood that the Messiah would live forever and never die. Why are you saying he will die? What Messiah are you talking about?"

35Jesus replied, "My light will shine out for you just a little while longer. Walk in it while you can, and go where you want to go before the darkness falls, for then it will be too late for you to find your way. 36Make use of the Light while there is still time; then you will become light bearers."

After saying these things, Jesus went away and was hidden from them.

A Thought: *Jesus knew his crucifixion lay ahead, and he dreaded it. He knew he would have to take the sins of the world on himself, and he knew this would separate him from his Father. He wanted to be delivered from this horrible death, but he knew that God sent him into the world to die for our sins, in our place. Jesus said no to his own desires in order to obey his Father and bring glory to him. Although we will never have to face such a difficult situation, we are still called to obedience. Whatever the Father asks, we should do his will and bring glory to his name.*

Paul's Charge to Timothy/ 2 Timothy 4:1–4

And so I solemnly urge you before God and before Christ Jesus—who will some day judge the living and the dead when he appears to set up his Kingdom— 2to preach the Word of God urgently at all times, whenever you get the chance, in season and out, when it is convenient and when it is not. Correct and rebuke your people when they need it, encourage them to do right, and all the time be feeding them patiently with God's Word.

3For there is going to come a time when people won't listen to the truth, but will go around looking for teachers who will tell them just what they want to hear. 4They won't listen to what the Bible says but will blithely follow their own misguided ideas.

A Thought: *It was important for Timothy to preach the gospel so that the Christian faith could spread throughout the world. We believe in Christ today because people like Timothy were faithful to their mission. It is still vitally important for the church to preach the gospel. Half the people who have ever lived are alive today, and most of them do not know Jesus. He is coming soon, and he wants to find a faithful church waiting for him. It may be inconvenient to take a stand for Christ or to tell others about his love, but preaching the Word of God is the most important responsibility the church has been given. Be prepared, courageous, and sensitive to God-given opportunities to share the Good News.*

Proverbs for Today/ 23:1–3

When dining with a rich man, be on your guard and don't stuff yourself, though it all tastes so good; for he is trying to bribe you, and no good is going to come of his invitation.

SEPTEMBER 11

Isaiah Predicted Unbelief/ John 12:37–50

But despite all the miracles Jesus had done, most of the people would not believe he was the Messiah. 38This is exactly what Isaiah the prophet had predicted: "Lord, who will believe us? Who will accept God's mighty miracles as proof?" 39But they couldn't believe, for as Isaiah also said: 40"God has blinded their eyes and hardened their hearts so that they can neither see nor understand nor turn to me to heal them." 41Isaiah was referring to Jesus when he made this prediction, for he had seen a vision of the Messiah's glory.

42However, even many of the Jewish leaders believed him to be the Messiah but wouldn't admit it to anyone because of their fear that the Pharisees would excommunicate them from the synagogue; 43for they loved the praise of men more than the praise of God.

44Jesus shouted to the crowds, "If you trust me, you are really trusting God. 45For when you see me, you are seeing the one who sent me. 46I have come as a Light to shine in this dark world, so that all who put their trust in me will no longer wander in the darkness. 47If anyone hears me and doesn't obey me, I am not his judge—for I have come to save the world and not to judge it. 48But all who reject me and my message will be judged at the Day of Judgment by the truths I have spoken. 49For these are not my own ideas, but I have told you what the Father said to tell you. 50And I know his instructions lead to eternal life; so whatever he tells me to say, I say!"

A THOUGHT: *Jesus had performed many miracles, but most people still didn't believe in him. Likewise, many today won't believe despite all God does. Don't be discouraged if your witness for Christ doesn't turn as many to him as you'd like. Your job is to continue as a faithful witness. You are not responsible for the decisions of others, but simply to reach out to others.*

Paul Realizes That His End Is Near/ 2 Timothy 4:5–8

Stand steady, and don't be afraid of suffering for the Lord. Bring others to Christ. Leave nothing undone that you ought to do.

6I say this because I won't be around to help you very much longer. My time has almost run out. Very soon now I will be on my way to heaven. 7I have fought long and hard for my Lord, and through it all I have kept true to him. And now the time has come for me to stop fighting and rest. 8In heaven a crown is waiting for me which the Lord, the righteous Judge, will give me on that great day of his return. And not just to me, but to all those whose lives show that they are eagerly looking forward to his coming back again.

A THOUGHT: *As he neared the end of his life, Paul could confidently say that he had been faithful to his call. Thus he faced death calmly; he knew he would be rewarded at Christ's Second Coming. Is your life preparing you for death? Do you share Paul's confident expectation of meeting Christ? The Good News is that the heavenly reward is not just for giants of the faith, like Paul, but for all who "are eagerly looking forward" to Jesus' Second Coming. Paul gave these words to encourage Timothy, and us, that no matter how difficult the fight seems—keep fighting. We will discover when we are with Jesus Christ that it was all worth it.*

Proverbs for Today/ 23:4–5

Don't weary yourself trying to get rich. Why waste your time? For riches can disappear as though they had the wings of a bird!

SEPTEMBER 12

Jesus Washes the Disciples' Feet/ John 13:1–20

Jesus knew on the evening of Passover Day that it would be his last night on earth before returning to his Father. During supper the devil had already suggested to Judas Iscariot, Simon's son, that this was the night to carry out his plan to betray Jesus. Jesus knew that the Father had given him everything and that he had come from God and would return to God. And how he loved his disciples! 4So he got up from the supper table, took off his robe, wrapped a towel around his loins, 5poured water into a basin, and began to wash the disciples' feet and to wipe them with the towel he had around him.

6When he came to Simon Peter, Peter said to him, "Master, you shouldn't be washing our feet like this!"

7Jesus replied, "You don't understand now why I am doing it; some day you will."

8"No," Peter protested, "you shall never wash my feet!"

"But if I don't, you can't be my partner," Jesus replied.

9Simon Peter exclaimed, "Then wash my hands and head as well—not just my feet!"

10Jesus replied, "One who has bathed all over needs only to have his feet washed to be entirely clean. Now you are clean—but that isn't true of everyone here." 11For Jesus knew who would betray him. That is what he meant when he said, "Not all of you are clean."

12After washing their feet he put on his robe again and sat down and asked, "Do you understand what I was doing? 13You call me 'Master' and 'Lord,' and you do well to say it, for it is true. 14And since I, the Lord and Teacher, have washed your feet, you ought to wash each other's feet. 15I have given you an example to follow: do as I have done to you. 16How true it is that a servant is not greater than his master. Nor is the messenger more important than the one who sends him. 17You know these things—now do them! That is the path of blessing.

18"I am not saying these things to all of you; I know so well each one of you I chose. The Scripture declares, 'One who eats supper with me will betray me,' and this will soon come true. 19I tell you this now so that when it happens, you will believe on me.

20"Truly, anyone welcoming my messenger is welcoming me. And to welcome me is to welcome the Father who sent me."

A THOUGHT: *Jesus was the model servant, and he showed this attitude to his disciples. Washing guests' feet was a job for household servants when guests arrived. But Jesus wrapped a towel around him, as the lowliest slave would do, and washed his disciples' feet. If even he, God in the flesh, is willing to serve with such humility, we, his followers, must also be servants, willing to serve in humility to bring glory to God. Are you willing to follow Christ's example of serving? Whom can you serve today?*

Paul's Final Instructions and Greetings/
2 Timothy 4:9–22

Please come as soon as you can, 10for Demas has left me. He loved the good things of this life and went to Thessalonica. Crescens has gone to Galatia, Titus to Dalmatia. 11Only Luke is with me. Bring Mark with you when you come, for I need him. 12(Tychicus is gone too, as I sent him to Ephesus.) 13When you come, be sure to bring the coat I left at Troas with Brother Carpus, and also the books, but especially the parchments.

14Alexander the coppersmith has done me much harm. The Lord will punish him, 15but be careful of him, for he fought against everything we said.

16The first time I was brought before the judge no one was here to help me. Everyone had run away. I hope that they will not be blamed for it. 17But the Lord stood with me and gave me the opportunity to boldly preach a whole sermon for all the world to hear. And he saved me from being thrown to the lions. 18Yes, and the Lord will always deliver me from all evil and will bring me into his heavenly Kingdom. To God be the glory forever and ever. Amen.

19Please say "hello" for me to Priscilla and Aquila and those living at the home of Onesiphorus. 20Erastus stayed at Corinth, and I left Trophimus sick at Miletus.

21Do try to be here before winter. Eubulus sends you greetings, and so do Pudens, Linus, Claudia, and all the others. 22May the Lord Jesus Christ be with your spirit.

Farewell,
Paul

A Thought: *Only Luke was with Paul at this time, and Paul was feeling lonely. Tychicus, one of his most trusted companions, had already left for Ephesus. He missed his young helpers Timothy and Mark. Mark, also called John and John Mark, had left Paul on his first missionary journey, and this had greatly angered Paul. But Mark later proved himself a worthy helper, and Paul recognized him as a good friend and trusted Christian leader. This list of Paul's coworkers should serve to remind us that Paul was not out to bring himself fame, he was a fellow servant of Christ. Paul felt the need of the body of Christ, he was not a spiritual lone ranger. We all have need of each other in the body of Christ. Let us remember that each part of the body is necessary for the building up of the whole.*

Proverbs for Today/ 23:6–8

Don't associate with evil men; don't long for their favors and gifts. Their kindness is a trick; they want to use you as their pawn. The delicious food they serve will turn sour in your stomach and you will vomit it, and have to take back your words of appreciation for their "kindness."

SEPTEMBER 13

Judas Betrays Jesus/ John 13:21–38

Now Jesus was in great anguish of spirit and exclaimed, "Yes, it is true—one of you will betray me." 22The disciples looked at each other, wondering whom he could mean. 23Since I was sitting next to Jesus at the table, being his closest friend, 24Simon Peter motioned to me to ask him who it was who would do this terrible deed.

25So I turned and asked him, "Lord, who is it?"

26He told me, "It is the one I honor by giving the bread dipped in the sauce."

And when he had dipped it, he gave it to Judas, son of Simon Iscariot.

27As soon as Judas had eaten it, Satan entered into him. Then Jesus told him, "Hurry—do it now."

28None of the others at the table knew what Jesus meant. 29Some thought that since Judas was their treasurer, Jesus was telling him to go and pay for the food or to give some money to the poor. 30Judas left at once, going out into the night.

31As soon as Judas left the room, Jesus said, "My time has come; the glory of God will soon surround me—and God shall receive great praise because of all that happens to me. 32And God shall give me his own glory, and this so very soon. 33Dear, dear children, how brief are these moments before I must go away and leave you! Then, though you search for me, you cannot come to me—just as I told the Jewish leaders.

34"And so I am giving a new commandment to you now— love each other just as much as I love you. 35Your strong love for each other will prove to the world that you are my disciples."

36Simon Peter said, "Master, where are you going?"

And Jesus replied, "You can't go with me now; but you will follow me later."

37"But why can't I come now?" he asked, "for I am ready to die for you."

38Jesus answered, "Die for me? No—three times before the cock crows tomorrow morning, you will deny that you even know me!

A THOUGHT: *Love is not simply warm feelings; it is instead an attitude that reveals itself in action. How can we love others as Christ loves us? We can demonstrate Christ's love by helping when it's not convenient, by giving when it hurts, by devoting energy to others' welfare rather than our own, by absorbing hurts from others without complaining or fighting back. This kind of loving is hard to do. That is why people will notice when you do it and will know you are empowered by a supernatural source—the Holy Spirit. We are called to be like Christ—a servant who came to give his life for many. Let us express this same kind of love to those around us.*

Titus Appointed to Strengthen the Churches/
Titus 1:1–6

From: Paul, the slave of God and the messenger of Jesus Christ.

I have been sent to bring faith to those God has chosen and to teach them to know God's truth—the kind of truth that changes lives—so that they can have eternal life, which God promised them before the world began—and he cannot lie. 3And now in his own good time he has revealed this Good News and permits me to tell it to everyone. By command of God our Savior I have been trusted to do this work for him.

4*To:* Titus, who is truly my son in the affairs of the Lord.

May God the Father and Christ Jesus our Savior give you his blessings and his peace.

5I left you there on the island of Crete so that you could do whatever was needed to help strengthen each of its churches, and I asked you to appoint pastors in every city who would follow the instructions I gave you. 6The men you choose must be well thought of for their good lives; they must have only one wife and their children must love the Lord and not have a reputation for being wild or disobedient to their parents.

A Thought: *In one short phrase, Paul gives us insight into his reason for living. He calls himself a slave (or servant) of God—that is, he was committed to obeying God. This obedience led him to spend his life telling others about Christ. How would you describe your purpose in life? To what are you devoted?*

Proverbs for Today/ 23:9–11

Don't waste your breath on a rebel. He will despise the wisest advice. □ Don't steal the land of defenseless orphans by moving their ancient boundary marks, for their Redeemer is strong; he himself will accuse you.

SEPTEMBER 14

Jesus Is the Way to the Father/ John 14:1–14

"Let not your heart be troubled. You are trusting God, now trust in me. 2,3There are many homes up there where my Father lives, and I am going to prepare them for your coming. When everything is ready, then I will come and get you, so that you can always be with me where I am. If this weren't so, I would tell you plainly. 4And you know where I am going and how to get there."

5"No, we don't," Thomas said. "We haven't any idea where you are going, so how can we know the way?"

6Jesus told him, "I am the Way—yes, and the Truth and the Life. No one can get to the Father except by means of me. 7If you had known who I am, then you would have known who my Father is. From now on you know him—and have seen him!"

8Philip said, "Sir, show us the Father and we will be satisfied."

9Jesus replied, "Don't you even yet know who I am, Philip, even after all this time I have been with you? Anyone who has seen me has seen the Father! So why are you asking to see him? 10Don't you believe that I am in the Father and the Father is in me? The words I say are not my own but are from my Father who lives in me. And he does his work through me. 11Just believe it—that

I am in the Father and the Father is in me. Or else believe it because of the mighty miracles you have seen me do.

12,13"In solemn truth I tell you, anyone believing in me shall do the same miracles I have done, and even greater ones, because I am going to be with the Father. You can ask him for *anything*, using my name, and I will do it, for this will bring praise to the Father because of what I, the Son, will do for you. 14Yes, ask *anything*, using my name, and I will do it!

A THOUGHT: *This is one of the most basic and important passages in Scripture. It asks, "How can I find God?" and answers, "Only through Jesus." Jesus is the Way because he is both God and man. By uniting our lives with his, we are united with God. Trust Jesus to take you to the Father, and all the benefits of being God's child will be yours.*

Requirements for Church Leadership/ Titus 1:7–16

These pastors must be men of blameless lives because they are God's ministers. They must not be proud or impatient; they must not be drunkards or fighters or greedy for money. 8They must enjoy having guests in their homes and must love all that is good. They must be sensible men, and fair. They must be clean minded and level headed. 9Their belief in the truth which they have been taught must be strong and steadfast, so that they will be able to teach it to others and show those who disagree with them where they are wrong.

10For there are many who refuse to obey; this is especially true among those who say that all Christians must obey the Jewish laws. But this is foolish talk; it blinds people to the truth, 11and it must be stopped. Already whole families have been turned away from the grace of God. Such teachers are only after your money. 12One of their own men, a prophet from Crete, has said about them, "These men of Crete are all liars; they are like lazy animals, living only to satisfy their stomachs." 13And this is true. So speak to the Christians there as sternly as necessary to make them strong in the faith, 14and to stop them from listening to Jewish folk tales and the demands of men who have turned their backs on the truth.

15A person who is pure of heart sees goodness and

purity in everything; but a person whose own heart is evil and untrusting finds evil in everything, for his dirty mind and rebellious heart color all he sees and hears. 16Such persons claim they know God, but from seeing the way they act, one knows they don't. They are rotten and disobedient, worthless so far as doing anything good is concerned.

A THOUGHT: *The Greek word for "pastors" in this passage is "elders." Paul briefly describes some qualifications that an elder should have. He gave Timothy a similar set of instructions for the church in Ephesus. Notice that most of the qualifications involve the elder's character, not his knowledge or skill. A person's lifestyle and relationships provide a window into his or her character. Consider these qualifications as you evaluate a person for a position of leadership. While it is important to have an elder or pastor who can effectively preach God's Word, it is even more important to have one who can live out God's Word and be an example for others to follow.*

Proverbs for Today/ 23:12
Don't refuse to accept criticism; get all the help you can.

SEPTEMBER 15

The Comforter/ John 14:15–31
"If you love me, obey me; and I will ask the Father and he will give you another Comforter, and he will never leave you. 17He is the Holy Spirit, the Spirit who leads into all truth. The world at large cannot receive him, for it isn't looking for him and doesn't recognize him. But you do, for he lives with you now and some day shall be in you. 18No, I will not abandon you or leave you as orphans in the storm—I will come to you. 19In just a little while I will be gone from the world, but I will still be present with you. For I will live again—and you will too. 20When I come back to life again, you will know that I am in my Father, and you in me, and I in you. 21The one who obeys me is the one who loves me; and because he loves me, my Father will love him; and I will too, and I will reveal myself to him."

22Judas (not Judas Iscariot, but his other disciple with

that name) said to him, "Sir, why are you going to reveal yourself only to us disciples and not to the world at large?"

23Jesus replied, "Because I will only reveal myself to those who love me and obey me. The Father will love them too, and we will come to them and live with them. 24Anyone who doesn't obey me doesn't love me. And remember, I am not making up this answer to your question! It is the answer given by the Father who sent me.

25"I am telling you these things now while I am still with you. 26But when the Father sends the Comforter instead of me—and by the Comforter I mean the Holy Spirit—he will teach you much, as well as remind you of everything I myself have told you.

27"I am leaving you with a gift—peace of mind and heart! And the peace I give isn't fragile like the peace the world gives. So don't be troubled or afraid. 28Remember what I told you—I am going away, but I will come back to you again. If you really love me, you will be very happy for me, for now I can go to the Father, who is greater than I am. 29I have told you these things before they happen so that when they do, you will believe [in me].

30"I don't have much more time to talk to you, for the evil prince of this world approaches. He has no power over me, 31but I will freely do what the Father requires of me so that the world will know that I love the Father. Come, let's be going.

A THOUGHT: *The disciples must have been perplexed, wondering how Jesus could leave them and still be with them. The Comforter—the Spirit of God himself—would come to care for and guide the disciples after Jesus was gone. This happened at Pentecost, shortly after Jesus ascended to heaven. The Holy Spirit is the very presence of God within all believers, helping us live as God wants.*

Community Life within the Church/ Titus 2:1–10

But as for you, speak up for the right living that goes along with true Christianity. 2Teach the older men to be serious and unruffled; they must be sensible, knowing and believing the truth and doing everything with love and patience.

3Teach the older women to be quiet and respectful in everything they do. They must not go around speaking evil of others and must not be heavy drinkers, but they should be teachers of goodness. 4These older women must train the younger women to live quietly, to love their husbands and their children, 5and to be sensible and clean minded, spending their time in their own homes, being kind and obedient to their husbands, so that the Christian faith can't be spoken against by those who know them.

6In the same way, urge the young men to behave carefully, taking life seriously. 7And here you yourself must be an example to them of good deeds of every kind. Let everything you do reflect your love of the truth and the fact that you are in dead earnest about it. 8Your conversation should be so sensible and logical that anyone who wants to argue will be ashamed of himself because there won't be anything to criticize in anything you say!

9Urge slaves to obey their masters and to try their best to satisfy them. They must not talk back, 10nor steal, but must show themselves to be entirely trustworthy. In this way they will make people want to believe in our Savior and God.

A THOUGHT: *In most churches there are people of all ages. This makes the church strong, but it also brings potential for problems. So Paul gives Titus counsel on how to help various types of people. The older people should teach the younger, by their words and by their example. Paul urged Titus to be a good example to those around him so that others might see his good deeds and imitate him. His life would give his words greater impact. If you want someone to act a certain way, be sure that you live that way yourself. Then you will earn the right to be heard.*

Proverbs for Today/ 23:13–14

Don't fail to correct your children; discipline won't hurt them! They won't die if you use a stick on them! Punishment will keep them out of hell.

SEPTEMBER 16

The Vine and the Branches/ John 15:1–15

"I am the true Vine, and my Father is the Gardener. 2He lops off every branch that doesn't produce. And he prunes those branches that bear fruit for even larger crops. 3He has already tended you by pruning you back for greater strength and usefulness by means of the commands I gave you. 4Take care to live in me, and let me live in you. For a branch can't produce fruit when severed from the vine. Nor can you be fruitful apart from me.

5"Yes, I am the Vine; you are the branches. Whoever lives in me and I in him shall produce a large crop of fruit. For apart from me you can't do a thing. 6If anyone separates from me, he is thrown away like a useless branch, withers, and is gathered into a pile with all the others and burned. 7But if you stay in me and obey my commands, you may ask any request you like, and it will be granted! 8My true disciples produce bountiful harvests. This brings great glory to my Father.

9"I have loved you even as the Father has loved me. Live within my love. 10When you obey me you are living in my love, just as I obey my Father and live in his love. 11I have told you this so that you will be filled with my joy. Yes, your cup of joy will overflow! 12I demand that you love each other as much as I love you. 13And here is how to measure it—the greatest love is shown when a person lays down his life for his friends; 14and you are my friends if you obey me. 15I no longer call you slaves, for a master doesn't confide in his slaves; now you are my friends, proved by the fact that I have told you everything the Father told me.

A THOUGHT: *Christ is the Vine, and God is the Gardener who cares for the branches to make them fruitful. The branches are all who claim to be followers of Christ. The fruitful branches are true believers who by their living union with Christ produce much fruit. But those who become unproductive will be separated from the Vine—such are the people who have turned back from Christ after making superficial commitments. The unproductive followers are as good as dead and will be cut off and cast aside.*

Salvation Is Available to Everyone/ Titus 2:11–15

For the free gift of eternal salvation is now being offered to everyone; 12and along with this gift comes the realization that God wants us to turn from godless living and sinful pleasures and to live good, God-fearing lives day after day, 13looking forward to that wonderful time we've been expecting, when his glory shall be seen—the glory of our great God and Savior Jesus Christ. 14He died under God's judgment against our sins, so that he could rescue us from constant falling into sin and make us his very own people, with cleansed hearts and real enthusiasm for doing kind things for others. 15You must teach these things and encourage your people to do them, correcting them when necessary as one who has every right to do so. Don't let anyone think that what you say is not important.

A THOUGHT: *The power to live the Christian life comes from Jesus Christ. Because Christ died and rescued us from sin, we are free from sin's control. Jesus gives us the power and understanding to live according to God's will, to look forward to his return, and to do good. To live in accordance with God's will, we must continually submit to the control of God's Spirit. As we submit to the Spirit we will find ourselves gradually being transformed into Christlikeness.*

Proverbs for Today/ 23:15–16

My son, how I will rejoice if you become a man of common sense. Yes, my heart will thrill to your thoughtful, wise words.

SEPTEMBER 17

Be Prepared for Persecution/ John 15:16–27

"You didn't choose me! I chose you! I appointed you to go and produce lovely fruit always, so that no matter what you ask for from the Father, using my name, he will give it to you. 17I demand that you love each other, 18for you get enough hate from the world! But then, it hated me before it hated you. 19The world would love you if you belonged to it; but you don't—for I chose you to come out of the world, and so it hates you. 20Do you remember what I told you? 'A slave isn't greater than his master!' So since they persecuted me, naturally they will persecute you. And if they had listened to me, they would listen to you! 21The people of the world will persecute you because you belong to me, for they don't know God who sent me.

22"They would not be guilty if I had not come and spoken to them. But now they have no excuse for their sin. 23Anyone hating me is also hating my Father. 24If I hadn't done such mighty miracles among them they would not be counted guilty. But as it is, they saw these miracles and yet they hated both of us—me and my Father. 25This has fulfilled what the prophets said concerning the Messiah, 'They hated me without reason.'

26"But I will send you the Comforter—the Holy Spirit, the source of all truth. He will come to you from the Father and will tell you all about me. 27And you also must tell everyone about me, because you have been with me from the beginning.

A THOUGHT: *Once again Jesus offers hope. The Holy Spirit gives strength to endure the hatred and evil in our world and the hostility many have toward Christ. This is especially comforting for those facing persecution.*

Be Obedient to the Government/ Titus 3:1–8

Remind your people to obey the government and its officers, and always to be obedient and ready for any honest work. 2They must not speak evil of anyone, nor quarrel, but be gentle and truly courteous to all.

3Once we, too, were foolish and disobedient; we were misled by others and became slaves to many evil pleasures and wicked desires. Our lives were full of resentment and envy. We hated others and they hated us.

4But when the time came for the kindness and love of God our Savior to appear, 5then he saved us—not because we were good enough to be saved, but because of his kindness and pity—by washing away our sins and giving us the new joy of the indwelling Holy Spirit 6whom he poured out upon us with wonderful fullness—and all because of what Jesus Christ our Savior did 7so that he could declare us good in God's eyes—all because of his great kindness; and now we can share in the wealth of the eternal life he gives us, and we are eagerly looking forward to receiving it. 8These things I have told you are all true. Insist on them so that Christians will be careful to do good deeds all the time, for this is not only right, but it brings results.

A Thought: *Paul summarizes what Christ does for us when he saves us. We move from a life full of sin to one led by God's Holy Spirit. All our sins, not merely some, are washed away. We gain eternal life with all its treasures. We have the fullness of the Holy Spirit, and he continually renews our hearts. None of this occurs because we earned or deserved it; it is all a gift of God's grace.*

Proverbs for Today/ 23:17–18

Don't envy evil men but continue to reverence the Lord all the time, for surely you have a wonderful future ahead of you. There is hope for you yet!

SEPTEMBER 18

The Promise to Send the Holy Spirit/ John 16:1–15

"I have told you these things so that you won't be staggered [by all that lies ahead.] 2For you will be excommunicated from the synagogues, and indeed the time is coming when those who kill you will think they are doing God a service. 3This is because they have never known the Father or me. 4Yes, I'm telling you these things now so that when they happen you will remember I warned you. I didn't tell you earlier because I was going to be with you for a while longer.

5"But now I am going away to the one who sent me; and none of you seems interested in the purpose of my going; none wonders why. 6Instead you are only filled with sorrow. 7But the fact of the matter is that it is best for you that I go away, for if I don't, the Comforter won't come. If I do, he will—for I will send him to you.

8"And when he has come he will convince the world of its sin, and of the availability of God's goodness, and of deliverance from judgment. 9The world's sin is unbelief in me; 10there is righteousness available because I go to the Father and you shall see me no more; 11there is deliverance from judgment because the prince of this world has already been judged.

12"Oh, there is so much more I want to tell you, but

you can't understand it now. 13When the Holy Spirit, who is truth, comes, he shall guide you into all truth, for he will not be presenting his own ideas, but will be passing on to you what he has heard. He will tell you about the future. 14He shall praise me and bring me great honor by showing you my glory. 15All the Father's glory is mine; this is what I mean when I say that he will show you my glory.

A THOUGHT: *In his last moments with his disciples, Jesus (1) warned them about further persecution, (2) told them where he was going, when he was leaving, and why, and (3) assured them they would not be left alone, but that the Spirit would come. He knew what lay ahead, and he did not want their faith shaken or destroyed. God wants you to know you are not alone in the world. You have the Holy Spirit to comfort you, teach you truth, and help you.*

Stay Away from Arguments/ Titus 3:9–15

Don't get involved in arguing over unanswerable questions and controversial theological ideas; keep out of arguments and quarrels about obedience to Jewish laws, for this kind of thing isn't worthwhile; it only does harm. 10If anyone is causing divisions among you, he should be given a first and second warning. After that have nothing more to do with him, 11for such a person has a wrong sense of values. He is sinning, and he knows it.

12I am planning to send either Artemas or Tychicus to you. As soon as one of them arrives, please try to meet me at Nicopolis as quickly as you can, for I have decided to stay there for the winter. 13Do everything you can to help Zenas the lawyer and Apollos with their trip; see that they are given everything they need. 14For our people must learn to help all who need their assistance, that their lives will be fruitful.

15Everybody here sends greetings. Please say "hello" to all of the Christian friends there. May God's blessings be with you all.

Sincerely,
Paul

A THOUGHT: *Paul warns Titus, as he warned Timothy, not to get involved in arguments over unanswerable or irrelevant questions. This does not mean we should refuse to study, discuss, and examine different interpretations of difficult Bible passages. Paul is warning against petty quarrels, not honest discussion that leads to wisdom. When foolish arguments develop, it is best to turn the discussion back to a track that is going somewhere or politely excuse yourself.*

Proverbs for Today/ 23:19–21

O my son, be wise and stay in God's paths; don't carouse with drunkards and gluttons, for they are on their way to poverty. And remember that too much sleep clothes a man with rags.

SEPTEMBER 19

Jesus Predicts His Death and Resurrection/ John 16:16–33

"In just a little while I will be gone, and you will see me no more; but just a little while after that, and you will see me again!"

17,18"Whatever is he saying?" some of his disciples asked. "What is this about 'going to the Father'? We don't know what he means."

19Jesus realized they wanted to ask him so he said, "Are you asking yourselves what I mean? 20The world will greatly rejoice over what is going to happen to me, and you will weep. But your weeping shall suddenly be turned to wonderful joy [when you see me again]. 21It will be the same joy as that of a woman in labor when her child is born—her anguish gives place to rapturous joy and the pain is forgotten. 22You have sorrow now, but I will see you again and then you will rejoice; and no one can rob you of that joy. 23At that time you won't need to ask me for anything, for you can go directly to the Father and ask him, and he will give you what you ask for because you use my name. 24You haven't tried this before, [but begin now]. Ask, using my name, and you will receive, and your cup of joy will overflow.

25"I have spoken of these matters very guardedly, but the time will come when this will not be necessary and I will tell you plainly all about the Father. 26Then you will present your petitions over my signature! And I won't need to ask the Father to grant you these requests, 27for the Father himself loves you dearly because you love me and believe that I came from the Father. 28Yes, I came from the Father into the world and will leave the world and return to the Father."

29"At last you are speaking plainly," his disciples said, "and not in riddles. 30Now we understand that you know everything and don't need anyone to tell you anything. From this we believe that you came from God."

31"Do you finally believe this?" Jesus asked. 32"But the time is coming—in fact, it is here—when you will be scattered, each one returning to his own home, leaving me alone. Yet I will not be alone, for the Father is with me. 33I have told you all this so that you will have peace of heart and mind. Here on earth you will have many trials and sorrows; but cheer up, for I have overcome the world."

A THOUGHT: *The disciples did not understand Jesus' statements concerning leaving them and going to the Father. He was speaking of the fulfillment of his own mission—to redeem mankind and establish a new relationship between the believer and God. Previously, people approached God through priests. After Jesus' resurrection, any believer could approach God directly. A new day has dawned and now all believers are priests, talking with God personally and directly. We approach God, not because of our own merit, but because Jesus, our great High Priest, has made us acceptable to God.*

Paul Gives Thanks for Philemon/ Philemon 1:1–7

From: Paul, in jail for preaching the Good News about Jesus Christ, and from Brother Timothy.

To: Philemon, our much loved fellow worker, and to the church that meets in your home, and to Apphia our sister, and to Archippus who like myself is a soldier of the cross.

3May God our Father and the Lord Jesus Christ give you his blessings and his peace.

4I always thank God when I am praying for you, dear Philemon, 5because I keep hearing of your love and trust in the Lord Jesus and in his people. 6And I pray that as you share your faith with others it will grip their lives too, as they see the wealth of good things in you that come from Christ Jesus. 7I myself have gained much joy and comfort from your love, my brother, because your kindness has so often refreshed the hearts of God's people.

A Thought: *Paul reflected on Philemon's kindness, love, and comfort. He had opened his heart and his home to the church. We should do likewise, opening ourselves and our homes to others, offering Christian fellowship to refresh people's spirits.*

Proverbs for Today/ 23:22
Listen to your father's advice and don't despise an old mother's experience.

SEPTEMBER 20

Jesus Prays for His Followers/ John 17:1–26
When Jesus had finished saying all these things he looked up to heaven and said, "Father, the time has come. Reveal the glory of your Son so that he can give the glory back to you. 2For you have given him authority over every man and woman in all the earth. He gives eternal life to each one you have given him. 3And this is the way to have eternal life—by knowing you, the only true God, and Jesus Christ, the one you sent to earth! 4I brought glory to you here on earth by doing everything you told me to. 5And now, Father, reveal my glory as I stand in your presence, the glory we shared before the world began.

6"I have told these men all about you. They were in the world, but then you gave them to me. Actually, they were always yours, and you gave them to me; and they have obeyed you. 7Now they know that everything I have is a gift from you, 8for I have passed on to them the commands you gave me; and they accepted them and know of a certainty that I came down to earth from you, and they believe you sent me.

9"My plea is not for the world but for those you have given me because they belong to you. 10And all of them, since they are mine, belong to you; and you have given them back to me with everything else of yours, and so *they are my glory!* 11Now I am leaving the world, and leaving them behind, and coming to you. Holy Father, keep them in your own care—all those you have given me—so that they will be united just as we are, with none missing. 12During my time here I have kept safe within your family all of these you gave me. I guarded them so that not one perished, except the son of hell, as the Scriptures foretold.

13"And now I am coming to you. I have told them many things while I was with them so that they would be filled with my joy. 14I have given them your commands. And the world hates them because they don't fit in with it, just as I don't. 15I'm not asking you to take them out of the world, but to keep them safe from Satan's power. 16They are not part of this world any more than I am. 17Make them pure and holy through teaching them your words of truth. 18As you sent me into the world, I am sending them into the world, 19and I consecrate myself to meet their need for growth in truth and holiness.

20"I am not praying for these alone but also for the future believers who will come to me because of the testimony of these. 21My prayer for all of them is that they will be of one heart and mind, just as you and I are, Father—that just as you are in me and I am in you, so they will be in us, and the world will believe you sent me.

22"I have given them the glory you gave me—the glorious unity of being one, as we are— 23I in them and you in me, all being perfected into one—so that the world will know you sent me and will understand that you love them as much as you love me. 24Father, I want them with me—these you've given me—so that they can see my glory. You gave me the glory because you loved me before the world began!

25"O righteous Father, the world doesn't know you, but I do; and these disciples know you sent me. 26And I have revealed you to them, and will keep on revealing you so that the mighty love you have for me may be in them, and I in them."

A THOUGHT: *Jesus' great desire for his disciples was that they become one. Jesus prayed for unity among the believers based on the oneness Jesus has with the Father. Christians can know unity among themselves if they are living in union with God. Are you helping to unify the body of Christ, the church? You can pray for other*

Christians, avoid gossip, build others up, work together in humility, give your time and money, lift up Christ, and refuse to get sidetracked by arguing over unimportant matters that too often divide us.

Paul's Plea for Onesimus/ Philemon 1:8–25

Now I want to ask a favor of you. I could demand it of you in the name of Christ because it is the right thing for you to do, but I love you and prefer just to ask you— I, Paul, an old man now, here in jail for the sake of Jesus Christ. 10My plea is that you show kindness to my child Onesimus, whom I won to the Lord while here in my chains. 11Onesimus (whose name means "Useful") hasn't been of much use to you in the past, but now he is going to be of real use to both of us. 12I am sending him back to you, and with him comes my own heart.

13I really wanted to keep him here with me while I am in these chains for preaching the Good News, and you would have been helping me through him, 14but I didn't want to do it without your consent. I didn't want you to be kind because you had to but because you wanted to. 15Perhaps you could think of it this way: that he ran away from you for a little while so that now he can be yours forever, 16no longer only a slave, but something much better—a beloved brother, especially to me. Now he will mean much more to you too, because he is not only a servant but also your brother in Christ.

17If I am really your friend, give him the same welcome you would give to me if I were the one who was coming. 18If he has harmed you in any way or stolen anything from you, charge me for it. 19I will pay it back (I, Paul, personally guarantee this by writing it here with my own hand) but I won't mention how much you owe me! The fact is, you even owe me your very soul! 20Yes, dear brother, give me joy with this loving act and my weary heart will praise the Lord.

21I've written you this letter because I am positive that you will do what I ask and even more!

22Please keep a guest room ready for me, for I am hoping that God will answer your prayers and let me come to you soon.

23Epaphras my fellow prisoner, who is also here for preaching Christ Jesus, sends you his greetings. 24So do

Mark, Aristarchus, Demas and Luke, my fellow workers.
25The blessings of our Lord Jesus Christ be upon your spirit.

Paul

A THOUGHT: *What a difference Onesimus' status as a Christian made in his relationship to Philemon. He was no longer merely a servant, he was also a brother. Now both Onesimus and Philemon were members of God's family—equals in Christ. A Christian's status as a member of God's family transcends all other distinctions among believers. Do you look down on any fellow Christians? Remember, they are your brothers and sisters, your equals before Christ. How you treat your brothers and sisters in Christ's family reflects your true Christian commitment.*

Proverbs for Today/ 23:23
Get the facts at any price, and hold on tightly to all the good sense you can get.

SEPTEMBER 21

Jesus Is Arrested in the Garden/ John 18:1–14
After saying these things Jesus crossed the Kidron ravine with his disciples and entered a grove of olive trees. 2Judas, the betrayer, knew this place, for Jesus had gone there many times with his disciples.

3The chief priests and Pharisees had given Judas a squad of soldiers and police to accompany him. Now with blazing torches, lanterns, and weapons they arrived at the olive grove.

4,5Jesus fully realized all that was going to happen to him. Stepping forward to meet them he asked, "Whom are you looking for?"

"Jesus of Nazareth," they replied.

"I am he," Jesus said. 6And as he said it, they all fell backwards to the ground!

7Once more he asked them, "Whom are you searching for?"

And again they replied, "Jesus of Nazareth."

8"I told you I am he," Jesus said; "and since I am the

one you are after, let these others go." 9He did this to carry out the prophecy he had just made, "I have not lost a single one of those you gave me. . . . "

10Then Simon Peter drew a sword and slashed off the right ear of Malchus, the High Priest's servant.

11But Jesus said to Peter, "Put your sword away. Shall I not drink from the cup the Father has given me?"

12So the Jewish police, with the soldiers and their lieutenant, arrested Jesus and tied him. 13First they took him to Annas, the father-in-law of Caiaphas, the High Priest that year. 14Caiaphas was the one who told the other Jewish leaders, "Better that one should die for all."

A THOUGHT: *Trying to protect Jesus, Peter pulled a sword and wounded one of the Temple police. But Jesus told him to put away his sword and allow God's plan to unfold. At times it is tempting to take matters into our own hands, to force the issue. Instead we must trust God to work out his plan. Think of it—if Peter would have had his way, Jesus would not have gone to the cross, and God's plan of redemption would have been halted.*

God's Son Is Greater Than Angels/ Hebrews 1:1–14

Long ago God spoke in many different ways to our fathers through the prophets [in visions, dreams, and even face to face], telling them little by little about his plans.

2But now in these days he has spoken to us through his Son to whom he has given everything, and through whom he made the world and everything there is.

3God's Son shines out with God's glory, and all that God's Son is and does marks him as God. He regulates the universe by the mighty power of his command. He is the one who died to cleanse us and clear our record of all sin, and then sat down in highest honor beside the great God of heaven.

4Thus he became far greater than the angels, as proved by the fact that his name "Son of God," which was passed on to him from his Father, is far greater than the names and titles of the angels. 5,6For God never said to any angel, "You are my Son, and today I have given you the honor that goes with that name." But God said it about Jesus. Another time he said, "I am his Father and he is my Son." And still another time—when his firstborn Son came to earth—God said, "Let all the angels of God worship him."

7God speaks of his angels as messengers swift as the wind and as servants made of flaming fire; 8but of his Son he says, "Your Kingdom, O God, will last forever and ever; its commands are always just and right. 9You love right and hate wrong; so God, even your God, has poured out more gladness upon you than on anyone else."

10God also called him "Lord" when he said, "Lord, in the beginning you made the earth, and the heavens are the work of your hands. 11They will disappear into nothingness, but you will remain forever. They will become worn out like old clothes, 12and some day you will fold them up and replace them. But you yourself will never change, and your years will never end."

13And did God ever say to an angel, as he does to his Son, "Sit here beside me in honor until I crush all your enemies beneath your feet"?

14No, for the angels are only spirit-messengers sent out to help and care for those who are to receive his salvation.

A THOUGHT: *God used many approaches to send his messages to people in Old Testament times. He spoke to Isaiah in visions, to Jacob in a dream, and to Abraham and Moses personally. Jewish people familiar with these stories would not have found it hard to believe that God was still revealing his will, but it was astonishing for them to think that God had revealed [himself] by speaking through his Son, Jesus Christ. Jesus is the fulfillment and culmination of God's many revelations through the centuries. He is the full revelation of God. You can have no clearer view of God than by looking at him. Jesus Christ is the complete embodiment of God.*

Proverbs for Today/ 23:24–25

The father of a godly man has cause for joy—what pleasure a wise son is! So give your parents joy!

SEPTEMBER 22

Peter's Denials/ John 18:15–27

Simon Peter followed along behind, as did another of the disciples who was acquainted with the High Priest. So that other disciple was permitted into the courtyard along with Jesus, 16while Peter stood outside the gate. Then the other disciple spoke to the girl watching at the gate, and she let Peter in. 17The girl asked Peter, "Aren't you one of Jesus' disciples?"

"No," he said, "I am not!"

18The police and the household servants were standing around a fire they had made, for it was cold. And Peter stood there with them, warming himself.

19Inside, the High Priest began asking Jesus about his followers and what he had been teaching them.

20Jesus replied, "What I teach is widely known, for I have preached regularly in the synagogue and Temple; I have been heard by all the Jewish leaders and teach nothing in private that I have not said in public. 21Why are you asking me this question? Ask those who heard me. You have some of them here. They know what I said."

22One of the soldiers standing there struck Jesus with his fist. "Is that the way to answer the High Priest?" he demanded.

23"If I lied, prove it," Jesus replied. "Should you hit a man for telling the truth?"

24Then Annas sent Jesus, bound, to Caiaphas the High Priest.

25Meanwhile, as Simon Peter was standing by the fire, he was asked again, "Aren't you one of his disciples?"

"Of course not," he replied.

26But one of the household slaves of the High Priest— a relative of the man whose ear Peter had cut off—asked, "Didn't I see you out there in the olive grove with Jesus?"

27Again Peter denied it. And immediately a rooster crowed.

A THOUGHT: *Imagine standing outside while Jesus, your Lord and Master, is questioned. Imagine watching this man, whom you have come to believe is the long-awaited Messiah, being abused and beaten. Naturally Peter was confused and afraid. It is a serious sin to deny Christ, but Jesus later forgave Peter. No sin is too great for Jesus to forgive if we are truly repentant. He will forgive even your worst sin if you turn from it and ask his pardon.*

Do Not Drift Away from the Truth/ Hebrews 2:1–4

So we must listen very carefully to the truths we have heard, or we may drift away from them. 2For since the messages from angels have always proved true and people have always been punished for disobeying them, 3what makes us think that we can escape if we are indifferent to this great salvation announced by the Lord Jesus himself, and passed on to us by those who heard him speak?

4God always has shown us that these messages are true by signs and wonders and various miracles and by giving certain special abilities from the Holy Spirit to those who believe; yes, God has assigned such gifts to each of us.

A Thought: *A central theme of Hebrews is that Christ is infinitely greater than all other proposed means to God. Your previous faith was good, the author said to his Jewish readers, but Christ is incomparably better. Just as Christ is greater than angels, so his message is more important than theirs. Don't turn your back on Christ in an attempt to escape your troubles. The only escape is to flee to him.*

Proverbs for Today/ 23:26–28

O my son, trust my advice—stay away from prostitutes. For a prostitute is a deep and narrow grave. Like a robber, she waits for her victims as one after another become unfaithful to their wives.

SEPTEMBER 23

Jesus Is Tried before Pilate/ John 18:28–40

Jesus' trial before Caiaphas ended in the early hours of the morning. Next he was taken to the palace of the Roman governor. His accusers wouldn't go in themselves for that would "defile" them, they said, and they wouldn't be allowed to eat the Passover lamb. 29So Pilate, the governor, went out to them and asked, "What is your charge against this man? What are you accusing him of doing?"

30"We wouldn't have arrested him if he weren't a criminal!" they retorted.

31"Then take him away and judge him yourselves by your own laws," Pilate told them.

"But we want him crucified," they demanded, "and your approval is required." 32This fulfilled Jesus' prediction concerning the method of his execution.

33Then Pilate went back into the palace and called for Jesus to be brought to him. "Are you the King of the Jews?" he asked him.

34"'King' as *you* use the word or as the *Jews* use it?" Jesus asked.

35"Am I a Jew?" Pilate retorted. "Your own people and their chief priests brought you here. Why? What have you done?"

36Then Jesus answered, "I am not an earthly king. If I were, my followers would have fought when I was arrested by the Jewish leaders. But my Kingdom is not of the world."

37Pilate replied, "But you are a king then?"

"Yes," Jesus said. "I was born for that purpose. And I came to bring truth to the world. All who love the truth are my followers."

38"What is truth?" Pilate exclaimed.Then he went out again to the people and told them, "He is not guilty of any crime. 39But you have a custom of asking me to release someone from prison each year at Passover. So if you want me to, I'll release the 'King of the Jews.'"

40But they screamed back. "No! Not this man, but Barabbas!" Barabbas was a robber.

A THOUGHT: *Pilate, the Roman governor at this time, was in charge of Judea (the region in which Jerusalem was located) from A.D. 26 to 36. Pilate was unpopular with the Jews because he had raided the Temple treasuries for money to build an aqueduct. He did not like the Jews, but when Jesus, the King of the Jews, stood before him, Pilate found him innocent. Pilate knew what was going on; he knew that the religious leaders hated Jesus, and he did not want to act as their executioner. They could not sentence Jesus to death themselves—permission had to come from a Roman leader. Jesus' life became a pawn in a political power struggle. Responding to threats from the mob, Pilate finally turned Jesus over to be crucified.*

Jesus' Suffering and Death Secured Salvation/ Hebrews 2:5–10

And the future world we are talking about will not be controlled by angels. 6No, for in the book of Psalms David says to God, "What is mere man that you are so concerned about him? And who is this Son of Man you honor so highly? 7For though you made him lower than the angels for a little while, now you have crowned him with glory and honor. 8And you have put him in complete charge of everything there is. Nothing is left out."

We have not yet seen all of this take place, 9but we do see Jesus—who for awhile was a little lower than the angels—crowned now by God with glory and honor because he suffered death for us. Yes, because of God's great kindness, Jesus tasted death for everyone in all the world.

10And it was right and proper that God, who made everything for his own glory, should allow Jesus to suffer, for in doing this he was bringing vast multitudes of God's people to heaven; for his suffering made Jesus a perfect Leader, one fit to bring them into their salvation.

A THOUGHT: *God's kindness led Christ to his death—what a startling juxtaposition of ideas! Yet kindness can and often does involve sacrifice and pain. Jesus did not come into the world to gain status or political power, but to suffer and die so that we could truly live. If this is difficult to understand, perhaps it is time to evaluate our own motives. Are we more interested in power or submission, domination or service, getting or giving? If kindness, not selfishness, motivates us, we too may have to suffer.*

Proverbs for Today/ 23:29–35

Whose heart is filled with anguish and sorrow? Who is always fighting and quarreling? Who is the man with bloodshot eyes and many wounds? It is the one who spends long hours in the taverns, trying out new mixtures. Don't let the sparkle and the smooth taste of strong wine deceive you. For in the end it bites like a poisonous serpent; it stings like an adder. You will see hallucinations and have delirium tremens, and you will say foolish, silly things that would embarrass you no end when sober. You will stagger like a sailor tossed at sea, clinging to a swaying mast. And afterwards you will say, "I didn't even know it when they beat me up. . . . Let's go and have another drink!"

SEPTEMBER 24

The People Demand Jesus' Crucifixion/
John 19:1–15

Then Pilate laid open Jesus' back with a leaded whip, 2and the soldiers made a crown of thorns and placed it on his head and robed him in royal purple. 3"Hail, 'King of the Jews!' " they mocked, and struck him with their fists.

4Pilate went outside again and said to the Jews, "I am going to bring him out to you now, but understand clearly that I find him *not guilty.*"

5Then Jesus came out wearing the crown of thorns and the purple robe. And Pilate said, "Behold the man!"

6At sight of him the chief priests and Jewish officials began yelling, "Crucify! Crucify!"

"You crucify him," Pilate said. "I find him *not guilty.*"

7They replied, "By our laws he ought to die because he called himself the Son of God."

8When Pilate heard this, he was more frightened than ever. 9He took Jesus back into the palace again and asked him, "Where are you from?" but Jesus gave no answer.

10"You won't talk to me?" Pilate demanded. "Don't you realize that I have the power to release you or to crucify you?"

11Then Jesus said, "You would have no power at all over me unless it were given to you from above. So those who brought me to you have the greater sin."

12Then Pilate tried to release him, but the Jewish leaders told him, "If you release this man, you are no friend of Caesar's. Anyone who declares himself a king is a rebel against Caesar."

13At these words Pilate brought Jesus out to them again and sat down at the judgment bench on the stone-paved platform. 14It was now about noon of the day before Passover.

And Pilate said to the Jews, "Here is your king!"

15"Away with him," they yelled. "Away with him—crucify him!"

"What? Crucify your king?" Pilate asked.

"We have no king but Caesar," the chief priests shouted back.

A THOUGHT: *The Jewish leaders were so desperate to get rid of Jesus that despite their intense hatred for Rome, they shouted, "We have no king but Caesar." How ironic that they feigned allegiance to Rome while rejecting their own Messiah! The priests had truly lost their reasons for being—instead of turning people to God, they claimed allegiance to Rome in order to kill their Messiah. And they encouraged the people to join them in their terrible sin.*

Christ Came As a Human Being/ Hebrews 2:11–15

We who have been made holy by Jesus, now have the same Father he has. That is why Jesus is not ashamed to call us his brothers. 12For he says in the book of Psalms, "I will talk to my brothers about God my Father, and together we will sing his praises." 13At another time he said, "I will put my trust in God along with my brothers." And at still another time, "See, here am I and the children God gave me."

14Since we, God's children, are human beings—made of flesh and blood—he became flesh and blood too by being born in human form; for only as a human being could he die and in dying break the power of the devil who had the power of death. 15Only in that way could he deliver those who through fear of death have been living all their lives as slaves to constant dread.

A THOUGHT: *Jesus had to be human so he could die, so he could overcome the same temptations we face, and so he could mediate between God and human beings. He identified with us so that we could identify with God. Christ's death reestablished our relationship with God. We are children of God because of what Christ did. Our hope of eternal life has been secured in Christ.*

Proverbs for Today/ 24:1–2

Don't envy godless men; don't even enjoy their company. For they spend their days plotting violence and cheating.

SEPTEMBER 25

Jesus Is Crucified/ John 19:16–30

Then Pilate gave Jesus to the soldiers to be crucified.
17So they had him at last, and he was taken out of the

city, carrying his cross to the place known as "The Skull," in Hebrew, "Golgotha." 18There they crucified him and two others with him, one on either side, with Jesus between them. 19And Pilate posted a sign over him reading, "Jesus of Nazareth, the King of the Jews." 20The place where Jesus was crucified was near the city; and the signboard was written in Hebrew, Latin, and Greek, so that many people read it.

21Then the chief priests said to Pilate, "Change it from 'The King of the Jews' to '*He said,* I am King of the Jews.'"

22Pilate replied, "What I have written, I have written. It stays exactly as it is."

23,24When the soldiers had crucified Jesus, they put his garments into four piles, one for each of them. But they said, "Let's not tear up his robe," for it was seamless. "Let's throw dice to see who gets it." This fulfilled the Scripture that says,

"They divided my clothes among them, and cast lots for my robe." 25So that is what they did.

Standing near the cross were Jesus' mother, Mary, his aunt, the wife of Cleopas, and Mary Magdalene. 26When Jesus saw his mother standing there beside me, his close friend, he said to her, "He is your son."

27And to me he said, "She is your mother!" And from then on I took her into my home.

28Jesus knew that everything was now finished, and to fulfill the Scriptures said, "I'm thirsty." 29A jar of sour wine was sitting there, so a sponge was soaked in it and put on a hyssop branch and held up to his lips.

30When Jesus had tasted it, he said, "It is finished," and bowed his head and dismissed his spirit.

A THOUGHT: *Crucifixion was a Roman form of punishment. The victim sentenced to this type of execution was forced to carry his cross along a main road to the execution site, as a warning to the people. Crosses and methods of crucifixion varied. Jesus was nailed to his cross; others were sometimes tied with ropes. Death came by suffocation, because the weight of the body made breathing difficult as the victim lost strength. Crucifixion was a hideously slow and painful death.*

Jesus was the final and ultimate sacrifice for sin. The word finished is the same as "paid in full." Jesus came to finish God's work of salvation, to pay the full penalty for our sins. With his

death, the complex sacrificial system ended because Jesus took all sin upon himself. Now we can freely approach God because of what Jesus did for us. Those who believe in Jesus' death and resurrection can live eternally with God and escape the death which comes from sin.

Jesus Is Our Merciful High Priest/ Hebrews 2:16—3:6

We all know he did not come as an angel but as a human being—yes, a Jew. 17And it was necessary for Jesus to be like us, his brothers, so that he could be our merciful and faithful High Priest before God, a Priest who would be both merciful to us and faithful to God in dealing with the sins of the people. 18For since he himself has now been through suffering and temptation, he knows what it is like when we suffer and are tempted, and he is wonderfully able to help us.

3:1Therefore, dear brothers whom God has set apart for himself—you who are chosen for heaven—I want you to think now about this Jesus who is God's Messenger and the High Priest of our faith.

2For Jesus was faithful to God who appointed him High Priest, just as Moses also faithfully served in God's house. 3But Jesus has far more glory than Moses, just as a man who builds a fine house gets more praise than his house does. 4And many people can build houses, but only God made everything.

5Well, Moses did a fine job working in God's house, but he was only a servant; and his work was mostly to illustrate and suggest those things that would happen later on. 6But Christ, God's faithful Son, is in complete charge of God's house. And we Christians are God's house—he lives in us!—if we keep up our courage firm to the end, and our joy and our trust in the Lord.

A THOUGHT: *In the Old Testament, the High Priest was the mediator between God and his people. His job was to regularly offer animal sacrifices according to the law and to intercede with God for the people's sins. Jesus Christ is now our High Priest. He has once and for all paid the penalty for all our sins by his own sacrificial death, and he continually intercedes on our behalf before God. We are released from sin's domination over us when we commit ourselves fully to Christ, trusting completely in what he has done for us.*

Proverbs for Today/ 24:3–4

Any enterprise is built by wise planning, becomes strong through common sense, and profits wonderfully by keeping abreast of the facts.

SEPTEMBER 26

Jesus' Burial/ John 19:31–42

The Jewish leaders didn't want the victims hanging there the next day, which was the Sabbath (and a very special Sabbath at that, for it was the Passover), so they asked Pilate to order the legs of the men broken to hasten death; then their bodies could be taken down. 32So the soldiers came and broke the legs of the two men crucified with Jesus; 33but when they came to him, they saw that he was dead already, so they didn't break his. 34However, one of the soldiers pierced his side with a spear, and blood and water flowed out. 35I saw all this myself and have given an accurate report so that you also can believe. 36,37The soldiers did this in fulfillment of the Scripture that says, "Not one of his bones shall be broken," and, "They shall look on him whom they pierced."

38Afterwards Joseph of Arimathea, who had been a secret disciple of Jesus for fear of the Jewish leaders, boldly asked Pilate for permission to take Jesus' body down; and Pilate told him to go ahead. So he came and took it away. 39Nicodemus, the man who had come to Jesus at night, came too, bringing a hundred pounds of embalming ointment made from myrrh and aloes. 40Together they wrapped Jesus' body in a long linen cloth saturated with the spices, as is the Jewish custom of burial. 41The place of crucifixion was near a grove of trees, where there was a new tomb, never used before. 42And so, because of the need for haste before the Sabbath, and because the tomb was close at hand, they laid him there.

A THOUGHT: *Joseph of Arimathea and Nicodemus were secret followers of Jesus. They were afraid to make this known because of their positions in the Jewish community. Joseph was a leader and honored member of the Supreme Court. Nicodemus, also a member of the Court, had come to Jesus by night and later tried to defend him before the other religious leaders. Yet they risked their reputations to bury Jesus. Are you a secret believer? Do you hide from your friends and fellow workers? This is an appropriate time to step out of hiding and let others know of your faith.*

God's Anger against the Israelites/ Hebrews 3:7–14

And since Christ is so much superior, the Holy Spirit warns us to listen to him, to be careful to hear his voice today and not let our hearts become set against him, as the people of Israel did. They steeled themselves against his love and complained against him in the desert while he was testing them. 9But God was patient with them forty years, though they tried his patience sorely; he kept right on doing his mighty miracles for them to see. 10"But," God says, "I was very angry with them, for their hearts were always looking somewhere else instead of up to me, and they never found the paths I wanted them to follow."

11Then God, full of this anger against them, bound himself with an oath that he would never let them come to his place of rest.

12Beware then of your own hearts, dear brothers, lest you find that they, too, are evil and unbelieving and are leading you away from the living God. 13Speak to each other about these things every day while there is still time, so that none of you will become hardened against God, being blinded by the glamor of sin. 14For if we are faithful to the end, trusting God just as we did when we first became Christians, we will share in all that belongs to Christ.

A THOUGHT: *Many times the Bible warns us not to harden our hearts. "Hardening our hearts" is an expression that means we have set ourselves against God to the point that we are no longer able to turn to him to be saved. Such hardheartedness begins when we refuse to obey God's revealed will. The Israelites became hardhearted when they disobeyed God's command to conquer the Promised Land. Let us be careful to obey God's Word and not allow our hearts to become hardened.*

Proverbs for Today/ 24:5

A wise man is mightier than a strong man. Wisdom is mightier than strength.

SEPTEMBER 27

The Resurrection of Jesus/ John 20:1–18

Early Sunday morning, while it was still dark, Mary Magdalene came to the tomb and found that the stone was rolled aside from the entrance.

2She ran and found Simon Peter and me and said, "They have taken the Lord's body out of the tomb, and I don't know where they have put him!"

3,4We ran to the tomb to see; I outran Peter and got there first, 5and stooped and looked in and saw the linen cloth lying there, but I didn't go in. 6Then Simon Peter arrived and went on inside. He also noticed the cloth lying there, 7while the swath that had covered Jesus' head was rolled up in a bundle and was lying at the side. 8Then I went in too, and saw, and believed [that he had risen]— 9for until then we hadn't realized that the Scriptures said he would come to life again!

10We went on home, 11and by that time Mary had returned to the tomb and was standing outside crying. And as she wept, she stooped and looked in 12and saw two white-robed angels sitting at the head and foot of the place where the body of Jesus had been lying.

13"Why are you crying?" the angels asked her.

"Because they have taken away my Lord," she replied, "and I don't know where they have put him."

14She glanced over her shoulder and saw someone standing behind her. It was Jesus, but she didn't recognize him!

15"Why are you crying?" he asked her. "Whom are you looking for?"

She thought he was the gardener. "Sir," she said, "if you have taken him away, tell me where you have put him, and I will go and get him."

16"Mary!" Jesus said. She turned toward him.

"Master!" she exclaimed.

17"Don't touch me," he cautioned, "for I haven't yet ascended to the Father. But go find my brothers and tell them that I ascend to my Father and your Father, my God and your God."

18Mary Magdalene found the disciples and told them,

"I have seen the Lord!" Then she gave them his message.

A THOUGHT: *Jesus' resurrection is the key to the Christian faith. Why? (1) "Just as he said," Jesus rose from the dead. We can be confident, therefore, that he will accomplish all he has promised. (2) Jesus' bodily resurrection shows us that the living Christ is the ruler of God's eternal Kingdom. (3) We can be certain of our own resurrection because he was resurrected. Death is not the end— there is future life. (4) The divine power that brought Jesus back to life is now available to us to bring our spiritually dead selves back to life. (5) The resurrection is the basis for the church's witness to the world.*

Now Is the Time to Listen to God/ Hebrews 3:15–19

But *now* is the time. Never forget the warning, "*Today* if you hear God's voice speaking to you, do not harden your hearts against him, as the people of Israel did when they rebelled against him in the desert."

16And who were those people I speak of, who heard God's voice speaking to them but then rebelled against him? They were the ones who came out of Egypt with Moses their leader. 17And who was it who made God angry for all those forty years? These same people who sinned and as a result died in the wilderness. 18And to whom was God speaking when he swore with an oath that they could never go into the land he had promised his people? He was speaking to all those who disobeyed him. 19And why couldn't they go in? Because they didn't trust him.

A THOUGHT: *The Israelites failed to enter the Promised Land because they lacked trust in God. They did not believe God would help them conquer the land; and lacking trust, they failed. So God sent them into the wilderness to wander for 40 years, an unhappy alternative to the wonderful gift he had planned for them. Lack of trust in God always prevents us from receiving his best.*

Proverbs for Today/ 24:6–7

Don't go to war without wise guidance; there is safety in many counselors. □ Wisdom is too much for a rebel. He'll not be chosen as a counselor!

SEPTEMBER 28

Resurrection Appearances/ John 20:19–31

That evening the disciples were meeting behind locked doors, in fear of the Jewish leaders, when suddenly Jesus was standing there among them! After greeting them, 20he showed them his hands and side. And how wonderful was their joy as they saw their Lord!

21He spoke to them again and said, "As the Father has sent me, even so I am sending you." 22Then he breathed on them and told them, "Receive the Holy Spirit. 23If you forgive anyone's sins, they are forgiven. If you refuse to forgive them, they are unforgiven."

24One of the disciples, Thomas, "The Twin," was not there at the time with the others. 25When they kept telling him, "We have seen the Lord," he replied, "I won't believe it unless I see the nail wounds in his hands—and put my fingers into them—and place my hand into his side."

26Eight days later the disciples were together again, and this time Thomas was with them. The doors were locked; but suddenly, as before, Jesus was standing among them and greeting them.

27Then he said to Thomas, "Put your finger into my hands. Put your hand into my side. Don't be faithless any longer. Believe!"

28"My Lord and my God!" Thomas said.

29Then Jesus told him, "You believe because you have seen me. But blessed are those who haven't seen me and believe anyway."

30,31Jesus' disciples saw him do many other miracles besides the ones told about in this book, but these are recorded so that you will believe that he is the Messiah, the Son of God, and that believing in him you will have life.

A THOUGHT: *Some people think they would believe in Jesus if they could see a definite sign or miracle. But Jesus says we are blessed if we believe without seeing. We have all the proof we need in the words of the Bible and the testimony of believers. A physical appearance would not make Jesus any more real to us than the reality of his presence in the body of Christ—the church.*

Entrance into God's Rest/ Hebrews 4:1–6

Although God's promise still stands—his promise that all may enter his place of rest—we ought to tremble with fear because some of you may be on the verge of failing to get there after all. 2For this wonderful news—the message that God wants to save us—has been given to us just as it was to those who lived in the time of Moses. But it didn't do them any good because they didn't believe it. They didn't mix it with faith. 3For only we who believe God can enter into his place of rest. He has said, "I have sworn in my anger that those who don't believe me will never get in," even though he has been ready and waiting for them since the world began.

4We know he is ready and waiting because it is written that God rested on the seventh day of creation, having finished all that he had planned to make.

5 Even so they didn't get in, for God finally said, "They shall never enter my rest." 6Yet the promise remains and some get in—but not those who had the first chance, for they disobeyed God and failed to enter.

A THOUGHT: *Some of the Jewish Christians who received this letter of Hebrews may have been on the verge of turning back from their promised rest in Christ, just as the people in Moses' day turned back from the Promised Land. In both cases, the difficulties of the present moment overshadowed the reality of God's promise, and people stopped believing that God was able to fulfill his promises. When we place our trust in our own efforts instead of in Christ, we too are in danger of turning back. Our own efforts are never adequate; only Christ can see us through.*

Proverbs for Today/ 24:8

To plan evil is as wrong as doing it.

SEPTEMBER 29

Jesus Appears to His Disciples Again/ John 21:1–14

Later Jesus appeared again to the disciples beside the Lake of Galilee. This is how it happened:

2A group of us were there—Simon Peter, Thomas, "The Twin," Nathanael from Cana in Galilee, my brother James and I and two other disciples.

3Simon Peter said, "I'm going fishing."

"We'll come too," we all said. We did, but caught nothing all night. 4At dawn we saw a man standing on the beach but couldn't see who he was.

5He called, "Any fish, boys?"

"No," we replied.

6Then he said, "Throw out your net on the right-hand side of the boat, and you'll get plenty of them!" So we did, and couldn't draw in the net because of the weight of the fish, there were so many!

7Then I said to Peter, "It is the Lord!" At that, Simon Peter put on his tunic (for he was stripped to the waist) and jumped into the water [and swam ashore]. 8The rest of us stayed in the boat and pulled the loaded net to the beach, about 300 feet away. 9When we got there, we saw that a fire was kindled and fish were frying over it, and there was bread.

10"Bring some of the fish you've just caught," Jesus said. 11So Simon Peter went out and dragged the net ashore. By his count there were 153 large fish; and yet the net hadn't torn.

12"Now come and have some breakfast!" Jesus said; and none of us dared ask him if he really was the Lord, for we were quite sure of it. 13Then Jesus went around serving us the bread and fish.

14This was the third time Jesus had appeared to us since his return from the dead.

A THOUGHT: *These disciples had been fishing all night long. They seem to have been discouraged by the lack of fish in their nets and the sustained confusion as to Jesus' death, even after the resurrection appearances. Jesus comes to them at this time and tells them to cast their net on the "right–hand side of the boat." When they hauled in the large catch, they were reminded of a similar incident which had occurred earlier in Jesus' ministry (recorded in Luke 5:1–10). The miracle of this great catch and its connection to the earlier event caused John to recognize Jesus as the figure on the beach. Jesus continued to appear to his disciples to comfort and encourage them. Jesus has this same kind of concern for all his followers. Let us take comfort in God's care when troubled times come.*

The Power of God's Word/ Hebrews 4:7-13

But he has set another time for coming in, and that time is now. He announced this through King David long years after man's first failure to enter, saying in the words already quoted, "Today when you hear him calling, do not harden your hearts against him."

8This new place of rest he is talking about does not mean the land of Israel that Joshua led them into. If that were what God meant, he would not have spoken long afterwards about "today" being the time to get in. 9So there is a full complete rest *still waiting* for the people of God. 10Christ has already entered there. He is resting from his work, just as God did after the creation. 11Let us do our best to go into that place of rest, too, being careful not to disobey God as the children of Israel did, thus failing to get in.

12For whatever God says to us is full of living power: it is sharper than the sharpest dagger, cutting swift and deep into our innermost thoughts and desires with all their parts, exposing us for what we really are. 13He knows about everyone, everywhere. Everything about us is bare and wide open to the all-seeing eyes of our living God; nothing can be hidden from him to whom we must explain all that we have done.

A THOUGHT: *The Word of God is not merely words from God, a vehicle for communicating ideas; it is living, life-changing, and dynamic as it works in us. With the incisiveness of a surgeon's knife, it reveals who we are and what we are not. It discerns what is within us, both good and evil. We must not only listen to the Word; we must let it shape our lives.*

Proverbs for Today/ 24:9-10

The rebel's schemes are sinful, and the mocker is the scourge of all mankind. □ You are a poor specimen if you can't stand the pressure of adversity.

SEPTEMBER 30

Jesus Commands Peter to Feed His Sheep/
John 21:15–25

After breakfast Jesus said to Simon Peter, "Simon, son of John, do you love me more than these others?"

"Yes," Peter replied, "You know I am your friend."

"Then feed my lambs," Jesus told him.

16Jesus repeated the question: "Simon, son of John, do you *really* love me?"

"Yes, Lord," Peter said, "you know I am your friend."

"Then take care of my sheep," Jesus said.

17Once more he asked him, "Simon, son of John, are you even my friend?"

Peter was grieved at the way Jesus asked the question this third time. "Lord, you know my heart; you know I am," he said.

Jesus said, "Then feed my little sheep. 18When you were young, you were able to do as you liked and go wherever you wanted to; but when you are old, you will stretch out your hands and others will direct you and take you where you don't want to go." 19Jesus said this to let him know what kind of death he would die to glorify God. Then Jesus told him, "Follow me."

20Peter turned around and saw the disciple Jesus loved following, the one who had leaned around at supper that time to ask Jesus, "Master, which of us will betray you?" 21Peter asked Jesus, "What about him, Lord? What sort of death will he die?"

22Jesus replied, "If I want him to live until I return, what is that to you? *You* follow me."

23So the rumor spread among the brotherhood that that disciple wouldn't die! But that isn't what Jesus said at all! He only said, "If I want him to live until I come, what is that to you?"

24*I am that disciple!* I saw these events and have recorded them here. And we all know that my account of these things is accurate.

25And I suppose that if all the other events in Jesus' life were written, the whole world could hardly contain the books!

A THOUGHT: *Jesus asked Peter three times if he loved him. The first time Jesus said, "Do you love [the Greek word here is agape: signifying volitional, self–sacrificial love] me more than these others?" The second time, Jesus focused on Peter alone and still used the Greek word agape. The third time, Jesus used the Greek word phileo, (signifying affection, affinity, or brotherly love) and asked, "Are you even my friend?" Each time Peter responded with the Greek word phileo. Jesus doesn't settle for quick, superficial answers. He has a way of getting to the heart of the matter. Peter had to face his true feelings and motives when confronted by Christ. How would you respond if Jesus asked you, "Do you love me?" Do you really love Jesus? Are you even his friend?*

Jesus Understands Our Weaknesses/
Hebrews 4:14—5:6

But Jesus the Son of God is our great High Priest who has gone to heaven itself to help us; therefore let us never stop trusting him. 15This High Priest of ours understands our weaknesses, since he had the same temptations we do, though he never once gave way to them and sinned. 16So let us come boldly to the very throne of God and stay there to receive his mercy and to find grace to help us in our times of need.

5:1The Jewish high priest is merely a man like anyone else, but he is chosen to speak for all other men in their dealings with God. He presents their gifts to God and offers to him the blood of animals that are sacrificed to cover the sins of the people and his own sins too. And because he is a man he can deal gently with other men, though they are foolish and ignorant, for he, too, is surrounded with the same temptations and understands their problems very well.

4Another thing to remember is that no one can be a high priest just because he wants to be. He has to be called by God for this work in the same way God chose Aaron.

5That is why Christ did not elect himself to the honor of being High Priest; no, he was chosen by God. God said to him, "My Son, today I have honored you." 6And another time God said to him, "You have been chosen to be a priest forever, with the same rank as Melchizedek."

A THOUGHT: *Jesus is like us because he experienced every kind of temptation we experience today. But he is different because, although he was tempted, he never sinned. Jesus is the only human being who has ever lived without committing sin. Now in heaven, he completely understands our weaknesses and temptations and offers forgiveness.*

Proverbs for Today/ 24:11–12

Rescue those who are unjustly sentenced to death; don't stand back and let them die. Don't try to disclaim responsibility by saying you didn't know about it. For God, who knows all hearts, knows yours, and he knows you knew! And he will reward everyone according to his deeds.

OCTOBER 1

Jesus Ascends to Heaven/ Acts 1:1–13

Dear friend who loves God:

In my first letter I told you about Jesus' life and teachings and how he returned to heaven after giving his chosen apostles further instructions from the Holy Spirit. 3During the forty days after his crucifixion he appeared to the apostles from time to time, actually alive, and proved to them in many ways that it was really he himself they were seeing. And on these occasions he talked to them about the Kingdom of God.

4In one of these meetings he told them not to leave Jerusalem until the Holy Spirit came upon them in fulfillment of the Father's promise, a matter he had previously discussed with them.

5"John baptized you with water," he reminded them, "but you shall be baptized with the Holy Spirit in just a few days."

6And another time when he appeared to them, they asked him, "Lord, are you going to free Israel [from Rome] now and restore us as an independent nation?"

7"The Father sets those dates," he replied, "and they are not for you to know. 8But when the Holy Spirit has come upon you, you will receive power to testify about me with great effect, to the people in Jerusalem, throughout Judea, in Samaria, and to the ends of the earth, about my death and resurrection."

9It was not long afterwards that he rose into the sky and disappeared into a cloud, leaving them staring after him. 10As they were straining their eyes for another glimpse, suddenly two white-robed men were standing there among them, 11and said, "Men of Galilee, why are you standing here staring at the sky? Jesus has gone away to heaven, and some day, just as he went, he will return!"

12They were at the Mount of Olives when this happened, so now they walked the half mile back to Jerusalem 13and held a prayer meeting in an upstairs room of the house where they were staying.

A THOUGHT: *After 40 days with his disciples, Jesus ascended into heaven. Two angels proclaimed to the disciples that one day Jesus would return in the same way he went—bodily and visibly. History is not haphazard; it is moving toward a specific point—the return of Jesus to judge and rule over the earth. We should be ready for his sudden return, not by standing around "gazing into the sky," but by working hard to share the gospel so others will be able to share in God's great blessings.*

Jesus Learned Obedience through Suffering/ Hebrews 5:7–10

Yet while Christ was here on earth he pleaded with God, praying with tears and agony of soul to the only one who would save him from [premature] death. And God heard his prayers because of his strong desire to obey God at all times.

8And even though Jesus was God's Son, he had to learn from experience what it was like to obey, when obeying meant suffering. 9It was after he had proved himself perfect in this experience that Jesus became the Giver of eternal salvation to all those who obey him. 10For remember that God has chosen him to be a High Priest with the same rank as Melchizedek.

A THOUGHT: *Jesus found no pleasure in suffering and dying, but he chose to endure pain and humiliation in order to obey his Father. At times we will choose to undergo trials, not because we want to suffer, but because we want to obey God. Let Jesus' obedience sustain you and encourage you in times of trial. You can face anything when you know Jesus Christ is with you.*

Proverbs for Today/ 24:13–14

My son, honey whets the appetite, and so does wisdom! When you enjoy becoming wise, there is hope for you! A bright future lies ahead!

OCTOBER 2

Matthias Is Chosen to Be an Apostle/ Acts 1:14–26

Here is the list of those who were present at the meeting:

Peter,
John, James,
Andrew,
Philip, Thomas,
Bartholomew,
Matthew,
James (son of Alphaeus),
Simon (also called "The Zealot"),
Judas (son of James),
and the brothers of Jesus.
Several women, including Jesus' mother, were also
there.

15This prayer meeting went on for several days. During this time, on a day when about 120 people were present, Peter stood up and addressed them as follows:

16"Brothers, it was necessary for the Scriptures to come true concerning Judas, who betrayed Jesus by guiding the mob to him, for this was predicted long ago by the Holy Spirit, speaking through King David. 17Judas was one of us, chosen to be an apostle just as we were. 18He bought a field with the money he received for his treachery and falling headlong there, he burst open, spilling out his bowels. 19The news of his death spread rapidly among all the people of Jerusalem, and they named the place 'The Field of Blood.' 20King David's prediction of this appears in the Book of Psalms, where he says, 'Let his home become desolate with no one living in it.' And again, 'Let his work be given to someone else to do.'

21,22"So now we must choose someone else to take Judas' place and to join us as witnesses of Jesus' resurrection. Let us select someone who has been with us constantly from our first association with the Lord—from the time he was baptized by John until the day he was taken from us into heaven."

23The assembly nominated two men: Joseph Justus (also

called Barsabbas) and Matthias. 24,25Then they all prayed for the right man to be chosen. "O Lord," they said, "you know every heart; show us which of these men you have chosen as an apostle to replace Judas the traitor, who has gone on to his proper place."

26Then they drew straws, and in this manner Matthias was chosen and became an apostle with the other eleven.

A THOUGHT: *The apostles had to choose a replacement for Judas Iscariot. They outlined specific criteria for making the choice. When the "finalists" had been chosen, the apostles prayed, asking God to guide the selection process. This gives us a good example of how to proceed when we are making important decisions. Set up criteria consistent with the Bible, examine the alternatives, and pray for wisdom and guidance to reach a wise decision.*

Maturity Versus Immaturity/ Hebrews 5:11–14

There is much more I would like to say along these lines, but you don't seem to listen, so it's hard to make you understand.

12,13You have been Christians a long time now, and you ought to be teaching others, but instead you have dropped back to the place where you need someone to teach you all over again the very first principles in God's Word. You are like babies who can drink only milk, not old enough for solid food. And when a person is still living on milk it shows he isn't very far along in the Christian life, and doesn't know much about the difference between right and wrong. He is still a baby-Christian! 14You will never be able to eat solid spiritual food and understand the deeper things of God's Word until you become better Christians and learn right from wrong by practicing doing right.

A THOUGHT: *In order to grow from a "baby" Christian to a "grown-up" Christian, we must learn discernment. By practice and exercise, we must train our consciences, our senses, our minds, and our bodies to distinguish right from wrong. Can you recognize temptation before it controls you? Can you tell correct use of Scripture from mistaken or shallow uses?*

Proverbs for Today/ 24:15–16

O evil man, leave the upright man alone, and quit trying to cheat him out of his rights. Don't you know that this

good man, though you trip him up seven times, will each
time rise again? But one calamity is enough to lay you
low.

OCTOBER 3

The Coming of the Holy Spirit at Pentecost/
Acts 2:1–13

Seven weeks had gone by since Jesus' death and resurrection, and the Day of Pentecost had now arrived. As
the believers met together that day, 2suddenly there was
a sound like the roaring of a mighty windstorm in the
skies above them and it filled the house where they were
meeting. 3Then, what looked like flames or tongues of
fire appeared and settled on their heads. 4And everyone
present was filled with the Holy Spirit and began speaking
in languages they didn't know, for the Holy Spirit gave
them this ability.

5Many godly Jews were in Jerusalem that day for the
religious celebrations, having arrived from many nations.
6And when they heard the roaring in the sky above the
house, crowds came running to see what it was all about,
and were stunned to hear their own languages being spoken
by the disciples.

7"How can this be?" they exclaimed. "For these men
are all from Galilee, 8and yet we hear them speaking all
the native languages of the lands where we were born!
9Here we are—Parthians, Medes, Elamites, men from
Mesopotamia, Judea, Cappadocia, Pontus, Ausia,
10Phrygia, Pamphylia, Egypt, the Cyrene language areas
of Libya, visitors from Rome—both Jews and Jewish converts—11Cretans, and Arabians. And we all hear these
men telling in our own languages about the mighty miracles
of God!"

12They stood there amazed and perplexed. "What can
this mean?" they asked each other.

13But others in the crowd were mocking. "They're drunk,
that's all!" they said.

A Thought: *God made his presence known to this group of believers in a spectacular way—roaring wind, fire, and his Holy Spirit. Would you like God to reveal himself to you in such recognizable ways? Beware of forcing your expectations on God. Elijah, the great prophet of the Old Testament, also needed a message from God. There was a mighty wind, then an earthquake, and finally a fire. But God's message came in a gentle whisper. God may use dramatic methods to work in your life—or he may speak in gentle whispers. Wait patiently and always listen for him.*

Go Beyond Elementary Principles/ Hebrews 6:1–6

Let us stop going over the same old ground again and again, always teaching those first lessons about Christ. Let us go on instead to other things and become mature in our understanding, as strong Christians ought to be. Surely we don't need to speak further about the foolishness of trying to be saved by being good, or about the necessity of faith in God; 2you don't need further instruction about baptism and spiritual gifts and the resurrection of the dead and eternal judgment.

3The Lord willing, we will go on now to other things.

4There is no use trying to bring you back to the Lord again if you have once understood the Good News and tasted for yourself the good things of heaven and shared in the Holy Spirit, 5and know how good the Word of God is, and felt the mighty powers of the world to come, 6and then have turned against God. You cannot bring yourself to repent again if you have nailed the Son of God to the cross again by rejecting him, holding him up to mocking and to public shame.

A Thought: *Certain basics are essential for all believers. Those principles that all Christians must know include repentance, baptism, faith, etc. We need to move on to a more complete theology, to a more profound understanding of the faith. Christians should be teaching new Christians the basics, and then, acting on what they know, new Christians should be learning even more from God's Word.*

Proverbs for Today/ 24:17–20

Do not rejoice when your enemy meets trouble. Let there be no gladness when he falls—for the Lord may be displeased with you and stop punishing him! Don't envy the wicked. Don't covet his riches. For the evil man has no future; his light will be snuffed out.

OCTOBER 4

Peter's Sermon/ Acts 2:14–39

Then Peter stepped forward with the eleven apostles, and shouted to the crowd, "Listen, all of you, visitors and residents of Jerusalem alike! 15Some of you are saying these men are drunk! It isn't true! It's much too early for that! People don't get drunk by 9 A.M.! 16No! What you see this morning was predicted centuries ago by the prophet Joel— 17'In the last days,' God said, 'I will pour out my Holy Spirit upon all mankind, and your sons and daughters shall prophesy, and your young men shall see visions, and your old men dream dreams. 18Yes, the Holy Spirit shall come upon all my servants, men and women alike, and they shall prophesy. 19And I will cause strange demonstrations in the heavens and on the earth—blood and fire and clouds of smoke; 20the sun shall turn black and the moon blood-red before that awesome Day of the Lord arrives. 21But anyone who asks for mercy from the Lord shall have it and shall be saved.'

22"O men of Israel, listen! God publicly endorsed Jesus of Nazareth by doing tremendous miracles through him, as you well know. 23But God, following his prearranged plan, let you use the Roman government to nail him to the cross and murder him. 24Then God released him from the horrors of death and brought him back to life again, for death could not keep this man within its grip.

25"King David quoted Jesus as saying:

'I know the Lord is always with me. He is helping me. God's mighty power supports me.

26'No wonder my heart is filled with joy and my tongue shouts his praises! For I know all will be well with me in death—

27'You will not leave my soul in hell or let the body of your Holy Son decay.

28'You will give me back my life, and give me wonderful joy in your presence.'

29"Dear brothers, think! David wasn't referring to himself when he spoke these words I have quoted, for he died and was buried, and his tomb is still here among us. 30But he was a prophet, and knew God had promised with an unbreakable oath that one of David's own descendants would [be the Messiah and] sit on David's throne. 31David was looking far into the future and predicting the Messiah's resurrection, and saying that the Messiah's soul would not be left in hell and his body would not decay. 32He was speaking of Jesus, and we all are witnesses that Jesus rose from the dead.

33"And now he sits on the throne of highest honor in heaven, next to God. And just as promised, the Father gave him the authority to send the Holy Spirit—with the results you are seeing and hearing today.

34"[No, David was not speaking of himself in these words of his I have quoted], for he never ascended into the skies. Moreover, he further stated, 'God spoke to my Lord, the Messiah, and said to him, Sit here in honor beside me 35until I bring your enemies into complete subjection.'

36"Therefore I clearly state to everyone in Israel that God has made this Jesus you crucified to be the Lord, the Messiah!"

37These words of Peter's moved them deeply, and they said to him and to the other apostles, "Brothers, what should we do?"

38And Peter replied, "Each one of you must turn from sin, return to God, and be baptized in the name of Jesus Christ for the forgiveness of your sins; then you also shall receive this gift, the Holy Spirit. 39For Christ promised him to each one of you who has been called by the Lord our God, and to your children and even to those in distant lands!"

A THOUGHT: *Peter had been an unstable leader during Jesus' ministry, letting his bravado be his downfall, even denying that he knew Jesus. But Christ forgave him and restored him after his denial. This is a new Peter, humble but bold. His confidence comes from the Holy Spirit, who makes him a powerful and dynamic speaker. Have you ever felt as if you've made such bad mistakes that God could never forgive and use you? No matter what sins you have committed, if you genuinely admit your sins to God and turn away from those sins, he promises to forgive them and make you useful for his kingdom. Allow him to forgive you and effectively use you in service for him.*

The Example of Abraham/ Hebrews 6:7–15

When a farmer's land has had many showers upon it and good crops come up, that land has experienced God's blessing upon it. 8But if it keeps on having crops of thistles and thorns, the land is considered no good and is ready for condemnation and burning off.

9Dear friends, even though I am talking like this I really don't believe that what I am saying applies to you. I am confident you are producing the good fruit that comes along with your salvation. 10For God is not unfair. How can he forget your hard work for him, or forget the way you used to show your love for him—and still do—by helping his children? 11And we are anxious that you keep right on loving others as long as life lasts, so that you will get your full reward.

12Then, knowing what lies ahead for you, you won't become bored with being a Christian, nor become spiritually dull and indifferent, but you will be anxious to follow the example of those who receive all that God has promised them because of their strong faith and patience.

13For instance, there was God's promise to Abraham: God took an oath in his own name, since there was no one greater to swear by, 14that he would bless Abraham again and again, and give him a son and make him the father of a great nation of people. 15Then Abraham waited patiently until finally God gave him a son, Isaac, just as he had promised.

A THOUGHT: *In the midst of difficult times we must remember God's promises. Abraham serves as an example of steadfast faith. God had promised Abraham that he would be the father of a great nation. Abraham waited patiently for many years until the birth of his son Isaac. Even this great event was marked by Abraham's faith, for Abraham trusted that God would keep his promise to make him the father of a great nation even though he could only "see it" by faith. He saw in Isaac the fulfillment of the promise which was to come. Our faith in God must be based on what God has done in the past. We trust God because he has been faithful to fulfill his promises to his people.*

Proverbs for Today/ 24:21–22

My son, watch your step before the Lord and the king, and don't associate with radicals. For you will go down with them to sudden disaster, and who knows where it all will end?

The Fellowship of the Jerusalem Church/
Acts 2:40–47

Then Peter preached a long sermon, telling about Jesus and strongly urging all his listeners to save themselves from the evils of their nation. 41And those who believed Peter were baptized—about 3,000 in all! 42They joined with the other believers in regular attendance at the apostles' teaching sessions and at the Communion services and prayer meetings.

43A deep sense of awe was on them all, and the apostles did many miracles.

44And all the believers met together constantly and shared everything with each other, 45selling their possessions and dividing with those in need. 46They worshiped together regularly at the Temple each day, met in small groups in homes for Communion, and shared their meals with great joy and thankfulness, 47praising God. The whole city was favorable to them, and each day God added to them all who were being saved.

A THOUGHT: *Because they recognized other believers as brothers and sisters in the family of God, the Christians in Jerusalem shared all they had so that all could benefit from God's blessings. It is tempting—especially if we have material wealth—to cut ourselves off from one another, each taking care of his own, each providing for and enjoying his own little piece of the world. But as part of God's spiritual family, we have a responsibility to help one another in every way possible. God's family works best when its members work together.*

The Assurance of God's Promises/ Hebrews 6:16–20

When a man takes an oath, he is calling upon someone greater than himself to force him to do what he has promised, or to punish him if he later refuses to do it; the oath ends all argument about it. 17God also bound himself with an oath, so that those he promised to help would be perfectly sure and never need to wonder whether he might change his plans.

18He has given us both his promise and his oath, two things we can completely count on, for it is impossible for God to tell a lie. Now all those who flee to him to save them can take new courage when they hear such assurances from God; now they can know without doubt that he will give them the salvation he has promised them.

19This certain hope of being saved is a strong and trustworthy anchor for our souls, connecting us with God himself behind the sacred curtains of heaven, 20where Christ has gone ahead to plead for us from his position as our High Priest, with the honor and rank of Melchizedek.

A THOUGHT: *God's promises are unchangeable and trustworthy because God is unchangeable and trustworthy. When God promised Abraham a son, he took an oath in his own name. The oath was as good as his name, and his name was as good as his divine nature. God embodies all truth, and he therefore cannot lie. Because God is truth, you can be secure in his promises; you don't need to wonder if he will change his plans. For the true seeker who comes to God in belief, God gives an unconditional promise of acceptance. When you ask God in all openness, honesty, and sincerity of heart to save you from your sins, he will do it. This assurance should give you courage and hope.*

Proverbs for Today/ 24:23–25

It is wrong to sentence the poor, and let the rich go free. □ He who says to the wicked, "You are innocent," shall be cursed by many people of many nations; but blessings shall be showered on those who rebuke sin fearlessly.

OCTOBER 6

Peter Heals a Man Who Could not Walk/
Acts 3:1–26

Peter and John went to the Temple one afternoon to take part in the three o'clock daily prayer meeting. 2As they approached the Temple, they saw a man lame from birth carried along the street and laid beside the Temple gate—the one called The Beautiful Gate—as was his custom every day. 3As Peter and John were passing by, he asked them for some money.

4They looked at him intently, and then Peter said, "Look here!"

5The lame man looked at them eagerly, expecting a gift.

6But Peter said, "We don't have any money for you! But I'll give you something else! I command you in the name of Jesus Christ of Nazareth, *walk!*"

7,8Then Peter took the lame man by the hand and pulled him to his feet. And as he did, the man's feet and ankle-bones were healed and strengthened so that he came up with a leap, stood there a moment and began walking! Then, walking, leaping, and praising God, he went into the Temple with them.

9When the people inside saw him walking and heard him praising God, 10and realized he was the lame beggar they had seen so often at The Beautiful Gate, they were inexpressibly surprised! 11They all rushed out to Solomon's Hall, where he was holding tightly to Peter and John! Everyone stood there awed by the wonderful thing that had happened.

12Peter saw his opportunity and addressed the crowd. "Men of Israel," he said, "what is so surprising about this? And why look at us as though we by our own power and godliness had made this man walk? 13For it is the God of Abraham, Isaac, Jacob and of all our ancestors who has brought glory to his servant Jesus by doing this. I refer to the Jesus whom you rejected before Pilate, despite Pilate's determination to release him. 14You didn't want him freed—this holy, righteous one. Instead you demanded the release of a murderer. 15And you killed the Author of Life; but God brought him back to life again. And John and I are witnesses of this fact, for after you killed him we saw him alive!

16"Jesus' name has healed this man—and you know how lame he was before. Faith in Jesus' name—faith given us from God—has caused this perfect healing.

17"Dear brothers, I realize that what you did to Jesus was done in ignorance; and the same can be said of your leaders. 18But God was fulfilling the prophecies that the Messiah must suffer all these things. 19Now change your mind and attitude to God and turn to him so he can cleanse away your sins and send you wonderful times of refreshment from the presence of the Lord 20and send Jesus your Messiah back to you again. 21,22For he must remain in heaven until the final recovery of all things from sin, as prophesied from ancient times. Moses, for instance, said long ago, 'The Lord God will raise up a Prophet among you, who will resemble me! Listen carefully to everything he tells you. 23Anyone who will not listen to him shall be utterly destroyed.'

24"Samuel and every prophet since have all spoken about what is going on today. 25You are the children of those prophets; and you are included in God's promise to your ancestors to bless the entire world through the Jewish race—that is the promise God gave to Abraham. 26And as soon as God had brought his servant to life again, he sent him first of all to you men of Israel, to bless you by turning you back from your sins."

A THOUGHT: *When we repent, God promises not only to wipe away our sin, but to bring spiritual refreshment. Repentance may at first seem painful because it is hard to give up certain sins. But God will give you a better way. As Hosea promised, "Let us press on to know him, and he will respond to us as surely as the coming of dawn or the rain of early spring" (Hosea 6:3). Do you feel a need to be refreshed?*

Melchizedek Is Greater Than the Levitical Priesthood/ Hebrews 7:1–11

This Melchizedek was king of the city of Salem, and also a priest of the Most High God. When Abraham was returning home after winning a great battle against many kings, Melchizedek met him and blessed him; 2then Abraham took a tenth of all he had won in the battle and gave it to Melchizedek.

Melchizedek's name means "Justice," so he is the King of Justice; and he is also the King of Peace because of the name of his city, Salem, which means "Peace." 3Melchizedek had no father or mother and there is no record of any of his ancestors. He was never born and he never died but his life is like that of the Son of God— a priest forever.

4See then how great this Melchizedek is:

(a)Even Abraham, the first and most honored of all God's chosen people, gave Melchizedek a tenth of the spoils he took from the kings he had been fighting. 5One could understand why Abraham would do this if Melchizedek had been a Jewish priest, for later on God's people were required by law to give gifts to help their priests because the priests were their relatives. 6But Melchizedek was not a relative, and yet Abraham paid him.

(b)Melchizedek placed a blessing upon mighty Abraham, 7and as everyone knows, a person who has the power to bless is always greater than the person he blesses.

8(c)The Jewish priests, though mortal, received tithes; but we are told that Melchizedek lives on.

9(d)One might even say that Levi himself (the ancestor of all Jewish priests, of all who receive tithes), paid tithes to Melchizedek through Abraham. 10For although Levi wasn't born yet, the seed from which he came was in Abraham when Abraham paid the tithes to Melchizedek.

11(e)If the Jewish priests and their laws had been able to save us, why then did God need to send Christ as a priest with the rank of Melchizedek, instead of sending someone with the rank of Aaron—the same rank all other priests had?

A Thought: *The writer of Hebrews uses this story about Melchizedek to show that there is someone greater even than Abraham, father of the Jewish nation, and Levi (Abraham's descendant). Therefore, the Jewish priesthood (made up of Levi's descendants) was inferior to Melchizedek's priesthood (a type of Christ's priesthood). Melchizedek is said to be a priest forever in Psalm 110:4, because his priesthood has no record of beginning or end—he was a priest of God in Salem (Jerusalem) long before the nation of Israel and the levitical system began. Christ is the culmination of Melchizedek's priesthood—Jesus is the ultimate High Priest, there is no greater priest.*

Proverbs for Today/ 24:26

It is an honor to receive a frank reply.

OCTOBER 7

Peter's Defense before the Jewish Supreme Court/ Acts 4:1–22

While Peter and John were talking to the people, the chief priests, the captain of the Temple police, and some of the Sadducees came over to them, 2very disturbed that Peter and John were claiming that Jesus had risen from the dead. 3They arrested them and since it was already evening, jailed them overnight. 4But many of the people who heard their message believed it, so that the number of believers now reached a new high of about 5,000 men!

5The next day it happened that the Council of all the Jewish leaders was in session in Jerusalem— 6Annas the High Priest was there, and Caiaphas, John, Alexander, and others of the High Priest's relatives. 7So the two disciples were brought in before them.

"By what power, or by whose authority have you done this?" the Council demanded.

8Then Peter, filled with the Holy Spirit, said to them, "Honorable leaders and elders of our nation, 9if you mean the good deed done to the cripple, and how he was healed, 10let me clearly state to you and to all the people of Israel that it was done in the name and power of Jesus from Nazareth, the Messiah, the man you crucified—but God raised back to life again. It is by his authority that this man stands here healed! 11For Jesus the Messiah is (the one referred to in the Scriptures when they speak of) a 'stone discarded by the builders which became the capstone of the arch.' 12There is salvation in no one else! Under all heaven there is no other name for men to call upon to save them."

13When the Council saw the boldness of Peter and John, and could see that they were obviously uneducated non-professionals, they were amazed and realized what being with Jesus had done for them! 14And the Council could hardly discredit the healing when the man they had healed was standing right there beside them! 15So they sent them out of the Council chamber and conferred among themselves.

16"What shall we do with these men?" they asked each other. "We can't deny that they have done a tremendous miracle, and everybody in Jerusalem knows about it. 17But perhaps we can stop them from spreading their propaganda. We'll tell them that if they do it again we'll really throw the book at them." 18So they called them back in, and told them never again to speak about Jesus.

19But Peter and John replied, "You decide whether God wants us to obey you instead of him! 20We cannot stop telling about the wonderful things we saw Jesus do and heard him say."

²¹The Council then threatened them further, and finally let them go because they didn't know how to punish them without starting a riot. For everyone was praising God for this wonderful miracle — ²²the healing of a man who had been lame for forty years.

A THOUGHT: *Not often will our witnessing send us to prison as it did Peter and John. Still, we run risks in trying to win others to Christ. We might be willing to face a night in prison if it would bring 2,000 people to Christ, but shouldn't we also be willing to suffer for even one? What do you risk in witnessing—vulnerability, rejection, persecution? We are sometimes afraid to share our faith in God because people might feel uncomfortable and disapprove. But Peter and John's zeal for the Lord was so strong that they could not keep quiet, even when threatened. If your courage to witness for God has weakened, pray that your boldness may increase. Whatever the risks, realize that nothing done for God is ever wasted. Remember Jesus' promise, "If anyone publicly acknowledges me as his friend, I will openly acknowledge him as my friend before my father who is in heaven" (Matthew 10:32).*

Jesus Is a High Priest Like Melchizedek/ Hebrews 7:12–22

And when God sends a new kind of priest, his law must be changed to permit it. As we all know, Christ did not belong to the priest-tribe of Levi, but came from the tribe of Judah, which had not been chosen for priesthood; Moses had never given them that work. ¹⁵So we can plainly see that God's method changed, for Christ, the new High Priest who came with the rank of Melchizedek, ¹⁶did not become a priest by meeting the old requirement of belonging to the tribe of Levi, but on the basis of power flowing from a life that cannot end. ¹⁷And the Psalmist points this out when he says of Christ, "You are a priest forever with the rank of Melchizedek."

¹⁸Yes, the old system of priesthood based on family lines was canceled because it didn't work. It was weak and useless for saving people. ¹⁹It never made anyone really right with God. But now we have a far better hope, for Christ makes us acceptable to God, and now we, may draw near to him.

²⁰God took an oath that Christ would always be a Priest, ²¹although he never said that of other priests. Only to Christ he said, "The Lord has sworn and will never change his mind: You are a Priest forever, with the rank of Melchize-

dek." 22Because of God's oath, Christ can guarantee forever the success of this new and better arrangement.

A THOUGHT: *Jesus' high-priestly role was superior to that of any priest of Levi, because the Messiah was a priest of a higher rank. The animal sacrifices under the old covenant had to be repeated, and they offered only temporary forgiveness; Christ's sacrifice was offered once, and it offers total and permanent forgiveness. Under the new covenant, the levitical priesthood was cancelled in favor of Christ's role as High Priest.*

Proverbs for Today/ 24:27

Develop your business first before building your house.

OCTOBER 8

The Jerusalem Believers Unite in Prayer/
Acts 4:23–37

As soon as they were freed, Peter and John found the other disciples and told them what the Council had said. 24Then all the believers united in this prayer:

"O Lord, Creator of heaven and earth and of the sea and everything in them— 25,26you spoke long ago by the Holy Spirit through our ancestor King David, your servant, saying, 'Why do the heathen rage against the Lord, and the foolish nations plan their little plots against Almighty God? The kings of the earth unite to fight against him, and against the anointed Son of God!'

27"That is what is happening here in this city today! For Herod the king, and Pontius Pilate the governor, and all the Romans—as well as the people of Israel—are united against Jesus, your anointed Son, your holy servant. 28They won't stop at anything that you in your wise power will let them do. 29And now, O Lord, hear their threats, and grant to your servants great boldness in their preaching, 30and send your healing power, and may miracles and wonders be done by the name of your holy servant Jesus."

31After this prayer, the building where they were meeting shook and they were all filled with the Holy Spirit and boldly preached God's message.

32All the believers were of one heart and mind, and no one felt that what he owned was his own; everyone was sharing. 33And the apostles preached powerful sermons about the resurrection of the Lord Jesus, and there was warm fellowship among all the believers, 34, 35and no poverty—for all who owned land or houses sold them and brought the money to the apostles to give to others in need.

36For instance, there was Joseph (the one the apostles nicknamed "Barny the Preacher"! He was of the tribe of Levi, from the island of Cyprus). 37He was one of those who sold a field he owned and brought the money to the apostles for distribution to those in need.

A THOUGHT: *Notice how the believers prayed. First they praised God; then they told God their specific problem and asked for his help. They did not ask God to remove the problem, but to help them deal with it. This is a model for us to follow when we pray. We may ask God to remove our problems, and he may choose to do so, but we must recognize that often he will leave the problem in place and give us the grace to deal with it.*

Jesus Is a Priest Forever/ Hebrews 7:23–28

Under the old arrangement there had to be many priests, so that when the older ones died off, the system could still be carried on by others who took their places.

24But Jesus lives forever and continues to be a Priest so that no one else is needed. 25He is able to save completely all who come to God through him. Since he will live forever, he will always be there to remind God that he has paid for their sins with his blood.

26He is, therefore, exactly the kind of High Priest we need; for he is holy and blameless, unstained by sin, undefiled by sinners, and to him has been given the place of honor in heaven. 27He never needs the daily blood of animal sacrifices, as other priests did, to cover over first their own sins and then the sins of the people; for he finished all sacrifices, once and for all, when he sacrificed himself on the cross. 28Under the old system, even the high priests were weak and sinful men who could not keep from doing wrong, but later God appointed by his oath his Son who is perfect forever.

A THOUGHT: *What does it mean that Jesus is able to save completely? No one else can add to what Jesus did to save us; our past, present, and future sins are all forgiven. As our High Priest, Christ is our advocate, the mediator between us and God. The Old Testament High Priest went before God once a year to plead for the forgiveness of the nation's sins; Christ makes perpetual intercession before God for us. Christ's presence in heaven with the Father assures us that our sins have been paid for and forgiven. If you are a Christian, remember that Christ has paid the price for your sins once and for all.*

Proverbs for Today/ 24:28–29

Don't testify spitefully against an innocent neighbor. Why lie about him? Don't say, "Now I can pay him back for all his meanness to me!"

OCTOBER 9

Ananias and Sapphira Are Judged/ Acts 5:1–11

But there was a man named Ananias (with his wife Sapphira) who sold some property, 2and brought only part of the money, claiming it was the full price. (His wife had agreed to this deception.)

3But Peter said, "Ananias, Satan has filled your heart. When you claimed this was the full price, you were lying to the Holy Spirit. 4The property was yours to sell or not, as you wished. And after selling it, it was yours to decide how much to give. How could you do a thing like this? You weren't lying to us, but to God."

5As soon as Ananias heard these words, he fell to the floor, dead! Everyone was terrified, 6and the younger men covered him with a sheet and took him out and buried him.

7About three hours later his wife came in, not knowing what had happened. 8Peter asked her, "Did you people sell your land for such and such a price?"

"Yes," she replied, "we did."

9And Peter said, "How could you and your husband even think of doing a thing like this—conspiring together to test the Spirit of God's ability to know what is going on? Just outside that door are the young men who buried your husband, and they will carry you out too."

10Instantly she fell to the floor, dead, and the young men came in and, seeing that she was dead, carried her out and buried her beside her husband. 11Terror gripped the entire church and all others who heard what had happened.

A THOUGHT: *The sin Ananias and Sapphira committed was not stinginess or holding back part of the money—they could choose whether or not to sell the land they owned and how much money to give. Their sin was lying to God and God's people—saying they gave the whole amount but holding back some for themselves, trying to make themselves appear more generous than they really were. This act was judged harshly because dishonesty and covetousness are destructive in a church, preventing the Holy Spirit from working effectively. When we lie to try to deceive God and his people about our relationship with him, we destroy our testimony for Christ.*

Christ, the Priest of a New Covenant/ Hebrews 8:1–6

What we are saying is this: Christ, whose priesthood we have just described, is our High Priest, and is in heaven at the place of greatest honor next to God himself. 2He ministers in the temple in heaven, the true place of worship built by the Lord and not by human hands.

3And since every high priest is appointed to offer gifts and sacrifices, Christ must make an offering too. 4The sacrifice he offers is far better than those offered by the earthly priests. (But even so, if he were here on earth he wouldn't even be permitted to be a priest, because down here the priests still follow the old Jewish system of sacrifices.) 5Their work is connected with a mere earthly model of the real tabernacle in heaven; for when Moses was getting ready to build the tabernacle, God warned him to follow exactly the pattern of the heavenly tabernacle as shown to him on Mount Sinai. 6But Christ, as a Minister in heaven, has been rewarded with a far more important work than those who serve under the old laws, because the new agreement which he passes on to us from God contains far more wonderful promises.

A THOUGHT: *This "new agreement" is also called the new covenant or new testament. It is new in allowing us to go directly to God through Christ, no longer having to rely on sacrificed animals and priests to gain God's forgiveness. This new arrangement is better because, while priests died, Christ lives forever. Priests and sacrifices could not save people, but Christ truly saves.*

Proverbs for Today/ 24:30–34

I walked by the field of a certain lazy fellow and saw that it was overgrown with thorns, and covered with weeds; and its walls were broken down. Then, as I looked, I learned this lesson: "A little extra sleep, A little more slumber, A little folding of the hands to rest" means that poverty will break in upon you suddenly like a robber, and violently like a bandit.

OCTOBER 10

An Angel Rescues the Apostles from Jail/ Acts 5:12–25

Meanwhile, the apostles were meeting regularly at the Temple in the area known as Solomon's Hall, and they did many remarkable miracles among the people. 13The other believers didn't dare join them, though, but all had the highest regard for them. 14And more and more believers were added to the Lord, crowds both of men and women. 15Sick people were brought out into the streets on beds and mats so that at least Peter's shadow would fall across some of them as he went by! 16And crowds came in from the Jerusalem suburbs, bringing their sick folk and those possessed by demons; and every one of them was healed.

17The High Priest and his relatives and friends among the Sadducees reacted with violent jealousy 18and arrested the apostles, and put them in the public jail.

19But an angel of the Lord came at night, opened the gates of the jail and brought them out. Then he told them, 20"Go over to the Temple and preach about this Life!"

21They arrived at the Temple about daybreak, and immediately began preaching! Later that morning the High Priest and his courtiers arrived at the Temple, and, convening the Jewish Council and the entire Senate, they sent for the apostles to be brought for trial. 22But when the police arrived at the jail, the men weren't there, so they returned to the Council and reported, 23"The jail doors were locked, and the guards were standing outside, but when we opened the gates, no one was there!"

24When the police captain and the chief priests heard this, they were frantic, wondering what would happen next and where all this would end! 25Then someone arrived with the news that the men they had jailed were out in the Temple, preaching to the people!

A THOUGHT: *The apostles had power to do miracles, great boldness in preaching, and God's presence in their lives; yet they were not free from being hated and persecuted. They were arrested and put in jail, beaten with rods and whips, and slandered by community leaders. Faith in God does not make troubles disappear; it makes troubles appear less fearsome because it puts them in the right perspective. You cannot expect everyone to react favorably when you share something as dynamic as your faith in Christ. Some will be jealous of you, frightened, or threatened. Expect some negative reactions. But remember that you must be more concerned about God's reactions than the reactions of other people.*

The Old Agreement Versus the New Agreement/ Hebrews 8:7–13

The old agreement didn't even work. If it had, there would have been no need for another to replace it. 8But God himself found fault with the old one, for he said, "The day will come when I will make a new agreement with the people of Israel and the people of Judah. 9This new agreement will not be like the old one I gave to their fathers on the day when I took them by the hand to lead them out of the land of Egypt; they did not keep their part in that agreement, so I had to cancel it. 10But this is the new agreement I will make with the people of Israel, says the Lord: I will write my laws in their minds so that they will know what I want them to do without my even telling them, and these laws will be in their hearts so that they will want to obey them, and I will be their God and they shall be my people. 11And no one then will need to speak to his friend or neighbor or brother, saying, 'You, too, should know the Lord,' because everyone, great and small, will know me already. 12And I will be merciful to them in their wrongdoings, and I will remember their sins no more."

13God speaks of these new promises, of this new agreement, as taking the place of the old one; for the old one is out of date now and has been put aside forever.

A THOUGHT: *This passage quotes from Jeremiah 31:31–34 and compares the new agreement with the old. The old agreement was the covenant of law between God and Israel. The new and better way is the covenant of grace—Christ's offer to forgive our sins and bring us to God through his sacrificial death. This agreement is new in extent—it goes beyond Israel and Judah to all the Gentile nations. It is new in application, since it is written in our hearts and minds. It offers a new way to forgiveness, not through animal sacrifice but through faith. Have you entered into this new agreement and begun walking in the better way?*

Proverbs for Today/ 25:1–5

These proverbs of Solomon were discovered and copied by the aides of King Hezekiah of Judah: It is God's privilege to conceal things, and the king's privilege to discover and invent. You cannot understand the height of heaven, the size of the earth, or all that goes on in the king's mind! □ When you remove dross from silver, you have sterling ready for the silversmith. When you remove corrupt men from the king's court, his reign will be just and fair.

OCTOBER 11

The Apostles Suffer Persecution/ Acts 5:26–42

The police captain went with his officers and arrested the apostles (without violence, for they were afraid the people would kill them if they roughed up the disciples) and brought them in before the Council.

28"Didn't we tell you never again to preach about this Jesus?" the High Priest demanded. "And instead you have filled all Jerusalem with your teaching and intend to bring the blame for this man's death on us!"

29But Peter and the apostles replied, "We must obey God rather than men. 30The God of our ancestors brought Jesus back to life again after you had killed him by hanging him on a cross. 31Then, with mighty power, God exalted him to be a Prince and Savior, so that the people of Israel would have an opportunity for repentance, and for their sins to be forgiven. 32And we are witnesses of these things, and so is the Holy Spirit, who is given by God to all who obey him."

33At this, the Council was furious, and decided to kill them. 34But one of their members, a Pharisee named Gamaliel (an expert on religious law and very popular with the people), stood up and requested that the apostles be sent outside the Council chamber while he talked.

35Then he addressed his colleagues as follows:

"Men of Israel, take care what you are planning to do to these men! 36Some time ago there was that fellow Theudas, who pretended to be someone great. About 400 others joined him, but he was killed, and his followers were harmlessly dispersed.

37"After him, at the time of the taxation, there was Judas of Galilee. He drew away some people as disciples, but he also died, and his followers scattered.

38"And so my advice is, leave these men alone. If what they teach and do is merely on their own, it will soon be overthrown. 39But if it is of God, you will not be able to stop them, lest you find yourselves fighting even against God."

40The Council accepted his advice, called in the apostles, had them beaten, and then told them never again to speak in the name of Jesus, and finally let them go. 41They left the Council chamber rejoicing that God had counted them worthy to suffer dishonor for his name. 42And every day, in the Temple and in their home Bible classes, they continued to teach and preach that Jesus is the Messiah.

A THOUGHT: *The apostles knew their priorities. While we should try to keep peace with everyone, conflict with the world and its authorities is sometimes inevitable for a Christian. There will be situations where you cannot obey both God and man. Then you must obey God and trust his Word. Let Jesus' words encourage you: "What happiness it is when others hate you and exclude you and insult you and smear your name because you are mine! When that happens, rejoice! Yes, leap for joy! For you will have a great reward awaiting you in heaven" (Luke 6:22, 23). We should live as Christ has asked, sharing our faith no matter what the cost. We may not be beaten or thrown in jail, but we may be ridiculed, ostracized, or slandered. To what extent are you willing to suffer for the sake of sharing the gospel with others?*

The Furniture of the Earthly Tabernacle/
Hebrews 9:1–10

Now in that first agreement between God and his people there were rules for worship and there was a sacred tent down here on earth. Inside this place of worship there were two rooms. The first one contained the golden candlestick and a table with special loaves of holy bread upon it; this part was called the Holy Place. ³Then there was a curtain and behind the curtain was a room called the Holy of Holies. ⁴In that room there were a golden incense-altar and the golden chest, called the ark of the covenant, completely covered on all sides with pure gold. Inside the ark were the tablets of stone with the Ten Commandments written on them, and a golden jar with some manna in it, and Aaron's wooden cane that budded. ⁵Above the golden chest were statues of angels called the cherubim—the guardians of God's glory—with their wings stretched out over the ark's golden cover, called the mercy seat. But enough of such details.

⁶Well, when all was ready the priests went in and out of the first room whenever they wanted to, doing their work. ⁷But only the high priest went into the inner room, and then only once a year, all alone, and always with blood which he sprinkled on the mercy seat as an offering to God to cover his own mistakes and sins, and the mistakes and sins of all the people.

⁸And the Holy Spirit uses all this to point out to us that under the old system the common people could not go into the Holy of Holies as long as the outer room and the entire system it represents were still in use.

⁹This has an important lesson for us today. For under the old system, gifts and sacrifices were offered, but these failed to cleanse the hearts of the people who brought them. 10 For the old system dealt only with certain rituals—what foods to eat and drink, rules for washing themselves, and rules about this and that. The people had to keep these rules to tide them over until Christ came with God's new and better way.

A THOUGHT: *The High Priest could enter the Holy of Holies, the innermost room of the Tabernacle one day each year to atone for the nation's sins—the Day of Atonement. The Holy of Holies was a small room that contained the ark of the covenant (a gold-covered chest containing the original stone tablets on which the Ten Commandments were written, a pot of manna, and Aaron's rod). The top of the chest served as the "mercy seat" (the altar) on which the blood was sprinkled by the High Priest on the Day of Atonement. The Holy of Holies was the most sacred spot on earth for the Jews. Only the High Priest could enter—the other priests and the common people were forbidden to come into the room. Their only access to God was through the High Priest who offered a sacrifice and used its blood to atone first for his own sins and then for the people's sins.*

Proverbs for Today/ 25:6–7

Don't demand an audience with the king as though you were some powerful prince. It is better to wait for an invitation rather than to be sent back to the end of the line, publicly disgraced!

OCTOBER 12

The Church Appoints Seven Deacons/ Acts 6:1–7

But with the believers multiplying rapidly, there were rumblings of discontent. Those who spoke only Greek complained that their widows were being discriminated against, that they were not being given as much food, in the daily distribution, as the widows who spoke Hebrew. ²So the Twelve called a meeting of all the believers.

"We should spend our time preaching, not administering a feeding program," they said. ³"Now look around among yourselves, dear brothers, and select seven men, wise and full of the Holy Spirit, who are well thought of by everyone; and we will put them in charge of this business. ⁴Then we can spend our time in prayer, preaching, and teaching."

⁵This sounded reasonable to the whole assembly, and they elected the following:

Stephen (a man unusually full of faith and the Holy Spirit),
Philip,
Prochorus,
Nicanor,

Timon,

Parmenas,

Nicolaus of Antioch (a Gentile convert to the Jewish faith, who had become a Christian).

6These seven were presented to the apostles, who prayed for them and laid their hands on them in blessing.

7God's message was preached in ever-widening circles, and the number of disciples increased vastly in Jerusalem; and many of the Jewish priests were converted too.

A THOUGHT: *As the early church increased in size, their needs also increased. One need was to organize the distribution of food to the needy. The apostles needed to focus on preaching, so they chose others to administer the food program. Each person has a necessary part to play in the life of the church. If you are in a position of leadership and find yourself bogged down, determine your God–given abilities and priorities and then find others to help. If you are not in leadership, you have gifts that can be used by God in various areas of the church's ministry. Offer these gifts in service to him.*

Our High Priest Died for Our Sins/
Hebrews 9:11–15

He came as High Priest of this better system which we now have. He went into that greater, perfect tabernacle in heaven, not made by men nor part of this world, 12and once for all took blood into that inner room, the Holy of Holies, and sprinkled it on the mercy seat; but it was not the blood of goats and calves. No, he took his own blood, and with it he, by himself, made sure of our eternal salvation.

13And if under the old system the blood of bulls and goats and the ashes of young cows could cleanse men's bodies from sin, 14just think how much more surely the blood of Christ will transform our lives and hearts. His sacrifice frees us from the worry of having to obey the old rules, and makes us want to serve the living God. For by the help of the eternal Holy Spirit, Christ willingly gave himself to God to die for our sins—he being perfect, without a single sin or fault. 15Christ came with this new agreement so that all who are invited may come and have forever all the wonders God has promised them. For Christ died to rescue them from the penalty of the sins they had committed while still under that old system.

A THOUGHT: *Though you know Christ, you may still be trying to make yourself good enough for God. But rules and rituals have never cleansed people's hearts. By Jesus' blood alone (1) our consciences are cleared, (2) we are freed from death and can live to serve God, and (3) we are freed from sin's power. If you are carrying a load of guilt because you can't be good enough for God, take another look at Jesus' death and what it means for you.*

Proverbs for Today/ 25:8–10

Don't be hot-headed and rush to court! You may start something you can't finish and go down before your neighbor in shameful defeat. So discuss the matter with him privately. Don't tell anyone else, lest he accuse you of slander and you can't withdraw what you said.

OCTOBER 13

Stephen's Speech before the Jewish Supreme Court/ Acts 6:8—7:16

Stephen, the man so full of faith and the Holy Spirit's power, did spectacular miracles among the people.

9But one day some of the men from the Jewish cult of "The Freedmen" started an argument with him, and they were soon joined by Jews from Cyrene, Alexandria in Egypt, and the Turkish provinces of Cilicia, and Ausia. 10But none of them was able to stand against Stephen's wisdom and spirit.

11So they brought in some men to lie about him, claiming they had heard Stephen curse Moses, and even God.

12This accusation roused the crowds to fury against Stephen, and the Jewish leaders arrested him and brought him before the Council. 13The lying witnesses testified again that Stephen was constantly speaking against the Temple and against the laws of Moses.

14They declared, "We have heard him say that this fellow Jesus of Nazareth will destroy the Temple, and throw out all of Moses' laws." 15At this point everyone in the

Council chamber saw Stephen's face become as radiant as an angel's!

7:1 Then the High Priest asked him, "Are these accusations true?"

2 This was Stephen's lengthy reply: "The glorious God appeared to our ancestor Abraham in Iraq before he moved to Syria, 3 and told him to leave his native land, to say good-bye to his relatives and to start out for a country that God would direct him to. 4 So he left the land of the Chaldeans and lived in Haran, in Syria, until his father died. Then God brought him here to the land of Israel, 5 but gave him no property of his own, not one little tract of land.

"However, God promised that eventually the whole country would belong to him and his descendants—though as yet he had no children! 6 But God also told him that these descendants of his would leave the land and live in a foreign country and there become slaves for 400 years. 7 'But I will punish the nation that enslaves them,' God told him, 'and afterwards my people will return to this land of Israel and worship me here.'

8 "God also gave Abraham the ceremony of circumcision at that time, as evidence of the covenant between God and the people of Abraham. And so Isaac, Abraham's son, was circumcised when he was eight days old. Isaac became the father of Jacob, and Jacob was the father of the twelve patriarchs of the Jewish nation. 9 These men were very jealous of Joseph and sold him to be a slave in Egypt. But God was with him, 10 and delivered him out of all of his anguish, and gave him favor before Pharaoh, king of Egypt. God also gave Joseph unusual wisdom, so that Pharaoh appointed him governor over all Egypt, as well as putting him in charge of all the affairs of the palace.

11 "But a famine developed in Egypt and Canaan and there was great misery for our ancestors. When their food was gone, 12 Jacob heard that there was still grain in Egypt, so he sent his sons to buy some. 13 The second time they went, Joseph revealed his identity to his brothers, and they were introduced to Pharaoh. 14 Then Joseph sent for his father Jacob and all his brothers' families to come to Egypt, seventy-five persons in all. 15 So Jacob came to

Egypt, where he died, and all his sons. [16]All of them were taken to Shechem and buried in the tomb Abraham bought from the sons of Hamor, Shechem's father.

A THOUGHT: *Around the world, the gospel has most often taken root in places prepared by the blood of martyrs. Before people can give their lives for the gospel, however, they must first live for the gospel. One way God trains his servants is to place them in insignificant positions. Their desire to serve Christ is translated into the reality of serving others. Stephen was an effective administrator and messenger before becoming a martyr. Stephen's life is a continual challenge to all Christians. Because he was the first to die for the faith, his sacrifice raises questions: How many risks do we take in being Jesus' followers? Would we be willing to die for him? Are we really willing to live for him?*

Sacrifice under the Old Agreement/
Hebrews 9:16–23

Now, if someone dies and leaves a will—a list of things to be given away to certain people when he dies—no one gets anything until it is proved that the person who wrote the will is dead. [17]The will goes into effect only after the death of the person who wrote it. While he is still alive no one can use it to get any of those things he has promised them.

[18]That is why blood was sprinkled [as proof of Christ's death] before even the first agreement could go into effect. [19]For after Moses had given the people all of God's laws, he took the blood of calves and goats, along with water, and sprinkled the blood over the book of God's laws and over all the people, using branches of hyssop bushes and scarlet wool to sprinkle with. [20]Then he said, "This is the blood that marks the beginning of the agreement between you and God, the agreement God commanded me to make with you." [21]And in the same way he sprinkled blood on the sacred tent and on whatever instruments were used for worship. [22]In fact we can say that under the old agreement almost everything was cleansed by sprinkling it with blood, and without the shedding of blood there is no forgiveness of sins.

[23]That is why the sacred tent down here on earth, and everything in it—all copied from things in heaven— all had to be made pure by Moses in this way, by being sprinkled with the blood of animals. But the real things

in heaven, of which these down here are copies, were made pure with far more precious offerings.

A THOUGHT: *Why does forgiveness require the shedding of blood? This is no arbitrary decree on the part of a bloodthirsty God, as some have supposed. There is no greater symbol of life than blood; blood keeps us alive. Jesus shed his blood—gave his life—for our sins so that we wouldn't have to experience spiritual death, which is eternal separation from God. Jesus is the source of life, not death, and he offered his own life so that we might live. After shedding his blood for us, he rose victorious from the grave and proclaimed victory over sin and death.*

Proverbs for Today/ 25:11–14

Timely advice is as lovely as gold apples in a silver basket. □ It is a badge of honor to accept valid criticism. □ A faithful employee is as refreshing as a cool day in the hot summertime. □ One who doesn't give the gift he promised is like a cloud blowing over a desert without dropping any rain.

OCTOBER 14

Stephen's Speech—the Life of Moses/ Acts 7:17–43

"As the time drew near when God would fulfill his promise to Abraham to free his descendants from slavery, the Jewish people greatly multiplied in Egypt; but then a king was crowned who had no respect for Joseph's memory. 19This king plotted against our race, forcing parents to abandon their children in the fields.

20"About that time Moses was born—a child of divine beauty. His parents hid him at home for three months, 21and when at last they could no longer keep him hidden, and had to abandon him, Pharaoh's daughter found him and adopted him as her own son, 22and taught him all the wisdom of the Egyptians, and he became a mighty prince and orator.

23"One day as he was nearing his fortieth birthday, it came into his mind to visit his brothers, the people of Israel. 24During this visit he saw an Egyptian mistreating a man of Israel. So Moses killed the Egyptian. 25Moses supposed his brothers would realize that God had sent him to help them, but they didn't.

26"The next day he visited them again and saw two men of Israel fighting. He tried to be a peacemaker. 'Gentlemen,' he said, 'you are brothers and shouldn't be fighting like this! It is wrong!'

27"But the man in the wrong told Moses to mind his own business. 'Who made *you* a ruler and judge over us?' he asked. 28'Are you going to kill me as you killed that Egyptian yesterday?'

29"At this, Moses fled the country, and lived in the land of Midian, where his two sons were born.

30"Forty years later, in the desert near Mount Sinai, an Angel appeared to him in a flame of fire in a bush. 31 Moses saw it and wondered what it was, and as he ran to see, the voice of the Lord called out to him, 32'I am the God of your ancestors—of Abraham, Isaac and Jacob.' Moses shook with terror and dared not look.

33"And the Lord said to him, 'Take off your shoes, for you are standing on holy ground. 34I have seen the anguish of my people in Egypt and have heard their cries. I have come down to deliver them. Come, I will send you to Egypt.' 35And so God sent back the same man his people had previously rejected by demanding, 'Who made *you* a ruler and judge over us?' Moses was sent to be their ruler and savior. 36And by means of many remarkable miracles he led them out of Egypt and through the Red Sea, and back and forth through the wilderness for forty years.

37"Moses himself told the people of Israel, 'God will raise up a Prophet much like me from among your brothers.' 38How true this proved to be, for in the wilderness, Moses was the go-between—the mediator between the people of Israel and the Angel who gave them the Law of God—the Living Word—on Mount Sinai.

39"But our fathers rejected Moses and wanted to return to Egypt. 40They told Aaron, 'Make idols for us, so that we will have gods to lead us back; for we don't know what has become of this Moses, who brought us out of Egypt.' 41So they made a calf-idol and sacrificed to it, and rejoiced in this thing they had made.

42"Then God turned away from them and gave them up, and let them serve the sun, moon and stars as their gods! In the book of Amos' prophecies the Lord God asks, 'Was it to me you were sacrificing during those forty years in the desert, Israel? 43No, your real interest was in your heathen gods—Sakkuth, and the star god Kaiway, and in all the images you made. So I will send you into captivity far away beyond Babylon.'

A THOUGHT: *Stephen's speech described Israel's relationship with God era by era. From Old Testament history he showed that the Jews had constantly rejected God's message and his prophets, and that this Council had rejected the Messiah, God's Son. He made three main points: (1) Israel's history is the history of God's acts in the world; (2) men worshiped God long before there was a temple, for God does not live in a temple; (3) Jesus' death was just one more example of Israel's rebellion and rejection of God. Stephen showed the religious leadership that they were just like their ancestors—they had rejected God's servant—this time, though, they had rejected God's own Son, the Messiah.*

Christ Conquered the Power of Sin/ Hebrews 9:24–28

For Christ has entered into heaven itself, to appear now before God as our Friend. It was not in the earthly place of worship that he did this, for that was merely a copy of the real temple in heaven. 25Nor has he offered himself again and again, as the high priest down here on earth offers animal blood in the Holy of Holies each year. 26If that had been necessary, then he would have had to die again and again, ever since the world began. But no! He came once for all, at the end of the age, to put away the power of sin forever by dying for us.

27And just as it is destined that men die only once, and after that comes judgment, 28so also Christ died only once as an offering for the sins of many people; and he will come again, but not to deal again with our sins.

This time he will come bringing salvation to all those who are eagerly and patiently waiting for him.

A THOUGHT: *All people die physically, but Christ died so that we would not have to die spiritually. His death affects our past, present, and future. He has forgiven our past sin; he has given us the Holy Spirit to help us deal with present sin; and he promises to return and raise us to eternal life in a world from which sin is banished.*

Proverbs for Today/ 25:15
Be patient and you will finally win, for a soft tongue can break hard bones.

OCTOBER 15

Stephen Is Martyred/ Acts 7:44–60
"Our ancestors carried along with them a portable Temple, or Tabernacle, through the wilderness. In it they kept the stone tablets with the Ten Commandments written on them. This building was constructed in exact accordance with the plan shown to Moses by the Angel. 45Years later, when Joshua led the battles against the Gentile nations, this Tabernacle was taken with them into their new territory, and used until the time of King David.

46"God blessed David greatly, and David asked for the privilege of building a permanent Temple for the God of Jacob. 47But it was Solomon who actually built it. 48,49However, God doesn't live in temples made by human hands. 'The heaven is my throne,' says the Lord through his prophets, 'and earth is my footstool. What kind of home could you build?' asks the Lord. 'Would I stay in it? 50Didn't I make both heaven and earth?'

51"You stiff-necked heathen! Must you forever resist the Holy Spirit? But your fathers did, and so do you! 52Name one prophet your ancestors didn't persecute! They even killed the ones who predicted the coming of the Righteous One—the Messiah whom you betrayed and murdered. 53Yes, and you deliberately destroyed God's Laws, though you received them from the hands of angels."

54The Jewish leaders were stung to fury by Stephen's accusation, and ground their teeth in rage. 55But Stephen, full of the Holy Spirit, gazed steadily upward into heaven and saw the glory of God and Jesus standing at God's right hand. 56And he told them, "Look, I see the heavens opened and Jesus the Messiah standing beside God, at his right hand!"

57Then they mobbed him, putting their hands over their ears, and drowning out his voice with their shouts, 58and dragged him out of the city to stone him. The official witnesses—the executioners—took off their coats and laid them at the feet of a young man named Paul.

59And as the murderous stones came hurtling at him, Stephen prayed, "Lord Jesus, receive my spirit." 60And he fell to his knees, shouting, "Lord, don't charge them with this sin!" and with that, he died.

A THOUGHT: *Stephen saw the glory of God and Jesus the Messiah standing at God's right hand. Stephen's vision supported Jesus' claim and angered the Jewish leaders who had condemned Jesus to death for blasphemy. They would not tolerate Stephen's words, so they mobbed him and killed him. Stephen was ready to suffer like Jesus, even to the point of asking forgiveness for his murderers. Such a forgiving response comes only from the Holy Spirit. The Spirit can also help us love our enemies as Stephen did. People may not kill us for witnessing about Christ, but they will let us know they don't want to hear the truth and will often try to silence us. Keep honoring God in your conduct and words; though many will turn against you and your message, some may turn to Christ.*

Christ Died Once for All/ Hebrews 10:1–10

The old system of Jewish laws gave only a dim foretaste of the good things Christ would do for us. The sacrifices under the old system were repeated again and again, year after year, but even so they could never save those who lived under their rules. 2If they could have, one offering would have been enough; the worshipers would have been cleansed once for all, and their feeling of guilt would be gone.

3But just the opposite happened: those yearly sacrifices reminded them of their disobedience and guilt instead of relieving their minds. 4For it is not possible for the blood of bulls and goats really to take away sins.

5That is why Christ said, as he came into the world, "O God, the blood of bulls and goats cannot satisfy you, so you have made ready this body of mine for me to lay as a sacrifice upon your altar. 6You were not satisfied with the animal sacrifices, slain and burnt before you as offerings for sin. 7Then I said, 'See, I have come to do your will, to lay down my life, just as the Scriptures said that I would.'"

8After Christ said this, about not being satisfied with the various sacrifices and offerings required under the old system, 9he then added, "Here I am. I have come to give my life."

He cancels the first system in favor of a far better one. 10Under this new plan we have been forgiven and made clean by Christ's dying for us once and for all.

A THOUGHT: *When people gathered for sacrifice on the Day of Atonement, they were reminded of their sins and felt guilty all over again. What they needed was forgiveness—the permanent, powerful, sin-destroying forgiveness we have from Christ. Once we have confessed a sin to him, we need never think of it again. He has forgiven it, and it no longer exists. Christ's sacrifice for sin is all sufficient—there is no sin it cannot cover.*

Proverbs for Today/ 25:16

Do you like honey? Don't eat too much of it, or it will make you sick!

OCTOBER 16

Many in Samaria Become Believers/ Acts 8:1–25

Paul was in complete agreement with the killing of Stephen.

And a great wave of persecution of the believers began that day, sweeping over the church in Jerusalem, and everyone except the apostles fled into Judea and Samaria. 2(But some godly Jews came and with great sorrow buried Stephen.) 3Paul was like a wild man, going everywhere to devastate the believers, even entering private homes and dragging out men and women alike and jailing them.

4But the believers who had fled Jerusalem went everywhere preaching the Good News about Jesus! 5Philip, for instance, went to the city of Samaria and told the people there about Christ. 6Crowds listened intently to what he had to say because of the miracles he did. 7Many evil spirits were cast out, screaming as they left their victims, and many who were paralyzed or lame were healed, 8so there was much joy in that city!

9,10,11A man named Simon had formerly been a sorcerer there for many years; he was a very influential, proud man because of the amazing things he could do—in fact, the Samaritan people often spoke of him as the Messiah. 12But now they believed Philip's message that Jesus was the Messiah, and his words concerning the Kingdom of God; and many men and women were baptized. 13Then Simon himself believed and was baptized and began following Philip wherever he went, and was amazed by the miracles he did.

14When the apostles back in Jerusalem heard that the people of Samaria had accepted God's message, they sent down Peter and John. 15As soon as they arrived, they began praying for these new Christians to receive the Holy Spirit, 16for as yet he had not come upon any of them. For they had only been baptized in the name of the Lord Jesus. 17Then Peter and John laid their hands upon these believers, and they received the Holy Spirit.

18When Simon saw this—that the Holy Spirit was given when the apostles placed their hands upon people's heads— he offered money to buy this power.

19"Let me have this power too," he exclaimed, "so that when I lay my hands on people, they will receive the Holy Spirit!"

20But Peter replied, "Your money perish with you for thinking God's gift can be bought! 21You can have no part in this, for your heart is not right before God. 22Turn from this great wickedness and pray. Perhaps God will yet forgive your evil thoughts— 23for I can see that there is jealousy and sin in your heart."

24"Pray for me," Simon exclaimed, "that these terrible things won't happen to me."

25After testifying and preaching in Samaria, Peter and John returned to Jerusalem, stopping at several Samaritan villages along the way to preach the Good News to them too.

A THOUGHT: *Persecution forced the believers out of their homes in Jerusalem, and with them went the gospel. Often we have to become uncomfortable before we'll move. Discomfort may be unwanted, but it is not always undesirable, for out of our hurting, God works his purposes. The next time you are tempted to complain about uncomfortable or painful circumstances, stop and ask if God may be preparing you for a special task.*

Christ Opened a New and Living Way/
Hebrews 10:11–22

Under the old agreement the priests stood before the altar day after day offering sacrifices that could never take away our sins. 12But Christ gave himself to God for our sins as one sacrifice for all time, and then sat down in the place of highest honor at God's right hand, 13waiting for his enemies to be laid under his feet. 14For by that one offering he made forever perfect in the sight of God all those whom he is making holy.

15And the Holy Spirit testifies that this is so, for he has said, 16"This is the agreement I will make with the people of Israel, though they broke their first agreement: I will write my laws into their minds so that they will always know my will, and I will put my laws in their hearts so that they will want to obey them." 17And then he adds, "I will never again remember their sins and lawless deeds."

18Now, when sins have once been forever forgiven and forgotten, there is no need to offer more sacrifices to get rid of them.

19And so, dear brothers, now we may walk right into the very Holy of Holies where God is, because of the blood of Jesus. 20This is the fresh, new, life-giving way which Christ has opened up for us by tearing the curtain— his human body—to let us into the holy presence of God.

21And since this great High Priest of ours rules over God's household, 22let us go right in, to God himself, with true hearts fully trusting him to receive us, because we have been sprinkled with Christ's blood to make us clean, and because our bodies have been washed with pure water.

A THOUGHT: *The Jewish Christians to whom this book was written were in danger of returning to the old Jewish system, which would say that Christ's sacrifice wasn't enough to forgive their sins. But adding anything to his sacrifice or taking anything from it denies its validity. But we have been made perfect (complete) in Christ. Through his death and resurrection, Christ once for all made his believers perfect in God's sight. Any system to win God's approval through good works is essentially rejecting the significance of Christ's death and spurning the Holy Spirit's work. Beware of anyone who tells you that Christ's sacrifice was incomplete or that something else is needed to make you acceptable to God, because this can lead you away from right faith and right living.*

Proverbs for Today/ 25:17
Don't visit your neighbor too often, or you will outwear your welcome!

OCTOBER 17

Philip Tells the Ethiopian Eunuch about Jesus/ Acts 8:26–40

But as for Philip, an angel of the Lord said to him, "Go over to the road that runs from Jerusalem through the Gaza Desert, arriving around noon." 27So he did, and who should be coming down the road but the Treasurer of Ethiopia, a eunuch of great authority under Candace the queen. He had gone to Jerusalem to worship at the Temple, 28and was now returning in his chariot, reading aloud from the book of the prophet Isaiah.

29The Holy Spirit said to Philip, "Go over and walk along beside the chariot."

30Philip ran over and heard what he was reading and asked, "Do you understand it?"

31"Of course not!" the man replied. "How can I when there is no one to instruct me?" And he begged Philip to come up into the chariot and sit with him.

32The passage of Scripture he had been reading from was this:

"He was led as a sheep to the slaughter, and as a lamb is silent before the shearers, so he opened not his mouth; 33in his humiliation, justice was denied him; and who can express the wickedness of the people of his generation? For his life is taken from the earth."

34The eunuch asked Philip, "Was Isaiah talking about himself or someone else?"

35So Philip began with this same Scripture and then used many others to tell him about Jesus.

36As they rode along, they came to a small body of water, and the eunuch said, "Look! Water! Why can't I be baptized?"

37"You can," Philip answered, "if you believe with all your heart."

And the eunuch replied, "I believe that Jesus Christ is the Son of God."

38He stopped the chariot, and they went down into the water and Philip baptized him. 39And when they came up out of the water, the Spirit of the Lord caught away Philip, and the eunuch never saw him again, but went on his way rejoicing. 40Meanwhile, Philip found himself at Azotus! He preached the Good News there and in every city along the way, as he traveled to Caesarea.

A THOUGHT: *Philip found the Ethiopian man reading the Scriptures, and he took advantage of this opportunity to explain the gospel by asking if the man understood what he was reading. Philip (1) followed the Spirit's leading, (2) began the discussion from where the man was—immersed in the prophecies of Isaiah, and (3) explained how Jesus Christ fulfilled Isaiah's prophecies. When we share the gospel, we should start where the other person's concerns are focused. Then we can bring the gospel to bear on those concerns.*

Let Us Serve One Another/ Hebrews 10:23–25

Now we can look forward to the salvation God has promised us. There is no longer any room for doubt, and we can tell others that salvation is ours, for there is no question that he will do what he says.

24In response to all he has done for us, let us outdo each other in being helpful and kind to each other and in doing good.

25Let us not neglect our church meetings, as some people do, but encourage and warn each other, especially now that the day of his coming back again is drawing near.

A THOUGHT: *To neglect Christian meetings is to give up the encouragement and help of other Christians. We gather together to share our faith and strengthen each other in the Lord. As we near the end of the age and as we get closer to the day when Christ will return, we may face many spiritual struggles, tribulations, and even persecution. Anti–Christian forces will grow in strength. Difficulties should never be excuses for missing church services. Rather, as difficulties arise, we should make an even greater effort to be faithful in attendance.*

Proverbs for Today/ 25:18–19

Telling lies about someone is as harmful as hitting him with an axe, or wounding him with a sword, or shooting him with a sharp arrow.   □ Putting confidence in an unreliable man is like chewing with a sore tooth, or trying to run on a broken foot.

OCTOBER 18

Paul's Conversion/ Acts 9:1–19a

But Paul, threatening with every breath and eager to destroy every Christian, went to the High Priest in Jerusalem. 2He requested a letter addressed to synagogues in Damascus, requiring their cooperation in the persecution of any believers he found there, both men and women, so that he could bring them in chains to Jerusalem.

3As he was nearing Damascus on this mission, suddenly a brilliant light from heaven spotted down upon him! 4He fell to the ground and heard a voice saying to him, "Paul! Paul! Why are you persecuting me?"

5"Who is speaking, sir?" Paul asked.

And the voice replied, "I am Jesus, the one you are persecuting! 6Now get up and go into the city and await my further instructions."

7The men with Paul stood speechless with surprise, for they heard the sound of someone's voice but saw no one! 8,9As Paul picked himself up off the ground, he found that he was blind. He had to be led into Damascus and was there three days, blind, going without food and water all that time.

10Now there was in Damascus a believer named Ananias. The Lord spoke to him in a vision, calling, "Ananias!"

"Yes, Lord!" he replied.

11And the Lord said, "Go over to Straight Street and find the house of a man named Judas and ask there for Paul of Tarsus. He is praying to me right now, for 12I have shown him a vision of a man named Ananias coming in and laying his hands on him so that he can see again!"

13"But Lord," exclaimed Ananias, "I have heard about the terrible things this man has done to the believers in Jerusalem! 14And we hear that he has arrest warrants with him from the chief priests, authorizing him to arrest every believer in Damascus!"

15But the Lord said, "Go and do what I say. For Paul is my chosen instrument to take my message to the nations and before kings, as well as to the people of Israel. 16And I will show him how much he must suffer for me."

17So Ananias went over and found Paul and laid his hands on him and said, "Brother Paul, the Lord Jesus, who appeared to you on the road, has sent me so that you may be filled with the Holy Spirit and get your sight back."

18Instantly (it was as though scales fell from his eyes) Paul could see, and was immediately baptized. 19Then he ate and was strengthened.

A THOUGHT: *As Paul traveled to Damascus, pursuing Christians, he was confronted by the risen Christ and brought face to face with the truth of the gospel. Sometimes God breaks into a life in a spectacular manner, and sometimes conversion is a quiet experience. Beware of people who insist you must have a particular type of conversion experience. The right way to come to faith in Jesus is whatever way God brings you.*

A Warning Against Apostasy/ Hebrews 10:26–31

If anyone sins deliberately by rejecting the Savior after knowing the truth of forgiveness, this sin is not covered by Christ's death; there is no way to get rid of it. 27There will be nothing to look forward to but the terrible punishment of God's awful anger which will consume all his enemies. 28A man who refused to obey the laws given by Moses was killed without mercy if there were two or three witnesses to his sin. 29Think how much more terrible the punishment will be for those who have trampled underfoot the Son of God and treated his cleansing blood as though it were common and unhallowed, and insulted and outraged the Holy Spirit who brings God's mercy to his people.

30For we know him who said, "Justice belongs to me; I will repay them"; who also said, "The Lord himself will handle these cases." 31It is a fearful thing to fall into the hands of the living God.

A THOUGHT: *When people deliberately reject Christ's offer of salvation, they reject God's most precious gift. They push away the work of the Holy Spirit, the one who communicates to us God's saving love. This warning was given to Jewish Christians who were tempted to reject Christ for Judaism, but it applies to anyone who rejects Christ for another religion or, having understood Christ's atoning work, deliberately turns away from it. The point is that there is no other acceptable sacrifice for sin than the death of Christ on the cross. If someone deliberately, intentionally, purposely rejects the sacrifice of Christ after clearly understanding the gospel teaching about it, then there is no other hope of salvation for that person, for God has not provided any other name under heaven by whom we could be saved.*

Proverbs for Today/ 25:20–22

Being happy-go-lucky around a person whose heart is heavy is as bad as stealing his jacket in cold weather, or rubbing salt in his wounds. □ If your enemy is hungry, give him food! If he is thirsty, give him something to drink! This will make him feel ashamed of himself, and God will reward you.

OCTOBER 19

Paul Preaches the Good News about Jesus/ Acts 9:19b–31

Paul stayed with the believers in Damascus for a few days 20and went at once to the synagogue to tell everyone there the Good News about Jesus—that he is indeed the Son of God!

21All who heard him were amazed. "Isn't this the same man who persecuted Jesus' followers so bitterly in Jerusalem?" they asked. "And we understand that he came here to arrest them all and take them in chains to the chief priests."

22Paul became more and more fervent in his preaching, and the Damascus Jews couldn't withstand his proofs that Jesus was indeed the Christ.

23After a while the Jewish leaders determined to kill him. 24But Paul was told about their plans, that they were watching the gates of the city day and night prepared to murder him. 25So during the night some of his converts let him down in a basket through an opening in the city wall!

26Upon arrival in Jerusalem he tried to meet with the believers, but they were all afraid of him. They thought he was faking! 27Then Barnabas brought him to the apostles and told them how Paul had seen the Lord on the way to Damascus, what the Lord had said to him, and all about his powerful preaching in the name of Jesus. 28Then they accepted him, and after that he was constantly with the believers 29 and preached boldly in the name of the Lord. But then some Greek-speaking Jews with whom he had argued plotted to murder him. 30However, when the other believers heard about his danger, they took him to Caesarea and then sent him to his home in Tarsus.

31Meanwhile, the church had peace throughout Judea, Galilee and Samaria, and grew in strength and numbers. The believers learned how to walk in the fear of the Lord and in the comfort of the Holy Spirit.

A THOUGHT: *Immediately after receiving his sight, Paul went to the synagogue to tell the Jews about Jesus Christ. Some Christians counsel new believers to wait until they are thoroughly grounded in their faith before attempting to share the gospel. Paul took time alone to learn about Jesus before beginning his worldwide ministry, but he did not wait to witness. Although we should not rush into a ministry unprepared, we do not need to wait before telling others what has happened to us.*

Remember Your Eternal Reward/ Hebrews 10:32–39

Don't ever forget those wonderful days when you first learned about Christ. Remember how you kept right on with the Lord even though it meant terrible suffering. 33Sometimes you were laughed at and beaten, and sometimes you watched and sympathized with others suffering the same things. 34You suffered with those thrown into jail, and you were actually joyful when all you owned was taken from you, knowing that better things were awaiting you in heaven, things that would be yours forever.

35Do not let this happy trust in the Lord die away, no matter what happens. Remember your reward! 36You need to keep on patiently doing God's will if you want him to do for you all that he has promised. 37His coming will not be delayed much longer. 38And those whose faith has made them good in God's sight must live by faith, trusting him in everything. Otherwise, if they shrink back, God will have no pleasure in them.

39But we have never turned our backs on God and sealed our fate. No, our faith in him assures our souls' salvation.

A THOUGHT: *Hebrews encourages believers, who are in the midst of persecution, to persevere in their Christian walk. We don't usually think of suffering as good, but suffering is part of our relationship with Christ—it impressess upon us a deeper Christlikeness. During times of great stress, we can be confident that God is with us. Knowing that Jesus is with us in our suffering, we can endure the pain and realize that ultimately we will find rest in Christ.*

Proverbs for Today/ 25:23–24

As surely as a wind from the north brings cold, just as surely a retort causes anger! ☐ It is better to live in a corner of an attic than in a beautiful home with a cranky, quarrelsome woman.

OCTOBER 20

Peter Heals Aeneas/ Acts 9:32–35

Peter traveled from place to place to visit them, and in his travels came to the believers in the town of Lydda. 33There he met a man named Aeneas, paralyzed and bedridden for eight years.

34Peter said to him, "Aeneas! Jesus Christ has healed you! Get up and make your bed." And he was healed instantly. 35Then the whole population of Lydda and Sharon turned to the Lord when they saw Aeneas walking around.

A THOUGHT: *Peter healed the paralyzed Aeneas by the authority of Jesus Christ. Healing in the "name" is not some magical formula, like "abracadabra," that causes healing everytime it's uttered. God cannot be manipulated! God chooses to answer the prayers of his people—and often God does heal. However, God is not bound to healing anyone. Here God uses Peter to demonstrate his power in the healing of Aeneas in order to open opportunities for the fledgling church to share the Good News. Many "turned to the Lord" as a result of Aeneas' healing. God works in diverse ways. We must not attempt to put God in a box by saying that he has to operate according to our preconceived notions. We must let God be God.*

Faith/ Hebrews 11:1–6

What is faith? It is the confident assurance that something we want is going to happen. It is the certainty that what we hope for is waiting for us, even though we cannot see it up ahead. ²Men of God in days of old were famous for their faith.

³By faith—by believing God—we know that the world and the stars—in fact, all things—were made at God's command; and that they were all made from things that can't be seen.

⁴It was by faith that Abel obeyed God and brought an offering that pleased God more than Cain's offering did. God accepted Abel and proved it by accepting his gift; and though Abel is long dead, we can still learn lessons from him about trusting God.

⁵Enoch trusted God too, and that is why God took him away to heaven without dying; suddenly he was gone because God took him. Before this happened God had said how pleased he was with Enoch. ⁶You can never please God without faith, without depending on him. Anyone who wants to come to God must believe that there is a God and that he rewards those who sincerely look for him.

A THOUGHT: *Two words describe our faith: confidence and certainty. These two qualities need a secure beginning and ending point. The beginning point of faith is believing in God's character—he is who he says. The end point is believing in God's promises—he will do what he says. We believe that God will fulfill his promises even though we don't see those promises materializing now—this is true faith.*

Proverbs for Today/ 25:25–27

Good news from far away is like cold water to the thirsty. ☐ If a godly man compromises with the wicked, it is like polluting a fountain or muddying a spring. ☐ Just as it is harmful to eat too much honey, so also it is bad for men to think about all the honors they deserve!

OCTOBER 21

Peter Raises Dorcas from the Dead/ Acts 9:36–43

In the city of Joppa there was a woman named Dorcas ("Gazelle"), a believer who was always doing kind things for others, especially for the poor. 37About this time she became ill and died. Her friends prepared her for burial and laid her in an upstairs room. 38But when they learned that Peter was nearby at Lydda, they sent two men to beg him to return with them to Joppa. 39This he did; as soon as he arrived, they took him upstairs where Dorcas lay. The room was filled with weeping widows who were showing one another the coats and other garments Dorcas had made for them. 40But Peter asked them all to leave the room; then he knelt and prayed. Turning to the body he said, "Get up, Dorcas," and she opened her eyes! And when she saw Peter, she sat up! 41He gave her his hand and helped her up and called in the believers and widows, presenting her to them.

42The news raced through the town, and many believed in the Lord. 43And Peter stayed a long time in Joppa, living with Simon, the tanner.

A THOUGHT: *Dorcas made an enormous impact on her community by "always doing kind things for others, especially for the poor." When she died, the room was filled with mourners, people she had helped. And when she was brought back to life, the news raced through the town. God uses great preachers like Peter and Paul, but he also uses those who have gifts of kindness like Dorcas. Rather than wishing you had other gifts, make good use of the gifts God has given you.*

The Faith of Noah, Abraham, and Sarah/ Hebrews 11:7–12

Noah was another who trusted God. When he heard God's warning about the future, Noah believed him even though there was then no sign of a flood, and wasting no time, he built the ark and saved his family. Noah's belief in God was in direct contrast to the sin and disbelief of the rest of the world—which refused to obey—and because of his faith he became one of those whom God has accepted.

8Abraham trusted God, and when God told him to leave home and go far away to another land which he promised to give him, Abraham obeyed. Away he went, not even knowing where he was going. ⁹And even when he reached God's promised land, he lived in tents like a mere visitor, as did Isaac and Jacob, to whom God gave the same promise. ¹⁰Abraham did this because he was confidently waiting for God to bring him to that strong heavenly city whose designer and builder is God.

¹¹Sarah, too, had faith, and because of this she was able to become a mother in spite of her old age, for she realized that God, who gave her his promise, would certainly do what he said. ¹²And so a whole nation came from Abraham, who was too old to have even one child—a nation with so many millions of people that, like the stars of the sky and the sand on the ocean shores, there is no way to count them.

A THOUGHT: *Noah experienced what it meant to be different from his neighbors. God commanded him to build a huge boat in the middle of dry land, and although God's command seemed foolish, Noah obeyed. Noah's obedience made him appear strange to his neighbors, just as the new beliefs of Jewish Christians made them stand out. As you obey God, don't be surprised if others consider you different. Your obedience makes their disobedience stand out. Remember, if God asks you to do something, he will give you the necessary strength to carry out that task.*

Proverbs for Today/ 25:28
A man without self-control is as defenseless as a city with broken-down walls.

OCTOBER 22

God Gives Visions to Peter and Cornelius/ Acts 10:1–23a
In Caesarea there lived a Roman army officer, Cornelius, a captain of an Italian regiment. ²He was a godly man, deeply reverent, as was his entire household. He gave generously to charity and was a man of prayer. ³While wide awake one afternoon he had a vision—it was about three o'clock—and in this vision he saw an angel of God coming toward him.

"Cornelius!" the angel said.

4Cornelius stared at him in terror. "What do you want, sir?" he asked the angel.

And the angel replied, "Your prayers and charities have not gone unnoticed by God! 5,6Now send some men to Joppa to find a man named Simon Peter, who is staying with Simon, the tanner, down by the shore, and ask him to come and visit you."

7As soon as the angel was gone, Cornelius called two of his household servants and a godly soldier, one of his personal bodyguard, 8and told them what had happened and sent them off to Joppa.

9,10The next day, as they were nearing the city, Peter went up on the flat roof of his house to pray. It was noon and he was hungry, but while lunch was being prepared, he fell into a trance. 11He saw the sky open, and a great canvas sheet, suspended by its four corners, settle to the ground. 12In the sheet were all sorts of animals, snakes and birds [forbidden to the Jews for food].

13Then a voice said to him, "Go kill and eat any of them you wish."

14"Never, Lord," Peter declared, "I have never in all my life eaten such creatures, for they are forbidden by our Jewish laws."

15The voice spoke again, "Don't contradict God! If he says something is kosher, then it is."

16The same vision was repeated three times. Then the sheet was pulled up again to heaven.

17Peter was very perplexed. What could the vision mean? What was he supposed to do?

Just then the men sent by Cornelius had found the house and were standing outside at the gate, 18inquiring whether this was the place where Simon Peter lived!

19Meanwhile, as Peter was puzzling over the vision, the Holy Spirit said to him, "Three men have come to see you. 20Go down and meet them and go with them. All is well, I have sent them."

21So Peter went down. "I'm the man you're looking for," he said. "Now what is it you want?"

22Then they told him about Cornelius the Roman officer, a good and godly man, well thought of by the Jews, and how an angel had instructed him to send for Peter to come and tell him what God wanted him to do.

23So Peter invited them in and lodged them overnight.

A THOUGHT: *According to Jewish law, certain foods were forbidden. The food laws made it hard for Jews to eat with Gentiles without risking defilement. In fact, the Gentiles themselves were often seen as "unclean." Peter's vision meant that he was not to look upon the Gentiles as inferior people whom God would not redeem. Before having the vision, Peter would have thought a Gentile Roman officer could not accept Christ. Afterward, he understood that he should go with the messengers into a Gentile home and tell Cornelius the Good News of salvation in Jesus Christ.*

Faith in God's Promises/ Hebrews 11:13–16

These men of faith I have mentioned died without ever receiving all that God had promised them; but they saw it all awaiting them on ahead and were glad, for they agreed that this earth was not their real home but that they were just strangers visiting down here. 14And quite obviously when they talked like that, they were looking forward to their real home in heaven.

15If they had wanted to, they could have gone back to the good things of this world. 16But they didn't want to. They were living for heaven. And now God is not ashamed to be called their God, for he has made a heavenly city for them.

A THOUGHT: *The people of faith listed here died without receiving all that God had promised, but they never lost their vision of heaven. Many Christians become frustrated and defeated because their needs, wants, expectations, and demands are not immediately met when they believe in Christ. They become impatient and want to quit. Are you discouraged because your goal seems far away? Take courage from these heroes of faith who lived and died without seeing the fruit of their faith on earth, and yet continued to believe.*

Proverbs for Today/ 26:1–2

Honor doesn't go with fools any more than snow with summertime or rain with harvest time! □ An undeserved curse has no effect. Its intended victim will be no more harmed by it than by a sparrow or swallow flitting through the sky.

OCTOBER 23

The Good News Is for Gentiles Also/
Acts 10:23b–48

The next day Peter went with [Cornelius' men], accompanied by some other believers from Joppa.

24They arrived in Caesarea the following day, and Cornelius was waiting for him, and had called together his relatives and close friends to meet Peter. 25As Peter entered his home, Cornelius fell to the floor before him in worship.

26But Peter said, "Stand up! I'm not a god!"

27So he got up and they talked together for a while and then went in where the others were assembled.

28Peter told them, "You know it is against the Jewish laws for me to come into a Gentile home like this. But God has shown me in a vision that I should never think of anyone as inferior. 29So I came as soon as I was sent for. Now tell me what you want."

30Cornelius replied, "Four days ago I was praying as usual at this time of the afternoon, when suddenly a man was standing before me clothed in a radiant robe! 31He told me, 'Cornelius, your prayers are heard and your charities have been noticed by God! 32Now send some men to Joppa and Summon Simon Peter, who is staying in the home of Simon, a tanner, down by the shore.' 33So I sent for you at once, and you have done well to come so soon. Now here we are, waiting before the Lord, anxious to hear what he has told you to tell us!"

34Then Peter replied, "I see very clearly that the Jews are not God's only favorites! 35In every nation he has those who worship him and do good deeds and are acceptable to him. 36,37I'm sure you have heard about the Good News for the people of Israel—that there is peace with God through Jesus, the Messiah, who is Lord of all creation. This message has spread all through Judea, beginning with John the Baptist in Galilee. 38And you no doubt know that Jesus of Nazareth was anointed by God with the Holy Spirit and with power, and he went around doing good and healing all who were possessed by demons, for God was with him.

39"And we apostles are witnesses of all he did throughout

Israel and in Jerusalem, where he was murdered on a cross. 40,41But God brought him back to life again three days later and showed him to certain witnesses God had selected beforehand—not to the general public, but to us who ate and drank with him after he rose from the dead. 42And he sent us to preach the Good News everywhere and to testify that Jesus is ordained of God to be the Judge of all—living and dead. 43And all the prophets have written about him, saying that everyone who believes in him will have their sins forgiven through his name."

44Even as Peter was saying these things, the Holy Spirit fell upon all those listening! 45The Jews who came with Peter were amazed that the gift of the Holy Spirit would be given to Gentiles too! 46,47But there could be no doubt about it, for they heard them speaking in tongues and praising God.

Peter asked, "Can anyone object to my baptizing them, now that they have received the Holy Spirit just as we did?" 48So he did, baptizing them in the name of Jesus, the Messiah. Afterwards Cornelius begged him to stay with them for several days.

A THOUGHT: *Perhaps the greatest barrier to the spread of the gospel in the first century was the Jewish-Gentile conflict. Most early believers were Jewish, and to them it was scandalous even to think of associating with Gentiles. But God told Peter to take the gospel to a Roman, and Peter obeyed despite his background and personal feelings. (Later he struggled with this again—see Galatians 2:12.) God was making it clear that the Gospel of Christ is for everyone! We cannot allow any barrier—language, culture, geography, economic class, or education—to keep us from spreading the gospel.*

God's Testing of Abraham/ Hebrews 11:17–20

While God was testing him, Abraham still trusted in God and his promises, and so he offered up his son Isaac, and was ready to slay him on the altar of sacrifice; 18yes, to slay even Isaac, through whom God had promised to give Abraham a whole nation of descendants!

19He believed that if Isaac died God would bring him back to life again; and that is just about what happened, for as far as Abraham was concerned, Isaac was doomed to death, but he came back again alive! 20It was by faith that Isaac knew God would give future blessings to his two sons, Jacob and Esau.

A THOUGHT: *Abraham was willing to give up his son when God commanded him to do so. God did not let Abraham take Isaac's life, because God gave the command to test Abraham's faith. Instead of taking Abraham's son, God gave him a whole nation of descendants through Isaac. If you are afraid to trust God with your most prized possession, dream, or person, pay attention to Abraham's example. Because Abraham was willing to give up everything for God, he received back more than he could have imagined. What we receive, however, is not always immediate, or in the form of material possessions. After all, material possessions should be among the least satisfying of rewards. Our best and greatest rewards await us in eternity.*

Proverbs for Today/ 26:3–5

Guide a horse with a whip, a donkey with a bridle, and a rebel with a rod to his back! When arguing with a rebel, don't use foolish arguments as he does, or you will become as foolish as he is! Prick his conceit with silly replies!

OCTOBER 24

Peter Defends His Preaching to the Gentiles/
Acts 11:1–18

Soon the news reached the apostles and other brothers in Judea that Gentiles also were being converted! 2But when Peter arrived back in Jerusalem, the Jewish believers argued with him.

3"You fellowshiped with Gentiles and even ate with them," they accused.

4Then Peter told them the whole story. 5"One day in Joppa," he said, "while I was praying, I saw a vision—a huge sheet, let down by its four corners from the sky. 6Inside the sheet were all sorts of animals, reptiles and birds [which we are not to eat]. 7And I heard a voice say, 'Kill and eat whatever you wish.'

8" 'Never, Lord,' I replied. 'For I have never yet eaten anything forbidden by our Jewish laws!'

9"But the voice came again, 'Don't say it isn't right when God declares it is!'

10"This happened *three times* before the sheet and all

it contained disappeared into heaven. 11Just then three men who had come to take me with them to Caesarea arrived at the house where I was staying! 12The Holy Spirit told me to go with them and not to worry about their being Gentiles! These six brothers here accompanied me, and we soon arrived at the home of the man who had sent the messengers. 13He told us how an angel had appeared to him and told him to send messengers to Joppa to find Simon Peter! 14'He will tell you how you and all your household can be saved!' the angel had told him.

15"Well, I began telling them the Good News, but just as I was getting started with my sermon, the Holy Spirit fell on them, just as he fell on us at the beginning! 16Then I thought of the Lord's words when he said, 'Yes, John baptized with water, but you shall be baptized with the Holy Spirit.' 17And since it was *God* who gave these Gentiles the same gift he gave us when we believed on the Lord Jesus Christ, who was I to argue?"

18When the others heard this, all their objections were answered and they began praising God! "Yes," they said, "God has given to the Gentiles, too, the privilege of turning to him and receiving eternal life!"

A THOUGHT: *God had promised throughout Scripture that he would reach the Gentiles. This began with God's promise to Abraham and became very specific in Malachi's statement that God's name "will be honored by the Gentiles from morning till night" (Malachi 1:11). But this was an extremely difficult truth for Jews, even Jewish believers, to accept. The Jewish believers understood that certain prophecies were fulfilled in Christ, but they overlooked other Old Testament teachings. Too often we are inclined to accept only the parts of God's Word that appeal to us, ignoring the teachings we don't like. We must accept all of God's Word as absolute truth.*

The Faith of Jacob, Joseph, and Moses' Parents/ Hebrews 11:21–23

By faith Jacob, when he was old and dying, blessed each of Joseph's two sons as he stood and prayed, leaning on the top of his cane.

22And it was by faith that Joseph, as he neared the end of his life, confidently spoke of God bringing the people of Israel out of Egypt; and he was so sure of it that he made them promise to carry his bones with them when they left!

23Moses' parents had faith too. When they saw that God had given them an unusual child, they trusted that God would save him from the death the king commanded, and they hid him for three months, and were not afraid.

A THOUGHT: *Jacob was Isaac's son and Abraham's grandson. Jacob's sons became the fathers of Israel's 12 tribes. Even when Jacob (also called "Israel") was dying in a strange land, he believed the promise that Abraham's descendants would be like the sand on the seashore and that Israel would become a great nation. True faith helps us see beyond the grave.*

Joseph, one of Jacob's sons, was sold into slavery by his jealous brothers. Eventually, Joseph was sold again, this time to an officer of the Pharaoh of Egypt. Because of his faithfulness to God, however, Joseph was given a top-ranking position in Egypt. Although Joseph could have used that position to build a personal empire, he remembered God's promise to Abraham. After he had been reconciled to his brothers, he brought his family to be near him, and requested that his bones be taken to the Promised Land when the Jews eventually left Egypt. Faith means trusting in God and doing what he wants, regardless of the circumstances.

Proverbs for Today/ 26:6–8

To trust a rebel to convey a message is as foolish as cutting off your feet and drinking poison! In the mouth of a fool a proverb becomes as useless as a paralyzed leg. Honoring a rebel will backfire like a stone tied to a slingshot!

OCTOBER 25

Barnabas and Paul Become Partners in Evangelism/ Acts 11:19–30

Meanwhile, the believers who fled from Jerusalem during the persecution after Stephen's death traveled as far as Phoenicia, Cyprus, and Antioch, scattering the Good News, but only to Jews. 20However, some of the believers who went to Antioch from Cyprus and Cyrene also gave their message about the Lord Jesus to some Greeks. 21And the Lord honored this effort so that large numbers of these Gentiles became believers.

22When the church at Jerusalem heard what had happened, they sent Barnabas to Antioch to help the new converts. 23When he arrived and saw the wonderful things God was doing, he was filled with excitement and joy, and encouraged the believers to stay close to the Lord, whatever the cost. 24Barnabas was a kindly person, full of the Holy Spirit and strong in faith. As a result large numbers of people were added to the Lord.

25Then Barnabas went on to Tarsus to hunt for Paul. 26When he found him, he brought him back to Antioch; and both of them stayed there for a full year, teaching the many new converts. (It was there at Antioch that the believers were first called "Christians.")

27During this time some prophets came down from Jerusalem to Antioch, 28and one of them, named Agabus, stood up in one of the meetings to predict by the Spirit that a great famine was coming upon the land of Israel. (This was fulfilled during the reign of Claudius.) 29So the believers decided to send relief to the Christians in Judea, each giving as much as he could. 30This they did, consigning their gifts to Barnabas and Paul to take to the elders of the church in Jerusalem.

A THOUGHT: *It was from Antioch that Christianity launched its worldwide mission and where the believers aggressively preached to the Gentiles. Philip had preached in Samaria, but the Samaritans were already partly Jewish; Peter preached to Cornelius, but he already worshiped God. Believers who scattered after the outbreak of persecution in Jerusalem, shared the gospel with other Jews in the various lands they fled to. But now the believers began actively sharing the Good News with Gentiles.*

The Faith of Moses/ Hebrews 11:24–29

It was by faith that Moses, when he grew up, refused to be treated as the grandson of the king, but chose to share ill-treatment with God's people instead of enjoying the fleeting pleasures of sin. 26He thought that it was better to suffer for the promised Christ than to own all the treasures of Egypt, for he was looking forward to the great reward that God would give him. 27And it was because he trusted God that he left the land of Egypt and wasn't afraid of the king's anger. Moses kept right on going; it seemed as though he could see God right there with him. 28 And it was because he believed God would save his people that he commanded them to kill a lamb as God had told them to and sprinkle the blood on the doorposts of their homes, so that God's terrible Angel of Death could not touch the oldest child in those homes, as he did among the Egyptians.

29The people of Israel trusted God and went right through the Red Sea as though they were on dry ground. But when the Egyptians chasing them tried it, they all were drowned.

A THOUGHT: *Moses became one of Israel's greatest leaders, a prophet and a lawgiver. But when he was born, his people were slaves in Egypt and the Egyptian officials had ordered that all Hebrew baby boys were to be killed. Moses was spared, however, and Pharaoh's daughter raised Moses in Pharaoh's own household! It took faith for Moses to give up his place in the palace, but he could do it because he saw the fleeting nature of great wealth and prestige. It is easy to be deceived by the temporary benefits of wealth, popularity, status, and achievement, and to be blind to the long-range benefits of God's Kingdom. Faith helps us look beyond the world's value system to see the eternal values of God's Kingdom.*

Proverbs for Today/ 26:9–12

A rebel will misapply an illustration so that its point will no more be felt than a thorn in the hand of a drunkard. □ The master may get better work from an untrained apprentice than from a skilled rebel! □ As a dog returns to his vomit, so a fool repeats his folly. □ There is one thing worse than a fool, and that is a man who is conceited.

OCTOBER 26

An Angel Rescues Peter from Prison/ Acts 12:1–25

About that time King Herod moved against some of the believers, 2and killed the apostle James (John's brother). 3When Herod saw how much this pleased the Jewish leaders, he arrested Peter during the Passover celebration 4and imprisoned him, placing him under the guard of sixteen soldiers. Herod's intention was to deliver Peter to the Jews for execution after the Passover. 5But earnest prayer was going up to God from the church for his safety all the time he was in prison.

6The night before he was to be executed, he was asleep, double-chained between two soldiers with others standing guard before the prison gate, 7when suddenly there was a light in the cell and an angel of the Lord stood beside Peter! The angel slapped him on the side to awaken him and said, "Quick! Get up!" And the chains fell off his wrists! 8Then the angel told him, "Get dressed and put on your shoes." And he did. "Now put on your coat and follow me!" the angel ordered.

9So Peter left the cell, following the angel. But all the time he thought it was a dream or vision, and didn't believe it was really happening. 10They passed the first and second cell blocks and came to the iron gate to the street, and this opened to them of its own accord! So they passed through and walked along together for a block, and then the angel left him.

11Peter finally realized what had happened! "It's really true!" he said to himself. "The Lord has sent his angel and saved me from Herod and from what the Jews were hoping to do to me!"

12After a little thought he went to the home of Mary, mother of John Mark, where many were gathered for a prayer meeting.

13He knocked at the door in the gate, and a girl named Rhoda came to open it. 14When she recognized Peter's voice, she was so overjoyed that she ran back inside to tell everyone that Peter was standing outside in the street. 15They didn't believe her. "You're out of your mind," they said. When she insisted they decided, "It must be his angel. [They must have killed him.]"

16Meanwhile Peter continued knocking. When they finally went out and opened the door, their surprise knew no bounds. 17He motioned for them to quiet down and told them what had happened and how the Lord had brought him out of jail. "Tell James and the others what happened," he said—and left for safer quarters.

18At dawn, the jail was in great commotion. What had happened to Peter? 19When Herod sent for him and found that he wasn't there, he had the sixteen guards arrested, court-martialed and sentenced to death. Afterwards he left to live in Caesarea for a while.

20While he was in Caesarea, a delegation from Tyre

and Sidon arrived to see him. He was highly displeased with the people of those two cities, but the delegates made friends with Blastus, the royal secretary, and asked for peace, for their cities were economically dependent upon trade with Herod's country. 21An appointment with Herod was granted, and when the day arrived he put on his royal robes, sat on his throne and made a speech to them. 22At its conclusion the people gave him a great ovation, shouting, "It is the voice of a god and not of a man!"

23Instantly, an angel of the Lord struck Herod with a sickness so that he was filled with maggots and died— because he accepted the people's worship instead of giving the glory to God.

24God's Good News was spreading rapidly and there were many new believers.

25Barnabas and Paul now visited Jerusalem and, as soon as they had finished their business, returned to Antioch, taking John Mark with them.

A THOUGHT: *In the midst of the plots, execution, and arrest, Luke injects the very important word "but." Herod's plan was to execute Peter, but the believers were praying for Peter's safety. The earnest prayer of the church significantly affected the outcome of these events. We know from the testimony of the Bible that prayer changes attitudes and events. So pray often and pray with confidence.*

Heroes of Faith/ Hebrews 11:30–40

It was faith that brought the walls of Jericho tumbling down after the people of Israel had walked around them seven days, as God had commanded them. 31By faith— because she believed in God and his power—Rahab the harlot did not die with all the others in her city when they refused to obey God, for she gave a friendly welcome to the spies.

32Well, how much more do I need to say? It would take too long to recount the stories of the faith of Gideon and Barak and Samson and Jephthah and David and Samuel and all the other prophets. 33These people all trusted God and as a result won battles, overthrew kingdoms, ruled their people well, and received what God had promised them; they were kept from harm in a den of lions, 34and in a fiery furnace. Some, through their faith, escaped death by the sword. Some were made strong again after they had been weak or sick. Others were given great power in battle; they made whole armies turn and run away. 35And some women, through faith, received their loved ones back again from death. But others trusted God and were beaten to death, preferring to die rather than turn from God and be free—trusting that they would rise to a better life afterwards.

36Some were laughed at and their backs cut open with whips, and others were chained in dungeons. 37, 38Some died by stoning and some by being sawed in two; others were promised freedom if they would renounce their faith, then were killed with the sword. Some went about in skins of sheep and goats, wandering over deserts and mountains, hiding in dens and caves. They were hungry and sick and ill-treated—too good for this world. 39And these men of faith, though they trusted God and won his approval, none of them received all that God had promised them; 40for God wanted them to wait and share the even better rewards that were prepared for us.

A THOUGHT: *These verses summarize the lives of other great men and women of faith. Some experienced outstanding victories, even over death. But others were severely mistreated, tortured, and even killed. Having a steadfast faith in God does not guarantee a happy, carefree life. On the contrary, our faith almost guarantees us some form of abuse from the world. While we are on earth, we may never see the purpose of our suffering. But we know that God will keep his promises to us. Is your faith based on the assurance that God will keep his promises to you?*

Proverbs for Today/ 26:13–16

The lazy man won't go out and work. "There might be a lion outside!" he says. He sticks to his bed like a door to its hinges! He is too tired even to lift his food from his dish to his mouth! Yet in his own opinion he is smarter than seven wise men.

OCTOBER 27

Barnabas and Paul Are Sent Out to Preach/
Acts 13:1–12

Among the prophets and teachers of the church at Antioch were Barnabas and Symeon (also called "The Black Man"), Lucius (from Cyrene), Manaen (the foster-brother of King Herod), and Paul. 2One day as these men were worshiping and fasting the Holy Spirit said, "Dedicate Barnabas and Paul for a special job I have for them." 3So after more fasting and prayer, the men laid their hands on them—and sent them on their way.

4Directed by the Holy Spirit they went to Seleucia and then sailed for Cyprus. 5There, in the town of Salamis, they went to the Jewish synagogue and preached. (John Mark went with them as their assistant.)

6,7Afterwards they preached from town to town across the entire island until finally they reached Paphos where they met a Jewish sorcerer, a fake prophet named Bar-Jesus. He had attached himself to the governor, Sergius Paulus, a man of considerable insight and understanding. The governor invited Barnabas and Paul to visit him, for he wanted to hear their message from God. 8But the sorcerer, Elymas (his name in Greek), interfered and urged the governor to pay no attention to what Paul and Barnabas said, trying to keep him from trusting the Lord.

9Then Paul, filled with the Holy Spirit, glared angrily at the sorcerer and said, 10"You son of the devil, full of every sort of trickery and villainy, enemy of all that is good, will you never end your opposition to the Lord? 11And now God has laid his hand of punishment upon you, and you will be stricken awhile with blindness."

Instantly mist and darkness fell upon him, and he began wandering around begging for someone to take his hand and lead him. 12When the governor saw what happened he believed and was astonished at the power of God's message.

A THOUGHT: *This was the beginning of Paul's first missionary journey. The church was involved in sending Paul and Barnabas, but it was God's plan. Why did Paul and Barnabas go where they did? (1) The Holy Spirit led them. (2) They followed the communi-*

cation routes of the Roman Empire—this made travel easier. (3) They visited key population and cultural centers to reach as many people as possible. (4) They went to cities with synagogues, speaking first to the Jews in hopes that they would see Jesus as the Messiah and help spread the Good News to everyone.

Let Us Run the Race God Has Set for Us/ Hebrews 12:1–4

Since we have such a huge crowd of men of faith watching us from the grandstands, let us strip off anything that slows us down or holds us back, and especially those sins that wrap themselves so tightly around our feet and trip us up; and let us run with patience the particular race that God has set before us.

2Keep your eyes on Jesus, our leader and instructor. He was willing to die a shameful death on the cross because of the joy he knew would be his afterwards; and now he sits in the place of honor by the throne of God.

3If you want to keep from becoming fainthearted and weary, think about his patience as sinful men did such terrible things to him. 4After all, you have never yet struggled against sin and temptation until you sweat great drops of blood.

A THOUGHT: *The Christian life involves hard work. It requires us to give up whatever endangers our relationship with God, to run patiently, and to struggle against sin with the power of the Holy Spirit. To live this life effectively, we must keep our eyes on Jesus. We stumble when we look away from him and at ourselves or the circumstances surrounding us. We are running Christ's race, not our own, and we must always keep him in sight.*

Proverbs for Today/ 26:17

Yanking a dog's ears is no more foolish than interfering in an argument that isn't any of your business.

OCTOBER 28

A Trip to Antioch of Pisidia/ Acts 13:13–23

Now Paul and those with him left Paphos by ship for Turkey, landing at the port town of Perga. There John deserted them and returned to Jerusalem. 14But Barnabas and Paul went on to Antioch, a city in the province of Pisidia.

On the Sabbath they went into the synagogue for the services. 15After the usual readings from the Books of Moses and from the Prophets, those in charge of the service sent them this message: "Brothers, if you have any word of instruction for us come and give it!"

16So Paul stood, waved a greeting to them and began. "Men of Israel," he said, "and all others here who reverence God, [let me begin my remarks with a bit of history].

17"The God of this nation Israel chose our ancestors and honored them in Egypt by gloriously leading them out of their slavery. 18And he nursed them through forty years of wandering around in the wilderness. 19,20Then he destroyed seven nations in Canaan, and gave Israel their land as an inheritance. Judges ruled for about 450 years, and were followed by Samuel the prophet.

21"Then the people begged for a king, and God gave them Saul (son of Kish), a man of the tribe of Benjamin, who reigned for forty years. 22But God removed him and replaced him with David as king, a man about whom God said, 'David (son of Jesse) is a man after my own heart, for he will obey me.' 23And it is one of King David's descendants, Jesus, who is God's promised Savior of Israel!

A THOUGHT: *When they went to a new town to witness for Christ, Paul and Barnabas went first to the synagogue. The Jews who went to the synagogue believed in God and diligently studied the Scriptures. Tragically, however, many could not accept Jesus as the promised Messiah because they had the wrong idea of what kind of Messiah he would be. He was not a military king who would overthrow Rome's control, but a servant king who would overthrow sin in people's hearts. (Only later, when he returns, will he overthrow the nations of the world.) Paul and Barnabas did not separate themselves from the synagogues but tried to show clearly that the Scriptures the Jews studied pointed to Jesus.*

God Disciplines All of His Children/
Hebrews 12:5–11

And have you quite forgotten the encouraging words God spoke to you, his child? He said, "My son, don't be angry when the Lord punishes you. Don't be discouraged when he has to show you where you are wrong. 6For when he punishes you, it proves that he loves you. When he whips you it proves you are really his child."

7Let God train you, for he is doing what any loving father does for his children. Whoever heard of a son who was never corrected? 8If God doesn't punish you when you need it, as other fathers punish their sons, then it means that you aren't really God's son at all—that you don't really belong in his family. 9Since we respect our fathers here on earth, though they punish us, should we not all the more cheerfully submit to God's training so that we can begin really to live?

10Our earthly fathers trained us for a few brief years, doing the best for us that they knew how, but God's correction is always right and for our best good, that we may share his holiness. 11Being punished isn't enjoyable while it is happening—it hurts! But afterwards we can see the result, a quiet growth in grace and character.

A THOUGHT: *Who loves his child more—the father who allows the child to do what will harm him, or the one who corrects, trains, and even punishes the child to help him learn what is right? We may respond to discipline in several ways: (1) we can accept it with resignation; (2) we can accept it with self-pity, thinking we really don't deserve it; (3) we can be angry and resent God for it; or (4) we can accept it gratefully as the appropriate response towards a loving Father. It's never pleasant to be corrected and disciplined by God, but his discipline is a sign of his deep love for you. When God corrects you, see it as proof of his love and ask him what he is trying to teach you.*

Proverbs for Today/ 26:18–19
A man who is caught lying to his neighbor and says, "I was just fooling," is like a madman throwing around fire-brands, arrows and death!

OCTOBER 29

Paul Preaches to the Jews of Antioch/
Acts 13:24–44
"But before Jesus came, John the Baptist preached the need for everyone in Israel to turn from sin to God. 25As

John was finishing his work he asked, 'Do you think I am the Messiah? No! But he is coming soon—and in comparison with him, I am utterly worthless.'

26"Brothers—you sons of Abraham, and also all of you Gentiles here who reverence God—this salvation is for all of us! 27The Jews in Jerusalem and their leaders fulfilled prophecy by killing Jesus; for they didn't recognize him, or realize that he is the one the prophets had written about, though they heard the prophets' words read every Sabbath. 28They found no just cause to execute him, but asked Pilate to have him killed anyway. 29When they had fulfilled all the prophecies concerning his death, he was taken from the cross and placed in a tomb.

30"But God brought him back to life again! 31And he was seen many times during the next few days by the men who had accompanied him to Jerusalem from Galilee— these men have constantly testified to this in public witness.

32,33"And now Barnabas and I are here to bring you this Good News—that God's promise to our ancestors has come true in our own time, in that God brought Jesus back to life again. This is what the second Psalm is talking about when it says concerning Jesus, 'Today I have honored you as my Son.'

34"For God had promised to bring him back to life again, no more to die. This is stated in the Scripture that says, 'I will do for you the wonderful thing I promised David.' 35In another Psalm he explained more fully, saying, 'God will not let his Holy One decay.' 36This was not a reference to David, for after David had served his generation according to the will of God, he died and was buried, and his body decayed. 37[No, it was a reference to another]—someone God brought back to life, whose body was not touched at all by the ravages of death.

38"Brothers! Listen! In this man Jesus, there is forgiveness for your sins! 39Everyone who trusts in him is freed from all guilt and declared righteous—something the Jewish law could never do. 40Oh, be careful! Don't let the prophets' words apply to you. For they said, 41'Look and perish, you despisers [of the truth], for I am doing something in your day—something that you won't believe when you hear it announced.'"

42As the people left the synagogue that day, they asked

Paul to return and speak to them again the next week. 43And many Jews and godly Gentiles who worshiped at the synagogue followed Paul and Barnabas down the street as the two men urged them to accept the mercies God was offering. 44The following week almost the entire city turned out to hear them preach the Word of God.

A THOUGHT: *Paul's message to the Jews in the synagogue in Antioch began with an emphasis on God's covenant with Israel. He began with a point of agreement, for all Jews were proud to be God's chosen people. Then Paul went on to explain how the Good News fulfilled this covenant, and some Jews found this message hard to take. This is the essence of the Good News—that forgiveness of sins and freedom from guilt are available to all people through faith in Christ—including you. Have you received this forgiveness? Are you refreshed by it each day?*

Commands for Christian Living/ Hebrews 12:12–17

So take a new grip with your tired hands, stand firm on your shaky legs, 13and mark out a straight, smooth path for your feet so that those who follow you, though weak and lame, will not fall and hurt themselves, but become strong.

14Try to stay out of all quarrels and seek to live a clean and holy life, for one who is not holy will not see the Lord. 15Look after each other so that not one of you will fail to find God's best blessings. Watch out that no bitterness takes root among you, for as it springs up it causes deep trouble, hurting many in their spiritual lives. 16Watch out that no one becomes involved in sexual sin or becomes careless about God as Esau did: he traded his rights as the oldest son for a single meal. 17And afterwards, when he wanted those rights back again, it was too late, even though he wept bitter tears of repentance. So remember, and be careful.

A THOUGHT: *We must not live with only our own survival in mind. Others will follow our example, and we have a responsibility to them if we claim to live for Christ. Does your example make it easier for others to believe, follow, and mature in Christ? Or would those who follow you end up confused and misled?*

Proverbs for Today/ 26:20

Fire goes out for lack of fuel, and tensions disappear when gossip stops.

OCTOBER 30

Arguments Against Paul and Barnabas/
Acts 13:45–52

But when the Jewish leaders saw the crowds, they were jealous, and cursed and argued against whatever Paul said.

46Then Paul and Barnabas spoke out boldly and declared, "It was necessary that this Good News from God should be given first to you Jews. But since you have rejected it, and shown yourselves unworthy of eternal life—well, we will offer it to Gentiles. 47For this is as the Lord commanded when he said, 'I have made you a light to the Gentiles, to lead them from the farthest corners of the earth to my salvation.'"

48When the Gentiles heard this, they were very glad and rejoiced in Paul's message; and as many as wanted eternal life, believed. 49So God's message spread all through that region.

50Then the Jewish leaders stirred up both the godly women and the civic leaders of the city and incited a mob against Paul and Barnabas, and ran them out of town. 51But they shook off the dust of their feet against the town and went on to the city of Iconium. 52And their converts were filled with joy and with the Holy Spirit.

A THOUGHT: *Instead of hearing the truth, these Jewish leaders ran Paul and Barnabas out of town. When confronted by a disturbing truth, people often turn away and refuse to listen. When God's Spirit points out needed changes in our lives, we must listen to him, or else we risk pushing the truth so far away that it no longer affects us.*

The Earthly and Heavenly Mount Zion/
Hebrews 12:18–24

You have not had to stand face to face with terror, flaming fire, gloom, darkness and a terrible storm, as the Israelites did at Mount Sinai when God gave them his laws. 19For there was an awesome trumpet blast, and a voice with a message so terrible that the people begged God to stop speaking. 20They staggered back under God's command that if even an animal touched the mountain it must die.

21Moses himself was so frightened at the sight that he shook with terrible fear.

22But you have come right up into Mount Zion, to the city of the living God, the heavenly Jerusalem, and to the gathering of countless happy angels; 23and to the church, composed of all those registered in heaven; and to God who is Judge of all; and to the spirits of the redeemed in heaven, already made perfect; 24and to Jesus himself, who has brought us his wonderful new agreement; and to the sprinkled blood which graciously forgives instead of crying out for vengeance as the blood of Abel did.

A THOUGHT: *There is a great contrast in the way people approached God under the old covenant and how people approach God under the new covenant. When God established the old covenant on Mount Sinai, the people experienced the terror of God. The Israelites saw God's awesome power demonstrated; they had to stand at a distance from the mountain. Only Moses was allowed to go up the mountain when he received the Ten Commandments. Under the new covenant, because of what Christ has done, Christians can enter directly into the presence of God without fear. Christ has made it possible to commune intimately with God the Father because he has secured the forgiveness of sin for his people. Let us come boldly before God on the basis of Christ's shed blood.*

Proverbs for Today/ 26:21–22

A quarrelsome man starts fights as easily as a match sets fire to paper. □ Gossip is a dainty morsel eaten with great relish.

OCTOBER 31

The Good News Is Preached at Iconium/
Acts 14:1–7

At Iconium, Paul and Barnabas went together to the synagogue and preached with such power that many—both Jews and Gentiles—believed.

2But the Jews who spurned God's message stirred up distrust among the Gentiles against Paul and Barnabas, saying all sorts of evil things about them. 3Nevertheless, they stayed there a long time, preaching boldly, and the

Lord proved their message was from him by giving them power to do great miracles. 4But the people of the city were divided in their opinion about them. Some agreed with the Jewish leaders, and some backed the apostles.

5,6When Paul and Barnabas learned of a plot to incite a mob of Gentiles, Jews, and Jewish leaders to attack and stone them, they fled for their lives, going to the cities of Lycaonia, Lystra, Derbe, and the surrounding area, 7and preaching the Good News there.

A Thought: *We may wish we could perform a miraculous act that would convince everyone once and for all that Jesus is the Lord, but we see here that even if we could, it wouldn't convince everyone. God gave these men power to do great miracles as proof, but people were still divided. Don't spend your time and energy wishing for miracles. Sow your seeds of Good News on the best ground you can find in the best way you can, and leave the convincing to the Holy Spirit.*

Serve God with Holy Fear and Awe/ Hebrews 12:25–29

So see to it that you obey him who is speaking to you. For if the people of Israel did not escape when they refused to listen to Moses, the earthly messenger, how terrible our danger if we refuse to listen to God who speaks to us from heaven! 26When he spoke from Mount Sinai his voice shook the earth, but, "Next time," he says, "I will not only shake the earth, but the heavens too." 27By this he means that he will sift out everything without solid foundations, so that only unshakable things will be left.

28Since we have a Kingdom nothing can destroy, let us please God by serving him with thankful hearts, and with holy fear and awe. 29For our God is a consuming fire.

A Thought: *Eventually the world will crumble, and only God's Kingdom will last. Those who follow Christ are part of this Kingdom, and they will withstand the shaking, sifting, and burning. When we feel unsure about the future, we can take confidence from these verses. Whatever happens here, our future is built on a solid foundation that cannot be destroyed. Don't put your confidence in that which will be destroyed; instead, build your life on Christ and his unshakable Kingdom.*

Proverbs for Today/ 26:23

Pretty words may hide a wicked heart, just as a pretty glaze covers a common clay pot.

Paul Is Stoned in Lystra/ Acts 14:8–20a

While Paul and Barnabas were at Lystra, they came upon a man with crippled feet who had been that way from birth, so he had never walked. 9He was listening as Paul preached, and Paul noticed him and realized he had faith to be healed. 10So Paul called to him, "Stand up!" and the man leaped to his feet and started walking!

11When the listening crowd saw what Paul had done, they shouted (in their local dialect, of course), "These men are gods in human bodies!" 12They decided that Barnabas was the Greek god Jupiter, and that Paul, because he was the chief speaker, was Mercury! 13The local priest of the Temple of Jupiter, located on the outskirts of the city, brought them cartloads of flowers and prepared to sacrifice oxen to them at the city gates before the crowds.

14But when Barnabas and Paul saw what was happening they ripped at their clothing in dismay and ran out among the people, shouting, 15"Men! What are you doing? We are merely human beings like yourselves! We have come to bring you the Good News that you are invited to turn from the worship of these foolish things and to pray instead to the living God who made heaven and earth and sea and everything in them. 16In bygone days he permitted the nations to go their own ways, 17but he never left himself without a witness; there were always his reminders—the kind things he did such as sending you rain and good crops and giving you food and gladness."

18But even so, Paul and Barnabas could scarcely restrain the people from sacrificing to them!

19Yet only a few days later, some Jews arrived from Antioch and Iconium and turned the crowds into a murderous mob that stoned Paul and dragged him out of the city, apparently dead. 20But as the believers stood around him, he got up and went back into the city!

A THOUGHT: *Paul and Barnabas were dedicated to sharing the Good News. They were not out for fame and fortune. Here they had a prime opportunity to get rich quick by capitalizing on the honor these Gentiles wanted to bestow upon them. These people considered Barnabas to be Jupiter (the Roman name for Zeus, the chief god in Greco–Roman mythology), and considered Paul to be Mercury (the Roman name for the Greek god Hermes). But Paul and Barnabas were terribly upset that these people would do such a thing. They were there to share the Good News about Jesus Christ—he alone is the way to the living God. Paul's dedication to sharing the Good News can be seen in the fact that after he was nearly stoned to death, he rose up and went back into the city to preach the gospel. We must sacrifice our own self–interests in order to share the Good News to the glory of God.*

Live Holy and Obedient Lives/ Hebrews 13:1–9

Continue to love each other with true brotherly love. 2Don't forget to be kind to strangers, for some who have done this have entertained angels without realizing it! 3Don't forget about those in jail. Suffer with them as though you were there yourself. Share the sorrow of those being mistreated, for you know what they are going through.

4Honor your marriage and its vows, and be pure; for God will surely punish all those who are immoral or commit adultery.

5Stay away from the love of money; be satisfied with what you have. For God has said, "I will never, *never* fail you nor forsake you." 6That is why we can say without any doubt or fear, "The Lord is my Helper and I am not afraid of anything that mere man can do to me."

7Remember your leaders who have taught you the Word of God. Think of all the good that has come from their lives, and try to trust the Lord as they do.

8Jesus Christ is the same yesterday, today, and forever. 9So do not be attracted by strange, new ideas. Your spiritual strength comes as a gift from God, not from ceremonial rules about eating certain foods—a method which, by the way, hasn't helped those who have tried it!

A THOUGHT: *Real love toward others produces tangible actions: (1) kindness to strangers; (2) sympathy for those who are in prison and those who have been mistreated; (3) respect for one's marriage vows; and (4) satisfaction with what you have. Make sure your love runs deep enough to affect your hospitality, sympathy, fidelity, and contentment.*

Proverbs for Today/ 26:24–26

A man with hate in his heart may sound pleasant enough, but don't believe him; for he is cursing you in his heart. Though he pretends to be so kind, his hatred will finally come to light for all to see.

Paul and Barnabas Return to Antioch/
Acts 14:20b–28

The next day Paul left with Barnabas for Derbe. 21After preaching the Good News there and making many disciples, they returned again to Lystra, Iconium and Antioch, 22where they helped the believers to grow in love for God and each other. They encouraged them to continue in the faith in spite of all the persecution, reminding them that they must enter into the Kingdom of God through many tribulations. 23Paul and Barnabas also appointed elders in every church and prayed for them with fasting, turning them over to the care of the Lord in whom they trusted.

24Then they traveled back through Pisidia to Pamphylia, 25preached again in Perga, and went on to Attalia.

26Finally they returned by ship to Antioch, where their journey had begun, and where they had been committed to God for the work now completed.

27Upon apprival they called together the believers and reported on their trip, telling how God had opened the door of faith to the Gentiles too. 28And they stayed there with the believers at Antioch for a long while.

A THOUGHT: *Paul and Barnabas returned to visit the believers in all the cities where they had recently been threatened and physically attacked. They knew the dangers they faced, yet they believed they had a responsibility to encourage the new believers. No matter how inconvenient or uncomfortable the task may seem, we must never fail to support new believers who need our help and encouragement.*

Let Us Suffer with Christ/ Hebrews 13:10–16

We have an altar—the cross where Christ was sacrificed—where those who continue to seek salvation by obeying Jewish laws can never be helped. 11Under the system of Jewish laws the high priest brought the blood of the slain animals into the sanctuary as a sacrifice for sin, and then the bodies of the animals were burned outside the city. 12That is why Jesus suffered and died outside the city, where his blood washed our sins away.

13So let us go out to him beyond the city walls [that is, outside the interests of this world, being willing to be despised] to suffer with him there, bearing his shame. 14For this world is not our home; we are looking forward to our everlasting home in heaven.

15With Jesus' help we will continually offer our sacrifice of praise to God by telling others of the glory of his name. 16Don't forget to do good and to share what you have with those in need, for such sacrifices are very pleasing to him.

A THOUGHT: *Verse 13 can also be translated, "Let us go to him outside the camp, and bear the disgrace he endured." The Jewish Christians were being ridiculed and persecuted by Jews who didn't believe in Jesus the Messiah. Most of the book of Hebrews tells them how much greater Christ is than the sacrificial system. Now the writer makes the point of his lengthy argument: It may be necessary to leave the "camp" and suffer with Christ. To be outside the camp meant to be unclean. But Jesus suffered humiliation and uncleanness outside the Jerusalem gates on their behalf. The time had come for Jewish Christians to declare their loyalty to Christ above any other loyalty, to choose to follow the Messiah whatever suffering that might entail. Is there anything holding us back from complete loyalty to Jesus Christ?*

Proverbs for Today/ 26:27

The man who sets a trap for others will get caught in it himself. Roll a boulder down on someone, and it will roll back and crush you.

NOVEMBER 3

The Jerusalem Church Council/ Acts 15:1–21

While Paul and Barnabas were at Antioch, some men from Judea arrived and began to teach the believers that unless they adhered to the ancient Jewish custom of circumcision, they could not be saved. 2Paul and Barnabas argued and discussed this with them at length, and finally the believers sent them to Jerusalem, accompanied by some local men, to talk to the apostles and elders there about this question. 3After the entire congregation had escorted them out of the city the delegates went on to Jerusalem, stopping along the way in the cities of Phoenicia and Samaria to visit the believers, telling them—much to everyone's joy—that the Gentiles, too, were being converted.

4Arriving in Jerusalem, they met with the church leaders—all the apostles and elders were present—and Paul and Barnabas reported on what God had been doing through their ministry. 5But then some of the men who had been Pharisees before their conversion stood to their feet and declared that all Gentile converts must be circumcised and required to follow all the Jewish customs and ceremonies.

6So the apostles and church elders set a further meeting to decide this question.

7At the meeting, after long discussion, Peter stood and addressed them as follows: "Brothers, you all know that God chose me from among you long ago to preach the Good News to the Gentiles, so that they also could believe. 8God, who knows men's hearts, confirmed the fact that he accepts Gentiles by giving them the Holy Spirit, just as he gave him to us. 9He made no distinction between them and us, for he cleansed their lives through faith, just as he did ours. 10And now are you going to correct God by burdening the Gentiles with a yoke that neither we nor our fathers were able to bear? 11Don't you believe that all are saved the same way, by the free gift of the Lord Jesus?"

12There was no further discussion, and everyone now listened as Barnabas and Paul told about the miracles God had done through them among the Gentiles.

13When they had finished, James took the floor. "Brothers," he said, "listen to me. 14Peter has told you about the time God first visited the Gentiles to take from them a people to bring honor to his name. 15And this fact of Gentile conversion agrees with what the prophets predicted. For instance, listen to this passage from the prophet Amos:

16'Afterwards' [says the Lord], 'I will return and renew the broken contract with David, 17so that Gentiles, too, will find the Lord—all those marked with my name.'

18That is what the Lord says, who reveals his plans made from the beginning.

19"And so my judgment is that we should not insist that the Gentiles who turn to God must obey our Jewish laws, 20except that we should write to them to refrain from eating meat sacrificed to idols, from all fornication, and also from eating unbled meat of strangled animals. 21For these things have been preached against in Jewish synagogues in every city on every Sabbath for many generations."

A THOUGHT: *The real problem for the Jewish Christians was not over whether Gentiles could be saved, but whether Gentiles had to adhere to the laws of Moses. The test of whether or not the law was being followed was circumcision. The Jewish Christians were worried because soon there would be more Gentile than Jewish Christians, and the Jews were afraid of weakening moral standards among believers if they did not follow Jewish laws. Paul, Barnabas, and the other church leaders believed that the Old Testament Law was very important, but it was not a prerequisite to salvation. The Law cannot save; only faith in Jesus Christ can save.*

Final Commands and a Benediction/ Hebrews 13:17–25

Obey your spiritual leaders and be willing to do what they say. For their work is to watch over your souls, and God will judge them on how well they do this. Give them reason to report joyfully about you to the Lord and not with sorrow, for then you will suffer for it too.

18Pray for us, for our conscience is clear and we want to keep it that way. 19I especially need your prayers right now so that I can come back to you sooner.

20,21And now may the God of peace, who brought again from the dead our Lord Jesus, equip you with all you need for doing his will. May he who became the great Shepherd of the sheep by an everlasting agreement between God and you, signed with his blood, produce in you through the power of Christ all that is pleasing to him. To him be glory forever and ever. Amen.

22Brethren, please listen patiently to what I have said in this letter, for it is a short one. 23I want you to know that Brother Timothy is now out of jail; if he comes here soon, I will come with him to see you. 24,25Give my greetings to all your leaders and to the other believers there. The

Christians from Italy who are here with me send you their love. God's grace be with you all.

Good-bye.

A THOUGHT: *The writer of Hebrews recognized the need for prayer. Christian leaders are especially vulnerable to criticism from others, pride if they succeed, depression if they fail, and Satan's constant efforts to nullify their work for God. They desperately need our prayers! For whom should you regularly pray?*

Proverbs for Today/ 26:28

Flattery is a form of hatred and wounds cruelly.

NOVEMBER 4

A Letter to Gentile Believers/ Acts 15:22–41

Then the apostles and elders and the whole congregation voted to send delegates to Antioch with Paul and Barnabas, to report on this decision. The men chosen were two of the church leaders—Judas (also called Barsabbas) and Silas.

23This is the letter they took along with them:

"From: The apostles, elders and brothers at Jerusalem.

"To: The Gentile brothers in Antioch, Syria and Cilicia. Greetings!

24"We understand that some believers from here have upset you and questioned your salvation, but they had no such instructions from us. 25So it seemed wise to us, having unanimously agreed on our decision, to send to you these two official representatives, along with our beloved Barnabas and Paul. 26These men—Judas and Silas, who have risked their lives for the sake of our Lord Jesus Christ—will confirm orally what we have decided concerning your question.

27,28,29"For it seemed good to the Holy Spirit and to us to lay no greater burden of Jewish laws on you than to abstain from eating food offered to idols and from unbled meat of strangled animals, and, of course, from fornication. If you do this, it is enough. Farewell."

30The four messengers went at once to Antioch, where

they called a general meeting of the Christians and gave them the letter. 31And there was great joy throughout the church that day as they read it.

32Then Judas and Silas, both being gifted speakers, preached long sermons to the believers, strengthening their faith. 33They stayed several days, and then Judas and Silas returned to Jerusalem taking greetings and appreciation to those who had sent them. 34,35Paul and Barnabas stayed on at Antioch to assist several others who were preaching and teaching there.

36Several days later Paul suggested to Barnabas that they return again to Turkey, and visit each city where they had preached before, to see how the new converts were getting along. 37Barnabas agreed, and wanted to take along John Mark. 38But Paul didn't like that idea at all, since John had deserted them in Pamphylia. 39Their disagreement over this was so sharp that they separated. Barnabas took Mark with him and sailed for Cyprus, 40,41while Paul chose Silas and, with the blessing of the believers, left for Syria and Cilicia, to encourage the churches there.

A THOUGHT: *Gentile believers did not have to abide by the Jewish law of circumcision, but they were asked by the council to stay away from idolatry, sexual immorality (a common part of idol worship), and eating the meat of animals which have not had all the blood drained out of them (reflecting the Levitical teaching that the life of an animal is in its blood). If Gentile Christians would abstain from these three practices, they would please God and get along better with fellow Jewish Christians. Of course, there were other actions inappropriate for believers, but the Jews were especially concerned about these three. This compromise kept the church from being uneccessarily hindered by the cultural differences between Jews and Gentiles. When we share our message across cultural and economic boundaries, we must be sure that the requirements for faith we set up are God's universal requirements, not our particular cultural expressions of Christianity.*

Trials Build Character/ James 1:1–4

From: James, a servant of God and of the Lord Jesus Christ.

To: Jewish Christians scattered everywhere. Greetings!

2Dear brothers, is your life full of difficulties and temptations? Then be happy, 3for when the way is rough, your patience has a chance to grow. 4So let it grow, and don't try to squirm out of your problems. For when your patience is finally in full bloom, then you will be ready for anything, strong in character, full and complete.

A THOUGHT: *We can't really know the depth of our own character until we see how we react under pressure. It is easy to be kind when everything is going well, but can we still be kind when others are treating us unfairly? Instead of complaining about our struggles, we should see them as opportunities for growth. Thank God for promising to be with you in rough times. Ask him to help you solve your problems or give you the strength to endure them. Then be patient. God will not leave you alone with your problems; he will stay close by and help you grow through the trials.*

Proverbs for Today/ 27:1–2

Don't brag about your plans for tomorrow—wait and see what happens. ☐ Don't praise yourself; let others do it!

NOVEMBER 5

A Second Missionary Journey/ Acts 16:1–10

Paul and Silas went first to Derbe and then on to Lystra where they met Timothy, a believer whose mother was a Christian Jewess but his father a Greek. 2Timothy was well thought of by the brothers in Lystra and Iconium, 3so Paul asked him to join them on their journey. In deference to the Jews of the area, he circumcised Timothy before they left, for everyone knew that his father was a Greek [and hadn't permitted this before]. 4Then they went from city to city, making known the decision concerning the Gentiles, as decided by the apostles and elders in Jerusalem. 5So the church grew daily in faith and numbers.

6Next they traveled through Phrygia and Galatia, because the Holy Spirit had told them not to go into the Turkish province of Ausia at that time. 7Then going along the borders of Mysia they headed north for the province of Bithynia, but again the Spirit of Jesus said no. 8So instead they went on through Mysia province to the city of Troas.

9That night Paul had a vision. In his dream he saw a man over in Macedonia, Greece, pleading with him, "Come over here and help us." 10Well, that settled it. We would go to Macedonia, for we could only conclude that God was sending us to preach the Good News there.

A THOUGHT: *We don't know how the Holy Spirit told Paul that he and his men were not to go into Asia. It may have been through a prophet, a vision, an inner conviction, or some other circumstance. To know God's will does not mean we must audibly hear his voice. He leads in different ways. When seeking God's will (1) make sure your plan is in harmony with God's Word; (2) ask mature Christians for their advice; (3) check your own motives—are you seeking to do what you want or what you believe God wants?— and (4) pray for God to open and close the doors of circumstances.*

God Supplies Wisdom to Those Who Ask/ James 1:5–8

If you want to know what God wants you to do, ask him, and he will gladly tell you, for he is always ready to give a bountiful supply of wisdom to all who ask him; he will not resent it. 6But when you ask him, be sure that you really expect him to tell you, for a doubtful mind will be as unsettled as a wave of the sea that is driven and tossed by the wind; 7,8and every decision you then make will be uncertain, as you turn first this way, and then that. If you don't ask with faith, don't expect the Lord to give you any solid answer.

A THOUGHT: *When James speaks of wisdom, he means practical discernment. Wisdom begins with respect for God, leads to right living, and results in increased ability to tell right from wrong. God is willing to give us this wisdom. We will be unable to receive it if our goals are self-centered instead of God-centered. To learn God's will, we need to ask him to reveal it to us, and then we must be willing to do what he tells us to do.*

Proverbs for Today/ 27:3

A rebel's frustrations are heavier than sand and rocks.

NOVEMBER 6

Lydia Is Converted/ Acts 16:11–15

We [Luke, Paul, and his companions] went aboard a boat at Troas, and sailed straight across to Samothrace, and the next day on to Neapolis, 12and finally reached Philippi, a Roman colony just inside the Macedonian border, and stayed there several days.

13On the Sabbath, we went a little way outside the city to a river bank where we understood some people met for prayer; and we taught the Scriptures to some women who came. 14One of them was Lydia, a saleswoman from Thyatira, a merchant of purple cloth. She was already a worshiper of God and, as she listened to us, the Lord opened her heart and she accepted all that Paul was saying. 15She was baptized along with all her household and asked us to be her guests. "If you agree that I am faithful to the Lord," she said, "come and stay at my home." And she urged us until we did.

A THOUGHT: *After following the Holy Spirit's leading into Macedonia, Paul made his first evangelistic contact with a small group of women. Paul never allowed sexual or cultural boundaries to keep him from preaching the gospel. He preached to these women, and Lydia, an influential merchant, believed. This threw open the door for ministry in that region. In the early church God often worked in and through women. We should be careful not to exclude any group from hearing the gospel, or participating in the ministry of the church.*

Happy Is the Person Who Endures Temptation/ James 1:9–18

A Christian who doesn't amount to much in this world should be glad, for he is great in the Lord's sight. 10,11But a rich man should be glad that his riches mean nothing to the Lord, for he will soon be gone, like a flower that has lost its beauty and fades away, withered—killed by the scorching summer sun. So it is with rich men. They will soon die and leave behind all their busy activities.

12Happy is the man who doesn't give in and do wrong when he is tempted, for afterwards he will get as his reward the crown of life that God has promised those who love him. 13And remember, when someone wants to do wrong it is never God who is tempting him, for God never wants to do wrong and never tempts anyone else to do it. 14Temptation is the pull of man's own evil thoughts and wishes. 15These evil thoughts lead to evil actions and afterwards to the death penalty from God. 16So don't be misled, dear brothers.

17But whatever is good and perfect comes to us from

God, the Creator of all light, and he shines forever without change or shadow. 18And it was a happy day for him when he gave us our new lives, through the truth of his Word, and we became, as it were, the first children in his new family.

A THOUGHT: *The rich should be glad wealth means nothing to God, because wealth is easily lost. The poor should be glad riches mean nothing to God, otherwise they would be considered unworthy. True wealth is found in an individual's spiritual life, not his or her financial assets. God is interested in what is lasting (our souls), not in what is temporary (our money and possessions). If wealth, power, and status mean nothing to God, why do we attribute so much importance to them and honor those who possess them? Do your material possessions give you a sense of purpose and a reason for living? If they were gone, what would be left? What you have in your heart, not your bank account, matters to God and endures for eternity.*

Proverbs for Today/ 27:4–6

Jealousy is more dangerous and cruel than anger. ☐ Open rebuke is better than hidden love! Wounds from a friend are better than kisses from an enemy!

NOVEMBER 7

The Conversion of the Philippian Jailer/ Acts 16:16–40

One day as we [Luke, Paul, and his companions] were going down to the place of prayer beside the river, we met a demon-possessed slave girl who was a fortune-teller, and earned much money for her masters. 17She followed along behind us shouting, "These men are servants of God and they have come to tell you how to have your sins forgiven."

18This went on day after day until Paul, in great distress, turned and spoke to the demon within her. "I command you in the name of Jesus Christ to come out of her," he said. And instantly it left her.

19Her masters' hopes of wealth were now shattered; they grabbed Paul and Silas and dragged them before the judges at the marketplace.

20,21"These Jews are corrupting our city," they shouted. "They are teaching the people to do things that are against the Roman laws."

22A mob was quickly formed against Paul and Silas, and the judges ordered them stripped and beaten with wooden whips. 23Again and again the rods slashed down across their bared backs; and afterwards they were thrown into prison. The jailer was threatened with death if they escaped, 24so he took no chances, but put them into the inner dungeon and clamped their feet into the stocks.

25Around midnight, as Paul and Silas were praying and singing hymns to the Lord—and the other prisoners were listening— 26suddenly there was a great earthquake; the prison was shaken to its foundations, all the doors flew open—and the chains of every prisoner fell off! 27The jailer wakened to see the prison doors wide open, and assuming the prisoners had escaped, he drew his sword to kill himself.

28But Paul yelled to him, "Don't do it! We are all here!"

29Trembling with fear, the jailer called for lights and ran to the dungeon and fell down before Paul and Silas. 30He brought them out and begged them, "Sirs, what must I do to be saved?"

31They replied, "Believe on the Lord Jesus and you will be saved, and your entire household."

32Then they told him and all his household the Good News from the Lord. 33That same hour he washed their stripes and he and all his family were baptized. 34Then he brought them up into his house and set a meal before them. How he and his household rejoiced because all were now believers! 35The next morning the judges sent police officers over to tell the jailer, "Let those men go!" 36So the jailer told Paul they were free to leave.

37But Paul replied, "Oh, no they don't! They have publicly beaten us without trial and jailed us—and we are Roman citizens! So now they want us to leave secretly? Never! Let them come themselves and release us!"

38The police officers reported to the judges, who feared for their lives when they heard Paul and Silas were Roman citizens. 39So they came to the jail and begged them to go, and brought them out and pled with them to leave the city. 40Paul and Silas then returned to the home of

Lydia where they met with the believers and preached to them once more before leaving town.

A Thought: *Paul and Silas were stripped, beaten, whipped, and placed in stocks in the inner prison dungeon. Despite this dismal situation, they praised God, praying and singing as the other prisoners listened. God caused an earthquake to occur which opened the prison doors and all the chains fastened around the prisoners fell off. The jailer immediately drew his sword to commit suicide because Roman soldiers were usually executed if a prisoner was allowed to escape, and the Philippian jailer knew that he would be held responsible. Paul intervened to prevent the jailer from killing himself. Paul shared the gospel with the jailer and he became a Christian. We must always be open to those opportunities that God opens up to share the Good News with others.*

Become a Doer of the Word/ James 1:19–27

Dear brothers, don't ever forget that it is best to listen much, speak little, and not become angry; 20for anger doesn't make us good, as God demands that we must be.

21So get rid of all that is wrong in your life, both inside and outside, and humbly be glad for the wonderful message we have received, for it is able to save our souls as it takes hold of our hearts.

22And remember, it is a message to obey, not just to listen to. So don't fool yourselves. 23For if a person just listens and doesn't obey, he is like a man looking at his face in a mirror; 24as soon as he walks away, he can't see himself anymore or remember what he looks like. 25But if anyone keeps looking steadily into God's law for free men, he will not only remember it but he will do what it says, and God will greatly bless him in everything he does.

26Anyone who says he is a Christian but doesn't control his sharp tongue is just fooling himself, and his religion isn't worth much. 27The Christian who is pure and without fault, from God the Father's point of view, is the one who takes care of orphans and widows, and who remains true to the Lord—not soiled and dirtied by his contacts with the world.

A Thought: *When we talk too much and listen too little, we communicate to others that we think our ideas are much more important than theirs. James wisely advises us to reverse this process. Put a mental stopwatch on your conversations and keep track of how much you talk and how much you listen. In your conversations, do others feel that their viewpoints and ideas have value?*

Proverbs for Today/ 27:7–9

Even honey seems tasteless to a man who is full; but if he is hungry, he'll eat anything! □ A man who strays from home is like a bird that wanders from its nest. □ Friendly suggestions are as pleasant as perfume.

NOVEMBER 8

Paul and Silas Continue Their Preaching Mission/ Acts 17:1–15

Now Paul and Silas traveled through the cities of Amphipolis and Apollonia and came to Thessalonica, where there was a Jewish synagogue. 2As was Paul's custom, he went there to preach, and for three Sabbaths in a row he opened the Scriptures to the people, 3explaining the prophecies about the sufferings of the Messiah and his coming back to life, and proving that Jesus is the Messiah. 4Some who listened were persuaded and became converts—including a large number of godly Greek men, and also many important women of the city.

5But the Jewish leaders were jealous and incited some worthless fellows from the streets to form a mob and start a riot. They attacked the home of Jason, planning to take Paul and Silas to the City Council for punishment.

6Not finding them there, they dragged out Jason and some of the other believers, and took them before the Council instead. "Paul and Silas have turned the rest of the world upside down, and now they are here disturbing our city," they shouted, 7"and Jason has let them into his home. They are all guilty of treason, for they claim another king, Jesus, instead of Caesar."

8,9The people of the city, as well as the judges, were concerned at these reports and let them go only after they had posted bail.

10That night the Christians hurried Paul and Silas to

Beroea, and, as usual, they went to the synagogue to preach. 11But the people of Beroea were more open minded than those in Thessalonica, and gladly listened to the message. They searched the Scriptures day by day to check up on Paul and Silas' statements to see if they were really so. 12As a result, many of them believed, including several prominent Greek women and many men also.

13But when the Jews in Thessalonica learned that Paul was preaching in Beroea, they went over and stirred up trouble. 14The believers acted at once, sending Paul on to the coast, while Silas and Timothy remained behind. 15Those accompanying Paul went on with him to Athens, and then returned to Beroea with a message for Silas and Timothy to hurry and join him.

A THOUGHT: *What a reputation these early Christians had; they truly "turned the world upside down!" The power of the gospel revolutionized lives, crossed all social barriers, threw open prison doors, caused people to care deeply for one another, and stirred them to worship God. Our world needs to be turned upside down, to be transformed. The gospel is not in the business of merely improving programs and conduct, but of dynamically transforming lives.*

Do Not Show Favor to the Rich/ James 2:1–9

Dear brothers, how can you claim that you belong to the Lord Jesus Christ, the Lord of glory, if you show favoritism to rich people and look down on poor people?

2If a man comes into your church dressed in expensive clothes and with valuable gold rings on his fingers, and at the same moment another man comes in who is poor and dressed in threadbare clothes, 3and you make a lot of fuss over the rich man and give him the best seat in the house and say to the poor man, "You can stand over there if you like, or else sit on the floor"—well, 4judging a man by his wealth shows that you are guided by wrong motives.

5Listen to me, dear brothers: God has chosen poor people to be rich in faith, and the Kingdom of Heaven is theirs, for that is the gift God has promised to all those who love him. 6And yet, of the two strangers, you have despised the poor man. Don't you realize that it is usually the rich men who pick on you and drag you into court?

7And all too often they are the ones who laugh at Jesus Christ, whose noble name you bear.

8Yes indeed, it is good when you truly obey our Lord's command, "You must love and help your neighbors just as much as you love and take care of yourself." 9But you are breaking this law of our Lord's when you favor the rich and fawn over them; it is sin.

A THOUGHT: *Often we treat a well-dressed, impressive-looking person better than someone who looks poor. We do this because we would rather identify with successful people than with apparent failures. We feel better about ourselves when we associate with people we admire. The irony, as James reminds us, is that the supposed winners may have gained their impressive lifestyle at our expense. In addition, the rich find it hard to identify with the Lord Jesus who came as a humble servant. Are you easily impressed by status, wealth, or fame? Are you partial to the "haves" while ignoring the "have nots"? This prejudice is sin. God views all people as equals, and if he favors anyone, it is the poor and the powerless. We should follow his example.*

Proverbs for Today/ 27:10
Never abandon a friend—either yours or your father's. Then you won't need to go to a distant relative for help in your time of need.

NOVEMBER 9

Paul's Sermon at the Mars Hill Forum/
Acts 17:16–34
While Paul was waiting for Silas and Timothy in Athens, he was deeply troubled by all the idols he saw everywhere throughout the city. 17He went to the synagogue for discussions with the Jews and the devout Gentiles, and spoke daily in the public square to all who happened to be there.

18He also had an encounter with some of the Epicurean and Stoic philosophers. Their reaction, when he told them about Jesus and his resurrection, was, "He's a dreamer," or, "He's pushing some foreign religion."

19But they invited him to the forum at Mars Hill. "Come

and tell us more about this new religion," they said, 20"for you are saying some rather startling things and we want to hear more." 21(I should explain that all the Athenians as well as the foreigners in Athens seemed to spend all their time discussing the latest new ideas!)

22So Paul, standing before them at the Mars Hill forum, addressed them as follows:

"Men of Athens, I notice that you are very religious, 23for as I was out walking I saw your many altars, and one of them had this inscription on it—'To the Unknown God.' You have been worshiping him without knowing who he is, and now I wish to tell you about him.

24"He made the world and everything in it, and since he is Lord of heaven and earth, he doesn't live in man-made temples; 25and human hands can't minister to his needs—for he has no needs! He himself gives life and breath to everything, and satisfies every need there is. 26He created all the people of the world from one man, Adam, and scattered the nations across the face of the earth. He decided beforehand which should rise and fall, and when. He determined their boundaries.

27"His purpose in all of this is that they should seek after God, and perhaps feel their way toward him and find him—though he is not far from any one of us. 28For in him we live and move and are! As one of your own poets says it, 'We are the sons of God.' 29If this is true, we shouldn't think of God as an idol made by men from gold or silver or chipped from stone. 30God tolerated man's past ignorance about these things, but now he commands everyone to put away idols and worship only him. 31For he has set a day for justly judging the world by the man he has appointed, and has pointed him out by bringing him back to life again."

32When they heard Paul speak of the resurrection of a person who had been dead, some laughed, but others said, "We want to hear more about this later." 33That ended Paul's discussion with them, 34but a few joined him and became believers. Among them was Dionysius, a member of the City Council, and a woman named Damaris, and others.

A THOUGHT: *Paul was well prepared to speak to this group. He came from Tarsus, an educational center, and had the training and knowledge to present his beliefs clearly and persuasively. Paul was a rabbi, taught by the finest scholar of his day, Gamaliel, and he had spent much of his life thinking and reasoning through the Scriptures.*

It is not enough to teach or preach with conviction. Like Paul, we must be prepared. The more we know about the Bible, what it means, and how to apply it to our lives, the more convincing our words will be. This does not mean we should avoid presenting the gospel until we feel adequately prepared. We should work with what we know, but always want to know more in order to reach more people and answer their questions and arguments more effectively.

Breaking One Commandment Violates the Whole Law/ James 2:10–13

And the person who keeps every law of God, but makes one little slip, is just as guilty as the person who has broken every law there is. 11For the God who said you must not marry a woman who already has a husband, also said you must not murder, so even though you have not broken the marriage laws by committing adultery, but have murdered someone, you have entirely broken God's laws and stand utterly guilty before him.

12You will be judged on whether or not you are doing what Christ wants you to. So watch what you do and what you think; 13for there will be no mercy to those who have shown no mercy. But if you have been merciful, then God's mercy toward you will win out over his judgment against you.

A THOUGHT: *It is easy to spot sins in others while we overlook or rationalize our own. James reminds us that if we've broken just one law, we are sinners. You can't break the law a little bit; if you have broken it at all, you need Christ to pay for your sin. Measure yourself, not someone else, against God's standards. Ask for forgiveness where you need it, and then renew your effort to show your faith by your actions.*

Proverbs for Today/ 27:11

My son, how happy I will be if you turn out to be sensible! It will be a public honor to me.

NOVEMBER 10

Paul Meets Priscilla and Aquila/ Acts 18:1–8

Then Paul left Athens and went to Corinth. 2,3There he
became acquainted with a Jew named Aquila, born in Pontus,
who had recently arrived from Italy with his wife, Priscilla.
They had been expelled from Italy as a result of Claudius
Caesar's order to deport all Jews from Rome. Paul lived
and worked with them, for they were tentmakers just
as he was.

4Each Sabbath found Paul at the synagogue, trying to
convince the Jews and Greeks alike. 5And after the arrival
of Silas and Timothy from Macedonia, Paul spent his full
time preaching and testifying to the Jews that Jesus is
the Messiah. 6But when the Jews opposed him and blasphemed, hurling abuse at Jesus, Paul shook off the dust
from his robe and said, "Your blood be upon your own
heads—I am innocent—from now on I will preach to the
Gentiles."

7After that he stayed with Titus Justus, a Gentile who
worshiped God and lived next door to the synagogue.
8However, Crispus, the leader of the synagogue, and all
his household believed in the Lord and were baptized—
as were many others in Corinth.

A THOUGHT: *Some couples know how to make the most of life.*
They complement each other, utilize each other's strengths, and
form an effective team. Their united efforts affect those around
them. Aquila and Priscilla were such a couple. They are never
mentioned separately in the Bible. In marriage and ministry, they
were together.

Priscilla and Aquila met Paul in Corinth during his second
missionary journey. They had just been expelled from Rome due
to Emperor Claudius' decree against the Jews. Their home was
as movable as the tents they made to support themselves. They
opened their home to Paul, and he joined them in tentmaking.
Paul shared with them his wealth of spiritual wisdom.

Genuine Faith Produces Good Works/
James 2:14–26

Dear brothers, what's the use of saying that you have
faith and are Christians if you aren't proving it by helping
others? Will *that* kind of faith save anyone? 15If you have

a friend who is in need of food and clothing, 16and you say to him, "Well, good-bye and God bless you; stay warm and eat hearty," and then don't give him clothes or food, what good does that do?

17So you see, it isn't enough just to have faith. You must also do good to prove that you have it. Faith that doesn't show itself by good works is no faith at all—it is dead and useless.

18But someone may well argue, "You say the way to God is by faith alone, plus nothing; well, I say that good works are important too, for without good works you can't prove whether you have faith or not; but anyone can see that I have faith by the way I act."

19Are there still some among you who hold that "only believing" is enough? Believing in one God? Well, remember that the demons believe this too—so strongly that they tremble in terror! 20Fool! When will you ever learn that "believing" is useless without *doing* what God wants you to? Faith that does not result in good deeds is not real faith.

21Don't you remember that even our father Abraham was declared good because of what he *did,* when he was willing to obey God, even if it meant offering his son Isaac to die on the altar? 22You see, he was trusting God so much that he was willing to do whatever God told him to; his faith was made complete by what he did, by his actions, his good deeds. 23And so it happened just as the Scriptures say, that Abraham trusted God, and the Lord declared him good in God's sight, and he was even called "the friend of God." 24So you see, a man is saved by what he does, as well as by what he believes.

25Rahab, the prostitute, is another example of this. She was saved because of what she did when she hid those messengers and sent them safely away by a different road. 26Just as the body is dead when there is no spirit in it, so faith is dead if it is not the kind that results in good deeds.

A THOUGHT: *Intellectual assent—agreement with a set of Christian teachings—is incomplete faith. True faith transforms our lives. If our lives remain unchanged, we don't truly believe the truths we claim to believe. Living the way God wants us to live does not earn our way into heaven, but it shows that our commitment to God is real. Godly conduct is not a substitute for, but a verification of our faith in Christ.*

Proverbs for Today/ 27:12

A sensible man watches for problems ahead and prepares to meet them. The simpleton never looks, and suffers the consequences.

NOVEMBER 11

Governor Gallio Releases Paul/ Acts 18:9–23

One night the Lord spoke to Paul in a vision and told him, "Don't be afraid! Speak out! Don't quit! 10For I am with you and no one can harm you. Many people here in this city belong to me." 11So Paul stayed there the next year and a half, teaching the truths of God.

12But when Gallio became governor of Achaia, the Jews rose in concerted action against Paul and brought him before the governor for judgment. 13They accused Paul of "persuading men to worship God in ways that are contrary to Roman law." 14But just as Paul started to make his defense, Gallio turned to his accusers and said, "Listen, you Jews, if this were a case involving some crime, I would be obliged to listen to you, 15but since it is merely a bunch of questions of semantics and personalities and your silly Jewish laws, you take care of it. I'm not interested and I'm not touching it." 16And he drove them out of the courtroom.

17Then the mob grabbed Sosthenes, the new leader of the synagogue, and beat him outside the courtroom. But Gallio couldn't have cared less.

18Paul stayed in the city several days after that and then said good-bye to the Christians and sailed for the coast of Syria, taking Priscilla and Aquila with him. At Cenchreae, Paul had his head shaved according to Jewish custom, for he had taken a vow. 19Arriving at the port of Ephesus, he left us aboard ship while he went over to the synagogue for a discussion with the Jews. 20They asked him to stay for a few days, but he felt that he had no time to lose.

21"I must by all means be at Jerusalem for the holiday,"

he said. But he promised to return to Ephesus later if God permitted; and so he set sail again.

22The next stop was at the port of Caesarea from where he visited the church [at Jerusalem] and then sailed on to Antioch. 23After spending some time there, he left for Turkey again, going through Galatia and Phrygia visiting all the believers, encouraging them and helping them grow in the Lord.

A THOUGHT: *The early Christians experienced persecution from every side. In this reading, the Roman governor did not want to get involved, yet he allowed the beating of Sosthenes to go on. In spite of all the disappointments and struggles Paul and his fellow workers shared the Good News. As Christians we are called to suffer for the Good News—Let us not shrink back when those times come, but rely on the power of the Holy Spirit.*

Controlling the Tongue/ James 3:1–12

Dear brothers, don't be too eager to tell others their faults, for we all make many mistakes; and when we teachers of religion, who should know better, do wrong, our punishment will be greater than it would be for others.

If anyone can control his tongue, it proves that he has perfect control over himself in every other way. 3We can make a large horse turn around and go wherever we want by means of a small bit in his mouth. 4And a tiny rudder makes a huge ship turn wherever the pilot wants it to go, even though the winds are strong.

5So also the tongue is a small thing, but what enormous damage it can do. A great forest can be set on fire by one tiny spark. 6And the tongue is a flame of fire. It is full of wickedness, and poisons every part of the body. And the tongue is set on fire by hell itself, and can turn our whole lives into a blazing flame of destruction and disaster.

7Men have trained, or can train, every kind of animal or bird that lives and every kind of reptile and fish, 8but no human being can tame the tongue. It is always ready to pour out its deadly poison. 9Sometimes it praises our heavenly Father, and sometimes it breaks out into curses against men who are made like God. 10And so blessing and cursing come pouring out of the same mouth. Dear brothers, surely this is not right! 11Does a spring of water bubble out first with fresh water and then with bitter water? 12Can you pick olives from a fig tree, or figs from a grape vine? No, and you can't draw fresh water from a salty pool.

A THOUGHT: *What you say and what you don't say are both important. Proper speech is not only saying the right words at the right time, but controlling your desire to say what you shouldn't. Examples of wrongly using the tongue include gossiping, putting others down, bragging, manipulating, false teaching, exaggerating, complaining, flattering, and lying. Before you speak, ask, "Is it true, is it necessary, and is it kind?"*

Proverbs for Today/ 27:13

The world's poorest credit risk is the man who agrees to pay a stranger's debts.

NOVEMBER 12

Priscilla and Aquila Teach Apollos about Jesus/ Acts 18:24–28

As it happened, a Jew named Apollos, a wonderful Bible teacher and preacher, had just arrived in Ephesus from Alexandria in Egypt. 25,26While he was in Egypt, someone had told him about John the Baptist and what John had said about Jesus, but that is all he knew. He had never heard the rest of the story! So he was preaching boldly and enthusiastically in the synagogue, "The Messiah is coming! Get ready to receive him!" Priscilla and Aquila were there and heard him—and it was a powerful sermon. Afterwards they met with him and explained what had happened to Jesus since the time of John, and all that it meant!

27Apollos had been thinking about going to Greece, and the believers encouraged him in this. They wrote to their fellow-believers there, telling them to welcome him. And upon his arrival in Greece, he was greatly used of God to strengthen the church, 28for he powerfully refuted all the Jewish arguments in public debate, showing by the Scriptures that Jesus is indeed the Messiah.

A THOUGHT: *Apollos had heard only what John the Baptist had said about Jesus, so his message was not the complete story. John focused on repentance from sin, the first step to faith in Christ. Apollos did not know about Jesus' life, crucifixion, and resurrection, nor did he know about the coming of the Holy Spirit. Priscilla and Aquila explained this to him.*

Heavenly Wisdom and Earthly Ambition/ James 3:13–18

If you are wise, live a life of steady goodness, so that only good deeds will pour forth. And if you don't brag about them, then you will be truly wise! 14And by all means don't brag about being wise and good if you are bitter and jealous and selfish; that is the worst sort of lie. 15For jealousy and selfishness are not God's kind of wisdom. Such things are earthly, unspiritual, inspired by the devil. 16For wherever there is jealousy or selfish ambition, there will be disorder and every other kind of evil.

17But the wisdom that comes from heaven is first of all pure and full of quiet gentleness. Then it is peace-loving and courteous. It allows discussion and is willing to yield to others; it is full of mercy and good deeds. It is wholehearted and straightforward and sincere. 18And those who are peacemakers will plant seeds of peace and reap a harvest of goodness.

A THOUGHT: *Have you ever known anyone who claimed to be wise, but acted foolishly? True wisdom can be measured by the depth of one's character. As you can identify a tree by the type of fruit it produces, you can evaluate your wisdom by the way you act. Foolishness leads to disorder, but wisdom leads to peace and goodness.*

Proverbs for Today/ 27:14

If you shout a pleasant greeting to a friend too early in the morning, he will count it as a curse!

NOVEMBER 13

Paul Preaches to John the Baptist's Disciples/ Acts 19:1–10

While Apollos was in Corinth, Paul traveled through Turkey and arrived in Ephesus, where he found several disciples.

2"Did you receive the Holy Spirit when you believed?" he asked them.

"No," they replied, "we don't know what you mean. What is the Holy Spirit?"

3"Then what beliefs did you acknowledge at your baptism?" he asked.

And they replied, "What John the Baptist taught."

4Then Paul pointed out to them that John's baptism was to demonstrate a desire to turn from sin to God and that those receiving his baptism must then go on to believe in Jesus, the one John said would come later.

5As soon as they heard this, they were baptized in the name of the Lord Jesus. 6Then, when Paul laid his hands upon their heads, the Holy Spirit came on them, and they spoke in other languages and prophesied. 7The men involved were about twelve in number.

8Then Paul went to the synagogue and preached boldly each Sabbath day for three months, telling what he believed and why, and persuading many to believe in Jesus. 9But some rejected his message and publicly spoke against Christ, so he left, refusing to preach to them again. Pulling out the believers, he began a separate meeting at the lecture hall of Tyrannus and preached there daily. 10This went on for the next two years, so that everyone in the Turkish province of Ausia—both Jews and Greeks—heard the Lord's message.

A THOUGHT: *John's baptism was a sign of repentance from sin only, not a sign of new life in Christ. Like Apollos, these Ephesian believers needed further instruction on the message and ministry of Jesus Christ. By faith they believed in Jesus as the Messiah, but they did not understand the significance of Jesus' death and resurrection or the work of the Holy Spirit. Therefore they had not experienced the presence and power of the Holy Spirit. Paul was quick to point out that salvation requires repentance and faith. People need to be confronted with their sin and their need to repent, but this is only half the story. They must also accept the Good News of forgiveness and new life through Jesus.*

God Strengthens the Humble and Opposes the Proud/ James 4:1–6

What is causing the quarrels and fights among you? Isn't it because there is a whole army of evil desires within you? 2You want what you don't have, so you kill to get it. You long for what others have, and can't afford it, so you start a fight to take it away from them. And yet the reason you don't have what you want is that you don't ask God for it. ³And even when you do ask you don't get it because your whole aim is wrong—you want only what will give *you* pleasure.

⁴You are like an unfaithful wife who loves her husband's enemies. Don't you realize that making friends with God's enemies—the evil pleasures of this world—makes you an enemy of God? I say it again, that if your aim is to enjoy the evil pleasure of the unsaved world, you cannot also be a friend of God. ⁵Or what do you think the Scripture means when it says that the Holy Spirit, whom God has placed within us, watches over us with tender jealousy? ⁶But he gives us more and more strength to stand against all such evil longings. As the Scripture says, God gives strength to the humble, but sets himself against the proud and haughty.

A THOUGHT: *Quarrels among believers are always harmful. James tells us that these quarrels result from evil desires within us—we want more possessions, more money, higher status, more recognition. We fight in order to get what we want. Instead of aggressively grabbing what we want, we should ask God to help us get rid of our selfish desires and trust him to give us what we really need. The cure for evil desires is humility. Pride makes us self-centered and leads us to conclude that we deserve all we can see, touch, or imagine. It creates greedy appetites for far more than we need. The antidote to self-centered desires is to humble ourselves before God, realizing that we need nothing except his approval. When his Holy Spirit fills us, we realize that the things we have coveted are only cheap substitutes for what God has to offer.*

Proverbs for Today/ 27:15–16

A constant dripping on a rainy day and a cranky woman are much alike! You can no more stop her complaints than you can stop the wind or hold onto anything with oil-slick hands.

NOVEMBER 14

Paul Casts Out Demons in Ephesus/ Acts 19:11–20

And God gave Paul the power to do unusual miracles, 12so that even when his handkerchiefs or parts of his clothing were placed upon sick people, they were healed, and any demons within them came out.

13A team of itinerant Jews who were traveling from town to town casting out demons planned to experiment by using the name of the Lord Jesus. The incantation they decided on was this: "I adjure you by Jesus, whom Paul preaches, to come out!" 14Seven sons of Sceva, a Jewish priest, were doing this. 15But when they tried it on a man possessed by a demon, the demon replied, "I know Jesus and I know Paul, but who are you?" 16And he leaped on two of them and beat them up, so that they fled out of his house naked and badly injured.

17The story of what happened spread quickly all through Ephesus, to Jews and Greeks alike; and a solemn fear descended on the city, and the name of the Lord Jesus was greatly honored. 18,19Many of the believers who had been practicing black magic confessed their deeds and brought their incantation books and charms and burned them at a public bonfire. (Someone estimated the value of the books at $10,000.) 20This indicates how deeply the whole area was stirred by God's message.

A THOUGHT: *Ephesus was considered a center for black magic and other occult practices. The people sought spells to give them wealth, happiness, and success in marriage. Superstition and sorcery were commonplace. God clearly forbids such practices in Scripture. You cannot be a believer and hold onto the occult, black magic, or sorcery. Once you begin to dabble in these areas, it is extremely easy to become obsessed by them because Satan is very powerful. But God's power is even greater. If you are mixed up in the occult, learn a lesson from the Ephesians and get rid of anything that lures you into such practices.*

Draw Near to God/ James 4:7–10

So give yourselves humbly to God. Resist the devil and he will flee from you. 8And when you draw close to God, God will draw close to you. Wash your hands, you sinners, and let your hearts be filled with God alone to make them pure and true to him. 9Let there be tears for the wrong things you have done. Let there be sorrow and sincere grief. Let there be sadness instead of laughter, and gloom instead of joy. 10Then when you realize your worthlessness before the Lord, he will lift you up, encourage and help you.

A THOUGHT: *How can you draw close to God? James gives five suggestions: (1) "Give yourselves humbly to God." Realize that you need his forgiveness, and be willing to follow him. (2) "Resist the devil." Don't allow him to entice and tempt you. (3) "Wash your hands" (that is, lead a pure life) and "let your hearts be filled with God." Be cleansed from sin, replacing it with God's purity. (4) Let there be tears, sorrow, and sincere grief for your sins. Don't be afraid to express deep heartfelt sorrow for them. (5) "Realize your worthlessness." Humble yourself before God, and he will lift you up.*

Proverbs for Today/ 27:17

A friendly discussion is as stimulating as the sparks that fly when iron strikes iron.

NOVEMBER 15

A Riot Erupts at Ephesus/ Acts 19:21–41

Afterwards, Paul felt impelled by the Holy Spirit to go across to Greece before returning to Jerusalem. "And after that," he said, "I must go on to Rome!" 22He sent his two assistants, Timothy and Erastus, on ahead to Greece while he stayed awhile longer in Turkey.

23But about that time, a big blowup developed in Ephesus concerning the Christians. 24It began with Demetrius, a silversmith who employed many craftsmen to manufacture silver shrines of the Greek goddess Diana. 25He called a meeting of his men, together with others employed in related trades, and addressed them as follows:

"Gentlemen, this business is our income. 26As you know so well from what you've seen and heard, this man Paul has persuaded many, many people that handmade gods aren't gods at all. As a result, our sales volume is going down! And this trend is evident not only here in Ephesus, but throughout the entire province! 27Of course, I am not only talking about the business aspects of this situation and our loss of income, but also of the possibility that the temple of the great goddess Diana will lose its influence, and that Diana—this magnificent goddess worshiped not only throughout this part of Turkey but all around the world—will be forgotten!"

28At this their anger boiled and they began shouting, "Great is Diana of the Ephesians!"

29A crowd began to gather and soon the city was filled with confusion. Everyone rushed to the amphitheater, dragging along Gaius and Aristarchus, Paul's traveling companions, for trial. 30Paul wanted to go in, but the disciples wouldn't let him. 31Some of the Roman officers of the province, friends of Paul, also sent a message to him, begging him not to risk his life by entering.

32Inside, the people were all shouting, some one thing and some another—everything was in confusion. In fact, most of them didn't even know why they were there.

33Alexander was spotted among the crowd by some of the Jews and dragged forward. He motioned for silence and tried to speak. 34But when the crowd realized he was a Jew, they started shouting again and kept it up for two hours: "Great is Diana of the Ephesians! Great is Diana of the Ephesians!"

35At last the mayor was able to quiet them down enough to speak. "Men of Ephesus," he said, "everyone knows that Ephesus is the center of the religion of the great Diana, whose image fell down to us from heaven. 36Since this is an indisputable fact, you shouldn't be disturbed no matter what is said, and should do nothing rash. 37Yet you have brought these men here who have stolen nothing from her temple and have not defamed her. 38If Demetrius and the craftsmen have a case against them, the courts are currently in session and the judges can take the case at once. Let them go through legal channels. 39And if there are complaints about other matters, they can be settled at the regular City Council meetings; 40for we are in danger of being called to account by the Roman government for today's riot, since there is no cause for it. And if Rome demands an explanation, I won't know what to say."

⁴¹Then he dismissed them, and they dispersed.

A THOUGHT: *When Paul preached in Ephesus, Demetrius and his fellow shrinemakers did not quarrel with his doctrine. Their anger boiled because his preaching threatened their profits. They made statues of the goddess Diana and her temple, and if people started believing in God and discarding their idols, their livelihood would suffer. Demetrius' strategy for stirring up a riot was to appeal to the people's love of money and then hide their greed behind the mask of patriotism and religious loyalty. The rioters couldn't see the selfish motives for their rioting—instead they saw themselves as heroes for the sake of their land and beliefs.*

Don't Criticize One Another/ James 4:11–12

Don't criticize and speak evil about each other, dear brothers. If you do, you will be fighting against God's law of loving one another, declaring it is wrong. But your job is not to decide whether this law is right or wrong, but to obey it. ¹²Only he who made the law can rightly judge among us. He alone decides to save us or destroy. So what right do you have to judge or criticize others?

A THOUGHT: *Jesus summarized the Old Testament Law as love to God and neighbor, and Paul said love demonstrated towards a neighbor fully satisfies the law. When we fail to love, we are actually breaking God's law. Examine your attitude and actions toward others. Do you build people up or tear them down? When you're ready to criticize someone, remember God's law of love and say something good about him or her instead. If you make this a habit, your tendency to find fault with others will diminish and your ability to obey God's Law will increase.*

Proverbs for Today/ 27:18–20

A workman may eat from the orchard he tends; anyone should be rewarded who protects another's interests. □ A mirror reflects a man's face, but what he is really like is shown by the kind of friends he chooses. □ Ambition and death are alike in this: neither is ever satisfied.

NOVEMBER 16

Paul Raises Eutychus from the Dead/ Acts 20:1–12

When it was all over, Paul sent for the disciples, preached a farewell message to them, said good-bye and left for Greece, 2preaching to the believers along the way, in all the cities he passed through. 3He was in Greece three months and was preparing to sail for Syria when he discovered a plot by the Jews against his life, so he decided to go north to Macedonia first.

4Several men were traveling with him, going as far as Turkey; they were Sopater of Beroea, the son of Pyrrhus; Aristarchus and Secundus, from Thessalonica; Gaius, from Derbe; and Timothy; and Tychicus and Trophimus, who were returning to their homes in Turkey, 5and had gone on ahead and were waiting for us at Troas. 6As soon as the Passover ceremonies ended, we boarded ship at Philippi in northern Greece and five days later arrived in Troas, Turkey, where we stayed a week.

7On Sunday, we gathered for a communion service, with Paul preaching. And since he was leaving the next day, he talked until midnight! 8 The upstairs room where we met was lighted with many flickering lamps; 9and as Paul spoke on and on, a young man named Eutychus, sitting on the window sill, went fast asleep and fell three stories to his death below. 10,11,12Paul went down and took him into his arms. "Don't worry," he said, "he's all right!" And he was! What a wave of awesome joy swept through the crowd! They all went back upstairs and ate the Lord's Supper together; then Paul preached another long sermon—so it was dawn when he finally left them!

A Thought: *The church at Troas experienced the power of God in Paul's preaching and also in Eutychus being raised from the dead. God displayed his great power as the Christians were together to share communion and hear the preaching of Paul. Although, God may not raise the dead in our midst, we may be confident that the Holy Spirit will be working among us where we are open to his ministry.*

Our Lives Are Like the Morning Fog/ James 4:13–17

Look here, you people who say, "Today or tomorrow we are going to such and such a town, stay there a year, and open up a profitable business." 14How do you know what is going to happen tomorrow? For the length of your lives is as uncertain as the morning fog—now you see it; soon it is gone. 15What you ought to say is, "If the Lord wants us to, we shall live and do this or that." 16Otherwise you will be bragging about your own plans, and such self-confidence never pleases God.

17Remember, too, that knowing what is right to do and then not doing it is sin.

A THOUGHT: *It is good to have goals, but goals can disappoint us if we leave God out of them. There is no point in making plans as though God does not exist, because the future is in his hands. What would you like to be doing ten years from now? One year from now? Tomorrow? How will you react if God steps in and rearranges your plans? Plan ahead, but hang on to your plans lightly. If you put God's desires at the center of your planning, you will not be disappointed.*

Proverbs for Today/ 27:21–22

The purity of silver and gold can be tested in a crucible, but a man is tested by his reaction to men's praise.   □ You can't separate a rebel from his foolishness though you crush him to powder.

NOVEMBER 17

Paul's Farewell Sermon to the Ephesian Elders/ Acts 20:13–38

Paul was going by land to Assos, and we went on ahead by ship. 14He joined us there and we sailed together to Mitylene; 15the next day we passed Chios; the next, we touched at Samos; and a day later we arrived at Miletus.

16Paul had decided against stopping at Ephesus this time, as he was hurrying to get to Jerusalem, if possible, for the celebration of Pentecost.

17But when we landed at Miletus, he sent a message to the elders of the church at Ephesus asking them to come down to the boat to meet him.

18When they arrived he told them, "You men know that from the day I set foot in Turkey until now 19I have done the Lord's work humbly—yes, and with tears—and have faced grave danger from the plots of the Jews against my life. 20Yet I never shrank from telling you the truth, either publicly or in your homes. 21I have had one message for Jews and Gentiles alike—the necessity of turning from sin to God through faith in our Lord Jesus Christ.

22"And now I am going to Jerusalem, drawn there irresistibly by the Holy Spirit, not knowing what awaits me, 23except that the Holy Spirit has told me in city after city that jail and suffering lie ahead. 24But life is worth nothing unless I use it for doing the work assigned me by the Lord Jesus—the work of telling others the Good News about God's mighty kindness and love.

25"And now I know that none of you among whom I went about teaching the Kingdom will ever see me again. 26Let me say plainly that no man's blood can be laid at my door, 27for I didn't shrink from declaring all God's message to you.

28"And now beware! Be sure that you feed and shepherd God's flock—his church, purchased with his blood—for the Holy Spirit is holding you responsible as overseers. 29I know full well that after I leave you, false teachers, like vicious wolves, will appear among you, not sparing the flock. 30Some of you yourselves will distort the truth in order to draw a following. 31Watch out! Remember the three years I was with you—my constant watchcare over you night and day and my many tears for you.

32"And now I entrust you to God and his care and to his wonderful words which are able to build your faith and give you all the inheritance of those who are set apart for himself.

33"I have never been hungry for money or fine clothing—34you know that these hands of mine worked to pay my own way and even to supply the needs of those who were with me. 35And I was a constant example to you in helping the poor; for I remembered the words of the Lord Jesus, 'It is more blessed to give than to receive.'"

36When he had finished speaking, he knelt and prayed with them, 37and they wept aloud as they embraced him in farewell, 38sorrowing most of all because he said that he would never see them again. Then they accompanied him down to the ship.

A THOUGHT: *The Ephesian elders were told to feed the believers under their care by teaching them God's Word, and to shepherd them by being examples of God's love. All leaders of the church carry these two major responsibilities—to nourish others with God's truth and to exemplify God's truth at work in their lives. God's truth must be talked out and lived out.*

Warnings to the Rich/ James 5:1–6

Look here, you rich men, now is the time to cry and groan with anguished grief because of all the terrible troubles ahead of you. 2Your wealth is even now rotting away, and your fine clothes are becoming mere moth-eaten rags. 3The value of your gold and silver is dropping fast, yet it will stand as evidence against you, and eat your flesh like fire. That is what you have stored up for yourselves, to receive on that coming day of judgment. 4For listen! Hear the cries of the field workers whom you have cheated of their pay. Their cries have reached the ears of the Lord of Hosts.

5You have spent your years here on earth having fun, satisfying your every whim, and now your fat hearts are ready for the slaughter. 6You have condemned and killed good men who had no power to defend themselves against you.

A THOUGHT: *James proclaims the worthlessness of riches, not the worthlessness of the rich. Today's money will be worthless when Christ returns, so we should spend our time accumulating treasures that will be worthwhile in God's eternal Kingdom. Money itself is not the problem; Christian leaders need money to live and support their families; missionaries need money to help them spread the gospel; churches need money to do their work effectively. It is the love of money that leads to evil. This is a warning to all Christians who are tempted to adopt worldly standards rather than God's standards.*

Proverbs for Today/ 27:23–27

Riches can disappear fast. And the king's crown doesn't stay in his family forever—so watch your business interests closely. Know the state of your flocks and your herds; then there will be lamb's wool enough for clothing, and goat's milk enough for food for all your household after the hay is harvested, and the new crop appears, and the mountain grasses are gathered in.

NOVEMBER 18

Paul Arrives in Jerusalem/ Acts 21:1–17

After parting from the Ephesian elders, we [Luke, Paul, and his companions] sailed straight to Cos. The next day we reached Rhodes and then went to Patara. 2There we boarded a ship sailing for the Syrian province of Phoenicia. 3We sighted the island of Cyprus, passed it on our left and landed at the harbor of Tyre, in Syria, where the ship unloaded. 4We went ashore, found the local believers and stayed with them a week. These disciples warned Paul—the Holy Spirit prophesying through them—not to go on to Jerusalem. 5At the end of the week when we returned to the ship, the entire congregation including wives and children walked down to the beach with us where we prayed and said our farewells. 6Then we went aboard and they returned home.

7The next stop after leaving Tyre was Ptolemais where we greeted the believers, but stayed only one day. 8Then we went on to Caesarea and stayed at the home of Philip the Evangelist, one of the first seven deacons. 9He had four unmarried daughters who had the gift of prophecy.

10During our stay of several days, a man named Agabus, who also had the gift of prophecy, arrived from Judea 11and visited us. He took Paul's belt, bound his own feet and hands with it and said, "The Holy Spirit declares, 'So shall the owner of this belt be bound by the Jews in Jerusalem and turned over to the Romans.'" 12Hearing this, all of us—the local believers and his traveling companions—begged Paul not to go on to Jerusalem.

13But he said, "Why all this weeping? You are breaking my heart! For I am ready not only to be jailed at Jerusalem, but also to die for the sake of the Lord Jesus." 14When it was clear that he wouldn't be dissuaded, we gave up and said, "The will of the Lord be done."

15So shortly afterwards, we packed our things and left for Jerusalem. 16Some disciples from Caesarea accompanied us, and on arrival we were guests at the home of Mnason, originally from Cyprus, one of the early believers; 17and all the believers at Jerusalem welcomed us cordially.

A Thought: *Paul knew he would be imprisoned in Jerusalem. His friends pleaded with him to not go there, but he knew he had to because God wanted him to. No one wants to face hardship or suffering, but a faithful disciple wants above all else to please God. Our desire to please God should overshadow our desire to avoid hardship and suffering. When we really want to do God's will, we must accept all that comes with it—even the pain. Then we can say with Paul, "The will of the Lord be done."*

Job, Our Example in Patient Suffering/ James 5:7–12

Now as for you, dear brothers who are waiting for the Lord's return, be patient, like a farmer who waits until the autumn for his precious harvest to ripen. 8Yes, be patient. And take courage, for the coming of the Lord is near.

9Don't grumble about each other, brothers. Are you yourselves above criticism? For see! The great Judge is coming. He is almost here. [Let him do whatever criticizing must be done.]

10For examples of patience in suffering, look at the Lord's prophets. 11We know how happy they are now because they stayed true to him then, even though they suffered greatly for it. Job is an example of a man who continued to trust the Lord in sorrow; from his experiences we can see how the Lord's plan finally ended in good, for he is full of tenderness and mercy.

12But most of all, dear brothers, do not swear either by heaven or earth or anything else; just say a simple yes or no, so that you will not sin and be condemned for it.

A Thought: *The farmer must wait patiently for his crops to grow, he cannot hurry the process. But he does not take the summer off and hope that all goes well in the fields. There is much work to do to ensure a good harvest. In the same way, we must wait patiently for Christ's return. We cannot make Christ return any sooner, but while we wait there is much work we can do to advance God's Kingdom. Both the farmer and the Christian must live by faith, looking toward the future reward for their labors. Don't live as if Christ will never come. Work faithfully to build his Kingdom, for the King will come when the time is ripe.*

Proverbs for Today/ 28:1

The wicked flee when no one is chasing them! But the godly are bold as lions!

NOVEMBER 19

A Great Riot in the Jerusalem Temple/
Acts 21:18–36

The second day Paul took us with him to meet with James and the elders of the Jerusalem church. 19After greetings were exchanged, Paul recounted the many things God had accomplished among the Gentiles through his work.

20They praised God but then said, "You know, dear brother, how many thousands of Jews have also believed, and they are all very insistent that Jewish believers must continue to follow the Jewish traditions and customs. 21Our Jewish Christians here at Jerusalem have been told that you are against the laws of Moses, against our Jewish customs, and that you forbid the circumcision of their children. 22Now what can be done? For they will certainly hear that you have come.

23"We suggest this: We have four men here who are preparing to shave their heads and take some vows. 24Go with them to the Temple and have your head shaved too—and pay for theirs to be shaved.

"Then everyone will know that you approve of this custom for the Hebrew Christians and that you yourself obey the Jewish laws and are in line with our thinking in these matters.

25"As for the Gentile Christians, we aren't asking them to follow these Jewish customs at all—except for the ones we wrote to them about: not to eat food offered to idols, not to eat unbled meat from strangled animals, and not to commit fornication."

26,27So Paul agreed to their request and the next day went with the men to the Temple for the ceremony, thus publicizing his vow to offer a sacrifice seven days later with the others.

The seven days were almost ended when some Jews from Turkey saw him in the Temple and roused a mob against him. They grabbed him, 28yelling, "Men of Israel! Help! Help! This is the man who preaches against our people and tells everybody to disobey the Jewish laws. He even talks against the Temple and defiles it by bringing

Gentiles in!" 29(For down in the city earlier that day, they had seen him with Trophimus, a Gentile from Ephesus in Turkey, and assumed that Paul had taken him into the Temple.)

30The whole population of the city was electrified by these accusations and a great riot followed. Paul was dragged out of the Temple, and immediately the gates were closed behind him. 31As they were killing him, word reached the commander of the Roman garrison that all Jerusalem was in an uproar. 32He quickly ordered out his soldiers and officers and ran down among the crowd. When the mob saw the troops coming, they quit beating Paul. 33The commander arrested him and ordered him bound with double chains. Then he asked the crowd who he was and what he had done. 34Some shouted one thing and some another. When he couldn't find out anything in all the uproar and confusion, he ordered Paul to be taken to the armory. 35As they reached the stairs, the mob grew so violent that the soldiers lifted Paul to their shoulders to protect him, 36and the crowd surged behind shouting, "Away with him, away with him!"

A THOUGHT: *There are two ways to think of the Old Testament Law. Paul rejects one and accepts the other. (1) Paul rejects the idea that the Old Testament Law brings salvation to those who keep it. Our salvation is freely given by God's gracious act. We receive it by faith. The Law is of no value for salvation except to show us our sin. (2) Paul accepts the view that the Old Testament laws prepared us for and taught us about the coming of Jesus Christ. Christ fulfilled the Law and released us from its burden of guilt. But the Law still teaches us many valuable principles and gives us guidelines for living. Paul was not observing the Law for salvation. He was keeping the Law because it served as an excellent guideline for righteous living. By keeping the Law, Paul also avoided offending the Jews he wished to reach with the gospel.*

Prayer Offered in Earnest Faith/ James 5:13–20

Is anyone among you suffering? He should keep on praying about it. And those who have reason to be thankful should continually be singing praises to the Lord.

14Is anyone sick? He should call for the elders of the church and they should pray over him and pour a little oil upon him, calling on the Lord to heal him. 15And their prayer, if offered in faith, will heal him, for the Lord will make him well; and if his sickness was caused by some sin, the Lord will forgive him.

16Admit your faults to one another and pray for each other so that you may be healed. The earnest prayer of a righteous man has great power and wonderful results. 17Elijah was as completely human as we are, and yet when he prayed earnestly that no rain would fall, none fell for the next three and one half years! 18Then he prayed again, this time that it *would* rain, and down it poured and the grass turned green and the gardens began to grow again.

19Dear brothers, if anyone has slipped away from God and no longer trusts the Lord and someone helps him understand the Truth again, 20that person who brings him back to God will have saved a wandering soul from death, bringing about the forgiveness of his many sins.

Sincerely,
James

A THOUGHT: *The Christian's most powerful resource is communion with God through prayer. The results are often greater than we thought were possible. Some people see prayer as a last resort to be tried when all else fails. This is backwards. Prayer should come first. Since God's power is infinitely greater than our own, it only makes sense to rely on it—especially because he encourages us to do so.*

Proverbs for Today/ 28:2
When there is moral rot within a nation, its government topples easily; but with honest, sensible leaders there is stability.

NOVEMBER 20

Paul Retells His Conversion/ Acts 21:37—22:16
As Paul was about to be taken inside, he said to the commander, "May I have a word with you?"

"Do you know Greek?" the commander asked, surprised. "Aren't you that Egyptian who led a rebellion a few years ago and took 4,000 members of the Assassins with him into the desert?"

39"No," Paul replied, "I am a Jew from Tarsus in Cilicia which is no small town. I request permission to talk to these people."

40The commander agreed, so Paul stood on the stairs and motioned to the people to be quiet; soon a deep silence enveloped the crowd, and he addressed them in Hebrew as follows:

22:1"Brothers and fathers, listen to me as I offer my defense." 2(When they heard him speaking in Hebrew, the silence was even greater.) 3"I am a Jew," he said, "born in Tarsus, a city in Cilicia, but educated here in Jerusalem under Gamaliel, at whose feet I learned to follow our Jewish laws and customs very carefully. I became very anxious to honor God in everything I did, just as you have tried to do today. 4And I persecuted the Christians, hounding them to death, binding and delivering both men and women to prison. 5The High Priest or any member of the Council can testify that this is so. For I asked them for letters to the Jewish leaders in Damascus, with instructions to let me bring any Christians I found to Jerusalem in chains to be punished.

6"As I was on the road, nearing Damascus, suddenly about noon a very bright light from heaven shone around me. 7And I fell to the ground and heard a voice saying to me, 'Saul, Saul, why are you persecuting me?'

8" 'Who is it speaking to me, sir?' I asked. And he replied, 'I am Jesus of Nazareth, the one you are persecuting.' 9The men with me saw the light but didn't understand what was said.

10"And I said, 'What shall I do, Lord?'

"And the Lord told me, 'Get up and go into Damascus, and there you will be told what awaits you in the years ahead.'

11"I was blinded by the intense light, and had to be led into Damascus by my companions. 12There a man named Ananias, as godly a man as you could find for obeying the law, and well thought of by all the Jews of Damascus, 13came to me, and standing beside me said, 'Brother Saul, receive your sight!' And that very hour I could see him!

14"Then he told me, 'The God of our fathers has chosen you to know his will and to see the Messiah and hear him speak. 15You are to take his message everywhere, telling what you have seen and heard. 16And now, why delay? Go and be baptized, and be cleansed from your sins, calling on the name of the Lord.'

A THOUGHT: *When Paul said "just as you have tried to do today," he acknowledged their sincere motives in trying to kill him and recognized that he would have done the same to Christian leaders some years earlier. Paul always tried to establish a common point of contact with his audience before launching into a full-scale defense of Christianity. When you witness for Christ, first identify yourself with your audience. They are much more likely to listen to you if they feel a common bond with you.*

Trials Refine Our Faith/ 1 Peter 1:1–7

From: Peter, Jesus Christ's missionary.

To: The Jewish Christians driven out of Jerusalem and scattered throughout Pontus, Galatia, Cappadocia, Asia minor, and Bithynia.

2Dear friends, God the Father chose you long ago and knew you would become his children. And the Holy Spirit has been at work in your hearts, cleansing you with the blood of Jesus Christ and making you to please him. May God bless you richly and grant you increasing freedom from all anxiety and fear.

3All honor to God, the God and Father of our Lord Jesus Christ; for it is his boundless mercy that has given us the privilege of being born again, so that we are now members of God's own family. Now we live in the hope of eternal life because Christ rose again from the dead. 4And God has reserved for his children the priceless gift of eternal life; it is kept in heaven for you, pure and undefiled, beyond the reach of change and decay. 5And God, in his mighty power, will make sure that you get there safely to receive it, because you are trusting him. It will be yours in that coming last day for all to see. 6So be truly glad! There is wonderful joy ahead, even though the going is rough for a while down here.

7These trials are only to test your faith, to see whether or not it is strong and pure. It is being tested as fire tests gold and purifies it—and your faith is far more precious to God than mere gold; so if your faith remains strong after being tried in the test tube of fiery trials, it will bring you much praise and glory and honor on the day of his return.

A Thought: *All believers face such trials when they let their light shine into the darkness. We must accept trials as part of the refining process that burns away impurities, preparing us to meet Christ. Trials teach us patience and help us grow to be the kind of people God wants us to be. As gold is heated, impurities float to the top and can be skimmed off. Steel is tempered or strengthened by heating it in fire. Likewise, our trials, struggles, and the persecutions we face strengthen our faith and make us more like Christ—useful to God for service in his Kingdom.*

Proverbs for Today/ 28:3–5

When a poor man oppresses those even poorer, he is like an unexpected flood sweeping away their last hope. □ To complain about the law is to praise wickedness. To obey the law is to fight evil. □ Evil men don't understand the importance of justice, but those who follow the Lord are much concerned about it.

NOVEMBER 21

Paul Is Sentenced to Be Whipped/ Acts 22:17–29

[Then Paul said] "One day after my return to Jerusalem, while I was praying in the Temple, I fell into a trance and saw a vision of God saying to me, 'Hurry! Leave Jerusalem, for the people here won't believe you when you give them my message.'

19" 'But Lord,' I argued, 'they certainly know that I imprisoned and beat those in every synagogue who believed on you. 20And when your witness Stephen was killed, I was standing there agreeing—keeping the coats they laid aside as they stoned him.'

21"But God said to me, 'Leave Jerusalem, for I will send you far away to the *Gentiles!*' "

22The crowd listened until Paul came to that word, then with one voice they shouted, "Away with such a fellow! Kill him! He isn't fit to live!" 23They yelled and threw their coats in the air and tossed up handfuls of dust.

24So the commander brought him inside and ordered him lashed with whips to make him confess his crime.

He wanted to find out why the crowd had become so furious!

25As they tied Paul down to lash him, Paul said to an officer standing there, "Is it legal for you to whip a Roman citizen who hasn't even been tried?"

26The officer went to the commander and asked, "What are you doing? This man is a Roman citizen!"

27So the commander went over and asked Paul, "Tell me, are you a Roman citizen?"

"Yes, I certainly am."

28"I am too," the commander muttered, "and it cost me plenty!"

"But I am a citizen by birth!"

29The soldiers standing ready to lash him, quickly disappeared when they heard Paul was a Roman citizen, and the commander was frightened because he had ordered him bound and whipped.

A THOUGHT: *God used Paul's persecution as an opportunity for him to witness. Now even his enemies were creating a platform for him to address the entire Jewish Council. If we are sensitive to the Holy Spirit's leading, we will notice increased opportunities to share our faith, even in the heat of opposition.*

The Hope of Eternal Life/ 1 Peter 1:8–13

You love him even though you have never seen him; though not seeing him, you trust him; and even now you are happy with the inexpressible joy that comes from heaven itself. 9And your further reward for trusting him will be the salvation of your souls.

10This salvation was something the prophets did not fully understand. Though they wrote about it, they had many questions as to what it all could mean. 11They wondered what the Spirit of Christ within them was talking about, for he told them to write down the events which, since then, have happened to Christ: his suffering, and his great glory afterwards. And they wondered when and to whom all this would happen.

12They were finally told that these things would not occur during their lifetime, but long years later, during yours. And now at last this Good News has been plainly announced to all of us. It was preached to us in the power of the same heaven-sent Holy Spirit who spoke to them;

and it is all so strange and wonderful that even the angels in heaven would give a great deal to know more about it.

13So now you can look forward soberly and intelligently to more of God's kindness to you when Jesus Christ returns.

A THOUGHT: *Although the plan of salvation was a mystery to the Old Testament prophets, they still suffered persecution and some died for God. Some Jewish Christians reading Peter's letter, by contrast, had seen Jesus for themselves and knew why he came. They based their assurance on Jesus' death and resurrection. With their firsthand knowledge and personal experience of Jesus, their faith should have been even stronger than that of the Old Testament prophets. We stand at a point in history where we have the testimony of the Old Testament and the New Testament. The nature of God's salvation in Christ has been clearly revealed in the pages of the New Testament. God kept his promise in the past—Jesus Christ, God's Messiah died to bring salvation to his people—and Christ will keep his promise to come again.*

Proverbs for Today/ 28:6–7

Better to be poor and honest than rich and a cheater. ▢ Young men who are wise obey the law; a son who is a member of a lawless gang is a shame to his father.

NOVEMBER 22

Paul Appears before the Sanhedrin/ Acts 22:30—23:11

The next day the commander freed Paul from his chains and ordered the chief priests into session with the Jewish Council. He had Paul brought in before them to try to find out what the trouble was all about.

23:1Gazing intently at the Council, Paul began:

"Brothers, I have always lived before God in all good conscience!"

2Instantly Ananias the High Priest commanded those close to Paul to slap him on the mouth.

3Paul said to him, "God shall slap you, you whitewashed pigpen. What kind of judge are you to break the law yourself by ordering me struck like that?"

4Those standing near Paul said to him, "Is that the way to talk to God's High Priest?"

5"I didn't realize he was the High Priest, brothers," Paul replied, "for the Scriptures say, 'Never speak evil of any of your rulers.'"

6Then Paul thought of something! Part of the Council were Sadducees, and part were Pharisees! So he shouted, "Brothers, I am a Pharisee, as were all my ancestors! And I am being tried here today because I believe in the resurrection of the dead!"

7This divided the Council right down the middle—the Pharisees against the Sadducees — 8for the Sadducees say there is no resurrection or angels or even eternal spirit within us, but the Pharisees believe in all of these.

9So a great clamor arose. Some of the Jewish leaders jumped up to argue that Paul was all right. "We see nothing wrong with him," they shouted. "Perhaps a spirit or angel spoke to him [there on the Damascus road]."

10The shouting grew louder and louder, and the men were tugging at Paul from both sides, pulling him this way and that. Finally the commander, fearing they would tear him apart, ordered his soldiers to take him away from them by force and bring him back to the armory.

11That night the Lord stood beside Paul and said, "Don't worry, Paul; just as you have told the people about me here in Jerusalem, so you must also in Rome."

A THOUGHT: *The Sadducees and Pharisees were both Jewish religious sects, but with strikingly different beliefs. While the Pharisees believed in a bodily resurrection, the Sadducees did not because they adhered only to the Old Testament books of Genesis through Deuteronomy, which contain no explicit teaching on resurrection. Paul's words moved the debate away from himself and toward the ongoing raging controversy between the Sadducees and Pharisees over the resurrection. The Jewish Council was split. God will help us when we are under fire for our faith. Like Paul, we should always be ready to present our testimony. The Holy Spirit will give us power to speak boldly.*

Be Holy, for God Is Holy/ 1 Peter 1:14–25

Obey God because you are his children; don't slip back into your old ways—doing evil because you knew no better. 15But be holy now in everything you do, just as the Lord is holy, who invited you to be his child. 16He himself has said, "You must be holy, for I am holy."

17And remember that your heavenly Father to whom you pray has no favorites when he judges. He will judge you with perfect justice for everything you do; so act in reverent fear of him from now on until you get to heaven. 18 God paid a ransom to save you from the impossible road to heaven which your fathers tried to take, and the ransom he paid was not mere gold or silver, as you very well know. 19But he paid for you with the precious lifeblood of Christ, the sinless, spotless Lamb of God. 20God chose him for this purpose long before the world began, but only recently was he brought into public view, in these last days, as a blessing to you.

21Because of this, your trust can be in God who raised Christ from the dead and gave him great glory. Now your faith and hope can rest in him alone. 22Now you can have real love for everyone because your souls have been cleansed from selfishness and hatred when you trusted Christ to save you; so see to it that you really do love each other warmly, with all your hearts.

23For you have a new life. It was not passed on to you from your parents, for the life they gave you will fade away. This new one will last forever, for it comes from Christ, God's ever-living Message to men. 24Yes, our natural lives will fade as grass does when it becomes all brown and dry. All our greatness is like a flower that droops and falls; 25but the Word of the Lord will last forever. And his message is the Good News that was preached to you.

A THOUGHT: *After people commit their lives to Christ, they still feel a pull back into their old ways. Peter tells us to be like our heavenly Father—holy in everything we do. Holiness means being totally devoted or dedicated to God, set aside for his special use, and set apart from sin and its influence. We're to be set apart and different, not blending in with the crowd, yet not being different just for the sake of being different. What makes us different are God's qualities in our lives. Our focus and priorities must be his. All this is in direct contrast to our old ways. We cannot become holy on our own, but God gives us his Holy Spirit to help us obey and to give us power to overcome sin. Don't use the excuse that you can't help slipping into sin. Call on God's power to free you from sin's grip.*

Proverbs for Today/ 28:8–10

Income from exploiting the poor will end up in the hands
of someone who pities them. □ God doesn't listen to
the prayers of those who flout the law. □ A curse on
those who lead astray the godly. But men who encourage
the upright to do good shall be given a worthwhile reward.

NOVEMBER 23

A Plot against Paul's Life/ Acts 23:12–35

The next morning some forty or more of the Jews got
together and bound themselves by a curse neither to eat
nor drink until they had killed Paul! 14Then they went to
the chief priests and elders and told them what they had
done. 15"Ask the commander to bring Paul back to the
Council again," they requested. "Pretend you want to
ask a few more questions. We will kill him on the way."

16But Paul's nephew got wind of their plan and came
to the armory and told Paul.

17Paul called one of the officers and said, "Take this
boy to the commander. He has something important to
tell him."

18So the officer did, explaining, "Paul, the prisoner,
called me over and asked me to bring this young man to
you to tell you something."

19The commander took the boy by the hand, and leading
him aside asked, "What is it you want to tell me, lad?"

20"Tomorrow," he told him, "the Jews are going to
ask you to bring Paul before the Council again, pretending
they want to get some more information. 21But don't do
it! There are more than forty men hiding along the road
ready to jump him and kill him. They have bound themselves
under a curse to neither eat nor drink till he is dead.
They are out there now, expecting you to agree to their
request."

22"Don't let a soul know you told me this," the commander
warned the boy as he left. 23,24Then the commander called

two of his officers and ordered, "Get 200 soldiers ready to leave for Caesarea at nine o'clock tonight! Take 200 spearmen and 70 mounted cavalry. Give Paul a horse to ride and get him safely to Governor Felix."

25Then he wrote this letter to the governor:

26"*From:* Claudius Lysias

"*To:* His Excellency, Governor Felix.

"Greetings!

27"This man was seized by the Jews and they were killing him when I sent the soldiers to rescue him, for I learned that he was a Roman citizen. 28Then I took him to their Council to try to find out what he had done. 29I soon discovered it was something about their Jewish beliefs, certainly nothing worthy of imprisonment or death. 30But when I was informed of a plot to kill him, I decided to send him on to you and will tell his accusers to bring their charges before you."

31So that night, as ordered, the soldiers took Paul to Antipatris. 32They returned to the armory the next morning, leaving him with the cavalry to take him on to Caesarea.

33When they arrived in Caesarea, they presented Paul and the letter to the governor. 34He read it and then asked Paul where he was from.

"Cilicia," Paul answered.

35"I will hear your case fully when your accusers arrive," the governor told him, and ordered him kept in the prison at King Herod's palace.

A THOUGHT: *The Roman commander ordered Paul sent to Caesarea. Jerusalem was the seat of Jewish government, but Caesarea was the Roman headquarters for the area. God works in amazing and amusing ways. There were many possible options which God could have chosen to get Paul to Caesarea, but he chose to use the Roman army to deliver Paul from his enemies. God's ways are not our ways—ours are limited, his are not. Don't limit God by asking him to respond your way. When God intervenes, anything can happen, with much greater effectiveness than any of us could anticipate or imagine.*

We Are Living Building Stones/ 1 Peter 2:1–10

So get rid of your feelings of hatred. Don't just pretend to be good! Be done with dishonesty and jealousy and talking about others behind their backs. 2,3Now that you realize how kind the Lord has been to you, put away all evil, deception, envy, and fraud. Long to grow up into the fullness of your salvation; cry for this as a baby cries for his milk.

4Come to Christ, who is the living Foundation of Rock upon which God builds; though men have spurned him, he is very precious to God who has chosen him above all others.

5And now you have become living building-stones for God's use in building his house. What's more, you are his holy priests; so come to him—[you who are acceptable to him because of Jesus Christ]—and offer to God those things that please him. 6As the Scriptures express it, "See, I am sending Christ to be the carefully chosen, precious Cornerstone of my church, and I will never disappoint those who trust in him."

7Yes, he is very precious to you who believe; and to those who reject him, well—"The same Stone that was rejected by the builders has become the Cornerstone, the most honored and important part of the building." 8And the Scriptures also say, "He is the Stone that some will stumble over, and the Rock that will make them fall." They will stumble because they will not listen to God's Word, nor obey it, and so this punishment must follow—that they will fall.

9But you are not like that, for you have been chosen by God himself—you are priests of the King, you are holy and pure, you are God's very own—all this so that you may show to others how God called you out of the darkness into his wonderful light. 10Once you were less than nothing; now you are God's own. Once you knew very little of God's kindness; now your very lives have been changed by it.

A Thought: *Peter portrays the church as a living Temple: Christ is the foundation, and each believer is a stone. Paul portrays it as a body: Christ is the head, and each believer is a member. Both pictures emphasize community. One stone is not a temple or even a wall; one bodily part is useless without the others. In our individualistic society, it is easy to imagine that we can "go it alone." But when God calls you to a task, remember that he is also calling others to work with you. Together your individual efforts can be multiplied. Look for those people and join with them to build a beautiful house for God.*

Proverbs for Today/ 28:11

Rich men are conceited, but their real poverty is evident to the poor.

NOVEMBER 24

Accusations Against Paul/ Acts 24:1–9

Five days later Ananias the High Priest arrived with some of the Jewish leaders and the lawyer Tertullus, to make their accusations against Paul. 2When Tertullus was called forward, he laid charges against Paul in the following address to the governor:

"Your Excellency, you have given quietness and peace to us Jews and have greatly reduced the discrimination against us. 3And for this we are very, very grateful to you. 4But lest I bore you, kindly give me your attention for only a moment as I briefly outline our case against this man. 5For we have found him to be a troublemaker, a man who is constantly inciting the Jews throughout the entire world to riots and rebellions against the Roman government. He is a ringleader of the sect known as the Nazarenes. 6Moreover, he was trying to defile the Temple when we arrested him.

"We would have given him what he justly deserves, 7but Lysias, the commander of the garrison, came and took him violently away from us, 8demanding that he be tried by Roman law. You can find out the truth of our accusations by examining him yourself."

9Then all the other Jews chimed in, declaring that everything Tertullus said was true.

A THOUGHT: *The accusers arrived—Ananias, the High Priest; Tertullus, the lawyer; and several Jewish leaders. They traveled 60 miles to Caesarea, the Roman center of government, to give their false accusations against Paul. Tertullus was a special orator called to present the religious leaders' case before the Roman governor. He made three accusations against Paul: (1) he was a renegade, inciting the Jews around the world; (2) he was the ringleader of an unrecognized religious sect, which was against Roman law; and (3) he had profaned the Temple. The religious leaders hoped that these accusations would persuade Felix to execute Paul to keep the peace in Palestine.*

Live According to God's Will/ 1 Peter 2:11–16

Dear brothers, you are only visitors here. Since your real home is in heaven I beg you to keep away from the evil pleasures of this world; they are not for you, for they fight against your very souls.

12Be careful how you behave among your unsaved neighbors; for then, even if they are suspicious of you and talk against you, they will end up praising God for your good works when Christ returns.

13For the Lord's sake, obey every law of your government: those of the king as head of the state, 14and those of the king's officers, for he has sent them to punish all who do wrong, and to honor those who do right.

15It is God's will that your good lives should silence those who foolishly condemn the Gospel without knowing what it can do for them, having never experienced its power. 16You are free from the law, but that doesn't mean you are free to do wrong. Live as those who are free to do only God's will at all times.

A THOUGHT: *When Peter told his readers to respect the civil government, he was probably speaking of the Roman Empire under Nero, a notoriously cruel tyrant. Obviously he was not telling believers to compromise their consciences; as Peter had told the High Priest years before, "We must obey God rather than men" (Acts 5:29). But in most aspects of their daily lives, it was possible and desirable for Christians to live according to the law of their land. Today, some Christians live in freedom while others live under repressive governments. All are commanded to cooperate with the rulers as far as conscience will allow. We are to do this "for the Lord's sake"—so that his Good News and his people will be respected. If we are to be persecuted, it should be for standing for God, and not for wantonly or selfishly breaking civil laws.*

Proverbs for Today/ 28:12–13

When the godly are successful, everyone is glad. When the wicked succeed, everyone is sad. □ A man who refuses to admit his mistakes can never be successful. But if he confesses and forsakes them, he gets another chance.

Paul's Defense before Governor Felix/
Acts 24:10–27

Now it was Paul's turn. The governor motioned for him to rise and speak.

Paul began: "I know, sir, that you have been a judge of Jewish affairs for many years, and this gives me confidence as I make my defense. 11You can quickly discover that it was no more than twelve days ago that I arrived in Jerusalem to worship at the Temple, 12and you will discover that I have never incited a riot in any synagogue or on the streets of any city; 13and these men certainly cannot prove the things they accuse me of doing.

14"But one thing I do confess, that I believe in the way of salvation, which they refer to as a sect; I follow that system of serving the God of our ancestors; I firmly believe in the Jewish law and everything written in the books of prophecy; 15and I believe, just as these men do, that there will be a resurrection of both the righteous and ungodly. 16Because of this I try with all my strength to always maintain a clear conscience before God and man.

17"After several years away, I returned to Jerusalem with money to aid the Jews, and to offer a sacrifice to God. 18My accusers saw me in the Temple as I was presenting my thank offering. I had shaved my head as their laws required, and there was no crowd around me, and no rioting! But some Jews from Turkey were there 19(who ought to be here if they have anything against me)—20but look! Ask these men right here what wrongdoing their Council found in me, 21except that I said one thing I shouldn't when I shouted out, 'I am here before the Council to defend myself for believing that the dead will rise again!' "

22Felix, who knew Christians didn't go around starting riots, told the Jews to wait for the arrival of Lysias, the garrison commander, and then he would decide the case. 23He ordered Paul to prison but instructed the guards to treat him gently and not to forbid any of his friends from visiting him or bringing him gifts to make his stay more comfortable.

24A few days later Felix came with Drusilla, his legal wife, a Jewess. Sending for Paul, they listened as he told them about faith in Christ Jesus. 25And as he reasoned with them about righteousness and self-control and the judgment to come, Felix was terrified.

"Go away for now," he replied, "and when I have a more convenient time, I'll call for you again."

26He also hoped that Paul would bribe him, so he sent for him from time to time and talked with him. 27Two years went by in this way; then Felix was succeeded by Porcius Festus. And because Felix wanted to gain favor with the Jews, he left Paul in chains.

A THOUGHT: *Paul's talk with Felix became so personal that Felix felt convicted. Felix, like Herod Antipas, had taken another man's wife. Paul's words were interesting to Felix until they focused on "righteousness and self-control and the judgment to come." Many people will be glad to discuss the gospel with you as long as it doesn't touch their lives too personally. When it does, some will resist or run away. But this is what the gospel is all about—God's power to change lives. The gospel is not effective until it moves from principles and doctrine into a life-changing dynamic.*

Suffering Is a Part of Our Christian Lives/ 1 Peter 2:17–25

Show respect for everyone. Love Christians everywhere. Fear God and honor the government.

18Servants, you must respect your masters and do whatever they tell you—not only if they are kind and reasonable, but even if they are tough and cruel. 19Praise the Lord if you are punished for doing right! 20Of course, you get no credit for being patient if you are beaten for doing wrong; but if you do right and suffer for it, and are patient beneath the blows, God is well pleased.

21This suffering is all part of the work God has given you. Christ, who suffered for you, is your example. Follow in his steps: 22He never sinned, never told a lie, 23never answered back when insulted; when he suffered he did not threaten to get even; he left his case in the hands of God who always judges fairly. 24He personally carried the load of our sins in his own body when he died on the cross, so that we can be finished with sin and live a good life from now on. For his wounds have healed ours! 25Like sheep you wandered away from God, but now you have returned to your Shepherd, the Guardian of your souls who keeps you safe from all attacks.

A THOUGHT: *There are many reasons for human suffering. Peter writes that suffering is part of the work God has given us to do. Christ never sinned, yet he suffered so that we could be set free. When we follow Christ's example and live for others, we too may suffer. Our goal should be to live as Christ lived and to face suffering as he did—with patience, calmness, and confidence that God is in control of the future.*

Proverbs for Today/ 28:14

Blessed is the man who reveres God, but the man who doesn't care is headed for serious trouble.

NOVEMBER 26

Paul Demands a Hearing before Caesar/
Acts 25:1–12

Three days after Festus arrived in Caesarea to take over his new responsibilities, he left for Jerusalem, 2where the chief priests and other Jewish leaders got hold of him and gave him their story about Paul. 3They begged him to bring Paul to Jerusalem at once. (Their plan was to waylay and kill him.) 4But Festus replied that since Paul was at Caesarea and he himself was returning there soon, 5those with authority in this affair should return with him for the trial.

6Eight or ten days later he returned to Caesarea and the following day opened Paul's trial.

7On Paul's arrival in court the Jews from Jerusalem gathered around, hurling many serious accusations which they couldn't prove. 8Paul denied the charges: "I am not guilty," he said. "I have not opposed the Jewish laws or desecrated the Temple or rebelled against the Roman government."

9Then Festus, anxious to please the Jews, asked him, "Are you willing to go to Jerusalem and stand trial before me?"

10,11But Paul replied, "No! I demand my privilege of a hearing before the Emperor himself. You know very well I am not guilty. If I have done something worthy of death, I don't refuse to die! But if I am innocent, neither you nor anyone else has a right to turn me over to these men to kill me. *I appeal to Caesar.*"

12Festus conferred with his advisors and then replied, "Very well! You have appealed to Caesar, and to Caesar you shall go!"

A THOUGHT: *Paul knew he was blameless of the charges against him and could appeal to Caesar's judgment. He knew his rights as a Roman citizen and as an innocent person. Paul had met his responsibilities as a Roman, and so he had the opportunity to claim Rome's protection. The good reputation and clear conscience that result from our walk with God can help us remain not only guilt-free before God, but blame–free before the world as well.*

Instructions for Wives/ 1 Peter 3:1–6

Wives, fit in with your husbands' plans; for then if they refuse to listen when you talk to them about the Lord, they will be won by your respectful, pure behavior. Your godly lives will speak to them better than any words.

3Don't be concerned about the outward beauty that depends on jewelry, or beautiful clothes, or hair arrangement. 4Be beautiful inside, in your hearts, with the lasting charm of a gentle and quiet spirit which is so precious to God. 5That kind of deep beauty was seen in the saintly women of old, who trusted God and fitted in with their husbands' plans.

6Sarah, for instance, obeyed her husband Abraham, honoring him as head of the house. And if you do the same, you will be following in her steps like good daughters and doing what is right; then you will not need to fear [offending your husbands].

A THOUGHT: *A changed life speaks loudly and clearly, and it is often the most effective way to influence a family member. Peter instructed Christian wives to develop inner beauty rather than being overly concerned about their outward appearance. Their husbands would be won by their love rather than by their looks. Live your Christian faith quietly and consistently in your home, and your family will see Christ in you.*

Proverbs for Today/ 28:15–16

A wicked ruler is as dangerous to the poor as a lion or bear attacking them. Only a stupid prince will oppress his people, but a king will have a long reign if he hates dishonesty and bribes.

NOVEMBER 27

Festus Explains Paul's Case/ Acts 25:13–27

A few days later King Agrippa arrived with Bernice for a visit with Festus. 14During their stay of several days Festus discussed Paul's case with the king. "There is a prisoner here," he told him, "whose case was left for me by Felix. 15When I was in Jerusalem, the chief priests and other Jewish leaders gave me their side of the story and asked me to have him killed. 16Of course I quickly pointed out to them that Roman law does not convict a man before he is tried. He is given an opportunity to defend himself face to face with his accusers.

17"When they came here for the trial, I called the case the very next day and ordered Paul brought in. 18But the accusations made against him weren't at all what I supposed they would be. 19It was something about their religion, and about someone called Jesus who died, but Paul insists is alive! 20I was perplexed as to how to decide a case of this kind and asked him whether he would be willing to stand trial on these charges in Jerusalem. 21But Paul appealed to Caesar! So I ordered him back to jail until I could arrange to get him to the Emperor."

22"I'd like to hear the man myself," Agrippa said.

And Festus replied, "You shall—tomorrow!"

23So the next day, after the king and Bernice had arrived at the courtroom with great pomp, accompanied by military officers and prominent men of the city, Festus ordered Paul brought in.

24Then Festus addressed the audience: "King Agrippa and all present," he said, "this is the man whose death is demanded both by the local Jews and by those in

Jerusalem! 25But in my opinion he has done nothing worthy of death. However, he appealed his case to Caesar, and I have no alternative but to send him. 26But what shall I write the Emperor? For there is no real charge against him! So I have brought him before you all, and especially you, King Agrippa, to examine him and then tell me what to write. 27For it doesn't seem reasonable to send a prisoner to the Emperor without any charges against him!"

A THOUGHT: *The fact that Paul was in prison, didn't stop him from making the most of his situation. Military officers and prominent city leaders met in the palace room with Agrippa to hear this case. Paul saw this new audience as yet another opportunity to present the gospel. Rather than complain about your present situation, seek for ways to use every opportunity to serve God and share him with others. Our problems may be opportunities in disguise.*

Instructions for Husbands/ 1 Peter 3:7–9

You husbands must be careful of your wives, being thoughtful of their needs and honoring them as the weaker sex. Remember that you and your wife are partners in receiving God's blessings, and if you don't treat her as you should, your prayers will not get ready answers.

8And now this word to all of you: You should be like one big happy family, full of sympathy toward each other, loving one another with tender hearts and humble minds. 9Don't repay evil for evil. Don't snap back at those who say unkind things about you. Instead, pray for God's help for them, for we are to be kind to others, and God will bless us for it.

A THOUGHT: *If a man does not treat his wife kindly, his prayers become ineffective, because a living relationship with God depends on right relationships with others. Jesus said that if you have a problem with a fellow believer, you must make things right with that person before coming to worship. This principle carries over into family relationships. Our relationship with God will suffer if we do not show a respect and love for others within our family. How we relate to others within our family is part of our relationship with God.*

Proverbs for Today/ 28:17–18

A murderer's conscience will drive him into hell. Don't stop him! □ Good men will be rescued from harm, but cheaters will be destroyed.

Paul's Defense before King Agrippa/ Acts 26:1–32

Then Agrippa said to Paul, "Go ahead. Tell us your story."

So Paul, with many gestures, presented his defense:

2"I am fortunate, King Agrippa," he began, "to be able to present my answer before you, 3for I know you are an expert on Jewish laws and customs. Now please listen patiently!

4"As the Jews are well aware, I was given a thorough Jewish training from my earliest childhood in Tarsus and later at Jerusalem, and I lived accordingly. 5If they would admit it, they know that I have always been the strictest of Pharisees when it comes to obedience to Jewish laws and customs. 6But the real reason behind their accusations is something else—it is because I am looking forward to the fulfillment of God's promise made to our ancestors. 7The twelve tribes of Israel strive night and day to attain this same hope I have! Yet, O King, for me it is a crime, they say! 8But is it a crime to believe in the resurrection of the dead? Does it seem incredible to you that God can bring men back to life again?

9"I used to believe that I ought to do many horrible things to the followers of Jesus of Nazareth. 10I imprisoned many of the saints in Jerusalem, as authorized by the High Priests; and when they were condemned to death, I cast my vote against them. 11I used torture to try to make Christians everywhere curse Christ. I was so violently opposed to them that I even hounded them in distant cities in foreign lands.

12"I was on such a mission to Damascus, armed with the authority and commission of the chief priests, 13 when one day about noon, sir, a light from heaven brighter than the sun shone down on me and my companions. 14We all fell down, and I heard a voice speaking to me in Hebrew, 'Saul, Saul, why are you persecuting me? You are only hurting yourself.'

15" 'Who are you, sir?' I asked.

"And the Lord replied, 'I am Jesus, the one you are persecuting. 16Now stand up! For I have appeared to you to appoint you as my servant and my witness. You are to tell the world about this experience and about the many other occasions when I shall appear to you. 17And I will protect you from both your own people and the Gentiles. Yes, I am going to send you to the Gentiles 18to open their eyes to their true condition so that they may repent and live in the light of God instead of in Satan's darkness, so that they may receive forgiveness for their sins and God's inheritance along with all people everywhere whose sins are cleansed away, who are set apart by faith in me.'

19"And so, O King Agrippa, I was not disobedient to that vision from heaven! 20I preached first to those in Damascus, then in Jerusalem and through Judea, and also to the Gentiles that all must forsake their sins and turn to God—and prove their repentance by doing good deeds. 21The Jews arrested me in the Temple for preaching this, and tried to kill me, 22but God protected me so that I am still alive today to tell these facts to everyone, both great and small. I teach nothing except what the prophets and Moses said— 23that the Messiah would suffer, and be the First to rise from the dead, to bring light to Jews and Gentiles alike."

24Suddenly Festus shouted, "Paul, you are insane. Your long studying has broken your mind!"

25But Paul replied, "I am not insane, Most Excellent Festus. I speak words of sober truth. 26And King Agrippa knows about these things. I speak frankly for I am sure these events are all familiar to him, for they were not done in a corner! 27King Agrippa, do you believe the prophets? But I know you do—"

28Agrippa interrupted him. "With trivial proofs like these, you expect me to become a Christian?"

29And Paul replied, "Would to God that whether my arguments are trivial or strong, both you and everyone here in this audience might become the same as I am, except for these chains."

30Then the king, the governor, Bernice, and all the others stood and left. 31As they talked it over afterwards they agreed, "This man hasn't done anything worthy of death or imprisonment."

32And Agrippa said to Festus, "He could be set free if he hadn't appealed to Caesar!"

A Thought: *Agrippa answered Paul's presentation with a sarcastic remark. Paul didn't react to the brush-off, but made a personal appeal to which he hoped all his listeners would respond. Paul's response is a good example for us as we tell others about God's plan of salvation. A sincere personal appeal or personal testimony can show the depth of our concern and break through hardened hearts. Paul's heart is revealed here in his defense: he was more concerned for the salvation of these strangers than for the removal of his own bonds. Ask God to help you share Paul's burning desire to see others come to him—a desire so strong that it overshadows your problems.*

Exhortations to Holy Living/ 1 Peter 3:10–15

If you want a happy, good life, keep control of your tongue, and guard your lips from telling lies. 11Turn away from evil and do good. Try to live in peace even if you must run after it to catch and hold it! 12For the Lord is watching his children, listening to their prayers; but the Lord's face is hard against those who do evil.

13Usually no one will hurt you for wanting to do good. 14But even if they should, you are to be envied, for God will reward you for it. 15Quietly trust yourself to Christ your Lord and if anybody asks why you believe as you do, be ready to tell him, and do it in a gentle and respectful way.

A Thought: *Some Christians believe faith is a personal matter that should be kept to oneself. It is true that we shouldn't be boisterous or obnoxious in sharing our faith, but we should always be ready to answer, gently and respectfully, when asked about our faith, our lifestyle, or our Christian perspective. Is your hope in Christ readily observable to others? Are you prepared to tell others what Christ has done in your life?*

Proverbs for Today/ 28:19–20

Hard work brings prosperity; playing around brings poverty. The man who wants to do right will get a rich reward. But the man who wants to get rich quick will quickly fail.

NOVEMBER 29

Paul Begins His Voyage to Rome/ Acts 27:1–15

Arrangements were finally made to start us [Luke, Paul, and his companions] on our way to Rome by ship; so Paul and several other prisoners were placed in the custody of an officer named Julius, a member of the imperial guard. 2We left on a boat which was scheduled to make several stops along the Turkish coast. I should add that Aristarchus, a Greek from Thessalonica, was with us.

3The next day when we docked at Sidon, Julius was very kind to Paul and let him go ashore to visit with friends and receive their hospitality. 4Putting to sea from there, we encountered headwinds that made it difficult to keep the ship on course, so we sailed north of Cyprus between the island and the mainland, 5 and passed along the coast of the provinces of Cilicia and Pamphylia, landing at Myra, in the province of Lycia. 6There our officer found an Egyptian ship from Alexandria, bound for Italy, and put us aboard.

7,8We had several days of rough sailing, and finally neared Cnidus; but the winds had become too strong, so we ran across to Crete, passing the port of Salome. Beating into the wind with great difficulty and moving slowly along the southern coast, we arrived at Fair Havens, near the city of Lasea. 9There we stayed for several days. The weather was becoming dangerous for long voyages by then, because it was late in the year, and Paul spoke to the ship's officers about it.

10"Sirs," he said, "I believe there is trouble ahead if we go on—perhaps shipwreck, loss of cargo, injuries, and death." 11But the officers in charge of the prisoners listened more to the ship's captain and the owner than to Paul. 12And since Fair Havens was an exposed harbor—a poor place to spend the winter—most of the crew advised trying to go further up the coast to Phoenix, in order to winter there; Phoenix was a good harbor with only a north-west and southwest exposure.

13Just then a light wind began blowing from the south, and it looked like a perfect day for the trip; so they pulled up anchor and sailed along close to shore.

14,15But shortly afterwards, the weather changed abruptly and a heavy wind of typhoon strength (a "northeaster," they called it) caught the ship and blew it out to sea. They tried at first to face back to shore but couldn't, so they gave up and let the ship run before the gale.

A THOUGHT: *Ships in ancient times had no compasses and navigated by the stars. Overcast weather made sailing almost impossible and very dangerous. Sailing was doubtful in September and impossible by November. Paul had warned the ship's officers about the possibility of trouble ahead, but they decided to follow the advice of the ship's captain instead of heeding Paul's warning. As Paul predicted, a storm overtook the ship and blew it off course. Yet in the midst of all the difficulties God was with Paul and protected all the crew as well.*

Do Right, Even When You Suffer For It/
1 Peter 3:16–22

Do what is right; then if men speak against you, calling you evil names, they will become ashamed of themselves for falsely accusing you when you have only done what is good. 17Remember, if God wants you to suffer, it is better to suffer for doing good than for doing wrong!

18Christ also suffered. He died once for the sins of all us guilty sinners, although he himself was innocent of any sin at any time, that he might bring us safely home to God. But though his body died, his spirit lived on, 19and it was in the spirit that he visited the spirits in prison, and preached to them— 20spirits of those who, long before in the days of Noah, had refused to listen to God, though he waited patiently for them while Noah was building the ark. Yet only eight persons were saved from drowning in that terrible flood. 21(That, by the way, is what baptism pictures for us: In baptism we show that we have been saved from death and doom by the resurrection of Christ; not because our bodies are washed clean by the water, but because in being baptized we are turning to God and asking him to cleanse our *hearts* from sin.) 22And now Christ is in heaven, sitting in the place of honor next to God the Father, with all the angels and powers of heaven bowing before him and obeying him.

A THOUGHT: *You may not be able to keep people from attacking you, but you can at least stop supplying them with justification for their actions. If we suffer for wrongdoing we should humbly endure it as just punishment. When we suffer for doing what is right, then we are given the opportunity to suffer as Christ suffered. Since Jesus suffered injustice, his followers should expect to suffer injustice as well. It is a privilege to suffer for Christ, even though it is not at all a pleasant experience. Let us keep our conduct above criticism, so that when we do suffer, our suffering can be a testimony to those around us.*

Proverbs for Today/ 28:21–22

Giving preferred treatment to rich people is a clear case of selling one's soul for a piece of bread. ◻ Trying to get rich quick is evil and leads to poverty.

NOVEMBER 30

Paul Is Shipwrecked on the Way to Rome/ Acts 27:16–44

We [Luke, Paul, and his companions] finally sailed behind a small island named Clauda, where with great difficulty we hoisted aboard the lifeboat that was being towed behind us, 17and then banded the ship with ropes to strengthen the hull. The sailors were afraid of being driven across to the quicksands of the African coast, so they lowered the topsails and were thus driven before the wind.

18The next day as the seas grew higher, the crew began throwing the cargo overboard. 19The following day they threw out the tackle and anything else they could lay their hands on. 20The terrible storm raged unabated many days, until at last all hope was gone.

21No one had eaten for a long time, but finally Paul called the crew together and said, "Men, you should have listened to me in the first place and not left Fair Havens— you would have avoided all this injury and loss! 22But cheer up! Not one of us will lose our lives, even though the ship will go down.

23"For last night an angel of the God to whom I belong and whom I serve stood beside me, 24and said, 'Don't be afraid, Paul—for you will surely stand trial before Caesar! What's more, God has granted your request and will save the lives of all those sailing with you.' 25So take courage! For I believe God! It will be just as he said! 26But we will be shipwrecked on an island."

27About midnight on the fourteenth night of the storm, as we were being driven to and fro on the Adriatic Sea, the sailors suspected land was near. 28They sounded, and found 120 feet of water below them. A little later they sounded again, and found only ninety feet. 29At this rate they knew they would soon be driven ashore; and fearing rocks along the coast, they threw out four anchors from the stern and prayed for daylight.

30Some of the sailors planned to abandon the ship, and lowered the emergency boat as though they were going to put out anchors from the prow. 31But Paul said to the soldiers and commanding officer, "You will all die unless everyone stays aboard." 32So the soldiers cut the ropes and let the boat fall off.

33As the darkness gave way to the early morning light, Paul begged everyone to eat. "You haven't touched food for two weeks," he said. 34"Please eat something now for your own good! For not a hair of your heads shall perish!"

35Then he took some hardtack and gave thanks to God before them all, and broke off a piece and ate it. 36Suddenly everyone felt better and began eating, 37all two hundred seventy-six of us—for that is the number we had aboard. 38After eating, the crew lightened the ship further by throwing all the wheat overboard.

39When it was day, they didn't recognize the coastline, but noticed a bay with a beach and wondered whether they could get between the rocks and be driven up onto the beach. 40They finally decided to try. Cutting off the anchors and leaving them in the sea, they lowered the rudders, raised the foresail and headed ashore. 41But the ship hit a sandbar and ran aground. The bow of the ship stuck fast, while the stern was exposed to the violence of the waves and began to break apart.

42The soldiers advised their commanding officer to let them kill the prisoners lest any of them swim ashore and escape. 43But Julius wanted to spare Paul, so he told them no. Then he ordered all who could swim to jump overboard and make for land, 44and the rest to try for it on planks and debris from the broken ship. So everyone escaped safely ashore!

A THOUGHT: *God was faithful to the promise he had made to Paul by way of the angel—everyone arrived safely on shore. God is sovereign over all the affairs of nature and people. We can take comfort in the promises of God even when the circumstances do not seem to indicate that God will fulfill his promises. We must remember that the story is never over until the final chapter is closed. Difficult times will come, but they are not the ultimate end for Christians, for we have the hope of the resurrection and life eternal ahead of us. The next time you find yourself in difficult circumstances, trust God to bring you through them—he is faithful.*

Be Ready to Suffer for Christ/ 1 Peter 4:1–6

Since Christ suffered and underwent pain, you must have the same attitude he did; you must be ready to suffer, too. For remember, when your body suffers, sin loses its power, 2and you won't be spending the rest of your life chasing after evil desires, but will be anxious to do the will of God. 3You have had enough in the past of the evil things the godless enjoy—sex sin, lust, getting drunk, wild parties, drinking bouts, and the worship of idols, and other terrible sins.

4Of course, your former friends will be very surprised when you don't eagerly join them any more in the wicked things they do, and they will laugh at you in contempt and scorn. 5But just remember that they must face the Judge of all, living and dead; they will be punished for the way they have lived. 6That is why the Good News was preached even to those who were dead—killed by the flood—so that although their bodies were punished with death, they could still live in their spirits as God lives.

A THOUGHT: *Some people will do anything to avoid pain. As followers of Christ, however, we should be willing and prepared to do God's will and to suffer for it if necessary. Sin loses its power when we suffer if we focus on Christ and what he wants us to do. When our bodies are in pain or our lives are in jeopardy, our real values show up clearly, and sinful pleasures seem less important.*

Proverbs for Today/ 28:23–24

In the end, people appreciate frankness more than flattery. □ A man who robs his parents and says, "What's wrong with that?" is no better than a murderer.

DECEMBER 1

Paul Survives a Bite from a Poisonous Snake/
Acts 28:1–10

We [Luke, Paul, and his companions] soon learned that we were on the island of Malta. The people of the island were very kind to us, building a bonfire on the beach to welcome and warm us in the rain and cold.

3As Paul gathered an armful of sticks to lay on the fire, a poisonous snake, driven out by the heat, fastened itself onto his hand! 4The people of the island saw it hanging there and said to each other, "A murderer, no doubt! Though he escaped the sea, justice will not permit him to live!"

5But Paul shook off the snake into the fire and was unharmed. 6The people waited for him to begin swelling or suddenly fall dead; but when they had waited a long time and no harm came to him, they changed their minds and decided he was a god.

7Near the shore where we landed was an estate belonging to Publius, the governor of the island. He welcomed us courteously and fed us for three days. 8As it happened, Publius' father was ill with fever and dysentery. Paul went in and prayed for him, and laying his hands on him, healed him! 9Then all the other sick people in the island came and were cured. 10As a result we were showered with gifts, and when the time came to sail, people put on board all sorts of things we would need for the trip.

A THOUGHT: *God had promised safe passage to Paul, and he allowed neither sea nor serpent stop his servant. The snake that bit Paul, though poisonous, was unable to harm him. God still had work for Paul to do. Our lives are in God's hands, to continue or end in his good timing.*

Use Your Gifts to Serve Others/ 1 Peter 4:7–11

The end of the world is coming soon. Therefore be earnest, thoughtful men of prayer. 8Most important of all, continue to show deep love for each other, for love makes up for many of your faults. 9Cheerfully share your home with those who need a meal or a place to stay for the night.

10God has given each of you some special abilities; be

sure to use them to help each other, passing on to others God's many kinds of blessings. 11Are you called to preach? Then preach as though God himself were speaking through you. Are you called to help others? Do it with all the strength and energy that God supplies, so that God will be glorified through Jesus Christ—to him be glory and power forever and ever. Amen.

A THOUGHT: *Some people, well aware of their abilities, believe they have the right to use them as they please. Others feel they have no special talents at all. To both groups Peter addresses these verses. Peter says, everyone has some abilities; find yours and use them. All our abilities should be dedicated to others, he points out; none are for our own exclusive enjoyment. We must use the gifts which God has given to us to serve others.*

Proverbs for Today/ 28:25–26

Greed causes fighting; trusting God leads to prosperity. □ A man is a fool to trust himself! But those who use God's wisdom are safe.

DECEMBER 2

Paul Lives under Guard in Rome/ Acts 28:11–31

It was three months after the shipwreck before we [Luke, Paul, and his companions] set sail again, and this time it was in *The Twin Brothers* of Alexandria, a ship that had wintered at the island. 12Our first stop was Syracuse, where we stayed three days. 13From there we circled around to Rhegium; a day later a south wind began blowing, so the following day we arrived at Puteoli, 14where we found some believers! They begged us to stay with them seven days. Then we went on to Rome.

15The brothers in Rome had heard we were coming and came to meet us at the Forum on the Appian Way. Others joined us at The Three Taverns. When Paul saw them, he thanked God and took courage.

16When we arrived in Rome, Paul was permitted to live wherever he wanted to, though guarded by a soldier.

17Three days after his arrival, he called together the

local Jewish leaders and spoke to them as follows:

"Brothers, I was arrested by the Jews in Jerusalem and handed over to the Roman government for prosecution, even though I had harmed no one nor violated the customs of our ancestors. 18The Romans gave me a trial and wanted to release me, for they found no cause for the death sentence demanded by the Jewish leaders. 19But when the Jews protested the decision, I felt it necessary, with no malice against them, to appeal to Caesar. 20I asked you to come here today so we could get acquainted and I could tell you that it is because I believe the Messiah has come that I am bound with this chain."

21They replied, "We have heard nothing against you! We have had no letters from Judea or reports from those arriving from Jerusalem. 22But we want to hear what you believe, for the only thing we know about these Christians is that they are denounced everywhere!"

23So a time was set and on that day large numbers came to his house. He told them about the Kingdom of God and taught them about Jesus from the Scriptures—from the five books of Moses and the books of prophecy. He began lecturing in the morning and went on into the evening!

24Some believed, and some didn't. 25But after they had argued back and forth among themselves, they left with this final word from Paul ringing in their ears: "The Holy Spirit was right when he said through Isaiah the prophet,

26" 'Say to the Jews, "You will hear and see but not understand, 27for your hearts are too fat and your ears don't listen and you have closed your eyes against understanding, for you don't want to see and hear and understand and turn to me to heal you." ' 28,29So I want you to realize that this salvation from God is available to the Gentiles too, and they will accept it."

30Paul lived for the next two years in his rented house and welcomed all who visited him, 31telling them with all boldness about the Kingdom of God and about the Lord Jesus Christ; and no one tried to stop him.

A THOUGHT: *Paul wanted to preach the gospel in Rome, and he eventually got there—in chains, through shipwreck, and after many trials. Although he may have wished for an easier passage, he knew that God had blessed him greatly in allowing him to meet the believers in Rome and preach the message to both Jews and Gentiles in that great city. God "worked all things for good" (Romans 8:28) for Paul, and you can trust him to do the same for you. God may not make you comfortable or secure, but he will provide the opportunity to do his work.*

We Are Partners with Christ in Suffering/ 1 Peter 4:12–19

Dear friends, don't be bewildered or surprised when you go through the fiery trials ahead, for this is no strange, unusual thing that is going to happen to you. 13Instead, be really glad—because these trials will make you partners with Christ in his suffering, and afterwards you will have the wonderful joy of sharing his glory in that coming day when it will be displayed.

14Be happy if you are cursed and insulted for being a Christian, for when that happens the Spirit of God will come upon you with great glory. 15Don't let me hear of your suffering for murdering or stealing or making trouble or being a busybody and prying into other people's affairs. 16But it is no shame to suffer for being a Christian. Praise God for the privilege of being in Christ's family and being called by his wonderful name! 17For the time has come for judgment, and it must begin first among God's own children. And if even we who are Christians must be judged, what terrible fate awaits those who have never believed in the Lord? 18If the righteous are barely saved, what chance will the godless have?

19So if you are suffering according to God's will, keep on doing what is right and trust yourself to the God who made you, for he will never fail you.

A THOUGHT: *Again Peter brings to mind Jesus' words: "When you are reviled and persecuted and lied about because you are my followers—wonderful!" (Matthew 5:11). It is never shameful to suffer for Christ, and he will send his Spirit to strengthen those who are persecuted for their faith. This does not mean that all suffering is good, however. Sometimes a person will grumble, "He's just picking on me because I'm a Christian," when it's obvious to everyone else that it is the person's own unpleasant behavior that is the cause of his problems. It may take careful thought or wise counsel to determine the real cause of our suffering. We can be assured, however, that whenever we suffer because of our loyalty to Christ, he will be with us all the way.*

Proverbs for Today/ 28:27–28
If you give to the poor, your needs will be supplied! But
a curse upon those who close their eyes to poverty. □ When the wicked prosper, good men go away;
when the wicked meet disaster, good men return.

DECEMBER 3

A Greeting and a Doxology/ Revelation 1:1–9a
This book unveils some of the future activities soon to
occur in the life of Jesus Christ. God permitted him to
reveal these things to his servant John in a vision; and
then an angel was sent from heaven to explain the vision's
meaning. ²John wrote it all down—the words of God and
Jesus Christ and everything he heard and saw.

³If you read this prophecy aloud to the church, you
will receive a special blessing from the Lord. Those who
listen to it being read and do what it says will also be
blessed. For the time is near when these things will all
come true.

⁴*From:* John
To: The seven churches in Turkey.
Dear Friends:
May you have grace and peace from God who is, and
was, and is to come! and from the seven-fold Spirit before
his throne; ⁵and from Jesus Christ who faithfully reveals
all truth to us. He was the first to rise from death, to
die no more. He is far greater than any king in all the
earth. All praise to him who always loves us and who
set us free from our sins by pouring out his lifeblood for
us. ⁶He has gathered us into his Kingdom and made us
priests of God his Father. Give to him everlasting glory!
He rules forever! Amen!

⁷See! He is arriving, surrounded by clouds; and every
eye shall see him—yes, and those who pierced him. And
the nations will weep in sorrow and in terror when he
comes. Yes! Amen! Let it be so!

8"I am the A and the Z, the Beginning and the Ending of all things," says God, who is the Lord, the All Powerful One who is, and was, and is coming again!

9It is I, your brother John, a fellow sufferer for the Lord's sake, who am writing this letter to you. I, too, have shared the patience Jesus gives, and we shall share his Kingdom!

A THOUGHT: *Jesus gave his message to John in a vision, allowing him to see and record certain future events so they could be an encouragement to all believers. The vision includes many signs and symbols, because they well convey the essence of what is to happen. What John saw, in most cases, was indescribable, so he used illustrations to show what it was like. When reading this symbolic language, don't think you have to understand every detail— John didn't. Instead, realize that John's imagery is used to show us that Christ is indeed the glorious and victorious Lord of all.*

Exhortations Concerning Church Leadership/
1 Peter 5:1–7

And now, a word to you elders of the church. I, too, am an elder; with my own eyes I saw Christ dying on the cross; and I, too, will share his glory and his honor when he returns. Fellow elders, this is my plea to you: 2Feed the flock of God; care for it willingly, not grudgingly; not for what you will get out of it, but because you are eager to serve the Lord. 3Don't be tyrants, but lead them by your good example, 4and when the Head Shepherd comes, your reward will be a never-ending share in his glory and honor.

5You younger men, follow the leadership of those who are older. And all of you serve each other with humble spirits, for God gives special blessings to those who are humble, but sets himself against those who are proud. 6If you will humble yourselves under the mighty hand of God, in his good time he will lift you up.

7Let him have all your worries and cares, for he is always thinking about you and watching everything that concerns you.

A THOUGHT: *Peter describes several characteristics of good leaders in the church: (1) they realize they are caring for God's flock, not their own; (2) they lead out of eagerness to serve, not out of obligation; (3) they are concerned for what they can give, not for what they can get; (4) they lead by example, not force. All of us lead others in some way. Whatever your role, your leadership should be in line with these characteristics.*

Proverbs for Today/ 29:1
The man who is often reproved but refuses to accept criticism will suddenly be broken and never have another chance.

DECEMBER 4

John Has a Vision on the Lord's Day/
Revelation 1:9b–20
I was on the island of Patmos, exiled there for preaching the Word of God, and for telling what I knew about Jesus Christ. 10It was the Lord's Day and I was worshiping, when suddenly I heard a loud voice behind me, a voice that sounded like a trumpet blast, 11saying, "I am A and Z, the First and Last!" And then I heard him say, "Write down everything you see, and send your letter to the seven churches in Turkey: to the church in Ephesus, the one in Smyrna, and those in Pergamos, Thyatira, Sardis, Philadelphia, and Laodicea."

12When I turned to see who was speaking, there behind me were seven candlesticks of gold. 13And standing among them was one who looked like Jesus who called himself the Son of Man, wearing a long robe circled with a golden band across his chest. 14His hair was white as wool or snow, and his eyes penetrated like flames of fire. 15His feet gleamed like burnished bronze, and his voice thundered like the waves against the shore. 16He held seven stars in his right hand and a sharp, double-bladed sword in his mouth, and his face shone like the power of the sun in unclouded brilliance.

17,18When I saw him, I fell at his feet as dead; but he laid his right hand on me and said, "Don't be afraid! Though I am the First and Last, the Living One who died, who is now alive forevermore, who has the keys of hell and death—don't be afraid! 19Write down what you have just seen, and what will soon be shown to you. 20This is the meaning of the seven stars you saw in my right hand, and the seven golden candlesticks: The seven stars are the leaders of the seven churches, and the seven candlesticks are the churches themselves.

A THOUGHT: *John describes himself as a "fellow sufferer for the Lord's sake," indicating that the church was undergoing intense persecution as he was writing this letter. The whole church, as the body of Christ, should experience joy and suffering together. Follow John's example in your relationships with other Christians: identify with them, encourage them to be steadfast and faithful, and remind them of their future reward with God.*

Stand Firm in the Midst of Suffering/ 1 Peter 5:8–14

Be careful—watch out for attacks from Satan, your great enemy. He prowls around like a hungry, roaring lion, looking for some victim to tear apart. 9Stand firm when he attacks. Trust the Lord; and remember that other Christians all around the world are going through these sufferings too.

10After you have suffered a little while, our God, who is full of kindness through Christ, will give you his eternal glory. He personally will come and pick you up, and set you firmly in place, and make you stronger than ever. 11To him be all power over all things, forever and ever. Amen.

12I am sending this note to you through the courtesy of Silvanus who is, in my opinion, a very faithful brother. I hope I have encouraged you by this letter for I have given you a true statement of the way God blesses. What I have told you here should help you to stand firmly in his love.

13The church here in Rome—she is your sister in the Lord—sends you her greetings; so does my son Mark. 14Give each other the handshake of Christian love. Peace be to all of you who are in Christ.

A THOUGHT: *When we are suffering, we feel as though our pain will never end. Peter shows these faithful Christians the wider perspective. In comparison with eternity, their suffering would last only "a little while." Some of Peter's readers would be picked up, set in place, and strengthened in their own lifetimes. Others would be released from their suffering through death. All of God's faithful followers, however, are assured of Christ's eternal glory—endless, joyful life in which suffering plays no part at all.*

Proverbs for Today/ 29:2–4

With good men in authority, the people rejoice; but with
the wicked in power, they groan. □ A wise son makes
his father happy, but a lad who hangs around with prostitutes
disgraces him. □ A just king gives stability to his nation,
but one who demands bribes destroys it.

DECEMBER 5

The Letter to the Church in Ephesus/
Revelation 2:1–7

*"Write a letter to the leader of the church at Ephesus and
tell him this:*

"I write to inform you of a message from him who
walks among the churches and holds their leaders in his
right hand.

"He says to you: 2I know how many good things you
are doing. I have watched your hard work and your patience;
I know you don't tolerate sin among your members, and
you have carefully examined the claims of those who say
they are apostles but aren't. You have found out how
they lie. 3You have patiently suffered for me without quitting.

4"Yet there is one thing wrong; you don't love me as
at first! 5Think about those times of your first love (how
different now!) and turn back to me again and work as
you did before; or else I will come and remove your candlestick from its place among the churches.

6"But there is this about you that is good: You hate
the deeds of the licentious Nicolaitans, just as I do.

7"Let this message sink into the ears of anyone who
listens to what the Spirit is saying to the churches: To
everyone who is victorious, I will give fruit from the Tree
of Life in the Paradise of God.

A THOUGHT: *The church at Ephesus is commended for (1) working
hard, (2) being patient, (3) resisting sin, (4) critically examining
the claims of false apostles, and (5) suffering patiently without
quitting. Every church should have these characteristics. But these*

good things should spring from our love for Jesus Christ. The Ephesians had lost their first love, and they may have been in danger of falling into legalism. Work for God is not lasting unless it is based on love for God and others.

Seek to Know God and His Will/ 2 Peter 1:1–11

From: Simon Peter, a servant and missionary of Jesus Christ.

To: all of you who have our kind of faith. The faith I speak of is the kind that Jesus Christ our God and Savior gives to us. How precious it is, and how just and good he is to give this same faith to each of us.

2Do you want more and more of God's kindness and peace? Then learn to know him better and better. 3For as you know him better, he will give you, through his great power, everything you need for living a truly good life: he even shares his own glory and his own goodness with us! 4And by that same mighty power he has given us all the other rich and wonderful blessings he promised; for instance, the promise to save us from the lust and rottenness all around us, and to give us his own character.

5But to obtain these gifts, you need more than faith; you must also work hard to be good, and even that is not enough. For then you must learn to know God better and discover what he wants you to do. 6Next, learn to put aside your own desires so that you will become patient and godly, gladly letting God have his way with you. 7This will make possible the next step, which is for you to enjoy other people and to like them, and finally you will grow to love them deeply. 8The more you go on in this way, the more you will grow strong spiritually and become fruitful and useful to our Lord Jesus Christ. 9But anyone who fails to go after these additions to faith is blind indeed, or at least very shortsighted, and has forgotten that God delivered him from the old life of sin so that now he can live a strong, good life for the Lord.

10So, dear brothers, work hard to prove that you really are among those God has called and chosen, and then you will never stumble or fall away. 11And God will open wide the gates of heaven for you to enter into the eternal kingdom of our Lord and Savior Jesus Christ.

A Thought: *Many believers want more of God's kindness and peace, but they are unwilling to put forth the effort to get to know* him better. *To enjoy the privileges God offers us freely, we have to combine hard work with complete trust. In order to get to know God's will for our lives, we must faithfully obey what he has already revealed as his will in the Scriptures. As we internalize the Scriptures, the Holy Spirit transforms us into greater and greater Christlikeness—God's kindness and peace are then made realities in our lives.*

Proverbs for Today/ 29:5–8

Flattery is a trap; evil men are caught in it, but good men stay away and sing for joy. □ The good man knows the poor man's rights; the godless don't care. □ Fools start fights everywhere while wise men try to keep peace.

DECEMBER 6

The Letter to the Church in Smyrna/
Revelation 2:8–11

"To the leader of the church in Smyrna write this letter:
   "This message is from him who is the First and Last, who was dead and then came back to life.

⁹"I know how much you suffer for the Lord, and I know all about your poverty (but you have heavenly riches!). I know the slander of those opposing you, who say that they are Jews—the children of God—but they aren't, for they support the cause of Satan. ¹⁰Stop being afraid of what you are about to suffer—for the devil will soon throw some of you into prison to test you. You will be persecuted for 'ten days.' Remain faithful even when facing death and I will give you the crown of life—an unending, glorious future. ¹¹Let everyone who can hear, listen to what the Spirit is saying to the churches: He who is victorious shall not be hurt by the Second Death.

A THOUGHT: *Everyone would like to feel good and live comfortably, but pain is part of life—and it is not easy to suffer, no matter what the cause. Jesus commended the church at Smyrna for their faith in the midst of suffering. He then encouraged them that they need not fear the future if they remained faithful. If you are experiencing difficult times, don't let them turn you away from God. Instead let them draw you toward greater faithfulness. Trust him and remember your heavenly reward.*

Peter Is an Eyewitness of Christ/ 2 Peter 1:12–18

I plan to keep on reminding you of these things even though you already know them and are really getting along quite well! 13,14But the Lord Jesus Christ has showed me that my days here on earth are numbered, and I am soon to die. As long as I am still here I intend to keep sending these reminders to you, 15hoping to impress them so clearly upon you that you will remember them long after I have gone.

16For we have not been telling you fairy tales when we explained to you the power of our Lord Jesus Christ and his coming again. My own eyes have seen his splendor and his glory: 17,18I was there on the holy mountain when he shone out with honor given him by God his Father; I heard that glorious, majestic voice calling down from heaven, saying, "This is my much-loved Son; I am well pleased with him."

A THOUGHT: *Outstanding coaches constantly review the basics of the sport with their teams, and good athletes can execute the fundamentals consistently well. In our spiritual lives we must not neglect the basics of our faith when we go on to study deeper truths. Just as an athlete needs constant practice, we need constant reminders of the fundamentals of our faith and of how we came to believe in the first place. Don't allow yourself to be bored or impatient with messages on the basics of the Christian life. Instead, take the attitude of an athlete who continues to practice and refine the basics even as he learns more advanced skills.*

Proverbs for Today/ 29:9–11

There's no use arguing with a fool. He only rages and scoffs, and tempers flare. □ The godly pray for those who long to kill them. □ A rebel shouts in anger; a wise man holds his temper in and cools it.

|DECEMBER 7

The Letter to the Church in Pergamos/ Revelation 2:12–17

"Write this letter to the leader of the church in Pergamos:
"This message is from him who wields the sharp and

double-bladed sword. 13I am fully aware that you live in the city where Satan's throne is, at the center of satanic worship; and yet you have remained loyal to me, and refused to deny me, even when Antipas, my faithful witness, was martyred among you by Satan's devotees.

14"And yet I have a few things against you. You tolerate some among you who do as Balaam did when he taught Balak how to ruin the people of Israel by involving them in sexual sin and encouraging them to go to idol feasts. 15Yes, you have some of these very same followers of Balaam among you!

16"Change your mind and attitude, or else I will come to you suddenly and fight against them with the sword of my mouth.

17"Let everyone who can hear, listen to what the Spirit is saying to the churches: Every one who is victorious shall eat of the hidden manna, the secret nourishment from heaven; and I will give to each a white stone, and on the stone will be engraved a new name that no one else knows except the one receiving it.

A THOUGHT: *As the center for four idolatrous cults, Pergamos is called "the city where Satan's throne is." Surrounded by Satanic worship, the church at Pergamos refused to deny Christ even when Satan's worshipers martyred one of their members. There is no room for heresy and moral impurity among Christians. Your town may not participate in idol feasts, but it probably has pornography, sexual sin, cheating, gossiping, and lying. Don't tolerate sin under the pressure to be open-minded. Standing firm against Satan's attractive temptations is never easy, but the alternative is deadly.*

God Inspired the Message of the Prophets/
2 Peter 1:19—2:11

So we have seen and proved that what the prophets said came true. You will do well to pay close attention to everything they have written, for, like lights shining into dark corners, their words help us to understand many things that otherwise would be dark and difficult. But when you consider the wonderful truth of the prophets' words, then the light will dawn in your souls and Christ the Morning Star will shine in your hearts. 20,21For no prophecy recorded in Scripture was ever thought up by the prophet himself. It was the Holy Spirit within these godly men who gave them true messages from God.

2:1But there were false prophets, too, in those days, just as there will be false teachers among you. They will cleverly tell their lies about God, turning against even their Master who bought them; but theirs will be a swift and terrible end. 2Many will follow their evil teaching that there is nothing wrong with sexual sin. And because of them Christ and his way will be scoffed at.

3These teachers in their greed will tell you anything to get hold of your money. But God condemned them long ago and their destruction is on the way. 4For God did not spare even the angels who sinned, but threw them into hell, chained in gloomy caves and darkness until the judgment day. 5And he did not spare any of the people who lived in ancient times before the flood except Noah, the one man who spoke up for God, and his family of seven. At that time God completely destroyed the whole world of ungodly men with the vast flood. 6Later, he turned the cities of Sodom and Gomorrah into heaps of ashes and blotted them off the face of the earth, making them an example for all the ungodly in the future to look back upon and fear.

7,8But at the same time the Lord rescued Lot out of Sodom because he was a good man, sick of the terrible wickedness he saw everywhere around him day after day. 9So also the Lord can rescue you and me from the temptations that surround us, and continue to punish the ungodly until the day of final judgment comes. 10He is especially hard on those who follow their own evil, lustful thoughts, and those who are proud and willful, daring even to scoff at the Glorious Ones without so much as trembling, 11although the angels in heaven who stand in the very presence of the Lord, and are far greater in power and strength than these false teachers, never speak out disrespectfully against these evil Mighty Ones.

A THOUGHT: *Jesus had told the disciples that false teachers would come. Peter had heard these words, and now he was seeing them come true. Just as false prophets had contradicted the true prophets in Old Testament times, telling people only what they wanted to hear, so false teachers twisted Christ's teachings and the words of his apostles. These teachers belittled the significance of Jesus' life, death, and resurrection. Some claimed he couldn't be God; others claimed he couldn't have been a real man. They allowed and even* encouraged all kinds of wrong and immoral acts, especially sexual sin. Though these false teachers were popular, Peter warned that they would be destroyed. We should beware of those who make such claims against God's Word today. Let us avoid those who seek their own profit, their own glory, cause divisions within the church, and deny the truths of God's inspired Word.

Proverbs for Today/ 29:12–14

A wicked ruler will have wicked aides on his staff. □ Rich and poor are alike in this: each depends on God for light. □ A king who is fair to the poor shall have a long reign.

DECEMBER 8

The Letter to the Church in Thyatira/ Revelation 2:18–29

"Write this letter to the leader of the church in Thyatira:

"This is a message from the Son of God, whose eyes penetrate like flames of fire, whose feet are like glowing brass.

19"I am aware of all your good deeds—your kindness to the poor, your gifts and service to them; also I know your love and faith and patience, and I can see your constant improvement in all these things.

20"Yet I have this against you: You are permitting that woman Jezebel, who calls herself a prophetess, to teach my servants that sex sin is not a serious matter; she urges them to practice immorality and to eat meat that has been sacrificed to idols. 21I gave her time to change her mind and attitude, but she refused. 22Pay attention now to what I am saying: I will lay her upon a sickbed of intense affliction, along with all her immoral followers, unless they turn again to me, repenting of their sin with her; 23and I will strike her children dead. And all the churches shall know that I am he who searches deep within men's hearts, and minds; I will give to each of you whatever you deserve.

24,25"As for the rest of you in Thyatira who have not

followed this false teaching ('deeper truths,' as they call them—depths of Satan, really), I will ask nothing further of you; only hold tightly to what you have until I come.

26"To every one who overcomes—who to the very end keeps on doing things that please me—I will give power over the nations. 27You will rule them with a rod of iron just as my Father gave me the authority to rule them; they will be shattered like a pot of clay that is broken into tiny pieces. 28And I will give you the Morning Star!

29"Let all who can hear, listen to what the Spirit says to the churches.

A THOUGHT: *Obedience to Christ always involves a change of attitude. When we are converted, a battle begins inside us as Satan tries to keep us from changing. John records this example from Jezebel's life to show the importance of changes in attitude. Our attitudes powerfully influence our behavior. Which of your attitudes would Jesus highlight as needing change? If you're having trouble doing right in an area of your life, perhaps you need a change of attitude.*

Beware of False Teachers/ 2 Peter 2:12–22

But false teachers are fools—no better than animals. They do whatever they feel like; born only to be caught and killed, they laugh at the terrifying powers of the underworld which they know so little about; and they will be destroyed along with all the demons and powers of hell.

13That is the pay these teachers will have for their sin. For they live in evil pleasures day after day. They are a disgrace and a stain among you, deceiving you by living in foul sin on the side while they join your love feasts as though they were honest men. 14No woman can escape their sinful stare, and of adultery they never have enough. They make a game of luring unstable women. They train themselves to be greedy; and are doomed and cursed. 15They have gone off the road and become lost like Balaam, the son of Beor, who fell in love with the money he could make by doing wrong; 16but Balaam was stopped from his mad course when his donkey spoke to him with a human voice, scolding and rebuking him.

17These men are as useless as dried-up springs of water, promising much and delivering nothing; they are as unstable as clouds driven by the storm winds. They are doomed to the eternal pits of darkness. 18They proudly boast about their sins and conquests, and, using lust as their bait, they lure back into sin those who have just escaped from such wicked living.

19"You aren't saved by being good," they say, "so you might as well be bad. Do what you like, be free."

But these very teachers who offer this "freedom" from law are themselves slaves to sin and destruction. For a man is a slave to whatever controls him. 20And when a person has escaped from the wicked ways of the world by learning about our Lord and Savior Jesus Christ, and then gets tangled up with sin and becomes its slave again, he is worse off than he was before. 21It would be better if he had never known about Christ at all than to learn of him and then afterwards turn his back on the holy commandments that were given to him. 22There is an old saying that "A dog comes back to what he has vomited, and a pig is washed only to come back and wallow in the mud again." That is the way it is with those who turn again to their sin.

A THOUGHT: *Many believe freedom means doing anything you want. But no one is ever completely free in that sense. If we refuse to follow God, we will follow our own sinful desires and become enslaved to what our bodies want. If we submit our lives to Christ, he will free us from slavery to sin. Christ frees us to serve him, which always results in our ultimate good.*

Proverbs for Today/ 29:15–17

Scolding and spanking a child helps him to learn. Left to himself, he brings shame to his mother. □ When rulers are wicked, their people are too; but good men will live to see the tyrant's downfall. □ Discipline your son and he will give you happiness and peace of mind.

DECEMBER 9

The Letter to the Church in Sardis/
Revelation 3:1–6

"To the leader of the church in Sardis write this letter:
   "This message is sent to you by the one who has the

seven-fold Spirit of God and the seven stars.

"I know your reputation as a live and active church, but you are dead. 2Now wake up! Strengthen what little remains—for even what is left is at the point of death. Your deeds are far from right in the sight of God. 3Go back to what you heard and believed at first; hold to it firmly and turn to me again. Unless you do, I will come suddenly upon you, unexpected as a thief, and punish you.

4"Yet even there in Sardis some haven't soiled their garments with the world's filth; they shall walk with me in white, for they are worthy. 5Everyone who conquers will be clothed in white, and I will not erase his name from the Book of Life, but I will announce before my Father and his angels that he is mine.

6"Let all who can hear, listen to what the Spirit is saying to the churches.

A THOUGHT: *The church at Sardis was urged to hold on to the Christian truth they had heard when they first believed in Christ, to get back to the basics of the faith. It is important to grow in our knowledge of the Lord, to deepen our understanding through careful study. But no matter how much we learn, we must never abandon the basic truths about Jesus. Jesus will always be God's Son, and his sacrifice for our sins is permanent. No new truth from God will ever contradict these biblical teachings.*

Scoffers in the Last Days/ 2 Peter 3:1–7

This is my second letter to you, dear brothers, and in both of them I have tried to remind you—if you will let me—about facts you already know: facts you learned from the holy prophets and from us apostles who brought you the words of our Lord and Savior.

3First, I want to remind you that in the last days there will come scoffers who will do every wrong they can think of, and laugh at the truth. 4This will be their line of argument: "So Jesus promised to come back, did he? Then where is he? He'll never come! Why, as far back as anyone can remember everything has remained exactly as it was since the first day of creation."

5,6They deliberately forget this fact: that God did destroy the world with a mighty flood, long after he had made the heavens by the word of his command, and had used

the waters to form the earth and surround it. 7And God
has commanded that the earth and the heavens be stored
away for a great bonfire at the judgment day, when all
ungodly men will perish.

A THOUGHT: *Scoffers in the last days would say Jesus was never
coming back, but Peter refutes their argument by explaining God's
mastery over time. The "last days" are the time between Christ's
first and second comings; thus we, like Peter, live in the last days.
We must do the work to which God has called us and believe he
will return as he promised. God is not on man's time schedule,
but man is bound within God's schedule.*

Proverbs for Today/ 29:18

Where there is ignorance of God, crime runs wild; but
what a wonderful thing it is for a nation to know and
keep his laws.

DECEMBER 10

The Letter to the Church in Philadelphia/
Revelation 3:7–13

"Write this letter to the leader of the church in Philadelphia.

"This message is sent to you by the one who is holy
and true, and has the key of David to open what no one
can shut and to shut what no one can open.

8"I know you well; you aren't strong, but you have
tried to obey and have not denied my Name. Therefore
I have opened a door to you that no one can shut.

9"Note this: I will force those supporting the causes
of Satan while claiming to be mine (but they aren't—they
are lying) to fall at your feet and acknowledge that you
are the ones I love.

10"Because you have patiently obeyed me despite the
persecution, therefore I will protect you from the time
of Great Tribulation and temptation, which will come upon
the world to test everyone alive. 11Look, I am coming
soon! Hold tightly to the little strength you have—so that
no one will take away your crown.

12"As for the one who conquers, I will make him a

pillar in the temple of my God; he will be secure, and will go out no more; and I will write my God's Name on him, and he will be a citizen in the city of my God—the New Jerusalem, coming down from heaven from my God; and he will have my new Name inscribed upon him.

13"Let all who can hear, listen to what the Spirit is saying to the churches.

A THOUGHT: *Christians have differing gifts, abilities, experience, and maturity. God doesn't expect us all to be the same, but he does expect us to persevere in using our assets for him. The Philadelphians are commended for their effort to obey and encouraged to hold tightly to whatever strength they have. You may be a new believer and feel that your faith and spiritual strength are small. Use what you have to live for Christ, and God will commend you.*

The Day of the Lord/ 2 Peter 3:8–13

But don't forget this, dear friends, that a day or a thousand years from now is like tomorrow to the Lord. 9He isn't really being slow about his promised return, even though it sometimes seems that way. But he is waiting, for the good reason that he is not willing that any should perish, and he is giving more time for sinners to repent. 10The day of the Lord is surely coming, as unexpectedly as a thief, and then the heavens will pass away with a terrible noise and the heavenly bodies will disappear in fire, and the earth and everything on it will be burned up.

11And so since everything around us is going to melt away, what holy, godly lives we should be living! 12You should look forward to that day and hurry it along—the day when God will set the heavens on fire, and the heavenly bodies will melt and disappear in flames. 13But we are looking forward to God's promise of new heavens and a new earth afterwards, where there will be only goodness.

A THOUGHT: *God may have seemed slow in keeping his promise of return to these believers as they faced persecution every day and longed to be delivered. But God is not slow; he just is not on our timetable. Jesus is waiting so that more sinners will repent and turn to him. We must not sit and wait for him, but live with the realization that time is short and we have important work to do. Be ready to meet him any time, even today; yet plan your course of service as if he may not return for many years.*

Proverbs for Today/ 29:19–20
Sometimes mere words are not enough—discipline is needed. For the words may not be heeded. □ There is more hope for a fool than for a man of quick temper.

DECEMBER 11

The Letter to the Church in Laodicea/
Revelation 3:14–22

"Write this letter to the leader of the church in Laodicea:
"This message is from the one who stands firm, the faithful and true Witness [of all that is or was or evermore shall be], the primeval source of God's creation:

15"I know you well—you are neither hot nor cold; I wish you were one or the other! 16But since you are merely lukewarm, I will spit you out of my mouth!

17"You say, 'I am rich, with everything I want; I don't need a thing!' And you don't realize that spiritually you are wretched and miserable and poor and blind and naked.

18"My advice to you is to buy pure gold from me, gold purified by fire—only then will you truly be rich. And to purchase from me white garments, clean and pure, so you won't be naked and ashamed; and to get medicine from me to heal your eyes and give you back your sight. 19I continually discipline and punish everyone I love; so I must punish you, unless you turn from your indifference and become enthusiastic about the things of God.

20"Look! I have been standing at the door and I am constantly knocking. If anyone hears me calling him and opens the door, I will come in and fellowship with him and he with me. 21I will let every one who conquers sit beside me on my throne, just as I took my place with my Father on his throne when I had conquered. 22Let those who can hear, listen to what the Spirit is saying to the churches."

A THOUGHT: *Some believers falsely assume that an abundance of material possessions is a sign of God's spiritual blessing. Laodicea was a wealthy city, and the church was also wealthy. But what the Laodiceans could see and buy had become more valuable to them than what is unseen and eternal. Wealth, luxury, and ease can make people feel confident, satisfied, and complacent. But no matter how much you possess or how much money you make, you have nothing if you don't have a vital relationship with Christ. How does your current level of wealth affect your spiritual desire? Instead of centering your life primarily on comfort and luxury, find your true riches in Christ.*

Prepare For Christ's Coming/ 2 Peter 3:14–18

Dear friends, while you are waiting for these things to happen and for him to come, try hard to live without sinning; and be at peace with everyone so that he will be pleased with you when he returns.

15,16And remember why he is waiting. He is giving us time to get his message of salvation out to others. Our wise and beloved brother Paul has talked about these same things in many of his letters. Some of his comments are not easy to understand, and there are people who are deliberately stupid, and always demand some unusual interpretation—they have twisted his letters around to mean something quite different from what he meant, just as they do the other parts of the Scripture—and the result is disaster for them.

17I am warning you ahead of time, dear brothers, so that you can watch out and not be carried away by the mistakes of these wicked men, lest you yourselves become mixed up too. 18But grow in spiritual strength and become better acquainted with our Lord and Savior Jesus Christ. To him be all glory and splendid honor, both now and forevermore. Good-bye.

Peter

A THOUGHT: *We should not become lazy and complacent because Christ has not yet returned. Instead, our lives should express our eager expectation of his coming. What would you like to be doing when Christ returns? Is that the way you are living each day?*

Proverbs for Today/ 29:21–22

Pamper a servant from childhood, and he will expect you to treat him as a son! □ A hot-tempered man starts fights and gets into all kinds of trouble.

DECEMBER 12

A Vision of God's Throne/ Revelation 4:1–11

Then as I looked, I saw a door standing open in heaven, and the same voice I had heard before, that sounded like a mighty trumpet blast, spoke to me and said, "Come up here and I will show you what must happen in the future!"

2And instantly I was, in spirit, there in heaven and saw—oh, the glory of it!—a throne and someone sitting on it! 3Great bursts of light flashed forth from him as from a glittering diamond, or from a shining ruby, and a rainbow glowing like an emerald encircled his throne. 4Twenty-four smaller thrones surrounded his, with twenty-four Elders sitting on them; all were clothed in white, with golden crowns upon their heads. 5Lightning and thunder issued from the throne, and there were voices in the thunder. Directly in front of his throne were seven lighted lamps representing the seven-fold Spirit of God. 6Spread out before it was a shiny crystal sea. Four Living Beings, dotted front and back with eyes, stood at the throne's four sides. 7The first of these Living Beings was in the form of a lion; the second looked like an ox; the third had the face of a man; and the fourth, the form of an eagle, with wings spread out as though in flight. 8Each of these Living Beings had six wings, and the central sections of their wings were covered with eyes. Day after day and night after night they kept on saying, "Holy, holy, holy, Lord God Almighty—the one who was, and is, and is to come."

9And when the Living Beings gave glory and honor and thanks to the one sitting on the throne, who lives forever and ever, 10the twenty-four Elders fell down before him and worshiped him, the Eternal Living One, and cast their crowns before the throne, singing, 11"O Lord, you are worthy to receive the glory and the honor and the power, for you have created all things. They were created and called into being by your act of will."

A THOUGHT: *Who are these 24 elders? Since there were 12 tribes of Israel in the Old Testament and 12 apostles in the New Testament, the 24 elders in this vision probably represent all the redeemed of*

God for all time (both before and after Christ's death and resurrection). They symbolize all those—both Jews and Gentiles—who are now part of God's family. The 24 elders show us that all the redeemed of the Lord are worshiping him—all beings in heaven and earth will praise and honor God because he is the Creator and Sustainer of everything.

An Eyewitness of the Incarnate Christ/ 1 John 1:1–4

Christ was alive when the world began, yet I myself have seen him with my own eyes and listened to him speak. I have touched him with my own hands. He is God's message of life. 2This one who is life from God has been shown to us and we guarantee that we have seen him; I am speaking of Christ, who is eternal Life. He was with the Father and then was shown to us. 3Again I say, we are telling you about what we ourselves have actually seen and heard, so that you may share the fellowship and the joys we have with the Father and with Jesus Christ his son. 4And if you do as I say in this letter, then you, too, will be full of joy, and so will we.

A THOUGHT: *As an eyewitness to Jesus' ministry, John was qualified to teach the truth about him. The readers of this letter had not seen and heard Jesus themselves, but they could trust that what John wrote was accurate. We are like those second- and third-generation Christians. Though we have not personally seen, heard, or touched Jesus, we have the New Testament record of his eyewitnesses, and we can trust that they spoke the truth about him.*

Proverbs for Today/ 29:23

Pride ends in a fall, while humility brings honor.

DECEMBER 13

The Scroll and the Lamb/ Revelation 5:1–14

And I saw a scroll in the right hand of the one who was sitting on the throne, a scroll with writing on the inside and on the back, and sealed with seven seals. 2A mighty angel with a loud voice was shouting out this question: "Who is worthy to break the seals on this scroll, and to unroll it?" ³But no one in all heaven or earth or from among the dead was permitted to open and read it.

⁴Then I wept with disappointment because no one anywhere was worthy; no one could tell us what it said.

⁵But one of the twenty-four Elders said to me, "Stop crying, for look! The Lion of the tribe of Judah, the Root of David, has conquered, and proved himself worthy to open the scroll and to break its seven seals."

⁶I looked and saw a Lamb standing there before the twenty-four Elders, in front of the throne and the Living Beings, and on the Lamb were wounds that once had caused his death. He had seven horns and seven eyes, which represent the seven-fold Spirit of God, sent out into every part of the world. ⁷He stepped forward and took the scroll from the right hand of the one sitting upon the throne. ⁸And as he took the scroll, the twenty-four Elders fell down before the Lamb, each with a harp and golden vials filled with incense—the prayers of God's people!

⁹They were singing him a new song with these words: "You are worthy to take the scroll and break its seals and open it; for you were slain, and your blood has bought people from every nation as gifts for God. ¹⁰And you have gathered them into a kingdom and made them priests of our God; they shall reign upon the earth."

¹¹Then in my vision I heard the singing of millions of angels surrounding the throne and the Living Beings and the Elders: ¹²"The Lamb is worthy" (loudly they sang it!) "—the Lamb who was slain. He is worthy to receive the power, and the riches, and the wisdom, and the strength, and the honor, and the glory, and the blessing."

¹³And then I heard everyone in heaven and earth, and from the dead beneath the earth and in the sea, exclaiming, "The blessing and the honor and the glory and the power belong to the one sitting on the throne, and to the Lamb forever and ever." ¹⁴And the four Living Beings kept saying, "Amen!" And the twenty-four Elders fell down and worshiped him.

A THOUGHT: *Jesus Christ is pictured as both a Lion (symbolizing his authority and power) and a Lamb (symbolizing his humble submission to God's will). One of the Elders calls John to look at the Lion, but when John looks he sees a Lamb. It is the Lamb, not the Lion, that becomes the focus in this vision. Christ the Lamb was the perfect sacrifice for the sins of all mankind; therefore, only he can save us from the terrible events revealed by the scroll. Christ the Lamb won the greatest battle of all—defeating all the forces of evil and death by submitting humbly to God's will and dying on the cross, the perfect sacrifice for sin. Christ the Lion will be victorious because of what Christ the Lamb has already done. We will enjoy the rewards of victory not because of our power and might, but because we belong to God.*

Forgiveness through the Blood of Jesus/ 1 John 1:5–10

This is the message God has given us to pass on to you: that God is Light and in him is no darkness at all. 6So if we say we are his friends, but go on living in spiritual darkness and sin, we are lying. 7But if we are living in the light of God's presence, just as Christ does, then we have wonderful fellowship and joy with each other, and the blood of Jesus his Son cleanses us from every sin.

8If we say that we have no sin, we are only fooling ourselves, and refusing to accept the truth. 9But if we confess our sins to him, he can be depended on to forgive us and to cleanse us from every wrong. [And it is perfectly proper for God to do this for us because Christ died to wash away our sins.] 10If we claim we have not sinned, we are lying and calling God a liar, *for he says we have sinned.*

A THOUGHT: *Confession is supposed to free us to enjoy fellowship with Christ. It should ease our consciences and lighten our cares. But some Christians do not understand how it works. They feel so guilty that they confess the same sins over and over, and then wonder if they might have forgotten something. Other Christians believe God forgives them when they confess their sins, but if they died with unconfessed sins, they would be forever lost. These Christians do not understand that God wants to forgive us. He allowed his beloved Son to die just so he could pardon us. When we come to Christ, he forgives all the sins we have committed or will ever commit. We don't need to confess the same sins all over again, and we don't need to fear that he will cast us out if we don't keep our slate perfectly clear at all moments. Of course we want to continue to confess our sins, but not because we think failure to do so will make us lose our salvation. Our hope in Christ is secure. Instead, we confess our sins so that we can enjoy maximum fellowship and joy with him.*

True confession also involves a commitment not to continue in sin. We are not genuinely confessing our sins before God if we

*plan to commit the sin again and just want temporary forgiveness.
We must pray for strength to defeat the temptation the next time it
appears.*

Proverbs for Today/ 29:24–25

A man who assists a thief must really hate himself! For
he knows the consequence but does it anyway. □ Fear
of man is a dangerous trap, but to trust in God means
safety.

DECEMBER 14

The Lamb Opens the Seals/ Revelation 6:1–17

As I watched, the Lamb broke the first seal and began
to unroll the scroll. Then one of the four Living Beings,
with a voice that sounded like thunder, said, "Come!"

2I looked, and there in front of me was a white horse.
Its rider carried a bow, and a crown was placed upon
his head; he rode out to conquer in many battles and
win the war.

3Then he unrolled the scroll to the second seal, and
broke it open too. And I heard the second Living Being
say, "Come!"

4This time a red horse rode out. Its rider was given a
long sword and the authority to banish peace and bring
anarchy to the earth; war and killing broke out everywhere.

5When he had broken the third seal, I heard the third
Living Being say, "Come!" And I saw a black horse, with
its rider holding a pair of balances in his hand. 6And a
voice from among the four Living Beings said, "A loaf of
bread for $20, or three pounds of barley flour, but there
is no olive oil or wine."

7And when the fourth seal was broken, I heard the
fourth Living Being say, "Come!" 8And now I saw a pale
horse, and its rider's name was Death. And there followed
after him another horse whose rider's name was Hell.
They were given control of one-fourth of the earth, to
kill with war and famine and disease and wild animals.

9And when he broke open the fifth seal, I saw an altar, and underneath it all the souls of those who had been martyred for preaching the Word of God and for being faithful in their witnessing. 10They called loudly to the Lord and said, "O Sovereign Lord, holy and true, how long will it be before you judge the people of the earth for what they've done to us? When will you avenge our blood against those living on the earth?" 11White robes were given to each of them, and they were told to rest a little longer until their other brothers, fellow servants of Jesus, had been martyred on the earth and joined them.

12I watched as he broke the sixth seal, and there was a vast earthquake; and the sun became dark like black cloth, and the moon was blood-red. 13Then the stars of heaven appeared to be falling to earth—like green fruit from fig trees buffeted by mighty winds. 14And the starry heavens disappeared as though rolled up like a scroll and taken away; and every mountain and island shook and shifted. 15The kings of the earth, and world leaders and rich men, and high-ranking military officers, and all men great and small, slave and free, hid themselves in the caves and rocks of the mountains, 16and cried to the mountains to crush them. "Fall on us," they pleaded, "and hide us from the face of the one sitting on the throne, and from the anger of the Lamb, 17because the great day of their anger has come, and who can survive it?"

A THOUGHT: *Four horses appear as the first four seals are broken. The horses represent God's judgment of peoples' sin and rebellion. God is directing human history—even using his enemies to unknowingly accomplish his purposes. The four horsemen are given control of one-fourth of the earth, indicating that God is still limiting his judgment—it is not yet complete. With these judgments there is still time for people to turn to Christ and away from their sin. In this case, the limited punishment not only demonstrates God's wrath against sin, but also his merciful love in giving people yet another opportunity to turn to him before he brings final judgment.*

Our Advocate before the Father/ 1 John 2:1–6

My little children, I am telling you this so that you will stay away from sin. But if you sin, there is someone to plead for you before the Father. His name is Jesus Christ, the one who is all that is good and who pleases God completely. 2He is the one who took God's wrath against our sins upon himself, and brought us into fellowship with God; and he is the forgiveness for our sins, and not only ours but all the world's.

3And how can we be sure that we belong to him? By looking within ourselves: are we really trying to do what he wants us to?

4Someone may say, "I am a Christian; I am on my way to heaven; I belong to Christ." But if he doesn't do what Christ tells him to, he is a liar. 5But those who do what Christ tells them to will learn to love God more and more. That is the way to know whether or not you are a Christian. 6Anyone who says he is a Christian should live as Christ did.

A THOUGHT: *To people who are feeling guilty and condemned, John offers reassurance. They know they have sinned, and Satan (called "the Accuser of our brothers" in Revelation 12:10) is demanding the death penalty. When you feel this way, don't give up hope— the best defense attorney in the universe is pleading your case. Jesus Christ, your advocate, is the Judge's Son. He has already suffered the Judge's penalty in your place. You can't be tried again for a case that is no longer on the docket. United with Jesus, you are as safe as he is. Don't be afraid to ask him to plead your case—he has already won it.*

Proverbs for Today/ 29:26–27

Do you want justice? Don't fawn on the judge, but ask the Lord for it! □ The good hate the badness of the wicked. The wicked hate the goodness of the good.

DECEMBER 15

144,000 Are Marked by God/ Revelation 7:1–17

Then I saw four angels standing at the four corners of the earth, holding back the four winds from blowing, so that not a leaf rustled in the trees, and the ocean became as smooth as glass. 2And I saw another angel coming from the east, carrying the Great Seal of the Living God. And he shouted out to those four angels who had been given power to injure earth and sea, 3"Wait! Don't do anything yet—hurt neither earth nor sea nor trees—until we have placed the Seal of God upon the foreheads of his servants."

4-8How many were given this mark? I heard the number—it was 144,000; out of all twelve tribes of Israel, as listed here:

Judah	12,000
Reuben	12,000
Gad	12,000
Asher	12,000
Naphtali	12,000
Manasseh	12,000
Simeon	12,000
Levi	12,000
Issachar	12,000
Zebulun	12,000
Joseph	12,000
Benjamin	12,000

9After this I saw a vast crowd, too great to count, from all nations and provinces and languages, standing in front of the throne and before the Lamb, clothed in white, with palm branches in their hands. 10And they were shouting with a mighty shout, "Salvation comes from our God upon the throne, and from the Lamb."

11And now all the angels were crowding around the throne and around the Elders and the four Living Beings, and falling face down before the throne and worshiping God. 12"Amen!" they said. "Blessing, and glory, and wisdom, and thanksgiving, and honor, and power, and might, be to our God forever and forever. Amen!"

13Then one of the twenty-four Elders asked me, "Do you know who these are, who are clothed in white, and where they come from?"

14"No, sir," I replied. "Please tell me."

"These are the ones coming out of the Great Tribulation," he said; "they washed their robes and whitened them by the blood of the Lamb. 15That is why they are here before the throne of God, serving him day and night in his temple. The one sitting on the throne will shelter them; 16they will never be hungry again, nor thirsty, and they will be fully protected from the scorching noontime heat. 17For the Lamb standing in front of the throne will feed them and be their Shepherd and lead them to the springs of the Water of Life. And God will wipe their tears away."

A THOUGHT: *People try many methods to remove the guilt of sin— good works, intellectual pursuits, and even casting blame. The crowd in heaven however, praises God, saying, "Salvation comes from our God upon the throne, and from the Lamb." Salvation from sin's penalty can come only through Jesus Christ. Have you had the guilt of sin removed in the only way possible?*

Love One Another/ 1 John 2:7–11

Dear brothers, I am not writing out a new rule for you to obey, for it is an old one you have always had, right from the start. You have heard it all before. 8Yet it is always new, and works for you just as it did for Christ; and as we obey this commandment, *to love one another,* the darkness in our lives disappears and the new light of life in Christ shines in.

9Anyone who says he is walking in the light of Christ but dislikes his fellow man, is still in darkness. 10But whoever loves his fellow man is "walking in the light" and can see his way without stumbling around in darkness and sin. 11For he who dislikes his brother is wandering in spiritual darkness and doesn't know where he is going, for the darkness has made him blind so that he cannot see the way.

A THOUGHT: *The commandment to love is both old and new. It is old because it comes from the Old Testament, but it is new because Jesus interpreted it in a radically new way. In the Christian Church, love goes beyond respect to self-sacrifice and servanthood. In fact, it can be defined as "selfless giving." It reaches beyond friends to enemies and persecutors. Love should be the unifying force and the identifying mark of the Christian community. It is the key to walking in the light, because we cannot grow spiritually while we hate others. A growing relationship with God results in growing relationships with others.*

Proverbs for Today/ 30:1–4

These are the messages of Agur, son of Jakeh addressed to Ithiel and Ucal: I am tired out, O God, and ready to die. I am too stupid even to call myself a human being! I cannot understand man, let alone God. Who else but God goes back and forth to heaven? Who else holds the wind in his fists, and wraps up the oceans in his cloak? Who but God has created the world? If there is any other, what is his name—and his Son's name—if you know it?

DECEMBER 16

The Seventh Seal and the Trumpets/
Revelation 8:1-13

When the Lamb had broken the seventh seal, there was silence throughout all heaven for what seemed like half an hour. 2And I saw the seven angels that stand before God, and they were given seven trumpets.

3Then another angel with a golden censer came and stood at the altar; and a great quantity of incense was given to him to mix with the prayers of God's people, to offer upon the golden altar before the throne. 4And the perfume of the incense mixed with prayers ascended up to God from the altar where the angel had poured them out.

5Then the angel filled the censer with fire from the altar and threw it down upon the earth; and thunder crashed and rumbled, lightning flashed, and there was a terrible earthquake.

6Then the seven angels with the seven trumpets prepared to blow their mighty blasts.

7The first angel blew his trumpet, and hail and fire mixed with blood were thrown down upon the earth. One-third of the earth was set on fire so that one-third of the trees were burned, and all the green grass.

8,9Then the second angel blew his trumpet, and what appeared to be a huge burning mountain was thrown into the sea, destroying a third of all the ships; and a third of the sea turned red as blood; and a third of the fish were killed.

10The third angel blew, and a great flaming star fell from heaven upon a third of the rivers and springs. 11The star was called "Bitterness" because it poisoned a third of all the water on the earth and many people died.

12The fourth angel blew his trumpet and immediately

a third of the sun was blighted and darkened, and a third of the moon and the stars, so that the daylight was dimmed by a third, and the nighttime darkness deepened. 13As I watched, I saw a solitary eagle flying through the heavens crying loudly, "Woe, woe, woe to the people of the earth because of the terrible things that will soon happen when the three remaining angels blow their trumpets."

A THOUGHT: *When the seventh seal is opened, the seven trumpet judgments are revealed. The trumpet judgments, like the seal judgments, are only partial. God's final and complete judgment has not yet come. In God's mercy, he is drawing out his judgment in order that there will be sufficient time for people to repent and turn to him for salvation. If justice seems to be long in coming, we must learn to be patient, it is God's mercy that brings delay. Judgment is coming—be sure of that. We should thank God for the time he gives us to turn from sin, and work to help others turn as well.*

Do Not Love This Evil World/ 1 John 2:12–17

I am writing these things to all of you, my little children, because your sins have been forgiven in the name of Jesus our Savior. 13I am saying these things to you older men because you really know Christ, the one who has been alive from the beginning. And you young men, I am talking to you because you have won your battle with Satan. And I am writing to you younger boys and girls because you, too, have learned to know God our Father.

14And so I say to you fathers who know the eternal God, and to you young men who are strong, with God's Word in your hearts, and have won your struggle against Satan: 15Stop loving this evil world and all that it offers you, for when you love these things you show that you do not really love God; 16for all these worldly things, these evil desires—the craze for sex, the ambition to buy everything that appeals to you, and the pride that comes from wealth and importance—these are not from God. They are from this evil world itself. 17And this world is fading away, and these evil, forbidden things will go with it, but whoever keeps doing the will of God will live forever.

A THOUGHT: *Some people think worldliness has to do with external behavior—the people we associate with, the places we go, the activities in which we participate. This is not entirely accurate, for worldliness begins in the heart. It is characterized by these three attitudes: (1) lust—preoccupation with gratifying physical desires; (2) mate-*

rialism—craving and accumulating things, and (3) pride—obsession with one's status or importance. When the serpent tempted Eve, he tempted her in these areas. Also, when the devil tempted Jesus in the wilderness, these were his three areas of attack. By contrast, God values self-control, a spirit of generosity, and humble service. It is possible to avoid "worldly pleasures" while still harboring worldly attitudes in one's heart. It is also possible, like Jesus, to love sinners and spend time with them while maintaining the values of God's Kingdom. What values are most important to you? Do your actions reflect the world's values or God's values?

Proverbs for Today/ 30:5–6

Every word of God proves true. He defends all who come to him for protection. Do not add to his words, lest he rebuke you, and you be found a liar.

DECEMBER 17

Trumpets Announce God's Judgment/
Revelation 9:1–21

Then the fifth angel blew his trumpet and I saw one who was fallen to earth from heaven, and to him was given the key to the bottomless pit. 2When he opened it, smoke poured out as though from some huge furnace, and the sun and air were darkened by the smoke.

3Then locusts came from the smoke and descended onto the earth and were given power to sting like scorpions. 4They were told not to hurt the grass or plants or trees, but to attack those people who did not have the mark of God on their foreheads. 5They were not to kill them, but to torture them for five months with agony like the pain of scorpion stings. 6In those days men will try to kill themselves but won't be able to—death will not come. They will long to die—but death will flee away!

7The locusts looked like horses armored for battle. They had what looked like golden crowns on their heads, and their faces looked like men's. 8Their hair was long like women's, and their teeth were those of lions. 9They wore breastplates that seemed to be of iron, and their wings roared like an army of chariots rushing into battle. 10They had stinging tails like scorpions, and their power to hurt, given to them for five months, was in their tails. 11 Their king is the Prince of the bottomless pit whose name in Hebrew is Abaddon, and in Greek, Apollyon [and in English, the Destroyer]

12One terror now ends, but there are two more coming!

13The sixth angel blew his trumpet and I heard a voice speaking from the four horns of the golden altar that stands before the throne of God, 14saying to the sixth angel, "Release the four mighty demons held bound at the great River Euphrates." 15They had been kept in readiness for that year and month and day and hour, and now they were turned loose to kill a third of all mankind. 16They led an army of 200,000,000 warriors—I heard an announcement of how many there were.

17,18I saw their horses spread out before me in my vision; their riders wore fiery-red breastplates, though some were sky-blue and others yellow. The horses' heads looked much like lions', and smoke and fire and flaming sulphur billowed from their mouths, killing one-third of all mankind. 19Their power of death was not only in their mouths, but in their tails as well, for their tails were similar to serpents' heads that struck and bit with fatal wounds.

20But the men left alive after these plagues *still refused to worship God!* They would not renounce their demon-worship, nor their idols made of gold and silver, brass, stone, and wood—which neither see nor hear nor walk! 21Neither did they change their mind and attitude about all their murders and witchcraft, their immorality and theft.

A THOUGHT: *All the judgments God had sent to the earth were not enough to bring these people to repentance. People don't usually fall into immorality and evil suddenly—they slip into it a little at a time until, hardly realizing what has happened, they are irrevocably mired in their wicked ways. Those who allow sin to take root in their lives can find themselves in this predicament. Temptation entertained today becomes sin tomorrow, then a habit the next day, then death and separation from God forever. To think you could never become this evil is the first step toward becoming hard hearted.*

The Antichrist/ 1 John 2:18–27

Dear children, this world's last hour has come. You have heard about the Antichrist who is coming—the one who is against Christ—and already many such persons have appeared. This makes us all the more certain that the end of the world is near. 19These "against-Christ" people used to be members of our churches, but they never really belonged with us or else they would have stayed. When they left us it proved that they were not of us at all.

20But you are not like that, for the Holy Spirit has come upon you, and you know the truth. 21So I am not writing to you as to those who need to know the truth, but I warn you as those who can discern the difference between true and false.

22And who is the greatest liar? The one who says that Jesus is not Christ. Such a person is antichrist, for he does not believe in God the Father and in his Son. 23For a person who doesn't believe in Christ, God's Son, can't have God the Father either. But he who has Christ, God's Son, has God the Father also.

24So keep on believing what you have been taught from the beginning. If you do, you will always be in close fellowship with both God the Father and his Son. 25And he himself has promised us this: *eternal life.*

26These remarks of mine about the Antichrist are pointed at those who would dearly love to blindfold you and lead you astray. 27But you have received the Holy Spirit and he lives within you, in your hearts, so that you don't need anyone to teach you what is right. For he teaches you all things, and he is the Truth, and no liar; and so, just as he has said, you must live in Christ, never to depart from him.

A THOUGHT: *John is talking about the "last days," the time between Christ's first and second comings. The first-century readers of 1 John lived in the last days, and so do we. During this time, "anti-christs" (false teachers who pretend to be Christians and lure weak members away from Christ) will appear. Finally, just before the world ends, one great Antichrist will arise. We do not need to fear these evil people, however. The Holy Spirit shows us their errors, so we are not deceived. However, we must teach the Word of God clearly and carefully to the peripheral, weak members among us so they won't fall prey to these teachers "who come disguised as harmless sheep, but are wolves" (Matthew 7:15).*

Proverbs for Today/ 30:7–9

O God, I beg two favors from you before I die: First, help me never to tell a lie. Second, give me neither poverty

nor riches! Give me just enough to satisfy my needs!
For if I grow rich, I may become content without God.
And if I am too poor, I may steal, and thus insult God's
holy name.

DECEMBER 18

A Small Scroll/ Revelation 10:1–11

Then I saw another mighty angel coming down from heaven,
surrounded by a cloud, with a rainbow over his head;
his face shone like the sun and his feet flashed with fire.
2And he held open in his hand a small scroll. He set his
right foot on the sea and his left foot on the earth, 3and
gave a great shout—it was like the roar of a lion—and
the seven thunders crashed their reply.

4I was about to write what the thunders said when a
voice from heaven called to me, "Don't do it. Their words
are not to be revealed."

5Then the mighty angel standing on the sea and land
lifted his right hand to heaven, 6and swore by him who
lives forever and ever, who created heaven and everything
in it and the earth and all that it contains and the sea
and its inhabitants, that there should be no more delay,
7but that when the seventh angel blew his trumpet, then
God's veiled plan—mysterious through the ages ever since
it was announced by his servants the prophets—would
be fulfilled.

8Then the voice from heaven spoke to me again, "Go
and get the unrolled scroll from the mighty angel standing
there upon the sea and land."

9So I approached him and asked him to give me the
scroll. "Yes, take it and eat it," he said. "At first it will
taste like honey, but when you swallow it, it will make
your stomach sour!" 10So I took it from his hand, and
ate it! And just as he had said, it was sweet in my mouth
but it gave me a stomach ache when I swallowed it.

11Then he told me, "You must prophesy further about
many peoples, nations, tribes, and kings."

A Thought: *Throughout history people have wanted to know what would happen in the future, and God reveals some of it in this book. But John was stopped from revealing certain parts of his vision. An angel also told the prophet Daniel that some things he saw were not to be revealed yet to everyone, and Jesus told his disciples that the time of the end is known by no one but God. God has revealed all we need to know to live for him now. In our desire to be ready for the end, we must live holy lives before God, not speculation about the details and timing of the last days.*

We Are God's Children/ 1 John 2:28—3:6

And now, my little children, stay in happy fellowship with the Lord so that when he comes you will be sure that all is well, and will not have to be ashamed and shrink back from meeting him. 29Since we know that God is always good and does only right, we may rightly assume that all those who do right are his children.

3:1See how very much our heavenly Father loves us, for he allows us to be called his children—think of it—and we really *are!* But since most people don't know God, naturally they don't understand that we are his children. 2Yes, dear friends, we are already God's children, right now, and we can't even imagine what it is going to be like later on. But we do know this, that when he comes we will be like him, as a result of seeing him as he really is. 3And everyone who really believes this will try to stay pure because Christ is pure.

4But those who keep on sinning are against God, for every sin is done against the will of God. 5And you know that he became a man so that he could take away our sins, and that there is no sin in him, no missing of God's will at any time in any way. 6So if we stay close to him, obedient to him, we won't be sinning either; but as for those who keep on sinning, they should realize this: They sin because they have never really known him or become his.

A Thought: *The visible proof of being a Christian is right behavior. Many people do some good things but don't have faith in Jesus Christ. Others claim to have faith but rarely produce good works. A deficit in either faith or right behavior is cause for shame when Christ returns. Because true faith always results in good works, those who claim to have faith and who consistently live rightly are true believers. Good works cannot produce salvation, but they are necessary proof that true faith has actually occurred.*

Proverbs for Today/ 30:10
Never falsely accuse a man to his employer, lest he curse you for your sin.

DECEMBER 19

Two Witnesses/ Revelation 11:1–19

Now I was given a measuring stick and told to go and measure the temple of God, including the inner court where the altar stands, and to count the number of worshipers. 2"But do not measure the outer court," I was told, "for it has been turned over to the nations. They will trample the Holy City for forty-two months. 3And I will give power to my two witnesses to prophesy 1,260 days clothed in sackcloth."

4These two prophets are the two olive trees, and two candlesticks standing before the God of all the earth. 5Anyone trying to harm them will be killed by bursts of fire shooting from their mouths. 6They have power to shut the skies so that no rain will fall during the three and a half years they prophesy, and to turn rivers and oceans to blood, and to send every kind of plague upon the earth as often as they wish.

7When they complete the three and a half years of their solemn testimony, the tyrant who comes out of the bottomless pit will declare war against them and conquer and kill them; 8,9and for three and a half days their bodies will be exposed in the streets of Jerusalem (the city fittingly described as "Sodom" or "Egypt")—the very place where their Lord was crucified. No one will be allowed to bury them, and people from many nations will crowd around to gaze at them. 10And there will be a worldwide holiday—people everywhere will rejoice and give presents to each other and throw parties to celebrate the death of the two prophets who had tormented them so much!

11But after three and a half days, the spirit of life from God will enter them and they will stand up! And great fear will fall on everyone. 12Then a loud voice will shout from heaven, "Come up!" And they will rise to heaven in a cloud as their enemies watch.

13The same hour there will be a terrible earthquake that levels a tenth of the city, leaving 7,000 dead. Then everyone left will, in their terror, give glory to the God of heaven.

14The second woe is past, but the third quickly follows:

15For just then the seventh angel blew his trumpet, and there were loud voices shouting down from heaven, "The Kingdom of this world now belongs to our Lord, and to his Christ; and he shall reign forever and ever."

16And the twenty-four Elders sitting on their thrones before God threw themselves down in worship, saying, 17"We give thanks, Lord God Almighty, who is and was, for now you have assumed your great power and have begun to reign. 18The nations were angry with you, but now it is your turn to be angry with them. It is time to judge the dead, and reward your servants—prophets and people alike, all who fear your Name, both great and small—and to destroy those who have caused destruction upon the earth."

19Then, in heaven, the temple of God was opened and the ark of his covenant could be seen inside. Lightning flashed and thunder crashed and roared, and there was a great hailstorm and the world was shaken by a mighty earthquake.

A THOUGHT: *The whole world rejoices at the deaths of these two prophets, who have caused trouble by saying what the people didn't want to hear—words about their sin, their need for repentance, and the coming punishment. Sinful people hate those who call attention to their sin and who urge them to repent. They hated Christ, and they hate his followers. When you obey Christ and take a stand against sin, be prepared to draw the world's hatred. But remember that the great reward awaiting you in heaven far outweighs any suffering you face now.*

God's Children Do Not Continue in Sin/ 1 John 3:7–11

Oh, dear children, don't let anyone deceive you about this: if you are constantly doing what is good, it is because you *are* good, even as he is. 8But if you keep on sinning, it shows that you belong to Satan, who since he first began to sin has kept steadily at it. But the Son of God came to destroy these works of the devil. 9The person who has been born into God's family does not make a practice of sinning, because now God's life is in him; so he can't keep on sinning, for this new life has been born into him and controls him—he has been *born again.*

10So now we can tell who is a child of God and who belongs to Satan. Whoever is living a life of sin and doesn't love his brother shows that he is not in God's family; 11for the message to us from the beginning has been that we should love one another.

A THOUGHT: *There is a difference between committing a sin and remaining in sin. We all have areas where temptation is strong and habits are hard to conquer. We all struggle with particular sins, however, these verses are not directed at us, even if for the time we seem to "keep on sinning." John is not talking about people whose victories are still incomplete; he is talking about people who make a practice of sinning and look for ways to justify it.*

Three steps are necessary to find victory over prevailing sin: (1) one must seek the power of the Holy Spirit and the Word of God; (2) one must flee lustful desires; and (3) one needs the help of the body of Christ—accountability to others and the prayers of others.

Proverbs for Today/ 30:11–14

There are those who curse their father and mother, and feel themselves faultless despite their many sins. They are proud beyond description, arrogant, disdainful. They devour the poor with teeth as sharp as knives!

DECEMBER 20

The Woman and the Dragon/ Revelation 12:1–17

Then a great pageant appeared in heaven, portraying things to come. I saw a woman clothed with the sun, with the moon beneath her feet, and a crown of twelve stars on her head. 2She was pregnant and screamed in the pain of her labor, awaiting her delivery.

3Suddenly a red Dragon appeared, with seven heads and ten horns, and seven crowns on his heads. 4His tail drew along behind him a third of the stars, which he plunged to the earth. He stood before the woman as she was about to give birth to her child, ready to eat the baby as soon as it was born.

5She gave birth to a boy who was to rule all nations with a heavy hand, and he was caught up to God and to his throne. 6The woman fled into the wilderness, where God had prepared a place for her, to take care of her for 1,260 days.

7Then there was war in heaven; Michael and the angels under his command fought the Dragon and his hosts of fallen angels. 8And the Dragon lost the battle and was forced from heaven. 9This great Dragon—the ancient serpent called the devil, or Satan, the one deceiving the whole world—was thrown down onto the earth with all his army.

10Then I heard a loud voice shouting across the heavens, "It has happened at last! God's salvation and the power and the rule, and the authority of his Christ are finally here; for the Accuser of our brothers has been thrown down from heaven onto earth—he accused them day and night before our God. 11They defeated him by the blood of the Lamb, and by their testimony; for they did not love their lives but laid them down for him. 12Rejoice, O heavens! You citizens of heaven, rejoice! Be glad! But woe to you people of the world, for the devil has come down to you in great anger, knowing that he has little time."

13And when the Dragon found himself cast down to earth, he persecuted the woman who had given birth to the child. 14But she was given two wings like those of a great eagle, to fly into the wilderness to the place prepared for her, where she was cared for and protected from the Serpent, the Dragon, for three and a half years.

15And from the Serpent's mouth a vast flood of water gushed out and swept toward the woman in an effort to get rid of her; 16but the earth helped her by opening its mouth and swallowing the flood! 17Then the furious Dragon set out to attack the rest of her children—all who were keeping God's commandments and confessing that they belong to Jesus. He stood waiting on an ocean beach.

A THOUGHT: *The critical blow to Satan came when the Lamb, Jesus Christ, shed his blood for our sins. John says the war is still being waged, but the outcome is already determined. Satan and his followers have been defeated and will be destroyed. Nevertheless, Satan is battling daily to bring more into his ranks and to keep his own from defecting to God's side. Those who belong to Christ have gone into battle on God's side, and he has guaranteed them victory. God will not lose the war, but we must make certain not to lose the battle for our own souls. Don't waver in your commitment to Christ. A great spiritual battle is being fought, and there is no time for indecision.*

Effective Love/ 1 John 3:12–24

We are not to be like Cain, who belonged to Satan and killed his brother. Why did he kill him? Because Cain had been doing wrong and he knew very well that his brother's life was better than his. 13So don't be surprised, dear friends, if the world hates you.

14If we love other Christians it proves that we have been delivered from hell and given eternal life. But a person who doesn't have love for others is headed for eternal death. 15Anyone who hates his Christian brother is really a murderer at heart; and you know that no one wanting to murder has eternal life within. 16We know what real love is from Christ's example in dying for us. And so we also ought to lay down our lives for our Christian brothers.

17But if someone who is supposed to be a Christian has money enough to live well, and sees a brother in need, and won't help him—how can God's love be within *him?* 18Little children, let us stop just *saying* we love people; let us *really* love them, and *show it* by our *actions.* 19Then we will know for sure, by our actions, that we are on God's side, and our consciences will be clear, even when we stand before the Lord. 20But if we have bad consciences and feel that we have done wrong, the Lord will surely feel it even more, for he knows everything we do.

21But, dearly loved friends, if our consciences are clear, we can come to the Lord with perfect assurance and trust, 22and get whatever we ask for because we are obeying him and doing the things that please him. 23And this is what God says we must do: Believe on the name of his Son Jesus Christ, and love one another. 24Those who do what God says—they are living with God and he with them. We know this is true because the Holy Spirit he has given us tells us so.

A Thought: *Real love is an action, not a feeling. It produces selfless, sacrificial giving. The greatest act of love anyone can do is to give himself or herself for others. How can we lay down our lives? Sometimes it is easier to say we'll die for others than to truly live for them, which involves putting others' desires first. These verses give an example of how to lay down our lives for others— provide money to help meet others' needs. How clearly do your actions say you really love others? Are you as generous as you should be with your money, possessions, and time?*

Proverbs for Today/ 30:15–16

There are two things never satisfied, like a leech forever craving more: no, three things! no, four! Hell. The barren womb. A barren desert. Fire.

DECEMBER 21

A Creature from the Sea/ Revelation 13:1–18

And now, in my vision, I saw a strange Creature rising up out of the sea. It had seven heads and ten horns, and ten crowns upon its horns. And written on each head were blasphemous names, each one defying and insulting God. 2This Creature looked like a leopard but had bear's feet and a lion's mouth! And the Dragon gave him his own power and throne and great authority.

3I saw that one of his heads seemed wounded beyond recovery—but the fatal wound was healed! All the world marveled at this miracle and followed the Creature in awe. 4They worshiped the Dragon for giving him such power, and they worshiped the strange Creature. "Where is there anyone as great as he?" they exclaimed. "Who is able to fight against him?"

5Then the Dragon encouraged the Creature to speak great blasphemies against the Lord; and gave him authority to control the earth for forty-two months. 6All that time he blasphemed God's Name and his temple and all those living in heaven. 7The Dragon gave him power to fight against God's people and to overcome them, and to rule over all nations and language groups throughout the world.

8And all mankind—whose names were not written down before the founding of the world in the slain Lamb's Book of Life—worshiped the evil Creature.

9Anyone who can hear, listen carefully: 10The people of God who are destined for prison will be arrested and taken away; those destined for death will be killed. But do not be dismayed, for here is your opportunity for endurance and confidence.

11Then I saw another strange animal, this one coming up out of the earth, with two little horns like those of a lamb but a fearsome voice like the Dragon's. 12He exercised all the authority of the Creature whose death-wound had been healed, whom he required all the world to worship. 13He did unbelievable miracles such as making fire flame down to earth from the skies while everyone was watching. 14By doing these miracles, he was deceiving people everywhere. He could do these marvelous things whenever the first Creature was there to watch him. And he ordered the people of the world to make a great statue of the first Creature, who was fatally wounded and then came back to life. 15He was permitted to give breath to this statue and even make it speak! Then the statue ordered that anyone refusing to worship it must die!

16He required everyone—great and small, rich and poor, slave and free—to be tattooed with a certain mark on the right hand or on the forehead. 17And no one could get a job or even buy in any store without the permit of that mark, which was either the name of the Creature or the code number of his name. 18Here is a puzzle that calls for careful thought to solve it. Let those who are able, interpret this code: the numerical values of the letters in his name add to 666!

A THOUGHT: *Throughout the Bible we see miracles performed as proofs of God's power, love, and authority. But here we see counterfeit miracles performed to deceive. This is a reminder of Pharaoh's magicians, who duplicated Moses' signs in Egypt. True signs and miracles point us to Jesus Christ, but miracles alone can be deceptive. That is why we must ask of each miracle we see, "Is this consistent with what God says in the Bible?" The Creature here gains influence through the signs and then orders the people to worship a statue—a direct flouting of the second commandment. Allowing the Scriptures to guide our faith and practice will keep us from being deceived by false signs, however convincing they may appear. Any teaching that contradicts God's Word is false.*

The Incarnation—A Test for Truth/ 1 John 4:1–6

Dearly loved friends, don't always believe everything you hear just because someone says it is a message from God: test it first to see if it really is. For there are many false teachers around, ²and the way to find out if their message is from the Holy Spirit is to ask: Does it really agree that Jesus Christ, God's Son, actually became man with a human body? If so, then the message is from God. ³If not, the message is not from God but from one who is against Christ, like the "Antichrist" you have heard about who is going to come, and his attitude of enmity against Christ is already abroad in the world.

⁴Dear young friends, you belong to God and have already won your fight with those who are against Christ, because there is someone in your hearts who is stronger than any evil teacher in this wicked world. ⁵These men belong to this world, so, quite naturally, they are concerned about worldly affairs and the world pays attention to them. ⁶But we are children of God; that is why only those who have walked and talked with God will listen to us. Others won't. That is another way to know whether a message is really from God; for if it is, the world won't listen to it.

A THOUGHT: *Some people believe everything they read or hear. Unfortunately, many things printed and taught are not true. Christians should not be gullible. Verify every message you hear, even if the person who brings it says it's from God. If the message is truly from God, it will be consistent with Christ's teachings.*

Proverbs for Today/ 30:17

A man who mocks his father and despises his mother shall have his eye plucked out by ravens and eaten by vultures.

DECEMBER 22

The Lamb Stands on Mount Zion/ Revelation 14:1–7

Then I saw a Lamb standing on Mount Zion in Jerusalem, and with him were 144,000 who had his Name and his

Father's Name written on their foreheads. 2And I heard a sound from heaven like the roaring of a great waterfall or the rolling of mighty thunder. It was the singing of a choir accompanied by harps.

3This tremendous choir—144,000 strong—sang a wonderful new song in front of the throne of God and before the four Living Beings and the twenty-four Elders; and no one could sing this song except those 144,000 who had been redeemed from the earth. 4 For they are spiritually undefiled, pure as virgins, following the Lamb wherever he goes. They have been purchased from among the men on the earth as a consecrated offering to God and the Lamb. 5No falsehood can be charged against them; they are blameless.

6And I saw another angel flying through the heavens, carrying the everlasting Good News to preach to those on earth—to every nation, tribe, language and people.

7"Fear God," he shouted, "and extol his greatness. For the time has come when he will sit as Judge. Worship him who made the heaven and the earth, the sea and all its sources."

A THOUGHT: *Some believe these angels are offering a final, worldwide appeal for all people to recognize the one true God. No one will have the excuse of never hearing God's truth. Others, however, see this as an announcement of judgment rather than an appeal. The people of the world have had their chance to proclaim their allegiance to God, and now God's great judgment is about to begin. If you are reading this, you have already heard God's truth. You know that God's final judgment will not be put off forever. Have you joyfully received the everlasting Good News? Have you confessed your sins and trusted in Christ to save you? If so, you have nothing to fear from God's judgment. The Judge of all the earth is your Savior!*

Let Us Love One Another/ 1 John 4:7–15

Dear friends, let us practice loving each other, for love comes from God and those who are loving and kind show that they are the children of God, and that they are getting to know him better. 8But if a person isn't loving and kind, it shows that he doesn't know God—for God is love.

9God showed how much he loved us by sending his only Son into this wicked world to bring to us eternal life through his death. 10In this act we see what real love is: it is not our love for God, but his love for us when he sent his Son to satisfy God's anger against our sins.

11Dear friends, since God loved us as much as that, we surely ought to love each other too. 12For though we have never yet seen God, when we love each other God lives in us and his love within us grows ever stronger. 13And he has put his own Holy Spirit into our hearts as a proof to us that we are living with him and he with us. 14And furthermore, we have seen with our own eyes and now tell all the world that God sent his Son to be their Savior. 15Anyone who believes and says that Jesus is the Son of God has God living in him, and he is living with God.

A THOUGHT: *Everyone believes love is important, but we usually think of it as a feeling. In reality, love is a choice and an action. God is the source of our love: he loved us enough to sacrifice his Son for us. Jesus is our example of what it means to love; everything he did in life and death was supremely loving. The Holy Spirit gives us the power to love; he lives in our hearts and makes us more and more like Jesus. God's love always involves a choice and an action, and our love should be like his. How well is your love for God displayed, in the choices you make and the actions you take?*

Proverbs for Today/ 30:18–20

There are three things too wonderful for me to understand—no, four! How an eagle glides through the sky. How a serpent crawls upon a rock. How a ship finds its way across the heaving ocean. The growth of love between a man and a girl. There is another thing too: how a prostitute can sin and then say, "What's wrong with that?"

DECEMBER 23

Angels Announce the Judgment to Come/ Revelation 14:8–20

Then another angel followed him through the skies, saying, "Babylon is fallen, is fallen—that great city—because she seduced the nations of the world and made them share the wine of her intense impurity and sin."

9Then a third angel followed them shouting, "Anyone worshiping the Creature from the sea and his statue and accepting his mark on the forehead or the hand, 10must drink the wine of the anger of God; it is poured out undiluted into God's cup of wrath. And they will be tormented with fire and burning sulphur in the presence of the holy angels and the Lamb. 11The smoke of their torture rises forever and ever, and they will have no relief day or night, for they have worshiped the Creature and his statue, and have been tattooed with the code of his name. 12Let this encourage God's people to endure patiently every trial and persecution, for they are his saints who remain firm to the end in obedience to his commands and trust in Jesus."

13And I heard a voice in the heavens above me saying, "Write this down: At last the time has come for his martyrs to enter into their full reward. Yes, says the Spirit, they are blest indeed, for now they shall rest from all their toils and trials; for their good deeds follow them to heaven!" 14Then the scene changed and I saw a white cloud, and someone sitting on it who looked like Jesus, who was called "The Son of Man," with a crown of solid gold upon his head and a sharp sickle in his hand.

15Then an angel came from the temple and called out to him, "Begin to use the sickle, for the time has come for you to reap; the harvest is ripe on the earth." 16So the one sitting on the cloud swung his sickle over the earth, and the harvest was gathered in. 17After that another angel came from the temple in heaven, and he also had a sharp sickle.

18Just then the angel who has power to destroy the world with fire, shouted to the angel with the sickle, "Use your sickle now to cut off the clusters of grapes from the vines of the earth, for they are fully ripe for judgment." 19So the angel swung his sickle on the earth and loaded the grapes into the great winepress of God's wrath. 20And the grapes were trodden in the winepress outside the city, and blood flowed out in a stream 200 miles long and as high as a horse's bridle.

A THOUGHT: *This news about God's ultimate triumph should encourage God's people to remain firm through every trial and persecution. They can do this, God promises, by trusting in Jesus and obeying the commands in his Word. The secret to enduring, therefore, is trust and obedience. Trust God to give you patience to endure even the small, trials you face daily; obey him, even when obedience is unattractive or dangerous.*

God's Children Live in Love/ 1 John 4:16–21

We know how much God loves us because we have felt his love and because we believe him when he tells us that he loves us dearly. God is love, and anyone who lives in love is living with God and God is living in him. 17And as we live with Christ, our love grows more perfect and complete; so we will not be ashamed and embarrassed at the day of judgment, but can face him with confidence and joy, because he loves us and we love him too.

18We need have no fear of someone who loves us perfectly; his perfect love for us eliminates all dread of what he might do to us. If we are afraid, it is for fear of what he might do to us, and shows that we are not fully convinced that he really loves us. 19So you see, our love for him comes as a result of his loving us first.

20If anyone says "I love God," but keeps on hating his brother, he is a liar; for if he doesn't love his brother who is right there in front of him, how can he love God whom he has never seen? 21And God himself has said that one must love not only God, but his brother too.

A THOUGHT: *It is easy to say we love God when it doesn't cost us anything more than weekly attendance at religious services. But the real test of our love for God is how we treat the people right in front of us—our family members and fellow believers. We cannot truly love God while neglecting to love those who are created in his image.*

Proverbs for Today/ 30:21–23

There are three things that make the earth tremble— no, four it cannot stand: A slave who becomes a king. A rebel who prospers. A bitter woman when she finally marries. A servant girl who marries her mistress' husband.

The Song of Moses and the Lamb/
Revelation 15:1-8

And I saw in heaven another mighty pageant showing things to come: Seven angels were assigned to carry down to earth the seven last plagues—and then at last God's anger will be finished.

2Spread out before me was what seemed to be an ocean of fire and glass, and on it stood all those who had been victorious over the Evil Creature and his statue and his mark and number. All were holding harps of God, 3,4and they were singing the song of Moses, the servant of God, and the song of the Lamb:

"Great and marvelous
Are your doings,
Lord God Almighty.
Just and true
Are your ways,
O King of Ages.
Who shall not fear,
O Lord,
And glorify your Name?
For you alone are holy.
All nations will come
And worship before you,
For your righteous deeds
Have been disclosed."

5Then I looked and saw that the Holy of Holies of the temple in heaven was thrown wide open!

6The seven angels who were assigned to pour out the seven plagues then came from the temple, clothed in spotlessly white linen, with golden belts across their chests. 7And one of the four Living Beings handed each of them a golden flask filled with the terrible wrath of the Living God who lives forever and forever. 8The temple was filled with smoke from his glory and power; and no one could enter until the seven angels had completed pouring out the seven plagues.

A THOUGHT: *The song of Moses celebrated Israel's deliverance from Egypt. The song of the Lamb celebrates the ultimate deliverance of God's people from the power of Satan.*

The Holy of Holies was the innermost room in the Temple, where the ark of the covenant resided, (a symbol of God's presence among his people). This room was closed off from view by a great curtain. Only the High Priest could enter there, and only once a year on the Day of Atonement. The Holy of Holies was thrown open once before—at Christ's crucifixion, when the curtain was ripped from top to bottom. The wide open entrance into the Holy of Holies symbolizes the open access to God's very presence which Christians have on the basis of Jesus' shed blood. Those of us who are united with the sinless Christ, our High Priest, can approach God boldly, but unrepentant sinners will be unable to come into his presence.

Eternal Life Is in God's Son/ 1 John 5:1–15

If you believe that Jesus is the Christ—that he is God's Son and your Savior—then you are a child of God. And all who love the Father love his children too. 2So you can find out how much you love God's children—your brothers and sisters in the Lord—by how much you love and obey God. 3Loving God means doing what he tells us to do, and really, that isn't hard at all; 4for every child of God can obey him, defeating sin and evil pleasure by trusting Christ to help him.

5But who could possibly fight and win this battle except by believing that Jesus is truly the Son of God? 6, 7, 8And we know he is, because God said so with a voice from heaven when Jesus was baptized, and again as he was facing death —yes, not only at his baptism but also as he faced death. And the Holy Spirit, forever truthful, says it too. So we have these three witnesses: the voice of the Holy Spirit in our hearts, the voice from heaven at Christ's baptism, and the voice before he died. And they all say the same thing: that Jesus Christ is the Son of God. 9We believe men who witness in our courts, and so surely we can believe whatever God declares. And God declares that Jesus is his Son. 10All who believe this know in their hearts that it is true. If anyone doesn't believe this, he is actually calling God a liar, because he doesn't believe what God has said about his Son.

11And what is it that God has said? That he has given us eternal life, and that this life is in his Son. 12So whoever has God's Son has life; whoever does not have his Son, does not have life.

13I have written this to you who believe in the Son of God so that you may know you have eternal life. 14And we are sure of this, that he will listen to us whenever we ask him for anything in line with his will. 15And if we really know he is listening when we talk to him and make our requests, then we can be sure that he will answer us.

A THOUGHT: *Some people hope they will be given eternal life. John says we can know we have it. Our certainty is based on God's promise that he has given us eternal life through his Son. This is true whether you feel close to God or distant from him. Eternal life is not based on feelings, but on facts. You can know you have eternal life if you believe God's truth. If you lack assurance as to whether you are a Christian, ask yourself if you have honestly committed your life to him as your Savior and Lord. If so, you know by faith that you are indeed a child of God.*

Proverbs for Today/ 30:24–28

There are four things that are small but unusually wise: Ants: they aren't strong, but store up food for the winter. Cliff badgers: delicate little animals who protect themselves by living among the rocks. The locusts: though they have no leader, they stay together in swarms. The lizards: they are easy to catch and kill, yet are found even in king's palaces!

DECEMBER 25

Angels Pour Out Plagues upon the Earth/ Revelation 16:1–21

And I heard a mighty voice shouting from the temple to the seven angels, "Now go your ways and empty out the seven flasks of the wrath of God upon the earth."

2So the first angel left the temple and poured out his flask over the earth, and horrible, malignant sores broke out on everyone who had the mark of the Creature and was worshiping his statue.

3The second angel poured out his flask upon the oceans,

and they became like the watery blood of a dead man; and everything in all the oceans died.

4The third angel poured out his flask upon the rivers and springs and they became blood. 5And I heard this angel of the waters declaring, "You are just in sending this judgment, O Holy One, who is and was, 6for your saints and prophets have been martyred and their blood poured out upon the earth; and now, in turn, you have poured out the blood of those who murdered them; it is their just reward."

7And I heard the angel of the altar say, "Yes, Lord God Almighty, your punishments are just and true."

8Then the fourth angel poured out his flask upon the sun, causing it to scorch all men with its fire. 9Everyone was burned by this blast of heat, and they cursed the name of God who sent the plagues—they did not change their mind and attitude to give him glory.

10Then the fifth angel poured out his flask upon the throne of the Creature from the sea, and his kingdom was plunged into darkness. And his subjects gnawed their tongues in anguish, 11and cursed the God of heaven for their pains and sores, but they refused to repent of all their evil deeds.

12The sixth angel poured out his flask upon the great River Euphrates and it dried up so that the kings from the east could march their armies westward without hindrance. 13And I saw three evil spirits disguised as frogs leap from the mouth of the Dragon, the Creature, and his False Prophet. 14These miracle-working demons conferred with all the rulers of the world to gather them for battle against the Lord on that great coming Judgment Day of God Almighty.

15"Take note: I will come as unexpectedly as a thief! Blessed are all who are awaiting me, who keep their robes in readiness and will not need to walk naked and ashamed."

16And they gathered all the armies of the world near a place called, in Hebrew, Armageddon—the Mountain of Megiddo.

17Then the seventh angel poured out his flask into the air; and a mighty shout came from the throne of the temple in heaven, saying, "It is finished!" 18Then the thunder crashed and rolled, and lightning flashed; and there was a great earthquake of a magnitude unprecedented in human history. 19The great city of "Babylon" split into three sections, and cities around the world fell in heaps of rubble; and so all of "Babylon's" sins were remembered in God's thoughts, and she was punished to the last drop of anger in the cup of the wine of the fierceness of his wrath. 20And islands vanished, and mountains flattened out, 21and there was an incredible hailstorm from heaven; hailstones weighing a hundred pounds fell from the sky onto the people below, and they cursed God because of the terrible hail.

A THOUGHT: *Sinful men will unite to fight against God in a final display of rebellion. Many are already united against Christ and his people—those who stand for truth, peace, justice, and morality. Your personal battle with evil foreshadows the great battle pictured here, where God will meet evil and destroy it once and for all. Be strong and courageous as you battle against sin and evil: you are fighting on the winning side.*

God's Children Do Not Continue in Sin/
1 John 5:16–21

If you see a Christian sinning in a way that does not end in death, you should ask God to forgive him and God will give him life, unless he has sinned that one fatal sin. But there is that one sin which ends in death and if he has done that, there is no use praying for him. 17Every wrong is a sin, of course. I'm not talking about these ordinary sins; I am speaking of that one that ends in death.

18No one who has become part of God's family makes a practice of sinning, for Christ, God's Son, holds him securely and the devil cannot get his hands on him. 19We know that we are children of God and that all the rest of the world around us is under Satan's power and control. 20And we know that Christ, God's Son, has come to help us understand and find the true God. And now we are in God because we are in Jesus Christ his Son, who is the only true God; and he is eternal Life.

21Dear children, keep away from anything that might take God's place in your hearts. Amen.

Sincerely,
John

A THOUGHT: *Christians commit sins, of course, but they ask God to forgive them and then they continue serving him. God has freed them from their slavery to Satan, and he keeps them safe from Satan's continued attacks. The rest of the world does not have the Christian's freedom to obey God. Unless they come to Christ in faith, they have no choice but to obey Satan. There is no middle ground; people either belong to God and obey him, or they live under Satan's control.*

Proverbs for Today/ 30:29–31

There are three stately monarchs in the earth—no, four: The lion, king of the animals. He won't turn aside for anyone. The peacock. The male goat. A king as he leads his army.

DECEMBER 26

The Woman, A Symbol of Babylon/
Revelation 17:1–18

One of the seven angels who had poured out the plagues came over and talked with me. "Come with me," he said, "and I will show you what is going to happen to the Notorious Prostitute, who sits upon the many waters of the world. 2The kings of the world have had immoral relations with her, and the people of the earth have been made drunk by the wine of her immorality."

3So the angel took me in spirit into the wilderness. There I saw a woman sitting on a scarlet animal that had seven heads and ten horns, written all over with blasphemies against God. 4The woman wore purple and scarlet clothing and beautiful jewelry made of gold and precious gems and pearls, and held in her hand a golden goblet full of obscenities:

5A mysterious caption was written on her forehead: "Babylon the Great, Mother of Prostitutes and of Idol Worship Everywhere around the World."

6I could see that she was drunk—drunk with the blood of the martyrs of Jesus she had killed. I stared at her in horror.

7"Why are you so surprised?" the angel asked. "I'll

tell you who she is and what the animal she is riding represents. 8He was alive but isn't now. And yet, soon he will come up out of the bottomless pit and go to eternal destruction; and the people of earth, whose names have not been written in the Book of Life before the world began, will be dumbfounded at his reappearance after being dead.

9"And now think hard: his seven heads represent a certain city built on seven hills where this woman has her residence. 10They also represent seven kings. Five have already fallen, the sixth now reigns, and the seventh is yet to come, but his reign will be brief. 11The scarlet animal that died is the eighth king, having reigned before as one of the seven; after his second reign, he too, will go to his doom. 12His ten horns are ten kings who have not yet risen to power; they will be appointed to their kingdoms for one brief moment, to reign with him. 13They will all sign a treaty giving their power and strength to him. 14Together they will wage war against the Lamb, and the Lamb will conquer them; for he is Lord over all lords, and King of kings, and his people are the called and chosen and faithful ones.

15"The oceans, lakes and rivers that the woman is sitting on represent masses of people of every race and nation.

16"The scarlet animal and his ten horns—which represent ten kings who will reign with him—all hate the woman, and will attack her and leave her naked and ravaged by fire. 17For God will put a plan into their minds, a plan that will carry out his purposes: They will mutually agree to give their authority to the scarlet animal, so that the words of God will be fulfilled. 18And this woman you saw in your vision represents the great city that rules over the kings of the earth."

A Thought: *Throughout history people have been killed for their faith. Over the last century, millions have been killed by oppressive governments, and many of these were believers. The woman's drunkenness shows her pleasure in her evil accomplishments and her false feeling of triumph over the church. But every martyr who fell before her sword only strengthened the church. No matter what happens, we must trust that God is still in charge, and his plans will happen just as he says. He even uses people opposed to him to execute his will. Although he allows evil to permeate this present world, the new earth will never know sin.*

To Love One Another Is to Obey God/ 2 John 1:1–6

From: John, the old Elder of the church.

To: That dear woman Cyria, one of God's very own, and to her children whom I love so much, as does everyone else in the church. 2Since the Truth is in our hearts forever, 3God the Father and Jesus Christ his Son will bless us with great mercy and much peace, and with truth and love.

4How happy I am to find some of your children here, and to see that they are living as they should, following the Truth, obeying God's command.

5And now I want to urgently remind you, dear friends, of the old rule God gave us right from the beginning, that Christians should love one another. 6If we love God, we will do whatever he tells us to. And he has told us from the very first to love each other.

A THOUGHT: *The love Christians should have for one another is a recurrent New Testament theme. Love is not an option for Christians, it is a command. True obedience to God is measured by our love for others. We can show love in many ways: by accepting people regardless of their differences from us, by listening, helping, giving, serving, and refusing to judge. But just knowing God's command is not enough. We must put it into practice.*

Proverbs for Today/ 30:32

If you have been a fool by being proud or plotting evil, don't brag about it—cover your mouth with your hand in shame.

DECEMBER 27

The Fall of Babylon/ Revelation 18:1–24

After all this I saw another angel come down from heaven with great authority, and the earth grew bright with his splendor.

2He gave a mighty shout, "Babylon the Great is fallen, is fallen; she has become a den of demons, a haunt of devils and every kind of evil spirit. 3For all the nations have drunk the fatal wine of her intense immorality. The rulers of earth have enjoyed themselves with her, and businessmen throughout the world have grown rich from all her luxurious living."

⁴Then I heard another voice calling from heaven, "Come away from her, my people; do not take part in her sins, or you will be punished with her. ⁵For her sins are piled as high as heaven and God is ready to judge her for her crimes. ⁶Do to her as she has done to you, and more—give double penalty for all her evil deeds. She brewed many a cup of woe for others—give twice as much to her. ⁷She has lived in luxury and pleasure—match it now with torments and with sorrows. She boasts, 'I am queen upon my throne. I am no helpless widow. I will not experience sorrow.' ⁸Therefore the sorrows of death and mourning and famine shall overtake her in a single day, and she shall be utterly consumed by fire; for mighty is the Lord who judges her."

⁹And the world leaders, who took part in her immoral acts and enjoyed her favors, will mourn for her as they see the smoke rising from her charred remains. ¹⁰They will stand far off, trembling with fear and crying out, "Alas, Babylon, that mighty city! In one moment her judgment fell."

¹¹The merchants of the earth will weep and mourn for her, for there is no one left to buy their goods. ¹²She was their biggest customer for gold and silver, precious stones, pearls, finest linens, purple silks, and scarlet; and every kind of perfumed wood, and ivory goods and most expensive wooden carvings, and brass and iron and marble; ¹³and spices and perfumes and incense, ointment and frankincense, wine, olive oil, and fine flour; wheat, cattle, sheep, horses, chariots, and slaves—and even the souls of men.

¹⁴"All the fancy things you loved so much are gone," they cry. "The dainty luxuries and splendor that you prized so much will never be yours again. They are gone forever."

¹⁵And so the merchants who have become wealthy by selling her these things shall stand at a distance, fearing danger to themselves, weeping and crying, ¹⁶"Alas, that great city, so beautiful—like a woman clothed in finest purple and scarlet linens, decked out with gold and precious stones and pearls! ¹⁷In one moment, all the wealth of the city is gone!"

And all the shipowners and captains of the merchant

ships and crews will stand a long way off, 18crying as they watch the smoke ascend, and saying, "Where in all the world is there another city such as this?" 19And they will throw dust on their heads in their sorrow and say, "Alas, alas, for that great city! She made us all rich from her great wealth. And now in a single hour all is gone. . . . "

20But you, O heaven, rejoice over her fate; and you, O children of God and the prophets and the apostles! For at last God has given judgment against her for you.

21Then a mighty angel picked up a boulder shaped like a millstone and threw it into the ocean and shouted, "Babylon, that great city, shall be thrown away as I have thrown away this stone, and she shall disappear forever. 22Never again will the sound of music be there—no more pianos, saxophones, and trumpets. No industry of any kind will ever again exist there, and there will be no more milling of the grain. 23Dark, dark will be her nights; not even a lamp in a window will ever be seen again. No more joyous wedding bells and happy voices of the bridegrooms and the brides. Her businessmen were known around the world and she deceived all nations with her sorceries. 24And she was responsible for the blood of all the martyred prophets and the saints."

A THOUGHT: *Babylon "lived in luxury and pleasure." She boasted, "I am queen upon my throne. . . . I will not experience sorrow." The powerful, wealthy people of this world are susceptible to this same attitude. A person who is financially comfortable often feels invulnerable, secure, and in control, not in need of God or anyone else. This kind of attitude defies God, and his judgment against it is harsh. We are told to avoid "her sins." If you are financially secure, don't become complacent and deluded by the myth of self-sufficiency. Christians are warned to stay free from the enchantment of money, status, and the "good life." We are to live according to the values Christ lived by: service, giving, self-sacrifice, obedience, and truth. Use your resources to help others and advance God's Kingdom.*

Beware of False Teachers/ 2 John 1:7–13

Watch out for the false leaders—and there are many of them around—who don't believe that Jesus Christ came to earth as a human being with a body like ours. Such people are against the truth and against Christ. 8Beware of being like them, and losing the prize that you and I have been working so hard to get. See to it that you win your full reward from the Lord. 9For if you wander beyond the teaching of Christ, you will leave God behind; while if you are loyal to Christ's teachings, you will have God too. Then you will have both the Father and the Son.

10If anyone comes to teach you, and he doesn't believe what Christ taught, don't even invite him into your home. Don't encourage him in any way. 11If you do you will be a partner with him in his wickedness.

12Well, I would like to say much more, but I don't want to say it in this letter, for I hope to come to see you soon and then we can talk over these things together and have a joyous time.

13Greetings from the children of your sister—another choice child of God.

Sincerely,
John

A THOUGHT: *In John's day, many false teachers taught that spirit was good and matter was evil; therefore, they reasoned that Jesus could not have been both God and man. In strong terms, John warned against this kind of teaching. There are still many false teachers who promote an understanding of Jesus that is not biblical. They are dangerous because they twist the truth and undermine the foundations of Christian faith. They may use the right words but change the meanings. The way your teachers live shows a lot about what they believe about Christ.*

Proverbs for Today/ 30:33

As the churning of cream yields butter, and a blow to the nose causes bleeding, so anger causes quarrels.

DECEMBER 28

A Vast Crowd in Heaven Praises God/
Revelation 19:1–21

After this I heard the shouting of a vast crowd in heaven, "Hallelujah! Praise the Lord! Salvation is from our God. Honor and authority belong to him alone; 2for his judgments are just and true. He has punished the Great Prostitute who corrupted the earth with her sin; and he has avenged the murder of his servants."

3Again and again their voices rang, "Praise the Lord! The smoke from her burning ascends forever and forever!"

4Then the twenty-four Elders and four Living Beings fell down and worshiped God, who was sitting upon the throne, and said, "Amen! Hallelujah! Praise the Lord!"

5And out of the throne came a voice that said, "Praise our God, all you his servants, small and great, who fear him."

6Then I heard again what sounded like the shouting of a huge crowd, or like the waves of a hundred oceans crashing on the shore, or like the mighty rolling of great thunder, "Praise the Lord. For the Lord our God, the Almighty, reigns. 7Let us be glad and rejoice and honor him; for the time has come for the wedding banquet of the Lamb, and his bride has prepared herself. 8She is permitted to wear the cleanest and whitest and finest of linens." (Fine linen represents the good deeds done by the people of God.)

9And the angel dictated this sentence to me: "Blessed are those who are invited to the wedding feast of the Lamb." And he added, "God himself has stated this."

10Then I fell down at his feet to worship him, but he said, "No! Don't! For I am a servant of God just as you are, and as your brother Christians are, who testify of their faith in Jesus. Worship God. The purpose of all prophecy and of all I have shown you is to tell about Jesus."

11Then I saw heaven opened and a white horse standing there; and the one sitting on the horse was named "Faithful and True"—the one who justly punishes and makes war. 12His eyes were like flames, and on his head were many crowns. A name was written on his forehead, and only he knew its meaning. 13He was clothed with garments dipped in blood, and his title was "The Word of God." 14The armies of heaven, dressed in finest linen, white and clean, followed him on white horses.

15In his mouth he held a sharp sword to strike down the nations; he ruled them with an iron grip; and he trod the winepress of the fierceness of the wrath of Almighty God. 16On his robe and thigh was written this title: "King of Kings and Lord of Lords."

17Then I saw an angel standing in the sunshine, shouting loudly to the birds, "Come! Gather together for the supper of the Great God! 18Come and eat the flesh of kings, and captains, and great generals; of horses and riders; and of all humanity, both great and small, slave and free."

19Then I saw the Evil Creature gathering the governments of the earth and their armies to fight against the one sitting on the horse and his army. 20And the Evil Creature was captured, and with him the False Prophet, who could do mighty miracles when the Evil Creature was present—miracles that deceived all who had accepted the Evil Creature's mark, and who worshiped his statue. Both of them—the Evil Creature and his False Prophet—were thrown alive into the Lake of Fire that burns with sulphur. 21And their entire army was killed with the sharp sword in the mouth of the one riding the white horse, and all the birds of heaven were gorged with their flesh.

A THOUGHT: *Praise is the heartfelt response to God by those who love him. The more you get to know him and realize what he has done, the more you will respond with praise. Praise is at the heart of true worship. Let your praise of God flow out of your realization of who he is and how much he loves you.*

God's Children Do What Is Right/ 3 John 1:1–15

From: John, the Elder.

To: Dear Gaius, whom I truly love.

2Dear friend, I am praying that all is well with you and that your body is as healthy as I know your soul is. 3Some of the brothers traveling by have made me very happy by telling me that your life stays clean and true, and that you are living by the standards of the Gospel. 4I could have no greater joy than to hear such things about my children.

5Dear friend, you are doing a good work for God in taking care of the traveling teachers and missionaries who are passing through. 6They have told the church here of your friendship and your loving deeds. I am glad when you send them on their way with a generous gift. 7For they are traveling for the Lord, and take neither food, clothing, shelter, nor money from those who are not Christians, even though they have preached to them. 8So we ourselves should take care of them in order that we may become partners with them in the Lord's work.

9I sent a brief letter to the church about this, but proud

Diotrephes, who loves to push himself forward as the leader of the Christians there, does not admit my authority^r over him and refuses to listen to me. 10When I come I will tell you some of the things he is doing and what wicked things he is saying about me and what insulting language he is using. He not only refuses to welcome the missionary travelers himself, but tells others not to, and when they do he tries to put them out of the church.

11Dear friend, don't let this bad example influence you. Follow only what is good. Remember that those who do what is right prove that they are God's children; and those who continue in evil prove that they are far from God. 12But everyone, including Truth itself, speaks highly of Demetrius. I myself can say the same for him, and you know I speak the truth.

13I have much to say but I don't want to write it, 14for I hope to see you soon and then we will have much to talk about together. 15So good-bye for now. Friends here send their love, and please give each of the folks there a special greeting from me.

Sincerely,
John

A Thought: *In the early days of the church, traveling prophets, evangelists, and teachers were helped on their way by people like Gaius who housed and fed them. Hospitality is a lost art in many churches today. We would do well to invite more people for meals— fellow church members, young people, traveling missionaries, those in need, visitors. This is an active and much appreciated way to show your love. In fact it is probably more important today. Because of our individualistic, self-centered society, there are many lonely people who wonder if anyone cares whether they live or die. If you find such a lonely person, show him or her that you care!*

Proverbs for Today/ 31:1–7

These are the wise sayings of King Lemuel of Massa, taught to him at his mother's knee: O my son, whom I have dedicated to the Lord, do not spend your time with women—the royal pathway to destruction. And it is not for kings, O Lemuel, to drink wine and whiskey. For if they drink they may forget their duties and be unable to give justice to those who are oppressed. Hard liquor is for sick men at the brink of death, and wine for those in deep depression. Let them drink to forget their poverty and misery.

Satan Is Bound for a Thousand Years/
Revelation 20:1–15

Then I saw an angel come down from heaven with the key to the bottomless pit and a heavy chain in his hand. ²He seized the Dragon—that old Serpent, the devil, Satan—and bound him in chains for 1,000 years, ³and threw him into the bottomless pit, which he then shut and locked, so that he could not fool the nations any more until the thousand years were finished. Afterwards he would be released again for a little while.

⁴Then I saw thrones, and sitting on them were those who had been given the right to judge. And I saw the souls of those who had been beheaded for their testimony about Jesus, for proclaiming the Word of God, and who had not worshiped the Creature or his statue, nor accepted his mark on their foreheads or their hands. They had come to life again and now they reigned with Christ for a thousand years.

⁵This is the First Resurrection. (The rest of the dead did not come back to life until the thousand years had ended.) ⁶Blessed and holy are those who share in the First Resurrection. For them the Second Death holds no terrors, for they will be priests of God and of Christ, and shall reign with him a thousand years.

⁷When the thousand years end, Satan will be let out of his prison. ⁸He will go out to deceive the nations of the world and gather them together, with Gog and Magog, for battle—a mighty host, numberless as sand along the shore. ⁹They will go up across the broad plain of the earth and surround God's people and the beloved city of Jerusalem on every side. But fire from God in heaven will flash down on the attacking armies and consume them.

¹⁰Then the devil who had betrayed them will again be thrown into the Lake of Fire burning with sulphur where the Creature and False Prophet are, and they will be tormented day and night forever and ever.

¹¹And I saw a great white throne and the one who sat upon it, from whose face the earth and sky fled away,

but they found no place to hide. 12I saw the dead, great and small, standing before God; and The Books were opened, including the Book of Life. And the dead were judged according to the things written in The Books, each according to the deeds he had done. 13The oceans surrendered the bodies buried in them; and the earth and the underworld gave up the dead in them. Each was judged according to his deeds. 14And Death and Hell were thrown into the Lake of Fire. This is the Second Death—the Lake of Fire. 15And if anyone's name was not found recorded in the Book of Life, he was thrown into the Lake of Fire.

A THOUGHT: *Satan's power is not eternal—he will meet his end. He began his evil work in mankind at the beginning and continues it today, but he will be destroyed when he is thrown into the Lake of Fire. Satan will be released from the bottomless pit for a time, but he will never be released from the Lake of Fire. He will never be a threat to anyone again—his doom is sure.*

Defend God's Truth/ Jude 1:1–7

From: Jude, a servant of Jesus Christ, and a brother of James.

To: Christians everywhere—beloved of God and chosen by him. 2May you be given more and more of God's kindness, peace, and love.

3Dearly loved friends, I had been planning to write you some thoughts about the salvation God has given us, but now I find I must write of something else instead, urging you to stoutly defend the truth which God gave, once for all, to his people to keep without change through the years. 4I say this because some godless teachers have wormed their way in among you, saying that after we become Christians we can do just as we like without fear of God's punishment. The fate of such people was written long ago, for they have turned against our only Master and Lord, Jesus Christ.

5My answer to them is: Remember this fact—which you know already—that the Lord saved a whole nation of people out of the land of Egypt, and then killed every one of them who did not trust and obey him. 6And I remind you of those angels who were once pure and holy, but turned to a life of sin. Now God has them chained up in prisons of darkness, waiting for the judgment day. 7And don't forget the cities of Sodom and Gomorrah and their neighboring towns, all full of lust of every kind including lust of men for other men. Those cities were destroyed by fire and continue to be a warning to us that there is a hell in which sinners are punished.

A THOUGHT: *Many first-century false teachers taught that Christians could do whatever they liked without fear of God's punishment. They took a light view of God's holiness and his justice. Even today, some Christians minimize the sinfulness of sin, believing that how they live has little to do with their faith. They may do well to ask, "Does the way I live show that I am sincere about my faith?" Those who truly have faith will show it by their deep respect for God and their sincere desire to live according to the principles in his Word.*

Proverbs for Today/ 31:8–9

You should defend those who cannot help themselves. Yes, speak up for the poor and helpless, and see that they get justice.

DECEMBER 30

The New Jerusalem/ Revelation 21:1—22:7

Then I saw a new earth (with no oceans!) and a new sky, for the present earth and sky had disappeared. 2 And I, John, saw the Holy City, the new Jerusalem, coming down from God out of heaven. It was a glorious sight, beautiful as a bride at her wedding.

3I heard a loud shout from the throne saying, "Look, the home of God is now among men, and he will live with them and they will be his people; yes, God himself will be among them. 4He will wipe away all tears from their eyes, and there shall be no more death, nor sorrow, nor crying, nor pain. All of that has gone forever."

5And the one sitting on the throne said, "See, I am making all things new!" And then he said to me, "Write this down, for what I tell you is trustworthy and true: 6It is finished! I am the A and the Z—the Beginning and the End. I will give to the thirsty the springs of the Water of Life—as a gift! 7Everyone who conquers will inherit all these blessings, and I will be his God and he will be my son. 8But cowards who turn back from following me, and those who are unfaithful to me, and the corrupt, and murderers, and the immoral, and those conversing with demons, and idol worshipers and all liars—their doom is in the Lake that burns with fire and sulphur. This is the Second Death."

9Then one of the seven angels, who had emptied the flasks containing the seven last plagues, came and said to me, "Come with me and I will show you the bride, the Lamb's wife."

10In a vision he took me to a towering mountain peak and from there I watched that wondrous city, the holy Jerusalem, descending out of the skies from God. 11It was filled with the glory of God, and flashed and glowed like a precious gem, crystal clear like jasper. 12Its walls were broad and high, with twelve gates guarded by twelve angels. And the names of the twelve tribes of Israel were written on the gates. 13There were three gates on each side—north, south, east, and west. 14The walls had twelve foundation stones, and on them were written the names of the twelve apostles of the Lamb.

15The angel held in his hand a golden measuring stick to measure the city and its gates and walls. 16When he measured it, he found it was a square as wide as it was long; in fact it was in the form of a cube, for its height was exactly the same as its other dimensions—1,500 miles each way. 17Then he measured the thickness of the walls and found them to be 216 feet across (the angel called out these measurements to me, using standard units).

18,19,20The city itself was pure, transparent gold like glass! The wall was made of jasper, and was built on twelve layers of foundation stones inlaid with gems:

The first layer with jasper;
The second with sapphire;
The third with chalcedony;
The fourth with emerald;
The fifth with sardonyx;
The sixth layer with sardus;
The seventh with chrysolite;

The eighth with beryl;
The ninth with topaz;
The tenth with chrysoprase;
The eleventh with jacinth;
The twelfth with amethyst.

21The twelve gates were made of pearls—each gate from a single pearl! And the main street was pure, transparent gold, like glass.

22No temple could be seen in the city, for the Lord God Almighty and the Lamb are worshiped in it everywhere. 23And the city has no need of sun or moon to light it, for the glory of God and of the Lamb illuminate it. 24Its light will light the nations of the earth, and the rulers of the world will come and bring their glory to it. 25Its gates never close; they stay open all day long—and there is no night! 26And the glory and honor of all the nations shall be brought into it. 27Nothing evil will be permitted in it—no one immoral or dishonest—but only those whose names are written in the Lamb's Book of Life.

22:1And he pointed out to me a river of pure Water of Life, clear as crystal, flowing from the throne of God and the Lamb, 2coursing down the center of the main street. On each side of the river grew Trees of Life, bearing twelve crops of fruit, with a fresh crop each month; the leaves were used for medicine to heal the nations.

3There shall be nothing in the city which is evil; for the throne of God and of the Lamb will be there, and his servants will worship him. 4And they shall see his face; and his name shall be written on their foreheads. 5And there will be no night there—no need for lamps or sun—for the Lord God will be their light; and they shall reign forever and ever.

6,7Then the angel said to me, "These words are trustworthy and true: 'I am coming soon!' God, who tells his prophets what the future holds, has sent his angel to tell you this will happen soon. Blessed are those who believe it and all else written in the scroll."

A Thought: *Have you ever wondered what eternity will be like? The "Holy City, the new Jerusalem" is described as the place where God "will wipe away all tears." Forevermore, there will be no death, pain, sorrow, or crying. What a wonderful truth! No matter what you are going through, it's not the last word—God has written the final chapter, and it is about true fulfillment and eternal joy for those who love him. We do not know as much as we would like, but it is enough to know that eternity with God will be more wonderful than we can imagine.*

The Punishment of False Teachers/ Jude 1:8–16

Yet these false teachers carelessly go right on living their evil, immoral lives, degrading their bodies and laughing at those in authority over them, even scoffing at the Glorious Ones. 9Yet Michael, one of the mightiest of the angels, when he was arguing with Satan about Moses' body, did not dare to accuse even Satan, or jeer at him, but simply said, "The Lord rebuke you." 10But these men mock and curse at anything they do not understand, and, like animals, they do whatever they feel like, thereby ruining their souls.

11Woe upon them! For they follow the example of Cain who killed his brother; and, like Balaam, they will do anything for money; and like Korah, they have disobeyed God and will die under his curse.

12When these men join you at the love feasts of the church, they are evil smears among you, laughing and carrying on, gorging and stuffing themselves without a thought for others. They are like clouds blowing over dry land without giving rain, promising much, but producing nothing. They are like fruit trees without any fruit at picking time. They are not only dead, but doubly dead, for they have been pulled out, roots and all, to be burned.

13All they leave behind them is shame and disgrace like the dirty foam left along the beach by the wild waves. They wander around looking as bright as stars, but ahead of them is the everlasting gloom and darkness that God has prepared for them.

14Enoch, who lived seven generations after Adam, knew about these men and said this about them: "See, the Lord is coming with millions of his holy ones. 15He will bring the people of the world before him in judgment, to receive just punishment, and to prove the terrible things they have done in rebellion against God, revealing all they have said against him." 16These men are constant gripers, never satisfied, doing whatever evil they feel like; they are loudmouthed "show-offs," and when they show respect for others, it is only to get something from them in return.

A THOUGHT: *False teachers claimed that they possessed secret knowledge which gave them authority. Their "knowledge" of God was esoteric—mystical and beyond human understanding. In reality, the nature of God is beyond our understanding. But God, in his grace, has chosen to reveal himself to us—in his Word, and supremely in Jesus Christ. Therefore, we must seek to know all we can about what he has revealed, even though we cannot fully comprehend God with our finite human minds. Beware of those who claim to have all the answers and who belittle what they do not understand.*

Proverbs for Today/ 31:10–24

If you can find a truly good wife, she is worth more than precious gems! Her husband can trust her, and she will richly satisfy his needs. She will not hinder him, but help him all her life. She finds wool and flax and busily spins it. She buys imported foods, brought by ship from distant ports. She gets up before dawn to prepare breakfast for her household, and plans the day's work for her servant girls. She goes out to inspect a field, and buys it; with her own hands she plants a vineyard. She is energetic, a hard worker, and watches for bargains. She works far into the night! She sews for the poor, and generously helps those in need. She has no fear of winter for her household, for she has made warm clothes for all of them. She also upholsters with finest tapestry; her own clothing is beautifully made—a purple gown of pure linen. Her husband is well known, for he sits in the council chamber with the other civic leaders. She makes belted linen garments to sell to the merchants.

DECEMBER 31

The Promise of Jesus' Return/ Revelation 22:8–21

I, John, saw and heard all these things, and fell down to worship the angel who showed them to me; 9but again he said, "No, don't do anything like that. I, too, am a servant of Jesus as you are, and as your brothers the prophets are, as well as all those who heed the truth stated in this Book. Worship God alone."

10Then he instructed me, "Do not seal up what you have written, for the time of fulfillment is near. 11And when that time comes, all doing wrong will do it more and more; the vile will become more vile; good men will be better; those who are holy will continue on in greater holiness."

12"See, I am coming soon, and my reward is with me, to repay everyone according to the deeds he has done. 13I am the A and the Z, the Beginning and the End, the First and Last. 14Blessed forever are all who are washing their robes, to have the right to enter in through the gates of the city, and to eat the fruit from the Tree of Life.

15"Outside the city are those who have strayed away from God, and the sorcerers and the immoral and murderers and idolaters, and all who love to lie, and do so.

16"I, Jesus, have sent my angel to you to tell the churches all these things. I am both David's Root and his Descendant. I am the bright Morning Star. 17The Spirit and the bride say, 'Come.' Let each one who hears them say the same, 'Come.' Let the thirsty one come—anyone who wants to; let him come and drink the Water of Life without charge. 18And I solemnly declare to everyone who reads this book: If anyone adds anything to what is written here, God shall add to him the plagues described in this book. 19And if anyone subtracts any part of these prophecies, God shall take away his share in the Tree of Life, and in the Holy City just described.

20"He who has said all these things declares: Yes, I am coming soon!"

Amen! Come, Lord Jesus!

21The grace of our Lord Jesus Christ be with you all. Amen!

A THOUGHT: *The first of the Ten Commandments is "You may worship no other god than me" (Exodus 20:3). Jesus said that the greatest command of Moses' laws was "Love the Lord your God with all your heart, soul, and mind" (Matthew 22:37). Here, at the end of the Bible, this truth is reiterated. The angel instructs John to "worship God alone." God alone is worthy of our worship and adoration. He is above all creation, even the angels. Are there people, ideas, goals, or possessions that occupy the central place in your life, crowding God out? Worship God alone, allowing nothing to distract you from your devotion to him.*

Exhortations to Holy Living/ Jude 1:17–25

Dear friends, remember what the apostles of our Lord Jesus Christ told you, 18that in the last times there would come these scoffers whose whole purpose in life is to enjoy themselves in every evil way imaginable. 19They stir up arguments; they love the evil things of the world; they do not have the Holy Spirit living in them.

20But you, dear friends, must build up your lives ever more strongly upon the foundation of our holy faith, learning to pray in the power and strength of the Holy Spirit.

21Stay always within the boundaries where God's love can reach and bless you. Wait patiently for the eternal life that our Lord Jesus Christ in his mercy is going to give you. 22 Try to help those who argue against you. Be merciful to those who doubt. 23Save some by snatching them as from the very flames of hell itself. And as for others, help them to find the Lord by being kind to them, but be careful that you yourselves aren't pulled along into their sins. Hate every trace of their sin while being merciful to them as sinners.

24,25And now—all glory to him who alone is God, who saves us through Jesus Christ our Lord; yes, splendor and majesty, all power and authority are his from the beginning; his they are and his they evermore shall be. And he is able to keep you from slipping and falling away, and to bring you, sinless and perfect, into his glorious presence with mighty shouts of everlasting joy. Amen.
Jude

A THOUGHT: *In trying to find common ground with those to whom we witness, we must be careful not to fall into the quicksand of compromise. When reaching out to others, we must be sure our own footing is safe and secure. Be careful not to become so much like non-Christians that no one can tell who you are or what you believe. Influence them for Christ—don't allow them to influence you to sin!*

Proverbs for Today/ 31:25–31

She is a woman of strength and dignity, and has no fear of old age. When she speaks, her words are wise, and kindness is the rule for everything she says. She watches carefully all that goes on throughout her household, and is never lazy. Her children stand and bless her; so does her husband. He praises her with these words: "There are many fine women in the world, but you are the best of them all!" Charm can be deceptive and beauty doesn't last, but a woman who fears and reverences God shall be greatly praised. Praise her for the many fine things she does. These good deeds of hers shall bring her honor and recognition from people of importance.

The New Testament Talks about Life

Let him have all your worries and cares, for he is always thinking about you and watching everything that concerns you. 1 Peter 5:7

Agitation

"I am leaving you with a gift—peace of mind and heart! And the peace I give isn't fragile like the peace the world gives. So don't be troubled or afraid." *John 14:27*

Don't worry about anything; instead, pray about everything; tell God your needs and don't forget to thank him for his answers. If you do this you will experience God's peace, which is far more wonderful than the human mind can understand. His peace will keep your thoughts and hearts quiet and at rest as you trust in Christ Jesus. *Philippians 4:6, 7*

Anger

If you are angry, don't sin by nursing your grudge. Don't let the sun go down with you still angry—get over it quickly; for when you are angry you give a mighty foothold to the devil. *Ephesians 4:26, 27*

Dear brothers, don't ever forget that it is best to listen much, speak little, and not become angry; for anger doesn't make us good, as God demands that we must be. *James 1:19, 20*

Discouragement

"Let not your heart be troubled. You are trusting God, now trust in me. There are many homes up there where my father lives, and I am going to prepare them for your coming. When everything is ready, then I will come and get you, so that you can always be with me where I am." *John 14:1-3*

Eternal Life

Jesus told her, "I am the one who raises the dead and gives them life again. Anyone who believes in me, even though he died like anyone else, shall live again. He is given eternal life for believing in me and shall never perish. Do you believe this, Martha?" *John 11:25, 26*

For we know that when this tent we live in now is taken down— when we die and leave these bodies—we will have wonderful new bodies in heaven, homes that will be ours forevermore, made for us by God himself, and not by human hands. How weary we grow of our present bodies. . . . We want to slip into our new bodies so that these dying bodies will, as it were, be swallowed up by everlasting life. This is what God has prepared for us and, as a guarantee, he has given us his Holy Spirit.
2 Corinthians 5:1, 2, 4, 5

Yet what we suffer now is nothing compared to the glory he will give us later. *Romans 8:18*

Fear

God has said, "I will never, never fail you nor forsake you." That is why we can say without any doubt or fear, "The Lord is my Helper and I am not afraid of anything that mere man can do to me." *Hebrews 13:5, 6*

May God bless you richly and grant you increasing freedom from all anxiety and fear. *1 Peter 1:2*

Frustration

You need to keep on patiently doing God's will if you want him to do for you all that he has promised. *Hebrews 10:36*

Guilt

But if we confess our sins to him, he can be depended on to forgive us and to cleanse us from every wrong. [And it is perfectly proper for God to do this for us because Christ died to wash away our sins.] *1 John 1:9*

So overflowing is his kindness towards us that he took away all our sins through the blood of his Son, by whom we are saved. *Ephesians 1:7*

And I will be merciful to them in their wrongdoings, and I will remember their sins no more. *Hebrews 8:12*

Impatience

Now as for you, dear brothers who are waiting for the Lord's return, be patient, like a farmer who waits until the autumn for his precious harvest to ripen. Yes, be patient. And take courage, for the coming of the Lord is near. *James 5:7, 8*

Insecurity

What can we ever say to such wonderful things as these? If God is on our side, who can ever be against us? Since he did not spare even his own Son for us but gave him up for us all, won't he also surely give us everything else? *Romans 8:31, 32*

This is why we can say without any doubt or fear, "The Lord is my Helper and I am not afraid of anything that mere man can do to me." *Hebrews 13:6*

Insult

"Happy are those who are persecuted because they are good, for the Kingdom of Heaven is theirs. When you are reviled and persecuted and lied about because you are my followers—wonderful! Be happy about it! Be very glad! for a tremendous reward awaits you up in heaven. And remember, the ancient prophets were persecuted too. . . . But I say: Love your enemies! Pray for those who persecute you! In that way you will be acting as true sons of your Father in heaven. For he gives his sunlight to both the evil and the good, and sends rain on the just and on the unjust too." *Matthew 5:10-12, 44, 45*

Jealousy

And by all means don't brag about being wise and good if you are bitter and jealous and selfish; that is the worst sort of lie. For jealousy and selfishness are not God's kind of wisdom. Such things are earthly, unspiritual, inspired by the devil. For wherever there is jealousy or selfish ambition, there will be disorder and every other kind of evil. *James 3:14-16*

Loneliness

"No, I will not abandon you or leave you as orphans in the storm—I will come to you." *John 14:18*

Low Self-Esteem

". . . 'You must love others as much as yourself.' No other commandments are greater than these." *Mark 12:31*

As God's messenger I give each of you God's warning: Be honest in your estimate of yourselves, measuring your value by how much faith God has given you. Just as there are many parts to our bodies, so it is with Christ's body. We are all parts of it, and it takes every one of us to make it complete, for we each have different work to do. So we belong to each other, and each needs all the others. *Romans 12:3-5*

Pain

"Father, Father," he said, "everything is possible for you. Take away this cup from me. Yet I want your will, not mine."
Mark 14:36

These troubles and sufferings of ours are, after all, quite small and won't last very long. Yet this short time of distress will result

in God's richest blessing upon us forever and ever! . . . I was given a physical condition which has been a thorn in my flesh, a messenger from Satan to hurt and bother me, and prick my pride. Three different times I begged God to make me well again. Each time he said, "No. But I am with you; that is all you need. My power shows up best in weak people." Now I am glad to boast about how weak I am; I am glad to be a living demonstration of Christ's power. Since I know it is all for Christ's good, I am quite happy about "the thorn," and about insults and hardships, persecutions and difficulties; for when I am weak, then I am strong—the less I have, the more I depend on him.
2 Corinthians 4:17; 12:7-10

Sickness

Is anyone sick? He should call for the elders of the church and they should pray over him and pour a little oil upon him, calling on the Lord to heal him. And their prayer, if offered in faith, will heal him, for the Lord will make him well; and if his sickness was caused by some sin, the Lord will forgive him. *James 5:14, 15*

Suffering and Death

And now, dear brothers, I want you to know what happens to a Christian when he dies so that when it happens, you will not be full of sorrow, as those are who have no hope. For since we believe that Jesus died and then came back to life again, we can also believe that when Jesus returns, God will bring back with him all the Christians who have died. *1 Thessalonians 4:13, 14*

But I am telling you this strange and wonderful secret; we shall not all die, but we shall all be given new bodies! It will all happen in a moment, in the twinkling of an eye, when the last trumpet is blown. For there will be a trumpet blast from the sky and all the Christians who have died will suddenly become alive, with new bodies that will never, never die; and then we who are still alive shall suddenly have new bodies too. For our earthly bodies, the ones we have now that can die, must be transformed into heavenly bodies that cannot perish but will live forever. When this happens, then at last this Scripture will come true—

"Death is swallowed up in victory." O death, where then your victory? Where then your sting? *1 Corinthians 15:51-55*

Temptation

But remember this—the wrong desires that come into your life aren't anything new and different. Many others have faced exactly the same problems before you. And no temptation is irresistible. You can trust God to keep the temptation from becoming so strong that you can't stand up against it, for he has promised this and will do what he says. He will show you how to escape temptation's power so that you can bear up patiently against it. *1 Corinthians 10:13*

Happy is the man who doesn't give in and do wrong when he is tempted, for afterwards he will get as his reward the crown of life that God has promised those who love him. And remember, when someone wants to do wrong it is never God who is tempting him, for God never wants to do wrong and never tempts anyone else to do it. . . . So give yourselves humbly to God. Resist the devil and he will flee from you. *James 1:12, 13; 4:7*

For since he himself has now been through suffering and temptation, he knows what it is like when we suffer and are tempted, and he is wonderfully able to help us. *Hebrews 2:18*

Weariness

"Come to me and I will give you rest—all of you who work so hard beneath a heavy yoke. Wear my yoke—for it fits perfectly— and let me teach you; for I am gentle and humble, and you shall find rest for your souls; for I give you only light burdens." *Matthew 11:28-30*

Worry

Let him have all your worries and cares, for he is always thinking about you and watching everything that concerns you. *1 Peter 5:7*

Then turning to his disciples he said, "Don't worry about whether you have enough food to eat or clothes to wear. For life consists of far more than food and clothes. And besides, what's the use of worrying? What good does it do? Will it add a single day to your life? Of course not! And if worry can't even do such little things as that, what's the use of worrying over bigger things? Look at the lilies! They don't toil and spin, and yet Solomon in all his glory was not robed as well as they are. And if God provides clothing for the flowers that are here today and gone tomorrow, don't you suppose that he will provide clothing for you, you doubters?" *Luke 12:22-28*

The New Testament Talks about Relationships
"Your strong love for each other will prove to the world that you are my disciples." John 13:35

Friends

Don't be selfish; don't live to make a good impression on others. Be humble, thinking of others as better than yourself. Don't just think about your own affairs, but be interested in others, too, and in what they are doing. *Philippians 2:3, 4*

Injustice

Do what is right; then if men speak against you, calling you evil names, they will become ashamed of themselves for falsely accusing you when you have only done what is good. Remember, if God wants you to suffer, it is better to suffer for doing good than for doing wrong! Christ also suffered. He died once for the sins of all us guilty sinners, although he himself was innocent of any sin at any time, that he might bring us safely home to God.
1 Peter 3:16-18

After you have suffered a little while, our God, who is full of kindness through Christ, will give you his eternal glory. He personally will come and pick you up, and set you firmly in place, and make you stronger than ever. To him be all power over all things forever and ever. Amen. *1 Peter 5:10, 11*

Love

"I have loved you even as the Father has loved me. Live within my love. When you obey me you are living in my love, just as I obey my Father and live in his love. I have told you this so that you will be filled with my joy. Yes, your cup of joy will overflow! I demand that you love each other as much as I love you. And here is how to measure it—the greatest love is shown when a person lays down his life for his friends; and you are my friends if you obey me. I no longer call you slaves, for a master doesn't confide in his slaves; now you are my friends, proved by the fact that I have told you everything the Father told me. You didn't choose me! I chose you! I appointed you to go and produce lovely fruit always, so that no matter what you ask for from the Father, using my name, he will give it to you." *John 15:9-16*

"For God loved the world so much that he gave his only Son so that anyone who believes in him shall not perish but have eternal life." *John 3:16*

God showed how much he loved us by sending his only Son into this wicked world to bring to us eternal life through his death. In this act we see what real love is: it is not our love for God, but his love for us when he sent his Son to satisfy God's anger against our sins. . . . We know how much God loves us because we have felt his love and because we believe him when he tells us that he loves us dearly. God is love, and anyone who lives in love is living with God and God is living in him. And as we live with Christ, our love grows more perfect and complete; so we will not be ashamed and embarrassed at the day of judgment, but can face him with confidence and joy, because he loves us and we love him too. . . . If anyone says "I love God," but keeps on hating his brother, he is a liar; for if he doesn't love his brother who is right there in front of him, how can he love God whom he has never seen? And God himself has said that one must love not only God, but his brother too. *1 John 4:9-21*

Love is very patient and kind, never jealous or envious, never boastful or proud, never haughty or selfish or rude. Love does not demand its own way. It is not irritable or touchy. It does not hold grudges and will hardly even notice when others do it wrong. It is never glad about injustice, but rejoices whenever truth wins out. If you love someone you will be loyal to him no matter what the cost. You will always believe in him, always expect the best of him, and always stand your ground in defending him. . . . There are three things that remain—faith, hope, and love—and the greatest of these is love. *1 Corinthians 13:4-7, 13*

Marriage

Honor Christ by submitting to each other. You wives must submit to your husbands' leadership in the same way you submit to the Lord. . . . And you husbands, show the same kind of love to your wives as Christ showed to the Church when he died for her, to make her holy and clean, washed by baptism and God's Word; so that he could give her to himself as a glorious Church without a single spot or wrinkle or any other blemish, being holy and without a single fault. That is how husbands should treat their wives, loving them as parts of themselves. For since a man and his wife are now one, a man is really doing himself a favor and loving himself when he loves his wife. *Ephesians 5:21, 22, 25-28*

Wives, fit in with your husbands' plans; for then if they refuse to listen when you talk to them about the Lord, they will be won by your respectful, pure behavior. Your godly lives will speak to them better than any words. Don't be concerned about the outward beauty that depends on jewelry, or beautiful clothes, or hair arrangement. Be beautiful inside, in your hearts, with the lasting charm of a gentle and quiet spirit which is so precious to God. That kind of deep beauty was seen in the saintly women of old, who trusted God and fitted in with their husbands' plans. Sarah, for instance, obeyed her husband Abraham, honoring him as head of the house. And if you do the same, you will be following in her steps like good daughters and doing what is right; then you will not need to fear [offending your husbands]. You husbands must be careful of your wives, being thoughtful of their needs and honoring them as the weaker sex. Remember that you and your wife are partners in receiving God's blessings, and if you don't treat her as you should, your prayers will not get ready answers. *1 Peter 3:1-7*

A man should leave his father and mother, and be forever united to his wife. The two shall become one—no longer two, but one! And no man may divorce what God has joined together. Anyone who divorces his wife, except for fornication, and marries another, commits adultery. *Matthew 19:5, 9*

When a man divorces his wife to marry someone else, he commits adultery against her. And if a wife divorces her husband and remarries, she, too, commits adultery. *Mark 10:11, 12*

Parents and Children

Children, obey your parents; this is the right thing to do because God has placed them in authority over you. Honor your father and mother. This is the first of God's Ten Commandments that ends with a promise. And this is the promise: that if you honor your father and mother, yours will be a long life, full of blessing. And now a word to you parents. Don't keep on scolding and nagging your children, making them angry and resentful. Rather, bring them up with the loving discipline the Lord himself approves, with suggestions and godly advice. *Ephesians 6:1-4*

The New Testament Talks about the Future

We are all parts of one body, we have the same Spirit, and we have all been called to the same glorious future. Ephesians 4:4

Direction for Life

And remember, it is a message to obey, not just to listen to. So don't fool yourselves. For if a person just listens and doesn't obey, he is like a man looking at his face in a mirror; as soon as he walks away, he can't see himself any more or remember what he looks like. But if anyone keeps looking steadily into God's law for free men, he will not only remember it, but he will do what it says, and God will greatly bless him in everything he does. *James 1:22-25*

Money Management

And it is he who will supply all your needs from his riches in glory, because of what Christ Jesus has done for us. *Philippians 4:19*

Do you want to be truly rich? You already are if you are happy and good. After all, we didn't bring any money with us when we came into the world, and we can't carry away a single penny when we die. So we should be well satisfied without money if we have enough food and clothing. But people who long to be rich soon begin to do all kinds of wrong things to get money, things that hurt them and make them evil-minded and finally send them to hell itself. For the love of money is the first step toward all kinds of sin. Some people have even turned away from God because of their love for it, and as a result have pierced themselves with many sorrows. *1 Timothy 6:6-10*

Trust

I know how to live on almost nothing or with everything. I have learned the secret of contentment in every situation, whether it be a full stomach or hunger, plenty or want; for I can do everything

God asks me to with the help of Christ who gives me the strength and power. *Philippians 4:12, 13*

The New Testament Talks about Faith
Faith comes from listening to this Good News—the Good News about Christ. Romans 10:17

Being Born Again

Jesus replied, "With all the earnestness I possess I tell you this: Unless you are born again, you can never get into the Kingdom of God. . . . What I am telling you so earnestly is this: Unless one is born of water and the Spirit, he cannot enter the Kingdom of God. Men can only reproduce human life, but the Holy Spirit gives new life from heaven; so don't be surprised at my statement that you must be born again." *John 3:3, 5-7*

All honor to God, the God and Father of our Lord Jesus Christ; for it is his boundless mercy that has given us the privilege of being born again, so that we are now members of God's own family. *1 Peter 1:3*

The person who has been born into God's family does not make a practice of sinning, because now God's life is in him; so he can't keep on sinning, for this new life has been born into him and controls him—he has been *born again. 1 John 3:9*

Finding God

"His purpose in all of this is that they should seek after God, and perhaps feel their way toward him and find him—though he is not far from any one of us. For in him we live and move and are! As one of your own poets says it, 'We are the sons of God.'" *Acts 17:27, 28*

Knowing God

Dear friends, let us practice loving each other, for love comes from God and those who are loving and kind show that they are getting to know him better. But if a person isn't loving and kind, it shows that he doesn't know God—for God is love. *1 John 4:7, 8*

Knowing Jesus Christ

Before anything else existed, there was Christ, with God. He has always been alive and is himself God. He created everything there is—nothing exists that he didn't make. Eternal life is in him, and this life gives light to all mankind. His life is the light that shines through the darkness—and the darkness can never extinguish it. God sent John the Baptist as a witness to the fact that Jesus Christ is the true Light. John himself was not the Light; he was only a witness to identify it. Later on, the one who is the true Light arrived to shine on everyone coming into the world. But although he made the world, the world didn't recognize him when he came. Even in his own land and among his own people, the Jews, he was not accepted. Only a few would welcome and receive him. But to all who received him he gave the right to become children of God. All they needed to do was to trust him to save them. All those who believe this are reborn!—not a physical rebirth resulting from human passion or plan—but from the will of God. And Christ became a human being and lived here on earth among us and was full of loving forgiveness and truth. And some of us have seen his glory—the glory of the only Son of the heavenly Father! *John 1:1-14*

Christ is the exact likeness of the unseen God. He existed before God made anything at all, and, in fact, Christ himself is the Creator who made everything in heaven and earth, the things we can see and the things we can't; the spirit world with its kings and kingdoms, its rulers and authorities; all were made by Christ for his own use and glory. He was before all else began and it is his power that holds everything together. He is the Head of the body made up of his people—that is, his Church—which he began; and he is the Leader of all those who arise from the dead, so that he is first in everything; for God wanted all of himself to be in his Son. . . . You were dead in sins, and your sinful desires were not yet cut away. Then he gave you a share in the very life of Christ, for he forgave all your sins, and blotted out the charges proved against you, the list of his commandments which you had not obeyed. He took this list of sins and destroyed it by nailing it to Christ's cross. *Colossians 1:15-19, 2:13, 14*

God's Son shines out with God's glory, and all that God's Son is and does marks him as God. He regulates the universe by the mighty power of his command. He is the one who died to cleanse us and clear our record of all sin, and then sat down in highest honor beside the great God of heaven. . . . but of his Son he says, "Your kingdom, O God, will last forever and ever; its commands are always just and right." *Hebrews 1:3, 8*

Knowing the Holy Spirit

He has put his brand upon us—his mark of ownership—and given us his Holy Spirit in our hearts as guarantee that we belong to him, and as the first installment of all that he is going to give us. *2 Corinthians 1:22*

But you are not like that. You are controlled by your new nature if you have the Spirit of God living in you. (And remember that if anyone doesn't have the Spirit of Christ living in him, he is not a Christian at all.) Yet, even though Christ lives within you, your body will die because of sin; but your spirit will live, for Christ has pardoned it. And if the Spirit of God, who raised up Jesus from the dead, lives in you, he will make your dying bodies live again after you die, by means of this same Holy Spirit living within you. *Romans 8:9-11*

"If you love me, obey me; and I will ask the Father and he will give you another Comforter, and he will never leave you. He is the Holy Spirit, the Spirit who leads into all truth. The world at large cannot receive him, for it isn't looking for him and doesn't recognize him. But you do, for he lives with you now and some day shall be in you. . . . But when the Father sends the Comforter instead of me—and by the Comforter I mean the Holy Spirit—he will teach you much, as well as remind you of everything I myself have told you." *John 14:15-17, 26*

Prayer

Admit your faults to one another and pray for each other so that you may be healed. The earnest prayer of a righteous man has great power and wonderful results. *James 5:16*

"But if you stay in me and obey my commands, you may ask any request you like, and it will be granted!" *John 15:7*

"Ask, and you will be given what you ask for. Seek, and you will find. Knock, and the door will be opened. For everyone who asks, receives. Anyone who seeks, finds. If only you will knock, the door will open." *Matthew 7:7, 8*

If we confess our sins to him, he can be depended on to forgive us and to cleanse us from every wrong. *1 John 1:9*